A Study of Southwestern Archaeology

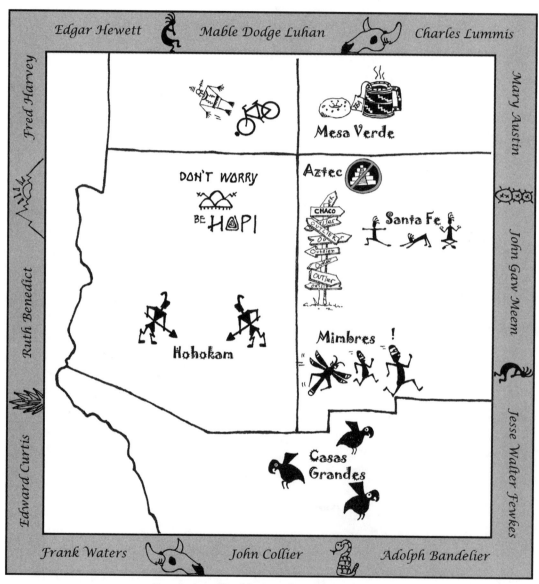

Frontispiece: "Pueblo Space." Artwork by Rod Buskas.
"Don't worry, be Hopi" attrib. Janice and Joe Day, Tsakurshovi Trading Post, Hopi.
Used with permission.

A Study of Southwestern Archaeology

STEPHEN H. LEKSON

THE UNIVERSITY OF UTAH PRESS
Salt Lake City

The Defiance House Man colophon is a registered trademark
of The University of Utah Press. It is based on a four-foot-tall
Ancient Puebloan pictograph (late PIII) near Glen Canyon, Utah.

LIBRARY OF CONGRESS CATALOGING-IN-PUBLICATION DATA

Names: Lekson, Stephen H., author.
Title: A study of Southwestern archaeology / Stephen H. Lekson.
Description: Salt Lake City : The University of Utah Press, [2018] | Includes
    bibliographical references and index. |
Identifiers: LCCN 2018026858 (print) | LCCN 2018029400 (ebook) |
    ISBN 9781607816423 | ISBN 9781607816416 (pbk. : alk. paper)
Subjects: LCSH: Chaco culture—Research—History. | Southwest,
    New—Antiquities—Research—History. | Chaco Canyon (N.M.)—Antiquities. |
    Hopi Indians—Antiquities. | Pueblo Indians—Antiquities. |
    Archaeology—Methodology—History.
Classification: LCC E99.C37 (ebook) | LCC E99.C37 L44 2018 (print) |
    DDC 979/.01—dc23
LC record available at https://lccn.loc.gov/2018026858

For friends met along the trail:
Adventures in archaeology from Chimney Rock
to Cerro de Moctezuma, from Laguna Plata to Fortaleza;
and somewhere near the heart of it, Cañada Alamosa.

For John Schelberg, Bob Powers,
Marcie Donaldson, and the Chaco Center.

And before:
The Upper Gila Project and the Redrock gang;
and Cynthia Irwin-Williams and the Salmon Ruins crew.

And after:
Staff and students on
UNM & ENMU & HSR & CDA & CU field projects;
and kindred spirits at Crow Canyon.

And through it all:
Cathy Cameron. Met along the trail.

Contents

An analytical table of contents and additional online content at
https://stevelekson.com/

Acknowledgments

My thanks for kindnesses contributing to the completion of this book: Larry Benson, Wesley Bernardini, Sally Cole, Janice and Joe Day, Severin Fowles, Robert Kelly, Timothy Kohler, Jay Miller, James Collins Moore, John Pohl, David Roberts, Joe Traugott, and Richard Wilshusen. Ruth and Ken Wright and Sean Rice generously supported the book's production. To all: Thanks!

Much of chapter 4 was written at the School for Advanced Research in Santa Fe; most of the rest was written at the University of Colorado, Boulder. For developmental editing, my thanks to Lynn Baca (MEREA Consulting). And thanks to the excellent people of the University of Utah Press: Reba Rauch and Patrick Hadley; and copyeditor Virginia Hoffman (Last Word Editorial Services) and Ina Gravitz Indexing Services. All of the above are innocent of my transgressions, real or imaginary.

Preface

We poets in our youth begin in gladness;
But in the end, despondency and sadness.

—with apologies to Agatha Christie (*A-Sitting on a Site*),
who apologized to Lewis Carroll (*Aged Aged Man*),
who apologized to William Wordsworth (*Leech Gatherer*)

Plan of the Last Book

If you are a Southwestern archaeologist, I wrote this book for you, but you may not enjoy reading it. I'm a Southwestern archaeologist, and I did not enjoy writing it. Its basic premise is also its dismal conclusion: It's almost impossible for American Anthropological Archaeology to do justice to the ancient Southwest— to get it right—because of biases we inherited from our intellectual forefathers/ foremothers. And because archaeology is deeply entangled in Southwestern popular culture and seriously estranged from Southwestern Indigenous peoples. All these make it hard to do good, accurate archaeology. Almost impossible.

But of course that depends on your definition of "archaeology." Now more than ever, archaeology appears to be whatever archaeologists want to do, whatever makes archaeologists happy (attrib. to Albert Spaulding).[1] My archaeology is history and science, using those terms in their narrow European Enlightenment meanings. More than that: I insist that archaeology must be history first, before it can be science. Unless we get the history right (more or less), we probably will do silly science: Ask the wrong questions and get irrelevant answers.

But history and science operate by very different rules: History makes arguments, science tests theories. A methodological conundrum: We think we know how to do science, but very few of us have thought about how to do narrative history—historiography for prehistory! Hereafter I will refer to the narrative history of ancient times with this awkward, hyphenated term: pre-history.[2] (Hereafter, sans hyphen prehistory = ancient times.)

The focus of this book is Southwestern archaeology, and its central case study is Chaco. The specific argument is that Southwestern archaeology has been getting Chaco wrong for over a century because of something I will call "Pueblo Space": Everything in the past must be Pueblo, Pueblo-ish, or leading logically to modern Pueblos. This bias—and it is a bias—comes from a variety of causes explored in chapter 1, which takes the story up to around the year 2000. Southwestern archaeologists (including, of course, your author) inherited this bias. Pueblo Space confines and distorts all that we do, in ways obvious and not so obvious. Some recent Chaco-related examples showing the continuing effect (post-Y2K) of Pueblo Space are discussed in chapter 2. In chapter 3, I present Chaco freed (I hope) from Pueblo Space, a new pre-history. To preview: Chaco was a small, secondary state with nobles and commoners, similar in structure to a particular, fairly common Mesoamerican model of its time; it had a small capital city at Chaco Canyon and a large region or hinterland encompassing several tens of thousands of people. There's nothing like that in Pueblo Space.

If we escape Pueblo Space, the science we can do with Southwestern data is rather different than what we currently do. I offer a few ideas using my version of Chaco for science in chapter 4. Chapter 5 reviews the current state of American Anthropological Archaeology as it impacts writing narrative pre-history. Finally, chapter 6 suggests possible beginnings for pre-historiography: Theories and methods that might (or might not) be useful for producing narrative history for ancient times.

There's a narrative arc or logic both to the book and to individual chapters, but it's messy and sprawling. As Albert Einstein reportedly said, "If you are out to describe the truth, leave elegance to the tailor." I'm sure I'm far short of truth, but to get anywhere at all, I had to abandon all hope of elegance.

"What Do You Want Us to Do?"

A question: Not Yali's to Dr. Diamond; nor the Bridge-keeper's Three to Arthur's knights; nor Dirty Harry's to the luckless punk. The question came from a graduate student at Arizona State University, after I'd given a colloquium arguing that Anthropology was not a good intellectual home for ancient North America. The audience consisted of the ASU Anthropology faculty and, behind them, a score of graduate students. A tough crowd: Murderers' Row up front and, back in the cheap seats, a seething pack of critically thinking students. And all of 'em (most of 'em) smarter than me. But after I told them that—oops—they had taken jobs in the wrong discipline, they treated me with restraint and generosity. Many good questions and—from the back of the hall—the one that titles this section: "What do you want us to do?" Good question! I was taken aback. I hadn't thought that far; I'd recognized a problem but I hadn't figured out how to solve it. My response at the time was tactical: "Nothing, until you get tenure!" (A growl of agreement from the ASU faculty.)

This book answers that question. What do I want young Southwesternists to do? Reinvent North American prehistory, somewhere outside or beyond or parallel to American Anthropology. Late in life I realized what my elders knew: That the archaeology of North America landed in Anthropology by accident, or by colonial design—which is worse (chapter 1). It didn't have to be that way. Archaeology could have been a stand-alone or, more likely, allied with History—as it is in many other countries—or allied with any of several other disciplines. At my university, archaeologists work in Art History, Classics, History, Religious Studies, Geology, Geography, and environmental institutes. "Archaeology is anthropology or it is nothing" (a '60s slogan we revisit in chapter 1)? Bosh—tell that to the Classics Department.

The archaeology of ancient North America sits firmly in the bosom of Anthropology (with rare appearances in Art History). And of course that won't change. But it's really interesting and useful to think: What if, back in the late nineteenth century, archaeology had been assigned to History—the most obvious alternative—rather than Anthropology?

And that, graduate students, is what I want you to do: Reinvent a North American pre-history that is fundamentally historical. As it should have been, from the beginning. You don't have to stop doing Anthropology or Science. But to do good science, first you must get the history right. Understand the baggage, recognize and control the bias, and see what wonderful new possibilities open up for the ancient Southwest.

Choking on Chaco

I lost my faith in American Anthropological Archaeology and reached my history epiphany in the late 1970s[3] while chewing on solid, dry data: Chaco Canyon. Chaco was not comfortable in what I've come to call Pueblo Space. But we forced Chaco to fit. That was puzzling; how had we painted ourselves into that corner? Thereafter, I thought and wrote about Chaco, protesting too much, perhaps; but the problem remained: It really seemed like we were getting Chaco wrong.

The first of many caveats: I don't think Chaco is important because I worked there; I worked there because it was obvious that Chaco was important. When I began at Chaco, in the early 1970s, one textbook of the times declared, "Less is really known of the area [Chaco] than almost any other southwestern district. It is amazing that so little work has been done there and so few significant reports published" (Martin and Plog 1973:108). That was then, this is now: Now we know a lot. The volumes of Chaco literature published in the last forty years would choke a team of Clydesdales, could they be persuaded to eat them.[4]

Yet Chaco remains a "mystery." Elsewhere (and everywhere) I've complained that Chaco constitutes an embarrassing failure for Southwestern archaeology. The archaeology of Chaco Canyon and its region is simple, easy to see, straightforward, and well researched. Yet we reach no resolution. It's not for lack of data: Over a century of research, remarkably well-preserved ruins, and thousands of precise tree-ring dates have made Chaco one of the best-known archaeological sites, inch for inch, in the world.

The fact that our interpretations are all over the map may or may not tell us something about Chaco, but I think that tells us much more about Southwestern archaeology. It is archaeology's job to figure things out, and we do that for most times and places in the ancient Southwest. But at Chaco, we've failed. And consequently, the interested public and Chambers of Commerce declare Chaco a marketable mystery, an economically useful enigma.

Göbekli Tepe is an enigma and a mystery; Poverty Point is an enigma and a mystery; Caral is an enigma and a mystery: Early and unprecedented monumental centers. Chaco was neither early nor unprecedented: Millennia of Native history—histories of empires and states!—preceded it. By Chaco's times, they pretty much had tried everything, worked things out, and settled down to a limited menu of workable variations. Chaco is not an enigma nor a mystery. In fact, Chaco is easily understood if one references fairly common social and political structures in contemporary Mesoamerica (chapter 3).

To make my argument, I use Chaco archaeology as a case study, an admonition, a foil—maybe a punching bag or piñata.[5] This is NOT a Chaco book, although (perhaps) you can (maybe) learn a bit about the place here. Or not.

A Study of Southwestern Archaeology

My title, of course, nods to Alfred Vincent Kidder's (1924) *Introduction to the Study of Southwestern Archaeology*—a masterful synthesis of the field in the early 1920s, almost a century ago and still in print! I am amazed by how much those old guys knew, how much they'd figured out, a century ago.

My title also nods to Walter W. Taylor's ill-fated dissertation, published in 1948 with the title "A Study of Archeology."[6] In it, newly minted PhD Taylor took aim at the status of American archaeology, and (more problematically) at the leaders of American archaeology of his time. His career, in consequence, suffered. (What was his advisor thinking?)

Taylor was at the beginning of his career, trying to make a name for himself. I'm at the end of my career, and I'm not concerned about personal consequences: Good, bad, or ugly. I am concerned, however, about Southwestern archaeology—my career for almost fifty years. Here are my fears and my hopes for its future.

In my early days in Southwestern archaeology, if I had something unsettling or contradictory to say, I made a joke of it. One constant (and not unfriendly) critic called me the Will Rogers of Southwestern archaeology. But another constant (and not unfriendly) critic advised me: If you don't take your work seriously, why should anyone else? So I changed my tone from comic to curmudgeon, from Will Rogers to Ambrose Bierce.[7] Arguments became more pointed and, sometimes, seemingly personal. But not ad hominem! Never ad hominem, save several of our early giants, impervious to my carping. Their reputations are well established and, more importantly, they're dead. I call out scholars' particular ideas and interpretations because those ideas are importantly wrong or right. Often those ideas are associated with or best articulated by a notable archaeologist, but I'm not aiming at personalities; I'm evaluating ideas.[8] (In chapter 5, I do poke a little fun at French philosophers, but most of those guys are also dead.)

Some of my suggestions may strike readers as conservative or reactionary, somehow out of tune in these troubling times. I cannot adjust my life span to the unaccountable whims of the American electorate. Almost all of this was written during the halcyon days of the Obama administration; sadly, it appears in the time of Trump, this strange new world of anger, arrogance, and ignorance. I hope I'm no part of that great American backslide, nor are my arguments. I may sound like a crabby old man, and the reason is simple: I AM a crabby old man. But, I hope, one with some useful ideas for moving the field forward. Which has always been my goal.

This will almost certainly be my last scholarly book on Southwestern archaeology. It is obviously NOT the last word on that endlessly fascinating subject!

Notes on Terms

Some of my terms are unattractive: Not the language we use, not in our discursive formation. In part, that's the point.

I use "Anasazi" when needed as archaeological jargon, especially in the early, historical chapters. I use "pre-history" to mean not a time before or lacking history, but rather the history of times that conventional historians will not or cannot address. I throw around terms like "city" and "state" even as more sophisticated colleagues wince and shun them as over-simple. I even raise "diffusion" from its shallow grave. If you don't like "pre-history," you'll hate this: Following David Lowenthal (1998), I use "history" to mean both what happened in the past and (capital H) the academic discipline that studies it, and I use "heritage" to mean uses of the past in the present. Bear with me at least until chapter 5, which (shall we say?) goes into more nuanced discussions of these words.

These are not the neologisms beloved by theorists. They are old, unfashionable terms revived precisely because Pueblo Space denied the Southwest their use back when we really needed them.[9] Ontogeny recapitulates phylogeny: The Southwest must catch up to the world beyond Pueblo Space before we can adopt methods and manners of more mature scholarship.

I will repeatedly use a long, awkward term: American Anthropological Archaeology in the Southwest. Ugly, but all those adjectives and modifiers are necessary. Let's look at them, one term at a time. *American*: The prehistory of the Southwest is largely the province of modern (United States of) Americans, plus some excellent Canadians and Mexicans! There's not a lot of interest and almost no investment in Southwestern research from scholars from Europe or Japan or elsewhere—again, with a few notable exceptions! *Anthropological*: North America's prehistory was entrusted to Anthropology, as noted above and revisited at length in chapter 1. *Archaeology*, of course, means…several different things, as we shall see. I address mainly the archaeology of the Academy and CRM—that is, Anthropological Archaeology—but other flavors appear from time to time in the book. Finally, *Southwest*: A region of the USA which oddly enough includes much of Chihuahua and Sonora and even a bit of Sinaloa—areas researched primarily by excellent Mexican archaeologists, all trained to value history.

"American Anthropological Archaeology in the Southwest" is a mouthful, so I'll shorten it to "Southwestern Archaeology" and sometimes just "Archaeology," but all those other adjectives should be remembered because it's a very particular beast. More than that: Along with Pueblo Space, those other terms are variously part of the problem. Both have serious baggage, as we shall see in chapter 1.

Apparatuses, Albatrosses, Aphorisms

Footnotes: I began using footnotes several books ago to unburden the text from long asides, some necessary, others not so much. And also, I'm sad to say, because too many readers of my earlier works failed to follow up my in-text citations and accused me of making stuff up. No kidding. Footnotes in *A History of the Ancient Southwest* bulked up: As many words in footnotes as in text. This was, in part, because I wanted that book to look like a history book; and in part to work out a problem that culminates here, in chapter 6: Any (interesting) archaeological statement requires many, many layers of subtext, side-stories, backstories, and even pretext. How to deliver all that without making the main text unreadable? For print: Footnotes and endnotes. The notes for this book are printed here, but they are also available online at uofupress.com.[10] We return to this question and some possible solutions in chapter 6.

I will not apologize for peculiar punctuation and crazed capitalizations. They are not arbitrary albatrosses. Over the years I've developed some quirks in my writing style, and I think they work. At least, they work for me; and help me slog through the often difficult task of writing. For the first but not last time: My book, my rules.

Quotes, faux quotes, epigrams, and attributions: Quoted text with proper citations (e.g., Smith 2000:100) are accurate—I hope—save minor editing for flow (omitting internal citations irrelevant for the arguments, compressing ellipses, etc.). Other quotes or epigrams "attributed to," "supposedly said," "reportedly wrote," or simply unattributed literary allusions may or may not be real. Indeed, many are well-known "quotes" which have been determined to be apocryphal; others are real. Aside from amusing myself and hopefully at least a few readers, there's a point to this, much like my use of artists' reconstructions for almost every illustration in *A History of the Ancient Southwest*, and the virtual absence of illustrations in this book. There are reasons for odd quotes and no pictures: But I'm not telling.

There is additional content online, originally written for this book but excluded as unnecessary to my central argument(s). If you don't see your Chaco study referenced here, check online at https://stevelekson.com/.

CHAPTER 1

Chaco in the Twentieth Century

*L'histoire n'est après tout qu'un ramas de tracasseries
qu'on fait aux morts.*
—attributed to Voltaire

Essential to science—to any systematic, rigorous scholarship—is identifying and controlling bias. Scientists constantly worry about their samples (representative?), their measurements (accurate?), and any uncontrolled bias that might compromise their observations or experiments. Historians, too, critically examine their sources for authenticity, accuracy, and agendas—that is, for uncontrolled bias. And, as humanists, historians also routinely examine themselves: What biases are they bringing to their work? Archaeology is both history and science; I will argue in this book it must first be history before it can be science. In both arenas, it is critical to understand bias.[1]

The premise developed in this chapter—which underwrites the rest of the book—is that American Anthropological Archaeology through the twentieth century presented an inaccurate history of the ancient Southwest because of unexamined (and therefore uncontrolled) biases. Note, please: This is the twentieth century! The twenty-first century will come in chapter 2. Current colleagues: Holster your pistols, sheave your knives, hang up your ropes. You'll want 'em later, in the next chapter.

In the twentieth century, archaeology invested impressive amounts of energy, money, and brain-power in the Southwest; and archaeology discovered wonderful things and amassed vast quantities of data. But the history and traditions of the field—American Anthropological Archaeology in the Southwest—slanted our understandings of those data away from the truth and toward an illusion I call "Pueblo Space." Pueblo Space is founded on a vague, idealized notion of how Pueblos work. When those notions are applied as proper limits for interpreting the past, we are in Pueblo Space. Where those notions came from and how they became the metes and bounds of prehistory are the central subjects of this chapter.

Pueblo Space was not the result of archaeologists being stupid, or lazy, or incompetent; rather, it was archaeologists doing their work well, within rules and conventions they inherited from earlier archaeologists. These become what Ian Hodder (2003:129) calls "taken-for-granted assumptions" and I less politely call bias.[2] After nearly fifty years in this racket, I'm pretty sure that several key rules and conventions—applied early and often—which I and my colleagues inherited, were simply wrong. Our regime of truth is off the mark.

Consider this thought experiment, paraphrased from Ian Tattersall's (2015) *Strange Case of the Rickety Cossack*, an account of paleoanthropology: If the entire Southwestern archaeological record were to be rediscovered tomorrow and analyzed by archaeologists with no horses already in the race, it is pretty certain we would emerge with a picture of Southwestern prehistory very different from the one we have inherited.[3]

I speak of archaeologists but I am interested in ideas, not individuals. In some cases these are inseparable; and in other cases I use individuals (Morgan, Hewett) to represent larger historical moments.[4] Indeed, in the early days, when Southwestern archaeology was small, a few individuals WERE the larger historical moments. As we move closer to the present, I begin to omit actual names and citations—separating ideas from egos. I name names in the twenty-first century; it's unavoidable. But I assure the reader that I am not shooting at straw men—or straw women.[5]

The point, of course, is to move the field forward. To do that, I fear, some portions of the received wisdom must be re-examined and, I'm pretty sure, discarded. If people identify strongly with those ideas, they may not want to see them go.

The history of Southwestern archaeology[6] is a record of discovering new things and discarding old notions—as it should be. New insights and new data transform or replace received versions of the past. For example, Hohokam in the 1930s rose as something new and alarming in a field then focused almost exclusively on the Pueblo past. Mogollon also challenged Anasazi's pride-of-place—and in that case, many Anasazi archaeologists pushed back (Reid and Whittlesey 2010). Let no new thing arise.

Conversely, archaeology is also cumulative—as it should be. With each new chapter, much that was old was brought forward, both substantive and conceptual. But with older, hard-won knowledge often come older, ill-conceived ideas. After several generations of repetition, those ideas become facts, or fact-like, or truthy—and difficult to separate from actual knowledge.

It is far easier to correct substantive errors than it is to correct conceptual bias. We can date and redate Chaco, but we can't rid ourselves of the preconceptions we bring to that polemically charged site. It may have started in the tenth century, it may have started in the ninth century, but by God we KNOW *a priori* that Chaco was an "intermediate society." That is, Chaco was not-a-state. That goes without saying, because we know *a priori* that all Native societies north of Mexico were intermediate not-a-states. The automatic assumption of "intermediate society" is an uncontrolled bias which will surface and resurface in chapters to follow.

My "twentieth century" stretches things a bit, from 1880 to 2000—plus a brief five-century run-up. The twentieth century was quite a century for South-western archaeology, with pauses for a couple of World Wars. In its first half, blockbuster set-piece excavations and heroic wide-ranging surveys: Pecos! Bonito! Awatovi! Hawikku! Snaketown! Then, after midcentury, even larger (if narrower) projects well funded through environmental and heritage laws: Glen Canyon! Black Mesa! Central Arizona Project! Dolores! Cochiti Dam! Remark-able projects by extraordinary archaeologists, amassing more data than you can possibly imagine. And throughout owing debts, increasingly distant and unac-knowledged/unexamined, to earlier nineteenth-century archaeologists.

And of course, late nineteenth-century archaeologists—O Pioneers!—had debts of their own. And so on and so on, as the philosopher says. So I begin with a brief five-century run-up—the global milieu that set the tone for national and regional histories.

In the Beginning, All the World Was America

We begin in 1492; twigs that were bent and things that were thought in earliest colonial times impacted, directly and indirectly, American Anthropological Ar-chaeology (a questing beast I describe in more detail below). The New World, in 1492, was quite a surprise for the Old World. The discovery of two new con-tinents gave Enlightenment thinkers much to ponder.[7] Like Locke, from whom this section's title is borrowed, Europe took stock of its marvelous new posses-sions, and the Natives. Did Indians have souls? If so, had they rights and consid-erations offered to Christians? Were they a model, a reminder of the ancient Old World, sans Genesis? Did they have history?[8]

Churchmen and *philosophes* pondered these questions, in cloisters and in coffee houses, and they formulated theories. Locke and Rousseau reached very different conclusions about the Natives of the New World. Their readers read, and argued.

A world away from Catholic cloisters and Enlightenment coffee houses, col-onists put conquest into practice. By the seventeenth century, the great Native empires of Central America were no more. By the eighteenth century, gone too were the Native Tribes in the Dutch, French, and British colonies, decimated by disease and displaced or removed to the West. Tribes on the California coast, colonized by Spain, fared as badly from disease and relocation. Plains groups—both old and newly minted—would hold out in the Great American Desert, largely uncolonized until the nineteenth century; those Indian Wars culminated in 1890 at Wounded Knee and ended in reservations.

The Southwest was different. The settled Native societies survived disease and colonial disruptions—most, but of course not all. The Pueblos famously stayed in place.[9]

We know the Indians we know. The colonists knew the Indians of their particular colonies. Northern Europe—English, Dutch, French—dismissed as "savages" the Natives of easternmost North America. The Spanish knew the cities and civilizations of Mexico and Peru—and, more distantly, the Pueblos of New Mexico. From New Mexico to Cuzco, the Spanish encountered cities and towns that more or less resembled European cities and towns. In contrast, the northern Europeans who colonized the eastern seaboard did not see cities and towns—the Native settlements did not remind the colonists of home. Colonial policies varied, north and south, to fit differing Natives and divergent colonial goals.

The English considered Indians as impediments. The best policy seemed to be removal or extermination. The Natives didn't make good slaves and were quickly replaced, in that role, by Africans. In the South—at least in Mexico— Spain worked with the Native peoples and institutions of government inherited from the conquered empires, and incorporated Natives in the new society—the vast majority of course in the lowest castes as peons, but Native nobility in all but the uppermost colonial classes. Spain had no doubts about European superiority but recognized Aztec and Inca civilizations as worthy of consideration.

After the American Revolution, the leading lights of the young United States (while open to ideas) thought at best that North American Indians were "natural men"—noble savages—and thus an interesting study; or at worst that Indians were simply unredeemable savages, to be removed or eradicated.[10] The Native Southwest, held by enemy Spanish, did not enter into Philadelphian conversations.

Some decades later the Southwest belonged to Mexico, forbidden fruit for foreigners (ask Zeb Pike). Even for Mexico itself, the Southwest seemed a distant frontier, so far from Mexico City, so near to St. Louis. Before the Mexican War of 1846–1848, most (but not all)[11] of the East Coast was effectively unaware of what would thereafter be the nation's new Southwest. It was the distant destination of a few hardy traders on the Santa Fe Trail, but nothing more. The Trail produced modest wealth but little illumination for correspondents in Boston and New York. The Mexican War, however, brought firsthand appreciation of the ancient civilizations of central Mexico, and reinforced the impressions offered by William Prescott's (1843) best-selling *History of the Conquest of Mexico*, which hinted at Aztec ruins in the newly acquired territory of Nuevo Mexico.

The founding of American Anthropology—synonymous, really, with the study of American Indians—came around mid-nineteenth century. Not Southwestern archaeology as such (the Southwest was then barely American), but American Anthropology, which included American Archaeology (these distinctions are important!).[12] Lewis Henry Morgan (1818–1881; Bieder 1986:194–246; Moses 2009) was not alone at the creation, but he is sometimes credited with being "the Father of American Anthropology." It's a complicated paternity: I hold Morgan as a (perhaps "the") Founder, and Franz Boas as more properly the Father in light of Franz's sizable intellectual progeny.[13] Boas trained many students, Morgan only a few: Adolph Bandelier, John Wesley Powell, and Edgar Hewett—none were formally his "students," but these three had more profound (early) effects on Southwestern archaeology than did all Franz's tribe.

Morgan—and this was critically important—established anthropology (and archaeology) as *science* through its inclusion, at his insistence, in the American Association for the Advancement of Science[14] (a tale to which we will return, below). Thus archaeology in the United States began as a science, while archaeology in Europe was widely associated with history—classical archaeology, for example, and the national archaeologies that rose in the late nineteenth century.[15]

Morgan himself became the most significant early interpreter of American Anthropological Archaeology, cited by Darwin, Marx, and Freud—among many others.[16] What did Morgan think about Indians and the Southwest?

Glass Ceilings and Iron Curtains

Morgan was fascinated by Native Americans. From an almost obsessive hobby, he turned more seriously to ethnology—first as a gentleman's avocation, later as profession—but as an independent scholar. He visited many western tribes— west being relative to the nineteenth-century East. His last field work (and his first in the Southwest) was at Aztec Ruins, where Morgan actually did a bit of dirt archaeology. Chaco itself had been mapped and photographed by a few expeditions, and displayed as models at the 1876 Centennial Exposition in Philadelphia,[17] but Morgan's may have been the first Anthropological study of a major Chaco site, which Aztec Ruins is.

Aztec Ruins's name, however, was a red flag to Morgan, a symptom of a particular disorder he wanted to cure: What he (and, soon thereafter, Charles Lummis and Edgar Hewett) called the "Romantic View" of ancient America. The Romantic View encompassed a range of speculations from mysterious Moundbuilders, to Lost Tribes of Israel, to wandering Phoenicians, and so forth;[18] but one trope demanded attention—and provoked Morgan's ire—because it was plausible and widely accepted: Aztecs created the monuments of the Southwest, and then left them for Mexico and glory. That's what Prescott had said; and most educated Easterners read and admired Prescott. Besides, Indians in the Southwest spoke openly of Moctezuma; prewar Mexican maps showed "Aztlan"—the Aztec homelands—about where Chaco sits.[19]

We took the Southwest from Mexico in 1846 in James Polk's war; and then we nationalized its ruins and its prehistory. Morgan (and his student Adolph Bandelier) demolished both Mexican claims and the Romantic View, and asserted that all ruins and all prehistory within the sovereign boundaries of the United States were the work of tribes now residing in the United States. No Phoenicians, no Aztecs, no Mexicans need apply. An Iron Curtain descended across the continent, from San Diego on the Pacific to Brownsville on the Gulf.[20] The United States of America's ancient past was to be understood on strictly American Anthropological terms.[21]

Morgan realized that the ruins at Aztec and Chaco and the mounds of the eastern United States evidenced antiquity—but not history. Native history—if any—was properly the purview of the ethnologist, perhaps embellished a little bit by archaeology. Morgan was adamant that the proper way to study the Indian's past was what he called "the Ethnological Method": That is, starting with ethnology and projecting backwards, logically. Native societies as historically known (or ethnographically "reconstructed") constituted the culmination or end-point of North American prehistory—one might say, tribes of the ethnographic present were the goal of that prehistory. The Ethnological Method would reveal how those societies evolved and developed to their ethnological end-points. Morgan, the father/founder of American Anthropology, laid down the law for Anthropological Archaeologists: "American archaeology must be studied ethnologically; i.e., from the institutions, usages, and mode of life of existing Indian tribes. It is by losing sight of this principle that American Archaeology is in such a low condition, or rather that we scarcely have such a science among us" (Morgan 1880:30).

For Southwestern archaeology, the Ethnological Method is a particularly sinister inherited bias. It assumes that historically or ethnologically known Pueblos were preordained endpoints for developmental histories; and that those histories could only be known through projection or reconstruction from the ethnographic present back into the past. That circular logic denies Native North America any hope of history. No rises, no falls, no deviations from a slow, gradual development from primitive pasts to the tribes encountered at colonization; in the Southwest, Pueblos. I will return to this grievance several times below, and at length in chapter 2.

Morgan thought—like Locke and many others—that the Native tribes of America represented fossilized or preserved versions of much earlier Old World societies. That is, the New World hinted at the primordial Old, ancient Europe of the Stone and Bronze Ages. Morgan developed a ranked series of social stages through which ancient history in Old and New Worlds evolved, from simpler to more complicated, from "savagery" through "barbarism" and finally "civilization"—which meant nations and states like Greece and Rome or, more appropriately, Victoria's England and Franz Joseph's Austria. Morgan was pretty sure that no New World society had ever advanced beyond "barbarism."[22] He certainly saw no "civilizations" in the New World—and that included the Aztec "empire," which he dismissed as Spanish colonial propaganda.[23]

Mexican archaeologists simply ignored (and continue to ignore) Morgan's mistaken pronouncements on Aztecs (Bernal 1980), but north of the border his views dominated and persuaded the small pool of intellectuals then interested in Native prehistory. Even his peculiar notions about Aztecs were widely shared in the American Academy through the first few decades of the twentieth century.

Aztecs were later restored to their former glory, even in gringo eyes. Okay: There were states and empires in old Mexico, but not OUR Natives. American Anthropological Archaeology firmly believed, henceforth and for always: No states north of Mexico! That became a given, a "taken-for-granted assumption," an unquestioned truth—in short, a bias. A Glass Ceiling was lowered over Native American prehistory. No Natives north of Mexico ever rose to the level of "state" or "civilization."

Morgan's views reflect nineteenth-century colonial bias and racist prejudices. He was a product of his times, as are we all; and his times were fairly rough on Indians. The United States was removing tribes as quickly and efficiently as possible, and occupying their lands. Morgan was not entirely happy about that, of course; but he was a part of a colonial society. Many (most?) White Victorian gentlemen were moderately, even benignly racist: "white man's burden" and all that. Morgan concluded that there were no "civilizations" in the New World in part because (he believed) Native Americans lacked the intellectual capacity to produce and sustain civilization (Harris 1968:137–140; Lekson 2010a). But he was still a great friend to Indians, a patron (as it were) of tribal peoples.

Morgan's pronouncements—Glass Ceiling and Iron Curtain—along with his insistence on the primacy of the Ethnological Method became Southwestern archaeology's ground rules, the first few planks of Pueblo Space. Morgan was not a professor; he did not train cohorts of graduate students, like Franz Boas. How did Morgan's ideas pervade the field? Two key, foundational Southwesternists were personally mentored by Morgan, and a third he influenced less directly but just as strongly. Adolph Bandelier worked for Morgan, John Wesley Powell worked with Morgan, and Edgar Hewett worshiped the ground Morgan walked on.[24] (Byron Cummings, Hewett's less-influential ur-archaeological contemporary in Arizona, was also deeply influenced by Morgan; see Bostwick 2006:17.) All three carried forward Morgan's convictions of the evils of romanticism, the primacy of the Ethnological Method, and the upper limits of Native social development well short of the state and civilization—somewhere in Morgan's Middle Barbarism.

Adolph Bandelier, Morgan's most influential student,[25] first questioned his mentor's deflating views of the Aztecs but later accepted them as Gospel—an almost religious conversion, of which Bandelier had several. In an 1885 address honoring Morgan, Bandelier insisted, "The Mexican aborigines [the Aztecs] never knew monarchy previous to the advent of Cortés!" (Bandelier 1885:9; exclamation point original). The Romantic View of the Aztec emperor was merely myth, a Spanish exaggeration. If the Aztecs, with their pyramids and cities, were demoted to communalism and Middle Barbarism, certainly no Native society north of Mexico, with their rude mounds and mud pueblos, could aspire to anything greater. For Bandelier and Powell and Hewett (in declining degrees of orthodoxy), all tribes everywhere in North America were ruled communally and democratically, by elected councils. Middle Barbarism.

Bandelier became Morgan's man in the field.[26] Morgan politicked to have his protégé Bandelier selected by the Archaeological Institute of America to investigate Southwestern ruins—in part, to determine if the Southwest was or was not the Aztec homeland.[27] Bandelier, predictably, came down hard against that Romantic View. After a truly heroic field survey—working one canyon over from Apache battles but somehow never quite making it to Chaco and the Four Corners—Bandelier's monumental *Final Report of Investigations among the Indians of the Southwestern United States* (published 1890–1892) set the tone for Southwestern archaeology. And a dull, flat tone it was, too. His conclusions:

> The picture which can be dimly traced into this past is a very modest and unpretending one. No great cataclysms of nature, no waves of destruction on a large scale, either natural or human, appear to have interrupted the slow and tedious development of the people before the Spaniards came. (Bandelier 1890–1892:592)[28]

John Wesley Powell did not work for Morgan, but he was a dyed-in-the-wool Morganite and (in effect) worked with the Founding Father. While Morgan inserted Anthropology into the Sciences, Powell largely created and then directed the government's Bureau of American Ethnology (BAE), one of two major centers of anthropological activities in the late nineteenth century. And he directed much of the BAE's energies towards the Southwest, rescuing Ethnology from its earlier excesses, such as Frank Hamilton Cushing's theatrical "My Adventures in Zuni."[29]

The other anthropological center was New York with the American Museum of Natural History and Columbia University; this was Franz Boas's territory. Boas did not much care for Morgan's evolutionary cultural stages (Savagery,

Barbarism, Civilization). Boas was more interested in getting into the field to ethnologize surviving Native cultures before they vanished, or changed, or otherwise lost their luster. With the ethnographically known tribes as the historical end-point, Boas shared Morgan's belief that North America was always "simple," and he shared Morgan's faith in the ethnological method as the best means of knowing their past—such as it was. His historical/archaeological interests were directed mainly towards how those tribes came to be, much like Morgan. Boas trained many American Anthropologists of the second and third generations, and inculcated both his version of the Glass Ceiling and the rock-ribbed efficacy of the Ethnological Method.[30]

Morgan laid down the law and to that, at least, Boas agreed: No states north of Mexico! Morgan influenced and Boas trained the turn-of-last-century's first crop of professional anthropologists, who themselves went on to teach at America's universities. Indeed, they taught the professors who taught the professors who taught the professors who taught the professors who taught me. And taught my colleagues. We all were taught Morgan's Glass Ceiling. Today, any suggestion of a Native state within the confines of the United States provokes derision and even censure. I'm not making this up; that was true through the twentieth century and remains largely true in today's American Anthropological Archaeology. Over the Lower 48, the Glass Ceiling remains firmly in place. (And over Alaska too, but perhaps not Hawaii!) The Glass Ceiling survives today in the almost automatic assertion that all ancient societies in the Southwest and Southeast were "intermediate" or "small-scale" or "midlevel" or "stateless" or "prestate"—all of which mean, awkwardly, "not-a-state."

Those were and are the ground rules, set before the start of the twentieth century: The Glass Ceiling and the Iron Curtain. The Glass Ceiling meant every Native society was not-a-state, and instead was tossed into a vast undifferentiated vat of "intermediate" societies. The Iron Curtain meant that no Native society north of Mexico had any significant connections in prehistory with the southern half of the continent and—more importantly—vice versa. In the Southwest, those biases were compounded and reinforced by the Ethnological Method (discussed below).

Those rules were strictly enforced in the Mississippi Valley where great pyramids became "mounds"[31]—as the poet said: A mound's a mound, for a' that. But the Curtain and the Ceiling were sometimes a bit awkward in the Southwest, with its well-known colonial connections to Old Mexico (deep? shallow?) and its impressive ruins—ancient "great houses" such as Casa Grande, Casas Grandes, and Chaco Canyon. We might dismiss the Mississippi's pyramids as mere mounds, but the Southwestern ruins looked uncomfortably like real architecture. The Southwest's "lost cities" inflamed (or at least intrigued) the public imagination, and it was necessary to repeatedly tamp down any romantic fires.

In short, to normalize Mesa Verde and Chaco and Taos. At first, this was done by dismissing modern Pueblos as crude copies of Spanish farming villages; but that dismissal melted away with the discovery of impressive pre-Columbian ruins at Mesa Verde and Chaco. Our engagement with "pueblo" architecture became...complicated. Pueblos and pueblo ruins looked like real buildings—and as we shall see, buildings in Santa Fe soon began to look like Pueblos, in a very deliberate creation of a unique Southwestern genius loci. We appropriated the architecture and slathered over it—like tan stucco dripped on a Santa Fe Victorian house—a carefully crafted White-wash: the Pueblo Mystique and Pueblo Style, to which we will soon turn. But first: What does "pueblo" mean?

¿ Qué es Pueblo?

One meaning—today and in the sixteenth century—of the Spanish word *pueblo* is "town," and that (we are told) was its application to the Native town-dwellers of the northern Southwest. One size fits all: They are all Pueblos.

The Tiwa speakers of Taos, the Keres speakers of Acoma, the Zuni speakers of Halona:wa, the Hopi speakers of Mishongnovi, and other groups in forty or so separate towns—more than 60,000 human beings today, speaking six different languages from four completely different language families. That's today. When the Spanish arrived around 1600 there was at least one more language and a lot more people, living in seventy-plus towns scattered over an area of 72,000 sq km (28,000 sq mi).[32] Each town (and each clan within each town) has its own particular history, customs, traditions, and so forth. For example, the social organizations and kinship systems of Hopi villages on the west are famously quite different from those of Rio Grande villages on the east. Is there a generic term that fits all those different societies? "Pueblo." Not a Native term: A colonial and later an anthropological category.

"Pueblo" and its changing meanings introduce a theme which will carry through chapter 2 and much of the rest of the book: How terms come into the Southwest and are changed by (the yet-to-be-defined) Pueblo Space—made to fit Pueblo Space. "Pueblo" began as an administrative term, became a faux-ethnic label, and ended up a brand. The shifting meaning of "pueblo" introduces Pueblo Space, its cause and its effects.

As the colonial frontier moved north from central Mexico, Spanish authorities contrasted farming towns and villages of *Indios Pueblo* to *Indios Barbaros* who moved much and planted little—Apaches and Navajos, for example.[33] One colonial administrative strategy worked for town-dwelling Pueblos, quite another worked (sometimes) for *Indios Barbaros*. So we have pueblos Pueblos, right? The town-dwelling Town Indians.

Things were probably a bit more complicated than that. "Pueblo" in early colonial Mexico meant more than just "town"; it also (and often) referenced the meaning "people": A community of people.[34] There was a town, of course—central in Spanish and (presumably) Native eyes—but "pueblo" went beyond the darkness at the edge of towns to encompass lands and resources and rural populations which comprised the actual community. Plus—very importantly—the social institutions which held it all together, including governance or *ayuntamiento*. So more than just town or even community: "Pueblo" meant polity.[35]

Was "Pueblo" *as a political unit* how the Spanish originally categorized the settled farming societies of Nuevo Mexico? Why not?—that's what the word meant early on, in Mexico. The Spanish clearly recognized that the world of the Indians of northern New Mexico expanded far beyond their towns (thus the early land grants) and the Spanish recognized that they had governance—they had captains, well or badly obeyed.

The Spanish, too, recognized the linguistic and cultural diversity of those many Pueblos. The term "pueblo" typically preceded an ethnic identity: "Pueblo de Acoma," for example. The pueblo of Chimayo was Hispanic; the pueblo of Cochiti was Native. Spanish and Mexican authorities knew which was which. With the influx of ignorant Americans, "Pueblo" became a broad but restricted identification of Native farming villages of New Mexico and northern Arizona (which remained a single administrative unit until Arizona calved off of New Mexico in 1863). The term "pueblo" then became an administrative/ethnic category, repurposed for American administration.

The Americans redefined all kinds of things. "Hopi," for example, was created by American fiat. An American official announced that twenty-plus Hopi-speaking towns were henceforth a single, unified tribe or nation. This came as news to the villagers; despite their shared language, the towns did not always get along (ask Awatovi).

As noted above, the various societies we call "Pueblo" vary famously in social structure, west to east. But (in our eyes) Pueblos are more like each other than they are like neighboring tribes (Navajos, Apaches, Utes, the Piman and Yuman tribes of southern Arizona, Plains peoples, and others). Crunched in a giant statistical matrix of ethnographic data on American Indian tribes, Pueblos cluster together.[36] So, despite their many differences, "Pueblo" has long been recognized in American Anthropology as a cultural unit.[37] For example, a standard reference, the *Atlas of World Cultures*, was structured largely on linguistic lines. An exception was made for Pueblos: "This province consists of peoples who are united by sedentary life in pueblos despite the diverse languages they speak."[38] There's a circularity here that reflects the shifting meaning of the word: Pueblos in their variety are "Pueblo" as an ethnicity.

Four languages in a Culture (in the old Anthropological usage) is rather remarkable, as Timothy Kohler notes in his thoughtful paper on this problem, "How the Pueblos Got Their Sprachbund":

The situation we see in the Pueblo Southwest contrasts with the common pattern across the traditional world…. worldwide, languages were more widespread than cultures; that is, in general, there were many cultures per language. In the Puebloan Southwest, by contrast, there were many languages per culture. This pattern therefore deserves some explanation. (Kohler 2013:213)[39]

There are, to be sure, strong similarities from Pueblo to Pueblo, including (and certainly not limited to) shared loan-words, clan names, social structures, and ideologies. And back into pre-history: A sameness across distance. Kohler sees two main causes for the shared cultural characteristics from 600 to 1300: Frequent movements between and among subregions and adaptation of varied populations to similar environments ("convergent evolution"), with the former—movement—perhaps more important than the latter.[40] Both were crucial, but I would add another, not insignificant: top-down effects of the Chaco-Aztec polity, and widespread reactions against it after 1300—a tale told in chapter 3.[41]

For American Anthropological Archaeology, "Pueblo" was the first but not the last term that came into the Southwest meaning one thing, then modified and bent to fit our needs and notions—as we will see in chapter 2. Fit to Pueblo Space. What is Pueblo Space, exactly? To get to Pueblo Space, we must follow "Pueblo" through a series of transubstantiations in the City of Holy Faith.

Pueblo Mystique, Pueblo Style

"Pueblo Space" has a tangled provenance, part Anthropology, part pop culture. Pop first: Pueblo Space derived from what critics and historians have called "Pueblo Mystique" and, later, "Santa Fe Style" or "Pueblo Style." These have only tenuous connections with Pueblo people; they were creations of White people in the late nineteenth and early twentieth centuries in Santa Fe (and, to some extent, in Chicago).

This section sketches cultural histories that could easily fill a book.[42] I will not attempt a full recounting of the modern intellectual, artistic, commercial, and political histories of northern New Mexico; I aim mainly at the effect of "Pueblo Mystique" on American Anthropological Archaeology. Archaeology played a key role in the creation of the Mystique, and archaeology was and continues to be recursively influenced by it, to the detriment of our interpretations and understandings.

I've borrowed "Pueblo Mystique" from historian Richard Frost's (1980) article "The Romantic Inflation of Pueblo Culture," but Frost was not the first or last to use the term, often with irony or even ridicule. I, too, ridicule the Mystique—but I am NOT ridiculing Pueblos, rather I am ridiculing what White people have said about Pueblos.

The Mystique impacts archaeology, but my archaeological colleagues are not bedazzled by it. We know hooey when we see it: Kokopellis, kachinas, kiva fireplaces, and all the claptrap of Santa Fe. But archaeology is still affected by the Pueblo Mystique: the baroque creation of the Gilded Age, over many decades has become a diffuse zeitgeist we paste on the past, the vague notions of Pueblo Space.[43] Mystique is mystical; Space is operational. First, a summary of Space; then a history of the Mystique, and its contribution to Space.

Pueblo Space, quite simply, is the boundaries and conventions within which Southwest archaeology operates. We eliminate ideas and speculations as outside the Space, outside the box. Elizabeth Brandt (1994:9) concisely defined the archaeological vision of Pueblos in the late twentieth century: "Pueblo societies as primarily egalitarian, small-scale, autonomous communities with simple decision-making, which lacked social ranking and centralized coercive political authority." Pueblo Space is that, plus a good bit of residual Mystique. The Mystique, then, encompassed all of Brandt's anthropological stuff, but adds the philosophical:

Self-sufficient, inward-looking
Communal, egalitarian
Spiritual, peaceful
Eternal, unchanging

I submit that Pueblo Space weaves those more ethereal qualities of the Pueblo Mystique in among the woofs and warps of Anthropological facts.

Those are all very good qualities, and I'm sure that Pueblo people aspire to them when possible. There can be no doubt that Pueblo societies are spiritual, humble, and communal. But, in a way, Pueblo peoples' qualities and intentions are irrelevant. The Mystique is by, for, and of White people. AGAIN: PLEASE NOTE THAT I AM NOT QUESTIONING OR DISPARAGING PUEBLOS; I AM QUESTIONING AND DISPARAGING WHITE PEOPLE—MY PEOPLE.

The Mystique holds that Pueblo philosophies are constituted in such a way that Pueblo people achieved all those good things; and if we understand those philosophies and adopt their principles, we White people can be all those things.[44] Through the years, the Mystique became more than marketing, more than philosophy: It became mystical. Pueblos are good to think.[45] That's a big part of Santa Fe Style: Just living in that Mystique brings peace,[46] and if it has a kiva fireplace and a dirt road, you can add a zero to the asking price. When I was a young man, Americans cured anomie with Jehovah and Jim Beam; then it was chardonnay and therapy; today it's Adderall and irony. In Santa Fe—the City Different—anomie is treated with drink, drugs, and irony, to be sure; but also with Pueblo Mystique and noodling flute music.

How we perceived, appreciated, and appropriated "Pueblo" in art, architecture, and letters is a matter of considerable study, a small but recognizable niche in cultural studies.[47] "The pueblos have proven to be endlessly malleable in the American imagination," notes Jerold Auerbach (2006). It began in the Gilded Age, with men of substance, community leaders of Santa Fe, in the very early twentieth century. A small group of White people in Santa Fe—including several famous archaeologists—created an idealized vision of "Pueblos" to sell New Mexico to the rest of the country and, perhaps, to the world.[48] They invented traditions to market their fair city.[49] Then railroad sharps in Chicago took it to the masses.

They invented an idealized notion of "Pueblo" that emphasized things they liked, ignored things they didn't, and layered on marketing notions that helped it all go down. Some of this invention embroidered or spun Anthropological facts, as far as non-Pueblo people can know Pueblo facts. Other inventions had little or nothing to do with actual Pueblos: The old Spanish corner fireplaces—*fogón*—became "kiva fireplaces." Pueblo people didn't ask to be idealized, even in false stereotype; and many Pueblo people I've spoken to are either amused or annoyed by it (e.g., Swentzell 2003).

"The American Southwest has functioned as an Anglo cultural fantasy for more than a century" (Goodman 2002). Through time, Pueblo Mystique became Pueblo Style. In the 1910s, 1920s, and 1930s, artists, architects, journalists, businessmen, educators, civic leaders, and other taste-makers deliberately created the Pueblo Style to market Santa Fe.[50] And—to a lesser degree—Taos. Archaeologists were present at the creation: Edgar Hewett, Kenneth Chapman (Munson 2008), Jesse Nusbaum (Shapiro 2017), Sylvanus Morley (Wilson 2014: 52–63), and others. More than merely present, archaeology drove the deeper myth-making which, recursively, now defines the area in which archaeology works—the Pueblo Space.

Edgar L. Hewett was at the center of it. Richard Frost calls Hewett "the leading institutional impresario of the Pueblo mystique," and he's quite right. Hewett was the big fish in the very small pond of New Mexico archaeology, both by personality and by default. Many archaeologists who worked in New Mexico and the Southwest came from and returned to the East Coast, to Washington or Boston or New York. Hewett stayed here—unless he was jet-setting on the slow coach to his several extraterritorial interests in California, Canada, and the Cosmos Club in the District of Columbia. Hewett built a cabal of local collaborators, initially Adolph Bandelier (Morgan's student and Hewett's mentor) and journalist Charles Lummis (Padget 1995; Thompson 2001). As noted above, their initial intentions were scholarly: They sought to defeat "the romantic school" of American pre-history (Bandelier 1885) and establish a scientific pre-history. By the late nineteenth century, Lost Tribes and Phoenicians were largely discredited; the romantic school's principle sin was the suggestion that Native societies north of Mexico might be something other than Morgan's communal democracies, and might indeed be related historically to Aztecs. Bandelier took care of that in his (1890–1892) *Final Report of Investigations among the Indians of the Southwestern United States* (see also Bandelier 1992) and decamped for Peru. Lummis (e.g., 1893) went west to L.A., where he founded the Southwest Museum. But he kept a journalistic oar in New Mexico's water.

That left Edgar Hewett in New Mexico, fighting the good fight, last of the three original amigos. Among Santa Fe's movers and shakers (a dozen? it was a small town), Hewett was impressive: Ex-president of the teacher's college in Las Vegas, New Mexico; Doctor of Science from the University of Geneva; a Washington, DC, player, responsible for the Antiquities Act of 1906;[51] and a cultural empire-builder.[52]

East Coast archaeologists didn't like him ("bumpkin" pretty much sums it up),[53] but what of that? They were far away in Cambridge or on DuPont Circle or around Central Park. In Santa Fe, Hewett was the archaeologist of record. A Western alpha male, strong but far from silent, Hewett emerged as "a seminal figure in the stylistic and cultural revolution that marked Santa Fe's development"; in particular, "his awareness of the role of archaeology, the broader place of anthropology and the arts...afforded him a leading place in the creation of a new direction for Santa Fe" (Tobias and Woodhouse 2001:73, 84). Richard Frost (1980:57) tells us that Hewett "convince[d] the civic leaders of Santa Fe that historically bona fide local color could be made profitable through his School of American Archaeology."

Santa Fe—the City Different[54]—has become a certified World Class Destination. But that's today: In the early decades of the twentieth century, Santa Fe was a dusty backwater. It was, of course, the capital of old New Mexico. But old New Mexico was no great prize: Low-value loot scooped up (along with Arizona) during the Mexican War so our railroads could run a southern, flat, snow-free route to higher-value California. The civilized coasts, East and West, wrinkled their patrician noses at the Southwest.[55] It was Mexican, it was Catholic, it was desert, it was savage. At the turn of the last century, almost no one beyond Anthropologists and Indian Agents cared much about Pueblo Indians, or knew anything about Chaco, although many had heard of Mesa Verde and its Aztec artifacts (Brandes 1960)!

Santa Fe itself in 1900 was famously old—older than Philadelphia!—but that's about all it had going for it: A jumble of winding, narrow streets, dusty or muddy depending on weather, lined by blank, mud-plastered walls with few doors or windows. Empty army quarters and a few dozen Victorian homes demonstrated the U.S. presence, along with assorted offices and stores. Santa Fe had no real industries beyond territorial government—a small establishment, and not a financial force. The decrepit Palace of the Governors, a courthouse, a plaza, and an incongruously ostentatious cathedral were the principal public monuments.[56] And five thousand souls—not much bigger than eleventh-century Chaco Canyon.

Santa Fe was backward and remote.[57] It was not even a stop on its own rail-road—the Atchison, Topeka, and Santa Fe. The AT&SF passed it by. A spur line ran from the station at Lamy fifteen miles to the capital. The city that bene-fited from the AT&SF was Albuquerque; the rails ran right through the city, separating Old Town from New Town. With twice as many people as Santa Fe, Albuquerque boasted electric street cars and the University of New Mexico.[58] It was thoroughly modern—at least, in the minds of its civic leaders. Those same civic leaders thought that perhaps it was time to shift the state capital from dusty, inaccessible, backwards-looking Santa Fe to booming bustling Albuquerque (Tobias and Woodhouse 2001:29–35).

The city fathers of Santa Fe were alarmed. Meetings were held, ideas pro-posed, actions planned. Let Albuquerque be the commercial hub, Santa Fe would be the cultural capital—and thus retain the political capital, too.[59] But... what culture? New Mexico famously boasted three: Anglo, Spanish, and Indian.

Albuquerque made its choice: Its Anglo culture was aggressively modern and progressive—at least in New Town. (Albuquerque later tore down most of Old Town.) Santa Fe couldn't compete with Anglo culture: Its Anglo heritage was shallow and transplanted, and not very impressive.[60] And, indeed, not very savory. The biggest Anglo news out of the capital was the Santa Fe Ring: A circle of businessmen and politicians who fleeced New Mexicans of all three cultures, equal opportunity robbers. The Ring's activities made the newspapers in New York. That was Santa Fe's Anglo culture, at the turn of last century: Nothing to brag about there.

Much more than Albuquerque, Santa Fe enjoyed its Spanish past, real and fictive.[61] Lummis was a huge fan of old New Mexico and its Spanish heritage (Lummis 1893). In Spanish heritage, Albuquerque was parvenu, a minor farm-ing village elevated by the AT&SF. Santa Fe decided to market its Hispanic, colonial past, and thus began the first branding of "Santa Fe Style." (I do not know when that term first appeared or who coined it.) The Santa Fe Style was originally Spanish—the first major marketing project was the restoration of the Governor's Palace, which was to look "as nearly as possible in harmony with the Spanish architecture of the period" (Tobias and Woodhouse 2001:73).[62] That enthusiasm carried over into Hewett's exhibit halls at the Panama-California Exposition in San Diego in 1915[63] and the New Mexico Art Museum in 1917—those buildings mimicked New Mexico Mission churches. Local interests made Colonial Spanish–revival style the Santa Fe standard.[64]

The old Spanish Fiesta was revived and reinvented (by Anglos) about that same time. The Fiesta was an autumn celebration of the 1692 reconquest of Santa Fe after the Pueblo Revolt expelled the Spanish—nothing to do with Anglos and hardly a happy event for Indians. The ancient and venerated icon

La Conquistadora (officially, Our Lady of the Rosary) was brought out from its chapel in Santa Fe's incongruous cathedral and paraded around the Plaza. Everybody had a good time. The Fiesta was an old (that is, real) tradition, but by the turn of the nineteenth century it was fading, and lapsed completely by World War I. After the war, the Fiesta was dusted off for marketing. "The Santa Fe Fiesta celebration, which was inactive between 1913 and 1918…was revived in 1919 and developed under the auspices of [Hewett's] Museum of New Mexico" (Lovato 2004:25). Although a few Indians participated, Hewett's Fiesta clearly intended—at least initially—to revive the old Spanish event.[65]

Santa Fe marketed its Spanish history to the world, but the world wasn't buying. We'd just fought a war with Spain, and there was that old Black Legend thing.[66] Anyway, if New Yorkers wanted Old Spanish, they could hop on Henry Flager's comfortable trains and ride down to Florida, where St. Augustine had a real Spanish *castillo*, real Spanish moss, and possibly a real Fountain of Youth! So, too, on the West Coast: if San Franciscans wanted Spanish, they had St. Junipero's Spanish missions, which were being restored, or Balboa Park (Christman 1985). Why go to New Mexico to see dusty, decrepit, flat-roofed mud adobes, when red tiles, arched doorways, bell towers, and Baroque frippery were an easy rail or auto ride away?

Santa Fe recalibrated. If not Spanish, then maybe Indian? Hewett and others shifted the emphasis from Hispanic to Native heritage. And specifically, to Pueblos.[67] Apaches and Navajos had name recognition, but perhaps not the sort to bring visitors—recall that the Indian Wars ended only in the 1890s. But Pueblos were not inherently newsworthy. The defeat of the "romantic school" had taken care of that: No Aztec civilizations, no pyramids, no monuments. Pueblos lived peacefully in small villages, farmed, and prayed in Catholic churches; many spoke Spanish, and much of their culture *looked* like New Mexican Spanish— which, as noted above, lacked the charm and refinement of California or Florida Spanish. Among the potential national audience, "apart from a pervasive belief that the Pueblos worshiped snakes and Montezuma, and were closely related to the Aztecs, there was little romance about them" (Frost 1980:5). Pueblos needed an agent, and Hewett was the man.[68] But no Montezuma, no Aztecs! Hewett insisted those be no part of his Pueblos.

Archaeology, not ethnology or art, led the way.[69] The Pueblo present could be made to seem exotic (worshiping snakes?), but the Pueblo past—if not Aztec—was surely mysterious. Edgar Hewett had many Pueblo friends and spent a lot of time at Pueblos, but—unlike the early anthropologists discussed in the next section—he considered himself first and foremost an archaeologist, not an ethnologist-turned-archaeologist (as were many of the pioneer archaeologists).

In Santa Fe, Hewett had built up a remarkable infrastructure for archaeology and ethnology. He took the Museum of New Mexico from a cupboard in the Governor's Palace to a regional showpiece.[70] Even more central to American

Anthropological Archaeology in the Southwest, Hewett hijacked the Archaeological Institute of America's proposed School of American Archaeology[71]—originally intended for Mexico City—and brought it to Santa Fe.[72] Two of the biggest culture clubs in town, and Hewett ran both.

The Pueblos present and past had to be made exceptional, marketable. Hewett and Lummis (and many others, such as Ruth Benedict and John Collier, discussed below) wrote books and essays and magazine articles emphasizing Pueblo exceptionalism[73]—a theme to which we will return. You won't see anything like this anywhere else in the United States—in the world—so come to New Mexico and see Pueblos! Fred Harvey (who we will also meet shortly) could take you from the modern comforts of the AT&SF sleeper car, and drive you into another, older, exotic world of the Pueblo Mystique.

Santa Fe went Pueblo.[74] The somewhat vague and certainly ethereal Pueblo Mystique was codified as Pueblo Style. "Pueblo" had indeed become a brand.

Local Hispanics largely withdrew from the Fiesta, leaving Anglos and—importantly—an uptick in invited Indians.[75] An Indian art market began as a sideshow but soon became a major feature of Fiesta, and then (much later) eclipsed it entirely (Bernstein 2012). The terraced Pueblo style entered Santa Fe architecture around 1917, and Spanish themes in Santa Fe style gave way to Pueblo by the 1930s—Santa Fe Style became Pueblo Style, as Santa Fe's signature look is usually called today (C. Wilson 1997:136–138). It went to absurd extremes: Mud-colored stucco cascaded over gabled Victorian houses, and faux *vigas* bristled from every roofline. More and more buildings nodded to terraced Pueblo forms rather than Spanish ranchos;[76] Acoma-style "kiva ladders" appeared everywhere, stairways to nowhere; *fogónes*, as noted above, became "kiva fireplaces." Hewett and Co. made it all Pueblo, all the time—and it worked! Santa Fe and the Pueblos that surround it became tourist destinations.

It wasn't just the Pueblo style, of course; it was the Pueblos themselves. Anybody anywhere could build Pueblo-style; two faux Pueblos were built around this time near Denver. But they were empty without people, Pueblo people.[77] Santa Fe had Pueblo people, and marketed them mercilessly.

What did Hewett actually think about Pueblo societies? Hewett was no ethnologist; he knew what he knew from personal observation, informed by Morgan's theories. Hewett was a public intellectual. He held Pueblos up as exemplars in uncertain times, in a world recovering from the horrors of World War I, economic depression, and the alarming rise of dictators. Hewett viewed the Pueblos as primordial democracies (or, perhaps, republics), city-states to rival ancient Athens. "No two villages nor group of villages ever came under a common authority or formed a state. There is not the faintest tradition of a 'ruler' over the whole body of Pueblos, nor an organization of the people of this vast area under a common government" (Hewett 1930:71). He probably knew better, but it made good copy.

Half of his 1930 book, *Ancient Life in the American Southwest* (written for the broader public), was devoted to Pueblos: Egalitarian and democratic and communal—Hewett was, after all, a doctrinaire Morganite.[78] "The perfectly ordered community was the aim and end and agency of government. All the people participated in all the community activities, government, building, worshiping, making war when combat became inevitable" (Hewett 1930:43). For Hewett, except when attacked by outsiders, Pueblos were actively peaceful. And prayerful: Hewett recognized and applauded the deep interconnections of religion and every aspect of Pueblo life. "The religious life of the Pueblos is the key to their existence. Their arts, industries, social structure, government, flow in orderly sequence from their beliefs concerning nature and deific power" (Hewett 1930: 74). He recounted an example of their contemplative ethos: "When matters of great moment were up for consideration in council it was his practice (common to head men of the village) to retire to that sanctuary (kiva or estufa) for days at a time" (Hewett 1930:94). He marked and marketed their spirituality. "The Pueblo world is a singularly inviting one. There is in it the simplicity and serenity and charm of a time to us long dead—with them, too sacred to let go. In it too, there is a suggestion of a world of spirituality and grace to which we have not yet attained" (Hewett 1930:161). And it worked: "By the 1920s, in the popular mind the Pueblos were the most interesting of the American Indian tribes" (Frost 1980:5).[79]

Low-hanging fruit. Hewett and Co., having pruned and watered that tree, plucked first.[80] But there was fruit aplenty left for Fred Harvey, with his chain of AT&SF railroad restaurants and hotel/museums, and his Indian Detours which took travelers into the backcountry—a carefully plotted backcountry.[81] AT&SF marketers buzzed from corporate headquarters in Chicago.[82] He built it, and they came: Tourism sparked civic and regional development; and even more so after automobile tourism replaced trains (Wrobel and Long 2001; Smith and Winkler 2005). The money did not exactly roll in, but Santa Fe rose in the national eye and regained its place atop the small world of New Mexico. Most importantly, it remained the state's capital. The City Fathers of Albuquerque lost that battle, and Santa Fe won.

But at what cost? Marta Weigle—in her article "Desert to Disney World"—acidly comments on the manipulation of the ancient Southwest: "In commodifying the Indian Southwest as a tourist or secular pilgrimage center, Santa Fe/Harvey corporate image-makers transformed it into an archaeological holy land" (Weigle 1989:133). Beyond the Pueblos themselves, Hewett saw the cultural and commercial possibilities of their mysterious past: Ruins, ruins, ruins.

The romance built around ancient ruins played a central role in the invention of the Southwest and the creation of Pueblo Space. "Some ancient societies, just like rock bands, attract groupies. While Egypt takes pride of place in this regard, the Classic Maya run a close second" (Webster 2006:129). The Southwest might well be third, however distant.

Ruins were interesting diversions on early Harvey Detours, but they could be made into objects of awe and wonder. The role of archaeological sites and ruins in the rise of Pueblo Space was...complicated. Everyone had heard of Mesa Verde, America's answer to King Tut; but that park (established in 1906) was in remote southwestern Colorado. Hewett had his eyes on the prize: Chaco Canyon, the most spectacular archaeological district in New Mexico. Largely due to Hewett's lobbying, Chaco became a Park Service unit in 1907; but it was perhaps even harder to visit, to reach, than Mesa Verde. Chaco could not serve Santa Fe's purposes until the midcentury rise of automobile tourism. And even then, Chaco was only for the hardy, more suited for Jeeps and Dodge trucks than Oldsmobiles and Chryslers.

Santa Fe was short on presentable ruins, ruins to rival Mesa Verde; the nearest gawk-worthy vanished cities were Pecos (a State Monument in 1935 and a National Monument in 1965), 25 miles to the east on the old Santa Fe Trail. The most visible parts of Pecos were historic, a town abandoned in the late nineteenth century. Its most impressive pile was a ruined Spanish church. Evocative, but not sufficiently mysterious: A church was, after all, a church.

The prehistoric archaeology of the Pajarito Plateau had far more mystery, which Hewett's ham-fisted excavations did little to elucidate. That was alright: What was required was mystification, not illumination. Pajarito sites could be (and were) called cliff-dwellings—but that only worked if you'd never seen real cliff-dwellings at Mesa Verde. Which was how Hewett wanted it to work: See Santa Fe, not Mesa Verde.

To be fair, Hewett promoted ruins in general[83]—he helped lay out the boundaries of Mesa Verde—but his particular cause (almost an obsession) was "Pajarito Park," the area of Hewett's most extensive field work while crafting Pueblo Style, long before his later campaigns at Chaco Canyon. Even prior to his work on the Antiquities Act, Hewett promoted an archaeological "Pajarito Park" in Washington.[84] Frustrated by Colorado's successful lobbying for Mesa Verde, Hewett pumped the Pajarito as having "the largest cliff houses," and for a while his Pajarito Park was renamed "Cliff Dwellers Park" (Mathien 1993:28). To little effect: After a long frustrating battle,[85] the Pajarito was made a much-reduced Bandelier National Monument in 1916. Bandelier became the ruins of choice for Santa Fe and its promoters, especially after good roads reached Los Alamos and the monument after World War II.

James Snead (2002:19) notes that ruins and archaeology "played a central role in the construction of a new identity for the Southwest."[86] Hewett's huckstering did the trick, but as more and better professionals entered the archaeological lists, Southwestern archaeology itself seemed to back away; by mid-century, archaeologists eschewed myth-making. Indeed, archaeological Culture History of that era was deliberately dry and dull. After Hewett's era, archaeologists seldom doubled as civic boosters. But the regional momentum was set: Pueblo Mystique and Pueblo Style seeped into archaeology, forming the social, economic, and intellectual environments in which archaeology worked. If Morgan's Ceiling, Curtain, and Ethnological Method were the framework of Pueblo Space, the interior décor was pure Pueblo Style. More on this—much more—below and in chapter 2.

The Pueblo Mystique affected American intellectual life at levels higher than lowly archaeology.[87] Two examples, out of many possible examples, follow: The first, Ruth Benedict, an anthropologist and public intellectual; the second, John Collier, an Indian expert and high-level federal administrator.

Ruth Benedict[88] was a Boas-trained ethnologist, part of a line or triangle (with various knots and entanglements, personal and professional) that included Margaret Mead and Ruth Bunzel. As a public anthropologist, Benedict was second in stature only to Mead. Benedict's (1934) enormously successful book, *Patterns of Culture*, brought Pueblo Mystique to intellectuals and educated readers around the world.

Benedict presented the Pueblos much as had Hewett—although she would not have welcomed that association. Benedict was a Boas-trained ethnographer. She had little use for the self-taught efforts of Edgar Hewett or indeed for archaeology, though her portrayal of Pueblos (in her case, Zuni) mirrored Hewett's. In sum: Spiritual, deeply engaged in community ceremony, sober, communal, egalitarian, peaceful[89]—much like the Mystique. *Patterns of Culture* sold well over a million copies in a dozen different languages.[90] It's still in print: *Patterns of Culture* was repeatedly republished—most recently in 2006—with a series of prefaces by eminent anthropologists (Franz Boas, Margaret Mead, Mary Catherine Bateson, Louise Lamphere). Benedict's ethnography has not stood the test of time, questioned and criticized by later ethnologists,[91] but her version of the Mystique reached millions and millions of readers and demonstrably influenced American intellectual life. By the legerdemain of the term "Pueblo"—an elastic and encompassing ethnicity—the characteristics she saw at Zuni were extended to all the many Pueblos.[92] The spirituality and grace appealed very strongly to writers and artists and everyday people disillusioned by the horrors of World War I.[93] Benedict's vision of the Southwest was arguably the most influential anthropological work to ever come out of the region.

Among those was John Collier, a social worker who rose, ultimately, to be Franklin Roosevelt's Commissioner of Indian Affairs (1933–1945) and creator of the "Indian New Deal"—arguably the most significant Indian administrator of the twentieth century.[94] In 1920, long before his D.C. gig, Collier was introduced to Taos Pueblo by Mabel Dodge Luhan (then Mabel Dodge Sterne, who deserves a chapter here but won't get it). He was entranced—and I use the word "entranced" with purpose. Earlier in life, Collier had a transcendent experience of a utopian future, brought on by his discovery, at age seventeen, of Walt Whitman (Collier 1947:19). He was looking for a reality to match Whitman's art. At Taos, he found his vision in the Pueblos.[95] "Collier was transported with joy: At last he was home.... Could not white civilization, war-torn and soul-sick, dying of individualism and materialism, learn from the Pueblo Indians? Collier believed it was necessary" (Frost 1980:59). He constantly promoted his rarified vision of the Pueblos, but did not actually publish books on the subject until the late forties—after the horrors of a Second World War.[96] Collier's *chef d'oeuvre* was *Patterns and Ceremonials of the Indians of the Southwest*, published in 1949 "in a limited, deluxe edition with more than a hundred lithographs." He revised and republished it in a mass-market paperback (sans lithographs) in 1962, as *On the Gleaming Way*. (As we shall see, the '60s saw a boom in popular books about the Pueblos.) Collier presented the Southwest and its Pueblos as "a magnetic center" drawing seekers from around the globe.[97] His admiration for the Pueblos was almost mystical: Their nonlinear sense of time, their deep spiritualism, their conservation of the land, and their communalism (which he refers to as "pluralistic unity"),[98] which he saw as the world's hope.[99] Democracy, he asserts, was the primordial state of all humanity; the communalism of village life. But in the twentieth century, "the local community, for most Western men, dissolved. The great society and world community, for all men, unattained.... There is no hope, except in the re-attainment of community" (Collier 1962:161). The Pueblos were more than a model; they were in fact the solution: "Here the structure and dynamics and inwardness of the ancient world-wide village community can be precisely known, and here can be known the processes of change which do not diminish, but deepen, the spiritual core" (Collier 1962:162). The Pueblo Mystique!

Writers like Benedict and Collier—public intellectuals—burnished the Mystique, and offered it to the reading public. The Mystique was about to go public, even global. The hand-crafted Pueblo Style of Hewett's Santa Fe would soon become a mass-market commodity.

Hippies and Hopis

Ruth Benedict's psycho-pastiche of Pueblos was, I believe, the most influential account from the Southwest written by a licensed, professional anthropologist. A few other accessible accounts—Hewett's, for example—were credentialed; and writers like Collier had cred if not credential.

But credentials were unnecessary: With Pueblo Mystique and Pueblo Style, "Pueblo" had gone public. Journalists and travel writers popularized Pueblos.

National Geographic ran picture spreads, and color plates of Neil Judd's excavations at Chaco and Earl Morris's at Canyon de Chelly. By midcentury, the Pueblos were national, and increasingly international: Gustaf Nordenskiöld brought Mesa Verde to Scandinavia in 1892; Aby Warburg (whom we meet again in chapter 6) pilgrimaged from Berlin to Hopi in 1895; Jung came to Taos in 1925 to meet with Pueblo elders, particularly a gentleman named Ochwiay Biano ("Chief Mountain Lake"). Jung concluded that Pueblo people had a firm grip on their archetypes. Not only the living Pueblos: The Cliff Dwellers of Mesa Verde were known around the world.

John Collier's *On the Gleaming Way* was only one of a flurry of midcentury popular accounts of the Pueblo Mystique. Gifted amateurs—Frank Waters, Harold Courlander, and Thomas Mails—produced persuasive, popular Pueblo portraits, most notably of Hopi.[100] Their accounts strayed far from ethnographic "truth" but this was the West: When legend becomes fact, print the legend.

Frank Waters (1902–1992) was a Southwestern novelist and the author of *Book of the Hopi* (1963). *Book of the Hopi* claimed to transcribe Hopi traditions told by Oscar White Bear Fredericks and other Hopi sources.[101] Raised in Colorado Springs, Waters visited Taos in the 1940s, where Mabel Dodge Luhan welcomed him into her circle. After a stint in the nuclear weapons business at Los Alamos (among other posts and positions), he lived out his life as a literary lion among Taoseños. Waters reportedly watched a hundred A-bombs bloom (Livingston 2013).

Waters dropped his bomb—*Book of the Hopi*—in 1963, the same year the Beatles dropped theirs ("I Want to Hold Your Hand"), Dylan his ("Blowin' in the Wind"), and Sam Cooke his ("A Change Is Gonna Come"). Early signs of the counterculture: A few years later, Hippies walked among us.

Hippies really liked Hopis—the Hopis of Waters's book.[102] Published by a good house (Penguin), it "had a cult following in the '60s" (Livingston 2013).[103] Patchouli pilgrims appeared on the Mesas—lost White brothers and sisters? The Hopi Traditionalist Movement and many individual tribal members were first polite, then manipulative, and finally exasperated.[104]

John Collier Jr., son of the visionary Commissioner of Indian Affairs, extolled Pueblo virtues in an early 'Frisco hippie 'zine through essays and poems. "Collier's [junior, channeling senior?] image of the Pueblo here—as self-possessed, peaceful, content, childlike, deeply rooted in place, spiritually connected to the natural world—neatly summarized the appeal of Indianness to the 'long-hair, Beatniks, and Hippies'" (S. Smith 2012:68). "Kivas" appeared in San Francisco vacant lots.

Enthusiasm produced plans for a "Hopi-Hippie Be-In" at the Grand Canyon during the summer solstice of 1967. A contingent of Hippies met with Hopi leaders at Hotevilla to pitch their Be-In. Hopis be out: "They had no interest whatsoever."[105] But despite this rebuff, counterculture infatuation with Hopi and Pueblos only grew.

Hippies from both coasts arrived in northern New Mexico to found communes "inspired, in part, by what they imagined Indian communities to be" (S. Smith 2012:114). Taos was far more attractive to the counterculture than stodgy old Santa Fe—but for my purposes Taos has been annexed into the Santa Fe Style/Pueblo Style. (Sorry.)

What Hippies did with Hopi religion and prophecies is less important, perhaps, than the pervasive influence of the Collier-esque (jr. and sr.) fantasized Hippie-Hopi that oozed out to the literati of that era: Happy peaceful people living in harmony with their environment. Zen gardeners. Or a Hindu/Hopi spin: Don't worry, be Hopi.[106]

Harold Courlander fired up a fresh batch of incense in 1971 with *Fourth World of the Hopis*. Courlander (1908–1996), a folklorist and successful novelist, started out in Detroit but ultimately landed in Bethesda, Maryland—apparently, no residencies in Taos or Santa Fe! His interests were global, reaching Africa and (most famously) the Caribbean. The Southwest was a side trip, but with consequential results. *Fourth World of the Hopis: The Epic Story of the Hopi Indians as Preserved in their Legends and Traditions* arrived a few years after the first Be-In and Woodstock. And shortly after Altamont. Flower Power had begun to wilt but the counterculture marched on; more militant, perhaps, but never losing its fascination with peaceful, communal Hopis. Those in and around the counterculture read *Fourth World* (and *Book of the Hopi*) and dreamed about pueblo-communes in New Mexico. A myth told often enough becomes the truth, and *Fourth World of the Hopis* retold those myths and reinforced those truths.

Hippy, with the passage of time, became New Agey. To each age its own Hopi, and New Agers (while studying the classics, Waters and Courlander)[107] pondered newfound texts, most notably tomes produced by Rev. Thomas E. Mails (1920–2001).[108] Mails was a man of the cloth, and also a skilled artist and aficionado of all things Indian. He was a serviceable writer but not as talented as Waters or Courlander. Mails's biggest Pueblo book, *The Pueblo Children of the Earth Mother*, hit the stands in 1983, a few years before the first (and, we were warned, possibly last) Harmonic Convergence. He followed with *Hotevilla: Hopi Shrine of the Covenant, Microcosm of the World* in 1995 and *The Hopi Survival Kit* in 1997. Those books revealed eschatological prophesies of four Hopi elders who, jolted by the Hiroshima and Nagasaki bombs, told us how our world would end. Timely. *Survival Kit* arrived shortly before the Y2K millennial meltdown, another predicted cosmic catastrophe that we (and Hopi) survived.

Bookended by bombs? Waters helped build them, Mails told us what they meant, cosmologically. Hopi helped Hippies and the rest of the Cold War duck-

and-cover generation deal with an A- and H-world. Hippies could not love the bomb but they could, perhaps, stop worrying and be Hopi.

Waters, Courlander, and Mails—these men were mystics, two novelists and an artistic religious. None were anthropologists (save *soi dissant*: We're all anthropologists now); and they certainly were not scientists, nor would wish to be.

Hell hath no fury like an Anthro scooped. (Consider the discipline's reaction to Jared Diamond.) Academic eyes rolled; professors railed. But Waters's and Courlander's and Mails's Hopis had far more impact on the thinking classes than any professional account (even more than Ruth Benedict's, I think), and reached a much broader national readership than any anthropologist—each of these authors wrote several Hopi books for mass-market publishers. Pueblo Space was planned and framed by Morgan, furnished in Santa Fe, but its exterior finish and fenestrations—looking in, looking out—came from the West: Hopi via Haight-Ashbury.

The Tyranny of Ethnology

Collier? Waters? Courlander? Mails? Who were these guys? Whatever they read in Haight-Ashbury, ethnography still ruled the academy. And especially for Pueblos: The Classic Ethnographies.

Recall that archaeology in nineteenth- and early twentieth-century Southwest was deeply subservient to ethnology.[109] "How did the Pueblos come to be?" was THE historical question; no thought was given to possible pre-histories that might not inform directly on the ethnological present. The past was Pueblo, and shallow, and presumably (mostly) event-less—"the slow and tedious development" of Bandelier. What pre-history there was could best be known through the Ethnological Method espoused by Morgan and by most ethnologists, who in the early twentieth century were steadfast in their certainty about their superiority over archaeology—an attitude that continued among Cultural Anthropologists well into the second half of the twentieth century.

The Ethnological Method reconstructed the past by reasoning back from the ethnographic present, puzzling out where moieties came from or the history of "the Keresan bridge," much as historical linguists modeled protolanguages. It was logical, and therefore parsimonious, and therefore suspect—for me, or for anyone with a bump of history.

The classic ethnologies were strong attractors. Florence Hawley trained many midcentury Southwestern archaeologists. In 1937 she maintained:

> At best, reconstruction of prehistory is dangerous, in that a consideration of every item of culture make-up is necessary for valid conclusions, and yet our only data on ancient social organization and its history must come from modern peoples. (Hawley 1937:506)

Her "modern peoples" are, of course, the Pueblos. Southwestern archaeology has long boasted this particular strength: The modern Pueblos who, as Kidder (1924:142) boasted, "preserve the ancient culture of the Southwest almost in its aboriginal purity."[110] Mid-twentieth-century archaeology looked to the classic Pueblo ethnographies as sacred texts.[111] Their contents filled in the many gaps, holes in archaeology-as-anthropology.

But through the second half of the twentieth century, "the disciplines of ethnology and archaeology drifted further apart" (Ware 2014:xxii). The remarkable discoveries of Cultural Resource Management and big projects like the National Park Service's Chaco Project discovered a past that seemed rather different from the ethnographic present (a subject to which we shortly return); archaeology jostled with ethnology for the driver's seat in knowing the ancient past. Perhaps archaeology had a voice independent of ethnology? With the rise of stridently scientific New Archaeology (below), the classic ethnographies were relegated to the reference section—seldom consulted but not ignored entirely.[112] Archaeology still needed some frame of reference, some sense of propriety, and thus fell back on very general notions of Pueblos: Pueblo Space.

In 1979, Linda Cordell and Fred Plog, in their "Escaping the Confines" manifesto (of which, more below), noted, "The existence of the modern Pueblos, *or some idealized version of them*, has had such a powerful effect on southwestern archaeologists that they have rarely looked beyond the literature relating to these groups for appropriate analogs" (Cordell and Plog 1979:406, emphasis added). Katherine Spielmann quoted this account and brought it forward twenty-five years: "Archaeologists have either expressed ambivalence about the utility of ethnographic information, or have relied on 'some idealized version' (Cordell and Plog 1979:406) of what they *thought* Pueblos were all about" (Spielmann 2005:195, emphasis original).

"Some idealized version": This, truly, is what I mean by Pueblo Space—vague, idealized notions of how Pueblos work, now and in the ancient past. These notions reflect, only distantly, ethnology—John Ware (2014) is quite correct: Southwestern archaeology is largely innocent of the Classic Ethnographies. Where then do these vague notions come from? "Introduction to Anthropology" courses, of course; but more directly, I think, these notions are recursively entangled with the culture of Santa Fe and Pueblo Mystique. For archaeologists of a certain age, even perhaps the quasi-hippie-dippy fantasies of Courlander and Waters.[113] My archaeologist readers will reject those assertions angrily and absolutely, perhaps throwing this book across the room. But they're true: As David Webster (2006; see note 43) observed of the analogous Maya Mystique, it's hard to see it when you're in it. The Pueblo Mystique is all around us, it's pervasive. And we archaeologists are, indeed, all in it—in Pueblo Space.

The repercussions will be discussed below; contemporary examples will come in chapter 2. For now, more history: How did archaeology—once the happy handmaiden of ethnology—drift away into its own Pueblo Space?

From its nineteenth-century beginnings through the first half of the twentieth century, archaeology was intellectually and professionally secondary to and dependent on ethnology—archaeology was the awkward, embarrassing younger sibling.[114] Archaeology in the Pueblo region, particularly, served mainly to confirm Ethnology and Ethnohistory, to accumulate pots for display, and perhaps to develop sites for tourism. Elsewhere, archaeology discovered Paleo-Indian, Hohokam, and Mogollon—non-Pueblo things not found in the Classic Pueblo Ethnographies; Southwestern archaeology could almost be an independent discipline—except in Pueblo Space.

To understand the power of Pueblo Space, we must dip back into (dive back into?) early disciplinary history and the parallel cultural history of Santa Fe and Pueblo Mystique. If Morgan and Boas could agree on anything, it would be that ethnology was the core of American Anthropology. The other subfields—linguistics, physical anthropology, and archaeology—were useful embellishments, but subservient to the ethnological study of living tribes and groups. Indeed, Peter Whiteley suggests that American "anthropology practically began at Hopi"—although Zuni and several Rio Grande Pueblos might contest that dubious honor.[115]

Almost all of the earliest pioneering Southwesternists operated either primarily or secondarily as ethnologists, although few were trained in that then-new field. Bandelier intruded into several Pueblos around Santa Fe; Frank Hamilton Cushing moved into Zuni;[116] Jesse Walter Fewkes inflicted himself upon the Hopi. All viewed their subsequent archaeological researches through the very thick lenses of Pueblos they knew. Fewkes, for example, transposed (his view of) Hopi to Mesa Verde, establishing canards that befuddle us to this day.

Bandelier and Cushing and Fewkes were essentially nineteenth-century men, although an aging Fewkes returned to the Southwest periodically until 1926. They accepted (critically or uncritically) Pueblo traditions of migration and other events in the distant or mythical past. Bandelier famously wrote a novel blending archaeology and the traditions recorded by ethnology: *The Delight Makers*, published in 1890—and still in print! We are all ethnologists now; or, rather, they were all ethnologists then (for a useful analysis, see Saxton 1981).

Morgan's Ethnological Method moved from the present back into the past, chasing the origins of particular tribes or societies or traits. Later variations on this theme were called "direct historic approach," "ethnographic analogy," and more recently, "up-streaming."[117] They all share a common, fatal fault: They move against time's arrow, from present to past; history moves from past to present. We will see, below and in chapter 2, how that gets us into trouble.

Edgar Hewett, a second-generation Morganite, was perhaps less rigorous in application of the Ethnological Method to the ancient past—he was not, after all, trained in ethnology.[118] His thinking was clearly aligned with his friend Charles Lummis's exhortation to "catch our archaeology alive."[119] Hewett was largely innocent of formal ethnology, but he was personally connected to many Pueblo leaders and artists, and transferred that knowledge to his archaeological work. So, too, Neil Judd, excavator of Pueblo Bonito, who was trained in classics by Byron Cummings and then in archaeology by Edgar Hewett. (It's kind of amazing that Judd ever managed to—never mind.) Thus Judd had very little training in ethnology as it was understood by Boas or Morgan; and (like Hewett) Judd learned about Indians from Indians.[120] During his excavations at Chaco, he relied on his friend Santiago Naranjo of Santa Clara Pueblo and other Pueblo workmen to interpret problematic finds. (Judd also was open to ideas about Chaco from Navajos.) Absent comparative training, Hewett and Judd's Anthropology was almost pure Indianology: Personal friendships with and fascinations about Pueblo peoples informed their work with cut-and-paste notions for material culture, religion, social structure, and traditional histories and migration stories.[121]

The next generation of archaeologists, joining the field early in the twentieth century, was more thoroughly inculcated in ethnological methods. Those young cohorts might have rough-and-tumble on-the-job training from Hewett or Dean Cummings (Hewett's Arizona contemporary), but they broadened their horizons by studying at proper anthropology departments back east or in California. For example, such staunch ethnographer/archaeologists as Florence Hawley and Bertha Dutton: Hawley got her degree at Chicago and Dutton at Columbia.

Then, in the mid-1920s, a countercurrent swept into the Southwest from the East: A New Archaeology (the *first* New Archaeology) spearheaded by Clark Wissler and younger archaeologists associated (at one time or another) with the American Museum of Natural History. The (first) New Archaeology eschewed Pueblo myths and traditions in favor of a chronological approach, letting the past speak for itself. While by no means disdainful of ethnological accounts, the New Archaeology emerged as a separate but equal discipline—the beginnings of archaeology's growing separation from ethnology. By the 1930s, Hewett's style of archaeology—part booster, part huckster, lots of fieldwork—faded before the onslaught of no-nonsense, science-minded Young Turks. Professionals—and especially academics—run in packs. They spoke to each other in jargon—branches, phases, foci—and spoke to the public not at all. Eventually, they called it Culture History. What would the public think of Culture History's graphs and charts? Not much: Bloodless and boring. Absent any compelling new narrative, the public (including intellectuals in other disciplines) continued with Hewett-era Pueblo Mystique.

That Santa Fe brand was by now well established, and nothing was (or is) going to stop it—certainly not academic archaeology. Culture History had little to say to the Mystique. In the 1930s, if archaeology deliberately turned boring, then ethnology stepped in to keep the Mystique boiling. The 1930s and 1940s were the golden age of Southwestern ethnography.[122] Leslie White, Elsie Clews Parsons, Robert Lowie, Mischa Titiev, Fred Eggan, Esther Goldfrank, and others all poked around Pueblos and published richly detailed accounts of Pueblo customs, habits, and beliefs.[123] They sometimes acknowledged archaeology but generally considered it an odd, intellectually thin field. "Archaeologists' gray matter is mostly under their fingernails," sniffed a distinguished ethnologist (repeated in my youth, perhaps apocryphal).

Ethnology remained the public face of Anthropology. And the ethnologists of that Golden Age hammered home the old refrain of Pueblo exceptionalism. And exceptionalism touted by academics fueled the Mystique touted by Santa Feans. Not all ethnologists wrote popular or public accounts, but several did (famously, Margaret Mead), none more importantly for our purposes than Ruth Benedict, whom we met above. Her book *Patterns of Culture* proclaimed Pueblo exceptionalism (and casually dismissed archaeology):

> Pueblo culture, therefore, has a long homogeneous history behind it, and we have special need of this knowledge of it because the cultural life of these peoples is so at variance with that of the rest of North America. Unfortunately archaeology cannot go further and tell us how it came about that here in this small region of America a culture gradually differentiated itself from all those that surround it and came always more and more drastically to express a consistent and particular attitude towards existence. (Benedict 1934[1989]:59)

"So at variance with that of the rest of North America"—and by North America, she meant ALL of it north of Panama, Aztecs and Mayas included. Benedict can't say enough about the exceptionalism of Pueblos: "Set off from the other [Native] peoples of North America and Mexico" and "the basic contrast between the Pueblos and the other cultures of North America" and "the major qualities that differentiate Pueblo culture from those of other American Indians" and so on and so on (Benedict 1934[1989]:78–79). Hewett and the Santa Fe boosters declared the Pueblos were exceptional in the sense that they were something you couldn't see anywhere else. Benedict the public intellectual agreed (with the idea, if not with the man who said it). Popular (and academic) accounts through the first half of the twentieth century repeated and repeated the refrain: Pueblos were unique, culturally, morally, philosophically. Michael Kabotie, a Hopi artist, once complained, "You white people have put Pueblos up on a pedestal, and I'm not sure we want to be there."

The merchants of Santa Fe smiled; they were fine with Pueblos and Pueblo pots on pedestals. The Indian Market chugged along until Nelson Rockefeller opened his Museum of Primitive Art in New York in 1954. The market took notice; and when Rockefeller's collection of tribal art went uptown to the Met in 1969, so did prices in Santa Fe. The Met opened the "Rockefeller wing" in 1982 (various sources give varied dates for these three events; I follow Conn 2010: 37–38).

The Indian Market had first opened in 1922 as part of Fiesta; after Rockefeller made primitive art legit, it went big time, left Fiesta behind, and became its own event. The Market saw "phenomenal growth" after 1970 (Bernstein 2012:115). Art and archaeology marched hand in hand in early and mid-twentieth-century Santa Fe, but perhaps less so after antiquities became a fine-arts commodity with its own annual market, paralleling Indian Market (e.g., Lekson 1997— among many others!).

Benedict said archaeology alone couldn't tell how Pueblo culture came to be. Ouch. The (first) New Archaeology returned the compliment and more or less ignored ethnology. Kate Spielmann points out: "From the 1920s at least through the 1950s, the analogies that were employed [in Southwestern archaeology] were remarkably free of actual southwestern ethnographic content."[124] The standard midcentury text, John McGregor's (1941, 1965) *Southwestern Archaeology*—a masterwork of Culture History—barely mentioned the Pueblos, and the classic ethnographies were conspicuous by their absence from his references. Culture History in archaeology—compiling tables and charts of who was where, when—wouldn't dent Pueblo Mystique or escape Pueblo Space.

The old master narrative, carried over from the late 1920s, was the coded and codified Pecos Classification, the stepwise progression from rude beginnings (Basketmaker II and III) through a linear evolution of gradual improvements (Pueblo I, Pueblo II, Pueblo III, Pueblo IV) to the pinnacle, the end point of Modern Pueblos (Pueblo V)—all framed within Pueblo Space. However rude and crude the beginnings, we know they were Pueblo-like or Pueblo-ish or Puebloid or Puebloan.

The steady progress from simpler to more complex betrays the same high Victorian faith in progress that underwrote Morgan and other cultural evolutionists. The Pecos past was different, in a Cultural Historical sense that phases and stages could be defined as beginning and ending and following each other. But not THAT different: The Pecos past was merely simpler and then (moving backward) simpler still, but leading forward inexorably to the ethnographic Pueblos.

It is worth considering the Pecos Classification for a few paragraphs. The Pecos Classification, promulgated in 1928 (Woodbury 1993:Chapters 1–3), was a creature of Culture History—indeed the foundation of Culture History for the Pueblos. It offered a Whiggish account of Pueblo pre-history, every day in every way, better and better—with one or two small slips. Stage by Pecos stage, step by step, the people-who-would-become-Pueblos acquired first corn, then pit houses, then pottery, then kivas, then masonry, then "pueblo-style" villages, then kachinas, and so forth until all the elements of the modern Pueblos cumulated and crystallized, complete and entire. It was not an entirely smooth ride: The "abandonment of the Four Corners"—perhaps Athabaskan hordes from the north, perhaps a drought—was in the end only a speed bump on the road to the Hopi, Zuni, Acoma, and the Rio Grande Pueblos. And the abandonment validated (if simplified) the elaborate Pueblo origin stories; all of those stories involved migrations, and there were migrations. Chambers of Commerce and tour companies in the Four Corners could tout "the Mystery of the Anasazi—where did they go?" but the Pecos Classification knew precisely where they went: the modern Pueblos. Which was where BMIII, PI, PII, PIV, and PIII had been destined to go.

While misfits and exceptions appeared early and often, the Pecos System remained the standard chronology—even through the iconoclasms of both first and second New Archaeology. Those Pecos pioneers were good: The basic Pecos framework continued in use and survives today over much of the Pueblo region because, for the most part, it was solid. Not over all of the Southwest, of course: Not all roads led to Pecos, or to Pueblos.[125] The old Culture History did its job, workmanlike and decidedly undramatic.

The second New Archaeology of the late 1960s and 1970s shook off the inertia of Culture History and loudly proclaimed itself a Science, capital "S." And, oddly, aggressively re-embraced anthropology: "Archaeology is Anthropology or it is nothing!" (Willey and Phillips 1958:2; but see Kubler 1975).

Odd, because ethnological Anthropology was just then sliding back from Science. New Archaeologists were thinking of Anthropology as the old Science of Man (HRAF, Leslie White, neo-evolution, and all that). But times changed: In the final decades of the twentieth century, ethnology rebranded itself as cultural anthropology, morphing from a (nominally) comparative discipline to a postmodern wallow in thick description. Not much there for archaeology, old or new.

Moreover, Cultural Anthropology (for many reasons) now avoided Indians. During the latter decades of the twentieth century conventional Indianology/ethnology withered generally (Nabokov 2002:94), and in the Southwest specifically; only a few cultural anthropologists continued to study the Pueblos.[126] One of the best of that vanishing breed is Peter Whiteley of the American Museum of Natural History, whose principal Southwestern focus has been Hopi. In 1993, Whiteley pondered "The End of Anthropology (at Hopi?)." He saw Southwestern ethnology becoming marginal within the larger discipline, and he urged a reinvention of a flagging field from "pure research" to "applied" anthropology; that is, anthropologists working with and for tribal groups, lending anthropological expertise to tribal problems and initiatives—at, of course, the tribes' request (a topic to which we briefly return in chapters 5 and 6).

Back to the future, and the 1960s and 1970s: After a few experiments in retroethnology—trying to determine social organization by looking at motifs on potsherds, for example—New Archaeology put the Classic Ethnographies back on the shelf and turned instead to the kind of grand anthropological comparative work that was already long out of style in Cultural Anthropology: global cross-cultural pattern-seeking. Southwestern Pueblos became cases or data points in a larger array of world cultures. Cultures of a certain type, of course: intermediate. We knew a priori that all Southwestern societies were intermediate: Pueblo Space defined the limits of polite discourse on the Southwestern past.

Until it didn't. Starting around 1980 and continuing through that decade, a splinter group developed around archaeologists Fred Plog and Steadman Upham (e.g., Plog and Cordell and Plog 1979; Upham 1982) that questioned the uncritical application of Pueblo ethnographies and Pueblo Space (not their term) to the ancient past. The clearest statement came in a today-obscure chapter in an Arizona State University publication, from which this section's title is taken: Steadman Upham's 1987 "Tyranny of Ethnographic Analogy." The title—for which Upham nods to Wobst (1978)—pretty much says it all.[127] Strong stuff: Game on, as Wayne once said.

It was an epic argument, fierce and bloody.[128] (Young archaeologists today hear the tale around the campfire, much like young audiences of Homer's day: Bored, dozing, catching a quarter, maybe less.) When the hurly burly was done, when the battle was lost or won, the backlash sent Southwestern archaeology scurrying back to the safety of Pueblo Space, back to the bosom of Classic Ethnographies. The return was muted at first, but talk of sodalities, curing societies, and other Pueblo apparatus increased through the final decades of the century.[129] (We will return to the triumph of Pueblo Space in chapter 2.)

Plog and Upham were more or less right, I think, but they chose the wrong case: They insisted that a fourteenth- to fifteenth-century pueblo then called Chavez Pass (now Nuvakwewtaqa) had very un-Pueblo "managerial elites." They lost that argument, but theirs was a weak case: They should have taken Chaco Canyon. While debates raged, rather pointlessly, over managerial elites at pueblos in Arizona, fieldwork in New Mexico was revealing something remarkably unlike anything in the ethnographies: a monumental regional center at Chaco Canyon, with a territory encompassing all of northwestern New Mexico—and even crossing sacred state lines (OMG!) into Colorado, Utah, and Arizona. Chaco's escape from Pueblo Space will be discussed in chapter 3.

Something lost in all the hubbub was how very different the Pueblo Southwest was before and after 1300—an approximate date that can be considered a Great Divide in southwestern pre-history.[130] Throughout, it was assumed that Pueblos after 1300 had something useful to offer our archaeological understandings of the Southwest prior to 1300. But 1300 marks the end of the Chaco-Aztec polity (chapter 3) and the "abandonment of the Four Corners"—the remarkable movement of tens of thousands of people out of their old homelands into the areas of the modern Pueblos (e.g., Ortman 2012) and beyond (e.g., Clark 2001; Hill et al. 2004; Lekson et al. 2002). This was—in the Southwest, indeed in human history—a remarkable event. Epochal.

The disruptions at 1300 left a clear mark on the archaeological record, beyond the emptying of the Four Corners and subsequent population spike in the modern Pueblo areas. Almost everything changed: settlement geography, village plans, domestic and ritual architecture, pottery, art (reviewed in Lekson 2009a: 192–198). At 1300, the centuries-old rigidly geometric black-on-white pottery designs of Chaco and Mesa Verde gave way to dynamic, polychromatic compositions; much the same happened on wall murals. (If you think this is a small thing, compare the murals at Lowry Pueblo of Pueblo II [Martin 1936], to the murals at Pottery Mound of Pueblo IV [Hibben 1975]; you don't need a weatherman, etc., and you don't need Erwin Panofsky to recognize that something BIG happened.) At 1300, the family pit structures (which we mistakenly call "kivas," see chapter 3) disappear; thereafter only a few large pit structures—these, real kivas—graced a village plaza. At 1300, the dispersed single-family farm houses of Chaco and Aztec's time quickly aggregated into compact apartment-like "pueblos." And so on and so on, as Žižek says.

The changes were marked and dramatic, and they had been noticed in the Pecos Classification; indeed, changes at about 1300 from Pueblo III to Pueblo IV was the most obvious and therefore least contested of the classification's several stage breaks. Frank H. H. Roberts (1935:7) even suggested a cultural climax in Pueblo II–III, followed around 1300 by a fall or collapse or diminution in Pueblo IV, which Roberts termed "Regressive Pueblo." "Regressive" was roundly rejected by archaeologists working in late PIV (nobody wants their site to be Regressive); but it also slipped from use because it did not fit the agenda of archaeologists under the spell of Pueblo Mystique, working in Pueblo Space.

Whatever. Around 1300, something really big happened. My interpretation (Lekson 1999a, 2006, 2009a, 2015a) is this: Pueblo people, after 1300, rejected the un-Pueblo social structures of the old Chaco-Aztec polity (chapter 3), and they deliberately (and literally) reinvented themselves as Pueblos—that is, as the kind of societies celebrated by Pueblo Space: independent farming villages;

self-sufficient, inward-looking; egalitarian, communal; and—who knows?—
spiritual, peaceful, eternal, and unchanging. Much of that is true of modern (and
ethnographic) Pueblos but archaeology shows us that package came together
after 1300. Benedict dismissed archaeology's contribution to the ethnology of
Pueblo exceptionalism: "Archaeology cannot go further and tell us how it came
about." Well, actually, archaeology can tell you a lot about how it came about; and
the story archaeology tells is nothing you'd learn from Classic Ethnographies or
from the Ethnographic Method. Archaeology shows us a Great Divide at 1300,
beyond which the Ethnographic Method probably cannot reach. But don't tell
that to early twentieth-century classic ethnographers, or to their later twentieth-
and early twenty-first-century devotees—whom we meet in chapter 2. For them,
ethnology is still the answer. No matter what the question.

Surveys of Chaco Canyon

Ethnography's tyranny smacked up against the Lords of Chaco, whom we meet
briefly here and more properly in chapter 3. New data and new ideas changed
the equation: New data from the dirt, new ideas from Boomers. Dirt archaeology: The Chaco Project, subject of this section, showed us that Chaco didn't fit
Pueblo Space. Boomers: Demographics forged new regimes of truth in American Anthropological Archaeology—New and Processual archaeologies, met
briefly above and again in the next section.

    The National Park Service's substantial Chaco Project, which ran from 1969
to 1986, was heir-apparent of the earlier equally ambitious Wetherill Mesa Project at Mesa Verde—a classic of old-style Culture History. Mesa Verde archaeology, then and now, remained dependent on a vague sort of ethnology; all NPS
interpretations, illustrations, dioramas, and so forth fit comfortably in Pueblo
Space. One of the key Wetherill Mesa archaeologists was Alden C. Hayes, whose
portfolio also included extensive excavations in the late 1960s at Gran Quivira
(today's Salinas National Monument; Hayes et al. 1981)—a Contact Period
Pueblo, for which ethnology and ethnohistory were essential. Thus Hayes came
to the Chaco Project with impeccable Culture History, Pueblo Space credentials: Mesa Verde and Rio Grande Pueblo. Chaco rocked his world:

> The aggregation of traits having no apparent root in previous Anasazi
> tradition is so great, and they appeared on the scene so rapidly, that it is
> difficult to see them as anything but "hard" diffusion through the agency
> of a group of determined political entrepreneurs, some of whom must
> have been physically present and in residence.… There is no place to
> look for the source except ultimately in Mexico. (Hayes 1981:62–63)

Chaco out of Pueblo Space! Better still: Chaco with real history! Hayes's
historical interpretation echoed the ideas of Charles Di Peso (e.g., 1974), who

controversially argued that Mesoamerican agents had directed Chaco's rise, and Paquimé's, and many other interesting events in the ancient Southwest. Coming from Hayes, a revered figure in Mesa Verde and Rio Grande Pueblo archaeology, Hayes's words were more of a gut-punch than Di Peso's, who, after all, worked in southern Arizona and Chihuahua.

Soon thereafter came a changing to the guard, from elder Hayes to younger Judge: W. James Judge, who replaced the retiring Hayes (and Robert Lister) as the principal of the Chaco Project. Judge represented a New Archaeology: Sampling, statistics, science, and so forth. (His first research at Chaco was a statistical sample survey of the canyon, precursor to Hayes's subsequent, traditional full-coverage survey.) While (happily) not a science-demagogue like some of the early New Archaeologists, Judge moved away from Culture History. Hayes's interpretations—Chaco was hot!—were of course acknowledged, but Mexico (and history) were downplayed in subsequent Chaco Project work (e.g., Judge 1989; Lekson 1983). But the evidence from the dirt was compelling, even conclusive: Chaco was not comfortable in Pueblo Space.[131] The arena for understanding Chaco's oddness shifted from Hayes's history to Judge's ecology: Judge, working on archetypical New Archaeology scales, proposed "The Development of a Complex Cultural Ecosystem in the Chaco Basin, New Mexico" (Judge 1979). Science, not history, could best explain the Chaco Phenomenon— a term coined at this time, but not by the Chaco Project; rather by Cynthia Irwin-Williams, during her excavations of Salmon Ruins, 1972–1980. And, despite some recent carping (Ware 2014:130), entirely appropriate: Chaco was a phenomenon beyond Pueblo Space.

Scientism

At its beginning, American Archaeology aligned with the natural sciences and not with history. Anthropology's (and Archaeology's) place among the sciences was secured by the leadership of the American Association for the Advancement of Science, founded in 1848—by one of those happy/unhappy coincidences, the same year as the Treaty of Guadalupe Hidalgo. Several of AAAS's early leaders were anthropologists: Frederic Ward Putnam (professor of American Archeology and Ethnology, Harvard University) was secretary from 1872 to 1897, after which he became president in 1898. Lewis Henry Morgan, whom we've already met, had been president of AAAS in 1880; John Wesley Powell in 1888—recall that his day job was running the Bureau of American Ethnology from its 1878 founding to 1902. Anthropologists were, apparently, welcome among the chemists, geologists, and physicists.

Thus Anthropological Archaeology entered America's intellectual pantheon cloaked in the vestments of science, and wore that garb proudly through the twentieth century. The robes were renewed from time to time: As discussed above, two "New" Archaeologies, first in the 1910s–1920s and again in the 1960s–1970s, polished the buttons and buffed the regalia. The first New Archaeology emphasized system, rigor, stratigraphy and chronology (Culture History) over whatever-it-was that Hewett and Cummings and those early tyros did.

Their hopes for the Southwest were dashed when the Stock Market crash of 1929 diverted Rockefeller's money away from the science-sounding Laboratory of Anthropology—the "New" kids' challenge in Santa Fe to Hewett's more humanist School of American Research. Depression was followed by war; war was followed by peace; and peace by love and marriage and the baby carriage.

The first Boomers arrived in 1946.[132] Twenty-four years later, those puling infants had PhDs. Theoretically, that is: The first postwar kids could have PhDs in 1970 if they went straight through, tarried not, and finished their doctorates in six years. In any event, from 1968 to 1980 a tsunami of Boomers finished college and (if they had nothing better to do) began postgraduate work. University faculties expanded almost but not quite in proportion to the incoming tide of Boomer students; and the best college jobs, of course, were already filled by old, musty, tenured professors. The new PhDs needed new agendas to market themselves (and, perhaps, to nudge those old guys into retirement). Or, more charitably, new markets for their agendas.

Hard science hit archaeology hard in the late 1960s. The 1920s New Archaeology had devolved, midcentury, into Culture History—sorting sites and phases into matrices of time and space. Not good enough for Boomers! In 1971, a manifesto announced the new sheriff in town: "Explanation in Archeology: An Explicitly Scientific Approach" (Watson et al. 1971). The bandwagon rolled, Boomers hopped on, and scores of articles and papers and books proclaimed a brave new scientific world. This second, 1970s New Archaeology declared archaeology a (capital-S) Science, along the model of physics: quantification, hypotheses-testing, falsification, and so on and so on: A nose-gay of scientific trappings. Young Turks of the day quoted Popper, much as Young Turks today cite Heidegger—neither of whom, as it turns out, are particularly relevant to archaeology. Through the 1970s and well into the 1980s, capital-S Science ruled American Archaeology.

For my argument, a key feature of capital-S Science was this: No room for history. History was dismissed as background noise, static filtered out to reveal Science, to discover processes. New Archaeology's goal (initially) was "covering laws" (think: thermodynamics); when we realized that wasn't likely to happen, a strategic retreat to universal processes (think: neo-evolution). Archaeology might never reach $E=mc^2$, but we could do band $\rightarrow$ tribe $\rightarrow$ chiefdom $\rightarrow$ state. History, with its quirks and contingencies, had no place here: Neo-evolutionary processes (for example) applied whatever the vagaries of local conditions. Capital-S Science archaeology rejected the older humanities alliances (or, at least, affinities) of Culture History, and became resolutely ahistorical. (In the Southwest, no one saw a need for history, save for the Contact Period: We knew that the past was a slow steady crawl out of the distant past up to Pueblo; no history there.) Science slid into process, and process mellowed into Processual-Plus; but a persistent residual was incredulity to narrative: American Anthropological Archaeology simply does not value history. This curious fact—it may seem an assertion, but it is a fact—is explored at some length in chapters 6 and 7. For the present, the take-home from this paragraph should be that for at least three academic generations, American Anthropological Archaeology more or less ignored history, historiography, and narrative. For a discipline that deals with the past, that seems odd. More, much more, on this in later chapters.

Federal laws created Cultural Resource Management (CRM) in the late 1960s and early 1970s. Just as Boomers rewrote archaeology's rules, CRM boomed and rewrote what archaeology was. Archaeology escaped the academy and became a business. The National Historic Preservation Act of 1966 (signed by President Lyndon Johnson) created the National Register of Historic Places and Section 106 (which specified what must be done if a Register property would be impacted by construction)—among other things.[133] President Richard Nixon's Executive Order 11593 of 1971 ("Protection and Enhancement of the Cultural Environment") extended legal protections beyond sites already on the National Register to sites *potentially eligible* for that status (an extension later confirmed in law)—and that made all the difference. The 1974 Archeological and Historic Preservation Act greatly enlarged the earlier Reservoir Salvage Act in ways that seriously upped the financial ante. Archaeology would never rival Department of Defense wrenches and toilet seats (not to mention bombers and capital ships) but archaeology was suddenly Big Money. Several years later, the Archaeological Resources Protection Act of 1979 (signed by President Jimmy Carter) added punitive teeth lacking in the old Antiquities Act of 1906 and language allowing agencies to determine who was qualified to excavate. Those qualifications mostly (but not entirely) involved college training and postgraduate degrees—and by happy coincidence the universities had been cranking out cohorts of freshly minted Boomer MAs and PhDs. More and more Boomers went into CRM—just then, conveniently, emerging as an industry.[134] The growing bureaucracies created by the federal legislation needed staffing, too; Boomer grads became Civil Servants regulating their classmates on the CRM side.

And, before too long, both CRM and regulatory archaeologists were thumbing their noses at academics. Government jobs were (almost) as cushy as university jobs, and often paid better. Today there are three or four archaeology jobs outside the academy (CRM, regulatory, etc.) for every tenured professor inside ivory towers.[135]

So, in the years after 1970: (1) A flood of Boomer archaeologists hit the job market; (2) American Anthropological Archaeology pumped itself up to be Science—real, hard-core science; (3) Boomers bought into science, beat the old Culture History guys over the head with it, and took it to newly vacated or newly created jobs on university faculties, in federal agencies, CRM firms, and anywhere else archaeologists could find work. Market saturation: American Anthropological Archaeology—which had always been, nominally, a natural science—moved deeper into science and further from history and humanities. Boomers baptized in science stayed loyal to their training; a few backsliders, but only a few. In the decades that followed, they trained cohorts of graduate students in science's iron regimen. They peer-reviewed books and journals, evaluated National Science Foundation grants, and analyzed CRM proposals—keeping American Anthropological Archaeology scientific, in form if not in function.

With the passage of time, the heated manifestos of New Archaeology's early days gave way to the more measured (and practical) programs of Processual Archaeology, but the hope for scientific rigor remained. And Southwestern archaeology bloomed. If the early twentieth century was the golden age of Ethnology, the last quarter of that century may have been something like that—gilded for sure, maybe even golden—for Southwestern archaeology: Big money, big projects, big results, and remarkable freedoms. Before Y2K, Southwestern archaeology was largely untroubled by Postmodernity (see chapter 6); not yet the angst of the Native American Graves Protection and Repatriation Act (NAGPRA, discussed below), which passed as law in 1990 but took a decade to take hold.

The science of New and Processual Archaeology was, in many ways, great: It opened the Southwest up to a broader world of cross-cultural comparisons, and the possibility of life beyond Pueblo Space. But the gravity of Pueblo Space was too strong: Flirtations with neo-evolutionary "chiefdoms" (as recounted in chapter 2) had no real chance. We knew—we just *knew*—that Pueblos weren't like that, nor was their past.

For a glorious span of time in the last decades of the twentieth century, the Southwest was a leader in method and theory, so long as the M&T was Science. The ancient Southwest became a "natural laboratory," or rather a series of small natural laboratories.[136] Adaptation replaced history; ancient people became ancient lab rats: The man in the maze/maize. What mattered were environment, ecology, biomass, crop production, population size—things we could measure. New Archaeology declared ideology epiphenomenal and social structure nearly so—bit of a relief, since those are hard to study. And, in any event, we knew all we needed to know about ideology and social structure from ethnology; or rather, from an archaeological précis of ethnography, our shared general vision of Pueblos, our vague notions, the Pueblo Space: Egalitarian, peaceful, all that stuff. We bragged that the Southwest's remarkable ethnographic record was a strength of the natural laboratory: We could set our controls to "egalitarian" and "peaceful" and proceed with our experiments, measuring and manipulating more empirical variables.

It was too good to last. Southwestern Anthropological Archaeologists of a certain age (my age) still speak of "hypothesis testing," "test expectations," "warranting arguments," "parsimony," and all the jargon of archaeological science. Even those who have shed those idioms still think like that. They want research that is controlled and unambiguous. In a word, they want certainty. So of course they were unmoved (if perhaps a bit unnerved) by the astonishing looseness of British interpretive archaeology (discussed in chapter 6), which first appeared in the Southwest in the late 1980s and early 1990s, Postmodernism-come-lately. But those ideas from across the pond made little practical impact; we shrugged and soldiered on.

The laboratory glitter of New Archaeology patinated to a less strident Processual Archaeology, but strong residuals of science remain—as may be expected after its decades-long domination of Southwestern archaeology. Now we are old: The Boomers retire, your author included. Taught to younger generations, residuals of Boomer science remain—as much scientism as science—but perhaps the time is right for new directions. Which new directions? Wait for chapters 5 and 6.

Law-like Statements: Land Claims and NAGPRA

During the years of Culture History and New/Processual Archaeology, we honored Pueblo Space but more or less ignored Pueblos. Indians were conspicuous by their absence, except as recorded by ethnologists. It took the might and majesty of the law to get archaeologists and Indians together at the table. The legal engagements came in two rounds: Land Claims and NAGPRA.

The first re-engagement was not so much at a table as before the judge's bench. The Indian Claims Act of 1946 allowed tribes to sue the federal government over lost lands, narrowly defined. Tribes would be recompensed for the value of lands at the time they were lost—that is, seventeenth- or eighteenth-century values, not today's. But that was better than nothing, so many tribes moved forward. The Indian Claims Act brought archaeologists back in contact with Indians working (for pay or pro bono) for or against the Pueblos, in both roles paying close attention to Pueblo oral histories and traditions—particularly those recorded in ethnographies and ethnohistories, which carried legal weight. Their findings (on both sides) are troves of ethnohistory; many were later published.[137] Steadman Upham cogently summarized the impact of the Land Claims work on Southwestern archaeology:

> The passage of the Indian Claims Act of 1946 set in motion a pattern of research that would span nearly two decades. The explicit goal of this research was to establish an unbroken chain of occupation from history to prehistory, thereby justifying Puebloan groups' claims to "ancestral" lands.... [This work] contributed to the now ingrained belief that living Pueblo groups represented a continuum of occupation on the Colorado Plateaus and that their customs, beliefs, practices, and organizational structure mirrored the past rather well. (Upham 1987:266)

In effect, legally sanctioning Pueblo Space. Pueblos and other tribes continue to challenge the federal government over land issues, understandably; but archaeologists were not so directly involved as in the land claims.

The second legal entanglement came in 1990, in a law aimed squarely at archaeology: The Native American Graves Protection and Repatriation Act of 1990, or NAGPRA. Tribes pointed to tens of thousands of their ancestors collected by anthropologists sitting in boxes on museum shelves, and demanded that those people be returned, be "repatriated."[138] That made sense to the public and to legislators—and, indeed, to many archaeologists. NAGPRA was duly passed and signed by President George H. W. Bush, and it fundamentally changed American Anthropological Archaeology.[139] Before NAPGRA, Indians were optional; archaeology could engage or ignore at its pleasure. After NAPGRA, Indians had a seat at the head table, at or very near the podium.

The regulations for exactly how NAGPRA would be implemented came five years later, in 1995. It took the federal agencies a while to staff up; it took CRM operations a while to sort out the regulations; it took museums a while to figure out how to consult with tribes. It was almost 2000 before the law really gained traction; thus we will meet NAGPRA again in postmillennial chapter 2, and its theoretical ramification in chapter 6. My concern here is with NAGPRA's methods: a clause in the bill that flipped American Anthropological Archaeology back to the first half of the twentieth century. After midcentury, we were taught (and this was written on our hearts): "Pots do not equal people." That is, material culture (and especially pottery, the fetish of our forefathers/mothers) was a highly suspect indicator of ethnicity or identity. For Boomers, this was law; for Millennials, not so much. In and out of NAGPRA, younger people started chasing Hopi clans and Rio Grande linguistic groups back into the vastly distant past. This became a genre, and accepted practice—as it had been in the 1940s, '50s, and '60s (e.g., Ford et al. 1972). Back, as I've said before, to the future, once o'er. Déjà vu all over again, as the poet said.

That effect of NAGPRA, passed in 1990, belongs in this chapter. At the heart of it, archaeologically, is the requirement for the government agency or the museum holding human remains to determine their "cultural affiliation"—a NAGPRA term—specifying a tribe or tribes to which remains and other NAGPRA items could be repatriated. From the regulations (CFR 43A10.2 e(1)):

> "Cultural affiliation" means that there is a relationship of shared group identity which can be reasonably traced historically or prehistorically between a present day Indian tribe or Native Hawaiian organization and an identifiable earlier group.

Under the law, tribes can assert affinities, but tribes cannot "determine cultural affiliation." The law makes that the task of the agency or museum archaeologist, who, by regulation, is required to consult with any and all tribes which may be affiliated.[140] There's a circular guessing game here, which often presupposes what is to be proven. All honor to the tribes: I have heard, more than a few times, tribal representatives deny affiliation to particular NAGPRA items based on their own information and criteria. They play it straight.

For Agency and museum archaeologists making determinations of cultural affiliation, the regulations specify the nature of evidence and the standards of proof (CFR 43A10.2 e(1)):

> Show cultural affiliation by a preponderance of the evidence based upon geographical, kinship, biological, archaeological, anthropological, linguistic, folkloric, oral traditional, historical, or other relevant information or expert opinion.

In the 1990s, science ruled American Anthropological Archaeology. We still tested hypotheses and had no truck with the philosophical convulsions then affecting the humanities (wait for chapter 6). In that context, NAGPRA procedures laid down in law and regulation were stunning atavisms, the kinds of evidence for the kinds of questions Southwestern archaeology had asked several decades before. Archaeologists involved in the Land Claims cases might have been comfortable with these requirements; New and Processual archaeologists certainly were not. NAGPRA dragged us back to our distant past—an archaeology that (we thought) was outdated before many 1990s practitioners were born.

How were the multiple lines of evidence to be used? As a simple checklist: "Preponderance of evidence" was a legal standard for NAGPRA, but no archaeologist used it in his/her daily work. It means, simply, that more evidence supports one conclusion than supports other possible conclusions. In NAGPRA, if more than half of the list of allowed evidence (geographical, kinship, biological, archaeological, anthropological, linguistic, folkloric, oral traditional, historical) supports a possible cultural affiliation, then that affiliation holds. We will meet "preponderance" again in chapter 6; not favorably.

My NAGPRA experiences spanned a decade, from 2003 to 2014 (Lekson 2010b). During that time, when doing NAGPRA I turned off the archaeology side of my brain. I could not (and still cannot) credit that a valid archaeological attribution of modern ethnicity could be made for ancient sites in the Southwest, and certainly not prior to the cataclysmic events around 1300. Above, I referred to 1300 as the "Great Divide"—what came before was markedly different than what came after. In the service of NAGPRA, I jumped back and forth blindly over the Great Divide scores of times and we got the job done. That job quite properly answered human rights, property law, Indian law, Red Power, but, in my opinion, had little or nothing to do with archaeology—save in the breach.

In both NAGPRA and academic work, I meet archaeologists who confidently argue that a particular thousand-year-old pit house was built by people speaking this particular Pueblo language, affiliated with those particular modern Pueblos. I'm pretty sure they are fooling themselves—in fact, I'm sure those assertions are specious—but they have the law on their side. Fight the law, and the law wins.

One thing I learned from NAGPRA was that the standards of proof are intriguingly different between science and law. We worry about "proving," with our thin archaeological evidence, a simple interpretation; nothing really important weighs in the balance. In law, equally light weight evidence can (or could, back in the day) get you hung by the neck until dead, dead, dead. Or, worse still, transported to the Antipodes. My point: The real world is far less formal and demanding than the rigid protocols of archaeological scientism. Those were lessons worth learning, which we will revisit in chapter 6.

Ritual über Alles

It's axiomatic to Pueblo Space that Pueblos are all about ritual. And since, with Pueblo Space, we know Pueblos are extraordinarily traditional—eternal and unchanging—it must always have been so: Ritual was forever paramount. "We know that ritual was always the most important thing"—according to a graduate student's paper at a national meeting (here, properly anonymous).

This seems a truism for ethnographic and modern Pueblos. Ritual and ceremony certainly dominate their social calendars. It may be worth considering that ritual was so prominent in Pueblo life in recent times because, after hundreds of years of colonial oppression, it's all they had left. That's a figure of speech, but not far off what I actually mean. Through three colonial regimes (Spanish, Mexican, American) we decimated their numbers, crushed their independence, took away their lands, destroyed their economies, imposed new languages and religions and governmental structures, and trained generations of their young away from traditional ways. Native leaders bemoaned these losses: more and more taken away, more and more lost. Ritual, in various forms, survived—some old, some new. It was not the only thing they could call their own, of course; but ritual was a big part of what remained uniquely *theirs* after wave after wave of devastating colonial onslaughts. This is not to suggest that Pueblo ritual and ceremony and "doings" are a sad remnant of past glories; not at all. But it is a fact (with which I assume most Indians would agree) that colonialism appropriated, subverted, controlled, demolished, and otherwise messed up very much of Pueblo life and society.

In any event: ethnographically and today, a very full ritual calendar![141] There are famous, formal, sometimes public ceremonies, kachina "dances." A multitude of curing and initiation ceremonies. Ceremonies adopted and adapted from Spanish Catholicism and Spanish paganism (think: matachines). As Severin Fowles points out, thoughts and actions we would call ritual, religion, or ceremony permeate every aspect of Pueblo life; the very category of "religion" makes no sense here. Fowles (2013), following Pueblo usage, calls these simply "doings."[142]

Most of Pueblo religious life is decidedly NOT public, at least not to non-Indians and especially to anthropologists; yet it is ritual and religion that seem foremost on the Southwestern archaeological mind.[143] Southwestern archaeology has become almost synonymous with ritual—we're (in)famous for it.

When I was trained (in the antediluvian 1970s and 1980s), ritual and religion were subsumed under ideology; and ideology was of no immediate application, an epiphenomenon. That was then, this is now: In the waning decades of the old millennium, the Southwest got religion. Now it's all ritual, all the time.

The Southwest's great awakening rose from a concatenation of circumstances (as Daniel Webster might put it) including the waning of scientism, the waxing of NAGPRA and Indigeneity, the remarkable reaffirmation of Pueblo Space, and a theoretical justification from Postprocessual archaeologies.

Postprocessual archaeology was the spawn of Postmodernism. Postmodernism proper impacted American Archaeology in the 1970s and 1980s, late in po-mo's life and lightly—in fact, almost not at all. Irony is a hard sell, out here in the bluff and hearty Old West. "Science studies" could not dethrone or defeat the Southwest's entrenched scientism. Those dangerously modern/postmodern/poststructural notions leaked through the dyke when Southwestern Boomers tired and retired; and thus the ancient Southwest met the French *philosophes* rather late, after most of the *philosophes* were long since dead and discredited (a sad story recounted in chapter 6). Postmodernism and poststructuralism manifested themselves as an exterior challenge: Postprocessual archaeology—British channeling the French—in the early 1980s. Our infection/infatuation was selective: Bits of Brits we liked, bits of Brits we didn't like. Small doses, here and there.

No more theory wars! Michelle Hegmon identified three Postprocessual themes that oozed over into Southwestern archaeology in the final decades of the twentieth century: symbols and meaning, agency, and gender (Hegmon 2003:217). I focus here on symbols and meaning, which include ideology, religion, and ritual. Hegmon defines three realms within symbols and meaning that Processual Archaeology borrowed from Postprocessual archaeologies: first "as intrinsic to many social and economic processes, sometimes as part of ritual behavior or religion"; second, symbolic "interpretations of all kinds and scales of archaeological evidence, ranging from portable material culture to architecture and landscapes"; and "A third realm of focus on symbols and meanings involves a revitalized interest in understanding pre-historic ideas and cosmologies, not just as part of social processes but also for their own sake" (Hegmon 2003:222). In the last decade of the twentieth century, the latter bloomed in Southwestern archaeology: the study of cosmologies and rituals for their own sake. And in the end: Ritual über alles.

Ritual and religion achieved full ascendency in Southwestern archaeology in the first decades of the twenty-first century (chapter 2); but the dam first cracked around 1990, with Charles Adams's (1991) *The Origin and Development of the Pueblo Kachina Cult* and notably—for this Chaco-centric book—with W. James Judge's (1989) pilgrimage model for Chaco, in his chapter in *Dynamics of Southwest Prehistory*.

Adams's work was good solid Southwestern stuff, beginning with the ethnographic present and chasing kachinas back into prehistory, and ending happily with process. Based on imagery and other evidence, he concluded that the "cult" crystalized in the fourteenth century in central Arizona in response to an influx of migrants from the Four Corners—that is, on the near side of the Great Divide. Makes sense to me, and to many other Southwestern archaeologists; it's fair to call Adams's book a classic.

W. James Judge's (1989) ideas about Chaco were, in some ways, more revolutionary. He proposed a ritual/ceremonial system for Chaco that was decidedly NOT Pueblo, just barely in Pueblo Space. He imported and then distorted a hypothetical model of "pilgrimage fairs" from Maya archaeology.[144] Judge was trying to explain the seemingly inexplicable distribution of material goods (turquoise, in particular, and other goods) and the concentration of monumental architecture at Chaco Canyon, within its larger region. Pilgrimage fairs would gather people from all around Chaco's world into Chaco Canyon at specified times, via the famous Chaco "roads." Ritual specialists/priests who organized all this pomp and circumstance lived in the Canyon, and took a little bit off the top for their expenses (room and board, incidental expenses, and so forth). Retreating from his earlier ecologically driven ideas about Chaco as a redistributive economy, Judge (following David Friedel 1981, the author of the Maya model) noted that "the overall structure of the system would have to be a widely shared religion" involving "formal pilgrimages.... As the system expanded, these pilgrimages would be attended by increasingly large numbers of people, involving increasingly complex ritual" (Judge 1989:242, again citing Friedel 1981:378). He explained the inexplicable by invoking ritual.

Thus Chaco became the gargantuan punchline for a very old joke Indians tell about archaeologists: In archaeology, any artifact that cannot be ascribed to some quotidian function is automatically deemed ritual. The way Indians tell this joke is much funnier than my telling; because in Chaco's case, I don't think it's funny, I think it is seriously wrong. Not that Chaco had no ritual. Of course it did, and perhaps Judge's pilgrimage. But there was much more to Chaco than that (chapter 3).

That kind of pilgrimage—thousands of people converging, Mecca-like, on a ritual center—is not something Pueblos do now or (as far as we can tell) ever did in the past.[145] Pueblos are famous for pilgrimages of small groups of people to distant places—say, an ocean, or a mountain, or a spring. In the ethnographic literature, however, there is no mention of a Pueblo ritual center to which masses of people periodically pilgrimaged (if that's a verb). More disturbing, the pilgrimage model requires (or, at least, specifies) an organized and even universalizing religion (Judge suggested a "widely shared religion")—things not conformable with Pueblo Space. (None of this disqualifies, for me, Judge's ideas; why should Chaco be limited to the Classic Ethnographies?)

So it was necessary for archaeology to expand Pueblo Space, not in response to new insights from the Pueblos but to accommodate new ideas we acquired from tough cases, particularly Chaco. It was an implicit admission that Chaco did not fit the Pueblo Space. But importantly Judge kept Chaco hovering near, if not safely in, Pueblo Space: Pilgrimage was ritual, and Pueblos are all about ritual, right? The concept of a ritual-based pilgrimage center conformed not to what Pueblos actually did, but to OUR notions of Pueblos cosmologies and spirituality. Pueblo Space, heir of Pueblo Mystique. Vague notions of how Pueblos should behave, present and past.

Judge was suggesting something not seen in ethnology. That was revolutionary. As noted above, a central pilgrimage center is not how Pueblo pilgrimage works. Judge's model strayed beyond old Pueblo Space (recall it was based on a Maya model!). But it never reached escape velocity: We expanded the Space to encompass it and the awesome gravitational pull of Pueblo Space brought "pilgrimage center" back, if not to a full grounding on earth then at least to an inner, habitable orbit.

Pueblos might not actually do "pilgrimage fairs" in the ethnographic present, but it seems like something (we think) that Pueblo people might have done in the distant past (we think). Judge's model was, with some effort, conformable to Pueblo Space; and it surely kept Chaco safely beneath the Glass Ceiling; and although the model itself came from Maya archaeology, it did not require actual trespass across the Iron Curtain. (Judge wasn't suggesting Mayans ran Chaco's pilgrimage center, or that Chaco priest-elites actually knew anything about the Maya.) More than a few archaeologists, and many NPS interpreters, and most of the engaged public jumped on board and Chaco became a pilgrimage center.

Pilgrimage, by century's end, was by far the most widely accepted version of Chaco.[146]

And there was a lot more ritual at Chaco than just pilgrimage. Look at all those kivas! A Park Service interpretation in the late 1970s suggested that Pueblo Bonito was more religious than Chetro Ketl because it had more kivas. It's almost impossible to make a rational case that the hundreds of smaller kivas (sometimes called "clan kivas") at Chaco were anything like the things archaeologists call kivas in modern or ethnographic Pueblos—an extended argument rehearsed in a footnote to chapter 3. We've known this since the 1980s and, for a while, thoughtful archaeologists backed off and referred to them as "round rooms." But Pueblo Space plus (I think) Pueblo Indian annoyance at losing a heritage marker for NAGPRA brought us back to old-time religion, and today most of us once again call 'em kivas, with all the ethnographic implications of that term. Many kivas mean much ritual. Ritual über alles.

And there's more: We are reverential when it is proposed that Chaco knew the heavens sufficiently well to have a calendar and to align buildings to celestial objects.[147] Ritual of course, right? Sure; but for an agricultural society, a calendar was also an economic necessity.[148] Cloaked in ritual, to be sure; but as Solomon reminds us: For everything there is a season, a time to plant and a time to pluck up that which is planted. Time came from the sun, the moon, the stars. The heavens were marvelous, but they were also very practical.

Ritual, shotgunned at the problem of Chaco, kept Chaco in Pueblo Space. If there was power at Chaco, we all seem to agree that power must have been ritual, not political.[149] The tipping point, for me, came in 1999 on the cusp of the Millennium, when Chaco was officially declared a "rituality."[150] That term emerged from a working conference, brilliantly organized by Jill Neitzel, comparing the ancient Southwest and the ancient Southeast.[151] Published by Robert Drennan and Norman Yoffee simultaneously, Yoffee cited and ceded precedence to Drennan, keeping "rituality" vague but clearly contrasting it to "polity" and—heaven forfend!—"state":

> The term "rituality," of course, suggests that the fundamental component of the existence of Chaco and of the Chacoan network was its elaborate ritual apparatus.... [T]he ritual nature of Chaco cannot be reduced to the handmaiden of economic and/or political institutions. The term "rituality" also implies that Chaco society (or societies) cannot readily be typed in neo-evolutionary terms as being somewhere on its way to statehood. (Yoffee et al. 1999:266)

Yoffee, whose influence was (rightly) extensive in the Southwest from Tucson to Santa Fe, promoted Drennan's "rituality."[152] It fit into Pueblo Space and found a receptive audience in both popular and academic prehistory. But, as we shall see in chapter 2, upon further reflection Drennan changed his mind about Chaco, and the Chaco rituality.

I say this: Ritual did not build Pueblo Bonito. To anticipate chapter 3, people built Pueblo Bonito: hundreds, probably thousands of people. Those people had to be recruited, organized, and fed. Their feeding was almost certainly beyond the capacities of Chaco Canyon's agricultural production. Logistics and organization were comprehensive, long-term, and far-reaching: Construction events took years to complete and tens of thousands of beams had to be brought from distant forests. And people recruited and almost certainly brought into the canyon—how? Communal? Coerced? Corvée? Labor-tax or barn-raising? As images go, a Mennonite barn-raising seems preferable to slaves hauling stones up Pharaoh's pyramid. Neither are Pueblo, exactly, but the barn-raising better suits Pueblo Space—our notions of what's appropriate for Pueblos and their ancestors.

Farmers raise neighbor's barns every few years in rotation around their community. Bonito's barn was being raised more or less continuously for a century—1020 to 1125, if not longer. It required far more labor than any local community could provide. Not just beams, but hundreds (perhaps thousands) of people were brought into the canyon from distant settlements. And Bonito is only one of a half-dozen really big buildings, all going up at once; plus scores of smaller Great Houses, all going up at once; and roads and ramps and stairways and platforms, all going up at once. And that's just inside Chaco Canyon! Building boomed throughout the region. A whole lotta shakin' going on, a whole lotta barn-raisings: not much time left to raise corn or kids. No, Chaco was bigger than a barn-raising. (Whose barn? What barn? My barn!) Some form of labor-tax seems both reasonable and likely, but that's not in the Pueblo Space. Nor is it ritual.[153]

Of course, no one ever claimed that ritual actually brought Pueblo Bonito into being: A priest waved feathers over a vacant lot in Chaco Canyon and up popped a huge building. No. But tagging Bonito "ritual" somehow obviates awkward questions about labor. And somehow finesses the monumental differences between Bonito et alia and commoner ("Bc" sites or Unit Pueblos) houses (chapter 3). Say "ritual" and all is forgiven.

Chaco is a specific case; today ritual permeates all archaeology in the Southwest, from Hohokam to Hovenweep. Ritual was essentially nothing in the 1970s archaeology, at the height of New Archaeology; now ritual is everything. Clearly there is much more to the story than Adams's work with kachinas and Judge's views on Chaco Canyon. Larger forces were at work. I see at least three: Postmodern influences on (and from) British archaeology (as suggested by Hegmon, above); NAGPRA and archaeology's re-engagement with Indians; and New Age religions. All three hit the Southwest around 1990. We've already briefly reviewed the influence of Postprocessual archaeology on Processual-Plus archaeology (more in chapters 5 and 6). Let's look at NAGPRA and New Agery.

NAGPRA (discussed above) gave legal standing to ritual, to the sacred. "Ritual" heretofore had been a residual archaeological category, but with NAGPRA the word "sacred" now achieved legal power, and was often in the air.

Another element—outside any sort of archaeology—also played a role: The rise of New Age religions in the late 1970s and early 1980s (Hanegraaff 1996:12). The Harmonic Convergence brought thousands of New Agers to Chaco Canyon in 1987.[154] Few archaeologists were/are New Agers, and most Indians I know resent New Age appropriations of Indian symbols and ceremonies. But New Agery was as much a part of archaeology of ritual—its milieu, Pueblo Space, if not its content—as the Taos School of painting was part of the original Pueblo Mystique.

NAGPRA and New Agery, and to a lesser degree Postprocessual archaeology: that trinity triumphed and in a trice Southwestern archaeology's stern materialism crumbled like third-world cement. In a stunning reversal, Southwestern archaeology leapt joyfully into the pond/quagmire of cosmology and ritual.[155] Yesterday: Droughts and carrying capacities. Today: Ritual über alles. Who would have guessed? Not me.

Getting the Southwest Wrong: Chaco in Pueblo Space

By century's end, Southwestern archaeology, like Scrooge's pal Marley, dragged heavy chains, holding it back. Some were old and rusty: the Glass Ceiling and the Iron Curtain and Ethnological Method (and archaeology's perceived inferiority to ethnology). Add Pueblo Mystique and you have Pueblo Space, setting firm limits on the possible. Those chains were old and rusty, worn so long we hardly noticed them.

Some chains were newer and shinier: Science and scientism downplayed or denied history; but the same scientism deflected the British invasion of Postprocessual ideas, save (most importantly) one, ritual. Like the poor or a chronic condition, ritual had always been with us; but with the harmonic convergence of Southwestern ceremony and British theory, ritual shot high into the ether. The explosion, near century's end, of ritual and ceremony was exciting, but also another chain around Chaco's neck. All those chains kept Chaco in Pueblo Space: Perhaps not quite a Pueblo, but resolutely—if vaguely—Pueblo-like.

Here's what we said about Chaco, around the turn of the century[156] (sans citations, to protect the innocent): Chaco was a pilgrimage center, a "rituality" suffused and sustained by ritual and ceremony. Perhaps with a semi-quasi-elite priesthood, but more likely not; and in any event, priestly power came from ritual knowledge, not from any mundane or earthly base. And that settled it: It's hard to argue with the ineffable.

The first generation of archaeologists after Morgan and Bandelier codified a simple, local Southwest in the Pecos System, still our metanarrative of choice for Pueblo pre-history. Under the Ceiling and behind the Wall, every day in every way more and more like Zuni! We may not believe it, exactly, but we use it. An unholy alliance of Santa Fe boosters, Chicago railroad sharps, and popular anthropologists created, between World Wars, an idealization of Pueblos which appealed strongly to the American imagination and which flavors our archaeology even today as what I've called Pueblo Space. Timeless, spiritual, nearly utopian societies—exceptional societies, unique in the US, the Continent, maybe in the world. Other Indigenous societies have been held as paragons of this and that, as Great Warriors or Noble Savages or whatever. But the Pueblos were America's team and, importantly, still on their lands *all around Santa Fe*! Their exceptionalism makes the extraordinary our default, as long as it fits or conforms to Pueblo Space. In Pueblo Space, Chaco-as-state is foreign, outré, even offensive; Chaco-as-pilgrimage-center is respectful, ritual, and acceptable.

The strange attractions of Pueblo Space trumped science, materialism, even data. Its biases gave us Chaco at the Millennium: a uniqueness, a pilgrimage center, a rituality. I don't think so; but in Pueblo Space, no one can hear you scream.

CHAPTER 2

Chaco in the Twenty-First Century

You can't teach an old dogma new tricks.
—attributed to Dorothy Parker

Chapter 1 sketched an intellectual history of Pueblo Space and Chaco, up to the year 2000, give or take a decade or two. This chapter is more disparate, or is that desperate? It begins by bringing Chaco up-to-date, happily working with (i.e., ripping off) excellent synthetic reviews by Barbara Mills (2002) and Gregson Schachner (2015). Then we pivot polemical, looking critically at several current interpretive trends: Violence/cannibalism; imagined communities; inalienable possessions; and house societies. I consider these in Pueblo Space: Specifically, how those recent interpretive concepts were imported into the Southwest from larger Anthropological theaters, in forms that fit Pueblo Space. Finally, I move to two recent bombshell books on Chaco, one grounded firmly in Pueblo Space (Ware 2014) and the other orbiting way out beyond that familiar place (Lekson 2015): Bombs away!

Nouveau Chaco

There's no end in sight for Chaco. Since the turn of the Millennium, Chaco publications have exploded like celebratory fireworks. Mills (2002) and Schachner (2015)—both discussed below—list publications from Y2K to 2014. What could be added in the short time since? A ton, as it turns out. On my desktop is a folder named "Chaco Recent Research" with PDFs from the last few years: Thirty-plus files, almost all post-2010 and many post-2014. There has been, of late, much remarkable new research, some of which is noted briefly below.[1]

Most (almost all! trust me) of this research seems to support the Chaco I've described elsewhere (Lekson 2009a, 2015a), which you'll meet in chapter 3: Chaco NOT in Pueblo Space. Headlines like "Ancient Chaco Society Was Ruled by a Matrilineal Dynasty" (Google it; reporting the work of Kennett and others 2017) make me happy, as does the mounting confirmation that Chaco indeed relocated to Aztec Ruins (chapters in Reed 2008), as does validation of Chaco as a regional center/consumer/black hole for pots, rocks, timbers, labor, and food (Benson et al. 2009; Benson 2010; Grimstead et al. 2015; Guiterman et al. 2016; Duff et al. 2012; and others). And a few hold-the-press shockers: It started a half-century earlier than we'd (I'd) thought (Plog and Heitman 2010); Chaco's first love was not the north, but the south (provenance of construction wood; Guiterman et al. 2016); and Chaco's (matrilineal) rulers were knocking back both Mesoamerican cacao and Mississippian "black drink" (Crown and others 2015). The knowledge and taste of Chaco elites were continental.

At the fateful year of 2000—exactly 1,000 years since something-or-other happened somewhere at Pueblo Bonito—almost everyone could see that Chaco did not fit the Classic Pueblo Ethnographies[2] (almost everyone: wait a few pages for John Ware's *Pueblo Social History*). But we still needed or wanted to keep Chaco in the Pueblo ballpark, in Pueblo Space. What have we done/are we doing with Chaco in this brave new millennium? A heck of a lot, as I've hinted above. Happily, two outstanding summary reviews of Chaco studies book-end its first post-Y2K decade: Barbara Mills (2002) and Gregson Schachner (2015).

Chaco, from Clinton to Bush to Obama, 2000–2015

Barbara Mills gave us an excellent summary of Chaco at (approximately) the Millennium in her 2002 review article, "Recent Research on Chaco: Changing Views on Economy, Ritual, and Society." Her review is commendably broad and encompassing; I focus here on the bits most relevant to my argument: Power, ritual, polity, and those sorts of things.

Mills stated that, ca. 2000, "the ritual center model dominates the recent literature on Chaco," but she noted "some cracks in the pilgrimage fair model are beginning to appear" (Mills 2002:79, 94). Judge's Mayan model was, perhaps, a bit too far away from Pueblo Space, too exotic. It fell out of favor with several influential schools of Southwestern archaeology (e.g., Plog and Watson 2012; in Plog and Heitman's 2015 edited volume, *Chaco Revisited*, the word "pilgrimage" does not merit an index entry). But "pilgrimage center" remained (and remains) the mainstream public interpretation of Chaco.

In her discussion of "Political Organization," Mills contrasted Judge's pilgrimage fair (already on the way out), to Lynne Sebastian's (1992) insistence on leadership of uncertain form, to claims for Chacoan statehood (for example, Lekson 1999a). She questions but does not dismiss pilgrimage, then comes down hard against the state, and ends in favor of a ritual center of uncertain organization—perhaps à la Sebastian. Mills is not inimical to leadership and hierarchy at Chaco (Mills 2002:100) but she sees leadership as diffused through multiple role-specific and locale-specific individuals, with hierarchy based on restricted ritual knowledge, as in Pueblos—a trope that has (we shall see) come to dominate discussions of power at Chaco:

> Although many issues are hotly debated, there is a growing consensus that power was not based in a centralized political organization and that ritual organization was a key factor in the replication of Chacoan architecture across a vast regional landscape. (Mills 2002:65)

Ritual hierarchies, perhaps—Pueblos have ritual hierarchies, so that's OK. But not political or economic hierarchies—Pueblos shun those. Mills at the Millennium predicted Chaco's future:

> The idea of ritual landscapes, pilgrimages, roads through time, and landscapes of memory might once have seemed difficult to pursue—in any area. Yet these are at the very cusp of new research on Chaco. New research that looks at social identity, leadership, status, and ritual organization is just beginning. In particular, the model of Chaco as a ritual center will require more definition and critical evaluation. (Mills 2002:101)

And so it came to pass. Things that once seemed difficult to know—ritual, religion, ideology—have in recent years become stock-in-trade for Chaco studies and for the Southwest in general. Those of a certain age (mine) watch in awe (and shock) as young archaeologists make sweeping, confident statements about ritual, religion, and cosmology—statements that would have been laughed off the floor and shown the door in the materialist twentieth century. It's hard to see the basis for such statements; have we developed bold new tools for peering into past people's hearts and minds? No, we have not. We use the same bag of archaeological tools and tricks we had at 2000, but we now have very different interests and attitudes. In any event, ritual came to dominate Chacoan discourse. A decade later, Mills noted with apparent alarm,

> We are in a very new situation now—one where ritual (the practice) and religion (beliefs) have become primary topics of interest, and we might be in danger of making political and economic organization epiphenomenal. (Mills 2015:250)

Ritual über alles—as we saw in chapter 1. Ritual has come to dominate Chaco and Southwestern archaeology to such an extent that archaeologists working elsewhere chuckle at our obsession. I've heard them, and I answered with a hollow laugh. Those working outside Pueblo Space don't understand its powerful influence: making the past conform to an idealized "Pueblo" present. We evangelized Chaco: First pilgrimage, then rituality, and ritual center—all (intentionally) vague but safely in Pueblo Space.

Complementing and updating Mills's overview ca. 2000, Gregson Schachner (2014) provides a review of Chaco archaeology a decade-plus into the new millennium, as part of a larger assessment of "Ancestral Pueblo Archaeology:

The Value of Synthesis." Again, as with Mills, his review is far broader and comprehensive than my use of it here. Schachner notes several major post-2000 projects: The Chaco Synthesis,[3] the Chaco Research Archive,[4] the Salmon Ruins Initiative,[5] the Chaco Stratigraphy Project,[6] and other worthy studies conducted independently of those larger efforts.[7] "These efforts produced many important advances that post-date Mills's (2002) review of Chaco archaeology…and warrant extensive discussion" (Schachner 2015:57).

Much had happened in the century's first fifteen years. Pilgrimage and ritual remain the dominant chords. "Most recent models depict Chaco Canyon as a pilgrimage destination at the center of an area of shared religious ideals" (Schachner 2015: 60), which he questions.[8] On the pilgrims plod…

Much like Mills, Schachner summarizes my arguments in the first edition of *Chaco Meridian* (Lekson 1999a) fairly: I argued that Chaco was a low-wattage state with or without pilgrimage (no matter). But, after his fair and frank assessment, he rejects state-level society at Chaco, in words I find brilliantly hopeful:

> Nearly all Southwest archaeologists would argue that many of the archaeological markers of state organization, such as clear, multitiered settlement hierarchies, institutionalized bureaucracies, and armies, are difficult to see in the Chaco region. On the other hand, many of these markers are signs of successful state creation. It may be useful to explore the possibility that failed experiments in these directions did occur. (Schachner 2015:61; internal citations omitted)

He suggests we've been holding Chaco up to inappropriate standards—that's quite true: A topic to which we return in chapter 4. Schachner himself notes that several lines of fairly robust evidence "make a strong argument for sociopolitical inequality and the ability of Chaco Canyon's residents to draw surplus labor and its products from surrounding areas" (Schachner 2015:57), quoting at length a comparative article by Richard Drennan and others (2010)—to which we shortly return. I am greatly encouraged by the direction Schachner (and others) seems to be heading—revisiting the political, but not ignoring ritual. The two, after all, are intertwined. Schachner recommends a course correction:

> Chaco archaeologists should investigate models of chiefly societies proposed by Earle (2001) and others that have largely been ignored by Southwest archaeologists. Although we may be skeptical of the label "redistribution," the "special pleading" made for Ancestral Pueblo societies noted by Drennan et al. (2010) has been counterproductive. Of course ritual is important and some aspects of overly standardized models may not fit, but I believe we have taken too many of the pathways to power

seen around the world off the table to investigate Chaco properly or make it amenable to comparison to other cases. (Schachner 2015:64)

Schachner was much influenced by a chapter by Robert Drennan, Christian Peterson, and Jake Fox (2010), "Degrees and Kinds of Inequality"—an essay every Southwesternist should read. I, too, am a big fan of this essay; it has brought me much comfort over the last several years.

As noted in chapter 1, Drennan first suggested the term "rituality" for Chaco in 1999 (a term subsequently promoted by Norman Yoffee), but by 2010 Drennan had second thoughts. "Degrees and Kinds of Inequality" is an intelligent look at the question by outside scholars unbeglamoured by Pueblo Mystique and safely outside Pueblo Space.

Drennan, Peterson, and Fox's (2010) study opens, in fact, with "the Pueblo Problem" (indeed, their eyes on Chaco): Pueblos are the exception to almost every rule. When we are looking for an example of a corporate quasi-complex society (to mix anthropological metaphors), it's almost always "Pueblos" that are offered up—to which I add: If and only if we somehow keep Chaco in Pueblo Space.

Turns out, that's hard to do. Drennan and his colleagues compare and contrast Chaco with a dozen ancient societies in the Old and New Worlds, all from the upper end of "intermediate"—a twilight zone where distinctions between nonstates and states blur. They focus on burial data, household archaeology, and public works. Chaco ranks in the top three on each measure for which it is compared, alongside Olmec and Sitio Conte, and those three come in well ahead of the rest of the pack of upper-intermediate sites in Columbia, the Mississippi Valley, China, and Oaxaca.[9] Drennan and his colleagues are perplexed.[10] To avoid the appearance of improper selectivity, I'll let Schachner summarize their argument:

> Drennan et al. (2010) note that the labor expenditures and burial investment at Pueblo Bonito in Chaco Canyon are comparable to and often exceed efforts in other contexts where the presence of hierarchical political organization and social inequality are largely unquestioned (e.g., La Venta, Moundville, Formative Oaxaca, etc.). They chide Southwest archaeologists for obfuscating what they see as fairly clear evidence of inequality and our relegation of ancient Pueblo societies to a "separate, but equal" status in comparisons with other societies. (Schachner 2015:57; internal citations omitted)

Amen. For more than two decades, our thinking about Chaco has been almost entirely ritual, safely within Pueblo Space. The time has come, as the walrus said, to speak of other things: Economy and politics, cannibals and kings.

Light-Bending Gravity of Pueblo Space versus
Mind-Bending Anomaly of Chaco

Pueblo Space is still with us today. Or more accurately, we still work inside it, and don't even know. Even a cursory reading of articles, chapters, theses, and so forth will find, almost everywhere, expressions such as "we know it was an intermediate society," or "nonhierachical explanations are more satisfactory," or "better explained as ritual," or—the diagnostic symptom, the red flag—"as suggested by Pueblo ethnographies" or "based on ethnographic information." These are not actual quotes, but a distillation offered to avoid a tedious parade of Pueblo Space dicta from darn near every interpretative Southwestern screed I've read, ever.[11] Surely, dear reader, you've noticed them, too?

It's not only the low-level nod-to-Pueblo homilies with which we pepper our papers, to please a thesis committee or a peer reviewer, or to punch the Indigeneity ticket. Pueblo Space works on much higher interpretive levels. In this section, four situations which demonstrate the ongoing effects of Pueblo Space: Violence/cannibalism; imagined communities; inalienable possessions; and house societies. The first is an internal controversy compressed in or by Pueblo Space; the last three are anthropological concepts imported into the Southwest, shaved down from their original definitions to fit Pueblo Space. (To be fair, most of the shaving happened elsewhere, before the reconfigured concept made its Southwestern debut.)

In one of chapter 1's many digressions (most of which will lead somewhere, eventually), I followed the word "pueblo" from a Spanish colonial administrative term ("town" or "polity"), to a quasi-ethnic label ("Pueblo Indians"), and finally a brand ("Pueblo Style"). "Pueblo" was perhaps the first but certainly not the last term transformed by what I'm calling Pueblo Space: Words that originally, elsewhere, meant one thing but changed when they entered the Southwest.

We have a history of taking concepts from other disciplines and trimming them to fit Pueblo Space; and of showing to the door concepts—even those that are part of archaeological discourse everywhere else in the world—that fail to fit the Space. A few older examples, more or less at random, before we focus on twenty-first-century themes. Let's start with Edgar: Hewett insisted that Pueblos were ur-republics, Greek city-states-that-were-not-states because states are not allowed in Pueblo Space. Benedict said Zuni was Apollonian—sticking a whittled-down version of Nietzsche's shtick in Pueblo Space. (Mad Aby Warburg, whom we meet in chapter 6, insisted the Hopi were Dionysian!) Neo-evolutionary schemes—assumed to be universal—made a brief appearance and then were denounced as improper, chased from Pueblo Space. In neo-evolutionary terms, Chaco should have been a straight-up chiefdom.[12] When pressed, neo-evolutionists offered concoctions tailored to (and by) Pueblo Space: Group-oriented, corporate chiefdoms sans chiefs, of which Pueblos are the prime example (e.g., Earle 2001). But there's no crying in baseball and no chiefdoms in Pueblo Space, so neither survived. Pilgrimage fairs (in chapter 1) originally were a Maya model: Kingly courts peregrinated from city to city, causing or following trade fairs. Brought to the Southwest, the concept was turned on its head (off with its head?): An egalitarian ritual center, where the people gathered for communal ritual, untroubled by Maya-manqué kings. A Maya Mecca minus monarchs. And so on and so on.

The reach of Pueblo Space is inclusive and encompassing, reaching even Hohokam and Mogollon, both supposedly separate but equal to the ancients formerly known as Anasazi. Lines of masked dancers atop Hohokam platform mounds? Pueblo cosmologies for Mimbres pit houses? I offer no citations to protect both innocent and guilty.

Cannibal Questions

I begin with an example that exposed the procrustean clip of Pueblo Space in almost farcical clarity: The cannibal controversies of the earliest 2000s.

In 1999 two books were published that exploded Pueblo Space: Christy and Jaqueline Turner's *Man Corn: Cannibalism and Violence in the Prehistoric American Southwest* and Steven LeBlanc's *Prehistoric Warfare in the American Southwest*.[13] Both were roundly condemned and sternly suppressed—especially *Man Corn*. Indians, understandably, weren't happy with *Man Corn* and all the media hoopla around it.[14] But the archaeological anger could only be described as righteous: The fury of an anthropologist when someone scorns his/her "people."

The reaction of Southwesternists showed the boundaries of the Space, and the censorious campaign against Turner showed the zeal with which archaeologists defended it. It was not my field's finest hour, and I will not rehash its ignominies here. It still goes on, with C-word-deniers denigrating the late Turner and Turner and their analyses—although the reality of ancient cannibalism has been firmly established (Marlar et al. 2000; White 1992). Turner blamed the ancient unpleasantness on Chaco, or rather on Mesoamerican thugs who founded Chaco, and then went on a murderous spree[15]—a prehistory with more drama than Di Peso's!—but his reading has not survived into current times.

Mills, in her 2002 Chaco review, dismissed Turner's Mesoamerican narrative as "grasping at straws" and welcomed "alternative explanations" of the evident violence (Mills 2002:95–96): "It is certain that violence took place in some areas of the Southwest, that this violence often took the form of bodily mutilation and occasionally consumption."

There were alternatives. Archaeologists attempted to normalize violence by suggesting that it was ritual retribution for witchcraft (not unknown, historically, among Pueblos), bringing it all back home to Pueblo Space (e.g., Darling 2008; Walker 1998). If it was something Pueblos once did but don't do now, then it's OK, right? Plus, it's ritual! Everything goes better with ritual.

Steven LeBlanc's book, detailing warfare over much of the Southwest before-during-and-after Chaco, was, in the end, accepted. We acknowledge that from time to time, butts were kicked and heads were cracked. But that (alas) very human behavior has been consistently downplayed in the Southwest.[16] LeBlanc noted (and Mills [2002] readily acknowledged), violence was not everywhere and every time, a war of all against all—as Hobbes once said (sounds more like Calvin?). Notably, during Chaco's salad days, violence diminished greatly, the so-called Pax Chaco.[17] I suggested, shortly after LeBlanc's book appeared, that the diminution of violence during Chaco's era probably reflected Chaco's peace-keeping or order-keeping function, enforced by periodic acts of violence (Lekson 2002), an argument to which we return shortly.

After LeBlanc's book, the evidence of widespread violence could no longer be swept under the rug. It was perhaps a first chip in Southwestern exceptionalism, the armor-scale Smaug lost at Dale. If there was war, red war, in the past then maybe Pueblo Space was insufficient to ancient history. As Schachner (2015:81) noted, "As in most human societies, various forms and intensities of violence were present throughout the Ancestral Pueblo sequence," and he called on Southwesternists to take war seriously and study it—which many have (e.g., Kohler et al. 2006; Kuckelman 2016; among others).

No more can we not study war. If we can study war—something not in Pueblo Space—what other surprises might the ancient Southwest hold? Pueblo Space: The force is very strong in that one, as the Emperor warned Lord Vader. How strong? We'll review three anthropological concepts—some old, some new—all recently imported into the Southwest, and into Pueblo Space: Imagined communities, inalienable possessions, and house societies.

Imagined Community

We will ease into this, with an idea that, so far, has made only a small splash in the Southwest. "Imagined community" was coined in 1983 by political scientist Benedict Anderson to explain how the citizens of modern nation-states—far too big for everyone to know everyone—maintain a fictive sense of community.

There was and remains enthusiasm for imagined communities in archaeology, riffing on the phrase—but seldom the actual meaning—of Benedict Anderson's influential book, *Imagined Communities: Reflections on the Origin and Spread of Nationalism* (Anderson 1983, 1991, 2006). Anderson's book is about nation-states and the top-down manipulation of their citizens/subjects to imagine they are a community—despite the multiethnic composition of modern

nations.[18] Anderson argues that the imagined community is a very modern conclusion of an evolutionary sequence of social forms: Religious communities →
dynastic realms → nationalisms. His imagined community is both the tool and
the creation of what he calls "print-capitalism"—with a complex but (in archaeological terms) shallow history in both Old and New Worlds.

Anderson's imagined community in modern nation-states was stretched on
the rack of social theory[19] to encompass, apparently, anything archaeologists
want to call "community" that differed from the old, conventional, face-to-face
settlement model. Archaeological interest was most publicly expressed by a
chapter by William Isbell in the edited volume *Archaeology of Communities:
A New World Perspective* (Canuto and Yaeger 2000). Isbell explored "What We
Should Be Studying: The 'Imagined Community' and the 'Natural Community'" (Isbell 2000:243–266); his analysis seems to have had some purchase
among Southwesternists, for example in a 2008 volume of collected papers, *The
Social Construction of Communities*, edited by Mark D. Varien and James M.
Potter. In their introduction:

> Isbell has argued that the best way to avoid using community as an essen-
> tialist concept is to abandon the concept that he labels "the natural com-
> munity" and instead focus on what he calls "the imagined community."…
> Isbell's discussion of the imagined community is genuinely interesting,
> but it is difficult to come away from it with a concise definition of the
> term. (Varien and Potter 2008:3)

And they steer away (wisely, I think) from the imaginary and towards "The
Social Production of Communities" (Varien and Potter 2008:1–18)—nodding
to Giddens more than to Anderson. Indeed, imagined communities are largely
absent from the thirteen chapters of the book, save Varien and Potter's brief
discussion and a longer engagement in Gregson Schachner's "Imagining Communities in the Cibola Past" (2008:171–190). Schachner attempts to apply Isbell's
version of "imagined community" to the distant past. He questions "why some
archaeologists have revived earlier models of community, especially when they
are poorly suited to modern social theory" (2008:173).

Anticipating chapter 6, I will respond preemptively: Modern social theory
is poorly suited to early communities. The imagined communities of Benedict
Anderson are useful in the intended contexts—modern nation-states—but not
perhaps to the times and places we study, unless the term is stretched beyond
recognition. Schachner acknowledges that Isbell's notion is "a concept which
has simultaneously intrigued and confused many archaeologists" (2008:173),
but tries bravely to save something from the wreckage. In the end, "the 'imagined' community perspective encourages archaeologists to view the origins and

maintenance of local social systems in new ways...[for example] how different settlement forms were associated with other axes of variation" (Schachner 2008: 190). And there is nothing wrong with that, but I'm not sure we need to twist Anderson's ideas about modern nation-states to get us there.

But...I'm intrigued. Anderson's original "imagined community" might possibly be applicable to Chaco. Save that thought: We will return to it at the end of this section.

Inalienable Possessions

"Inalienable Possessions" is another anthropological import, with far more effect than "imagined communities." Barbara Mills's (2004a) influential *American Anthropologist* article, "The Establishment and Defeat of Hierarchy: Inalienable Possessions and the History of Collective Prestige Structures in the Pueblo Southwest," brought Annette Weiner's (1992) concept of "inalienable possessions" to the Southwest and to Chaco.

Mills presents three classes of Chaco artifacts—altars, clothing, and staffs, viewed through the lens of Zuni ethnology—as something not unlike NAGPRA's "objects of cultural patrimony" or "sacred objects."[20] Mills (2004a:24) says, "Based on the ethnographic evidence...I expect that altar furniture was owned collectively, while ceremonial clothing and wands or staffs of office were individually owned objects, and that all three classes were used in collective rituals at different scales."

Mills continues:

Inalienable possessions are objects made to be kept (not exchanged), have symbolic and economic power that cannot be transferred, and are often used to authenticate the ritual authority of corporate groups.... I argue that inalienable goods are more useful than prestige goods for understanding the role of social valuables in many nonstate societies, especially those in which inequalities are based on ritual knowledge. (Mills 2004a:238)

Fair enough; but other interpretations are possible.[21] Let's see where we might go with the original notions of "inalienable possessions" and "defeat of hierarchy," both of which come from Annette Weiner's (1992) book *Inalienable Possessions: The Paradox of Keeping-While-Giving*.[22] In her text but not her title, Mills adjusts Weiner's term, from "possession"—which implies ownership—to the neutral "object." Mills makes other adjustments to Weiner's original formulation—adjustments she specifies very clearly.[23]

Weiner's "inalienable possessions"—called by her in an earlier 1985 article "inalienable wealth"—were part of a complex system of elite gifting and exchange; in fact, they were tools of political power in ranked societies.[24] "Possessions like these are what strong political hierarchy is made of" (Weiner 1992: 130). They were *possessions* of an individual or of "a family, descent groups, or dynasty" (Weiner 1992:6). According to Weiner (1985), they were inalienable in two senses: Historical association and past/current ownership. Historical connections—the key thing—were typically to an important place, a key event, or a legendary individual. Ownership was inalienable precisely because the things are so bloody important—until they become chips to be cashed for a higher (or lower) purpose. Weiner says,

> We are all familiar with the crowns of kings and queens—or antique furniture and paintings that proclaim a family's distinguished ancestry.... [C]ertain things assume a subjective value that place them above exchange value. When a Maori chief brandishes a sacred cloak she is showing that she is more than herself—that she is her ancestors. This is the power of cosmological authentication. (Weiner 1992:6)

I don't think that's what Mills means by "inalienable objects," at least by the end of her article. The concepts are parallel to be sure; but Mills's use, in the course of her argument, is tailored to Chaco in Pueblo Space—my phrase of course, not hers.

Weiner's "defeat of hierarchy" is a key part of Mills's argument. Mills certainly acknowledges that inalienable possessions can play a role in the rise of hierarchy (à la Weiner), but in the Southwest the hierarchic whack-a-mole pops up only to be hammered down. Mills says, in part by inalienable objects,

> they establish hierarchy by validating or legitimizing the identity and claims of individuals and groups who are unequal in terms of access to knowledge and resources. They can be actively used and circulated in contexts of competition between leaders vying for positions of esteem. However, they can also defeat hierarchy when used to promote communal identities, rather than the individual identities of particular leaders. Additionally, they may result in the defeat of hierarchy when the knowledge of how to make and use them is destroyed, as they often are when new cults are established, or in colonial situations of mercantilism and missionization. In the latter cases, these objects may be destroyed or may move from objects of inalienable value to commodities as they are bought and sold on the world market (Weiner 1992:103). The movement of objects between inalienability and alienability has always been present but has been accelerated in the postcolonial world. (Mills 2004a:240)

The first part of this quote is a fair paraphrase of Weiner. The latter argument about "communal identities" is mostly Mills.[25] For Weiner "the defeat of hierarchy is traceable to the various cultural constructions that are created in attempts to overcome the exchange and gender paradoxes of keeping-while-giving" (1992:99)—not to inalienable possessions. The existence, use, and circulation of inalienable objects causes or supports hierarchies, which are subverted not by "inalienable objects" (in Weiner's definition) but by "cultural constructions" (such as manipulations of gender roles, incest taboos, and descent rules).[26]

Recall that Mills sees ritual hierarchy at Chaco rather than hierarchy based on political power. Inalienable objects played a role in the rise of ritual hierarchy; but at Chaco and at later Pueblos, they were, in the end, manifestations of its defeat:

> They construct hierarchy by authenticating the ritual authority of groups and, as the Southwestern [Pueblo ethnographic] examples illustrate, the relative rankings of those groups. Beyond their role in the construction of hierarchy, however, is how they were used in defeating hierarchy. As repositories and validations of group identity, they serve as a system of checks and balances to individual aggrandizement and personal gain. (Mills 2004a:248)

This requires communal or institutional (sodality) appropriation of the objects and their reassociations—at which point, they cease to be "inalienable possessions" in Weiner's terms.

But I'm intrigued. Perhaps Weiner's original ideas can help us understand Chaco—just not the Chaco of Pueblo Space. Hold that idea, too; we will return to it at the end of this section.

House Societies

"House societies" appear to have even broader impact than "inalienable possessions" (e.g., Heitman 2015; Mills 2015; Plog 2015; Whiteley 2015). "House society" was first forwarded by Claude Lévi-Strauss (1975, 1983, 1992; published in English in 1982). It's odd that American archaeologists are flocking to old Lévi-Strauss, who practically invented structuralism. Long ago, Lévi-Strauss's structuralism received a thorough pounding from young French intellectuals looking to launch their careers: Poststructuralists! (We meet these *théoriciens*—not young anymore, mostly dead—in chapter 6.) We are all poststructuralists now. And yet, with house societies, we hark back to arch-structuralist Lévi-Strauss and his *sociétés à maisons. Plus ça change, plus c'est la même chose.*[27]

The house that Claude built has been extensively remodeled—flipped and rebuilt—by American Anthropological Archaeology.[28] And now applied to Chaco. Barbara Mills (as always!) provides the clearest definition of house society as used today. She notes four "principles that underlie the concept of the house society":

First, it involves heritability...which may include material and imma-terial property. Second, it occurs with others of like structure.... Third, the house should be considered a "moral person"...a living being, em-bodied by its architecture.... And finally, houses may be archaeologically identified on the basis of architectural permanence, ancestors, origins or primacy, and inalienable objects. (Mills 2015:254–255)

These aspects of house societies come from Lévi-Strauss; but the myriad makeovers (well outside the Southwest) between the original *sociétés à maisons* and today,[29] something critical to his original definition, was left behind: Hier-archy. Lévi-Strauss's house societies were all about nobles, "noble houses." Think: House of Windsor. *Vraiment*, Claude specified feudal houses or Japanese noble houses, while talking about our Northwest Coast:

In order to recognize the house [in Kwakiutl society], it would have been necessary for ethnologists to look toward history, that of medieval Europe of course, but also that of Japan of the Heian and following periods.... Confining ourselves to the Middle Ages, there is a striking resemblance...[to] one that comes from the pen of a European medieval-ist seeking to outline exactly what is a house.... We are, therefore, in the presence of one and the same institution: a corporate body holding an es-tate made up of both material and immaterial wealth, which perpetuates itself through the transmission of its names, its goods, and its titles down a real or imaginary line, considered legitimate as long as the continuity can express itself in the language of kinship or of affinity and, most often, both. (Lévi-Strauss 1982:174)

And he goes on to analyze Charlemagne, fictive kinships among kings and queens of the Hundred Years War (pp. 176–177), and European "house names— Bourbon, Orleans, Valois, Savoy, Orange, Hannover, etc." (p. 180).

This is what Lévi-Strauss meant by "house societies," which he saw as a miss-ing link between egalitarian societies and the state (my terms, not his). This is the very core of his formulation, but it's been edited out. That sort of quasi-evolutionary notion was distasteful, and was shed long before we brought house societies to the Southwest.[30] Anthropologists gutted Lévi-Strauss's house and remodeled it to suit their varied tastes.

Lévi-Strauss's original idea of house society has been popped, scraped, and rebuilt to fit Pueblo Space—which, to extend the metaphor, acts rather like Santa Fe's building code: Everything in Pueblo Style. (I cannot resist repeating the analogy of mud-colored stucco slathered over a Santa Fe Victorian; sorry.) To be fair, the work on Claude's Old House was done outside the Southwest; Southwestern usage picks the published version that best fits Pueblo Space, rather than the architect's original plan. And thereby legitimize Pueblo Space by appeal to the old, original French theorist. Claude said it and that settles it; but he didn't say *that*. Would he recognize the house that Lévi-Strauss built, applied to Chaco? Who can say? He's dead, and French.

But I'm intrigued. Claude might not recognize his remodeled house societies in Pueblo Space, but the original formulation might help us understand Chaco. Please keep that (fourth) thought in mind, but only just for a moment: We now return to these several ideas, as originally defined, applied to Chaco.

Violence (sensu LeBlanc 1999 and Lekson 2002), imagined communities (sensu Anderson 1983), inalienable possessions (sensu Weiner 1985, 1992), and house societies (sensu Lévi-Strauss 1992)—these concepts *in their original meanings* might, indeed, apply to Chaco. Not the Chaco of Pueblo Space, but the Chaco we will meet in chapter 3: A secondary state of several tens of thousands of people, with a small capital at Chaco Canyon and a territory the size of Indiana, ruled by a half-dozen princely families. Not your grandmother's Chaco. If Chaco was something like that (and it was), then the concepts imported into the Southwest and fitted to Pueblo Space might work better as their authors originally intended.

Violence: The violence that killed (and sometimes cannibalized) people was, I think, socially sanctioned. That is, it was an expected part of the social contract (the stuff in the nasty small print) and not a surprise raid, a random war, or a barbarian invasion. Executing witches, for example, would be socially sanctioned violence. (If you're lighter than a duck, all must admit: It's a fair cop.) Once, in a conference paper, I tried to point out that there were, apparently, an awful lot of witches, and that one man's witchcraft might be another man's *lèse-majesté*. "Witchcraft," broadly defined, means not playing by the rules; witches or tax evaders, the people were just as dead. (Those suggestions got me bounced from the session, on Southwestern violence: I was expelled from Pueblo Space.)

Extended families or even small settlements were rounded up, executed, and then systematically butchered, cut into pieces. Not a hit-and-run raid, but something drawn out and deliberate, by guys who knew what they were about. Perhaps this spectacle was public; certainly, people for miles around would know about it. But—and this is important!—settlement patterns did not change: People continued to live in isolated single-family farmsteads. At least initially, no defensive steps were taken. And we know they knew how to defend their settlements: Later, isolated farmsteads aggregated into large towns (sometimes walled), or shifted up into cliff overhangs, and so forth. But during Chaco's reign, when these violent events were less frequent than later, settlement patterns did not change: People did not react as if there was widespread war, or random violence, or indeed *anything out of the ordinary*. Not that mass executions were "ordinary," but apparently the knowledge of such executions did not alter the basic settlement patterns (and all that implies: Social structures, economies, lifestyles, etc.). I think that whoever did the killing had a socially sanctioned right to do so. That would be consistent with a state's use of power.

Imagined communities: Anderson's original "imagined community" might actually be applicable to Chaco. Chaco's region was far too big for everyone to know everyone, yet it constituted a kind of community—an imagined community maintained not through print (as in Anderson's argument), but other media like linear monuments we call roads, line-of-sight signaling systems, prestige economies, power structures, and so forth. And an overarching ideology, a social contract, a government. But, again, do we need Benedict Anderson to figure that out? I don't think we need Anderson, but maybe Anderson needs us: To understand the pre-history of "imagined communities," before print and the nation-state and modernity.

Inalienable possessions: Also called by Weiner "inalienable wealth," they were tools of political power in ranked societies. Recall that "possessions like these are what strong political hierarchy is made of" (Weiner 1992:130). They were owned by elite families or dynasties like "the crowns of kings and queens." Carefully crafted staffs stacked in a room at the heart of Pueblo Bonito might remind us of the now-treasured canes given by the Lincoln administration to governors of the various Pueblos: Visible symbols of authority.[31] Or we can upstream (push the present back into the past) ritual interpretations from ethnographic Zuni to Chaco; but—and this is important!—Chaco was not Zuni. Rather than project modern Pueblo ritual practices back to an ancient city-state, we perhaps should wonder how scepters for Chaco nobles became ritual staffs in an egalitarian pueblo: Repurposed, resymbolized, recontextualized. Elsewhere (Lekson 1999a, 2015a), I've discussed the most important macaw-feather object we have from Chaco's time: A magnificent feathered sash, or kilt, or cape—whatever it was, a rare item of apparel which probably marked its wearer as lordly. That connotation would be consistent with feather use in Chaco's time, throughout Mesoamerica and in much of the Southeast. Up-streaming, however, we might assert (as did a famous up-streamer at a conference) that macaw feathers at Chaco were probably attached to *pahos*, prayer sticks; that's what Pueblo people do today. But we have macaw regalia, not *pahos*, at Chaco. How did macaw feathers—symbols of power in Chaco's world—become Pueblo prayer flags? What history would redefine macaw feathers from symbols of power to an attribute of kachinas?

House societies: There may be merit in applying Lévi-Strauss's idea to Chaco, but perhaps not in the modified version that Southwestern enthusiasts have in mind. Let's deconstruct the house, *la maison*. *Maison* in French means house, yes; but it also means a firm or a brand: *Maison Dior, Maison Veuve Clicquot*. Great Houses are Chaco's brand, or more likely Chaco's competing brands: *Maison Bonito, Maison Alto*. Great Houses are both the archaeological problem and the archaeological solution. Without Great Houses, there would be no Chaco problem—no century of fieldwork, no libraries of reports, no debates and alarms and excursions. As explained in chapter 3, Chaco's Great Houses were (comparatively) monumental palaces. That reading works nicely with Lévi-Strauss's original notion of house societies: Noble houses, palaces perpetuating power over many generations. According to Lévi-Strauss, House Societies exist as multiples: Houses, not the house. That, too, fits Chaco with its half-dozen major Great Houses. And Lévi-Strauss's original house society works well for the Mesoamerican political structure I will suggest in chapter 3, the *altepetl*, as an ethnohistoric box for Chaco. And, finally, yes: Lévi-Strauss's house societies as a (not necessarily *the*) precursor to the state—an insight lost with the blanket rejection by today's house society enthusiasts of Lévi-Strauss's nearly neo-evolutionary thinking.

Bombs Away

Circa 2015, in addition to biographies or autobiographies of Elon Musk, Ruth Ginsberg, John Cleese, Willie Nelson, and Eleanor Roosevelt, two books were published of singular relevance to our topic: John Ware's *Pueblo Social History* and my *Chaco Meridian*, second edition. I will be harsh with one and gentle with the other. (Guess which?) Nothing personal, here or elsewhere in this chapter/book: I'm just arguing ideas, but sometimes ideas are closely identified with individuals, as is the case with both these books.

A Pueblo Social History: *Return of the Ethnological Method*

The old Ethnological Method (hereafter referred to as EM) espoused by Lewis Henry Morgan has returned, in a spectacular tour-de-force by John Ware (2014). Recall from chapter 1 that EM derives a form of "history"—reconstructing past social systems—by working logically back from the ethnographic present: Puzzling out possible developments of the social systems, kinship, and so forth attested by ethnography. The original EM evolved or coevolved into a standard American Anthropological Archaeological method, the direct historic approach: Starting (again) at the ethnohistorical present and chasing traits back into the past, moving from known to unknown. Both EM and the direct historic approach easily could (and perhaps should) be confused with up-streaming. We up-stream a lot in the Southwest, painting Pueblo institutions directly over archaeological problems. Well, sure: That all makes sense, right? Well, no: None of it makes sense; in fact, quite the opposite.

It's how we do things, how we've always done things. EM, the direct historic approach, and up-streaming were always present in Southwestern archaeology, even hovering over our 1970s science.[32] New Archaeology questioned everything—a few Young Turks even railed against the tyranny of ethnology (chapter 1)—but, as noted above, the force was strong with Pueblo Space. New Archaeologists no longer pored over Classic Ethnographies but they settled for a generalized Pueblo Space, asserting (for an unreferenced example) Pueblo-ish matrilineality at fourteenth-century ruins.

That's a generalized notion of how Pueblos work; not the detailed analysis of the Ethnological Method. Vague notions were easier than the puzzle logic of EM, so fewer and fewer people went the EM route. It's back: In a few ranging shots in chapters in 2015's *Chaco Revisited*,[33] and in a book of considerably more megatonage: John Ware's (2014) *A Pueblo Social History*. Ware, by page count, is EM's principal proponent and undisputed champion.

"If our goal is to plot the trajectory of a thrown ball, knowing where the ball lands is important because it tells us—with the help of a little calculus—something about the ball's flight path" (Ware 2014:11).[34] Reconstructing the ballistics of a ball—or, forensically, a gunshot—is a good metaphor for EM: Logically deducing the most likely path through time that would lead to the present, to the Pueblos.

But history is not a parabola, not a linear path. History is a maze of false starts, dead ends, parallel paths, all leading in (mostly) unpredictable ways. Our job is not to project a curve into the past that ends at a known spot in the present, nor to calculate the quickest path from some hypothetical point in the past up to Pueblos of the present. Our job is to know (as best we can) what *actually happened* in the past, and ponder how, from that point in the past, the knotted threads of history produced the present. Or not the knotted threads: How, from that point in the past, did the present NOT (directly) emerge?

Here's the logical problem: History moves not from present to past, but from past to present. EM, Direct Historic Approach, and up-streaming all move the other way, against time's arrow.

For example, EM assumes that our main, principal, overriding question is: Where did Pueblos come from? That's an OK question, but there was a heck of a lot more going on in the ancient Southwest than the varied historical threads that eventually became known, collectively, as Pueblos. The particular contingencies that created Pueblo societies are only a part of a larger historical field, much of which plays no direct part in the specific lineage or descent of Pueblos today. Many of those things may have shaped, deflected, bent those contingent lineages—we can't know "where Pueblos came from" without knowing the much broader historical nexus from which they eventually emerged.[35] Where did Pueblos come from? What was Chaco? Two very good, but very separate, questions.

The Ethnological Method ends with Pueblos so it must begin with Pueblos, or societies firmly in Pueblo Space. Let me be blunt: The logic is circular and the method (or more accurately, philosophy) is teleological. I expand on those problems later in this section. EM (and other up-streaming strategies) are logically suspect, but their appeal is very strong: The methods are safely within Pueblo Space. And again, it's how many Southwestern archaeologists have (uncritically) always done their business.[36]

John Ware thinks we've been looking for Chaco in all the wrong places: we have been misled by well-known ethnographies of Western Pueblos. For Chaco, it's the far more authoritarian Eastern (Rio Grande) Pueblos we should consider. (There's something in that. As recounted in chapter 1, there's more Hopi built into Pueblo Space today than, say, Ohkay Owinghe.) He calls Eastern Pueblos theocracies (as have others): "The governance of all Pueblo communities is deeply theocratic" (Ware 2014:23). In the ethnographies, priests and ceremonial leaders call the shots. The centralization of decision-making gives priests and spiritual leaders the role but not the look of lords.[37] Pueblo priests do not live noticeably better-off than others. Chaco nobles definitely did (discussed in chapter 3).

Working from the Classic Ethnographies of the Eastern Pueblos, Ware looks at Pueblo prehistory from Basketmaker to the present (or, rather, from the present back to Basketmaker) through

> the interaction of two species of nonresidential organizations: corporate kinship groups and ritual associations or sodalities. If we can understand how and why these two kinds of organizations emerged and how they interacted, contested, and negotiated common social, economic and political domains over the past 1,500 years, we should be able to explain much about the Pueblo social practices and institutions that have survived into modern times. (Ware 2014:xxiv)[38]

Can we actually see those things in archaeological evidence, and follow their dialectic over a millennium and a half? Ware thinks he can.[39] Consider an example ripped out of context, but I think fair: Basketmaker III and Pueblo I "sodalities originally emerged when the avunculate took control of ceremonies that validated the existence and status of corporate matri-descent groups" (Ware 2014:127).[40] I'm pretty sure I've never seen an avunculate in the dirt; and I used to be pretty good at this. Ware's interpretation, I think, comes less from archaeological data, and more from the calculus of the curve.

EM demands (and assumes) deep historical continuity. For that kind of continuity—for historical homology—Ware must argue his way over several Great Divides: 1300, for example (discussed in chapter 1 and again below), and, more importantly perhaps for Ware's faith in ethnographies, another Great Divide at 1600—the beginning of four centuries of colonization.[41] Spain, Mexico, and the United States caused demographic collapse,[42] displacement from lands and resources, disruption of governance, repression and replacement of language and religion—it was really ugly. Decimations through disease, lost lands, insults to ceremony, and the list, sadly, goes on and on. EM enthusiasts seem to insist all that misery and disaster does not much matter. EM minimizes colonialism, kind of wishes it away.

Indeed, EM sometimes verges on mystical in its faith in Pueblo exceptionalism and its transcendence of time, "which is fortunate for archaeologists attempting to tease out cause and effect in deep prehistory, *because it has probably always been that way*" (Ware 2014:121, emphasis added). That assumes what is to be proved and flies in the face of the evidence: Southwestern archaeology is a record of change, not stasis. Yet "the present is the key to the past," because, he insists, Pueblos are "the most resilient community organizations ever described by ethnologists" (Ware 2014:7, xx).

> For me, the most startling thing about Pueblos is that many of their traditional cultural practices, especially in the more conservative realms of kinship and religion, have been preserved despite four hundred years of unrelenting attempts to "modernize" them. (Ware 2014:xxvi, xxiv)

That's a constant in the Pueblo Space: Whatever else changed (not much), kinship and religion remain constant. I don't know about kinship (who does, really?) but the evidence is overwhelming that religion(s) in the Pueblo region changed, dramatically, over the course of prehistory and history. Most famously, of course, when Jesus came.[43] But another well-known, widely accepted watershed came around 1300, an earlier, famous Great Divide. Almost every aspect of iconography—pottery, rock art, murals, everything—changed dramatically. We don't know the details—we can NEVER know the details—but from its material expression it seems clear that religion changed. It's not obscure or subtle. Every Southwest archaeologist who is paying attention knows of this, as do most interested laymen. Ware glosses over this, dismisses the compelling evidence of change at 1300, almost without comment.[44]

As we've seen with other concepts earlier in this chapter, there's a slight bending of anthropology itself to fit Pueblo Space. Anthropology wouldn't make these almost mystical assertions elsewhere: Change is as important as continuity. But continuity becomes the working principle in Pueblo Space. "The extreme conservatism of Pueblo culture encourages such reasoning," says Ware (2014:7)—a circular logic, I think.

As justification, Ware cites (among others) Edward Dozier's 1970 essay, "Making Inferences from the Present to the Past." Dozier, of course, was from Santa Clara Pueblo and a distinguished anthropologist. In the essay Ware cites supporting the extreme conservatism of Pueblos, Dozier lists six cautions and conditions for making inferences from present to past; and it is worth quoting Dozier directly, with my exegesis in brackets:

1. "Temporal factor...The shorter the time gap between a prehistoric site and the living site, the more likely the inference will be a reliable one."
2. "The sociocultural level of the prehistoric and ethnologic group must be matched." [He warns against making inferences from to band-level vs tribal-level societies—in the jargon of the times.]
3. "It is important to compare societies having the same type of subsistence economy."
4. "Inferences about societies widely separated in space can be made only with extreme caution." [Dozier notes African matrilineal clans as being very different from Hopi matrilineal clans; he wants us to stay within our region.]
5. "Language should be given a low priority." [He offers the example of the immigration of Tewa-speakers at Hano, who are now considered Hopi; he cautions us] "not to impute languages (either language families or stocks) to specific prehistoric sites or prehistoric regions."
6. "Some measure of how conservative the ethnologic culture has been over time should be established, insofar as possible." (Dozier 1970a:204)

EM surely claims Dozier's number six, because Dozier came down in favor of Pueblo conservatism. To measure "how conservative," Dozier contrasts Pueblos versus Yaquis and determines that Pueblos are measurably more conservative because "we have historical knowledge that the impact of Spanish rule did not modify the Pueblos as profoundly as the Yaquis" (Dozier 1970a:205). That suggests that "conservatism" was not inherent, it was a response to external pressure; i.e., fending off the Spanish made a society more conservative, succumbing to the Spanish made it less conservative. But Dozier argues that "the conservatism of these [Rio Grande] Pueblos cannot be attributed to Spanish conquest and oppression. The same conservatism exists, for example, among the Hopi and Zuni Pueblo Indians who did not experience the forceful policies of Spanish civil and church authorities" (Dozier 1970a:205).

Dozier discounts a century of American impacts on Zuni and Hopi which, while not as colorful as the Spanish Black Legend, were a full palette of oppressions. But I think Dozier got it right: Pueblo conservatism is probably a survival tactic against colonialism, Spanish, Mexican, American.

So much for number six. I direct the reader's attention to numbers one through five. For rhetorical purposes, I take them in reverse order. Number five, thou shalt not impute languages to prehistoric sites or regions: This will come as a shock to our more enthusiastic NAGPRA practitioners, as this is pretty much what the law requires us to do. Number four, keep it close, source it locally: Farewell to Chaco's acephalous African chiefdoms!—fine with me, as long as we are talking about my "local," which (absent the Iron Curtain of chapter 1) is continental, as we shall shortly see. Number three, same subsistence economies:

For Chaco (and Hohokam), a strong case can be made for bulk-goods econo-mies (discussed in chapter 3) and for Hohokam (and perhaps Chaco) a strong case can be made for market economies. Pueblos today, of course, are enmeshed in a global cash economy but the "ethnographic" Pueblos of Pueblo Space are independent, self-sufficient farming villages. As we shall see in chapter 3, *Chaco was not that*. Are we comparing Pueblo apples to Chaco's cacao beans? Number two, "sociocultural level": Dozier used the language of the 1970s and abjured us to not project backwards from tribes to bands. I extend his argument in the same language: Don't project backwards from tribes to states. Chaco, as I will argue in chapter 3, was patently not of the same "sociocultural level" as Pueblos. Ware simply assumes it was: All Pueblos past and present were (in today's lan-guage) "intermediate." And, finally, Dozier's number one, temporal factors: To repeat, "the shorter the time gap between a prehistoric site and the living site, the more likely the inference will be a reliable one (Dozier 1970a:204)." Amen and hallelujah! Ware skies over or tunnels under two Great Divides (1300 and 1600), taking EM back to deep prehistory. We don't have Dozier to ask, alas, but I suspect that violates the "short time gap" principle.

I'm OK with measured, controlled projections—or better, comparisons—from ethnographic Pueblos back to 1450 (actually, another mini–Great Divide) and perhaps with great caution as far back as 1300—but not any further back in time. Ware pushes even further back, a thousand years to Basketmaker III; defi-nitely not a short time gap. The changes we know from archaeology are simply too great to be papered over by EM's insistence on continuity, its doctrine of continuity.

But let's stick with the later part of prehistory. Chaco is the problem, dis-cussed in chapter 3. After 1300, the Pueblos never built or created anything re-motely like Chaco—the elephant in the room or, rather, the elephant outside Pueblo Space. Ware recognizes this: "Granted that the Eastern Pueblos don't build monumental great houses, earthworks, and roads, and Eastern Pueblo rit-ualists eschew obvious symbols of rank" (in his chapter with Kelley Hays-Gilpin in *Chaco Revisited*; Ware and Hays-Gilpin 2015:331). To which he could add: Ethnographic Pueblos east or west never had a primary center several times bigger than any other settlement of its time. Nor have Pueblos east or west ever had a regional center like Chaco, pivotal to several scores of lesser settlements—indeed, encompassing almost all of the Pueblo world of its time. As we shall see in chapter 3, there are other dramatic differences; but consider Chaco as the center of a region the size of Indiana. No ethnographic Pueblo does that; it's not to be found in Classic Ethnographies or in Pueblo Space.

There's nothing in Pueblo ethnography that looks remotely like Chaco and its region as we know them, in either architecture or landscape. Ware attempts to surmount this insurmountable problem first by suggesting that remnants of ethnographic Pueblo social structures reflect entities or organizations that might have built Chaco. "Ritual sodalities do a pretty good job of accounting for the salient patterns. This hypothesis has the additional advantage—which few competing models enjoy—of linking Chaco with known ethnographic destinations in the Rio Grande" (Ware 2014:126). Pueblo sodalities could account for the salient patterns? Pueblo sodalities do many things well, like organizing village activities like ditch clearing but, as far as we know, they never built and administered anything the size and scale of Chaco—much less Chaco's unprecedented region.[45] Chaco's regional organization—whatever it was—was never replicated or repeated by Ware's Pueblos.[46]

So Ware tries to make Chaco go away. Not literally "go away," of course: There's a National Park/World Heritage site which seems fairly secure in its location. But Ware wants to deflate and devalue Chaco, to take it down several pegs.[47] His argument begins with a section subtitled "normalizing Chaco":

> Someone once labeled Chaco a "phenomenon" and, unfortunately, the label stuck. The term, I think, has encouraged scholars to conceptualize Chaco as a singularity that will be explained only if we can discover the appropriate social-political-economic box to put it in. I argue that Chaco will be understood in historical context or not at all. (Ware 2014:130)[48]

By "historical context" he means EM, which a priori limits Chaco to ethnographic Pueblo models.[49] Ware seems strangely quiet on Great Houses; he admits they exist but then waves them away. "Monumental construction in places like Chaco Canyon consists mostly of vernacular architecture writ large, suggesting that if anything was being memorialized by Chacoan great houses, it was the corporate group which occupied the front-oriented habitation unit" (Ware 2014:41). Yes, Great Houses began as scaled-up versions of traditional houses of its time (Pueblo I, Pueblo II); that insight is hardly new—first proposed thirty years ago, in fact (Lekson 1984, if I'm not mistaken). As discussed in chapter 3, Great Houses were quite deliberately different from other, "vernacular" houses. And by the mid-eleventh century Chaco's Great Houses evolved far beyond McMansions. Ware seems to accept that Great Houses started as scaled-up residences and ended up as something else—but what "something else"? In a word (mine, not his): Palaces. It's true: Wait for chapter 3.

Ware niggles at Chaco's region, and hints that it was a "non-system" (citing Kantner 2003). "There is so much variation in outlier architecture and community plans that the rules for inclusion in the outlier club have been hotly debated" (Ware 2014:124). Hotly debated three decades ago; not today.[50] In the 1980s, archaeologists who felt their turf was threatened, loudly proclaimed that there were no "Chaco outliers" on Mesa Verde, or in southeastern Utah, or in the Kayenta area.[51] Under the weight of accumulating data, those gated communities have since joined the larger world. The distribution of Great Houses—and of course their variation!—was well known by the 1990s. Reopening this closed case seems a bit…desperate.

If I seem harsh with *Pueblo Social History*, it's because much of this was settled twenty or thirty years ago, through a very great deal of hard work by many people in several projects.[52] I am almost moved to ad hominem here: Those data were hard-won, and Ware does not give them the respect they deserve. (Why? Some Santa Fe thing, I guess.) The archaeology is quite clear: Chaco, with its Great Houses, was the center of a sizable region defined by hundreds of smaller Great Houses (and that's just the tip of the iceberg; see chapter 3). Sorry, that genie can't be wished back into the bottle.

In the end, Ware's bombshell is—for me—a squib, a fizzle. It does not move the field forward; it drags Southwestern archaeology back from today to the 1920s, and rejects, negates, or ignores a great deal we have learned in between.

And this is my fundamental problem with *A Pueblo Social History*: Mystique trumps method. Ware projects Eastern Pueblo kinship and social structures— or their putative predecessors—back over tremendous disjunctures: Colonization at 1600 and the collapse of the Chaco-Aztec polity at 1300. In the face of mountains of hard evidence for sweeping change, Ware justifies these jumps on the basis of…what? His surety that Pueblos have always been intensely conservative and traditional, his insistence that "it has probably always been that way," his belief that Pueblo forms and practices *must be* deeply rooted—I call this "mystical," and so it is. The archaeological and historical evidence is overwhelmingly against such continuity. There were more things under the Southwestern sun than are dreamt of in the Classic Ethnographies.

There are more useful ways—that recognize the Great Divides—for engaging ethnography. Two excellent examples: Severin Fowles's 2013 *Archaeology of Doings*[53] and Scott Ortman's 2012 *Winds from the North: Tewa Origins and Historical Anthropology*.[54] Both recognize major disjunctions, the Great Divides between later periods and Chacoan times; and both accept and address Chaco's singularity.

In Fowles's and Ortman's books, and in classics like Charles Adams's (1991) *Origin and Development of the Pueblo Katsina Cult*, discontinuities matter as much or even more than continuities. Continuities are interesting and important, but discontinuities give us history. EM, up-streaming, and Pueblo Space negate history. In chapter 6, I discuss the "ceremony of forgetting" when Acoma people left White House (probably Chaco/Aztec) as a formal rejection of the un-Pueblo behaviors that led to White House's fall. That account relates *historical discontinuity*, something up-streamers and EM choose to overlook. Another dramatic example comes from Hopi accounts of *Pasiwvi* (Wupatki and the San Francisco Peaks):[55]

> Pasiwvi represents the cradle of modern Hopi culture, a place where a small group of ancestors developed the major principles of Hopi life, religion, and philosophy.... *This new life plan would be distinct from the complex religious ways that had until then held sway.* (Kuwanwisiwma et al. 2012:7, 9; emphasis mine)

Change, discontinuity: The past was different. Robert Drennan said, considering Chaco: "If we refuse to accept the possibility of documenting archaeologically societies that differ significantly from those known ethnographically or historically, why should we bother with such a difficult, time-consuming, and, yes, tedious chore as archaeology?" (Drennan 1999:258). Indeed.

Chaco Meridian *2.0: Beyond Pueblo Space*

In 2015, I published a second edition of *Chaco Meridian*. The earth did not stand still; two suns did not appear in the sky. The book was mostly a prequel to my original (1999) tale of political history, Chaco to Aztec to Paquimé. Those three principal sites of Pueblo II and Pueblo III and Pueblo IV were sequent, historically related, and on a meridian. Not a coincidence. Turns out, that business began way back in Basketmaker III and Pueblo I and lasted longer, through Pueblo V. The main argument of *Chaco Meridian* version 2.0 was that for every Pecos stage, from Basketmaker III to Pueblo V, the biggest, weirdest, most important sites were on or very near that blasted meridian. If that's intriguing, you'll have to read the book; that's not the story here. The story here came in an appendix stuck into *Chaco Meridian* 2.0 because it was too soon for a second edition of *History of the Ancient Southwest*—which is where the appendix properly belonged. To anticipate chapter 3, I argued that Chaco had much the same form and structure, and was of comparable size, to a well-known Mesoamerican political system, called *altepetl* (details in chapter 3). I did not say Chaco *was* an altepetl, I said it looked a lot like one. This model from ethnohistory fit Chaco pretty well—and it came from Chaco's time and place, loosely speaking. A decade ago, Lynne Sebastian—rejecting the exceptionalism of Pueblo Space— urged us to look at more ethnographic models until we'd find one which might work for Chaco.[56] I kept looking and found one that fit.

This was in many ways the culmination of over forty years of thinking about Chaco (not constantly, thank God). I'd convinced myself early on that Chaco was not of or in Pueblo Space (Lekson 1984:273). I concluded that Chaco probably had some sort of hereditary hierarchy, something like kings (Lekson 2006b:37).[57] But beyond that vague claim, I went no further until I put Chaco in its place: Post-Classic North America (Lekson 2009a). Then things clicked.

Bingo! *Altepetl*: But I stuck it into Appendix A of *Chaco Meridian* version 2.0, where only the brave or foolhardy will see it. But you'll see it, long-suffering reader, in chapter 3, only a few pages from here.

I thought I'd solved the Mystery of Chaco Canyon—not alone, of course: Using lots of other people's data, building on other people's hard work, helping myself to other people's ideas and insights. Answering questions, solving mysteries: That's what we get paid to do, to figure out the past. But…

The Mystery of Chaco Canyon

Many people—both in archaeology and in tourism—seem to prefer that Chaco remain an enigma, a mystery.[58] Mystery gets grants for professors and fills rooms for hoteliers. They don't particularly want Chaco solved.

From some archaeologists, we hear the clarion call "more data!" Cassandras claim we know too little about Chaco to draw any conclusions; that's nonsense. Chaco is the most thoroughly researched archaeological site north of Mexico. We have mountains of data. We could always know more, and new discoveries may (and should) change the game. But to say that we do not know enough, now, to draw conclusions about Chaco is an affront to archaeology. Archaeologists who insist we need more data before we can say anything useful about Chaco are bad archaeologists.

The appeal of mystery goes deeper than data, or any perceived lack thereof. The title of this section nods respectfully to Anna Sofaer's archaeoastronomical video of the same name, released in the penultimate millennial year of 1999—yikes Y2K! Sofaer's (1999) video, narrated by Robert Redford, both rode and drove a wave of mystification of Chaco—one response, I think, to the awkward fact that Chaco simply does not fit Pueblo Space. If it can't be a Pueblo, exactly, Chaco could always be a *mystery*.[59] Flute music works for both.

Chaco-as-mystery appears in many scholarly works on Chaco. Stephen Plog, in a recent judgment of Chaco research, opined that "key questions about Chaco remain unanswered" (Plog 2015:11).[60] Really? After a century of research? Maybe we don't like the answers we're getting. To pick on a friend and colleague, Scott Ortman (in his recent review of *Chaco Revisited*) referred to Chaco as "this most enigmatic of New World societies."[61] Why? Maybe Chaco's a mystery because archaeologists can't (or won't) agree; Chaco is therefore declared deeply mysterious.[62]

The excellent *Chaco Handbook*—an encyclopedia of all things Chacoan, written by Gwinn Vivian and Bruce Halpert—leads off with this solemn invocation:

> For generations, the ruins of Chaco Canyon have intrigued explorers
> and archaeologists. Yet, as they try to refine their explanations through

better technology, additional data, native perspectives, and creative theories, definitive answers often slip through their fingers. In the end, there have been few definitive answers to the most intriguing questions. For the present, the mystery of Chaco Canyon remains just that—a mystery. (Vivian and Halpert 2011:43)

One of the best popular books on Chaco (there are several good ones) is David Grant Noble's 2004 *In Search of Chaco: New Approaches to an Archaeological Enigma.* Noble is an articulate, thoughtful, well-versed observer of Southwestern archaeology. In his introduction to the volume, he fairly characterizes the then-current state of Chacoan studies:

> The people who study Chaco year after year—in the field, in the laboratory, in the library, at conferences, and in Native communities—are themselves a sort of phenomenon. They certainly have stick-to-itiveness, even when solutions to the Chacoan "mystery" seem out of reach.... They recognize that future generations will regard them as just a phase in the ever-unfolding discovery. This too is part of the Chaco phenomenon, which includes the Chacoans themselves, the scholars and writers, the artists, photographers, and musicians, the preservationists, the tourists, the modern pilgrims and even the readers of these pages.... The unknown still outweighs the known. In that sense, perhaps Chaco is a metaphor for our search for knowledge—the closer we get to it, the more elusive it becomes. (Noble 2004:xiv)

This is how we serve up Chaco: A few clues to a riddle, wrapped in a mystery, inside an enigma, as a great man once said about Russia. I find that embarrassing. To return to a theme introduced above: Consider Chaco as an archaeological site, investigated intensively for over a century—Chaco, acre per acre, has probably absorbed more archaeological energy than any other prehistoric site in the United States. And Chaco archaeology is (relatively) easy: Superb preservation, astonishing chronological control, a century of intensive research (see note 58). If—after all that investment of funds and brains, after all that destruction of the archaeological record—Chaco remains an enigma or a mystery, then Chaco goes down as an epic failure of Southwestern archaeology.

CHAPTER 3

A History of the Ancient Southwest

It is better to be vaguely right than precisely wrong.

—attributed to John Maynard Keynes
(but actually Carveth Read, in slightly different words)

Chaco saw its share of ritual, but Chaco was not a rituality. Nor was it a uniquity or a phenomenon or a mystery. It was not even Pueblo—in the generic sense of "Pueblo culture" or Pueblo Space. (I cannot repeat too often that I am NOT saying Chaco wasn't part of Pueblo history and heritage; of course it was.) Chaco was the capital of a small, wobbly city-state. Before we go into that murk, let's clear the air.

Ten Fun Facts about Chaco

Here is a list of ten take-'em-to-the-bank facts about Chaco. They are so solid that I count them all as axioms. I cannot imagine anyone questioning them. So, of course, every one of these cold hard facts has been tutted and innuendoed in lectures, or hooted in bar-room arguments, or (in a very few rare cases) challenged in print.

1. Great Houses are real, and really different.
   Great Houses constitute a readily identified architectural class, both qualitatively and quantitatively different from other Southwestern architecture. There was nothing else like them in the Southwest before, during, or after Chaco/Aztec.[1]
2. Great Houses were *houses*, but not many people lived in them.
   The initial design of early Great Houses is clearly based on the common Unit Pueblos, scaled up. Unit Pueblos were family houses. Great Houses were, literally, Great *Houses*. And that residential function continued through their careers, although most of the architectural mass of later Great Houses was NOT residential, it was storage: Houses plus warehouses, if you will.[2]
3. People living in Great Houses were...special.
   Great House people were bigger and healthier, and had a great many fancy

things that other people did not have. The men were buff with big muscles, the women did not work: No squatting facets, no corn grinding.[3]

4. Chaco was a stratified class society.

    The architecture is unambiguous: Great Houses versus Unit Pueblos. All sorts of schemes have been put forward to keep Chaco in Pueblo Space and avoid the obvious: An upper class lived in Great Houses, a lower class lived in Unit Pueblos.[4] Call 'em what they were: Nobles and commoners.

5. Outlier Great Houses are real and define Chaco's region.

    A definable class or taxon of small Great Houses, numbering at least 150, were distributed from Cedar Mesa on the northwest to Chimney Rock on the northeast, to the Hopi Mesas on the west, to the Rio Puerco on the east, to Reserve NM on the south—an area about the size of the state of Indiana.[5]

6. Road networks and line-of-site communication: Chaco's region was a system.

    Chaco's famous "roads" were both monuments and transportation corridors, freighted both with goods and with symbolism.[6] Chaco also, and importantly, had an extensive regional line-of-sight signaling system.[7] Chaco was not simply a "distribution" of pottery styles or architectural forms: It clearly was a networked *system* with transportation and communication technologies.

7. Chaco's region encompassed 60,000 people, and perhaps as many as 100,000 people.

    Chaco Canyon itself had between 2,100 and 2,700 permanent residents.[8] For its region, Dean and colleagues (1994) took an educated, reasonable guess at the San Juan Basin population at Chaco's peak: 55,000 people. The San Juan Basin was only half of Chaco's region. Double down on Dean: Something close to 100,000?[9]

8. Chaco had bulk and prestige economies.

    Bulk goods moved in (and perhaps out) within a 150 km radius from Chaco Canyon. Prestige goods moved farther, up to a 250 km radius from Chaco Canyon—and prestige came into Chaco from 1,000 km away.[10]

9. Chaco was not a great place to grow corn.

    Chaco was better for farming than the surrounding 40–50 km radius. That's the best you can say about it—and very faint praise. It's unlikely that Chaco grew its own food, enough to feed 2,500-odd people.[11]

10. Chaco was cosmopolitan.

    Chaco and its region were almost certainly multilingual, possibly multiethnic. Chaco itself was a magnet for curiosities: Regional rarities, and truly exotic baubles and trinkets from far distant lands. Chaco's rulers appropriated aspects of Mesoamerican nobility. Chaco was not a valley of hardscrabble farming villages.[12]

What Was Chaco, Really?

So what was Chaco? Nothing in Pueblo Space. Pueblos aren't big (a Pueblo reaches 2,500 people and almost invariably within a generation or two, it splits into two new villages—a topic to which we return in chapter 4). Pueblos don't have social classes, nobles and commoners. They aren't capitals, they don't have large political regions (Pueblos had large catchments for needed resources, but never large regions of secondary, subordinate settlements). The Pueblos of Pueblo Space are self-sufficient farming villages, famously inward-looking, and (today) shunning modernities. Chaco wasn't any of that. Almost everything was imported, much in bulk; and Chaco looked eagerly beyond its economic region to the southern civilizations and the Mississippi Valley.

Chaco, to be clear, was surely part of Pueblo history and heritage, but Chaco was not "Pueblo" in the sense of Pueblo Space. As argued at length in chapter 2, the Classic Ethnographies won't help us: You won't find Chaco in the ethnographies because Pueblo people, after 1300, never built anything remotely like Chaco. Attempts to explain Chaco using bits and pieces up-streamed from what we know of nineteenth-century Pueblo life won't do, either: For the same reason, non-starters. We must look elsewhere: Over the Ceiling, past the Curtain, beyond the Space.

The existence of classes at Chaco is critical. So important I will harp on it here and again, from a slightly different angle, in chapter 4. Social classes are stunningly obvious in the architecture—and have been, for eighty years (see Fun Fact #1; and the exasperated discussion below)—but this obvious fact remains a remarkably hard sell. American Anthropological Archaeologists, looking at Native societies north of Mexico, are fine with the idea of class-stratified societies in the Mississippi Valley and the Southeast (but not states!); but don't bring that junk to the Southwest, into Pueblo Space. We won't have it here. Consequently, Southwesternists don't think much about class (or states!). Class is really important. Let's ease into things:

F. Scott Fitzgerald sighed, "The rich are different from you and me." "Yes," snapped Hemingway, "they have more money."

This exchange never happened—Hemingway invented it for *Snows of Kilimanjaro*.[13] But it makes a useful point: Fitzgerald was talking about quality, Hemingway about quantity. Class is quality; wealth is quantity. We would do well to remember that when we think about social differentiation, elites, complexity, and that whole mare's nest of archaeological euphemisms for class society. Our gauge is often quantities: More of this, more of that, an extra production step in the pottery, more and better food. (Think: Gini Coefficient.) In the Southwest, we think those things define "elites"—people at the upper end of a continuous dimension of more or less stuff. But class was qualitative; our conventional measures might miss those differences.[14] Nobles and commoners were two very different sorts of humans. Kings could be divine; and a king remained a king, even if he/she had fallen on hard times. Think Oedipus; think Lear; think Viserys Targaryen. So, too, nobles in North America.[15]

We Americans can deal with our Rockefellers and Gates because they simply *have more money*. More stuff. Our dream is that anyone, from any background, can get more money, can get rich—or so we are told. But Americans are not sure how to deal with classes, with nobles and royalty. The lost Dauphin stumped Huck and Jim. Well, he *said* he was the Dauphin, and Jim and Huck treated him according to their dim notions of etiquette. And the Dauphin worked it for all it was worth, until a mob ran him out of town on a rail.[16]

The American Anthropological view is that aggrandizers rise from the great unwashed masses and must cajole, convince, or coerce people into following them. When I suggest nobles at Chaco, the immediate response from American Anthropological Archaeologists is something like this: How did they persuade people to follow them? What was in it for the nonelites? That's probably not how it worked.

Chaco rose after more than a millennium of nobles and commoners in Mesoamerica, and we can be sure the Southwest was aware of class distinctions. Every struggling Basketmaker III farmer probably knew something about nobles and commoners, far to the south. Only rumors, but still...How could they *not* know, when nobles and commoners had been ubiquitous, down south, for at least five centuries before Basketmaker III? We *know* they knew by Pueblo I, when Chaco got going: Chaco imported macaws and other trappings of southern nobility, and Chaco buried its Great House elites just like nobles, toasting their memories with a pint of Mayan cacao or a stiff shot of Black Drink (Crown and Hurst 2009; Crown and others 2015; Plog and Heitman 2010; Watson and others 2015). Their knowledge was continental.

Nobles were one kind of person, whose role it was to rule. Commoners were another kind of person, whose role it was to support nobles. That's a simplification, of course, but it's closer to the truth than American Anthropological Archaeology's notions of bottoms-up, quid-pro-quo, what's-in-it-for-the-plebs inequality.

In North America at the end of the first millennium CE there were noble-commoner class societies from the Gulf of Mexico through the Mississippi Valley to the Pacific coast, and of course south though all of Mexico to Panama and beyond. Variations on the noble-commoner theme played out across the (future) United States, from Chumash elites of California to Calusa nobles in Florida. The biggest noble-commoner society was Cahokia, the great Mississippian capital and Chaco's exact contemporary. Judging by the remnants the

French encountered much later among the Natchez, the lords of Cahokia were almost certainly royals and nobles, far removed from the commoners. Natchez nobles called them "stinkards."

Nobles and commoners from sea to shining sea. In that context, the absence—not the presence!—of nobles and commoners in the Southwest would be extraordinary. We should expect the Southwest to have stratified societies. And so it did, from 800 to 1300 at Chaco and Aztec. After 1300, that social system ended in the northern Southwest—a class revolt sans guillotines—but continued unabashed and unabated at Paquimé and quite possibly Classic Period Hohokam (Lekson 2009a). Chaco's commoners shed the nobility, voting with their feet or even perhaps more directly by political revolt, and reinvented themselves as Pueblos. Not unlike the egalitarian ideals enshrined in Pueblo Space. Understand that Chaco was a noble-commoner class society, and thereafter course of Pueblo history flows logically and comprehensibly (Lekson 2009a, 2015a:Appendix A). Without that Chaco, the Southwest becomes exceptional, extraordinary, unique—and the odds are, it wasn't.

The history of Mesoamerica—written by/for kings, of course—is largely the story of nobles ruling or finding places to rule. That was their job, and commoners apparently accepted it (or so the kings tell us). To anticipate chapter 4, that may offend American populist notions and our national charter, but remember: We're not talking about OUR past.

Nobles and commoners, class-stratified societies. Chaco was like that. Sort of like that, anyway.

What?! Where's the evidence?![17] The best evidence: 50,000 tons of rock and mud, stacked up thirty feet high over the area of a major league baseball field. I'm describing Pueblo Bonito—and also Chetro Ketl and Pueblo Alto and the rest. The major Great Houses constitute astonishing piles of evidence for class-stratified society at Chaco. What makes Pueblo Bonito so hard to see?

Walk through Bonito—the archetypical Great House. Cross the wash, and walk around the Bc sites—normal Pueblo II houses, so standard and alike we call them "Unit Pueblos." It's not subtle; there's nothing difficult about this. The contrast is obvious and absolute: The architecture of a class society. It's not only *more* stuff, as Hemingway insists; it's *different* stuff, as Fitzgerald would have it. Great Houses are "more" than Bc sites—more of just about everything. But, importantly, the two are qualitatively different: Bc sites are vernacular, Great Houses are Architecture. Indeed, Great Houses can properly be called palaces (Lekson 2006).

The architectural evidence seems, to me, unambiguous: A higher class in the Great Houses, a lower class in Bc Unit Pueblos. Given Chaco's place and time, Chaco's context, there's no reason not to say: Nobles and commoners. No reason...save Pueblo Space. Say "nobles" at Cahokia and heads nod; say "nobles" at Chaco and eyes roll.

Great Houses are the stumbling block of pilgrimage models and indeed any ritual-centric model of Chaco. I've never heard a rational, convincing argument for why we should believe that Great Houses were "ritual structures."[18] Great Houses are huge, obvious, unmistakable evidence of an elite class, of nobles; yet reviews of Chaco routinely conclude that there were no elite/nobles because "there are no palaces."[19] Ouch. Again: What is it about Pueblo Bonito that makes it so hard to see?

Chaco beyond Pueblo Space: Solving the Mystery

We know a LOT about Chaco; that deck of cards is stacked full. Lay a few on the table, and as the kings and queens hit the felt, it's pretty clear what Chaco was. But it's not what people want Chaco to be.

In 2009's *A History of the Ancient Southwest*, I shocked the children by calling Chaco a "city" and its leaders "kings."[20] Forget shop-worn "chiefs" or vapid "elites"! Call a spade a spade and a king a king. This is important: We'll revisit kings in chapter 4.

One salient fact about Chaco was that there were a half-dozen major Great Houses—elite residences or palaces—over the length of the central canyon. No one Great House was an obvious first among equals, a paramount over princes.[21] Were there multiple kings? Five kings? Six kings? (That's dangerous talk in the Old West; flash five kings and you might get shot.)

I first looked at northern Italy in the Renaissance, where multiple princely houses competitively coexisted in towns like Florence and Sienna—except when they didn't, just like Romeo and Juliet. It was great fun to read about those places and times, but *Firenze era troppo*, the city of Dante, too much a stretch, like plopping an African acephalous chiefdom on Chaco. Something closer, in time and place. Not Pueblo obviously, but…what? *A History of the Ancient Southwest* summarized histories contemporary with the Southwest's, from the Mississippi Valley to Mesoamerica. That sort of context was surely useful to understanding the Southwest—and perhaps useful for understanding Chaco Canyon. I read broadly (and sometimes deeply) in Mesoamerican ethnohistory, especially for West Mexico and the Tarascans. Nothing there with a half-dozen princely families, multiple kings. When I discussed this with a colleague, Dr. Gerardo Gutierrez,[22] he directed my attention (late in 2010) to Nahua polities called *altepetl*. Bingo! Not to say that Chaco in the eleventh century was a point-for-point replica of Nahua city-states of late Postclassic and early Colonial times. But the basic structure and functions of *altepetl* fit Chaco well—and the model was relatively close to Chaco in time and space. *Altepetl* was not an anthropological theory like "complex chiefdom" or "house society"; it was not a model ripped from a distant time and place, like African chiefdoms or the House of Borgias; it was not a strained homology from Pueblo ethnology, like Ware's theocracies; it was not an invention, something new under the sun, like a rituality or pilgrimage center. The Nahua *altepetl* (hereafter un-italicized) was something real from Chaco's world (that is, the North America which Chaco knew), and there is a real possibility of historical connections, however distant and uncertain direction.[23] It was *relevant*—probably.

The altepetl argument logically should have been the last chapter of 2009's *A History of the Ancient Southwest.* But I found out about it after that book was published; so I attached it as an appendix to the second edition of *Chaco Meridian*; which you should read, but here's a brief summary:[24]

The altepetl encompassed a central capital and farming lands around it: Both city and countryside. At the capital, a half-dozen noble extended families occupied separate palaces, amid public architecture and an urban population of commoners. Far more commoners lived in countryside farming villages, many with smaller palaces of secondary nobility, for a total population of 2,000 to 40,000 people. The king was first-among-equals, elected by the nobility from one of the half-dozen highest noble families. (The nature of the "election" was probably not what we'd envision.) The office was not strong nor did it descend in a kingly line. When the king died, another election named a king from a different princely house. This "rotating" or "shared" governance prevented any single princely family from ascending to a strong hereditary kingship. A hierarchical tributary system moved goods and services up through the secondary and higher nobles and king. Particular commoner families owed tribute to particular noble families, who then owed tribute to the royal nobility. Tribute or tax was not onerous: A few bushels of corn, a week's work, some other good or service. The central "city" had from fewer than 1,000 to perhaps 5,000 people in a settlement of about 100 ha; secondary centers were an order of magnitude smaller. "Cities" were defined by civic architecture and monuments, and most importantly by the clustered noble houses or palaces, each of which controlled groups of commoner families localized in territorial *calpulli*—but sometimes complexly scattered throughout the altepetl. An altepetl on average covered a compact area of about 75 square km.

The Fun Facts about Chaco work well for altepetl: Similar in form and structure, similar in population and scale. The most obvious difference is territorial area: Altepetl 75 square km, Chaco 100,000 square km. That difference, I think, was environmental. Central Mexico is a great place to farm, highly productive, and a lot of people can live on relatively little land. The Southwest is (technically) a stinking desert, so farmers must seek scattered patches of decent farmland (springs, confluences, etc.). Chaco stretched the altepetl form over space to its modulus of rupture,[25] and then made it work by inventing or repurposing technologies of distance: "Roads" and line-of-site communication systems, which linked distant outlier communities back to the Canyon.

Our data on altepetl come from ethnohistories and a few precolonial sources, several centuries after Chaco. Is that a problem? Maybe, but the obvious alternatives are Pueblo Space from modern Santa Fe, or Classic Ethnographies from six or seven centuries after Chaco. And neither works for Chaco. The ethnographic Pueblos subsequently never did anything like Chaco. Nahua did something rather like Chaco; indeed, they had dozens of 'em.

You might object to trading one categorical box for another, Pueblo Space for altepetl. "Let Chaco be Chaco"—that is, a uniquity, one-and-done. I say: Horse feathers! Chaco came near the end of at least a thousand years of political history in North America. Chaco did not invent this stuff, nor most likely was Chaco anything new under the sun. Why shouldn't there be a "box" into which Chaco fits—not perfectly, but comfortably?

The box into which Chaco fits is not welcome in the Southwest. Altepetl were states, city-states (Smith 2008a). But go with me here: If Chaco was something like an altepetl, how would that change the science that we do—or can do—in the Southwest? How would that change the Southwest's role in larger social science conversations? In the next chapter (chapter 4), I explore some new uses for Southwestern archaeology that could open up, if we open that box. Gump's box of chocolates or Pandora's box of evils? Which, in the original, was not Pandora's box, but a giant wine jar. Drink up, it's about to get weird…

A Science of the Ancient Southwest

He put all his reliance
In courage and defiance
And risked his life for science.
Hooray for Captain Spaulding!

—attributed to Mrs. Rittenhouse

And now, a bit of science![1] Archaeology in the Southwest stands steadfast for science. That's a very good thing, despite my reservations about residual scientism—the intrusion of the forms of science where they don't belong—in chapters 1 and 5. So, it's not that Southwestern archaeology is not "doing" science, applying Southwestern data to questions of broader interest. Of course we are! To drop a few names (citations come later), the Village Ecodynamics Project, the Southwestern Social Networks Project, and several ambitious Arizona State University programs[2] do great science and reach wide scientific audiences. As so do many others. We know how to do this: Science R Us. But…

But, almost without exception, the science we do—hypotheses, models, and interpretations—assumes that Southwestern societies were politically simple, nothing like states. We do our science in Pueblo Space. What would happen if we did not make that assumption—if our science escaped Pueblo Space? This chapter presents ideas and suggestions about how a new model of the Southwest might shift our science. To write chapter 4, I shook the moths out of my lab coat, cleaned up my calipers, and rosined up my slide rule. Back off, man; I'm a scientist.[3]

If the Chaco presented in chapter 3 is more or less correct, then we can perhaps use that history for generalizing analyses and statements—perhaps we can do a different sort of science with that New Model ancient Southwest.

Three questions: Is my history more or less correct? And, what do I mean by science? And, what is all this mumbo jumbo about using history to do science?

First question: Is my history correct? I address problems of historical methods for ancient times—pre-historiography—in chapter 6. But for now, I'm pretty sure that the Chaco of chapter 3 is more correct than anything else currently on offer, closer than the views presented in chapters 1 and 2, because my foundational assumptions are more realistic: *My Chaco is not confined to Pueblo Space.* (Emphasis added.) And that makes all the difference.

Second question: What do I mean by science? My answer is not couched in philosophy-of-science; it's a low-bar, low-brow, lowest-common-denominator definition. What I am calling "science"—the best, perhaps, archaeology can hope for—is empirically based, rationally founded, logically structured, generalizing statements about some order or pattern (or definable disorder) in this gloriously, terrifyingly messy world. Science is necessarily reductionist, simplifying the complicated; and thus the opposite of history, which revels in complication. It would be useful, but perhaps not entirely necessary, if those scientific generalizing statements could be evaluated—if only as "more likely" or "less likely" than competing generalizing statements. If this sounds like what's left of the old bombed-out shell of Processual archaeology, that's because I'm what's left of an old bombed-out shell of a Processualist.

The third question—using that new history to do science—is explored in the rest of this chapter, in a series of themes. As noted above, Southwestern archaeology has been and is currently being used in generalizing, scientific studies. Most seem to focus on weather and war; that is, socioenvironmental questions and studies of violence. Indeed, the Southwest is famous for human-environment interaction and to a lesser degree warfare (see chapter 2). That turf is pretty well covered—although I'm sure those studies would reach different conclusions outside Pueblo Space—so I will not explore those topics further in this chapter. (I've already got enough people mad at me without engaging the current megaprojects.) Anyway, as the Government Agent might have told Indiana Jones: "We have top men working on weather and war right now. Top men." And, I might add, top women.

The topics addressed—scale, diffusion, states, cities, and cycles—are framed rather differently here than they would be with a conventional view of Southwestern prehistory. In fact, most of these topics would not be considered relevant to conventional Southwestern prehistory. Cities? States? Rises-and-falls? Not in Pueblo Space! Yet, there they are; or rather, there they were.

It will probably come as no surprise that none of the following sections resolves its particular issue or problem, or fully develops relevant theory or theories. These are exploratory essays, neither comprehensive nor conclusive; they frame the question, hopefully in new ways. Theorists of a certain stripe might call them provocations: An invitation to the dance, as it were. I present these essays not so much to solve these questions, but to draw attention to them and to demonstrate the possibilities of using Southwestern archaeology in new ways—getting the Southwest out into the world, as it were—given the Chaco presented in chapter 3.

My insistence/obsession on historicity shapes my exposition. My themes follow a narrative arc:

Scale: They needed government
Diffusion: They had models for government
States: They applied those models
Cities: They built a capital
Cycles: They collapsed

The history of chapter 3 (and Lekson 2009a) opens up new areas of research where the Southwest can do useful science. History leads us to scalar thresholds and the need for government; diffusion offers (historically) likely forms of government; applied, those forms become states; most states require capitals; and states almost always cycle and collapse. The history comes first, and in this chapter it also comes last: The structure of cycles is inherently historical. The history provides the data for science, and science in turn informs and reforms the history. What goes around comes around, as the singer sang.

These examples all focus, of course, on Chaco's history. Chaco by itself is mere local history; that history would be more useful when compared and contrasted to other cases: Hohokam, Casas Grandes, Cahokia, Aztatlan, you name it. For example, Hohokam. Chaco, in its serviceable but unspectacular environment, developed a mild case of political hierarchy. Hohokam, in an environmentally rich region (when tapped with technology), coordinated huge investments in infrastructure but—apparently—avoided Chaco's political afflictions. The contrast between Chaco and Hohokam could constitute a central question for Southwestern archaeological science, science using Southwestern prehistory. My point: *Of course* there are plenty of historically based questions that have little or nothing to do with Chaco. Help yourself.

Scale: They Needed Government

We have cognitive limits, hard-wired in our brains, for how many people we can actually know, how many people we can interact with, how many people we can handle before our fuses melt. Plug that factoid—an agent-based rule for "social channel capacity" (Turchin 2006:132)—into a network of several hundred people who are expected to interact (a school, a company, a community). Each member of that network has approximately the same cognitive limits. Interesting things might happen, mathematically, not just in people's heads but to the composition or dynamics of the group. And that's what we see, across many cultures:[4] When groups reach particular sizes, population thresholds are crossed and things happen. In archaeology, these thresholds or tipping points have been called "scalar thresholds" but the word "scalar" in this context is (useful) jargon. For most people, "scalar" means something else—it's a type of number—and only rarely is it used as an adjective "relating to scale or size."

I will try (unsuccessfully) to avoid it here and use plain words or, occasionally, the web-ish term "social channel capacity." To rephrase my melting-fuse metaphor: How many people can you handle before your head explodes? (For me, it's about two, maybe three; crowds make me twitchy.)

Size thresholds have been recognized—or hinted at—for many decades; they are of interest across a wide range of disciplines from philosophy to artificial intelligence[5] (hmmm; there's a joke here at philosophy's expense, but let it pass). Thresholds have a history in American Archaeology. Population thresholds were a small but significant theme in New and Processual archaeologies. Indeed, "packing densities"—the same thing—were central to Lewis Binford's last book, his 2001 magnum opus *Constructing Frames of Reference.* Today, the theoretically inclined dismiss them as "magic numbers": Numerical thresholds are reductionist, under-nuanced, overly scientific, whatever.[6]

Back to the future! Despite the current unpopularity of thresholds and "magic numbers," I think Southwestern archaeology can ally with evolutionary cognitive science and complexity science to perhaps resolve threshold issues— "resolve" as in "to make clearer," not as in "to solve." I'll discuss three thresholds here, in descending order: 2,500; 150; and 7: 2,500 is the "K-Rule"; 150 is "Dunbar's Number"; and 7 is the "Rule of Six (or Seven)." All three have applications in Chacoan and Puebloan prehistory.

K-Rule: 2,500

The ancient Southwest offers remarkably useful data for the study of population thresholds, particularly of or within communities or settlements.[7] My use of the term "community" means the settlement of potential daily, face-to-face interaction. Community does not mean you have to see everyone, every day; rather, there's the strong possibility of interactions between and among everyone, every day. In many parts of the Southwest, we can actually see ancient communities, and map them with some accuracy.

Here's a specific problem, useful for the ancient Southwest: How big can a community get before it requires governance—centralized, formal, institutional, hierarchical governance? Cross-cultural studies by me (Lekson 1985, 1990) and by Krisztina Kosse (1990, 1994, 1996, 2000) suggested that a fairly hard threshold exists at or somewhere just below about 2,500 people.[8] If a town had 2,500 or more people, very likely someone was in charge.[9] It was someone's job to direct, adjudicate, reconcile, ramrod, and otherwise interfere and intervene in peoples' lives. In short: A government. The obvious alternative—often taken—was to fission, splitting a too-big community into new, smaller, just-right communities. (For a recent consideration of fissioning in early villages: Bandy 2004.)

Kosse (and I) worked with a cross-cultural sample of permanent, independent, single-settlement societies. Permanence is important. It's quite possible for very large aggregations of people to exist briefly—as Colonel Custer discovered to his dismay at Little Bighorn—without governance. I've taken to calling 2,500 = governance the "Kosse rule" or the "K-Rule," in honor of Kosse, who died young.[10]

Of course, the actual value varies a few hundred people either side of 2,500—all figures in this essay should be understood as approximate, not absolute. They are, after all, statistics. However, if a permanent settlement or community reached or exceeded (approximately) 2,500 people, it almost always will have permanent, institutional, centralized, hierarchical governance: A chieftain, a mayor, a king, whatever. Even in the ancient Southwest.[11]

The K-Rule gives us a good indicator of political complexity in archaeological situations—independent of baubles and burials—and I was happy to use it as a tool to understand the ancient past. In the distant past (and, alas, in the present) arguments raged over whether Chaco was or was not "complex"—that is, had a government—addressing exactly the same data with very different conclusions. In a word or two: "yes" and "no." I thought a new line of evidence—population thresholds—might resolve the issue. For me, it did. Chaco was right on the K-Rule.

At some point in its career—say, around 1100—Chaco Canyon was home to between 2,100 and 2,700 people. That's my estimate, made thirty years ago in *Great Pueblo Architecture of Chaco Canyon* (Lekson 1984:272) and recapitulated here in chapter 4. As noted in chapter 3, it's very likely that Chaco was at the high end of that range, or maybe even a bit higher: 2,700+? That should get the job done: Chaco probably had a government.

Why was Chaco not bigger? I don't know, but I can suggest some ways to think about this question. In the cross-cultural samples, 2,500 was a hard upper limit for "simple" settlements (that is, lacking formal institutions of governance) but once past 2,500, surely the sky's the limit? (Not really; we will discuss Roland Fletcher's limits of settlement growth, below.) Why didn't Chaco bloat up to rival Cahokia or any of the medium-sized Mesoamerican city-states? As we shall see before this chapter ends, Chaco at about 2,500 (or more likely 2,700) was larger than many of the smaller Aztec-period regional capitals. Let's stick to Cahokia (which we will meet more fully in a following section) with population estimates of 10,000 to 20,000 (Pauketat 2009a).

Cahokia was bigger than most European cities of its time. It bulked up in an interesting way: Sucking in population from the surrounding countryside (Slater et al. 2014). It achieved its size by more or less emptying its hinterlands. Cahokia could do that because it was smack in the middle of some of the finest farmlands in North America: The American Bottom. Chaco, however, was not in a happy place for farming (see chapter 3). Provisioning the 2,500 in the canyon was probably a major chore—that alone may "explain" why Chaco Canyon never went Big. If we consider Chaco and Cahokia as polities, they were not so far apart in terms of regional population: Cahokia's and Chaco's polities were in the several tens of thousands, with Cahokia densely concentrated in the core urban area and Chaco spread out thinly across an agriculturally patchy landscape. (By the end of this chapter, I hope we will be thinking of the kind of science we could do if we recognize Chaco as a city-state, an altepetl-like whole of both countryside and urban center.)

Back to the K-rule. When I first worked with these data, I suggested that some sort of mental "hard wiring"[12]—what today is called "social channel capacity"—might underlie the K-Rule, but I didn't pursue that line of thought. Kosse took it further and theorized that the 2,500 limit was some sort of cognitive threshold or tipping point. In a community of that size, people's brains overloaded and they required new levels of sociopolitical structure for things to work. If there are basic limits to social channel capacity, it should be possible to model the madness mathematically. Kosse explored the emergent order of complexity theory—specifically the work of Stuart Kauffman at the Santa Fe Institute on emergent order or self-organization—"order for free" that developed from underlying principles (which could be described mathematically) within a field of agents or entities which were otherwise non- or minimally ordered.[13] As these interacting, nonlinear variables progressed, thresholds were reached in which order emerged; that is, a sort of quantum change from dis-order to a more stable, structured order. For Kauffman, the nonlinear and near-chaotic dynamics complemented or even completed the linear concepts of Darwinian evolution, which he finds insufficient for explanation of order observed in the biological universe. Working from Kauffman's mathematical models, Kosse derived a series of thresholds.[14] Only three of those concern us here: 2,500; 150; and 7. Now 2,500—the K-Rule—has already proved its usefulness, I think. Then we step down to 150 (Dunbar's Number) and then down again to 7 (the Rule of Six [or Seven]).

Dunbar's Number: 150

Dunbar's Number is the number of people a person can actually know or work with effectively as individuals: About 150. It is named for Robin I.M. Dunbar, a central figure in evolutionary cognitive neuroscience. Dunbar noticed that in primates (apes, monkeys, chimps, etc.) the size of a social group in the wild was closely correlated with the size of their brain's neocortex relative to the total brain size. Bigger the neocortex, bigger the group. Humans have really big neocortexes. Extrapolating from his primate data, Dunbar suggested that humans can know—really know, as individuals—only about 150 people (Dunbar 1995; see also Dunbar 1992, 1993, 1998, 2010; Dunbar et al. 2010; Hill and Dunbar 2003; for a recent positive appraisal, West 2017:304–309; for a less enthusiastic review, De Ruiter et al. 2014). Five thousand cyber-friends on Facebook don't count.

Dunbar's research is most accessible in his 2010 book, *How Many Friends Does One Person Need?: Dunbar's Number and Other Evolutionary Quirks.* He looks to prehistory: Dunbar sees evidence for a 150-person limit in the size of corporate groups in simple societies, such as clans and in Neolithic and Medieval villages.[15] He looks at modern organizations too: "Once you start to look for them, groups of about this size turn up everywhere," citing Christmas card lists, business organization theory, military unit size, and so forth (Dunbar 2010). The number is situational: You can know more than 150 people in nested or overlapping networks, but the upper limit on how many people you can deal with socially or work with effectively at one time is 150. Not simultaneously!— that would be six or seven (discussed below)—but as an element in a larger, sequential organization or group, of about 150.

Dunbar offers two explanations: (1) "memory overload" (we can only interact effectively with 150 people) or (2) "information constraint on the quality of the relationships involved." It is not, he concludes, simply a question of memory:

> It seems equally unlikely that the problem lies with a pure memory constraint, though memory capacity obviously must impose some kind of upper limit on the number of relationships that an animal can have. There are three reasons for this claim. First, in humans at least, memory for faces is an order of magnitude larger than the predicted cognitive group size: Humans are said to be able to attach names to around 2,000 faces but have a cognitive group size of only about 150. Second, there is no intrinsic reason to suppose that memory per se is the issue. The social brain hypothesis is about the ability to manipulate information, not simply to remember it. Third, and perhaps most significantly, memories appear to be stored mainly in the temporal lobes, whereas recent PET scan studies implicate the prefrontal neocortex, notably Brodman area 8, as the area for social skills and, specifically, theory of mind. (Dunbar 1998:184)

It is the *quality* of the relationship, the strength and nature of the personal knowledge. We might remember many hundreds of names and faces, but we can *really know* only about 150 people as individuals. Beyond 150, we have to categorize, put people into groups based on kinship, social strata, costume clues, linguistic keys, places of residence, or other dimensions that work in our particular society.[16] A step on the road to K-rule.

Dunbar's Number works at Chaco, in the size of groups that used Great Kivas. We don't know much (anything?) about what went on in Great Kivas—

despite the Park Service piping in "kiva music" at Aztec Ruin's reconstructed structure and guidebook hints at ceremony and ritual. We know that many people could sit on what is clearly a bench around the circumference of the Great Kiva, and they could view something going on at the center of the structure (unless they got cheap seats behind the pillars).

Consider Casa Rinconada. Its interior above-bench circumference is 200 feet. By modern ergonomic standards (18-inch seat width), Casa Rinconada can seat about 130 to 135 people.[17] Of course those are modern standards; readers who have attended events at Pueblos know that Pueblo proxemics can be tight. Two hundred people might possibly jam around Casa Rinconada's bench; but surely that's the absolute maximum, or very close to it.

We can safely assume that Great Kivas were designed with the thought and planning that typified Chacoan architecture. They had a pretty good idea of function, capacity, audience, and so forth before they laid out Casa Rinconada. If the building was planned—and of course it was—then it's likely that Casa Rinconada was intended to seat between 125 and 200 people—simple averaging gives us about 160. I suggest that the intended maximum size of the assembly that met in Chacoan Great Kivas was about 150 to 160—Dunbar's Number!

There are a surprising number of Great Kivas at Chaco, probably as many as 12 in simultaneous use during the height of the Bonito phase. Another thought experiment: Assume that Great Kivas were designed to seat 150 heads-of-households/lineages, and those (extended) households numbered between 10 and 20 people (Nimkoff and Middleton 1960; Pasternak et al. 1976), and all Great Kivas were in simultaneous use. We can then extrapolate from 12 Great Kivas × 150 heads-of-households × (10+20 / 2) persons per household = 27,000 people. Far too many for Chaco Canyon! But not far off the order of magnitude of Chaco's central region which numbered in the several tens of thousands of people. We will return of this head-of-household business shortly.

Please note, again, that I am not offering these as "real" figures—I am trying to estimate frames of reference, scales at which we should be thinking about Great Kivas in Chaco Canyon, and Chaco itself. In any event, it seems likely that the Great Kivas of Chaco Canyon serviced a larger region—there are far too many Great Kivas for Chaco itself (unless Great Kivas were used in sequence—that is, each had a specific function or use—which is of course possible).

Ruth Van Dyke (2007b) suggested that Chaco in effect "captured" Great Kivas from settlements in its interior region, forcing those settlements to come to the Canyon to do whatever they did in Great Kivas. Van Dyke may be onto something. Perhaps Chaco's dozen Great Kivas serviced different constituencies from both inside and outside the Canyon. Half of the twelve Great Kivas are located outside the enclosed plazas of the Great Houses, and surely that placement—in or out of the plaza—meant something. Perhaps Great Kivas inside the plazas serviced Chaco Great House residents; but 150 is higher than the total population—men, women, and children—of most individual Great Houses, and (with the head-of-household model) 150 times extended family seems way out of line. Someone smarter than me will have to figure out the constituencies of in-plaza Great Kivas; but presumably the users of those Great Kivas had close ties to the specific Great House. (Secondary nobility from the outlier communities?) Other, outside-the-plaza Great Kivas presumably serviced someone else; who? Or something else; what? Perhaps different Great Kivas were for different functions: Interior, Agriculture, Defense, State, Treasury, etc.

Think about scales, rather than absolute numbers: We know of about 150 Pueblo II Great Houses outside Chaco Canyon (the total is around 200, of which about 50 are pre- or post-Chaco); about 150 people could fit in a Great Kiva; and Dunbar's Number is 150. There may be something to these numbers, although relations of elements in the preceding sentence are not, at this point, clear to me. Drill down into the micro-world of the Rule of Six (or Seven).

Rule of Six (or Seven)

The Rule of Six is a rule of thumb in business for the maximum effective span of control; that is, the number of people a manager can simultaneously manage. This is the magic number most often invoked in the Southwest; it's good to recall that the Rule of Six (or Seven) began as an old factory shop–floor rule of thumb for how many workers a floor boss could simultaneously supervise.[18] Not too many, as it turns out. Six stamping machines, or six looms, or six lathes, or six die presses all banging away at once, all requiring constant supervision. Drive you crazy.

Business units of more than six tend to be divided and grouped into small subunits, leading to dendritic hierarchies branching at nodes of six. Note that the Rule of Six refers to simultaneous face-to-face interactions: Direct, personal, face-to-face management before the advent of information technologies made management more efficient and therefore broadened or "flattened" business organizational structures.

Gregory Johnson introduced the Rule of Six into archaeology in 1978.[19] Four decades later, Johnson's pioneering work still has legs: Around the Millennium, it was developed in a Southwestern example by Wesley Bernardini (1996).[20] Bernardini applied the Rule of Six to adults (leaving children out of the mangle), and posits four levels of integration known from Pueblo models: "Four transition points for a decision-making hierarchy structured by adult-, household-, clan-, and phratry-level decision-making units at population sizes of roughly 9, 36, 170, and 570 adults" (Bernardini 1996:385). (Happily, these are not far off Kosse's K=2 threshold series, stopping short of the K-Rule at 2,500.)

Perhaps the Rule of Six and Dunbar's Number are the kind of rules we need for agent-based models to generate order and hierarchy, bottom up.[21] Complexity may well be an emergent property, how complexity is initially established. I'd like to think so. But until such models emerge, I'll stick with top-down hierarchy—which is how complexity works, once it's established.

Resolving/Revolving Thresholds

How do we get from the Rule of Six to Dunbar's Number to the K-Rule? Can we build a bottom-up model of complexity/hierarchy? Is there a function or multiplier to get from 7 to 150 to 2,500? (For interesting approaches to the problem, see Kohler et al. 2012, and Blanton and Fargher 2008.) Mathematically, Kosse (building on Stuart Kauffman's work) derived both the Rule of Six and a threshold at 150 and the K-Rule 2,500, from a K=2 network. So there may indeed be a mathematical relationship. But, despite the fact that the Rule of Six has a degree of currency in American Anthropological Archaeology, I think it might be less relevant to the emergence of complexity and government than Dunbar's Number and the K-Rule. The Rule of Six is about how many people you can deal with simultaneously. Dunbar's Number is about how many people you can deal with—that is, do, make, or break deals—period. I'm guessing Dunbar's Number will be more useful than the Rule of Six.

Here are two working assumptions (mine, not Dunbar's) and one conundrum: (1) small groups make decisions through consensus: councils, assemblies, etc., with situational leadership but without permanent ruler roles; (2) consensus requires some degree of mutual social knowledge among all actors—it's pretty hard to reach consensus with strangers. And the conundrum: Dunbar's Number suggests that the largest group in which everyone could know everyone else was about 150 people. Thus, we might expect governance to appear above 150, but the K-Rule says 2,500. What gives?

Not all 2,500 people in a community "matter," politically. Kids, for example, don't have a lot of political clout. How many people are actually involved in community decision-making? How many "players" are in the pool? This brings us back to the idea of "head-of-household" briefly touched on, above, when considering Great Kivas and Dunbar's Number.

Let's assume that governance is normally a matter for adults (despite recent events in Washington, which suggest the contrary). And usually, sad to say, governance is very often the business of adult males. (Or females: Chaco was not a matriarchy, but it was matrilineal; Kennett et al. 2017.)

How many adult male (or female) "players" could there be in a community of 2,500, the K-Rule threshold? Southwestern populations averaged about 60:40 adults:kids, so we reduce 2,500 to 1,500 adults. For this exercise, let's assume 50:50 male:female, so that reduces 1,500 to 750. Of course, it's not that simple.

At Paquimé, the ratio of men to women was 40:60; Chaco was more balanced, but for a key age range of 15 to 25 years, there were far more women than men, two males to nine females (gender imbalance of this kind probably indicates slavery). A 40:60 ratio would, of course, further reduce the number of potential male players. But let's work with 750: That's the pool of all adult males. An assembly of 750 equals would be unworkable—five times Dunbar's Number. But all adult males are not equal. There are elders and there are young adults who have yet to prove themselves. I think we can assume that not all 750 were players. Again, we need a multiplier that will get this figure down to Dunbar—or in this case, a Dunbar divisor.

Maybe players didn't need to know everybody—every snot-nosed kid, every superannuated grandparent, every shiftless brother-in-law. Maybe they needed to know *families*, the basic social units. To know families, players needed to know only heads-of-households, heads-of-families, heads-of-lineages (this insight came from my colleague Dr. Catherine M. Cameron, who actually knows astonishing details about many more people than Dunbar would have expected—really big neocortex, perhaps). How many heads-of-households in a community of 2,500? That depends, of course, on how big families were.

Recall the discussion above of nuclear versus extended families. Our typical family—a "nuclear family"—is 2 adults, 2.5 kids, and a dog. Assuming a 5-person unit, 2,500 people would constitute 500 "nuclear families"—well beyond Dunbar's Number. Families in many societies are much larger and more inclusive, with a head couple, multiple nuclear families of their offspring, an odd uncle or aunt, some kids picked up from relatives who had too many kids, etc. Extended families range from 10 to 20 people, about 15 people on average. Bernardini (1996) estimated that a thirteenth-century Unit Pueblo—a demonstrable household—was, on average, about 13 people: 8 adults and 5 kids. That's pretty close to 15, a figure that works for an extended family. If extended families averaged 13 to 15 people, then a community of 2,500 would have around 200 heads-of-households, possibly fewer.

Recall Dunbar's Number: 150. Now 500 or 750 are far beyond the cognitive comfort level; 200 is much closer, but still a bit high. With 200 active players, one-quarter of the assembly are effectively strangers. Another threshold, the K-rule extended to extended families: When the number of players significantly exceeded 150—say, pushing 200—things fell apart. Time for a king. Two paths to oppression!

There are endless permutations and possibilities for theoretical family size and theoretical numbers of adult male/female players. I've assumed that single heads-of-households or lineages were the only players; that's a dangerous assumption, since other social roles, not defined by kinship, no doubt "played" as well: Priests, warriors, whatever. I suspect that the pool of players in a community of 2,500 was often (perhaps always) above—but not far above—Dunbar's Number.

I do not claim that these thought experiments and number games "solve" the K-Rule, but I think they "resolve" it a bit. The addition of other functions and factors (perhaps a role for the Rule of Six?) may lead us, ultimately, to a workable mathematical model of the K-Rule and the rise of hierarchical governance. I continue to work on this, but I am hopeful that younger minds will turn to the problem, or some version of it, and solve it.

Is this simply glib numerology, or might it matter? I wouldn't trouble with it (or trouble you with it) if I didn't think this probably matters. It matters when few make decisions that impact many. I side with Robert Carniero (1981): When a few people could make decisions for a community (or other collective), a key evolutionary tipping point had tipped—toward the state, in all its infinite varieties. Call it a chiefdom (as Carniero did) if that goes down easier, but it's really a tiny little state embryo. When tiny little states grow up to become big brutish states, they can spin off in a number of different, historically contingent directions (Yoffee 2005); but it all starts with a few ruling the many (Trigger 2003).[22]

K-Rule Scofflaws

One of the Southwest's most interesting assets are late, large Southwestern towns which bumped up against the K-Rule but kept their playing fields level. That is, they got big without becoming polities. A few towns approached K-Rule (and, indeed, a few actually topped it, as I discuss below). But they kept their worlds safe for democracy (sort of)[23] and avoided the K-Rule trap. That's interesting and worth study!

Southwestern archaeology has a marvelous database of communities.[24] We do villages well in the Southwest: How they formed, where they were, what they looked like, how long they lasted. Many we can map, in some detail, without the annoyances of excavation. We have a sizable library of towns, and a long history of estimating their populations. Many (most?) of these towns can be assumed to be communities—that is, the potential daily face-to-face groups that form the basis of the K-Rule. And a few of those towns got big.

Long ago, Art Rohn (1983) remarked that both ancient towns and modern Pueblos seldom if ever exceeded 2,500 people. As they approached that size, they fissioned or split into smaller, more manageable "daughter" communities. Rohn may have been overgenerous in his size estimates—he was working with big Mesa Verde sites, for which there are more recent and probably more accurate estimates. The largest Mesa Verde town (Yellow Jacket) topped out at 1,360 (Kuckelman 2003). (But Rohn's recognition of a "ceiling" at around 2,500 people for ancient and modern Pueblo villages certainly influenced my thinking on the K-Rule.) In general, large prehistoric Southwestern settlements (and large modern Pueblos) seldom exceeded 1,500 people.

In the Chaco/Aztec era, "outlier" communities ranged from a hundred to a few hundred people, about the same size as the biggest eleventh-century Mimbres villages, which had about 300 people.[25] In the decades following the fall of the Chaco/Aztec polity (that is, early Pueblo IV), new towns reached remarkably large sizes, most notably around Zuni and Hopi, on the Rio Chama, and along the Rio Grande (Adams and Duff 2004:Appendix: Site Information). But only a few exceeded 1,500 rooms, which (using an old Southwestern convention of one room = one person) would be about 1,500 people. Sapawe, the very largest Pueblo IV town on the Rio Chama, may have had as many as 2,300 people. Sapawe—like almost all of the largest Pueblo IV towns—lasted only a few generations before fissioning into "daughter" villages. Thereafter the big "mother" villages, like Sapawe, fell rapidly into ruin.

Intriguingly, Paul and Suzanne Fish (2007:46) suggested an average size for Hohokam platform mound communities in the Phoenix Basin not far off 2,500: "2,300 to 5,800 members [per community], bracketing our estimate of 2,400 to 3,000 people for the Marana Community near Tucson." Of course, there are about a dozen such "communities"—contiguous, jammed together like hexagons in a bee hive—in the Phoenix Basin, for a total population in the several tens of thousands. A topic which returns in a later section, on "Cities," of this chapter.

Historic Pueblos, with a few notable exceptions, were typically fewer than 1,000–1,500 people, and most often 500 or fewer people.[26] A few Pueblos exceeded the K-Rule, specifically Zuni, Awatovi, and Orayvi. They had interesting reasons and there were interesting results.

Zuni was the largest of all historic Pueblos, but its large size was a response to the Spanish. Five separate Pueblos relocated, circling the wagons for defense, at Zuni. It remained, through the historic period and today, a large town. Zuni's Native government (as described by Frank Hamilton Cushing) was centralized in a small council of leaders who ruled from a special house, at the center of the (Zuni) world. I once used Zuni's "Masters of the Great House" as a model for how Chaco might have worked, until I found something better—or rather, more apt and appropriate, the Mesoamerican altepetl (chapter 3). Zuni's experiment in governance was almost immediately superseded first by Spain, then by Mexico and the United States—kings over the hill: Zuni exceeded the K-rule, but it was part of a larger, colonial government.

The Hopi town of Awatovi, at and after Spanish contact, exceeded 2,500 people. In 1701 it was destroyed by warriors from other Hopi towns. Awatovi's survivors were scattered among the other Hopi towns: A forced fission. Hopi avoided close attention from the Spanish; there was a king or, rather, his representative in Santa Fe, but Santa Fe was a long, long way from the Hopi mesas.

The Hopi town of Orayvi (Oraibi) flirted with supra-2,500 population levels through the nineteenth century. In 1906, Orayvi famously and fractiously split into two smaller communities.

With the imposition of outside political controls—Spanish, Mexican, American—the K-Rule ceiling is lifted and all bets are off. Pueblos—like Zuni, and several Rio Grande towns—could get big without formal hierarchies because there was a royal governor or an Indian agent in Santa Fe representing, in practical ways, centralized governance. So the K-rule rules: The king over the hill.

Jumping the Gun/Jumping the Shark: Chaco and Paquimé

Chaco and Paquimé were two Southwestern sites for which we can safely assume centralized, formal, elaborate, institutional, hierarchical governance. Turn the question on its head: How big were they? As discussed in chapter 3, in 1984 I estimated 2,100 to 2,700 permanent residents at Chaco—conveniently straddling the K-Rule, before that rule was formalized. But as also noted, if we use an extended family figure of 13 people instead of the smaller family size favored in the 1980s, that figure would increase significantly. I think downtown Chaco was at or over the K-rule. Throw in the suburbs, settlements tightly surrounding downtown Chaco, and they were way over the limit (the "Chaco Halo" of Michael Marshall and David Doyel, most accessible in Mathien 2005:258–259).

Paquimé, according to Charles Di Peso (who excavated the site; Di Peso 1974) had a peak population of about 4,700—well over the K-Rule. Michael Whalen and others (2010) more recently argued that Paquimé was, in fact, only half the site Di Peso saw.[27] I tend to trust the excavator; but maybe Di Peso was wrong and Whalen is right. Halving Di Peso drops Paquimé's population to around 2,350—bumping up against the K-Rule threshold! In fact, Whalen (et al. 2010) estimates 2,500. Chaco-size, right on the cusp.

I think that Chaco and Paquimé both probably exceeded 2,500 for several generations, larger than any other Pueblo settlement of their times and almost all precontact Pueblo towns that followed. In both cases, governance might have "emerged" as a function of the K-Rule. But there is excellent and abundant evidence that both polities were heavily influenced by Mesoamerica. That is, both were probably secondary states (discussed later in this chapter, in sections on "Diffusion" and "States"). I'm not suggesting a Mesoamerican king-over-the-hill, but rather a different, less processual dynamic: History, contingency.

Something approaching 2,500 people is sufficient and necessary for governance—in the logical use of those words. That many people jammed into a community for a long term must have a king, or a council, or some other form of centralized decision-making. But formal governance happened in much smaller settlements, presumably NOT as an emergent property. Kosse (and I) found hierarchical institutional governance in communities as small as 500—but, significantly, not smaller.[28] A population of 500, I think, marks a size at which governance becomes possible, sustainable, and sufficient, but not really necessary—in the everyday uses of those words. Historically, some form of "borrowed" governance below K-Rule (perhaps at 500?)—rather than emergent order-for-free at 2,000—may be the route to the Southwest's K-Rule triumphs: Chaco and Paquimé. Both ultimately reached or exceeded the K-Rule but both had the institutions in place before they reached that threshold because both were secondary states. Chaco grew gradually, from three Great Houses at about 850–900 to 1000–1020 when Great House construction boomed. Chaco, I think, became political long before it reached K-Rule thresholds (see also Plog and Heitman 2010).

Here's a K-Rule history for Chaco: (1) Chaco represented the last in a string of theretofore unsuccessful attempts by Great House families (*nobles manqué*?) to establish polities in the northern San Juan and perhaps elsewhere; (2) at relatively low population totals—500 to 1000?—the polity "took," and rooted in Chaco Canyon during the late 800s and early 900s, with three major noble families (Pueblo Bonito, Peñasco Blanco, and Una Vida); (3) starting around 1000, new noble families joined Chaco and built their Great Houses (and attached commoners built Unit Pueblos) until Chaco approached and probably broached the K-Rule threshold; (4) political life was then locked-in, fixed, and necessary: Governance was there to stay—for a century or so.

Paquimé was both secondary and big—as far as we can tell, very close to the K-Rule almost from its inception. There was a local run-up (and a lot of outside help) but when the city itself appeared, it rose fast shortly after 1300 (Lekson 2015a:Appendix B; Whalen and Minnis 2009:44). Whatever its origins, Paquimé's size "locked in" the need for political structure almost from its inception.

History and Science

The history (my history: Lekson 2009a) tells us that several societies in the Southwest pushed through the Glass Ceiling and became polities. That is, they needed and got governments. Southwestern polities were small, perhaps not notably successful, probably not particularly significant; but they might be useful to social science, because in a field of more or less comparable Southwestern societies, some became polities while others didn't. That's interesting. Chaco had no business being a state but (as we shall see) it was; Hohokam should have been a state—and a respectable one at that—but (we think) it wasn't; and, famously, the Pueblos themselves deliberately avoided the state altogether, after the unpleasant experience of Chaco-Aztec. Those societies were all bumping along right at the threshold, near the tipping point. What a remarkable set of cases to compare, contrast, and generalize! If we get the history right, we have an opportunity to explore scales and thresholds at the very beginning of political life. "Beginning" but certainly not "invention." Political complexity did not evolve at Chaco or Paquimé (or, for that matter, Cahokia) because that development happened a thousand years earlier, a thousand kilometers away. The next section explores another aspect of the Southwest's ancient history that offers us more chances to learn and generalize: Secondary states, and their diffusion.

Diffusion: They Had Models for Government

A fairly recent issue of *American Anthropologist* reviewed "Archaeology in 2012." Jennifer Kahn highlighted "movement of people, ideas, and things across landscapes," with a picture of a Polynesian canoe on the journal's cover. She offered examples from around the world—but none from the Southwest.

This is odd, because the ancient Southwest was famously engaged with Mesoamerica. As discussed in chapter 1, early explorers speculated that its ruins were, in fact, Mesoamerican: Aztlán the ancient homeland of the Aztecs! Dour Adolph Bandelier, the region's first real archaeologist, denied those dreams. He concluded that Southwestern ruins were (merely) ancestral pueblos of the modern Pueblos. No Mexicans need apply; the Iron Curtain. But in the early decades of the twentieth century, excavations, particularly at Chaco Canyon, discovered undeniably Mesoamerican items, in surprising quantities and qualities. More followed. Their significance has been debated for decades, but their existence is simply a fact of ancient Southwestern life at Chaco and elsewhere.[29]

Exotic objects pose a puzzle for Pueblo Space—which typically lessens their impact by insisting there were only a few, those probably came from down-the-line indirect exchanges, they were repurposed for Pueblo rituals, and so forth. Like much else (chapter 2), Mesoamerican objects change, strangely but predictably, when they enter Pueblo Space. More reasonably, as Ben Nelson points out, exotica were symbols of power in their homelands, and almost certainly did the same work in the Southwest—not baubles or oddities—reinterpreted of course by Southwestern societies to serve local needs (Nelson 2006).

Elements of local Southwestern iconography also suggest southern sources. I have heard those motifs etc. dismissed as mere "diffusion of ideas" without much thought of how, historically, such ideas "move," who moves them, and what else might move with them. Institutions? Ideas about social order? Models for governance? In this section, my focus is on "movement of people, ideas, and things across landscapes"—and institutions, particularly social institutions, over distance.

Social institutions are not material objects or attributes of iconography. Certainly, they may be represented by objects and art styles, but I like architecture.

Identical temples and ball courts at Chichen Itza and Tula are a famous case, strong evidence that some hanky-panky linked these distant capitals (e.g., Kowalski and Kristan-Graham 2011). But the evidence need not be so obvious. The architectural *structure*—not the walls and roofs, but the layouts and patterns—of a society can also evidence connection. I argued in chapter 3 that Chaco's architecture, while owing little to Mesoamerica in form or fabric, reflects the structure of a Mesoamerican social institution, the altepetl.

Today we call these "cultural connections"; long ago they were called "diffusion." (My revival of the old term is deliberate; we've been down this road before, and sadly got lost.) Diffusion can be directional, from a core to a periphery. It may also be worth thinking of diffusion as Brownian or colloidal: Suffusion over area, in the manner of an archaeological "horizon." That begs the historical question but avoids the difficulties/opprobrium of core periphery.

This section explores some of our assumptions about diffusion in the ancient New World which differ from our perceptions about cultural connections in the ancient Old World. It's axiomatic that New and Old Worlds differed in many significant ways. Historian Peter Watson (2011) called the differences between Old and New Worlds, "the Great Divide" (a different use than mine), surely the grandest "natural experiment of history"—to borrow another book title, this from Jared Diamond and James Robinson (2011)—and of course Diamond famously riffed on these themes (Diamond 1997). Those differences were grist for several mills: Foundational texts of the Enlightenment, social evolutionary philosophy and even (a bit) Marxism, and the ethical underpinnings of American nation-building. And we live today with the consequences.

For American Anthropological Archaeology, one consequence has been the assumption that cultural connections and diffusion were necessarily limited, that Indians were not cosmopolitan. As argued in chapter 1, our views on what Indians could or could not do were shaped by a century of bias. These people got around a whole lot more than we'd (like to) think. To recalibrate, it might be useful to look at cultural connections and diffusion in the Old World as illustrative of what ancient human societies actually did and then ask ourselves: What if Indians did those things too? Dust off diffusion and see what it can do for us. First, a hasty history of diffusion in archaeology; then, a rapid review of diffusion in modern scholarship; thereafter, a concise case study from ancient North America; and finally, some sketchy suggestions of how we might proceed.

Where We've Been

Diffusion was a major focus, even a defining feature, of early anthropology, a sure shibboleth of Victorian times. In the Old World, diffusion under many names drove and drives prehistory, from V. Gordon Childe[30] to Kristian Kristiansen (discussed below). Diffusion remained a constant interest—if not always a central theme—in Old World social sciences and history, particularly in England and Germany. Not so much in the New World. Diffusion, today, is mostly absent from American Archaeology text books. When it appears, it's usually a cautionary historical footnote (for a recent review, see Storey and Jones 2011). It wasn't always so.

In the United States in the 1920s through the 1950s, diffusion was a particular leitmotif of the Berkeley School of cultural geography, led by Carl O. Sauer. Alfred Kroeber published an important essay on "Stimulus Diffusion" in *American Anthropologist* in 1940. "Stimulus Diffusion" marked an interest in the topic that carried through the historical social sciences—and particularly archaeology—through midcentury.[31]

The culmination or climax of diffusion in American Anthropological Archaeology came in two monumental tomes by Charles Di Peso and James A. Ford. Di Peso's (1974) eight-volume *Casas Grandes: A Fallen Trading Center of the Gran Chichimeca* argued that much of the prehistory of the Southwest (Mesa Verde, Chaco Canyon, etc.) was the result of active manipulation and diffusion from Mesoamerica. Ford's (1969) monumental *A Comparison of the Formative Cultures of the Americas: Diffusion or the Psychic Unity of Mankind*, published by the Smithsonian Institution, did much the same for the Southeast (Cahokia, Moundville, etc.). Indeed, Ford went further: After an exhaustive analysis of traits, timings, and distributions, Ford concluded that trans-Pacific contacts ignited the Formative, which thereafter diffused among and between the American continents. The late '60s to early '70s was bad timing for both Ford and Di Peso: These two expansive studies of diffusion arrived just as New Archaeology turned its back on diffusion and migration (and history).[32]

Diffusion and migration were specifically rejected by aggressively scientific New Archaeology in the 1970s. Both were exiled to the gulag of "non-explanations." Marvin Harris, a key theoretical figure of that time, ranted: "as soon as we admit, as the archaeology of the New World now compels, that independent invention has occurred on a massive scale, diffusion is not only superfluous, but the very incarnation of antiscience" (Harris 1968:378). (In Europe, migration and diffusion were also set aside, replaced not by American hypothesis-testing but by smaller scales, local issues, tending your own garden.)

Time changes everything, as the poet said. In 2007, the Society for American Archaeology presented its Book Award to Kristian Kristiansen and Thomas Larsson's (2005) magnificent study of diffusion in Bronze Age Europe. The word "diffusion" was not used (it remains déclassé) but Kristiansen welcomed the return of "forbidden" subjects like migration and long-distance dynamics.[33] In a word: Diffusion.

Within the last academic generation, migration (diffusion's evil twin) resurfaced in the Southwest. Perhaps first in a session on Mesa Verde–Rio Grande at the Fourth Southwest Symposium, then in CRM Salado projects in the Tonto Basin, and later still in the legal requirements of NAGPRA.[34] Turns out, migration matters. Today migration has become mainstream, with a number of dissertations and monographs and edited volumes and exam questions.[35] After renewed study, we found that migration was complicated, with ranges of variation across multiple axes.

If migration could be usefully rehabilitated, what about diffusion? There's a need. We have gotten very good at sourcing pottery, chipped stone, and even people; and it's pretty obvious there was more to it than trade and exchange.[36] But diffusion remains a hard sell.

From the 1970s through the present, diffusion on almost any scale has remained in exile. Michelle Hegmon's (2003) influential call for theoretical consilience among American Anthropological Archaeologists:

> New Archaeologists rejected "particularistic" explanations based on diffusion and migration. Although their reasoning made theoretical sense—*diffusion is not an explanation*—the result was a lack of attention to significant events such as large-scale population movements.... Archaeologists have again turned considerable attention toward the movement of people and apparent spread of traits. (Hegmon 2003:227–228; my emphasis)

In Europe, diffusion was never really banished; so now that it's back, big-time, under various names and guises, there are intellectual tools for dealing with it. Given American Anthropological Archaeology's long exile of diffusion, current American interests—while real—are understandably tentative and exploratory. (Network Analysis is a great start! See chapter 5.) We don't have the inclinations and tools, so we have not reached the critical mass of interest that would spark sustained engagement with methods and theory in diffusion.

Do the differing attitudes toward diffusion and long-distance interactions reflect real differences between Old and New World prehistories? Of course, the Old World and New World were "different"—they are in two different hemispheres, for starters—but perhaps they were, in fact, profoundly and importantly different, negating methodological transfers.

That belief underwrote Jared Diamond's (1997) *Guns, Germs and Steel*, and Peter Watson's (2011) *Great Divide*—they made their arguments by comparing the two worlds—as portrayed by New and Old World archaeology. And, if true, that difference would be fundamentally interesting. But to some degree—a large degree?—the perceived differences are the result of different methodologies—history in the Old World, anthropological archaeology in the New World (as discussed in chapter 1). Those methodological differences should be recognized and resolved before any meaningful conclusions are reached.

What Others Do: World History and Globalization

Globalization—transnational, long-distance cultural connections—emerged as a field of study in the 1980s. It famously excludes the New World before Columbus, before it was connected to and influenced by the Old World. Fair enough, I suppose, for modern times, but are globalization and cultural connections really *new* in the New World, or in the Old World for that matter? Is globalization necessarily modern, industrial, and (initially) Eurocentric?

A growing thread of historical scholarship looks back beyond modernity—for example, historians Robert McNeill and William H. McNeill's (2003) *The Human Web: A Bird's-Eye View of Human History*. And a thin but persistent theme of archaeological scholarship pushed things back even further: Hemispheric scales. Gunder Frank (Frank and Gills 1996) moved Immanuel Wallerstein's (1974 and subsequent works) modern "World-Systems" (a template for globalization) back deep into protohistory, positing a Eurasian world system as early as Ur.

Many globalization scholars reject premodern applications, protesting that modern technologies define globalization. That claim underwrites exceptionalist intellectual strategies, declaring premodern history (conveniently) irrelevant to the study of globalization. Recently, however, an important globalization scholar, Nayan Chanda, of the Yale Center for the Study of Globalization, has come to question that exceptionalism, in *Bound Together: How Traders, Preachers, Adventurers and Warriors Shaped Globalization* (2007). Chanda starts the clock with the African exodus, humans leaving the mother continent to populate the world. Chanda follows those connections, with ellipses and lacuna, into the present and on to the future. For him, at least, globalization is not solely modern; it has a history and pre-history.

Justin Jennings's (2011) *Globalizations in the Ancient World* is a recent landmark study that does, indeed, include Cahokia, but not, alas, Chaco. (Pueblo Space: The Southwest did not do such things.) Increasingly, globalization is seen as not necessarily modern, nor industrial, nor European: Premodern Asia and Africa were densely connected, as many studies attest.

We know the Old World was deeply and intricately interconnected, long before the Age of Discovery, long before modernity. Not only through quotidian "trade and exchange," but through active exploration. Phoenicians rounded Africa around 600 BCE, two millennia before Vasco de Gama. Polynesians reached Hawaii by 500 CE, more than a millennium before Captain Cook. Vikings settled in North America, briefly, 500 years before Cristoforo Colombo came and went, briefly. China mapped the East Indies by 1450, a century before Magellan's survivors blundered through the archipelagos.

A distinct historical subdiscipline focuses on cultural connections: World History.[37] World History is not simply collections or aggregations of regional or national histories; rather, World History's goal is to examine cultural connections between and among the regions. World History of premodern times has focused on Eurasia and north Africa, showing definitively how interconnected the cultures of those land masses were, back into deep pre-history; e.g., Jerry Bentley's (1993) seminal *Old World Encounters: Cross-Cultural Contacts and Exchanges in Pre-Modern Times* and libraries of later texts and journal (e.g., Manning 2003; Stuchtey and Fuchs 2003). World History makes it clear that long-distance dynamics were always important and occasionally transformative in the histories of societies and nations throughout Eurasia and Africa. Importantly, World History corrects the perception that within the Old World cultural connectivity was an exclusive or defining property of Europe. It is nearly impossible to think of a civilization in Asia, Africa, and Oceania which did not value and was not shaped by long-distance connectivity.

Why not North America?

North America enters most World Systems[38] and nearly all World History narratives only after Christopher Columbus blundered into the Caribbean and Europe discovered the New World. As Victor Mair wryly noted: "One is tempted to regard it as a kind of Eurocentric religion, the central tenet of faith being that—until it was discovered by modern Europeans—no place on earth had meaningful contacts with any other distant place" (Mair 2006:12).

Turn the comparison on its head: If the Old World—with its rich documentary evidence—is any indication, interactions suggested by exotic objects in the Southwest are probably just the tip of the iceberg. Diffusion both directional and Brownian might have been the rule, not the exception. Perhaps the difference between Old and New World is methodological, a matter of different evidence. The New World lacks the documents that inform Old World globalization studies and World History; what if the Old World was similarly mute?

How might we operationalize that notion? What would that look like? I suggest we begin by comparing apples and oranges, first within our continent and then between our Worlds, Old and New...

A Brave New World: Chaco, Cahokia, and Mesoamerica

Here's an example of the possible importance of diffusion for North America, focusing on two major Native American sites—Chaco and Cahokia—in what are now the United States, and the high civilizations of Mesoamerica, in Mexico. At the millennium, most American Anthropological Archaeologists were lukewarm, at best, about continental-scale hanky-panky, with most of what little interest there was coming from the Southwest (e.g., Cowgill, Hegmon, and Milner 2002). I take it as read that the three knew about each other—although Chaco and Cahokia are places while Mesoamerica, of course, is a region of many places.

"Mesoamerica" was a vast and complex region, encompassing many different states and civilizations. I use the term here for those parts of Mesoamerica most likely engaged respectively with Chaco in the US Southwest (west Mexico), and Cahokia in the Mississippi valley and the Southeast (Huasteca).[39] States, empires, and civilizations flourished and fell in those Mesoamericas for many centuries before Chaco and Cahokia.

We've had plenty—too much?—of Chaco (chapter 3); no need for more here. Cahokia (AD 900–1250) had a parallel career, but on a much larger scale and with greater historical impact. Tim Pauketat describes Cahokia:

> about the size of an average ancient Mesopotamian city-state (albeit spread out quite a bit more), close to that of early Andean capitals (Moche, Tiwanaku, Wari), and bigger than the initial capital built atop Monte Albán.... [Cahokia was centered on] a flat public square 1,600-plus feet in length and 900-plus feet in width...edged with the finest of buildings astride the largest of earthen pyramids: the main platform at the Grand Plaza's northern end, the awesome Monk's Mound. This black packed-earth pyramid of pyramids...rivals the largest in Mexico and Peru. (Pauketat 2009a:26, 34)

Quite a place. Unlike Chaco, Cahokia inherited long traditions of monumental architecture—"mounds"[40]—and the use of exotic materials and art styles, from earlier Poverty Point (Late Archaic) and Hopewell civilizations that rose and fell in the eastern United States. At the same time as Chaco, the city of Cahokia rose rapidly, drawing in populations from the surrounding region, until the city became larger than most Mesoamerican and European cities of its time. Strong cultural connections ranged from the Great Plains to the Atlantic and Gulf Coast. Nobles of such power that they could properly be called kings ruled or attempted to rule Cahokia's core area, in the American Bottom near St. Louis, Missouri—bigger than many Mesoamerican states but smaller than Chaco's region. Cahokia faded by 1250 and by 1300 the great city was essentially empty. (Again, contemporaneous with Chaco-Aztec.) Secondary Mississippian centers—smaller versions of Cahokia—popped up all over the eastern United States, surviving right up to European colonization.

Archaeologists stoutly deny that anything Mesoamerican appeared at Cahokia or in the Mississippi valley, but I will (safely) assert and assume that the lords of Cahokia were fully aware of Mesoamerica.[41] Mesoamerica at this time—the early and middle Postclassic—was a complicated place (Smith and Berdan 2003). There was no single, monolithic "Mesoamerica"—unless someone revives the currently unfashionable Toltec Empire. As suggested above, the Southwest most likely connected with West Mexico (which some would not include in "Mesoamerica") while the Mississippi valley probably consorted with the civilizations of the Huasteca region of northeast Mexico. Those were the nearest neighbors. There are material linkages—cold hard data—between the Southwest and West Mexico (Nelson 2009), and between Mississippian and Huastec Teeneks of northeastern Mexico—Mississippian forms in Huastec contexts (chapters in White 2005; White and Weinstein 2008).[42]

But Postclassic political shenanigans often played out over much longer distances—remarkable distances!—leaping over mundane middle ground to reach a distant area of interest. Most famously, for this period: Tula and Chichen Itza (e.g., Kowalski and Kristan-Graham 2011); although the nature of the interaction is hotly debated, no one denies the cultural connections between those two great Postclassic centers, 1,000+ km apart.

For elite interactions, for ideologies, for things not contained or constrained by tumpline economies, distance was no great difficulty. Indeed, as Mary Helms (1988, 1992) told us long ago, for ancient elites *distance was desirable.* Objects and actions at distance enhanced elite knowledge and prestige. Kings were supposed to not only know what was going on elsewhere; in many narratives kings were supposed to BE from elsewhere. Marshall Sahlins's (2008) important essay on "stranger-kings" identifies this pattern across the globe. (See also Sahlins 2017.)

We've known about macaws in the Southwest for over a century. More than likely, the macaws were NOT from west Mexico but farther south and farther east, perhaps the Maya country (Gilman et al. 2014). Recent research brings cacao to Chaco (Crown and Hurst 2009; Crown et al. 2015; Washburn et al. 2011; Washburn et al. 2014) and maybe Maya ideologies to Mimbres (Gilman et al. 2014). Neither cacao nor macaws nor Maya myths came from the Southwest's nearest neighbors; all originated in far distant lands. Kings and rulers played on these scales; if we accept that the Southwest had state-level societies, we don't have to dissemble with strained claims for "down-the-line" trade. (That's surely not going to work for macaws.)

I strongly suspect the more that we look, the more we will see of these out-of-place products. I recently saw two Ramos Polychrome effigy jars in a museum in Villahermosa, Tabasco. They came from farther up the coast, in the Huasteca area. There's Pachuca obsidian at Bandelier National Monument; my museum has a photo of an obsidian prismatic blade core from a Mimbres site.

As noted above, Mississippian forms are found in the Huasteca. But, so far, exotic Mesoamerican materials have not been found (or recognized) at Cahokia and other Mississippian centers, save a single piece of Mexican obsidian at the Mississippian gateway center at Spiro, Oklahoma (Barker et al. 2002). I recently saw open-work "lace" textiles from Spiro Mounds, which surely look Hohokam—or Mexican. The more we look, the more we'll find?

Of Chaco, Cahokia, and Mesoamerica, Chaco (AD 900–1125) was clearly the junior partner, in part because the corn agriculture that fueled Cahokia and Mesoamerica was risky and uncertain in Southwestern deserts. Cahokia looked very much like a Mesoamerican city built without the stone masonry: Pyramids around a plaza. Chaco had the stone masonry, but looked nothing like a Meso-american town: Its Great Houses were clearly part of the Pueblo tradition of building, and there's nothing like them in Mesoamerica. These qualities were not superficial: Simplified to architectural plans and elevations, there can be no question which—Chaco or Cahokia—was more similar to a Mesoamerican city.[43] And Cahokia was huge; Chaco was small.

If Chaco was a knock-off *altepetl*, Cahokia was the real deal: A peer to Tamtok and other great cities of northeast Mesoamerica (Stresser-Péan and Stresser-Péan 2001; Faust and Richter 2015). Yet Chaco had notable quantities of Mesoamerican objects, while Cahokia (to date) has produced no Mesoamerican materials. Why?

Peter Peregrine and I hypothesized that Chaco, a starter-kit kingdom on the edge of empire, needed anything it could use to legitimize its fledgling nobil-ity—precarious because of the harsh Chacoan environment. With turquoise and Mesoamerican prestige goods, Chaco nobles could reinforce their legitimacy (again, see Helms 1988, 1992).

Cahokia, on the other hand, built on a long history of Eastern Woodlands monumentality and exotic exchange, and did not need foreign props to legiti-mize its power (Peregrine and Lekson 2012). The lords of Cahokia employed and manipulated symbols of power which had long precursors in the memories of societies which came under Cahokia's sway: Copper, shell, mica, obsidian, and so forth. But that's not enough: We want cacao, macaws, and Mesoamerican bells, like the Southwest.

Maybe Cahokia didn't need cacao: They had Black Drink (Crown et al. 2015), which, it seems, Cahokia exported to Chaco and to who-knows-where else?

Maybe Cahokia didn't need macaws: They had some pretty remarkable birds, with the Mississippi valley flyway between Central/South America and Canada and the Gulf Coast. Mississippian and earlier Hopewell art (and archi-tecture: Effigy mounds) were obsessed with birds and bird forms (Brown 2007; Krech 2009). Perhaps they liked the birds they liked—Mississippians leaned towards raptors—and didn't need tropical plumage.

Maybe Cahokia didn't need Mesoamerican copper bells: There was a long tradition of fancy copperwork before and during Cahokia's time (Goodman and Cantwell 1984; Trevelyan 2015).[44]

Diffusion, diagnosed archaeologically, would have Chaco on the receiving end of Mesoamerican things, and Cahokia innocent of any Mesoamerican taint. Yet the scenario presented here, if correct, has Chaco actively seeking selected elements of Mesoamerican civilizations, while Cahokia could legitimately be considered a peer—even an equal?—of that northeastern Mesoamerican world.

Diffusion—at least of high-end items and their ideological entanglements—seems to have been purposeful and politically directed. This was not simple trade-and-exchange, oozing traits from one area to another; nor was it a cult, spread from convert to convert like an epidemic. To be sure, diffusion probably was wrapped up with trade and ritual. But at heart, cultural connections between Chaco and Mesoamerica, and between Cahokia and Mesoamerica, may have been political, and reflected the differing sociopolitical histories of Chaco and Cahokia.

Peregrine and I argued that in the New World—and particularly in North America—cultural connections should be assumed rather than treated as extraordinary claims, requiring extraordinary proof. Then, by comparing Chaco and Cahokia, we can recognize patterns and implications of diffusion which might otherwise go unnoticed or, worse still, be ignored because our methods are currently unequal to the task.

Where We Should Be

We can attack the methodological problem on two fronts, the Old World and the New World. Cultural connections and diffusion in the Old World are studied as history, and much of its content comes from documents. Historicity on the right scales gives us World History and Globalization; and the conclusion that, in the Old World, cultural connections were normal, not remarkable, in historical periods and therefore quite likely in prehistory.

The New World's ancient past is not history but rather anthropology, and lacks conventional documents. The earliest written accounts tell us of systems almost certainly disrupted by colonization. The biases of American Anthropological Archaeology compounded by a limited evidentiary base (objects, not documents) lead us to conclude that cultural connections were rare and exceptional both in recent and (therefore) ancient times.

That may be the case, but it might also be the case that different perceptions of Old and New World cultural connections come, at least in part, from the biases of American Anthropological Archaeology and the lack of literate societies in the New World north of Mexico. Comparing diffusion and cultural connections, and *how they are studied* in Old and New Worlds could perhaps rectify that.

How to find common denominators—an analytical language—which might correct for differing methodologies in Old versus New World? I suggest a "calibrating" research program for the Old World and a substantive research program for our part of the New World.[45]

For the Old World: Strip the record of its documentary advantages. Knowing what we know about cultural connections from documents, etc., consider the archaeology purely as archaeology: The distributions of artifacts, architecture, and landscape; that is, material patterns, not documents. How would the archaeological record alone suggest or support the cultural connections we know from documents? Such an exercise would be like ethnoarchaeology of the ancients: We'd know, for example, how the Roman empire actually worked (the ethno- part); the documentary record would "calibrate" the material distribution of goods and objects (the -archaeology part). We'd know what the material remains of a mighty empire looked like; we could then compare those to other material remains; say, for example, the Bell-beaker expansion, or one of the horse empires, or some other widespread distribution. How are the archaeological signatures different? How are they similar? How much would we know about Classical "world systems," for example, from archaeology without its corresponding ancient literature, inscriptions, coins?

Such calibrating studies of preindustrial societies across Europe, Asia, and Africa could create comparability between Old World (literate) and New World (nonliterate) situations.[46]

The potential utility of such studies for New World scholars seems obvious. But Old World scholars might wonder: What's in it for them? Why ignore documents, if you have 'em? I submit that the "natural experiment" of New versus Old World is of such transcendent importance—it helped launch the Enlightenment and altered the trajectory of World History—that global questions should be of interest to Old World scholars. Were New and Old Worlds so different? Or are their differences at least in part a function of differing data and methods?

The New World: To understand cultural connections and diffusion in the New World, first and foremost, we must recognize that the New World in fact had history and that understanding that history is fundamental to everything else archaeological. Such as social and political institutions. Both Chaco and Cahokia have been the subject of dozens—perhaps hundreds—of scientific studies (monographs, articles, theses, and term papers); variations on the theme of "evolution of sociopolitical complexity" or "development of complexity" framed locally, the evolution of complexity *at* Chaco, or *at* Cahokia. Framing the question locally overlooks the fact that sociopolitical complexity had already "evolved" long before Chaco and Cahokia, far to the south in Mesoamerica. At least a millennium before Chaco and Cahokia, Mesoamerica had kings, nobles, and commoners, all the apparatus of the state. And as I've argued already, we can be confident that the people of Chaco and Cahokia—and their antecedents for many centuries—were cognizant of those developments far to the south. They knew their historical context, even if we chose to ignore it. Complexity may or may not have "evolved" at Chaco and Cahokia; but it seems almost certain that fundamental forms and principles diffused from Mesoamerica to those later, northern centers.

History and Science

My history of the ancient Southwest (Lekson 2009a) razes (or raises?) the Iron Curtain. More importantly, that history—inspired by World History—allows the kind of continental-scale dynamics and interconnections that apparently characterized almost everywhere else in the world, but which American Anthropological Archaeology has largely denied to Natives north of Mexico.

While we have accurate ways to source material objects, we lack a robust intellectual framework for long-distance intellectual or conceptual interactions: Perhaps we should reconsider diffusion, and all archaeology did with it years ago, as a starting point. And we might look at the better brands of World History both for inspiration and methods. That could be very exciting: History and science might intertwine like the caduceus, or move from one to the other like the double helix.

States: They Applied Those Models

A couple of years ago in a large Southwestern city, a notable archaeologist gave an informal talk to a well-read audience. (The lecture was captured on video.) During the Q&A, a member of the audience asked a question appropriate to the evening's topic.

> *Question:* "What do you think of Steve Lekson's theory that the Southwest and the Southeast were secondary Mesoamerican states?"
> *Answer:* "Well in a way I think that's a fair characterization…that statement, while interesting at one level, is also an over-simplification."

The ellipsis in the answer eliminates a digression and does no violence to the gist of the notable archaeologist's response, which was, essentially, "yes, but it's complicated." When I watched that video, I did not shed tears of joy but I did reward myself with one of Boulder's better beers. The notable archaeologist may have been simply being polite, but still it was something to celebrate.[47] It's not that—for whatever reason—I *want* Chaco to be a state, and it's not that I think there's something *good* about "state" that ancient people aspired to.[48] It's simply that, based on the evidence, it's pretty clear that's what Chaco *was*. After a century of archaeologists mucking around Chaco, I want us to get it right. But Pueblo Space makes that difficult.

I'd been lobbying for statehood for Chaco (and Cahokia) for years.[49] Easier to get recognition for Chaco from the UN[50] than to get Southwestern archaeology to admit the possibility that Chaco had a state-level government. But if you dropped Chaco anywhere else on the planet, local archaeologists would look it over briefly and conclude: "Another petty state. Ho-hum." Because it sits in the Southwest—in Pueblo Space—many (most?) archaeologists both within and beyond the region simply cannot imagine or countenance such a thing. Claims that Chaco was state-like are rejected out of hand, or dismissed as shameless social climbing. I speak, here, from unpleasant personal experiences.

Well—what's a state? Most of us old guys learned from Henry Wright and Gregory Johnson (1975) that a state was a society with top-down decision-makers—say, kings—at several administrative removes from the working stiffs (peasants, commoners, serfs, whatever). States were all about layers of hierarchy. Since we took Archaeology 101, states got more complicated, more variable (e.g., Blanton and Fargher 2008). Southwesternists mostly do not keep up on such things. Why would we? We know the Southwest had no states.

I'd like to propose a working definition that acknowledges (must I say it?) today's more nuanced notions of "state," but that also (must I admit it?) plays to my argument: States had permanent, institutional, central governments with recognized rulers, social classes, a core ideology, and a capital/region.[51] That's a definition that should satisfy most archaeologists—but it won't satisfy every "state." Even way back in the day, they knew that one size did not fit all: "There are many kinds of states, including those that form on the margins of extant states" (Wright and Johnson 1975:267). And that's what I'm talking about here: "Secondary states."

"Secondary state" is archaeology jargon.[52] For my dubious purposes, "secondary" means derivative, subsequent, copied. "State" means a polity with a government, as described above. A "secondary state" is a state that was formed or caused or inspired through interaction with an existing state.

A decade before the notable archaeologist allowed that maybe Chaco was a secondary state, a panel of very distinguished archaeologists sat in judgment on prehistoric Puebloan achievements: "We can't even pretend [they] formed states." (Yoffee, Fish, and Milner 1999:262). That dismissive conclusion appeared the same year that *Chaco Meridian* was published, 1999, in which I suggested that ancient Southwesterners could form state-like entities—if they wanted to.

In chapter 1 I argued that our longstanding prohibition against Native states north of Mexico was a sad legacy of racist, colonial biases among the founding fathers of American Anthropology: The Glass Ceiling, "no states north of Mexico." That pronouncement is both *a priori* and Procrustean. It presumes both what we will know and what we can know. Know this: There *were* states north of Mexico!

Cahokia, for Example

Drop Chaco (for now) and consider Cahokia. To review: In the eleventh and twelfth and thirteenth centuries, Cahokia was a great city on the Mississippi, with a population of several tens of thousands and the largest pyramid north of Teotihuacan. Its power (whatever that was) reached at least 300 miles, from Cahokia to Aztalan, Wisconsin, in the north, and to Spiro, Oklahoma, and Macon,

Georgia, in the south—although its actual polity was the central core of that vast area. Its rulers were buried with enormous pomp and great circumstance. Whatever your definitions of "state," Cahokia can be excluded by only twisted logic and special pleading. Yet with very few exceptions, Eastern archaeologists are just as opposed to statehood for Cahokia as Southwestern archaeologists are to states at Chaco or Aztec or Paquimé.[53] Suggestions, in the 1990s, of a Cahokia-centered "Ramey State" (named after the most notable Cahokia pottery type, Ramey Incised; itself named for the farming family who owned much of the site) were hooted down.[54] Cahokia was demoted to a typical "chiefdom," as known from ethnohistorical accounts. In a key study, Cahokia was presented as "an unusually large version of the Mississippian chiefdoms that developed elsewhere in eastern North America" (Milner 1998:176).[55] This struck me, at the time, as astoundingly wrong: Cahokia was a state.

Tim Pauketat published in 2007 a book tackling this quandary: *Chiefdoms and Other Archaeological Delusions*.[56] His solution: He leaps over both "chiefdoms" and (red flag!) "states" to claim Cahokia was a *civilization*—a polity.[57] Avoiding the "S" word, but taking its territory.

Chaco, Maybe

In *A History of the Ancient Southwest* (2009a), I stopped dodging the issue: Chaco was a state, part of the North American world of states and empires.[58] "I insist on 'states' because North American polities must be so designated to occupy the same intellectual space as their peer polities across the border in Mexico" (Lekson 2009a:223). This was not social climbing, by Chaco or by me, but a tactical move to allow Chaco to operate outside Pueblo Space. Chaco and Aztec and Paquimé (and Hohokam and Cahokia) merit seats at the table with other small modest humble ordinary garden-variety states or statelike entities. Not at the table's head with the Big Four or Big Seven (or however many Primary/Archaic States make your list). Not even midtable with the empires. Down at the boot end with junior states, city-states, Medieval principalities, jungle kingdoms. The Southwestern polities sit below the salt, near the door—but at the table!

If we can escape Pueblo Space and allow Chaco to be a state, new horizons beckon, new borders can be crossed. Recall Lynne Sebastian's complaint against Chacoan uniquity: In attempting to understand Chaco, she insisted (correctly) that we had not looked at enough boxes or anthropological categories, and we should keep looking. We could look among states and state-like entities—although that was not Sebastian's intention. As we saw in chapter 3, if the Glass Ceiling is lifted we needn't look very far to find something that fits Chaco. Just outside Pueblo Space—a bit above the Glass Ceiling and not far south of the Iron Curtain—there were historically and culturally appropriate ancient societies that appear to "solve" the "mystery of Chaco." OK: Chaco found its box. OK: So what?

Secondary States

The notion of "primary" (or "pristine" or "archaic") states and "secondary" states was introduced into American Anthropological Archaeology through Morton Fried's (1967) *The Evolution of Political Society*. Primary/pristine/archaic states—and there were only a few, in Mesopotamia, Egypt, China, Mexico, and Peru—developed completely on their own, and their evolution (according to Fried) followed a series of more or less similar stages under a particular set of conditions (which need not distract us here). Secondary states—99 percent plus of all states that ever were, are now, or ever will be—were something else again. Something else to avoid.

Primary states got all the love; for archaeology, primary states were the prize, the brass ring, the Oscar-Emmy–Palme d'Or, the Pulitzer-McArthur-Nobel. (More superlatives appear at the end of this section.) So many people have offered theories of primary state formation that you could write a book analyzing their various schools and lineages. Secondary states? Not so much. You could perhaps write an extended essay on why we've ignored 99 percent plus of historic and pre-historic political formations. But no one would read it.

Primary states were evolutionary miracles; secondary states were historical by-products. Perhaps a limited set of processes created primary states (Fried 1967; Feinman and Marcus 1998; Flannery and Marcus 2012); perhaps primary states rose in multiple ways (Yoffee 2005). Secondary-state formations were exponentially more varied: Willa Cather supposedly said there were only two or three human stories, but secondary states have a thousand tales to tell. That's the kind of chaos and complication that begs for science and simplification: Can we discern commonalities and processes in all those varied secondary states? Beats me: Only a few people have tried to figure 'em out, compared to throngs that propose laws and patterns for primary states.

In evaluating and interpreting Chaco and Cahokia, many archaeologists compare them to the primary/pristine/archaic states, because that's the literature that's ready to hand. And, of course, our North American candidates are found wanting. That's silly. In defense of my colleagues and my field, there aren't anthropological textbooks on secondary states (in Political Science, yes; but Political Science's "secondary" is not Anthropology's "secondary"). Not many journal articles or book chapters tackle the issue head-on, explicitly. I'll review a few here, before suggesting a course of action.

Morton Fried (1967) thought most secondary states resulted from the expansion of primary states, or direct interactions with primary states. It's worth quoting Fried here:

Secondary states emerge through processes quite different from those that give rise to the pristine states. It is unfortunate that all real examples of state formation available for first-hand investigation are of secondary type. All too often, students of such state formation have assumed that, except for the inevitable unique elements that mark any particular case, the process of developing stateship they observe is the one that must always transpire.... [My argument] has been an attempt to controvert that view. (Fried 1967:242)

He wrote his book (and it's a classic) in large part to demonstrate that the rules for pristine/primary/archaic states need NOT apply to secondary states, and vice versa. Fried's ideas about primary states haven't aged well, but his insights on *secondary states* remain largely valid—though generally ignored. Fried thought primary-state expansion caused nonstate societies either to become secondary states (usually imposed by the primary state) or to tribalize. Most importantly, Fried insisted that primary states and secondary states were different animals and followed different rules.

Ten years after Fried's discussion, Barbara Price (1978) took a swing at secondary states in a book chapter titled "Secondary State Formation: An Explanatory Model." Her essay was in New Archaeology's language—for every age its own rhetoric:

It is paradoxical that there have been numerous studies of individual secondary states, including many which emphasize process and dynamics: all contemporary, all ethnographic-present, and the bulk of ethnohistorically documented states are secondary. Moreover, all direct, non-analogical, non-retrodictive knowledge of pristine states is in fact derived only from archaeology. Yet there has been almost no systematic theoretical treatment of the secondary state as a regular and lawful phenomenon. (Price 1978:161)

She avoids ubiquitous artifacts such as pottery and focuses on architecture (which makes good sense to me!): "A building, if appropriately analyzed, is thus theoretically capable of providing information on a fairly wide range of problems.... Probably the most powerful class of data to use in sociocultural explanation is settlement pattern" (Price 1978:165). Especially housing—which makes a lot of sense for Chaco. "Differential housing, however, represents instead the differential ability of individuals or coresident groups to dip into the total energy flow and divert some of it to private use," but she emphasizes that it's got to be LOTS more energy for a (relatively) FEW houses (Price 1978:169).

In the end, Price follows Fried: Secondary states are the result of expansion or aggression by primary states on nearby nonstate societies: "With the exception of situations of historical succession, secondary states are formed as a result of expansion of other states, themselves either pristine or secondary" (Price 1978:179). For example, Teotihuacan's expansion into Guatemala at Kaminaljuyu and Tikal (Price 1978:170–175).

"Historical succession" is an interesting development in our thinking on secondary states (in addition to Price, see also Marcus 1998). Some secondary states developed as successors to primary states, when they fell and splintered; while other secondary states developed from interactions with primary states. Now we're getting somewhere, learning something about the myriad secondary states that have, heretofore, been swept together into a single bin, and then under the rug. And there's a third, nonstate option, noted by Fried: Nonstate societies impacted by primary states could tribalize (Price 1978:179).

Interest in secondary states—what little interest there was—waned in the 1980s and 1990s; far fewer articles appeared with that term in the title. There were plenty of case studies of secondary states even if, in North America, researchers didn't know that they were studying secondary states (we called them "chiefdoms"). But not much synthesis. At century's end, state studies were dominated (as ever) by works on primary or pristine or archaic states: *Archaic States* (edited by Gary Feinman and Joyce Marcus 1998), followed by Norman Yoffee's (2005) rejoinder *Myths of the Archaic State*, and an unrelated masterpiece, Bruce Trigger's (2003) *Understanding Early Civilizations*, all carried us into the new millennium. Archaic, early—the focus remained on primary states. Understandably, of course. Yet all three volumes brought up the subject of secondary states, only to let it drop.[59]

After that long pause, there now seems to be an uptick of interest in secondary states.[60] Joyce Marcus (2004) authored a much-cited chapter, "Primary and Secondary State Formation in Southern Mesoamerica," in a volume on the Mayan site of Copan, which she (and others) see as a secondary state created by the imposition (possibly violent) of a foreign king or lord. "Founded perhaps 300 years after the primary states of the Petén, Copan became a secondary state with the arrival of a prince from the royal house of one of the preexisting states" (Marcus 2004:373). Her ideas move us a few more steps beyond the Fried model of secondary-state formation from the aggressions or expansions of primary states:

> During the Early Classic (AD 200–600), many parts of the Maya region achieved statehood. Not all these occurrences, however, conform to what theorists call primar*y state* formation. That term is usually reserved for cases where a state forms from simpler chiefly societies in the absence of a preexisting state that could serve as model. Once the first state has formed in a region, second*ary state*s based on the preexisting model could arise

through a number of processes. In some cases neighboring chiefly centers might join forces and reorganize themselves to avoid being absorbed
by an expanding primary state. In other cases a nearby chiefdom, desiring greater power, might ask an established state to send it a prince from
the latter's royal house. (Marcus 2004:357–358; original emphasis)

The latter suggestion—"a nearby chiefdom, desiring greater power"—is an
interesting wrinkle in secondary-state studies. In this age of agency, it grants a
degree of power to the secondary-state-to-be: Maybe they *wanted* to become a
state! I'll return to this point shortly.

A very useful later work on secondary states was an article in *American Anthropologist* by William A. Parkinson and Michael L. Galaty (2007), "Secondary
States in Perspective: An Integrated Approach to State Formation in the Prehistoric Aegean." They are perhaps a bit too encompassing, touching the bases on
a wide range of current archaeological fads and fancies, but their core message
is solid. They urge us

to distinguish between primary states (sensu stricto), which emerged
from less complex sociopolitical forms such as chiefdoms, in isolation
and with no evidence of interaction with more mature states, and first-
generation secondary states, which emerged from local competing corporate groups through interaction with more mature societies. (Parkinson
and Galaty 2007:125)

Following Price, they distinguish between "secondary-by-interaction" (that
is, secondary) versus "secondary-by-history" (that is, successor states) (Parkinson and Galaty 2007:124–125). Another important distinction, another angle
we can try on secondary states. Chaco and Cahokia were most likely secondary
"by-interaction," not "successor states"—neither Chaco nor Cahokia replaced
earlier states (I think). I suspect that the trajectories of historically successor
states differ from interaction secondary states: *That's a very good area for study*.

That distinction, one of several, shows us that the catch-all category "secondary states" needs attention. We have a thousand archaeological histories (case
studies) of next-generation states (some disguised as chiefdoms), and we could
hope that there are patterns among those many histories: *Another good area
for study*.

Kent Flannery and Joyce Marcus (2012:503–514) in their book *The Creation
of Inequality* follow the generational histories of statehood in central Mexico,
from the primary "Big Bang" of Teotihuacan at 500 CE; to "second-generation
states" that rose from the balkanized remains of Teotihuacan's realm after the
great city's fall, around 800 CE; to "third-generation states" which coalesced
around eleventh- and twelfth-century Tula; and "fourth-generation states" of
1200–1300, myriad small "petty states" which they call—wait for it!—*altepetl*:

Some small kingdoms of this era had an administrative hierarchy of no more than three levels [that is, a "chiefdom" for those of you keeping a Neo-evolutionary scorecard]. Having previously crossed the Rubicon to monarchy, however, these societies had no intention of giving up the trappings of kingship. Each attempted to maintain its own royal heritage, however modest its territory. (Flannery and Marcus 2012:510)[61]

Kingship, like rock-n-roll, will never die. Hey: Maybe it's all about kings! Bruce Trigger, in his magisterial *Understanding Early Civilizations* (2003:71–91), makes the case that all early civilizations had kings—even Teotihuacan and the Indus Valley cities (famous candidates for acephalous civilizations). "All early civilizations probably had monarchs, even if kingship was defined somewhat differently and the actual political power exercised by such rulers varied considerably from one to another" (Trigger 2003:73). Trigger's caveat is critical: When we say "king" in the Southwest, the word conjures up visions of Louis XIV or Nero or Ivan the Terrible: Despots and tyrants.[62] Kingship also includes the fourth-generation monarchs of modest territories, whose political power varied from some to little. But a king's a king, for a' that.

Game of Thrones

It matters that we are American. Let's play counterfactuals, my paraphrase of Carl Sauer's old question: What if the pre-history of North America had been written in Spanish, coming out of Mexican and Caribbean scholarly institutions?[63] North American prehistory was written in English, by staunchly antimonarchist republicans (the form of government, not the political party). What if the prehistory of North America had been written in Spanish by court historians working for the viceroy (counterfactualing away 1810 and the Grito de Dolores), instead of being written by self-made scientists working for the Bureau of American Ethnology? I won't answer that question; I leave it to you.

A return, briefly, to the Hemingway-Fitzgerald exchange of chapter 3, jacked up a notch: From class to kings. We had a king, once. We scraped him off in 1776. But our discarded king was still a king, over the water: The English monarchy tottered on and did rather well, later on—colonialism can be very profitable for the colonizer. The French got rid of their king about ten years after we did, but it didn't stick. They—and the rest of Europe—removed and restored kings and emperors on and off well into the next century.[64] England still has a queen, Spain a king, Japan an emperor. They are not quaint vestiges attracting tourists; those monarchies have deep meanings that Americans can hardly imagine.

Indeed, it's almost impossible for Americans to conceive a king or a monarchy as a part of government. Throughout prehistory, however, it's safe to say that for most people, it was hard to imagine life without a king. Kingship (in scores of local variations) was nearly universal (Trigger 2003).

Americans cannot fathom that anyone, anywhere would suffer a king, much less want one. Whatever their social realities, most Americans are nominally egalitarian, populist, democratic.[65] It's our bias by birthright—and not all biases are bad! But, when thinking about other times and places, it IS a bias, and maybe a bad one. We should consider how that rock-hard, copper-bottomed belief (which we inhaled with our first whiff of Independence Day fireworks) affects our archaeological theories and concepts. Egalitarianism, populism, and democracy pervade American Anthropological Archaeology's thinking on the evolution or emergence of governments (indeed, help form Pueblo Space). We think kings are an unnatural abrogation of universal human rights, primordial freedoms that (we think) existed until ecology, economy, demography, threat, or whatever forced free-range Noble Savages to accept and submit to a king/tyrant.

Three American questions: The second-from-the-top American question is: "Who put you in charge?" In the case of kings, the answer would be: God. One does not question God; thus the third-from-the-top American question may not apply: "What's in it for me?" There probably isn't anything in it for you or, at least, not much. That's not how class/kingship works. Americans don't get that: We prefer rational actors to divine rights; quid pro quo, et cetera. The top, number-one American question, of course, is: "If you're so smart, why aren't you rich?" And that's the point: Kings can be dumb and rich. Kings are rich because they are kings; they can be rich idiots or figureheads. Kings can also be out of work. Remember Huck, Jim, and the Lost Dauphin: All they're required to be is royal, and thereby different from Huck and Jim, from you and me. Identify and control our biases: One of which is our national aversion to monarchy.

A European question: Why not kings? *"It's good to have a king"*—as Felipe Fernández-Armesto (an Oxford historian to whom I'm partial) titled his review of Flannery and Marcus's (2012) *Creation of Inequality.* Fernández-Armesto, while admitting the book's many virtues, did not like it. His principal objection was what he saw as pervasive American bias against kingship. I will not paraphrase Fernández-Armesto, I will quote him. He is a far better writer than I am, and it is important for you, American reader, to hear this from a liberal, intelligent, non-American:[66]

> In the U.S., however, the advantages of a hereditary system elude most people's attention, perhaps because Americans are so used to seeing themselves as models for the world. "Why can't others be more like us?" is the implicit question. The often unnoticed answer is: "Why should they be?" The latest evidence for this curious myopia is a redoubtable book by two excellent American archaeologists, Kent Flannery and Joyce Marcus.... They start by assuming that hereditary elites are hard to explain, whereas it would be more pertinent to see egalitarian communities

as strange and problematic. The authors take Rousseau as their exemplar, though they seem to have misread him: Like Rousseau, they assume that natural inequalities—distributions of innate talents and skills—are morally superior to the hierarchies of rank that constitute civil inequalities. But as far as we know, for most societies, the reverse seems true: It is less dangerous to defer to rich or noble superiors than to trust the strength, cunning or eloquence of some naturally endowed Führer-figure.

Missing from such an analysis is an explanation both simpler and more persuasive: Hereditary leadership, like other forms of widely replicated culture, occurs frequently because it works well and benefits most people in the societies that adopt it, at least for a while. Indeed, humans have an amazing fertility, by comparison with other cultural animals, in devising political hierarchies. (Fernández-Armesto 2012)

Neither Fernández-Armesto nor I advocate monarchy. He is (and I am) identifying a pervasive American bias that, as he points out in his review, undercuts our archaeology. We would like to think that people accepted kings only out of necessity. Because Americans find kingship unnatural, we think would-be kings must persuade a community of rational actors that kingship is in their (the community's) best interest.[67] That is not how it works. After centuries and millennia, kings and monarchies became the nature of things across most of the agricultural areas of the continent. Kings needed commoners and commoners needed kings. A functioning New World polity needed both.

Kings and commoners were the natural order—and egalitarian agricultural societies were…what? Perhaps not, as we would like to believe, a stage on some evolutionary path to complexity, a precursor to polity. Pueblos are the archetypical, oft-cited example of egalitarian agricultural societies. When you are trying to fill in that cell for "corporate/symbolic" in your dual-processual matrix (Blanton et al. 1996)—or indeed any scheme that needs big egalitarian farming villages—Pueblos are the go-to example. But Pueblos developed in reaction to and rejection of noble-commoner polities at Chaco and Aztec. They had kings but scraped 'em off, around 1300.

But in the chaos and violence that ensued, they lived in very big towns, without kings. Without kings, without government, those towns were unstable—after a few decades of moving, fissioning, fighting—until the Spanish arrived, with the Castilian-Catholic clampdown.

Once and Future Kings

Kings in the Southwest? Homegrown? Imported? A bit of both? "A nearby chiefdom, desiring greater power." Maybe the Southwest needed kings. Or *wanted kings*. Ancient Southwestern societies are often portrayed as pawns of their environment, not so much dust in the wind as weeds in the rain. Rains start, they grow; rains stop, they wither. But in times of adequate rainfall—indeed, at all times!—they could make choices, change courses, decide things. They could act.

Governments act. Often not wisely, and often not well. (I'll return to that point presently.) We, heirs of the Enlightenment, would like to think that individuals act—and of course they do and did. "Agency" is the capacity of individuals to act independently and to make their own free choices—a popular theme in American Archaeology, if a tad presentist.[68] Still, agency's allure is strong in American Anthropological Archaeology: Especially bottom-up, populist agency.

American Anthropological Archaeology likes bottom-up agency, and (whenever possible) downplays or ignores top-down agency. For example, Mesoamerican archaeology had long favored the spectacular monuments and elite burials. But with the rise of agency, Americanist approaches welcomed a respite from Maya elites and embraced the common man/woman/child with "household archaeology."[69] Time to find out how the other half lived, how they resisted oppression, and so forth.

In the Southwest, we already have a really good handle on commoners, on household archaeology. That's all we've done for over a century: Commoners R Us. For the longest time, we didn't realize there were elites to study. Maybe it's time to find out how the one percent lived, and how they used their agency and power. For rulers have agency, too, probably more effective than any peasant's. What about top-down agency?

Rulers can reinvent themselves, step up to a higher level, real or imagined. (They can also be trundled off to the guillotine, but let's not worry about that right now.) "A nearby chiefdom, desiring greater power" can become a state—a secondary state—through choice, through top-down agency.[70] Most thinking about secondary states (what little there is, sampled above) derives from the actions and agency of primary states or existing mature states: Older states expanded and created secondary states. But what about the actions and agency of nonstate groups, out on the edges of distant empires? It is quite possible for "chiefs" or rulers or powerful persons on the periphery to reference and adopt the structures and trappings of established states and create a knock-off, starter-kit kingdom—that is, a secondary state. It's my impression that this was a common thing worldwide, and the origin of many secondary states (Helms 1988, 1992; Schortman and Urban 1998; Nelson 2006; Lekson 2009a). The question needs work.

History and Science

Chaco was a secondary state.

Secondary states perforce must be studied historically, in larger historical contexts. *A* was caused by *B. A* reflected *B. A* rejected *B.* Those are all historical statements, so we have to get the history right. Ninety-nine percent of the states we study were secondary—and we have not much theory, not many methods for dealing with them, scientifically.[71]

Archaeology has done a dandy job with primary states, all half-dozen of them. Primary states were the Holy Grail (to extend the riff: The Lost Ark, the Crystal Skull) of archaeology even before archaeology was an organized field. New and Processual Archaeologies sought to codify and routinize primary states by defining evolutionary pathways in which primary states emerged and then generalizing from that to all states—Flannery and Marcus's (2012) *Creation of Inequality* seems a sort of culmination of that approach. But Norman Yoffee (2005) and Bruce Trigger (2003), in studies of great intellectual weight and erudition, argued that even the half-dozen primary states varied greatly in their historical contexts and trajectories. It is still possible to generalize, but perhaps rather differently than Flannery and Marcus.

And all these beg the question of secondary states: Were there patterns and regularities in the historical transmission of state-level political systems? We have only begun to think about that. It's a daunting task: So many secondary states, so little time.

Pare the universe back to a continent. We can handle a continent, maybe. North America, entire. What a fine scientific use for the ancient Southwest: A strong case to compare to Mississippian, and perhaps to contrast with the Intermediate Zone and Caribbean and other peripheries of Mesoamerica. Maybe the Mississippi Valley was a core, not a periphery; the Southwest, more periphery than core. Cahokia and the "chiefdoms" that followed it were "secondary" in a very different way than Chaco.[72] Surely state-level societies of the Intermediate Zone had still other historical trajectories, different historical engagements with Mesoamerica's primary states, and massive secondary-by-succession states and empires. We can begin to use such differences between and among small states on the fringes of Mesoamerica to contribute to the notably understudied phenomenon of secondary states. North America offers a remarkable case for study: Compare and contrast, triangulate and debate (chapter 6).

Patterns and similarities? Divergences and differences? Either or all outcomes must surely inform on a general picture or theory of secondary states. Each secondary state has its history to be sure, but in the aggregate, there's got to be some great science waiting to be done.

Cities: They Built a Capital

There are libraries and libraries of books about cities, ancient and modern. And hundreds of journals and websites. Urbanism has its own philosophies, theories, and methodologies—indeed, its own disciplines and subdisciplines in both sciences and humanities. As with most things, I favor systematic comparative studies[73]—"systematic" in that things are actually measured and compared along various dimensions; unlike "Great Cities" coffee-table books, which don't attempt analysis but simply illustrate their subjects. (I like those too!) We will return to systematic comparative studies at the end of this section. How might Chaco fit into such efforts?

I argued above that Chaco as a regional polity was a secondary state. Now I want Chaco Canyon itself to be a city—indeed, a capital. This might seem like a cart-horse problem, but it's possible to have a state without a city.[74] Or cities without states.[75] Whatever Chaco writ large may or may not have been, Chaco writ small could still be a city. Chaco was a state with a capital city; but if you don't want to buy the whole package, consider the installment plan.

There are basically three ways to define cities: (1) required criteria—the laundry list; (2) demographic size (large) and density (high); and (3) regional relationships: A city is central to, provides services for, and transforms its region. I will argue against number one, laundry lists; their criteria and traits pretty much ensure all cities will look more or less European. Of the other two (big and dense, regional center): I'm leaning towards number three, but I'm willing to entertain number two—a city really ought to have a fair number of people.[76]

Number one, the laundry list, by definition truncates the very variation we should be studying. If cities must have A, B, and C, then all cities available for study will have A, B, and C. And the lists were almost always based, initially at least, on western cases. Manhattan might not be a good model for every ancient city: Not all roads led to Rome. There's more to urbanism than London, Paris, and Tokyo. Urbanism in the Southwest could be interesting: A different kind of city.

Within the spectrum of Southwestern urbanism (discussed below), I argue that Chaco was a political capital—one kind of city. Chaco should be considered a city (and a capital), both to get Chaco's particular history right, and for the comparative opportunities that result. No one listens to me, so in this section I appeal to authority! Three of my favorite urbanists: Amos Rapoport, Roland Fletcher, and Michael Smith. To preview: Rapoport makes Chaco a capital; Fletcher identifies Chaco as a particular (and particularly interesting) urban form—"low-density, agrarian-based city"; and Smith reviews that particular form in continental contexts historically relevant and appropriate for Chaco. Rapoport and Fletcher actually name Chaco; Smith does not.

Amos Rapoport Declares Chaco a Capital

Amos Rapoport had a long and productive career as Professor of Architecture and Urban Planning at the University of Wisconsin–Milwaukee, studying (among other things) what is termed "vernacular architecture," ancient and modern.[77] His essay "On the Nature of Capitals and Their Physical Expression" (Rapoport 1993) is a short but dense, grandly longitudinal, cross-cultural essay. Rapoport deliberately does not define the term "capital." No laundry lists. He summarizes his observations of a large, disparate collection. He is not provincial; Cahokia is a capital, Zimbabwe is a capital, London is a capital. Notably, Chaco is listed as a capital, without comment; it's just one of the gang, another example in the files (Rapoport 1993:35–36).[78] Rapoport recognizes differences, of course, between "early" and modern capitals, but he also sees commonalities:

> Many definitions [of capital] are rather ethnocentric and "tempocentric."…However, their commonalities are significant: strong and lasting centrality (e.g., as transactional centres, or centres of government and administration); exceptionally wide interests; images that symbolize national identity, status and power, so that resources are lavished over them; pre-eminence over other cities; exercise of control…and, above all, their function in the organization of territory. (Rapoport 1993:32)

Capitals exert control through a variety and often a redundancy of means: Education, military, administration of justice, resources, information, legitimation, and almost universally often through (1) "rituals and ceremonials, especially those significant for the entire society, legitimating the ruler and reinforcing cohesion" and (2) through architectural "continuity with the past, through site, name, myths of origin, tombs and so forth" (Rapoport 1993:33). Rapoport is particularly interested in the kinds and styles of buildings found in a capital, their built environments:

> In the central enclaves of traditional capitals, the culturally relevant elements used in all built environments receive their highest and strongest expression…. Although always culture-specific, regularities can be found: location; size and scale; restricted visual or physical access; elevation or height; special materials, colours, decoration or artistic elaboration; courts and gates; platforms; etc. (Rapoport 1993:35)

Rapoport emphasized the critical importance of ritual and ceremony in traditional capitals. Traditional capitals are planned and built as settings for mass theater and drama "impressing large audiences" (Rapoport 1993:36), often assembled through pilgrimage or something like pilgrimage.[79] The capital itself, or areas within it, are often sacred places. This may be particularly true of early capitals, "proto-capitals," which were literally designed to reflect cosmologies

> attempting to re-create a cosmic or divine order on earth, a reflection, however imperfect, of celestial archetypes…. [I]t is achieved through participation in the symbolism of the centre, expressed by the axis mundi; geomantic and other techniques of orientation are necessary to define sacred space in opposition to profane; this often involves an emphasis on cardinal directions. (Rapoport 1993:44)[80]

They often began as ceremonial centers, and grew to be capitals (and here he specifically includes both Chaco and Cahokia): "Organizing centres, then cities, began with a spiritual, ritual or sacred role—as ceremonial centres. Capitals in particular retained that ceremonial character" (Rapoport 1993:45). That is, proto-capitals often "grew" out of ceremonial centers.

A final observation, which segues into the next section's discussion of Roland Fletcher. Rapoport notes that not all capitals were embedded in or coterminal with great cities. He makes a useful distinction between "dispersed" capitals and ceremonial centers (that is, with a zone of settlements dispersed around the center) and "compact" capitals (e.g., capitals in a dense urban center) (Rapoport 1993:Figure 2). Chaco was the former. What are we to think of "dispersed" cities?

Roland Fletcher Urbanizes Chaco

Roland Fletcher is Professor of Theoretical and World Archaeology at the University of Sidney. In 1995, he published a remarkable book, *The Limits of Settlement Growth,* based on population and area information on over 300 settlements and cities through time and space.[81] There's nothing else quite like it.[82] Fletcher's data are presented as graphs of population on the X-axis and density on the Y-axis, and lo and behold, patterns appear: "I-limits" of density stress; "C-limits" of communication stress; and a "T-threshold" of density (about 10 persons/ha) below which neither I- nor C-limits apply. I-limits are predictably rather flat (around 1,000 persons/ha); C-limits are multiple, with one key limit at 100 ha and another at 100 sq km.

Obviously, Fletcher's analysis is much more complicated than I'm presenting here. I-limits and C-limits lead Fletcher into all sorts of interesting territory—but it's the T-threshold that's of most interest here. An extended quote is in order. Low-density cities, below the T-threshold, are

> settlements in which demands of communication are so slight that there is no constraint on settlement growth. Such settlements can reach an enormous size, well in excess of the size limit of their communication assemblage, but they obtain these sizes only by following a trajectory to very low residential densities below the T-limit. Possible examples which bypassed the 100 ha limit are Cahokia in the Mississippi Bottoms in the fourteenth to sixteenth centuries AD, and Chaco Canyon in the twelfth to thirteenth centuries AD. They are smaller-scale equivalents, relative to the 100 ha limit, of Tikal and Angkor relative to the 100 sq km limit. (Fletcher 1995:117)[83]

The existence of "bypass" settlements solves "a disturbing epistemological problem" (Fletcher 1995:121) and reminds us that there's variety to urbanization—

no laundry lists. But not endless variety. Fletcher sees repeated strategies or patterns of urbanization. Chaco and Cahokia are offered as examples of one type of urbanization: "Low-density, agrarian-based urbanism," cities incorporating kitchen gardens and fields within the urban fabric. Low-density urbanism was not a Western or modern style of city-making—Rapoport's troublesome "dispersed cities"? According to Fletcher (2009:2) in a later article, "low-density agrarian cities…dominated lowland Mesoamerica, Sri Lanka and mainland South-East Asia between the late first millennium BCE and the mid-second millennium CE [and] represent a distinctive path to urban life"—in those cases, in tropical forest environments. Many (most?) archaeologists might not be comfortable with that. A recent conventional summary of the archaeology of urbanism still insists on "dense packing or crowding of residential and nonresidential structures" (Marcus and Sabloff 2008:13) among other listed requisites.[84] But "low-density agrarian city" seems to be a real thing—a cluster of cases on Fletcher's continuum—found in many times and places.

Chaco incorporated gardens and fields (Vivian et al. 2006) but, as I argued in chapter 3, those probably were insufficient for supplying it with food. That's not necessary for low-density urbanism: Much of a low-density city is garden space, but a city is a city, and requires a hinterland.

Chaco and Cahokia were invited to a session exploring "low-density urbanism" at the 2013 Society for American Archaeology meetings, alongside European and Asian low-density cities. (Chaco brought along a friend: Phoenix Basin Hohokam, of which more below.)

So Chaco and other Southwestern centers were urban, but in ways we are not used to; they were low-density, agrarian-based, dispersed cities. Relevant here, Michael E. Smith states that in Mesoamerica "most ancient cities fall into [Fletcher's] low-density group" (Isendahl and Smith 2013:133).[85] To which and to whom we now turn…

Michael Smith Puts Chaco in Context (or in Its Place)

Teotihuacan and Tenochtitlan "bookend" Native urbanism in central Mesoamerica. Teotihuacan—which flourished from 100 BCE to 600 CE—was enormous: 100,000 people (more or less) packed into 20 sq km of orthogonal cityscape, with huge pyramids (the biggest pyramids south of Cahokia!), palaces, avenues, all the good stuff (except a ball court?).[86] It was Mesoamerica's first great city, truly a Big Bang. Much of subsequent Mesoamerican history can only be understood in light of Teotihuacan's rise and—just as importantly—its fall (e.g., Nelson 2000, who traces the ripples of its fall all the way to the Southwest).

Tenochtitlan was the Aztec capital conquered by doughty Cortes, a thousand years after Teotihuacan. Tenochtitlan, built (perhaps in the fourteenth century CE) on an artificially enlarged island in the middle of Lake Texcoco, had 100,000-plus people crammed into 13.5 sq km, with additional tens of thousands in the adjoining city of Tlatelolco (Isendahl and Smith 2013:138; cf. Smith 2008a: Table 2.1). Its pyramids and palaces were not as enormous as Teotihuacan's (or Cahokia's), but Tenochtitlan's monuments still astonished Cortes and his boys. The conquistadors recognized the Aztec capital as a city—in every European sense. Tenochtitlan was much larger than most European cities of its time!

Teotihuacan and Tenochtitlan conform to Western notions of urbanism— large populations, high density, stormy, husky, brawling, and so forth. But most Mesoamerican (and North American) cities did not fit the Western model. Contemporary with the two huge bookend cities, and in the many centuries between the fall of one and the rise of the other, most Mesoamerican cities were not big and dense, but rather small and not very crowded.

Michael Smith (2008a) compiled remarkably useful data on Aztec "city-state capitals." "The median Aztec city-state capital had a population of 4750 people living in an area of 108 ha (with a median density of 50 persons/ha)" (Isendahl and Smith 2013:139). Those are median values: Many cities were of course much smaller. The smallest Aztec city-state capitals on Smith's (2008a:Table 2.1) list were Coatlan and Cuxcomate, each with 800 people in 15-ha settlements. That's about the size of a Pueblo IV village.[87]

Size matters, but it's not everything. Recall, beyond the discredited laundry list, there are two other ways to think about cities: The conventional demographic (big and dense) and an emerging regional (service/transform a region) approaches. Most Mesoamerican capital cities qualify under the latter, but maybe not the former: They served and transformed their regions, but they were neither large nor populous. In the Aztec era (and arguably for earlier periods, too), their regions are pretty well understood in the altepetl. As described in chapter 3, an altepetl consisted of a center/capital and a small region of secondary centers and farmsteads. The altepetl was both city and countryside; it was not possible to separate rural and urban.[88] Sort of "low-density agrarian," you might say.

Isendahl and Smith (2013) applied Fletcher's model to Mesoamerican cities, concluding that most Mesoamerican cities were low-density agrarian forms. "Agrarian-based" in part explains the "low-density," the incorporation of substantial gardens and farmplots within the urban fabric. Houses were separated by fields but still close enough together to represent a coherent settlement with "urban agriculture."[89] This was not the case at Teotihuacan or Tenochtitlan— proper big and dense Western-style cities—both of which were provisioned from countrysides or nearby "truck-garden" towns, via market economies (again, a proper European model of urbanism).

Most of Fletcher's examples of "low-density agrarian-based" cities come from the tropics. There, they are sustainable (Fletcher 2009; Isendahl and Smith 2013). At Chaco's latitude, in Chaco's desert, maybe not. For farming, Chaco Canyon was "iffy" at best (chapter 3). Consider, however, Chaco's famous—if problematic—fields. Gwinn Vivian tells us that small, carefully constructed farmplots filled most of the gaps between buildings, at least on Chaco's north side, for almost the whole length of the canyon (see Vivian et al. 2006:Figure 2.2):

> The north-side farmers were remarkably consistent in the ways they collected, diverted and spread the water that flowed [from rainfall] off the slickrock and into short side canyons. They constructed earthen or masonry diversion dams near the mouths of these drainages to channel the runoff into canals. At the ends of the canals they built headgates to further channel the floodwater onto fields. To ensure that all plants received equal water, the farmers gridded their fields into rectangular plots separated by low earth borders...averaging seventy-five by forty-five feet. (Vivian 2004:11)

Field systems were part of Chaco's urban fabric—whatever their function (they were architecture in a complex cityscape, a fact we should not overlook; Lekson 2006), and however successful they may or (more likely) may not have been for provisioning Chaco. So Chaco could be considered (following Fletcher) a low-density, agrarian-based city—much like the small Mesoamerican capital it was trying to be.

Words like "city" and "urban" are red flags for most Southwestern archaeologists, taboo terms. No cities in Pueblo Space (except the City Different!). We don't study cities; why should we?[90] Consequently, we tend to think about cities in old, conventional terms—laundry lists, big and dense, and so forth. Say "city" and we think of the big ones. Compare Chaco to Teotihuacan or Tenochtitlan and of course Chaco is found wanting. QED no city, right?

No! Set those two megalopolises (and those antique criteria) aside. Without Teotihuacan and Tenochtitlan, the next largest remaining Mesoamerican cities were Cahokia-sized; median and smaller Mesoamerican cities were, in both size and form, rather Chaco-like. Those less-than-behemoth cities were defined not entirely by size or by density, but more by their role in regions. Chaco and Cahokia were capitals, central to, servicing, and transforming their regions.

Rapoport makes Chaco a capital—a particular kind of capital. Fletcher makes Chaco urban—a non-Western form of low-density urbanism. Michael Smith shows us that if Chaco was "low-density agrarian-based," it was far from unique in North America; rather, such cities characterized much Mesoamerican urbanism. Smith may not make Chaco a city, but that's my takeaway.[91]

Sunbelt Cities

Montezuma's Castle and Cliff Palace began as cowboy enthusiasms, fanciful names for dramatic ruins. Today those names are only tourist bait. The Park Service greets you with denials and corrections: It's NOT a castle, it's NOT a palace, and Montezuma never slept here.

Ignorance excuses the excesses of early "archaeology." We know better now. Ruins are more fitly named for a nearby creek or peak or, better still, a Native name. In fact, most sites today are simply numbered: LA 49 or 5MT5.

Similarly, "city" is seldom used in our region's archaeology, save with irony. The word does not fit our version of the ancient Southwest. "La Ciudad," a site under Phoenix, was named early, safely exoticized in Spanish. "Lost City" near Las Vegas, Nevada, was another early appellation, too far from Santa Fe to draw the wrath of archaeological arbiters. (Besides, what happens in Vegas stays in Vegas.) "Abandoned cities of Mesa Verde" and "Ancient City of the Sun" might be found on the web and in glossy magazines, but never in proper archaeological reports.

City? That claim has been made for several Southwestern sites: Paquimé (aka Casas Grandes) by Charles Di Peso (1974); "budding urban settlements in the northern San Juan" by Art Rohn (1983); Phoenix Basin Hohokam by anonymous Park Service text writers; and for Chaco Canyon by me, among others. And every time, the claim has been stoutly denied or (more often) ignored. No cities here. The case for Chaco has been made above. Here, I briefly review Paquimé, the San Juan, and Phoenix.

Paquimé

Charles Di Peso boldly proclaimed Paquimé a city in his monumental 1974 report. He spoke of "urban renewal" (a phrase then current in American cities); thereafter "the city of Paquimé prospered and reached the zenith of its development…a massive, multistoried, high-rise apartment house covering some 36 hectares" (Di Peso 1974:313) with a population of almost 5,000 people. By most definitions, 5,000 people on 36 ha qualify easily as a city (that's a density of 138/ha: pushing Teo numbers!). And beyond demographic criteria, Di Peso's Paquimé performed specialized functions in relation to a broader hinterland: It was a trading center and a political capital. Recent work has not been kind to Di Peso's Paquimé. Indeed, even his name for the site—a name reported in early Spanish accounts—was for a long time largely abandoned, replaced by the more pedestrian Casas Grandes.[92] As noted earlier in this chapter, Michael Whalen and colleagues (2010) recently halved the great city, cutting it down to size. Even if only half the place it used to be, Paquimé was still a great and possibly powerful city, the center and capital of a region of considerable size. With a population of several thousand people, a massed concentration of elite housing, ball courts, (small) pyramids, and assorted other monuments, Paquimé was a city—as I'm using that term here.[93]

San Juan

Art Rohn raised a few eyebrows in 1981 when he presented a paper on "Budding Urban Centers in the Northern San Juan." Rohn (1983:178) concluded: "By the thirteenth century some Pueblo settlements in the Northern San Juan had reached the threshold of true urban size." He was referring to a score of very large settlements dotting the fields and plains west of Cortez, Colorado. These sites were literally overshadowed by the famous cliff-dwellings of nearby Mesa Verde; but the large sites on the plains of Cortez were much larger than any sites in the National Park, and contained far more people in ancient times than did their contemporaries Mesa Verde (e.g., Varien and Wilshusen 2002). The largest was Yellow Jacket, about 45 km (27 miles) northwest of Cliff Palace. As noted above, in 1981 Rohn estimated a population at Yellow Jacket of 1,500, later upped to 2,700 (Ferguson and Rohn 1986). More recent research at Yellow Jacket reduced the estimated population to half Rohn's numbers, but it's still a big settlement.[94] As mentioned earlier, Rohn presciently recognized a threshold at about 2,000 to 2,500 "as a demarcation between a small urban settlement or pueblo and a large one or city" (Ferguson and Rohn 1986:177). He saw the budding urban centers of Mesa Verde banging up against that threshold but never quite crossing it. Rohn also worked with a conventional laundry list of criteria (craft specialization, markets, waste removal, transportation, political complexity) most of which he did not find at Yellow Jacket or other Cortez sites—so his cities budded but never flowered. I agree: Yellow Jacket was not a city, it was a big farming village. It never performed specialized functions in relation to a broader hinterland required for urbanism. The site was briefly interpreted as a "Four Corners Anasazi Ceremonial Center" (Lange and others 1986) based on its very large number of "kivas" (almost 200!). But "kivas" were a canard—a good index of population but not particularly ceremonial.[95] Yellow Jacket was not a regional ceremonial center, but instead a village in the hinterlands, first of eleventh-century Chaco Canyon and later of twelfth- to thirteenth-century Aztec Ruins. Chaco's influence was marked by an eleventh-century Chacoan Great House, and Aztec's by a twelfth-century bi-walled Great Tower (Lekson 2009a:158–161).

Phoenix

The Phoenix Basin was the epicenter of Hohokam, both historically and geographically (Fish and Fish 2007). (Phoenix, today, is the biggest city in the Southwest.) But "city" is almost never used in Hohokam archaeology—though "urban" creeps in, from time to time. Two of the more important compendia on

Hohokam settlement were titled *The Hohokam Village* (Doyel 1987) and *The Hohokam Village, Revisited* (Doyel et al. 2000). It takes a village to be Hohokam. Archaeology conventionally sees the Phoenix Basin as a dozen or more independent villages or communities, united only through the (important) requirements of administration of canals, each of which ran through multiple settlements.[96] The scales of political control for communities were calculated through partitioning Phoenix into Thiessen polygons centered on major platform mounds (Fish 1996). In this model, each platform-mound village controlled only the territory halfway to the next nearest platform mound; thus, scales were small and safely nonurban.[97] The estimated population for each platform-mound community was about 2,500 (or a bit more)—and may have solved the K-rule problem by compartmentalizing population into big, more or less freestanding neighborhoods (see Smith 2010b). In the aggregate, however, those dozen-plus communities represented several tens of thousands of people, spread over 200+ sq km of the Phoenix Basin, with irrigated farmlands separating one community core from another. Each platform-mound site may have constituted a separate political and economic unit, or Phoenix might have been a vast, segmented urban settlement, very much like Roland Fletcher's "low-density, agrarian-based urbanism"—and more accurately than Chaco's agriculturally problematic status as an "agrarian-based" city. Consider that Fletcher's cases, which confound the conventional Western big and dense model of urbanism, come mainly from tropical environments. Those cities extend up to 1,000 sq km or more, encompassing high proportions of productive agricultural lands (and consequently relatively low densities of population). Phoenix is famously not tropical; but the ancient investment in canal irrigation created agricultural potentials that approached tropical (agricultural) conditions, transforming the stinking desert to garden spot. As far as the crops knew, the valley of the sun was rather like a rainforest. One very conspicuous difference, of course, is the absence of a monumental center. Nothing in Phoenix provides an obvious counterpart to Tikal's pyramids and palaces, or to Angkor Wat's temple complex. We can assume that nothing comparably colossal will emerge from beneath Phoenix to surprise us; what we see is probably what we get. But recall: Cities without the state! Perhaps a monumental core is not necessary. Fletcher's "low-density, agrarian-based" model of Phoenix might transform Hohokam's core from a valley of villages to a large, unconventional, low-density proto-city.

History and Science

Urbanism in the Southwest: What's the score? One hit (Chaco), one strike-out (Yellow Jacket), one under review (Paquimé), and, perhaps, one whole new ballgame (Phoenix). Recognizing urbanism in the Southwest requires a very different reading of history than we get in textbooks. A history outside Pueblo Space.

It seems clear (to me at least) that "city" belongs in the Southwestern archaeology's lexicon. Urbanism could become a useful focus for future Southwestern research. More importantly, the Southwest may have something to contribute to larger studies of urbanism. That would be science.

Cycles: They Collapsed

This section is about the rise and fall of governments, the filling and emptying of regions, and the climax and collapse of societies in the past. Falls, disruptions, and collapse are of interest in the present—as evidenced by books like Turchin's (2003) *Historical Dynamics: Why States Rise and Fall*, Diamond's (2005) *Collapse*, Morris's (2010) *Why the West Rules—For Now*, or Acemoglu and Robinson's (2012) *Why Nations Fail*, and many more. Books like these are read by engaged citizens and policy-makers, and many involve archaeology—even, sometimes, the Southwest.

Chaco collapsed; in a word, Chaco failed. Failed to continue, except as a memory and heritage for Pueblo people. Go there now: Chaco is an empty place, managed by the National Park Service for its "wilderness characteristics." Whatever Chaco was, it's no longer there. It certainly looks like Chaco ended, Chaco collapsed.

That's not allowed in Pueblo Space! Early understandings saw a steady rise, and at no great angle. "No great cataclysms, no waves of destruction, either natural or human," according to Bandelier—who never visited the Four Corners. And then the Pecos Classification: Steady on from simple beginnings through intermediate stages to ultimately becoming Pueblos. No real falls (beyond a few speed-bump migrations), until the Spanish arrived. Not even then: Pueblos pride themselves on their perseverance through foreign colonization. And on our side, Pueblo Space avoids collapse: Eternal, unchanging, and so on and so on.

An inconvenient fact: The "Abandonment of the Four Corners"—the collapse formerly known as "The Mystery of the Anasazi." Vacant cliff dwellings and empty Great Houses contributed greatly to the marketing of the Southwest, especially after the rise of automobile tourism after the Second World War (see chapter 1). "Abandonment" and "Pueblo Mystique" perversely coexist; it all made good copy for travel magazines and, later, the web.

In archaeology, midcentury Culture History noted the Four Corners event (and others like it: the Hohokam collapse, the Mimbres collapse, etc.). The shift from Pueblo III to Pueblo IV evidently meant more than migrations; it was a historical event driven by invading marauders, epic droughts, whatever. The Pueblo rise became a series of rises and falls. "Collapse" and "abandonment" were key questions for Culture History and were further developed in New and early Processual Archaeology, tied almost always to environmental problem (droughts up north, floods down south).[98]

Today, we are uncomfortable with such terms. "Collapse" has been stricken from our lexicon or euphemized to extinction—in large part, I fear, in reaction to Jared Diamond's (2005) book of that name, discussed at some length later in this section. "Abandonment" has been abandoned,[99] rephrased as "depopulation" and other kinder, simpler terms. "Today, Southwestern archaeologists are more apt to call the end of occupation of a particular area a reorganization or a migration, rather than a 'collapse.'" (Mills 2002:97; see also Cameron 1995; Nelson 1999, 2000; Spielmann 1998). In resilience theory, collapse becomes "release"—its symbol Ω.[100] Ω—the calamity formerly known as "collapse." We proceed for a few pages without the C-word; and then it rises anew.

In the current terminology, Chaco declined, ceased to function, readjusted, reorganized, it Ω. But think with pride of what came before the fall! Things had to be good, better, and best before a bust went bad. Should we not tell those stories? Rises and falls are a staple in Mesoamerican pre-history. Mississippian chiefdoms famously "cycled" (e.g., Anderson 1994; see also Gavrilets et al. 2010). Why should the Southwest be different? In part, because Pueblo Space is changeless and eternal.

In the real world of "kings-and-battles" history beyond the Southwest, what goes up must/may/could come down. Things go up and down and up again and down again, a pattern explored in theories of cycles. Cycles can by mystical—Yeats's gyre?—but they can also be very practical: Business cycles, dear to Dismal Science, fear for investors.

Cycles of Conquest

There are many kinds of historical cycles, and they vary in lengths from lifetimes to centuries. These undulations ripple across disciplines from economics to history to sociology.[101] They are not, however, widely used in American Anthropological Archaeology.[102] Thomas Hall is a sociologist/anthropologist, who has written very useful things about the Southwest (Hall 1989). As a sociologist,[103] he likes cycles: Hall (2009) hits the cycle and lists a series:

> Kondratieff cycles (about 50 years)
> hegemonic cycles (about 100 years)
> "long waves" (about 200 years)
> Khaldun cycles (about 300 years)
> dark age cycles (about 600 years)

With such a conveniently progressive range of spans, one or another cycle should fit your data; the whole subject could easily devolve into some sort of fluid numerology. But most cycles come with explanations, and a well-theorized cycle tells us more than simply a wavelength of rise and fall. Cycles can have explanatory utility. Surf's up: Let's ride a few of those waves.

Which waves? "Kondratieff cycles" refer to economic ups and downs of Western industrial history after 1800.[104] "Hegemonic cycles" (from International Relations), too, are specific to modern history, as are "Long Waves" (a sort of Kondratieff tsunami). Of more useful application, "Khaldun cycles" (Turchin and Hall 2003; Hall and Turchin 2007) and "Dark Age cycles" (Chew 2001, 2007) have already been applied to ancient times.

Ibn Khaldun was a fourteenth-century Tunisian historian, so his notions certainly predated modernity.[105] Below, we will explore at some length an archaeological application of Khaldun to the ancient Southwest and describe it there. That leaves "Dark Age cycles," the ultimate pessimist's guide to the universe. Let us hope we never meet the Dark Age cycle. But we should look for 'em in the past.

The reader will be relieved to learn that I will not hunt through the Southwestern chronology looking for cyclic "fits"—as I did with "thresholds." Rather, I review cycles in recent American Anthropological Archaeology in the Southwest.

In the Southwest, cycles constitute a thin genre, themselves cyclic: A burst of enthusiasm in the 1980s, followed by a fallow period, and then an uptick in the 2010s. In what I consider a seminal book, Michael Berry (1984) showed, by cycles in histograms of tree-ring dates, that the Pecos Stages were valid. That's fine, but he went further in a prescient attempt at Big Data. Berry contrasted Colorado Plateau tree-rings to Hohokam 14C dates and noted that the two distributions were complementary: When there were many dates on the Plateau, there were few dates in the deserts, and vice versa. He concluded that populations shifted back and forth from desert to Plateau, presumably reflecting climatic shifts. A very neat piece of work, in my opinion (both at the time and in retrospect). Not everyone agreed: The book was savaged and, alas, faded from view.

The idea of cyclic boom-bust-boom-bust keyed to Pecos stages was independently advanced by Steadman Upham (1984) as "adaptive diversity"—societies switching between agricultural economies and less complex hunter-gatherer economies—and by Stuart and Gauthier (1981) as "power-efficiency" cycles marking each Pecos stage. Neither notion was wildly popular, and they too have not had the influence we might have hoped.[106]

Cycles cycled back into vogue! Berry revisited and largely vindicated his work in the North (Berry and Benson 2009), and more recently Bocinsky and colleagues (2016) plough the same fields: Construction tree-ring dates track well on the Pecos stages, with cycles of many dates followed by punctuations of far fewer dates (see also Arakawa 2012 and Kuckelman 2016). Boom and bust, indeed; although Bocinsky and colleagues rephrase the cycles as "exploration" followed by "exploitation" in each Pecos stage.

Before moving on to Tim Kohler's recent work with cycles in the Southwest, we must meet the cyclist he cites: Biologist Peter Turchin. (I have no idea if Turchin bikes.) Turchin is perhaps the most vocal recent champion of historical cycles ("secular cycles," aka Turchin cycles), most accessibly in three books: *Secular Cycles* (Turchin and Nefedov 2009); *War and Peace and War: The Life Cycles of Imperial Nations* (Turchin 2006); and *Historical Dynamics: Why States Rise and Fall* (Turchin 2003). (We meet Turchin again in chapter 6 with "Clio-dynamics," his stridently scientific approach to History.)

Turchin's *Secular Cycles* builds on Khaldun's medieval work.[107] A secular cycle begins with a "benign *integrative phase*" as population grows and elites prosper. Population growth benefits elites and nobles—up to a point. When population exceeds carrying capacity (Turchin's term, to be understood loosely), the polity enters a "troubled *disintegrative phase*." Elites accustomed to plenty must do with less, and they turn on each other over diminishing resources; that is, "*instability*." Political disorder drives population decrease and societal collapse. According to Turchin, "the typical period of a complete cycle…is around two or three centuries. I call these majestic oscillations in demographic, economic, and social structures of agrarian societies *secular cycles* (Turchin 2006:8, original emphasis). Note that Turchin's cycles are inherently political.

Cycling in the ancient Southeastern chiefdoms has also been understood as inherently political—"Cycling in the Complexity of Early Societies" (Anderson 1994). Turchin's cycles require political structure—elites, nobles, rulers. The Southeast had those: Chiefs and chiefdoms galore. So Turchin cycles make sense in the Southeast, and in fact have been usefully employed there (Gravilets, Anderson, and Turchin 2010).

Turchin Applied

Timothy Kohler and his colleagues (Kohler, Cole, and Cuipe 2009) applied Turchin's cycles in the Mesa Verde region, as part of the Village Ecodynamics Project (hereafter, VEP; the Great Sage Plains around Cortez, Colorado). They work with a version called the "Turchin-Korotayev model" (Turchin and Korotayev 2006) of cyclic population growth and violence.

Mesa Verde, of course, resides pleasantly in Pueblo Space (and, in the hearts and minds of the Park Service, probably always will), with all that entails and excludes. One of the most important exclusions, of course, is politics. Kohler and Co. factor in the political! Here is their précis of the VEP culture history for later periods:

> A major population influx in the mid- to late 1000s brought with it the earliest structures reminiscent of the great houses of Chaco Canyon and its surrounding area, some 170 kilometers south-southeast of our study area. A few archaeologists (e.g., Wilcox 1999) interpret Chaco's

fluorescence following an internal reorganization around 1030 as that of an expansionist, tributary state, though many others are more cautious.... The polity centered on Chaco Canyon went into decline in the mid-1100s, causing turmoil in our study area, though study area populations continued to grow. In the mid-1200s, many community centers in our area relocated to canyon head locations, and many of these are walled. Local populations began to decline by about 1260, and the area was completely depopulated by farmers sometime in the 1280s. (Kohler and others 2009:280)

Chaco acts as a political force to be reckoned with and an exterior factor, messing with Mesa Verde. Chaco-style politics was not native to the region; it was "exogenous." Kohler, Cole, and Cuipe reformulate Turchin's model, thus: "Population growth eventually causes an increase in instability, with a lag, whereas increased instability, with a lag, eventually leads to decreases in population size" (Kohler et al. 2009:277). Kohler's "instability" glosses Turchin's explicitly *political* triggers.

So: Population peaks should precede peaks in violence ("with a lag"). When were those respective peaks? The VEP data answer that question in admirable detail (Kohler et al. 2009:Figure 19.3). For population: A first, minor population peak followed by decline at about 850; a major peak with steady, relatively high growth began in the very late 900s or 1000 CE, accelerated markedly about 1080 CE, and peaked about 1225 CE, crashing thereafter with almost complete depopulation by 1300 CE. For violence: Increased violence followed the first population peak (850), as predicted by the model; but violence peaked in the mid- to late-1100s—before the second population peak.

Thus, "we find relative strong support for the Turchin-Korotayev model... during the first population cycle, when exogenous factors appear to have been weak.... The apparent failures of the model during the second population cycle may be due to the relative strengths of exogenous factors in our area" (Kohler et al. 2009:287–288).

And they specify the exogenous factor: Chaco. And an aggressive Chaco: "resistance (ultimately unsuccessful) to Chacoan expansion" (Kohler et al. 2009: 289). They continue:

The circa 1080s immigration (spanning the period from 1060 to 1100) represents the first successful Chacoan intrusions into the area.... The slight decrease in violence in the early 1100s, if real, represents as close to a "Pax Chacoensis" as our area ever experiences.... The collapse of the Chacoan system in the mid-1100s brought violence to unprecedented levels...as old (but apparently resented) power structures fell apart. (Kohler et al. 2009:289)

This was followed by relative peace in the early 1200s. Things finally fell completely apart in the late 1200s, with violence galore.

In my history (Lekson 2009a), Chaco directly affected Mesa Verde through the eleventh century. The center of government then shifted north to Aztec Ruins (Lekson 2015a), starting in the 1080s and fully by about 1110 CE. As indicated earlier in a discussion of Yellow Jacket, one marker for Aztec's region were bi-wall and tri-wall structures; and by that measure, Aztec's sphere of influence encompassed the area being studied by the VEP. How would Turchin's cycles work, with first Chaco and then Aztec active as "exogamous influences"?

Dancing to Khaldun's Tune

Here's how: Start with the Chaco of chapter 3—an altepetl-like polity with a half-dozen noble "Houses"—and add Aztec Ruins as Chaco's successor capital. Turchin's Khaldun/secular cycle assumes metaethnic political entities. Chaco was probably a metaethnic polity, encompassing several languages within its region (an "imagined community"? See chapter 2). Chaco itself rose in part as a geopolitical reaction to the explosive growth of the Hohokam Colonial period (Lekson 2009a). The boundary between Chaco and Hohokam certainly constituted a "major ethnic boundary"—another key element of Turchin's model, which defines the metaethnic polity. One Imagined Community to the north, another to the south? The widespread distribution of uniform Great Houses, roads, ceramic styles (Dogozshi; Neitzel and others 2002), and so forth that spread over the northern Southwest stood in sharp contrast to the powerful, homogenous Hohokam region of ball courts, palettes, and buffwares. Chaco's region (which included the entire Mesa Verde area) would have had a high degree of what Turchin calls *asabiyah* (after Ibn Khaldun; see note 107)—coherence in collective actions.

Kohler and his colleagues suggested an early role for Chaco in their area: Mesa Verde populations resisted Chacoan incursions in the early 1000s. Their evidence is indirect: They see no "structures in our area that look 'Chacoan'" at this time, but they suggest that elevated violence might reflect resistance to Chaco. Independently, I concluded that Chacoan buildings appeared north of the San Juan River, including the Mesa Verde region, as early as 1000 CE (Lekson 2015a:Appendix B). Our interpretations converge, perhaps.

Recall that the first ca. 900 CE peak of violence in the VEP followed peak population, as Turchin predicts; that is, the violence occurred during a time of population decline. Indeed, violence may have contributed to that decline. From a nadir at about 950 CE, population rose remarkably to a second peak at about 1250, three times the size of the first, tenth-century peak. Kohler and his colleagues suggest in-migration at ca. 1080 of large numbers of people, presumably bearing Chacoan credentials.

The in-migration evident in the VEP and the larger Mesa Verde region was not unique. All around the edges of Chaco's region, the eleventh century saw marked increases in populations and the appearance of Anasazi hallmarks: Corn agriculture, masonry pueblos, and black-on-white and corrugated pottery. To the west, Virgin Anasazi; to the east, the population jump of Late Developmental Rio Grande, and the conspicuous shift from pithouse to pueblo; to the south, Mimbres populations doubled (or tripled?), and switched from Hohokam-inspired pit houses to Anasazi-like pueblos and pottery (Lekson, ed. 2006); and to the north, Mesa Verde was repopulated, with Chaco's corona reaching perhaps as far as central Utah's Fremont (Lekson 2014).

Everywhere around Chaco, people who had formerly minded their own business suddenly chose to look like Chacoan commoners—that is, like Pueblos; and everywhere around Chaco, population skyrocketed. This used to be called the "Pueblo II Expansion"—to return to an antique use of the Pecos classification. The Pueblo II Expansion is no longer a popular concept, but the empirical pattern it described remains. (Those old guys were good.)

In Turchin's terms, this was the *"integrative phase"* in which population grew and elites prospered. Population growth benefited Chaco and its noble families—up to a point. All went well through the twelfth century; Chaco had sufficient power to build a new capital at Aztec Ruins. The "carrying capacity" (Turchin's term) of Chaco's immediate hinterlands took a big hit with a drought from 1130 to 1180, and Chaco entered Turchin's "troubled *disintegrative phase*." Chaco's noble families, accustomed to plenty, did with less; and turned on each other over diminishing resources—Turchin's "instability." We see early signs of inter-elite competition with the conversion of Pueblo Bonito from a solstitial/lunar cosmology to a solar/cardinal cosmology in the early twelfth century (Lekson 2009a:127, 238; 2015a)—probably a symptom of a larger power struggle among and between the noble Houses. The shift to Aztec may well have been spurred by competitions between princely "Houses."

It is conventionally stated that Chaco "collapsed" around 1130; but the Chaco polity actually continued at Aztec Ruins through the thirteenth century. Great House construction continued through the twelfth century at the new capital, Aztec Ruins, and in the VEP area and elsewhere in the Mesa Verde region. Total population continued to climb, peaking at about 1250.

The VEP area stood in much the same relation to Aztec as had the Chuska Valley to Chaco. Both Chuska and the VEP were breadbaskets, the prime agricultural lands within Chaco's and Aztec's regions, respectively.

The politically driven *disintegrative phase* came ultimately from Aztec Ruins, in a climate of violence inherited from the "Pueblo II expansion" of the late eleventh century and the 1130–1180 drought. Noble consumption overshot commoner production—how much the commoners either could or would produce.

Nobles turned on nobles and perhaps commoners turned on nobles; and the result was the remarkable violence of the twelfth century—Turchin's *disintegrative phase*. From Chaco rise to Aztec's end spanned almost three centuries; recall Turchin: "The typical period of a complete cycle…is around two or three centuries."

Then the nobles left (Lekson 1999a, 2015a)—went south—and peace returned (Kohler et al. 2009). Not so much "peace" as the absence of war, due to the absence of warriors and everyone else. Beginning in the mid-1200s, whole towns left the Mesa Verde area, voting with their feet for a system not subject to the political instability of Chacoan polities and Turchin's secular cycles. They reinvented themselves as Pueblos, constructing the Pueblo lifestyle of Pueblo IV and Pueblo V. Thus the archaeologists' goal—whence Pueblos?—was reached, but not by a linear progression; more accurately, by the cyclic rise and fall of polities. And far to the south, the cycle began again at Paquimé.

In my words, not Turchin's or Kohler's: In-migration, big bang, hegemony, collapse, out-migration, and balkanization. Rise and fall. That cycle fits both Chaco and Cahokia. Both involved influxes of population; a big bang where a (relatively) large city rises in regions hitherto city-free; one or two centuries of regional hegemony; collapse; out-migration ("Abandonment of the Four Corners" for Chaco; "the Vacant Quarter" for Cahokia); and balkanization (the rise of Pueblos and the rapid spread and cycling of small Mississippian "chiefdoms"). Each and every stage is much larger, more dramatic, more spectacular at Cahokia than at Chaco, but the parallels are there.

The End of Rise and Fall?

Southwestern archaeology is pretty good with rises, not so good with falls. We have richly textured accounts of how Chaco rose, replete with agency, contingency, ritual, and (of course) favorable rainfall. The fact that these several accounts are sometimes contradictory takes nothing away from their narrative grip. But there is surprisingly little on Chaco's fall.[108] The most notable exception was Joseph Tainter's (1988) remarkable *Collapse of Complex Societies*—an economic model featuring Chaco as a case study among other complex societies—which has more or less vanished from the current Chacoan literature.[109] Another victim of Pueblo Space, I think: We know Chaco was not complex, so Tainter's assumptions are (from Pueblo Space) flawed.

When it comes to falls, our *deus ex machinae* are limited to Mars and Jupiter: War and weather, the usual suspects. For the Four Corners, marauding Athabaskans were the first bad guys, but after the invention of dendrochronology (and more importantly dendroclimatology) blame shifted to precipitation or lack thereof. Dendroclimatology has become the tail wagging the dog of Southwestern pre-history.

This makes a certain amount of sense—the Southwest is, after all, a desert. But drought can be dealt with. Irrigate! Mimbres and Casas Grandes and Hohokam in the dry southern deserts, and Fremont on the edges of the Great Basin—lands of permanent, institutional drought—took water from rivers and ran it onto their fields. Not an easy task but (on the evidence) clearly doable. Then why didn't Chaco do it?—not at Chaco, of course, but in areas in Chaco's vast region with real rivers. There are hints of canals at Chaco Canyon, although their effectiveness for subsistence farming seems unlikely—there wasn't much water to tap (see chapter 3). There is stronger evidence of ancient canals at Aztec Ruins, where a river ran through it. But that's it: Other divertible rivers ran through the Four Corners (and especially the Chaco/Aztec region), yet none of those parched and starving people thought to redirect organized labor—the labor that built Great Houses, roads, and so forth—to the task of diverting the Piedra, Los Pinos, La Plata, Animas, Mancos, and McElmo creeks onto their farm fields.

Why not? Agency in the breach: They knew about irrigation (e.g., Friedman et al. 2003; Vivian et al. 2006), but decided not to. They chose, instead, to fail; or rather they chose to end Chacoan society by complete out-migration, a jailbreak which began long before the final droughts. It wasn't (only) rainfall. They voted with their feet and Chaco/Aztec collapsed.

Collapse Happens

The end of the cycle? Collapse: Back to the "C" word.

Collapse is a topic of central interest to archaeology, but which archaeology abhors when addressed by nonarchaeologists, such as Jared Diamond.[110] I was puzzled and somewhat embarrassed by the reactions of many archaeologists to Jared Diamond's *Guns, Germs and Steel* (1997) and *Collapse* (2005). Diamond reaches large and potentially influential readerships, and he uses archaeology to make points that inform or might even influence policy! Since the points he made were debatable but not evil, that seemed to me a good thing.[111]

Diamond likes (or liked) archaeology,[112] and he reaches far more readers than any American archaeologist, with the possible exception of Brian Fagan. He writes quality books, Pulitzer Prize books.[113]

What was archaeology's reaction to Diamond's books? In a word: Outrage. *Guns, Germs and Steel* became (and remains) a favorite target in graduate seminars across the country.[114] We flay it, dismember it! We beat on grad students' cubicles, and then throw in the bloody remains.

Collapse (subtitled *How Societies Choose to Fail or Succeed*) came in for higher-level attention: Senior scholars dissected and demolished it. Joe Tainter, who had written an influential earlier study of the subject (*The Collapse of Complex Societies*, 1988), wrote scathing reviews in several venues (Tainter 2005,

2006, 2008). Patricia McAnany and Norman Yoffee assembled a posse and a volume, *Questioning Collapse*, which grew out of their session at the Society for American Archaeology annual meeting addressing "the issues swirling around the popular writings of Jared Diamond" (McAnany and Yoffee 2010:2).[115]

Tainter has one view, Yoffee another, Diamond yet another on what collapse is and how best to explain it. We should not expect one cause, or even a single direction in which to look for multiple causes, because collapse encompasses demography, polity, economy, geography—and more. If population plummets, that's collapse. If a regime topples, that's collapse. If the economy tanks, that's collapse. If a region empties, that's collapse. But it's quite possible to imagine these four situations independently, or in combination, or in sequence. And all might cascade from entirely separate proximate causes. And, as K. R. Dark reminds us, "It must be remembered that 'catastrophic collapse' of this sort [in a rise and fall cycle] may not seem 'catastrophic' (or even collapse), in the conventional use of these terms, to those involved or other contemporary observers" (Dark 1998:123).

Joe Tainter, in one of his reviews, used a phrase I like a lot: "Collapse happens." I'm not sure Tainter used it with approval, but it's true: Collapse happens. Collapse is cyclic, the downside of cycles. In our drudgy, un-Whiggish world, "up" almost always entails "down." (Think: Market correction.) While overall trends in social history are undeniably upward (by most measures), the shorter-term human polities average only two or three centuries. Boom brings bust.

Archaeology, with its backward gaze, sees societies and civilizations wax and wane. If they wane with a bang and not a whimper, call it collapse. Or depopulation or release or Ω. However we euphemize the fall of Chaco-Aztec and the dramatic depopulation of the Four Corners, the facts seem clear. Chaco was a polity, a state; and that state vanished from the Pueblo Southwest. Its region supported several tens of thousands of people in the early 1200s, and a century later that region was essentially empty. That event or series of events was accompanied by political disorder, warfare, and economic disaster punctuated (but not caused) by a final Great Drought. Cities fell, governments crumbled, and traditions and cosmologies swerved. All that's missing, really, are rains of fire, plagues of frogs, and convulsions of the earth. It's hard to imagine a more complete collapse.[116]

Unless it's the decline of Classic period Hohokam. In the thirteenth century, the Phoenix Basin (the lower Salt River and its confluence with the Gila River) was teeming with people, several tens of thousands. They did wonderful things—developments economic, political, and artistic—that, in my opinion, overshadowed Chaco; all supported by a truly remarkable infrastructure of irrigation canals. By 1450, only a few ragged settlements remained. Of course, that story is contested (all interesting narratives are contested), but David Abbott's

2003 book, *Centuries of Decline during the Hohokam Classic Period*, tells a pretty grim tale. It's hard to imagine a more complete collapse.

Unless it's the fall of Paquimé and Casas Grandes. The city rose around 1300. There is no indication that it survived long after 1450. What became of the extraordinary, cosmopolitan people who built and ruled Casas Grandes? That society was, in many ways, the most remarkable ever seen in the Pueblo Southwest—rivaled only by Hohokam. Paquimé and the Casas Grandes polity marked a clear apex in Southwestern pre-history. But after only 150 years, that society collapsed. Charles Di Peso (1974), who excavated the site, thought the place was sacked.[117] Maybe he was wrong, but when the Spanish arrived, about a century after Paquimé's fall, all that was left were ruins and a few local legends. It's hard to imagine a more dramatic and significant collapse.

Unless it's the end of Mimbres…but enough, enough, enough. My point is clear, I hope: The Southwest has much to offer for the study of cycles and, consequently, of collapse. As Jared Diamond recognized, in those books of his. With the passage of time and the cooling of passions, perhaps collapse may return as something to be studied; perhaps it already has (Kohler and Bocinsky 2017).

History and Science

Cycles are inherently historical, and at the same time they are sciency. American Anthropological Archaeology in the Southwest muffles rises and falls in Pueblo Space, but actually they were rather loud and sometimes dramatic. As in: crash, boom. Moreover, the historic cycles were multiple, parallel, and interconnected (Lekson 2009a, 2015a): Hohokam rose; Hohokam fell while Chaco rose; and then Chaco fell as Paquimé rose; and so on and so on.

Looks like cycles to me. But which waves, what modulations, what amplifications? Thanks in large part to our remarkable chronological controls, the history of the ancient Southwest lends itself to rigorous, generalizing studies of cycles—and I mentioned a few, above. And in return, our scientific, generalizing understanding of cycles could fill out our history by giving us trajectories to connect events. Historical blanks and lacuna will be filled as we better understand the trajectories of cycles. History leads us to science, and science back to history, and from better history we can build better scientific generalizations. Full circle: It's a cycle.

The Science of Secondary City-States

"You tried your best and you failed miserably. The lesson is: Never try" (attributed to Homer). "Never try": Good advice for me, better advice for Homer's Hector. He got on the wrong side of Zeus and caught it in the neck.[118] But, as another poet said: What would you be if you didn't even try…. You have to try. I insisted that Chaco was a secondary state, and my fate? A thousand cuts in professor's lectures, graduate seminars, term papers, and final exams (correct answer: false). Or worse: Stony silence. But then there's that notable archaeologist we met many pages back who, when asked, "What about secondary states?" replied, "Well, maybe." A spot of blue sky from the bottom of my deep hole.

I dug my hole even deeper, suggesting that Chaco was structured along the lines of an altepetl. But I do not insist on that identity. If altepetl seems too precise, then perhaps a more general category, like city-state. My desk dictionary (a 1998 Merriam-Webster) defines city-state as "an autonomous state consisting of a city and surrounding territory."[119] If Chaco was a city—which it was—and if Chaco had a surrounding territory—which it did—then it is reasonable to call Chaco a city-state.

So what? Does this get us anywhere? It might. If we move Chaco out of Pueblo Space and into new territory, we can do very different science; as I hope the examples in this chapter have demonstrated. Escaped from Pueblo Space, Chaco could enter the comparative lists and shed its awkward status as an exceptional phenomenon, a uniquity. All the time and treasure we've spent on that small New Mexico canyon can be justified by Chaco contributions to bigger questions and larger issues.

City-states have been the subject of long and sustained cross-cultural study.[120] Although the idea of city-state has been around for a long time, not everyone is a fan. One group of archaeological urbanists, led by Joyce Marcus (Marcus and Feinman 1998), "would like to see [city-state] phased out."[121] But Bruce Trigger (2003), trying to understand early civilizations, thinks city-states are essential. He sees two basic types of states: City-states and territorial states.[122] And Norman Yoffee (1997)—our urbane arbiter of all things urban—accepts "city-states," broadly (and simply) defined as a small state with a single city/capital (my words, not his). City-states (says Yoffee) resist and in fact need no precise, prescriptive definition.[123] Michael Smith (2008a) has no qualms in calling basic Nahua political units "city-states." I generally defer to Trigger and Yoffee and Smith in such matters: "City-state" stands.

City-states occur in antiquity on every continent save Antarctica, Australia, and—we are told—America north of Mexico. But the natives of North America, as we have seen in chapters 1 and 2, have been viewed through biased lenses. If we set those old foggy goggles on the shelf, are there any city-state candidates north of Mexico? Chaco, for one. Cahokia, for another. I'll brook no quibbling about Cahokia: It was indeed a city and a state, and while its influence spanned half a continent, its polity proper was local: The American Bottoms and their surroundings. Like the classical city-states, most of its population lived in the urban area. That's not the case for Chaco, where the center had less than a tenth—probably less than a twentieth—of the total population in Chaco's polity. That's not a disqualification; it's an interesting difference to which we will return.

Some might object that city-states do not occur in isolation, they need polities to peer with, other city-states bubbling and frothing in the cauldron ("peer polities": Renfrew and Cherry 1986). If Chaco and Cahokia were city-states, they were city-states out on the edges, on the rim of the boiling pot. Chaco was by any measure "out there" and—if we ignore the intriguing problem of Hohokam—it stood alone in its region. As perhaps was Cahokia, although the ancient history of the Mississippi valley saw rises and falls before Cahokia: Poverty Point ca. 1200 BCE and Hopewell ca. 500 CE. I submit that Chaco and Cahokia offer two examples of relatively (and usefully) isolated city-states, connected to peers but at clinically safe distances. West Mexicans probably visited Chaco, Huastecans probably visited Cahokia, and the lords of Chaco and Cahokia doubtless paid return visits. But the nobility of both Chaco and Cahokia were almost certainly locals, putting on airs.

Is there a trajectory, or trajectories for the rise and fall of city-states?[124] Cycles of city-states? Chaco and Cahokia could provide remarkably detailed, expensively developed data to address that question. As noted before, their two careers ran in close parallel. But their paths also diverged: Chaco was a small administrative center for a widely dispersed population, Cahokia was a black hole sucking in population from all around its region. Ah, but perhaps that reflects differences in environment and productivity, patchy agricultural lands, and there we go, off and running! Compare and contrast! And something globally useful might emerge out of our investments in the archaeologies of America north of Mexico. This is not to denigrate the current scientific contributions of Southwestern archaeology (noted here and in chapter 6)—Not at all! Great stuff!—but to insist on a corrective of scale: Escaping Pueblo Space (these were NOT "intermediate" societies) changes both the questions we'll ask and the answers we'll get.

I do not pretend that my science essays in this chapter are correct, or that they solve the problems they pose. You may quibble, question, or quash my science; but I do insist that these directions are worth pursuing, and they can only be pursued if we escape Pueblo Space and understand that Chaco was not an "intermediate" society, it was not not-a-state, it was not a rituality. Chaco was a small polity—a secondary city-state—like (and unlike) hundreds of other small polities in the southern latitudes of eleventh-century North America. How to make a polity in the central Mesa Verde region?[125] Leave Pueblo Space and Oh, the places we'll go!

CHAPTER 5

An Appraisal of the Ancient Southwest

I've been thrown out of better books than this.

—attributed to Texas Guinan

At the turn of the Millennium, Patty Jo Watson—one of our wisest—posed this question: "Does Americanist archaeology have a future in the twenty-first century?" Her answer was not altogether reassuring:

> Yes, of course it does, but it will be so different from its traditional configuration that practitioners whose careers spanned a major portion of the twentieth century might have difficulty recognizing it as their own discipline. (Watson 2003:141)

Nearly two decades into the twenty-first century, Watson's prophecy has not quite come to pass in the Southwest. Processual-Plus plods on, and that's mostly a good thing; but it's showing signs of wear, fraying at the edges.

As I write this, environmental conservation and regulation are under attack at the national level. It's quite possible that historic preservation laws could be reversed or weakened. If CRM diminished or disappeared, Southwestern archaeology would take a huge hit: Most of what we know about Hohokam, for example, came from CRM. But archaeology would survive, because ruins are integral to tourism and the region's economy (a tale told in chapter 1). There will still be demand; but what will we supply?

We can expect astonishing new technical developments. New and wonderful gadgets: New ways to date, new ways to source, new ways to link, and so forth. The whole field could become DNA-driven, like Biology; or modeling and simulation might replace actual fieldwork, as in some environmental and climatological sciences. But so far, gadget science remains ancillary to what archaeology does. We use gadgets much as Art History or Sotheby's uses gadgets: As tools. The gee-whiz science stuff is (extremely) helpful, but it is not archaeology's core, which is history—even if American Anthropological Archaeology doesn't quite realize it. Absent a time-traveling DeLorean, archaeology should survive as storytelling, history telling. Because the heart of archaeology—history, I insist—is not technical, it is narrative.

We could, perhaps, destroy ourselves with theory. The Southwest seems largely impervious to the flightier fancies of archaeological theory, but the Ontological Turn might do us in. I save those cheerless ruminations for chapter 6. Southwestern archaeology, firm in the bosom of science, should survive theory's repeated attacks on reason. Even a historicized Southwestern archaeology—as I propose in chapter 6—should have enough residual scientism to ward off the worst of theory, like garlic repels a vampire.

But Professor Watson was surely right (as always): Southwestern archaeology has changed and will continue to change. Hopefully not through the loss of CRM, or the rise of the machines, or the ascendance of addled theory, but from external political forces. Most notably: Indians.

Indians have been conspicuous by their absence in most of this book, but in this chapter, Indians are everywhere.[1] This segregation is not out of any disrespect for Indian tribes; rather, the organization of this book reflects my firm belief that archaeology is not, inherently, a Native American enterprise. If Europe had not invaded, I doubt that anything like American Anthropological Archaeology would be going on today in North America. That's not a disrespectful judgment; I think that Native America would develop scholarly ways to deal with its past that differ significantly from European Enlightenment-based "-ologies," reflecting instead Native conventions and choices and ways of knowing. But Europe did invade North America; and today tribes engage with archaeology because (1) archaeology has no shame, and (2) various laws make archaeology unavoidable.

Indians have no reason to be fond of archaeology and anthropology. Many influential Indians particularly dislike archaeology. As tribes gain more and more political power, things might get awkward for archaeology, especially in the Southwest—for various reasons I will discuss below.

At century's end, American Anthropological Archaeology took a one-two punch: NAGPRA and Postmodernity.[2] Just when we might have shaken off Pueblo Space and reached new understandings of Chaco, those blows boxed us right back into that corner. NAGPRA was a straight up, honest jab to the jaw. We should have seen it coming, but when it landed: Lights out. Ammonia salts, back on our feet, stagger on. Postmodernity was a self-inflicted sucker punch, or punches: A rain of tiny taps to the brainpan that did cumulative damage. NAGPRA is a more or less straightforward law, and has become business as usual; but the after-effects of Postmodernity are more nebulous and sinister—like Chronic Traumatic Encephalopathy in contact sports. I'm not making light of head injuries. It really is that bad, I think, for Southwestern archaeology: Postmodernity's epistemic relativism subverts the authority and, ultimately, even the necessity of our field. NAGPRA we can live with: Paying debts we surely owe. Last century's Postmodernity and its current Post-postmodern theoretical entanglements could kill us, a threat serious enough to merit angst-laden soliloquies in chapter 6. So: Indians (and other archaeological current events) in this chapter; Theory (and other archaeological futures) in the next chapter.

I begin this chapter by differentiating heritage, history, and science. I then ask and answer a series of questions: Whose heritage? Whose history? Whose science? And—perhaps most importantly: Who is our audience? For me, the question of audience is a question of purpose: Why do archaeology?

But, before we begin, a preemptive defense. (Normally I'd do this sort of thing in footnotes, but it's too important.) I realize that my terms and definitions and conclusions may sound like I slept through the last thirty years, ignorant of Indians, NAGPRA, decolonization, and Indigenous concerns. That's not the case. I was, if not at the heart of those things, deep in their currents, woke in their wake. My *bona fides* were summarized in an article commissioned for *Museum Anthropology* on the occasion of NAGPRA turning twenty (Lekson 2010b)—a journal few archaeologists read, of course.[3]

Theory mavens may think I'm ignorant and oblivious of their developments, too. No: I read a lot of theory.[4] I read theory in Anthropology/Archaeology and Museology and History and certain Sciences. I used to read a fair amount of Architecture and Design theory; today, not so much. Together, that covers a lot of theoretical ground. I'm just not impressed by the theory I get from the Theoretical Archaeology Group and its fellow travelers. They'll get more attention in chapter 6, but I'm sure they will feel neglected here in chapter 5. Patience: Your turn is next.

So, no: I'm not ignorant, I'm opinionated. I hope, reasonably well-informed opinions.

Heritage, History, Science…and Anthropology

I use these terms in fairly specific ways which, I believe, are true to the dictionary; but I admit they are particular to my argument. To preview, simply:

- *Heritage* is the uses to which we put the past, in the present. Heritage is often, perhaps always, political.
- *History* is the (Western) intellectual discipline by which we know, however imperfectly, what actually happened in the past—insofar as we can know it. History, rightly done, tries not to be political; and often fails, but the goal remains. *Pre-history*, as I use it here, is narrative History of ancient nonliterate times; History without documents.
- *Science* is the (Western) intellectual discipline by which we learn, with some certainty, about how things work—the world, the universe, and everything on and in them.

- *Anthropology* is…what, exactly? American Anthropology today is fractured and disparate. And, I will argue, not a good home for the study of the prehistory of North America.

As with "Pueblo Mystique" and "Pueblo Space" (way back in chapter 1), a caveat so important I shout it in caps: PLEASE UNDERSTAND THAT I AM NOT SAYING HISTORY IS RIGHT (OR BETTER) AND HERITAGE IS WRONG (OR WORSE); THEY ARE TWO FUNDAMENTALLY DIFFERENT THINGS WITH DIFFERENT PURPOSES AND DIFFERENT AUDIENCES.

Heritage (and the Spoils of History)

Heritage? History? What's the difference? History is what happened in the past. Heritage is how the past is used in the present—for cultural, social, political, or other purposes. In this, I follow David Lowenthal (1985, 1999, 2015); and for my argument, that distinction is crucial.[5] My book, my rules.

Let's look at heritage first. The title of this section nods to David Lowenthal's (1998) other, less-read book, *The Heritage Crusade and the Spoils of History*, his account of the modern rise of "heritage" and its triumphs over history in Europe and America.[6] Lowenthal provides a useful—I would say critical—context for understanding historic preservation and Indian heritage laws in the United States. Ideas about Indian heritage—and, importantly, laws and regulations—came from earnest efforts of Indians and their allies, to be sure; but they are framed in the context of Euro-American ideas about heritage. (See also Thurley 2013.)

Heritage explains why things are the way they are. Or, justified by appeal to the past, how we would like things to be in the future. Heritage is how a group or society identifies itself by reference to a real or managed or fictive past.[7] All groups and societies and nation-states do this—an assertion, but a safe one for Anthropological readers.

My distinction of history and heritage (again, following Lowenthal) should not be construed to mean heritage is lesser than history. Heritage is often far more powerful than history; heritage puts history to work.

With the passage of time and a parade of agendas, heritage has displaced history in many arenas of archaeological interest. For us (and for U.S.), what once were members of the old National Register of Historic Places have been elevated to the newer, more progressive World Heritage List. Note the shift from "Historic" to "Heritage." Take Chaco, for example.[8] Heritage has different content for different user groups: Chaco's heritage is one thing for Pueblo people, another for New Agers, and yet another for the World Heritage list.

In the small world of the Southwest, we have seen in chapter 1 how early twentieth-century White Santa Feans (and others, in Taos and Chicago) exploited their region's Spanish heritage and, when that failed to sell, frothed up a

Native American heritage to create the Pueblo Mystique and the Pueblo Style, which sold very well indeed. At century's end, heritage was reappropriated by the non-Whites in those asymmetries. Hispanics took back their Fiesta, and Indians took back their narratives. (Fiesta and what it entails has only a tenuous relevance to pre-history, so I'll table Hispano/Chicano/Latino issues for now; complications arise when decolonizing colonists.)

Indian heritage, obviously, directly impacts pre-history (and, recursively, archaeology impacts Indian heritage). NAGPRA became law in 1990, a harbinger of rising decolonizing times and tides. Among anthropological taste-makers, there was (and is) much enthusiasm for shifting authority from hegemonic institutions to the subaltern. Legal and anthropological opinion swung away from hidebound conventional archaeology and toward Native control of the past.[9] In the Southwest, this is very evident in public interpretations by National Parks, popular press, PBS, and so forth. Gone were professorial talking heads, everywhere were Indian voices. (Not a bad thing, but a sign of the times.) In American Anthropological Archaeology, those interests emerged as Indigenous Archaeology—discussed briefly below and more fully later in the chapter.

Late twentieth- and early twenty-first-century collaborations between archaeology and Indians often produced parallel narratives—multivocalities—with conventional archaeology's take accompanied by Native interpretations or vice versa, depending on your preference—and sometimes other interested parties. A common, effective tactic, but often dissonant. I've participated in museum exhibits in which rock art (for example) was interpreted by Indians, archaeologists, river guides, artists, New Agers, and so forth; not chorus or concert, but cacophony. Rock art was everyone's heritage. Fine, perhaps, for a book or video or webpage, but in a point-of-contact public interpretation, the two main messages—archaeological and Native—got lost in the ruckus. (We return to this riddle below.)

Voice and authority in the regulatory realm is shifting to tribes, through various laws and regulations (correctly) requiring consultation; and culminating—in a way—with the creation of Tribal Historic Preservation Officers (the key role in the elaborate federal CRM regulatory apparatus). The tribes' power over heritage and history has yet to be fully realized or understood by archaeology. It could be considerable: A past Tribal Historic Preservation Officer of the Navajo Nation—with thousands of Anasazi sites, large and small—declared that the term "Ancestral Pueblo" was forbidden for archaeological permittees working on Navajo lands, and that all ancient material remains on the Navajo tribal lands were without exception to be considered ancestral to Navajo. That's an impressive use of heritage. I do not know if the policy remains in place; my point is that tribes now have that level of authority over heritage—and history.

History

History, as I've use it in this book, has two meanings: Imprecisely, what actually happened in the past; more precisely (and usually with a capital "H"), the Western intellectual discipline for knowing that past.[10] Here, I'm thinking about the latter, capital-"H" History. A dictionary definition: "A chronological record of significant events often with an explanation of their causes" with these additions: Empirical, critical, rational—all in their dictionary definitions. History is in the details: The unique situations that create one damn thing after another. So History, like most humanities, complicates things for a good end: Knowing the past in ways understandable to us, in the present. I know that's a pretty low bar. My too-simple use of "history"—conventional Western narrative History—would send an academic Historian into fits. But there it is—as Emperor Joseph might have said. Again, my book, my rules.

We are told that there are many ways to know the past. I disagree. There are many ways to *understand* the past—that's heritage; but there are demonstrably better ways to *know* the past—that's History. History is (supposed to be) rational, empirical, evidence-based, systematic, self-critical, correctable, and eschews the supernatural. Its (immediate) goal is to particularize and complicate: To lay out all the messy details of what happened. Its (ultimate) goal is to make the past known to a specific audience which expects rational, empirical, etc.—and to make the past *understandable* to that audience. Those attributes are not necessarily true of the alternatives to History.

Academic History suffers a bit from lingering, third- or fourth-generation Post-postmodernism (discussed in chapter 6). But History survived: "Most historians have simply moved on, incorporating insights from postmodern positions but not feeling obliged to take a stand on its epistemological claims" (Hunt 2014:39). A famous incident in Euro-American historiography provided an epiphany so far absent, for Archaeology. The crisis came in a court case about Holocaust denial and was described by Jeremy Popkin in his excellent history of History:

> The year 2000 was marked particularly by an unusual public courtroom case [the David Irving case] in which the issue of whether the methods of professional historical scholarship are in fact adequate to establish the truth about the past became a central issue…. [The deniers] sometimes seized on the assertions about the impossibility of achieving absolute truth in history put forward by postmodernist historical theorists such as Hayden White…. The 2000 trial reaffirmed most historians' conviction that the search for historical truth was too important to be abandoned… [and] reassured historians that postmodern critiques had not in fact

undermined their discipline's ability to establish certain truths about the past. (Popkin 2015:166–170)

Despite the doubt and despair of much current theory, History indeed can "know" the past with varying degrees of certainty. The judges took that decision out of the hands and minds of academics and philosophers, and settled it. In a very real and legally binding sense, as the would-be father-in-law told Sir Lancelot.

Science

If my notions of heritage and history are overly simple, my ideas about science are an insult to Newton, Darwin, and Einstein. (Sorry, boys.) The bar is very low (and does not require a capital "S"): Science is rational, empirical, evidence-based, systematic, self-critical, correctable, and eschews the supernatural. Much like my definition of History. But, unlike History, science's goal is to generalize and simplify: Discovering and analyzing order or patterns or definable disorder in this gloriously, terrifyingly messy world, and rendering them understandable. Science makes empirically grounded arguments of wider interest and relevance. It would be nice, but perhaps not entirely necessary, if those generalizing statements could be evaluated—if only as "more likely" or "less likely" than competing generalizing statements but even better as "true" or "false."

If we can find patterns or processes or sequences or shapes in the complicated particulars of the history of the ancient Southwest (as in chapter 4), that should help us understand similar (or different) situations in the histories of other places and times; and to me, that sounds like science.

…and Anthropology?

My ideas about heritage, history, and science are simple; my notion of Anthropology is…complicated. Born in Euro-American *fin-de-siècle* enthusiasms, young Anthropology made an astonishing claim to everything human, to be understood both scientifically and humanistically, everywhere, at every time. Taken literally, Anthropology would subsume dozens of university departments—history, law, art history, languages, and so forth. That's more than silly, it's impossible. So the anthropological sorting hat has, like Hogwarts, only four Houses: cultural, biological, linguistic, and archaeological.

Early on, they pulled together; today, they pull apart. Anthropological factions dabble in heritage, history, medicine, and science, while others produce poetry, fiction, film, and interpretive dance. Spread that range of methods over Anthropology's enormous field of study—everything human, everywhere—and disunity results. Perhaps Anthropology is whatever Anthropologists do, but that's not a definition of a discipline. Rather, the opposite: Indiscipline.

I no longer understand what American Anthropology is or does or should do. Is it detached, objective scholarship? Is it advocacy and activism? That fundamental split in today's Anthropology spills over to archaeology; many archaeologists would like to be activists and advocates.[11] What is Anthropology? I don't know.

But I care: As I argued at length in chapter 1, I am convinced that American Anthropology is not now, and never was, a good home for the prehistory of North America. (See also Gumerman and Phillips 1978; Smith 2010a, 2011a; Smith et al. 2012; chapters in Engelhardt and Rieger 2017 offer palliatives: Band-Aids for a gaping wound?) I am NOT saying that Anthropology is a poor fit for the archaeology of ancient hominids, or Mesopotamia, or Mount Vernon—although the first might be happier in Evolutionary Biology, the second in Classics, and the third in History. (Anthropology does not even seem *necessary* for those three examples.) But as presented in chapter 1, American Anthropology has been a disaster for the study of the pre-history of North America and, even more, the pre-history of the Southwest.

So it comes as a bit of a surprise that, in today's Southwest, archaeology is about the last man standing from Anthropology's original million-dollar quartet: Cultural, biological, linguistics, and archaeology. The Southwest was once a hotbed, even a hothouse, for all four. Now, no.

Cultural anthropology or ethnology has all but vanished from the Southwest. In 1969, Vine Deloria blasted cultural anthropology's intrusions into Native communities in *Custer Died for Your Sins: An Indian Manifesto*. Ethnologists noticed.[12] Severin Fowles and Barbara Mills observe: "After 1969, the volume of new ethnographic publications on the native Southwest peoples declined precipitously."[13] Today, almost any new ethnography—and there isn't much—serves legal or regulatory needs. It's fair to say that without the requirements of CRM and to a much lesser extent applied anthropology in the service of tribes, there would be almost no conventional cultural anthropology of the Native Southwest.

Biological anthropology—in particular its prehistoric arm, bioarchaeology—has not vanished entirely thanks to CRM (and some curious decisions by several museums), but it is greatly diminished.[14] While applied biological anthropology addresses modern health and wellness issues, bioarchaeology cannot be considered a growth industry in the Southwest.

Linguistics survives mainly in efforts to preserve Native languages; that is, applied anthropology. Historical linguistics—of potential value to prehistory—has very few active practitioners (e.g., Hill 2007). Some archaeologists have sought out training in historical linguistics to fill the void (e.g., Ortman 2012). But many tribes do not want their languages studied by outsiders.

For reasons both pragmatic and programmatic, I would move Southwestern pre-history out from under anthropology's aegis. For reasons both pragmatic and programmatic, that won't happen. Institutional inertia and intellectual traditions will maintain status quo, and American archaeologists will be trained in academic departments of Anthropology, and will identify themselves as such. That's not a good place for a practical Southwestern pre-historian to be; maybe we can think our way out of it (chapter 6).

Who Fibs, Who Lies, Who Tells the Story?

A Hamiltonian joke: No one is fibbing or lying, but the root question—who tells the story?—remains. Archaeology tells one (or several) versions of history. In-dians tell (insofar as they wish us to hear) other versions.[15] Multivocality seems a reasonable compromise, but—as hinted above—whose voices in the chorus? Despite NAGPRA's naïve but draconian notions of cultural affiliation, it's com-plicated.

Chaco is a case in point: The canyon itself and most of its interior region lie on Navajo lands. Indeed, many Navajo families lived in the canyon until the Park Service ran them out in the 1960s. As noted in the Appendix, Navajo traditional histories recount events at Chaco in remarkable detail. Pueblo her-itage—of course!—also claims Chaco. (More accurately plural: Pueblos' heri-tages also claim Chaco.) With NAGPRA, Chaco became the center of a difficult custody fight, still unresolved. It once had been the Navajo position that Chaco was indeed Pueblo, but also Navajo. Several of the Pueblos hold that Chaco was entirely Pueblo and that Navajo should have little say in its ancient history.[16] The argument reflects not only tradition and heritage, but also modern political and economic conundrums, pitting Pueblo against Navajo, Navajo against Pueblo.

For a cosmopolitan place like Chaco, who tells the story? In a newly pro-duced (2015) video at the Aztec Ruins visitor center, a young Native American woman[17] complains about archaeology's unwanted "revisionist history." Indians know their history, she protests; they have no need for archaeology. Well, then… who does? Archaeology still has stories to tell, but to whom? Who is archaeol-ogy's audience?

Whose Heritage?

Soldier on with Chaco. Many tribes claim Chaco as their heritage. So, too, do many Mexican-Americans, as Aztlán. New Agers, wilderness buffs,[18] and ama-teur astronomers all claim pieces of Chaco. And of course archaeologists.

And more: Chambers of Commerce in nearby cities cherish Chaco, and build roads to increase traffic through their business districts and into the Canyon. Chaco is a strong State interest, for New Mexico—under Edgar Lee Hewett, the University of New Mexico actually owned much of the canyon.[19] In 1907 Chaco became a National Monument, upgraded in 1980 to a National Park.

In 1987 Chaco was elevated to a UNESCO World Heritage site. Chaco's heritage became global—everyone's heritage. That's a lot of heritage-holders.[20]

Among Native or would-be Native groups, it appears that in public interpretations, Pueblo heritage comes first, closely followed by Navajo heritage, with Chicano Aztlán heritage a distant third. Aztec dancers have performed at Great House sites outside Chaco; to my knowledge, not yet in the Canyon.

New Agers get special consideration but must defer to Indian concerns.[21] On particular astroreligious days, aging New Agers or young "Spiritual but Not Religious" swarm to Chaco by the thousands. (In Pueblo Space are many mansions, and some reek of patchouli.)

For the nation and the world, these matters of local heritage are interesting but not an overriding issue. Its ruins—not its history or heritage—made Chaco a National Park and a World Heritage Site. The aesthetics of Chaco's architecture gained our attention long before its history or heritage came into the focus. Part of the "romantic view" that annoyed early archaeologists was just that: The view, the pleasure of ruins.[22] Chaco is a draw for architectural and art enthusiasts—its buildings regularly feature in "Great Architecture of the World" coffee-table books.

The National Park Service must balance all these competing and sometimes conflicting heritage claims, while preserving the ruins and landscape "for the continued benefit and enjoyment of all Americans" and, now, the world. It's not easy. For example, the NPS spends lots of money saving the ruins from further ruination, keeping them upright. But stabilization of Chaco's ruins runs counter to many Indians' notions of heritage. I know Indians who feel that the buildings should be allowed to crumble and complete their journey. So, yes: It's complicated.

In this tangle of heritage claims, what is archaeology's actual role? Archaeology, if it's doing its job, should acknowledge and respect heritage—and recognize it as the political, social, religious, etc. use of the past in the present. Our French friends (chapter 6) tell us that archaeology, like everything, is political. We already knew that: Another bias to identify and control as best we can, as we go about the business of pre-history. Because archaeology is History and maybe science; if it becomes heritage, then it is no longer archaeology.

Many American archaeologists support the heritage claims of descendent communities, affiliated tribes (sometimes stridently, discussed below with Indigenous Archaeology). But nothing is lost and perhaps something gained by considering the question more broadly: As noted above, heritage claims on Chaco are far more complicated and ramified than the too-simple requirements of NAGPRA. As cosmopolitan archaeologists—"cosmopolitan" in its original, uncorrupted sense—we owe consideration to Chaco's many other constituencies: Regional, national, and global—past, present, and future. This is not to challenge NAGPRA or the heritage claims of Southwestern peoples; simply to point out that archaeology's audiences are broader than that.

In these postcolonial times, we might forget what might be considered our "primary" constituency: The ancient peoples whose histories we study. Surely tribes take precedence? Under the law, yes; in our scholarship, perhaps not. In my NAGPRA role, I agreed that Chaco and its region are affiliated with all the Pueblos, a shared group identity. (That did not please the Navajo Nation.) Human remains went home to the Pueblos making the claims. And that was the right thing to do. In my archaeology role, I would argue that Chaco was affiliated with regional and continental cultures; its noble families shared a group identity with Mesoamerica and perhaps emphatically NOT with the commoners—who later became Pueblos. Chaco is part of Pueblo history and heritage, to be sure (and Navajo history and heritage—an admission too late to assuage the Nation, I fear). But it is not unreasonable to wonder if Chaco's noble families were also involved in the history and heritage of the Postclassic South. I would never let such conclusions interfere with NAGPRA's repatriation; that's an ethical responsibility. But I insist that much of what made Chaco, Chaco might not be affiliated with Pueblos or Navajos. "Might not be": That's a scholarly imperative. We cannot foreclose reasonable alternatives.

The pre-histories we write about those ancients for archaeology's modern audience must acknowledge later heritage claims but not be constrained by them. We owe descendants respect; we owe the ancient past honesty—historical honesty, insofar as we can accomplish that. Not that the ancients would approve of our versions of their pre-history; probably not. They probably had their own court historians, telling narratives the way they wanted them told.

Indians and Indigenous archaeologists will object that such a statement implies, offensively, that archaeologists are somehow the only accredited interpreters of the Native American past. That misses my point: Archaeologists are the accredited interpreters of *archaeological pre-history*; but not of heritage or traditional history, which of course belong to Native groups. Archaeologists should never claim to speak for Native heritage[23]—a slippery slope for Indigenous Archaeology.

Whose heritage? It depends: Who's at the table? Who is archaeology's audience?

Whose History?

Having presented a too-simple definition of "History," I now compound my errors by contrasting three kinds of history: Conventional Western narrative history; Native traditional history; and an academic hybrid, Indigenous History/ Indigenous Archaeology.

Conventional History

Conventional History: Western narratives of the past constructed from evidence through rational, empirical, systematic, critical, cumulative, correctable methods. My notions of History are unapologetically rooted in the Enlightenment[24] (why would one apologize for being Enlightened?), with a nod to the "noble dream" of objectivity (Novick 1998). That should be the goal of archaeological pre-history. You might scoff and say: Impossible! I would cough and say: Why not try?

History went through an existential Postmodern crisis and emerged bloodied but unbowed. I repeat Popkin (2015:170; above): "Postmodern critiques had not in fact undermined their discipline's ability to establish certain truths about the past."[25] Even if the Dark Side had won, and conventional History no longer existed, it would be necessary for archaeology to invent it. I agree absolutely with Norman Yoffee about the necessity of a conventional pre-history:

> History is not a hyper-particularist collection of oddments of the past—what historians call antiquarianism—but is a method of explaining causes and effects. The version of world history that I have been calling social evolutionary theory in fact requires a revivified comparative method that importantly includes comparisons of developmental sequences. Such investigations must include appraisals of what social changes occurred in the past as well as those that did not occur. The goal of these new rules of the game is to understand the past on its own terms, insofar as this can be imagined. I do not say the game is easy; I do think we've made a good start. (Yoffee 2005:195)

To repeat: Why not try? What's lost by trying? But, how to go about it. I offer ideas in chapter 6; but for now, I must distance myself from a mind-meld of Native traditions and conventional history, which is what many of my colleagues assume I mean when I say "history." That's not what I have in mind.

Alice Kehoe (e.g., 1998) has thought deeply about the causes and consequences of ahistoricity in American Anthropological Archaeology. In *America Before the European Invasions* (Kehoe 2002:239–242), she includes a section "How Should an Archaeologist Construct a History?" To summarize, she says, not with science but with a humanism informed by Native American traditional histories,

> toward more humanistic interpretations of archaeological data.... Efforts to link contemporary First Nations knowledge to archaeological material, and develop research questions from their perspective as well as conventional Western standpoints, increasingly find approval in the profession. (Kehoe 2002:242)

That's not quite what I have in mind. Most archaeologists with whom I have discussed my notions of pre-history assume I am talking about archaeology brought into agreement or congruence with Native traditional histories. I'm not, although I value Native traditional histories. To which we now turn…

Native Traditional Histories/Heritage

Traditional histories used to be called myths and legends. Those terms today feel dismissive.[26] Native traditional histories—insofar as we can know them—offer a remarkable corpus of information for narrative pre-history. A great deal of historical information, but also a great deal of other information serving other (very important) purposes—most of which non-Natives will ever know. In a word: Heritage. And there's not a thing in the world wrong with that!

In chapter 6 I will discuss methods for archaeology to acknowledge traditional histories. But it's necessary to maintain the separation. Peter Nabokov (a central figure in this chapter), in his essay "Native Views of History," described Native traditions and archaeological prehistory as "genres passing in the night" (1996:2).[27] One can inform the other, but they are two very distinct bodies of knowledge, with different ontologies, different temporalities, and—importantly—different purposes and different audiences. Traditions—Native heritage—serve the needs of Native communities. Conventional Western history serves the needs of conventional (or unconventional) Westerners—or anyone with Western ontological leanings. The twain may meet, but they won't change their spots. Nor should they.

Why don't you ask us?—Indians often chide archaeologists with that question. I've asked. And I've learned. My education began in 1991, when gentlemen from two different Rio Grande Pueblos told me this about Chaco (in close paraphrase): "We know all about Chaco. We don't talk about it. Bad things happened there." I was working in Santa Fe, for the Museum of New Mexico—at or very near the black hole at the center of Pueblo Mystique and Pueblo Space. "Bad things happened there": That information vanished in the vortex and never appeared in programming or exhibits at the Museum. But it opened my eyes (and ears) to accounts of Chaco as something that might not fit Pueblo Space. I continued to ask Indians—diffidently and, I hope, politely—and over the course of several decades here's what I learned: There is at least as much variation in Natives' accounts of Chaco as in archaeologists' accounts of Chaco. A range of these are summarized in the Appendix. In conversations and dialogues and recorded accounts, Native views of Chaco range from a place where Pueblo clans did Pueblo ceremonies, to a creation of non-Puebloan outsiders, to the city that sent kachina battalions marching on the Pueblos, to a place where bad things happened not to be spoken of, to the center of a cruel despot who enslaved the nations. Variation does not negate Native accounts, any more than variation negates archaeological accounts. Within the frameworks of traditional history, they could all be perceived as (locally) true—tales told, like Faulkner's Compsons, from the perspectives and heritages of their several tellers.

More than a few Native traditional histories suggest a Chaco outside Pueblo Space—that "space" defined, recall, by non-Indians. Others conform to our notions of what's proper and, predictably, those stories appear more often in both technical and public interpretations. In collaborative practice and consultations, those are often the stories offered by Pueblo officials for public consumption: Generic, eventless accounts that we can fit into Pueblo Space (again, our category, not theirs).

In brief: Clans migrate in, perform ceremonies (undescribed), and migrate out. There are examples in the Appendix. I do not mean this dismissively; that narrative structure is shared by almost all the Pueblo migration histories which I have been fortunate enough to hear or read, and I'm sure it is (or they are) true. I think those sparse narratives are all that Pueblos want outsiders to know. Severin Fowles notes that "there is no escaping the reality that history is primarily composed among the Pueblos in what we would call a sacred idiom, and this can result in a tension between the desire for public acknowledgment of the authority of oral histories and the desire to keep the details of those histories private" (Fowles 2013:45). A point to which we return, briefly below and at more length in chapter 6.

Pueblo traditional histories as they are told in-house offer much more incidents and events, conflict and struggle, *sturm und drang*. These meatier stories are typically not available to outsiders. A recent and controversial example: Acoma origin stories. Acoma origin stories are available in old reports, with richly detailed events and characters (among them the story of White House; see Appendix). Those versions were originally published midcentury as "The Origin Myth of Acoma Pueblo and Other Records" by Matthew W. Stirling (1946) in the (then and now) rather obscure *Bureau of American Ethnology Bulletin* 135. (The 1946 BAE version is in the public domain and has been available online for years; which does nothing to alleviate its obscurity.)

Very recently the "Origin Myth" was edited by Peter Nabokov and republished by the huge international house Penguin (Hunt 2015). Nabokov identified and credited the original Acoma author as Edward Proctor Hunt, or "Day Break."[28]

The publicity attendant on Nabokov's 2015 version 'roused the ire of Acoma and its allies.[29] Their complaints were many, but the heart of the matter appears to be the global publication by a major house of a fully rendered traditional history—that went far beyond migrations and unspecified ceremonies. That knowledge, reportedly, was not general even among the people of Acoma. That level of detail was restricted to particular individuals or offices or age-grades, to be preserved and used as events required. To have a full version out in print for all the world to read violated both structure and process of traditional history. Acoma was officially furious. Then-governor Fred Vallo published an angry denunciation in the *Santa Fe New Mexican*:

> Hunt never had the permission of the pueblo to impart any Acoma sacred information to anyone, much less to the Bureau of Ethnology for publication. The pueblo has always considered this publication by the Bureau of Ethnology to be a fundamental breach of trust by the United States. It is a glaring example of the unfortunate and ugly incidents of the late 19th century involving archaeologists and anthropologists, personified by the likes of Frank Cushing at Zuni. The O*rigin Myth of the Pueblo of Acoma is th*e intellectual property of the pueblo, not the property of the United States, and surely not the property of Hunt or Nabokov to reproduce. (Vallo 2015)

The proprietary nature of traditional histories is, I think, acutely true for Chaco. Bad things happened there: Remembering while forgetting.[30] Pueblo people surely retain strong memories of Chaco, but it is my impression that those memories are not necessarily exemplary of how Pueblo people wish to live today.

Traditional histories are revealed very carefully, as occasions warrant on a need-to-know basis—and non-Indians don't need to know. At least, that's my take, after years of working on Chaco, with and without Indians. I once presented an early, tentative, timid version of my history of Chaco to that park's Native American Advisory Board. (This would have been in the mid-1990s.) I don't think I used the word "king" but I made it clear that the archaeology strongly suggested elites and nonelites. They sat silent, until one Pueblo leader said, we do not wish for you to write about that. What then should I write about? I asked. Daily life, he replied: Farming, grinding corn, making pottery, the seasons, migrations.

He did not say I was wrong (too polite for that) but rather that my take on the topic was unneeded and unwelcome. After *Chaco Meridian* and *A History of the Ancient Southwest*, Pueblo people from east and west have told me, in effect, that I was not right but I was getting close, and they did not want their kids hearing this stuff from a White guy. That's their job, not mine.

An ethical issue: My job is to figure out the past, and to write pre-history. Again: Why don't you ask us? Again: I did. And I used what I was told in combination with what the archaeology told me to construct a narrative history—I did my job—and Indians did not like it. Native accounts were not offered to inform my interpretation; they were offered to replace my interpretation. Which brings us to…

Indigenous History/Archaeology

Archaeology is not Indigenous.

That statement, while perhaps confrontational, is surely true: Archaeology is a Western Euro-American (now global) undertaking, founded on the critical, empirical, universal, and rational principles of the Enlightenment. Archaeology is not Indigenous, any more than physics or economics or political science are Indigenous. Many Indigenous people and more than a few non-Indigenous archaeologists are not comfortable with that provenance, so they are trying to change archaeology, to make it Indigenous. But then it would no longer be archaeology.

This is obviously a highly complicated and contentious topic, and I will not do it justice in the brief discussion that follows. My main point is this: Insofar as it has been practiced in the Southwest, Indigenous Archaeology seems to reinforce Pueblo Space in American Anthropological Archaeology. That may (or may not) be fine for Indigenous Archaeology, but I submit it's bad for knowing pre-history. I will return to that theme at the end of this section.

Indigenous History and Indigenous Archaeology—two different things—attempt to meld conventional academic History and Archaeology with Native traditions and ways of knowing.[31] The strongest advocates of Indigenous History—the older, more developed of the two—are Native American academics. The most vocal promoters of Indigenous Archaeology, at least so far, are almost all non-Native archaeologists.[32] Which maybe tells us something: Indian scholars gravitate toward History (and other fields), but avoid archaeology.

What does Indigenous History look like? Susan A. Miller (Seminole), a strong advocate, explains her vision:

> Indigenous historians see their work as a service to their people and to Indigenous people generally.... Indigenous methodology privileges traditional tribal historical narratives and upholds Indigenous lifeways over those of nation-states.... With time, American Indian Indigenous historiography is likely to rely more heavily on traditional texts such as songs, dances, and landscapes, and the teachings of Indigenous institutions such as drum groups and craft circles, which function much as seminars on Indigenous knowledge. (Miller and Riding In 2011:3–4)[33]

Some advocates suggest that a fully Indigenous History should be communicated (print? speech?) only in Indigenous languages. That would, of course, rather limit its audience. And that's probably the idea.

Indigenous Archaeology began with a less radical agenda than Indigenous History, perhaps because it was pushed more by archaeologists, and less by Indians. The original idea was fairly simple: Collaboration between archaeology and Indigenous people.[34] To a great degree, the idea of collaboration builds upon consultations with tribes required by NAGPRA and various other historic preservation laws. While seldom cheerful, those exchanges opened fruitful communications between archaeology and Native communities.

Indigenous Archaeology now wants to push beyond those limited, formal engagements. In what ways? Its enthusiasts admit (and admire) that it's all over the map.[35] Some edges are fairly radical, and its adherents can be zealous: Indigenous Archaeology is sometimes presented as a moral imperative, washing away the sins of colonialism.[36] And sometimes inimical to conventional archaeology. Dorothy Lippert (Choctaw) of the National Museum of Natural History's Repatriation Office calls for "the destruction of an idealized view of what archaeological study represents. The landscape of archaeology after repatriation laws is different. We are in a new world, one in which Native people [are seen] as active participants in the understanding of this environment" (Lippert 2008:120).

The most radical Indigenous Archaeology calls for archaeology to set aside science and Western rationalism and somehow think like Indians; or—more realistically—let Indians do the thinking.[37] (We will revisit this swerve of the Ontological Turn in chapter 6.) Epistemic capitulation: Going Native? Larry Zimmerman, an outspoken advocate, apparently called for "a different kind of science, between the boundaries of Western ways of knowing and Indian ways of knowing" (Zimmerman quoted by George Johnson [1996], quoted by Allison Wylie 2014:73). Indigenous Archaeology would be a "sea change" in the discipline—so said Alison Wylie, archaeology's favorite philosopher, in an oft-cited 2014 essay.[38] This rhetoric elevates local political situations to a global paradigm shift.[39] Sea change indeed: Larry Zimmerman, in a polemical essay "On Archaeological Ethics and Letting Go," seems to reduce archaeologists to heritage technicians (my words, not his),[40] working at and for the service of tribes: "Archaeologists just need to realize who the real boss is, and archaeology will be better served when we figure out it isn't us!" (Zimmerman 2012:188).[41]

Indigenous Archaeology seems to me to be as much about archaeologists coming to grips with the (very real) sins of our past, as about Indian-initiated efforts to inject Native voice into conventional archaeology.[42] Significantly, that appears to reverse the situation with Indigenous History, which was primarily promoted by Native American scholars. There are today several Indigenous advocates for Indigenous Archaeology, and their voices are articulate and compelling. But I do not sense the enthusiasm tribal people seem to have for Indigenous History. It's my experience, after forty years of interactions on many levels with many Indians, that Native Americans generally have little enthusiasm for archaeology.[43] A Pueblo man—sympathetic to archaeology—said: "Back home, archaeology is a four-letter word."

It's my impression that most tribes wouldn't touch archaeology with a ten-foot pole except as required by CRM regulations—which, of course, are White peoples' laws, coming from European ideas about heritage.[44] For non-CRM archaeology, many tribes have strong policies against "discretionary digging"—that is, archaeological research.

So I say: Archaeology is not Indigenous. Archaeology is a Western (and now global) discipline. While (hopefully) thinking globally, Southwestern archaeology still operates locally—and currently that's a tough neighborhood. As proponents of Indigenous Archaeology rightly point out, consultation and collaboration can be rewarding and productive; it's certainly become routine in the Southwest. And, in my opinion, completely justified and understandable. Time to pay the rent, as the poet said.

Indigenous Archaeology is much more interesting and important than I have presented it here, but my focus is very specific: Indigenous Archaeology, as practiced in the Southwest, reinforces Pueblo Space. Recall the public versus proprietary narratives of Native traditional history. The proprietary stories are full of incident; the public stories are purposefully general. The general versions fit well in Pueblo Space, American Anthropological Archaeology's slant on the ancient Southwest. As one enthusiast of Indigenous Archaeology put it:

> Temporalizing and historicizing the ethnographic echo is a key agenda concern of Indigenous archaeology, as it is fundamental to demonstrating the relevancy and utility of archaeology to Indigenous communities. (McNiven 2016:33)

The "ethnographic echo" bounces around inside Pueblo Space. Indigenous Archaeology also tends to conflate Indian temporalities with archaeologists' (very proper) respect for Indian heritage. Thus, a common product of Indigenous Archaeology: Time Immemorial, eternal, unchanging. Whatever their heritage values, claims of Time Immemorial reinforce Pueblo Space: It has always been thus.

Indigenous Archaeology is a local response to local political issues. It will differ in method and content from Indigenous place to Indigenous place, from postcolonial situation to postcolonial situation. The particulars of the Southwestern situation differ from Northern Plains situations, or Pacific Coast situations, or Australian situations. Each situation requires tactics and strategies tailored to local conditions and concerns. Who are the stakeholders, who is the audience?

Archaeology as a discipline is not local or specific to the Southwest. It's an international, even transnational, endeavor. And archaeologists are its authors; taking that word literally, we are the authorities. Indigenous critics say archaeologists do not want to give up control of the narrative. Yes, that's correct. I don't want archaeology to give up control of the archaeological narrative in the Southwest or in Mesopotamia or in Olduvai Gorge. Just as I don't want Indians to give up control of their heritage/history. Ships that pass in the night, hopefully steered away from collision.

Which again begs the question: Who is our audience?

Whose Science?

"Normal science" in Southwestern archaeology is the work we routinely see in *American Antiquity* and *Kiva* and sometimes in *PNAS* or *Science*. Normal science is based on the received Culture Histories, matrices of who was where when. That's the grist it grinds but there's a problem: I think normal science is working with flawed history. Chapter 4 explored new kinds of science we might do based on narrative prehistory rather than Culture History. Still, my history or Culture History, Southwestern archaeology seems safe in the bosom of science.

My interest, in this section, is: Whose science? Broader impacts, as it were.

What Natives Know

In early global enthusiasms for Indigeneity of the 1970s and 1980s, partisans made bold claims for Native knowledge: It was science! This required considerable flexibility in the definition of *science*. Indigenous science was science because it constituted "systematic and comprehensive schemes for understanding the world" or "a systematic approach to acquiring knowledge of the natural world"—leading to awkward constructions like "traditional science knowledge systems."[45] These claims were typically made by non-Natives on behalf of Indigenous groups. One wonders if many Indigenous groups really wanted their knowledge to be identified with Western science—or appropriated by Big Pharma.

The term "Indigenous science" continues in use in some quarters, but it does not seem to be a contender for any science we might do with archaeology or pre-history. Indigenous science is almost entirely biological and environmental; I am not aware of any claims (for example) for an Indigenous particle physics. Where Indigenous Archaeology/History might contest and Native heritage might contradict conventional narrative History, Indigenous science—to the best of my knowledge—has little to say about pre-history or to the kind of science we do with pre-history: The origins of inequality, or the evolution of political complexity, for example.

Science is Angling in the Mud[46]

Is archaeology science? The histories that archaeology writes can and should be used to do science, but it would take a very flexible definition of science to make archaeology itself a standalone science or scientific discipline. So: No, I don't think archaeology is a science. It's part of humanities, much like History; and, like History, archaeology's narratives can be used for science, by archaeologists so inclined and by scientists from other disciplines.

Most (but not all) of our archaeological science comes from elsewhere, not unlike most of our theory. (Think: Evolution, adaptation, resilience, networks, and so on and so on.) We are not shy—nor should we be—about inserting borrowed science ideas into our archaeology. Scientists in other disciplines use our pre-histories in the service of larger questions. Tim Kohler—an archaeologist who does science very well—recently asked: "Who cannot name at least one biologist, economist, ecologist or Big Historian who has come to be as well known as a comparative interpreter of archaeological data as for research in his home discipline?" (Kohler 2012:325–326).

Wait, wait...don't tell me: Jared Diamond! Diamond's use of archaeology and archaeology's very hard use of Diamond were central to the discussion of "collapse" in chapter 4. I am delighted when scientists like Diamond use Chaco to make a larger point. But I'm sad because they use the wrong Chaco. They (quite reasonably) use the consensus Chaco, the received Chaco: The Chaco of Pueblo Space.

Chapter 3 demonstrated that Chaco makes a great deal more sense if you add kingship to the mix. Chaco becomes understandable, it clicks. But making Chaco a polity also, oddly enough, makes it much less interesting, less phenomenal. "We have garden-variety 'early states' stacked ten deep under the lab table." Chaco's on that pile, just another garden-variety early state (actually, not so early). That Chaco might not appeal so much to Diamond and future non-archaeological big-picture science writers: It's no longer exceptional. My guess is that archaeology will have to do its own science with Chaco (and the larger Southwest). Which, of course, we do: Chapter 4 offered examples, a few of my tentative attempts, and, more importantly, major initiatives such as the Village Ecodynamics Project, the Southwestern Social Network Project, and others.

I'm sure that I alienated academic colleagues by expressing mild appreciation for Jared Diamond's work. Perhaps I could better illustrate what I have in mind with a Chaco science book by a genuine Southwestern academic.

Anasazi America is a book by David E. Stuart published in 2000 with a second edition in 2014. Stuart is a cultural anthropologist by training with archaeological interests, and now emeritus Provost at the University of New Mexico.

Anasazi America is cited in only a half-dozen of the scores of post-2000 Chaco studies (e.g., Paul Reed 2004; Mathien 2005; Neitzel 2003; Van Dyke 2007a). It did not make the cut for the encyclopedic *Chaco Handbook* (Vivian and Hilpert 2002, 2012). And it figures not at all in Chaco's theory bush-wars. Curious.

Stuart presents his view of Chaco (alas, the Chaco of Pueblo Space) and extrapolates—scientifically, as I use that term here—from Chaco's rise and fall to modern-day America. That is, he uses Chaco to make empirically grounded arguments of wider interest and relevance—not just cautionary tales. For broader impacts, *Anasazi America* is in my opinion the best Chaco book ever written. Books and studies like *Anasazi America* are what I hope we can produce from Chaco and from the Southwest.[47]

But for what audience? For what audience?

Who Is Our Audience?

The Southwest is a good place to think about archaeology's audience: The ancient Southwest is a publicly traded commodity. I consider "audience" here as readerships, but my comments cross media. Let's list a few audiences. Other archaeologists, descendant communities, and larger publics—of which there are at least three: Other scholars, Southwest fans/aficionados, and the broader reading public.

Indians chide us: You archaeologists only write for each other. Well…yes, that's true; archaeologists (like any specialists) mostly write for other specialist archaeologists. Students write theses for a star chamber of frowning faculty. Professors write for their peers, who review them for tenure (one book and four articles) and later for promotion (two articles or book chapters each year). (These are fictitious standards; but most universities have some such standards.) CRM professionals write reports, deliverables delivered to clients and State Historic Preservation Offices for review. As long as CRM escapes congressional ire and people continue to move to sunbelt cities, we will have a great many CRM reports; no one could read them all.[48] Most are routine; but more than a few CRM projects and reports have been transformative: Dolores, Animas–La Plata, scores of big Hohokam projects—among many others.[49]

Yes, archaeologists write mainly for each other. How many others? Southwestern archaeologists have a captive audience: Ourselves. At a guess, there are about 1,500 of us, probably more.[50] A big audience, but not huge.

Archaeologists elsewhere—non-Southwesternists—read Southwestern work more selectively. For all its local glory, the Southwest does not travel well. It is, I fear, perceived by many other archaeologists as a minor archaeology: Overhyped, overfunded, and overexposed. It is my impression that Southwest most often informs other archaeologists' work as the bright particular example of the little egalitarian society that could—Pueblo Space. (Perhaps I should not urge us to abandon Pueblo Space, it may be our most popular export.)

Descendant communities, we tell ourselves, are our most important audiences; but Indians are not so much an audience as a constituency. A disenfranchised constituency: Represented by not-my-representatives.[51] "We don't need any revisionist history." Yet many Indians I've known read archaeology with real interest, if often with exasperation. (Vine Deloria Jr. read a lot of archaeology, and didn't much care for it.) So yes, Indians are an audience.

Larger audiences comprise at least three demographics (as the advertising people say): We turn now to conventional audiences of scholars, aficionados, and the reading public.

Scholars and scientists in other disciplines pay attention to Southwestern archaeology—thanks, I think, in large part to the allure of Santa Fe and the Pueblo Mystique. Consider the Santa Fe Institute (SFI; a high-profile, high-power think tank), which, by design, is energetically cross-disciplinary and, by happy accident, embraces archaeology.[52] SFI's faculty includes several prominent Southwestern archaeologists, among the physicists and economists and biologists. This is a two-way street: Southwestern archaeological institutions cross disciplinary boundaries to engage nonarchaeological scholars, as do many individual Southwesternists.[53]

Southwestern fans and aficionados: The Pueblo Mystique was designed to capture public attention, and it works. There is no need to belabor the Southwest's appeal to its fan base (in which I include the wonderful avocational archaeology community and state archaeological societies). Here's a clue: Technical or academic archaeology books typically sell a few hundred copies; popular or even semipopular Southwestern archaeology books move thousands. Tourism bureaus of New Mexico and Arizona could provide figures on visitors, but the audiences I'm thinking of are only a portion of the vacation throngs. Not everyone who visits Mesa Verde is interested in archaeology. At the same time, the audience of fans/aficionados is larger, globally; many love the Southwest but seldom visit. I would not venture a number but I'm sure it's many times greater than archaeological readership (Southwestern or otherwise) even adding nonarchaeologist scholarly audiences.

It's my impression, from browsing bookstores for fifty years, that the ancient Southwest presented to fans and the broader reading public is boring: Corn, beans, squash, and spirituality—Pueblo Space. That would be OK if the Southwest was, in fact, boring; but it wasn't. The archaeology is very clear on that point.

I submit that, after our captive audiences of "other archaeologists," Southwest aficionados and the broader reading public should be our primary concern: Creating new knowledge about the past, and making it understandable to educated consumers in the present.

This assertion is critical to my argument, and to the argument that runs through this book. I have no numbers, no analysis to back this up; my identification of "broader reading public" as our primary audience is an assertion, an opinion—but an assertion and opinion I feel qualified to make: For thirty years, I've made the broader reading public a significant part of my professional life, and for thirty years I've experimented with reaching all these various audiences. I know something about this.[54]

We will, of course, continue writing for each other, Southwestern archaeologists writing for 1,500-plus Southwestern archaeologists. But I am convinced that if some of us (more of us?) write intelligently for broader readerships, we will also service scientists and nonarchaeological scholars, and of course Native audiences. Focusing on Southwestern archaeology's biggest audiences—aficionados and broader readerships—should "scoop up" those other key audiences. Insofar as they care to be scooped.

In my experience, nonspecialist audiences—aficionados and intelligent readers—are not particularly interested in Anthropological theory or our attempts at science. They want to know: *What happened in history?* Once people get past archaeology-as-treasure-hunt (and dinosaurs), that's what they think archaeology does: History! *And they are right*, archaeology must be first and foremost history, not (only) to cater to our markets but, as I've argued at length, because that's what archaeology is supposed to do. More than that: History in the conventional Western tradition, the "common ontology" (chapter 6); history that makes the past understandable to *us* and to those larger audiences.

Indians and proponents of Indigenous Archaeology complain that archaeology sets itself up to be the only people who can speak for the past, for history. In a carefully limited way, that's true: Archaeology is the best way to speak for archaeological pre-history. Circular, perhaps; but archaeology is a discipline founded in Western Enlightenment forms of knowledge-production, and ceases to be archaeology if it moves too far away from those forms. (I will have more to say, sternly, along these lines in chapter 6.) There are other ways to speak for the ancients—to understand the past—but they are not archaeology's ways.

Other ways are valid, for other audiences. I believe that the ancient Southwest deserves and requires at least two parallel narratives: Archaeological prehistory and Native heritage, insofar as Indians care to share that heritage. And when the two conflict—as, perhaps, at Chaco? That conundrum could (and should) entangle graduate seminars for years to come. We must be truthful historians, honest brokers of prehistory; but we also want to respect Native heritage.

What is to be done? Method and theory! And maybe some mojo…

CHAPTER 6

A Future for the Ancient Southwest

I never meta-narrative I didn't like.

—attributed to Will Rogers

Method, theory, and…mojo? I'll save the last for last, and deal here with more familiar method and theory. Most archaeology graduate programs have a course called "Method and Theory." I've yet to find such a course, or textbook, that addresses the theory and methods of pre-historiography: History without documents. This chapter is a hint of a sketch of an outline of what pre-historiography might look like.

Standard archaeological "Culture History" is not History. Culture History tells us who was where when, and it's essential. We can't move forward without it. But it's static: It's not dynamic, not causal, not narrative.

Archaeologists might object (as some have) that we already "do" History, even if we don't explicitly teach pre-historiography. Yes: A few of us do. But, in my experience, most of American Anthropological Archaeology remains largely and happily ahistorical, uncomfortable with History and its vagaries. I will offer examples (including, as always, Chaco) of how archaeology seems to lack a bump of history, a historical sensibility.

I reverse the M&T order with theory first and method second, because method matters more. Archaeology has plenty of theory—more than enough! But, as far as I can tell, a near absence of pre-historiography. So, easy stuff first: Theory.

Theories of Everything

I see three kinds of "theory": in the real world, theory-as-speculation (1); and in our world, scientific theory (2) and arts and humanities theory (3).[1] Despite the protestations of many (mostly on the humanities' side), scientific and humanist theory really are different. Science theory thinks about how the world works; humanist theory thinks about how to think about how the world works. Alas, much of archaeology is dismissed by our several audiences with the other, more general usage: Theory as mere speculation.

167

How to differentiate? In yet another lark of typographic excess, I handle three theories thus: (1) theory as speculation (small "t"); (2) Theory in science (capital "T"); and (3) *théorie* in the arts and humanities (pardon my French). I had to call them something, and small "t," capital "T," and Francophonic *théorie* seemed preferable to Theory Type I, Theory Type II, and Theory Type III. So: Science Theory, humanities *théorie*, and theory-as-speculation. All through the provincial lens of Southwestern archaeology: A philosophical selfie.

Capital-"T" Theory

Science Theory (capital "T," meant to be pompous) means: Your ideas about how the world works.[2] It helps if your ideas are material and rational, not mystical; and it helps if their relationships can be described syllogistically or logically or mathematically. Those ideas must have a close correspondence to the empirical world, and it's useful (but not absolutely mandatory) that those ideas can be evaluated. (Think: String Theory.) Some Theories can be formally tested (for example, by experiment); some cannot. But all Theory can be judged against evidence. Capital-"T" Theories that have survived repeated evaluations and the tests of time—like evolution—might as well be called "facts." Scientific Theory is not speculation, it is knowledge-building; and I am all for it.

Archaeology always, from its earliest days, claimed to be scientific: An organized, disciplined, scholarly endeavor, in contrast to mere antiquarianism. That's a loose use of the term "science," and not quite what I have in mind; by "science," I mean what physicists do. American Anthropological Archaeologists started taking science very seriously fifty years ago. Physics envy. New Archaeology spouted Hempel and Popper and made law-like pronouncements on the logic of hypothesis formulation, test implications, and so forth. Even at the time, it seemed kind of silly.

Those ante[science]bellum pretensions have gone with the wind. We can't do what physicists do. We've hung up our lab coats, but Capital-"T" Theory still has a solid place in Southwestern archaeology: Ideas about how the world works. Those ideas are often not precisely testable but, if they are linked to the empirical world, they can be evaluated against evidence. Theory needn't be inductive or deductive or abductive; to be useful, it only has to work. (Which is sort of abductive-ish, I guess.)

I feel very strongly that Theory should drive archaeology. Not perhaps its daily operations, but its ultimate goals. If we are not investigating how the world works, why are we doing this? Without Theory, archaeology becomes an academic pastime—a dilettante's interest in ancient things. (As we shall see, some threads of *théorie* urge exactly that outcome.)

Alas, for a depressingly broad segment of archaeology, scientific Theory is yesterday's papers. *Théorie* seized the day.

Théorie

Since the 1990s, science Theory has been progressively overshadowed by a very different use of the word "theory" from the arts and humanities: Philosophical musings of many stripes, often with political or social agendas ("critical theory"),[3] but all loosely united in incredulity to metanarratives and hostility to positivism; celebrating epistemic pluralism and relativism; and insisting on the social construction of this and that. Its original provenance was largely Gallic[4]— last century's Poststructuralism—so I refer to these disparate notions, bundled together, as "*théorie*," hereafter mostly not italicized.

A few decades ago these were Postmodern. We are now well-past-post (indeed, nearly past "human") and in many academic disciplines, those once-radical postmodern notions have become business as usual. What's new, at least in archaeology, is the emergence of théorie as a subdicipline, almost a way of life.[5] That's just weird. (Of which, more below.) First: What is théorie?

Short answer: Just about anything you want it to be.

Longer answer: Philosophical théorie in the arts and humanities means, thinking about how to think about how the world works. It can be pretty vague: Théorie, according to archaeologists Michael Shanks and Christopher Tilley, "is reflection, critique, performance, a theatre for action, an act and object of contemplation" (Shanks and Tilley 1988:25). (Think: Thing Theory.) Shanks—an easy target—is a vocal proponent of Symmetrical Archaeology (a recent development that I will not attempt to summarize here); he disassociates this théorie from anything remotely causal, or methodological, or useful: "Symmetrical archaeology is not a new kind of archaeology. It is not a new theory. It is not another borrowed methodology…. Symmetrical archaeology is an attitude."[6] OK; What are we supposed to do with that?

Probably nothing. Théorie is not a huge problem in the stodgy old Southwest, save for two virulent strains discussed below.[7] Residual scientism may be a bigger issue. Scientism is hard on History, it makes History difficult. Théorie is not inimical to History—but, strangely, théorie did all it could to demolish History as a discipline. A cautionary tale for Southwestern archaeology?

Théorie is here *pour la longue durée*, so here I theorize théorie. I've been watching it closely for thirty years (a theme to which I return at the conclusion of this section). At least three academic generations have been trained to believe that théorie is part of our landscape—they no longer realize that théorie was and remains a choice. As Murray Gell-Mann is said to have said, "You don't have to read this stuff."

But I do, and I am alarmed by two relatively recent threads of theory: The Ontological Turn (their term) and New Antiquarianism (my term). In brief: The Ontological Turn questions the "common ontology" (Western rationalism) dragging us into yet another round of epistemic relativism; New Antiquarianism spins archaeology back to old antiquarianism, the pointless pondering of old pots. After letting off some general theoretical steam, I will focus on those two, which pose clear and present dangers to Southwestern archaeology.

Beginning in the 1970s, American departments of literature and art history began to experiment with French Poststructural thinking.[8] One thing led to another, experiment became habit, and habit became addiction. By the 1990s, it even reached American Anthropological Archaeology. A definable body of French theory began to dominate the discourse, as some might say.[9] This, at a time when those same French theorists were fading fast in *la Patrie*: The American obsession came as a surprise to French *savants*.[10]

French Poststructuralism was all Greek to me and to many others. Opacity was a virtue for French philosophers; writing clearly and simply was *pas intel-lectuelle*.[11] Beyond the fact that it's intentionally obtuse, it's difficult to gener-alize about the several threads of Poststructuralism: They were only united in being post–Lévi-Strauss. The most potentially damaging to American Anthro-pological Archaeology were those which rejected Enlightenment empiricism for epistemological relativism—French philosophers like Jacque Derrida, Michel Foucault, and Jean-François Lyotard. Your guess—anybody's guess—is as good as mine, because there's no real world out there and even if there was, we have no way to know it. (My paraphrase, of course—they said it in dense, impene-trable French, which we read in dense, impenetrable translations.) Archaeologi-cal *théoriciens* quickly realized that primrose path led to academic irrelevance, and stepped away from the epistemological abyss.[12] They were putting their own jobs at risk, and many had families to feed. But (as we shall see): It's back, in the Ontological Turn.

I gave théorie a serious shot early on, but it didn't seem to be going anywhere I wanted to go. After the Sokal Hoax in 1996, I checked in every few months be-cause théorie is a moving target. It's all about new ideas! A parade of intellectual bandwagons upon which *théoriciens* jump, strut their stuff, and then hop off.[13] This makes life difficult when théorie buffs complain that those not so inclined do not engage with théorie's issues and arguments. Which issues, exactly? What part of kaleidoscopic, hydra-headed, many-splendored théorie to engage?[14] Théorie is so changeable, so intentionally diverse, that we have a surprising number of book-length compendia on "Archaeological Theory," simply to lead innocent students through *le labyrinthe*.[15]

I am bemused by the intrusion of théorie for théorie's sake into archaeol-ogy, of all places. I repeat: Archaeology, of all places. Are we all metaphysicians now? Matthew Johnson notes, "It's possible for an archaeologist to call himself 'a theorist'—that is, someone who deals in theory" (Johnson 2011). A British Classical archaeologist noted, ruefully, curricular devolvement from "courses in archaeological method and theory...later theory and method, or even just theory" (Laurence 2012:xi–xii). TAG, the Theoretical Archaeology Group, is reportedly the largest annual archaeological conclave in the U.K. (I've attended several American TAGS—smaller but energetic, if occasionally sliding into self-parody.)

Hypertrophy of the theoretical, withering of the real—to paraphrase Walter Russell Mead (2010). Playing at philosophy[16] has, for some archaeologists, become more important than actually learning about the past. If we can't know the past, perhaps we can talk it to death.

Oh well, *à chacon son gout.* A noted Yankee philosopher said: "People who like this sort of thing will find this the sort of thing they like"—attributed to Lincoln but probably Artemas Ward (whose humor was the sort of humor that Lincoln liked). There must be something to théorie because some very smart people are involved. And there's a lot of 'em: The vector is sizable.

This is key: Théorie is of and for the present.[17] Or so I think. Insofar as archaeological théorie addresses contemporary philosophical issues, it is on firm ground. (Well, maybe not *firm.*) When contemporary philosophies are foisted upon the ancient past, the ground gives way.[18]

Speculative Realism, Feminism, New Materialism, Symmetrical Archaeology, Cosmopolitanism, the Ontological Turn, New Antiquarianism—these are philosophies very much for us, today. Indeed, many threads of theory have critical political agendas—which is fine for us now, but maybe not jammed back into somebody else's prehistory. (I return to this theme, of théorie in the present, below.)

I have much in common, politically, with my théorie friends. But I do not see how (most) théorie helps us with our principal task: Discovering new knowledge about the past, knowing the past.[19] Much théorie is inimical, even antagonistic, to that positivist pursuit. Théorie's previous "turns"—linguistic, historical, material, and so forth—were not the sharp turn of *die Kehre* but random deflections, wobbling ultimately...where? Somewhere nice, one hopes. But two new threads are of particular concern (that is, alarm) for the Southwest: The Ontological Turn and New Antiquarianism.

The Ontological Turn

The Ontological Turn is much on the minds of TAGers. Its roots (and proper place, I think) are in ethnology, but it's seeping into archaeology. It is almost absent from Southwestern archaeology, so far; but ontology saturates Indigenous Archaeology and (at several removes) philosophical discussions behind NAGPRA. And these are of considerable consequence in the Southwest, even if many Southwesternists are blissfully unaware. More on this later.

The Ontological Turn is really several turns done up in a knot. Various authors have rather different ideas about "ontology." They boil down to two:[20] (1) ontologies for how Other people think; and (2) a working ontology proposed for archaeology—relational ontologies—largely inimical to our modern, Western "common ontology."

Ontology 1 is very close to the old anthropological notion of "world view" or even the more idealized definitions of "culture."[21] That is: The notions and logics and thought processes that characterize a particular group or society. Not everyone thinks the way we do. This apparently came as a shock to younger American archaeologists (whose Introduction to Anthropology class may have avoided antique terms like "culture"), and to British archaeologists of every age who never took an Introduction to Anthropology class. The "Others" studied by ethnology have "other" ontologies that we can learn about (and learn from); but we rush to impose some idealized versions of "other" ontologies on the defenseless ancients—whose minds surely we can never know.[22]

Would not an ancient Ontology have to be cast in the language of the people (remember the Linguistic Turn?). Most archaeologists don't know the languages of living Native communities,[23] and we haven't a clue about languages in the distant past, like Chaco.[24] Absent their languages, how can we know their ontologies?

The goal of Ontology 1 may be worthy. What did they think? How did they think it? But it is really difficult, maybe impossible—absent some sort of archaeological Ouija board—to get there without veering off into mysticism.

Ontology 2 challenges the "common ontology"—how we (archaeologists, everyone) think. Followed in one direction, Ontology 2 suggests that Other ontologies might work better than ours. (For what? That's not clear yet.) Whatever their intended work, Relational or Symmetrical ontologies (and other big arcs of the Turn) seem familiar, like reanimated zombies of old, dead epistemological relativism, attacking yet again Western science. I have no use for epistemic relativism.[25] Neither should you: If you think you're leaning that way, read Boghossin (2006) twice and call me in the morning. Yet we have a hard time shaking it off. Ian Hodder, way back in 2003, devoted a chapter to "Whose rationality?"[26] If you have to ask, you can't afford it…or perhaps, if you have to ask, we can't afford you.

Ontology 2 would be simply another round of théorie tub-thumping (or, over here, bandwagoning) except that Ontology 2 has philosophical implications for Indigenous Archaeology (discussed in chapter 5) and NAGPRA. If, on general philosophical grounds, archaeological théorie admits epistemic relativism, then why should we, specifically, not follow the advocates of Indigeneity and shift archaeology from its traditional configuration to something difficult to recognize as a discipline—to paraphrase Watson (2003). Ontology 2 could do that: Destroy archaeology as we know it.[27] I don't think that's a useful outcome.

At some point, we will probably see a repeat of the academic cycle from earlier rounds of relativism: A realization that Ontology 2 might make archaeology irrelevant, with jobs at stake; followed by a pragmatic philosophical retreat (or another, slightly less dangerous Turn). If this was all (only, merely) academic, that would probably be the trajectory. But in the Southwest, we have NAGPRA and tribal concerns with decidedly nonacademic applications.

Challenge the "Common Ontology" of Western rationalism, and replace it with…what? Something Other, something non-Western, something Native? Well, yes: "Treating non-western thought as a form of theory [to]…create new ways of understanding the past" (Harris and Cipolla 2017:11).[28] Thus the Ontological Turn—by happy accident?—curves to intersect NAGPRA and Indigenous Archaeology. Indians certainly did not need the Ontological Turn to get that job done; they did it themselves. But for archaeologists, the Ontological Turn provides philosophical validation for our new normal, and for things yet to come.

New Antiquarianism

Perhaps archaeology is not meant to be a useful field or discipline for building knowledge. Perhaps the past—or its material traces—is there simply to be considered and enjoyed (or not) in the present. This is the New Antiquarianism.

Théorie directs us to think about ancient things, in the present. And for some *théoriciens* that takes a decidedly artistic, emotional, Romantic turn: Appreciation of ruins and artifacts for our personal aesthetic pleasure: Antiquarianism. Michael Shanks (e.g., 2008) is one the most influential academic proponent of New Antiquarianism (my term), which I extend to the several branches of théorie that obsess on the relationship of archaeologists to ancient objects in the present, the present, *toujours* the present.

For the Southwest, what we might call "vulgar antiquarianism" is not academic. Not by a long shot. We deal with big-time looters and high-end collectors: Supply and demand in Pueblo Space. That whole industry is built around the contemplation of old objects in the present, and indeed justifies itself as aesthetic antiquarianism. Do we really want to jump on *that* bandwagon, with those guys? If théorie allows everybody to enjoy ancient objects in their own aesthetics, what do we do with looters and collectors? Their ancient interests—fiscal and aesthetic—may be allowed by théorie, but are ethically repugnant; and often illegal.

While the antiquities market is a clear and present danger, academic Antiquarianism is less obviously objectionable but (I fear) no less threatening to archaeology as a discipline. One of the most elaborately developed arguments for antiquarianism comes from—*sacré bleu!*—a French *théoricien* who is…[drumroll] an archaeologist! I pick (and pick on) Frenchman Laurent Olivier, rather than an Anglophone proponent, because I am very unlikely to meet Olivier in an elevator at a conference.[29] And his work hints at the follies to which théorie and New Antiquarianism surely lead.

Laurent Olivier is curator of the Department of Celtic and Gallic Archaeology at the National Museum of Archaeology in Saint-Germain-en-Laye. His 2011 book *The Dark Abyss of Time: Archaeology and Memory*—an object of interest to TAGers—hammers home the point that théorie (while all over the map) is decisively about the present.[30] "What the archaeologist brings to the surface is not so much an object recalling some clearly delimited time period of the past, as the evolving memory of that past, whose meaning can be determined only by and in the present" (Olivier 2011:xvi). He nods to the usual suspects in French Poststructural théorie (Deleuze and the gang) but spends far more time with older, odder thinkers. He opens with a pair of standards, draws an unlikely third, and then plays a wild-card fourth: Darwin and Freud, Walter Benjamin, and Aby Warburg, who gets most of a chapter in *The Dark Abyss of Time*![31]

Olivier's first, last, and constantly repeated complaint is history, or historicity. Not the kind of narrative I'm pushing for, but simply the very idea of history. He doesn't seem to like it. "As Walter Benjamin has pointed out, conventional history, or more precisely put, the traditionally historicist perception of history, drains time of its substance.... We have to abandon the historicist's 'empty, homogeneous' time in favor of the full, heterogeneous time of newness.... [The latter] reveals another approach to time, a dizzying, dangerous approach. It is an understanding of time that situates its subject in the present, recognizing it to be the node where past, present, and yet-to-come intertwine" (Olivier 2011:184).[32]

He denies (of course) that the past is knowable, although he notes that archaeology operates as if it were knowable.[33] Rather than attempting to recount the past, we should focus not on people or their histories, but on objects as "memory" of past times, in the present. Olivier, again: "Considering artifacts, as we need to do, as symptoms of a constantly reconstructed memory rather than as objects that bear witness to some past, has opened uncharted paths for archaeologists."[34] This isn't history, or art history, or even art criticism. It's Romanticism. Shannon Lee Dawdy, in her fulsome introduction to *Abyss of Time*, declares: "We are on the verge of a new romantic era.... Romanticism, long enough rejected because misunderstood as a retrograde nostalgia, is due for a return in the wake of too much destructive rationalism" (Dawdy 2011:ix).

Romanticism may be attractive—we share the sorrows of young Werther—but rationalism gets things done. I will argue that to justify its existence and extend its life, Southwestern archaeology needs to get things done. When an Indians asks, "why do archaeologists desecrate my ancestors?" please don't tell him/her about your philosophical need to connect aesthetically with ancient objects.

Olivier offers a statement I will use to end this section: "Archaeology has struggled to find a path of its own, *other than that of recounting the past*" (Olivier 2011:xv, my emphasis). Laurent, riddle me this: What's wrong with recounting the past? That's what archaeology is supposed to do! It's a damned tricky business and—at least in my experience—hard work. As George Kubler many years ago said: "Knowing the past is as astonishing as knowing the stars" (1962). But both stars and past can be known.

I argue that knowing the past, recounting the past, is the right and proper goal of our field. I don't see how théorie gets us there; the hermeneutic circle spiraling inward in tighter and tighter loops until...poof.[35] It's not clear where théorie is going, if it will ever get there, or if it even wants to get there. "Theory has no conclusion, no end point, no moment of completion" (Harris and Cipolla 2017:193). That's not something to brag about.

By and large, théorie seems a sad diversion from serious work. They've had three decades of théorie: What have they produced? A more nuanced account? (I'd gladly trade murky layers of nuance for the clarity that théorie delighted to darken.) Thirty years of labor to bring forth *The Dark Abyss of Time*?

Culture History had the floor for about three decades, maybe four. (Of course it's still around.) Processual archaeology had its day in the sun, from the 1970s to the 1990s—thirty years or so. (Of course it's still around, too.) Then théorie. Maybe thirty years of théorie is enough?

Time for something new? Maybe getting on with the job of human history—in my opinion, the thing that best justifies the continued existence of archaeology. Terry Eagleton (2003) argued persuasively for life *After Theory*. And Kristian Kristiansen (2014) calls for a post-post-processual "third paradigm" in archaeology. Can we imagine a future incredulity to metaphysics? "Let's work without theorizing; it is the only way to make life bearable," advised Martin in *Candide*.

Small "t" theory

The general, popular usage of "theory" means speculation, variously idle or vacuous. "Theory-as-speculation" subverts science Theory ("evolution is only a theory") and dismisses humanities théorie ("ivory tower theory"). Small-"t" theory, however, is where the rubber meets the road: The general use of theory—speculation or worse—applies all too often to archaeology in areas that actually matter: Policy, law, real life. Theory capital "T" influences like-minded scientists; théorie engages like-minded *théoriciens*; but small-"t" theory—when used by congressional staffers, Park Service interpreters, or Native American intellectuals—can gut our whole enterprise. Hard-won knowledge is too easily dismissed: "That's just a theory..." Or, even worse: "That's just YOUR theory..."

Lowercase "t" theory—speculation—lies in the public domain. But, to a great extent, so does Southwestern archaeology. In one memorable month and a half a few years back, among my regular duties I did a couple of public tours and a lot of NAGPRA. On the tours—for the Crow Canyon Archaeological Center and for the Archaeological Conservancy, as I recall—several very intelligent participants said (smiling) variations on this theme: Archaeologists are only guessing. Small "t" theory. At several NAGPRA consultations, tribal representatives offered variations on this theme: Archaeology is evil. Those dual messages made a deep impression on me, almost made me change careers.

Archaeology as lowercase "t" theory—speculation, guessing—is a constant trope throughout the Southwest, where the archaeology itself is a constant trope. It's part of Pueblo Space: "We will never know…" "We can only guess…" "Archaeology cannot tell us…"—clichés as common as "mystery" and "vanished." They add value to Pueblo Space: Mystery sells. They also bleed into public discourse, and discredit archaeology.

And we, archaeologists, buy into it too! "Chaco" rarely appears in public print without "mystery," accompanied by amused references to various archaeological "theories" or speculations. In chapter 2 I argued that after a century of hard work and good thinking, and many millions of dollars sunk into holes in the ground, "the mystery of Chaco Canyon" should be an affront to any right-thinking archaeologist. But, as I also noted in chapter 2, archaeology does not seem to want Chaco "solved."

Once upon a time, public interpretation reflected the archaeological canon of its time: Archaeologists seemed fairly sure of their work and public providers respected that authority, up to a point. That changed amid the convulsions of Postmodernity and Culture Wars in the 1990s. Then and now in the twenty-first century, park rangers and interpreters (washed in the waters of constructivism) invite the public to speculate, maintaining that their guesses—lowercase "t" theories—are as good as those of the archaeologists.[36] And archaeologists, unprompted, will say: "I'm only guessing, of course"—when actually their statements are well-informed if tentative conclusions. In fact we aren't "guessing": We are making arguments informed from evidence—like historians or scientists.[37] Lowercase "t" theory undermines archaeology's authority.

Authority? In a rare and seemingly random conjunction, both academic théorie and American populism challenge authority. But think what the term means in scholarship: An expert, not an autarch. Every archaeologist has labored to become expert in fieldwork, analysis, interpretation, or all three. Every archaeologist has worked to acquire expertise in the prehistory of one or more regions. Archaeologists know a heck of a lot about many things, more than nonarchaeologists know about those things. So our guesses should be a lot better than their guesses.[38] We're experts: We must—as the poet said—recover our mojo, reclaim our authority. To do that, we need new methods. Those come in the next section.

Methods in the Madness

I wrote *A History of the Ancient Southwest*, in part, as an experiment in pre-historiography: Making up methods on the fly. A few other Southwesternists, over the years, have attempted pre-history, as I use that term here. I've always respected the historicity of David Wilcox (e.g., 1999; Wilcox et al. 2007) and Steven LeBlanc (e.g., 1989, 1999); and there are others. It is my impression, how-ever, that Southwestern archaeology and the larger field of American Anthro-pological Archaeology have not greatly valued their historical efforts or mine. I offer this comment not as a complaint (well, maybe a little), but as an index of American Anthropological Archaeology's ambivalence towards history: "Just-so stories" pretty much sums it up.[39]

Two recent and important articles that are fair barometers of the value we place on science, and the value we place on history:[40] "Grand Challenges for Ar-chaeology" by a group of fifteen eminent scholars (Kintigh et al. 2014a, 2014b), and "Key Issues and Topics in the Archaeology of the American Southwest and Northwestern Mexico" as seen by four outstanding Southwesternists (Plog et al. 2015). I have no quarrel with either, they are fine examples of orthodox American Anthropological Archaeology science; but I note that *history as a question* is essentially absent from both. History and pre-historiography are not considered "Grand Challenges" for American archaeology.[41] (I disagree.) In "Key Issues and Topics"—focused on the Southwest—history is allowed, but only late: "Culture history with an emphasis on the fifteenth and early sixteenth centuries" (Plog et al. 2015:3).[42] It seems that with colonization and the promise of Spanish docu-ments, we can perhaps do some history, and with Native migration stories maybe push things back a bit into the late protohistoric. But not before. (I disagree.)

With a few notable exceptions, discussed below, American Anthropological Archaeology has not concerned itself overmuch with pre-historiography.[43] We will have to build our own tools for analyzing, synthesizing, and producing pre-history. How would we do that?[44] Probably not Science. As noted in chapter 5, scientists don't write history; historians write history. As also noted in chapter 5, more than a few historians are pushing back into pre-historic times; but the tools of their trade remain (largely) documentary—papers. We'll have to roll our own.

This section has three parts. In the first part, "History and American An-thropological Archaeology," I summarize (1) recent attempts by archaeology to grapple with history within scientific frameworks, and (2) recent archaeological approaches within humanistic frameworks. In the second part of this section, I explore "Pre-historiography": Methods for writing narrative history from archaeological data. In the third and final part of this section, "Standards of Proof, Levels of Certainty," I explore methods for evaluating those narratives.

History in American Anthropological Archaeology

American Anthropological Archaeology has in the past sometimes addressed history and historiography—and happily, there seems to be an uptick in the topic! I briefly review several scientific takes on history: Eventful Archaeology, Path Dependence, and Cliodynamics. (Several other names you might expect to see here appear, instead, below in a discussion of more humanistic approaches.)

"Eventful Archaeology" comes from Robin A. Beck Jr., Douglas J. Bolender, James A. Brown, and Timothy K. Earle (2007) in a *Current Anthropology* article "Eventful Archaeology: The Place of Space in Structural Transformation." (See also Bolender 2010.) Following the theoretical framework of sociologist William Sewell (2005; himself building on Giddens), they define "event" as something that causes a radical change; in their term, a "rupture"—an unfortunate word and one of théorie's ugliest lexical sins. An archaeological rupture is a marked material change in a sequence; but events are a bit more complicated:

> Events...occur in three stages: (1) a sequence of context dependent happenings produces (2) multiple ruptures in the articulation of resources and schemas, creating (3) the opportunity for creative rearticulation within novel frames of reference. (Beck et al. 2007:835)

Events are consequential: "Ruptures" restructure society. Dramatic, epochal events (of course) are a fixture of conventional history, and they can form a framework for narrative. But historically significant events might fail to cause the sort of "ruptures" Beck and colleagues are after. The equation of "event" with major structural change implies that business as usual is ahistorical: Events are history, stasis is process.[45] This may be a useful compromise for processual archaeology coming to grips with history. The kinds of change seen in archaeology's rearview mirror as "ruptures" can be gradual and cumulative—as Beck and colleagues note—or sudden and catastrophic. Even stasis requires historical action, too: Gears must be greased to keep the machine purring along. But here's my point: You have to know the history *first* to tell what's a rupture and what's not. And it's not clear how Eventful Archaeology would do that.

Path Dependence is a concept originally developed in economics, which has been imported into a particular type of history (e.g., David 2007; Cliodynamics, of which more below) and, selectively, into archaeology. Michelle Hegmon, the chief Southwestern proponent:

Path dependence connotes a sense of becoming increasingly stuck in a particular way of doing things, and theories of path dependence attempt to explain how this happens, how the omnipresent past influences, weighs upon, and sometimes imposes nightmarish constraints on the present. (Hegmon 2017)

Hegmon, elsewhere: "We view path dependence as trajectories that are increasingly difficult to exit, because momentum and/or self-reinforcing processes create lock-in" (Hegmon et al. 2016:175). Stuck in a rut for the *longue durée*? In economics such a gummed-up situation was called "lock-in" and it constitutes one of many meanings Hodder proposes for his "entanglements." Technically, however, Path Dependence describes a condition or pattern, which can be analyzed and even mathematically expressed.

Paul David, looking at complex systems in historical narratives, notes that Path Dependence describes, but does not discover: "'Path dependence' is merely the label for a particular class of dynamic phenomena, not a theory to account for the way in which such systems behave" (David 2007:92). Again, *you must already know the history* before you can differentiate a rut from a trend or a process. What came before? What happened after? What are the contemporary restraints or impacts?

In the Southwest, Path Dependence has been applied to Hohokam canal systems: Infrastructure which subsequently shaped both Hohokam landscape and Hohokam history (Hegmon et al. 2016). That entanglement was fundamentally economic; while I'm sure much ritual and ideology accompanied canals, their engineering was solid and earthly. An example of ideological Path Dependence might be the Chaco Meridian. In both cases (and in other applications I've seen), Path Dependence requires us to know the path—that is, the historical narrative—before its concepts can be applied. Again: How do we do that? What's our pre-historiography?

Cliodynamics is sharply associated with Peter Turchin. (We met Turchin in chapter 4.) In his 2008 manifesto in *Nature*, "Arise 'Cliodyamics,'" Turchin announces his program: "Let history continue to focus on the particular. Cliodynamics, meanwhile, will develop unifying theories and test them with data generated by history [and] archaeology.... To truly learn from history, we must transform it into a science" (Turchin 2008:34–35). Turchin has high hopes: "Ultimately the aim is to discover general principles that explain the functioning and dynamics of actual historical societies."[46]

Turchin has not won many converts among conventional historians. "Cliodynamics is viewed with deep skepticism by most academic historians" (Spinney 2012:24). But the list of its science allies is impressive, including the Santa Fe

Institute and Human Relations Area Files; and a Cliodynamics Lab was established at the University of Hertfordshire in 2015.[47] While archaeologists of a certain age (mine) will sense a bit of déjà vu from New Archaeology, Cliodynamics (or something like it) seems here to stay.

A key point: Cliodynamics does not generate historical narratives, it analyzes existing narratives, looking for patterns and cycles. Cliodynamics "asks historians to explore the archives, or archaeologists to dig up data, and determine which theory's predictions best fit the data" (Turchin 2008:35; see also Krakauer 2007). Cliodynamics applies to existing histories.

Eventful Archaeology and Path Dependence and Cliodynamics all require us *to know the history before we do the science.* Quite correct, of course, but it leaves us wondering, still: How do we write history?

A handful of archaeologists have grappled with the problem from a more humanistic perspective, with varying success.[48]

History is most often lumped with Humanities, but sometimes with Social Sciences. With the "historical turn" in the social sciences came at least three varyingly humanistic approaches to archaeological historiography: Processual-Plus, Historical Processualism, and *Annales.* Michelle Hegmon's (2003) Processual-Plus quite properly admits history, and then attempts to control it scientifically through "path dependence" and various forms of "cliodynamics." That's all very well, but Processual-Plus is largely silent on actual pre-historiography.

History is center stage in Timothy Pauketat's (2001) Historical Processualism. But not as narrative. History melds with process and théorie: "History is the process of cultural construction through practice" (Pauketat 2001:87). While I do not share Pauketat's emphasis on agency and enthusiasm for religion and ritual,[49] I recognize Historical Processualism as a terrific methodological middle ground, and a real breakthrough.[50] I am a BIG fan, and so are many others.[51] Charles Cobb (2014) rebrands it Neohistorical Archaeology (see also Cobb 2005). Among many archaeologists taking this route in the eastern United States, I note with particular awe and envy Ken Sassaman's (2010) *The Eastern Archaic, Historicized.*[52] Not simply as an outstanding demonstration of the method, but also for its (correct) insistence that historicity applies to very deep and very distant times; in his case, the Archaic.[53]

More than a few American Anthropological Archaeologists were attracted to mid-twentieth-century French Annales School historiography, particularly the temporal rhythms of Fernand Braudel (e.g., Bintliff 1991, 2008; Knapp 2009). (Braudel's *longue durée*—somewhat predictably—has been invoked for Pueblo Space's famous changelessness.) But the full Annales program has not gained wide popularity in the Southwest or in American Anthropological Archaeology—it is, after all, history, not science.[54]

It is reassuring to know that there are other, very able archaeologists thinking about this, about history and why it matters: Michelle Hegmon, Severin Fowles, Timothy Pauketat, Ken Sassaman, Charles Cobb, and Alice Kehoe, among others mentioned throughout this book. And more importantly, perhaps, thinking about *how to do it*: How to write history. It's my impression that most of us, now, are making up methods as we move forward (or would that be backward?)—catching our historiography on the run, as it were. Whatever works. Someday pre-historiography (maybe by some other, nicer name) will be routinely taught in Method and Theory classes—but not yet.

We've seen what happens when archaeologists dabble in art history, without system or method: An iconological donnybrook. Just so with pre-history. Let's explore methods before we spin yarns. We need rules—or, more what you'd call "guidelines" than actual rules, as Captain Barbossa clarified the Code.

History and Pre-historiography: Same Logic, Different Data

To do any of those things—Path Dependence, Cliodynamics, Annales, whatever—we first need narrative histories.[55] "Narrative" has been hijacked, as have so many other innocent words, by théorie.[56] It is possible to speak of a "narrative turn"[57]—almost anything can be turned to the Dark Side. Let us be done with overtheorizing, and keep it simple: A narrative is a chronological story of events linked causally.[58] *A* caused *B* but didn't cause *C*. Normal narratives might have a beginning, a middle, and an end but archaeological narratives are probably exempt from that structure. Like a fragment of DNA, archaeological narratives will usually be segments of longer strings.

I will assert with great confidence that all archaeologists use narratives: Sequent accounts of what happened when, and why. For many (most?) American Anthropological Archaeologists, those narratives are not explicit, much less published. We carry these stories in our heads. Bring an archaeologist to the bar, buy him/her a couple, and ask this question: "What do you think actually happened?" They will have an answer, they will tell a narrative. It is specious to pretend that those internal narratives—fully developed, tentative, or inchoate—do not influence our archaeology.[59] Our peers review and critique almost every product we produce, from reports and articles to monographs. Why not put our narratives out there for all to see? We should be comparing and critiquing narratives much as we compare and critique chronologies.

Whatever else comes from this book—my last hurrah—I challenge my colleagues to make their narratives known. Make YOUR narratives known! It's not enough to declare vague theoretical alliances: "My work is informed by feminist theory, subaltern studies, and structuration" or "I follow evolutionary ecology." You owe it to us and to them (the ancients) to also lay out your actual notions of prehistory, your narratives. The exercise would be of benefit not only to us and to them, but also perhaps to you.

To repeat my argument made in earlier chapters: Formal narratives should be fundamental to our work. I believe that archaeology's primary focus should be producing histories of ancient times on our continent. Once we have workable histories, then we can and should use that history for science.

What sort of history? Academic historians long ago tired of "kings-and-battles histories"—a dismissive term for conventional narratives of Great Men/Women and Great Events. They wanted something new: Théorie, social history, microhistory, whatever. But these academic experiments are necessarily framed in (or against) existing "kings-and-battles history," the accepted narratives for particular places and times. That is, Historians already have narratives to work with or work against. The Southwest has yet to settle on that kind of history, its narrative history, its "chronologically tight, sequential stories." (The Pecos sequence is not narrative. Culture History is not narrative.) We have only one regional narrative history (mine) and I'm sure you will agree it needs work. New Histories must be written, however that plays out: Kings-and-battles, cabbages-and-kings, corn-beans-and-squash, none-of-the-above.

In European archaeology, the need for narrative appears to be assumed. After they verified a few hoary quasihistorical narratives (Troy and Knossos at *fin de siècle*), archaeology in the Old World busied itself with internal affairs and wrote narratives of Eurasian prehistory, for example Childe's (1942) *What Happened in History*. And thereafter, they revised and rewrote them (Think: "Radiocarbon Revolution"). Narrative is what they do, what they always did.[60]

Here's some relevant European historiographic théorie from Matthew Johnson—a very smart guy—who devotes a short chapter in his 300-page *Archaeological Theory: An Introduction* to "Archaeology and History" (Johnson 2010: 185–198).[61] He begins by briefly considering "Traditional History" (which here I call conventional History, to distinguish it from Native Traditional Histories; so I've taken the liberty of substituting my term for his):

> Coupled with an empiricist and inductivist approach to the material went a stress on history as a narrative of political events. [Conventional] historians told a story. [Conventional] history books often have a beginning, a middle and an end to their plots. Indeed, it can be argued that while [conventional] historians protested (and protest) that they have no theory, in fact they follow literary rules of narrative and emplotment that have been ably characterized by historical theorist Hayden White.[62] [Conventional] political history of this kind continues to be written to the present day. However, there has been a widening of historical thinking. (Johnson 2010:186)

After describing a few of these historical theories (Annales, etc.), he concludes with the rather depressing observation that théorie has so fragmented the discipline of History and "the human sciences as a whole" that there is no point in appealing to history or any other discipline's methods. "There is no salvation for archaeological thought in turning to the methods of another discipline, since the unity of methods professed by that discipline is invariably illusory" (Johnson 2010:189). That is: Théorie (intentionally) made a mess of academic History; therefore, we can't appeal to history without specifying what kind of "history" we mean.

Fair enough. What I mean is Johnson's "traditional [conventional] history." That is, "a narrative of political events." That antique art continues to be practiced by a diminished but still vital segment of academic historians and by wider and more widely read public historians. Can we actually do that for prehistory? You betcha! Years ago, Fernand Braudel proclaimed *avec vigueur patriotique*:

> Never say that prehistory is not history. Never say that there was "no such thing" as Gaul before Gaul, or France before France, or seek to deny that many features of both Gaul and France can be explained by the millennia dating from before the Roman conquest.... At one time, historians used to stake their reputations on exploring from both sides the artificial frontiers erected between antiquity and the Middle Ages, or between the Middle Ages and the modern period. The great challenge of our time must surely be the divide between prehistory and history. (Braudel 1990:21)

More than a few historians seem interested in enlarging their portfolios and moving back into our turf, into the "pre."[63] Big History (discussed in chapter 4) repeatedly and unapologetically poaches prehistory.[64] Perhaps prehistory is too important to be left to the archaeologists?[65]

Archaeology (famously) reaches out to many other disciplines but, strangely, not often to history. Ian Morris—a right-thinking Classical archaeologist—is perplexed: "Archaeologists seem uniquely insulated from historical thought, despite being the only other academic group defined by an obsessive focus on the human past" (Morris 2000:19).[66] What Morris said for European Archaeology[67]—which began and remains notably historical—goes double, triple, quadruple for American Anthropological Archaeology, which (as discussed in chapter 1) shunned history for perceived strengths of the Science of Man—to use an antiquated, gendered formulation.

I submit that there is no difference in the logics of history and pre-history, only differences in data. Historians assemble and assess data (source criticism), build chronologies of events, synthesize and interpret causes and meanings, and produce narratives. Archaeologists routinely do all that—except narrative—but with different data.[68]

We need to think this through, something like the analytical historiography of the first fifty pages of Hayden White's (1973) *Metahistory*.[69] Mark Pluciennik (1999) attempted something along these lines for archaeological narrative: "Narratives have been and are the dominant form in which the past is presented, yet for historical philosophical reasons there has been a tendency to analyze them only insofar as they can be treated as a form of explanation or knowledge analogous to that [of] science" (Pluciennik 1999:668). He analyzes narrative, for example identifying "the constituents of narrative": "Characters" (which can be collectives); "events"; "plots"; "scales, contexts, explanations." It's a useful start. But I'd like to see an analysis of narrative that isn't so worried about Bourdieu looking over its shoulder.

Let's start simply, and save théorie for later, or never. For now, be an under-nuanced, overconfident American realist: there IS a knowable past.[70] And if there isn't a real past, then—as Voltaire is said to have said of God—it would be necessary to create one. Otherwise, archaeology seems irrelevant.

"Why, then, has it taken so long to initiate an explicit inquiry into archaeological historiography?" ask Severin Fowles and Barbara Mills in their introduction to the 2017 *Oxford Handbook of Southwest Archaeology*. Why, indeed. I attempted an archaeological historiography in that same volume (Lekson 2017) and I expand that essay here.

Tools of the Trade

A History of the Ancient Southwest, written a decade ago, continued an experiment begun in 1999's *Chaco Meridian*, exploring historiography for pre-history. I stumbled through the process, making up tricks and techniques and methods as suggested by or required by the data. First, history of what? (Not thematically, but analytically.) Second, a few ground rules, three now semi-infamous dicta: "No coincidences"; "Everybody knew everything"; and "Distances can be dealt with." Third and lastly, a throwaway tag which is, in fact, a method: "Connect the dots." That last might be the most important, methodologically. But we'll work through them all, briefly.

History of What?

Aggregates, not individuals! Some historians argue that history is essentially biography. Not economic or environmental historians, or any historian dealing with *longues durées* and large areas; but still, at its heart, history has documents written by or about people, and those people can be known, analyzed, interrogated, corrected, and so forth to greater or lesser degrees. Micro-history is all about individuals or small groups of individuals. Archaeology works with aggregates, with meso- and macro-history. And on geographic scales. Our narratives will have far more in common with historical geography than, for example, with biography.[71] Critics carp about my taxonomic units acting as players, agents, historical figures: Chaco rose, Mimbres fell, Hohokam expanded, and so forth.[72] Promoting phases and cultures to protagonists seems old school. That's how they wrote in the 1940s. Well, yes: It's a bit of a reverse (much like NAGPRA's antiquated notions of archaeology) but—like NAGPRA—it's necessary.

I chose political history; that is, narratives of what we, today, would call political institutions and actions.[73] Who knows what they called it then? (We'd have to know the ancient ontology, and I'm pretty sure that's impossible.) In any event, I chose politics because it's a lot easier to see political institutions than it is to see, for example, ideologies or ontologies. Leadership manifests itself, often, in architecture and landscapes. Ideologies float above all that—although they certainly influence the built environment. Economics would be another good place to start, or technology. We can see all those things. Of course the ancients did not separate church and state, but I wasn't writing history for them (or their descendants) but for us, today—as discussed in chapter 5. Our histories should make sense of the past for us, now; not for the them, then. Be they friends, Romans, countrymen, or Chacoans.[74]

Ground Rules

A decade on, *A History of the Ancient Southwest*'s ground rules have (for me) become self-evident truths, almost axioms.[75] Not so for everyone, of course; so I will briefly revisit them here. I do this in part because they have caused me grief, not so much for their content but for their titles. More than a few of my colleagues read the titles but read no further.[76]

No Coincidences

Of course there are coincidences! The problem is that with Culture History—and the Processual and Processual-Plus program underwritten by Culture History—EVERYTHING is a coincidence. Contemporaneous or sequential causal connections are, to say the least, discouraged. What if we turned that on its head? Events big enough to be archaeologically visible almost certainly had historical contexts and causes and consequences—and by "events" I mean everything from a phase to a volcanic eruption. What if our assumption was that archaeological events were, more often than not, a historical nexus of other archaeological events? My "no coincidences" is not unlike Fernand Braudel's (1990) *conjunctures*: The operational simultaneity of events or trends over the broader field.[77]

A thumbnail example: Chaco rose as Hohokam fell. Mimbres was contemporary with both; early Mimbres was clearly cozy with Hohokam and later Mimbres looked a lot like Chaco. If we silo Hohokam, Chaco, and Mimbres—which we tend to do—these things are merely coincidences; if we look at them ensemble, they are history (Lekson 2009a). No coincidences!

Everybody Knew Everything

Of course everyone did NOT know everything. Doctor-Colonel Irina Spalko got to know everything the Crystal Skull knew, and look what happened to her (and, alas, to the franchise). No, not everything; but they knew a lot more than we've customarily given them credit for. American Anthropological Archaeology's early notions of Native savvy and intelligence were not flattering. Ancient Indians—it was assumed—knew little about their continent beyond their immediate (small) environs. Historic and ethnologic accounts tell of communications and direct actions crossing half the continent, but those were generally explained as reactions to colonialism. For prehistory—before Europeans galvanized the continent—rock-solid evidence (say, an exotic artifact) was required to suggest broader information, and even then was typically minimalized or dismissed as "down-the-line exchange"—our sure cure for the inconveniently out of place. Our assumptions put Native Americans in the lowest percentile among humans for geo-curiosity. As discussed in chapter 4, World History studies human networking, and everywhere World History looks, it finds extensive networks. Except in ancient America north of Mexico.

Another thumbnail: Let's assume that *everybody knew everything* regionally. F'rinstance, everyone in the Southwest was aware—more or less, with varying levels of specificity—of great cities and civilizations to the south, even while Southwestern peoples themselves were first figuring out how to be villagers. (Southwest-Mesoamerican "contacts" started long before Chaco.) Indeed, they did not have to "invent" villages; people had done that several thousand years before villages appeared in the Southwest (Lekson 2012). By the fifth or sixth century (and probably long before), the most solitary, poor, nasty, brutish Southwestern hunter-gatherer would know about cities. Or rumors of cities. So, too, kings and nobles, known at least in the abstract.

Distances Can Be Dealt With

Alice Kehoe's tagline—and a basic premise of World History. Distances intimidate American Anthropological Archaeology, but distance did not intimidate ancient North Americans.[78] PaleoIndians sprinted back and forth across the continent. Hopewell demonstrated what hunter-gatherer-horticulturists could do, gathering goodies across half the continent. A millennium earlier Poverty Point, and a millennium later Mississippian and Southwestern "exchange systems" or "interaction spheres," were comparable in scale and scope. Two thousand years of conspicuous exoticism.

And, of course, long-distance interactions came with the territory in Mesoamerica; in fact one could say that long-distance interactions defined that territory, from Mother Cultures to International Styles. And particularly in the post-Classic period, which was the era of Mesoamerica contemporary with

Chaco and post-Chaco. So: Distances, in ancient North America, could be dealt with.

A thumbnail: Chocolate at Chaco! The recent discovery of cacao at Chaco and other Southwestern sites (Crown and Hurst 2009) tops a growing pile of evidence of long-distance hanky-panky. Cacao came from the lower Gulf Coast or the Pacific Coast of West Mexico: Something like 2,000 km airline from Chaco. Cacao in itself is a wonderful discovery and, on the larger scale, cacao is perhaps the final sand grain atop the pile that starts the cascade. Cacao makes it possible for heretofore isolationist (or uninterested) archaeologists to accept the inevitable: The Southwest was part of the greater Mesoamerican world. Readers may scowl and mutter: "We've always known that!" True: We've had spectacular evidence for South in the North for over a century. Sure, we've always known, but (with a few largely unsuccessful exceptions) *we have not acted on that knowledge, historically.* We've ignored, minimized, normalized these things, and swept them under the rug. Throughout the twentieth century and into the twenty-first century, we contextualized our research not in reference to greater North America, but more comfortably within Pueblo Space. That seems to be changing.

My three assumptions, ground rules: No coincidences; everybody knew everything; distances can be dealt with. My method in *A History of the Ancient Southwest*? "Connect the dots."

Connecting the Dots

I originally equated dot-connecting with 1990s British Interpretive Archaeology (minus the rhetorical blather)—correctly, I think. Today, I would emphasize that dot-connecting is the essence of thinking historically: "This" caused "that," and "that" could not have happened without a prior "the other," and so forth. And some dots—maybe most dots—don't connect. That's important to know, too. But it's causal connections that give us narrative lines: Not the disconnected phase sequences which characterized classic Culture History. Rather, a dynamic history over the long term (but perhaps not the *longue durée*) with causes and effects, plus a few squibs and MacGuffins. F'rinstance: Pueblo worldviews arose in rejection of and reaction to Chaco.

Connecting the dots may require some connective creativity, but not manipulation of the facts. Mark Twain misquoted Herodotus: "Very few things happen at the right time, and the rest do not happen at all; the conscientious historian will correct those defects." Not the practical pre-historian, who must respect the timing of facts, and the facts themselves.

Connecting the dots is *what history does*. Historians have a word for it: Colligation. Dictionary definitions of "colligation" revolve around connecting together isolated things and facts by a material or intellectual appliance. The historical use is more specialized but it's close to what I have in mind. From C. Behan McCullagh's essay on "Colligation": "Sometimes historians write, not to answer a question, but to display a pattern which gives each of those events meaning and significance, and which sometimes helps to explain them. The practice of producing patterns like this is called 'colligation'" (McCullagh 2009: 152). And George Kubler (over half a century ago!) in *The Shape of Time: Remarks on the History of Things* (1962): "Unless he is an annalist or a chronicler, the historian communicates a pattern which was invisible to his subjects when they lived it, and unknown to his contemporaries before he detected it" (Kubler 1962:13).

How to connect the dots? How to colligate? I propose three tools: triangulation, commensuration, and models/counterfactuals.

The first of three tools: *Triangulation*. My use of "triangulation" harks back to land-surveying and geodetic work: "Fixing" historical events at the intersections of a mesh of viewpoints—prior, post, peer events.[79] If event *X* is our focus, what do we know about what came *prior*, before *X*? What happened *post*, after *X*? What *peer* events were contemporarily with *X*?

A thumbnail, from Chaco: The regional center at Chaco seemed to arise de novo, without precedent in the Southwest. And it appeared to end just as abruptly, with no issue. With more data, we know now that the first fledging steps towards Chaco's class structure and regional supremacy happened not at Chaco Canyon, but a century earlier and 100 miles to the north—Chaco's "prior." Construction ceased at Chaco around 1125; this date has been conventionally used as signaling Chaco's fall. But we now know that Chaco did not "fall" or collapse, but rather, at about 1090, deliberately shifted north to build a new successor capital at the misnamed Aztec Ruins. Aztec Ruins—Chaco's "post"—continued Chaco's regional role in the Southwest. And what of Chaco's "peers," its contemporaries? A remarkable civilization known as Hohokam rose and fell in the desert 250 miles south of Chaco: Rose as the earliest stirrings of Chacoan political structure emerged and fell as Chaco itself rose and expanded. That timing was probably not coincidental. By "triangulating" Chaco—prior, post, and peer events—we have a much richer historical account.[80]

The second tool: *Commensuration*. Comparison, comparison, comparison—relentless comparisons. Comparison is archaeology's most robust logic.[81] We may not be able to determine the nature of an event simply by studying it, analyzing it, theorizing it. But we can reliably determine that *A* was bigger than *B*, or longer, or shorter, or denser, or less organized, etc. Some dimensions are mathematical and therefore universal; others will be rooted in Eurocentric experiences and concepts. As long as we acknowledge and track those biases, I'd say all's fair in apples and oranges—and in oranges and potatoes. By building up a matrix of comparisons, we add meaning to the mesh of triangulations.

An example, again from North America, Chaco and Cahokia, whom we met in chapter 4. Chaco embraced Mesoamerican political and ideological symbolism, to legitimize its centrality and importance. Cahokia, on the other hand, was enormously larger than Chaco (and many Mesoamerican cities) and needed no Mesoamerican embellishments to cement its status. Comparisons of their scale demonstrate this: Cahokia was perhaps ten times larger than Chaco in population. Cahokia's regional impact was enormously larger than Chaco's: Cahokia's world encompassed perhaps ten eastern states, any one of which is larger than Chaco's region. (But Cahokia's core area, its area of actual political control, was probably smaller than Chaco's.) Cahokia's control of labor, building huge pyramids, dwarfs Chaco's monuments. In almost every dimension we can compare, Cahokia was larger than Chaco. Yet Chaco had many exotic Mesoamerican elements, while Cahokia had few or none. We can be certain that Chaco and Cahokia were fully aware of Mesoamerica; but their different engagements led Peter Peregrine and I to conclude Chaco needed Mesoamerica while Cahokia did not (chapter 4; Peregrine and Lekson 2012).

An example from the Southwest: Catherine Cameron and Andrew Duff's (2008) comparison of post-Chaco trajectories in the north and the south of the old Chaco World. The north had an ineffective successor capital at Aztec Ruins; the political turmoil caused defensive aggregation of commoners into large Mesa Verde villages. The south was beyond Aztec's reach, and the older pattern of "outlier" Great Houses surrounded by communities of commoners persisted long after Chaco's end—eventually giving way to large aggregated villages, perhaps as northern turmoil spread southward.

And, finally, the third tool(s): *Models* and *counterfactuals*.[82] In the Southwest, computer models or simulations of ancient societies have reached a high degree of development. Success is measured by how close the models parallel our ideas about what happened in the ancient Southwest—that is, the events as we perceive them. An example: Chaco ended with a shift of the capital to Aztec Ruins followed a century later by the total depopulation of the region. Tens of thousands of people out-migrated, presumably in response to well-documented climatic deterioration. The most sophisticated models of demography in Chaco's region, however, show that the region—despite climatic deterioration—could have supported up to half of the original population. That is, all those ancient people did not have to leave. This model—a form of counterfactual—suggests that the out-migration was as much a political as an economic or environmental event.

Most models are agent based and bottom up, and therefore dependent on how we believe that ancient peoples behaved—that is, their human nature. *Homo ludens*? *Homo economicus*? *Homo horribilis*? Those assumptions make all the difference in how models play out, suggesting a role for counterfactuals—historical what-ifs. What if we recalibrate our models on the assumption that people were aggressive, or aggrandizing, or altruistic? What if we impose top-down assumptions—anathema in agent-based models and much American Anthropological Archaeological thinking—how would the New World look? I submit that many New World large-scale archaeological and ethnohistorical patterns and distributions, currently euphemized as "horizons" or "styles" or "culture areas" would look rather like Old World *oikoumene*, trading spheres, economies, and even (gasp!) empires. More counterfactuals.

Ross Hassig provided a review of counterfactuals in archaeological application:

> The fundamental question underlying counterfactual speculation is whether past events could have taken a different course than the one they did, with the answer having implications for both historical and ethnographic research. While the response to this question is necessarily hypothetical, a counterfactual approach attempts to show plausible instances in which the road not taken very well could have been, with significant consequences for the subsequent course of history, whether the ending point of interest is the past or today. One goal, then, is to use counterfactual analysis to "proof" one's interpretation by altering the presumed cause and attempting to determine whether or not the outcome would be changed as a result. (Hassig 2001:58)

Here's an example, relevant to the argument of this book—indeed, not only relevant, but inspirational! Recall Gordon Vivian's observation "if Chaco had continued…" presented in chapter 2, note 2. That's a counterfactual! Vivian reached the painful conclusion that "the continuation of the direction taken by the Chaco group would have carried it even farther out of the stream of development that culminated in the Rio Grande" (Vivian and Mathews 1965:115). Vivian could reasonably imagine that Chaco *if it continued* was headed in a direction that led away from Pueblo Space. The counterfactual insight was therefore that Chaco *did not* continue. But Vivian's insight was ignored in almost all subsequent Chaco literature, keeping Chaco in Pueblo Space.

Many historians disdain counterfactuals, dismissing them as parlor games.[83] But I submit that any careful historian or pre-historian will use counterfactuals at least in their abbreviated form of "what if?" Before reaching a narrative conclusion, the careful prehistorian will consider a range of likely (and unlikely) what-ifs. "I think it was thus, but what if I'm wrong and instead of thus, it was that? Or that? Or that?" That part of the process seldom makes it into print; some of it should.

Counterfactuals, like models, should be used with caution and discretion. Initial assumptions and counterfacts could easily degenerate into the sort of what-would-I-expect-to-see delusions of scientism. Because initial conditions have ramifying effects, I suggest that both models and counterfactuals should be kept short, only a few time increments or a few causal steps. The long elaborate models of VEP—although brilliantly conceived—become something like black boxes, with input and output but the interior processes hidden, as it were, from sight. Rather like Bayesianism. Similarly, counterfactuals can become historical fantasies—indeed, a genre called "alternate histories." (Think *Man in the High Castle*.) Hassig argues "for a useful role for counterfactual analysis, *not in writing fiction*, but in assessing pivotal causation and proofing [evaluating] causal arguments" (2001:57, emphasis added).

For American archaeologists the very idea of "fiction" makes the skin crawl—OMG! Just-so stories! But if one keeps an open mind, we might learn some useful things (both positive and negative) from historical fiction.[84] Because thinking briefly about historical fiction may throw a bit of light down the Ontological Rabbit Hole.

Insofar as it is grounded on historical fact, historical fiction is not entirely fiction. I'm not talking about swashbucklers or bodice-rippers or fantasies, but good historical fiction. Think Patrick O'Brien or Mary Renault or even that old reprobate George McDonald Fraser. I'm not defending these as great literature but as convincing historical reconstructions. Surely pre-history and good historical fiction will share some methodological chops.[85] Both interpret, extrapolate from facts to sequences, causes, and narratives.

Where the two genres differ most strikingly is in plot and characters. Fiction (unless postmodern) must have a plot that carries a story and resolves the issues. History does not have to do those things, because history is often rather random. As Mark Twain supposedly said: "It's no wonder that truth is stranger than fiction. Fiction has to make sense." History does not: Things can simply end or dribble off or remain unresolved. Perhaps more importantly, pre-history can't rely on characters. Historical fiction uses characters to move the plot along, or uses the plot to move the characters, or uses characters to otherwise enthrall the reader. Characters and their thoughts and motivations make historical fiction work. And that's a huge difference: Archaeological pre-history can't do much with characters; we can't do thoughts and motivations.[86]

Aggregates, not individuals. Having cultures or collectives as characters makes for a boring novel, but better prehistory. It stays closer to the data—but not too close![87]

Matters of Style

History is a literature. Hayden White, one of the leading American historiographers, insisted that published history may not be "true" but it can be "poetic" (1973). That's a hard sell to science-leaning American Anthropological Archaeologists—or even, perhaps, to those beguiled by théorie. So I am NOT advocating that our prehistory becomes only literature. But, as David Lowenthal reminds us: "An intelligible past demands inventive retelling" (2015:341). Style matters. Not more than substance, but style is a key element of historiography. Environmental historian William Cronon:

> Historians have never abandoned our commitment to narrative storytelling as an essential rhetorical and analytical tool for conveying historical knowledge. This is consistent with our preferred styles of causal explanation, our periodizing impulses, our commitment to thick description and contextualization—but it also reflects the sense many of us share that history at its very best remains a form of literature, as much an art as a science. Historians have not forgotten that Clio was among the nine Muses of Greek mythology, and we are proud that her patronage of history sets our discipline apart from most others in the modern academy. (Cronon 2004:5–6)

American Anthropological Archaeologists seem ambivalent about style. Most American Anthropological Archaeologists believe that proper, scientific style is dull. Just the facts, ma'am (attributed to laconic Sgt. Joe Friday, LAPD, although he never actually said it; the glib Stan Freberg did). At the left end of the dial, *théoriciens* very much value style, sometimes over substance. One risks rhetorical whiplash moving from "Resource Breadth and Niche Creation in Pre-Pottery Neolithic: The Phytolith Evidence" to "Ontological Entanglements of Animism in Bronze-Age Croatia: Irony or Anomie?" in the same professional journal.

What style for narrative prehistory? I urge (but do not practice) plain speaking: One damn thing after another, this led to that: "Kings-and-battles" if such there were. Why not model our work on good "popular" history, Pulitzer Prize history? Doris Kearns Goodwin, David McCullough, Barbara Tuchman, Simon Schama—you know the ones to read. The difference between an assistant professor of cultural history and a good popular historian isn't only that the popular historian makes a lot more money; a successful popular historian also makes more of a difference. There would be no Miranda's Hamilton without Chernow's Hamilton. Who is our audience? Once past the profession itself, the reading public (chapter 5). Give 'em something good to read.

Write arguments to persuade, in plain English. Avoid academese. Avoid théorie gibberish: Do not give ammunition to archaeology's enemies. And, by writing clearly, confirm the field's value to archaeology's friends. The medium is a large part of the message: So mind your language!

Native Accounts: Trust, but Verify

Many people (archaeologists, Indians, and civilians) assume when I talk about "writing prehistory" I am talking about working with Pueblo traditional histories, tracing migrations and so forth. There has been a steady trickle of excellent work along these lines over the years, and more recently an explosion of new scholarship.[88]

But that's not what I have in mind. Archaeology is history—pre-history—or it is nothing. And pre-history is pre-history: Not the adoption or reconciliation of traditional accounts, but the extension of Western historiography to ancient times, absent documents. Pueblo traditional histories are one line of evidence, to be scrutinized and evaluated like other lines of evidence.[89] That's perhaps not the kind of thing one should say in postcolonial times: If these necessary preliminaries raise your ire and boil your blood, skip this section. Move along, nothing to see here.

Doveryai, no proveryai: A Russian proverb President Reagan dropped on Secretary Gorbachev while cutting a deal on nuclear missiles. In NAGPRA, tribal traditions and archaeology are evidentiary equals. But in archaeological pre-historiography, that is probably not the case. Pre-history should respect but not revere Native heritage, traditional histories.[90] Trust, but verify.

It is essential to keep in mind the distinction between history and heritage made in chapter 5. "History" is what happened in the past, understood in Western terms, or (if you like) ontologies. "Heritage" is the uses of the past in the present and covers a wide range, including "traditional histories." In that framework, history and heritage (traditional histories) are rather different things. Of course these are all White Guy categories; they are all English words, and they all represent "common" Western ontologies. That's the line I'm following.

Traditional histories comprise various genres and forms, but the traditional histories most often shared by Natives with non-Natives are usually origin or migration stories: Part cosmology, part philosophy, part poetry, part history.[91]

As in everything else in Southwestern archaeology, it is salutary to think outside Pueblo Space. How do archaeologists in other parts of the world deal with traditional histories and heritage accounts? That varies from place to place, and from archaeology to archaeology.[92]

One of the most useful reviews of the archaeological use of traditional history/heritage comes from Michael Smith (2011b), who critiqued Native traditional histories of Tula and Chichén Itzá—or rather, archaeologists' use of those traditional histories. His entire essay is well worth reading by every practicing Southwestern archaeologist.[93] After summarizing a number of recent, systematic studies of traditional or oral history, he concludes:

> Mesoamericanists should heed the call of Peter R. Schmidt for archaeologists to "set aside the literal and facile treatments of oral histories" (Schmidt 1990:270).... Just as scholars now accept the revisionist interpretation of documents like the Sumerian king lists, it is time for Mesoamericanists to acknowledge the mythological nature of colonial-period native history, at least for the earliest periods. (Smith 2011b:478)

In the Southwest, archaeology's attitude toward traditional histories has varied over the years. Robert Lowie famously pronounced, "I cannot attach to oral traditions any historical value whatsoever under any conditions whatsoever" (1915:598). Today we are more open-minded if not open-handed, but still selective about what parts of Pueblo traditions (as we know them) we accept, and which we reject.[94] The criteria often appear to be conformities to Pueblo Space: If it fits Pueblo Space, we use it; otherwise, it's a myth. We accept migration stories but ignore stories that suggest behaviors outside Pueblo Space: People with power over people, wars, and so forth.[95] And of course we politely ignore the pervasive supernatural.

While it may strike some readers as impolite or impolitic, here are a few considerations for working with traditional histories in the Southwest (building in part on Smith 2011b):

Traditional histories have different senses of time. Conventional Western history follows sequential, linear time. Many Native traditions do not—I speak here of historical time, not quotidian time. Although they proceed as narratives, the sense of time in traditional histories can be strikingly nonlinear.[96] While conflation of past and present may comfort proponents of up-streaming and the ethnological method, it poses difficulties for critical pre-historiography. How much, in any account, is past and how much is present?

Traditional histories have decay rates. Claims have been made for great antiquity,[97] but it would be mystical to believe that traditional histories accurately represent events of great antiquity in any detail.[98] This is a salient feature of Pueblo Space: Traditions handed down from time immemorial. Intriguingly, there is reason to think that less stratified societies—as in Pueblo Space—transmit more accurate information than societies with "court histories."[99]

Traditional histories are often closely linked to landscape features, which operate as markers or reminders of events.[100] The cliffs were CliffsNotes. This may be why Navajo accounts of Chaco are detailed and full of incidents specific to places, while Pueblo accounts tend to be more general—at least, Pueblo accounts I have heard.[101]

Traditional histories may be restricted or redacted. As discussed in chapter 5 (the controversies over "Origin Myth of Acoma Pueblo"), traditional accounts are largely kept by tribes for tribes, and not available for the practical pre-historian. Official accounts—written for the public by tribal officials—are often sparse narratives of migration, establishing a presence or claim. Moreover, some parts of the traditional histories are reserved from other tribal people by those entrusted with that knowledge, to be shared only on a need-to-know basis or at particular times.[102] Archaeologists access those accounts in successful collaborations (usually doing research beneficial to the tribe) but cannot use that knowledge in any but the most general, thematic way. This reduces us largely to published ethnographic accounts, Ware's classic ethnographies. As we've seen with the Nabokov controversy (in chapter 5), those published accounts are not always authorized by the tribes. And there's more.

Traditional histories recorded by anthropologists may be bogus.[103] It's complicated. Anthropologists—never popular among Pueblos—asked Natives questions. Natives gave them answers. Anthropologists asked for stories. Natives told them stories. Sometimes bogus: Tales today tell about how great-uncle so-and-so gave that pompous anthropologist a complete line of hooey (my words, not theirs). Stories of punked anthros are sufficiently numerous that some of them must be true. Even the classic Ethnographies? Who knows? *Doveryai, no proveryai.*

Traditional histories have different notions of precision and accuracy. There is truth, and there is Truth. Some traditional histories are king's lists and chronicles (not in the Southwest!) and require veracity or at least verisimilitude. Other traditional histories are teaching tools or parables. Great accuracy is not demanded to get a point across.[104]

Traditional histories have political implications. The loss of Native lands needs no rehearsal here. All tribes are keenly attuned to land issues and to other legal matters.[105] Traditional histories, and especially migration stories, are geographic. And that geography generally extends far beyond today's reservations, grants, and nations. Those seem to be the parts of traditional histories one hears most often: This clan was here, that clan was there. Making migration a matter of record seems to have no downside: Land Claims and NAGPRA relied heavily on published accounts in addition, of course, to oral testimony.[106]

Traditional histories are, most importantly, heritage. They invoke the past to make sense of the present, to educate and enculturate the young.[107] To explain the present, they can and perhaps must change with circumstances (e.g., Nabokov 2002:98–101).

Of course, many of these things could be said of conventional Western history: History is certainly political; history is shaped by its times; history can be fooled by false accounts; history can be redacted or restricted. Indeed, history can slip into heritage—a constant concern for the critical reader. But these are generalities: Every discourse (we are told) is political, a reflection of its times, potentially false, potentially private. The clear differences between conventional and traditional histories are not minor: Linear versus cyclic (nonlinear); written and fixed versus oral and malleable. But, moreover, history (like archaeology) is based on European Enlightenment values: Critical, empirical, universal, rational, and—importantly—open to correction. These are not heritage qualities.

Traditional histories and Western histories are genres that pass in the night—to repeat a phrase from chapter 5. Based on vastly different epistemologies and ontologies, they are largely incommensurable. And one cannot replace the other, because they are constructed for very different purposes, and—most importantly—for very different audiences.

Who is the audience? That, again, is the heart of the matter. Native traditions are heritage for a Native audience. Conventional history is narratives for a universal audience.

Standards of Proof, Levels of Certainty

One review of *A History of the Ancient Southwest* posed a statement straight out of science: "There is no way to know how much of this history Lekson has gotten right." That, of course, is true of history in general.

We must allow (and welcome) multiple versions of historical events and then judge them comparatively, which are plausible and then which are more than likely true. It will not be possible to demonstrate, scientifically, which of several competing well-founded, well-argued histories is in any absolute sense "correct." Peter Turchin (2013) pondered the Decline and Fall: "More than two hundred explanations have been proposed for why the Roman Empire fell. But we still don't know which of these hypotheses are plausible, and which should be rejected." A reader of history must be a reader of histories, as Jacque Barzun said.

Multiple narratives are not necessarily evil: Two (or three or four or more) different arguments for the fall of Rome may be cumulatively useful. Gibbon for this, Toyenbee for that, Tainter for the other.[108] Like theory, all history is local?

How do we evaluate archaeological statements? How do we decide what to accept?[109] ("Believe" and "belief" should not enter too often into archaeological discourse.)[110] It too often comes down to your personal choice: You are or are not convinced. But in an arena of unrecognized bias—in this case, Pueblo Space—should it be left *entirely* up to you? Because bias trumps facts. As Pat Moynihan is said to have said: You are entitled to your own opinion, but not your own facts.[111] Might there be some way to tag elements of an argument—"facts"—for their reliability? Something other than your opinion or my opinion; something factual, however vaguely factual?

Facts are one part of the problem (to which we will return!). Argument is the other. We argue from facts, and our argument interprets the facts and tells the story, or history.

History is persuasion, not hypothesis-testing. I described my methods (emerging and inchoate in *Chaco Meridian* and *History of the Ancient Southwest*) as "argument and persuasion"—and was roundly criticized for it.[112] But argument is the rhetoric of history: Historical arguments must *convince*: Persuasion, convincement.[113]

I have presented, for example, what I consider to be very strong factual arguments to colleagues content in Pueblo Space, who responded "I am not convinced," and walked away from the argument. What does one say to that? I myself am convinced to my very bones that "I am not convinced," in these cases, actually means: "Your argument is headed in inconvenient directions, beyond Pueblo Space: Therefore, I consider it an extraordinary argument; therefore, I demand some sort of hard-to-imagine smoking-gun proof; therefore, I am not convinced." Convincement is the final verdict, "I am not convinced" the Fore-closer of All Argument.

So…let me (try to) convince you that convincement is not simply a matter of belief, but perhaps a workable method. I will first look at business as usual: Ad hominem and peer review; then sample statistical certainty; and end with a brief legal brief.

Convincement: "To the Man" and Juries of Peers

Ad hominem is generally taken to mean arguing negatively against an idea by attacking the proponent of that idea. For example: "His ideas about economics are lousy because he wears silly shoes." But I use the term here more broadly and a bit more positively, in its literal sense "to the man/woman." That is, the qualities of the person; and those could be good qualities. In this sense, appeal to authority is ad hominem: Professor X is known to be brilliant; Professor X said it; so I believe it and that settles it.

We routinely use ad hominem—both positive and negative—to evaluate competing historical narratives. Two best-selling biographies of Ulysses Grant, both using the same documentary resources and both winning awards—present very different interpretations of the man. Grant was quietly great, Grant was a bloodthirsty bum.[114] Most readers, I think, would go ad hominem on the authors. Who's the bigger name? Who is pushing what agenda? And so forth.

Ad hominem becomes our court of first resort. And it actually matters be-yond the simple sorting of wheat and chaff. Ad hominem often decides who is invited to the seminar, who contributes to the edited volume, who sits on the committee making policy. Most such guest lists are harmless, but a few influence the course of the field.[115]

Our traditional authority is peer review—in effect inverted ad hominem.[116] (Peer review is used in CRM as quality control and in laboratory research; here I focus on its role in academic publication.) "Peer" is ad hominem—in a good way. Someone (an editor) judges Dr. X, Prof. Y, and Curator Z to be my (or your) peer: That is, someone of your professional status who knows as much/enough about the subject matter. That's mild ad hominem, a muted appeal to authority. That panel of peers judges whether the work in question is up to snuff. The edi-tor or publisher, however, typically is free to accept, reject, or otherwise modify the peer panel's verdict.[117]

Peer review has come under critique for various reasons. But it's a necessary evil or, if not evil exactly, a necessary archaism, a part of academic performance/ ritual seen as a hallmark of good scholarship and good science. That's how we've always done it, and we can't (at present) devise anything better.[118]

Peer review tends to truncate. (Truncate what?) The jury of peers can be seen as a sort of bell curve. (Of what? Don't worry about *what* exactly: Just go with me here.) Draw a dozen reviewers at random and they should cluster around some central tendency. Maybe that's the "what." Statistically, their reviews should eliminate the tails, two or three deviations out from the central tendency—thinking that deviates too far from the normal "what." Let's say the left tail is wackos, and the right tail represents equally deviant but possibly useful new thinking. Both are truncated: Left tail, good riddance; right tail, maybe something lost. Peer review effectively eliminates garbage but may also lose the promise of new ideas or original thinking.[119] Pueblo Space is a strong central tendency of the metaphorical bell curve: It keeps Chaco in mid-quartiles, in Pueblo Space.[120]

That can be a real barrier to convincement: You can't assess what you don't read, or evaluate an argument you never hear.

Taking Measures: Lies, Damn Lies, and Statistics[121]

What about statistical certainty/uncertainty? There's no statistic for narrative argument, for plausibility, for convincement. Is there?

There are serious (but marginal) proposals that history could be written using Bayesian logic and procedures.[122] I suppose it's worth considering. Bayesian approaches (when they are honest) put your biases—"priors"—out in the open for all to see.[123] Because desktops can handle the calculations, we are all Bayesians now, but what really goes on inside our machines while Oxcal is chugging away? A black box, spinning iterations of immense complexity. "We run the risk that such [Bayesian] software will be reduced to the status of black boxes" (Buck and Meson 2015:567). I know what's happening theoretically, schematically; but I could never replicate the process myself, nor could you, most likely. Much as we might want to be, we can't be in the RAM where it happens.

Bayesian analysis would dress up our history with quantified probabilities, but its basic tenets are subjective. "Choosing between explanations based on the notion of probability as a degree of belief in your head, rather than an objective property of the real world, is known as the Bayesian approach" (Hand 2014: 228). When the priors are fairly straightforward, as with 14C dates in Harris matrices, both the process and the results make a great deal of sense: Using our knowledge of stratigraphy and chronology to prune unruly radiocarbon to an acceptable topiary of time. And that has been Bayes's greatest strength, to date: Chronology-building with 14C. But other applications are possible (Ortman et al. 2007) and perhaps the most intriguing possible future applications are those where Bayesian biases (priors) become explicitly part of archaeological discourse. To be "good Bayesians" (we are told) requires us to "take an unapologetically subjective, Bayesian approach to scientific reasoning—not least since we are human, biased, and fallible" (Buck and Meson 2015:570). Wear our biases on our sleeves, as it were. Much as humanists and social scientists take (and misuse) concepts from physics—I once heard Heisenberg's Uncertainty Principal invoked as a justification of epistemic relativism—we might easily decide that if bias is OK for 14C chronology, then it's OK in other arenas, such as narrative discourse. And that may be true, as long as bias is acknowledged explicitly and rigorously as Harris-matrix Bayesian priors.

Normal frequentist statistics avoid the Bayesian hanky-panky. These, or something like them, could be bent to our purposes. The heated climate of climate change forced scientists to assign numerical certainty to statements and arguments—dressed up like statistical confidence. The lack of such a system allowed deniers to cast doubt on the science: One scientist's "disaster" was another scientist's "adverse impact." Deniers cried: Pox on 'em both. This was true even within a single, multiauthored report, for example the "Second Report of the Intergovernmental Panel on Climate Change" (1995), which was criticized for the lack of a graded or statistical system of certainty. The IPCC itself later proposed seven grades of scientific probability (IPCC 2001) and other agencies jumped right in, perhaps most influentially, a scale of certainty/uncertainty proposed by the National Research Council of the National Academy of Science.[124] *Confidence about Facts* were graded on five levels from "very low" to "very high." *Likelihood of an Outcome* was more finely divided, with ten levels from "exceptionally unlikely" to "virtually certain." These are subjective judgments, although crude statistical probabilities are given as guidelines—"virtually certain" should mean something like "more than 99 chances out of 100."[125]

Because prediction ("likelihood of an outcome") is often statistical, it is amenable to confidence-interval-like quantification. "Confidence about Facts" reflects a more qualitative assessment, even if expressed in numerical terms.[126] We will return to these systems below; with another iteration that tried to equate statistical certainty with legal standards.

Findings of Fact: Legal Standards

There are other avenues for marking up our histories and laying out their logics. As noted above, historical arguments are much more like legal arguments[127] than they are like scientific experiments.[128] (Indeed, there are legal tests and criteria for science itself, the Daubert Rule.)[129]

Law provides some insights, and perhaps opportunities for building methodology, pre-historiography.[130] Aspects of legal practice have been proposed for archaeological methods; Roger M. Thomas explores "Evidence, Archaeology and Law" and there is a more fully developed attempt in Anderson and Twining, "Law and Archaeology: Modified Wigmorean Analysis" (e.g., Thomas 2015; Anderson and Twining 2015). A Wigmore Analysis is sort of a Harris Matrix for arguments:

The chart method is essentially a way of structuring arguments, so that a complex case can be made more manageable by breaking it up into sectors and identifying which evidence is potentially relevant to one or more sectors, while maintaining a coherent picture of the whole.... It is very useful in identifying with precision the weak points in an argument.... It is less useful for communicating or presenting an argument to an audience.... This is where persuasive storytelling and other methods come into their own. (Anderson and Twining 2015:283)

Ah! It all comes down to "persuasive storytelling" which, in law, is not a "just-so" defect but a courtroom skill to be acquired and admired. What makes a legal argument persuasive? Evidence, rhetoric and [drumroll!] standards of proof. Probable cause, reasonable doubt, and so forth. (One of the most famous of which, of course, is "if it doesn't fit, you must acquit.")

An accessible recent attempt to apply legal standards to scientific arguments comes from Charles Weiss, retired professor of Science, Technology and International Affairs at Georgetown University. Weiss's (2003) framework was an attempt to standardize languages of certainty/uncertainty which varied (fatally) within the "Second Report of the Intergovernmental Panel on Climate Change" (1995), discussed above. It's worth considering here because it demonstrates how complicated this problem is, or could be. Weiss correlates a hierarchy of legal standards (culled from both civil and criminal law) with "informal scientific levels of certainty" (in italics, below) and Bayesian probabilities, abstracted from Weiss (2003:Tables 1 and 3), and added by me in brackets:

0. Impossible—a defense, not a standard of proof [0%]
1. No reasonable grounds for suspicion—inchoate hunch (no action); *unlikely* [<1%]
2. Reasonable grounds for suspicion—substantial possibility (stop and frisk, for example); *possible* [1–10%]
3. Probable cause for arrest—less evidence than required for conviction (arrest, search warrant, etc.); *plausible* [10–33%]
4. Clear indication—(a proposed standard for body cavity and X-Ray searches); *attractive but unproven* [33–50%]
5. Preponderance of the evidence—more probable than not (the standard for most civil cases); *more likely true than untrue* [50–67%]
6. Substantial and credible evidence—evidence might support a conclusion (impeachments); *probable* [67–80%]
7. Clear showing—clear likelihood (for example, for preliminary injunction); *very probable* [80–90%]
8. Clear and convincing evidence—clear, unequivocal, convincing leading to a

firm belief that the allegation is true (criminal sentencing, severe civil cases such as deportation); *substantially proven* [90–99%]

9. Beyond reasonable doubt—a reasonable person would not hesitate to act, no real possibility that he is not guilty (criminal conviction); *rigorously proven* [>99%]

10. Beyond any doubt—not a legal standard; *fundamental theory* [100%]

Numbers 1 and 2 get you out of jail, free. Numbers 3 and 4 could get you pulled over, arrested, and possibly charged. But they are field judgments for law enforcement and may not be relevant to archaeological historiography.

Working up from the bottom isn't getting us anywhere; let's go top-down and jump to the highest standard: Number 10 "Beyond any doubt" and Number 9 "Beyond a reasonable doubt." Too high! "Beyond any doubt" is essentially scientific certainty, and that won't fly—even in science. "Beyond reasonable doubt?" As Dr. Jones wisely told us, "there's always another explanation" in archaeology, another plausible alternative(s) that should, for any reasonable person, constitute doubt. The highest standards, Numbers 9 and 10, seem beyond archaeology's reach.

That leaves the midfield, Numbers 5 through 8: (5) preponderance of evidence, (6) substantial and credible evidence, (7) clear showing, and (8) clear and convincing evidence.

Number 5 "preponderance of evidence" means simply: More likely than not, better than a 50-50 chance. That may seem like a low bar, but "preponderance of evidence" will break you in a civil case. (O.J. avoided criminal charges—"reasonable doubt"—but in the later civil case "preponderance of evidence" ruined him, financially.) In fact, we already use "preponderance of evidence" in NAGPRA: "Preponderance of evidence" can empty a museum.[131] But still, it's only more likely than not. Number 6 "substantial and credible" also seems useful: "Such evidence as a reasonable mind *might* accept as adequate to support a conclusion" (emphasis added). Skipping over Number 7 "clear showing" (a standard used only for injunctions), let's consider Number 8 "clear and convincing"—the best, I think, archaeology can possibly hope for.[132]

"Clear and convincing" has two components: "Clear" evidentiary statements and "convincing" argument. Perhaps we can separate (essential) evidence/data from the (necessary) rhetoric of argument.

The evidence is generally not much in doubt: Pueblo Bonito is Pueblo Bonito, a giant pile of sandstone and mud and wooden beams at 36° 03' north, 107° 57' west.[133] And there's my "Ten Fun Facts about Chaco," back in chapter 3. "Some circumstantial evidence is very strong, as when you find a trout in the milk," said the Sage of Walden (aka Hank the Crank) regarding his suspicion that the milkman was watering down his product.[134] The vast majority of archaeological facts are circumstantial—at several removes from direct evidence. We almost never, ever have a smoking gun, so we shouldn't hold our evidence up to that impossible standard. We must judge facts.

People judge facts. Rules and standards of law assume a "reasonable man" (or woman, of course) *without undue bias*. Pueblo Space is bias. As long as Southwestern archaeology operates in the Pueblo Space, Chaco (and other interesting entities) will not get a fair trial. We might be clear but in the face of bias, we can never be convincing. So all this discussion of "standards of proof" is simply merely small-"t" theory. One might say: Academic.

But let's assume (I hope correctly) that we can bust out of Pueblo Space. How might we apply something like standards to our evidence and to our arguments?

Grading the evidence: At simplest, we could annotate our certainty, for others to evaluate our interpretations. Fact #1 I'm absolutely sure about; Fact #2 I'm just guessing about; Fact #3 is pure speculation; and so on. I think some of my "Ten Fun Facts about Chaco" are unassailable while others could be subject to revision. I can grade them on my "certainty": A = damn-sure certain; B = fairly confident; C = probably, possibly, maybe; D = wasting your time. With short parenthetical notes.

1. Great Houses are real, and really different = A (a rock-hard verity)
2. Great Houses were *houses*, but not many people lived in them = B– (some reasonable dissent)
3. People living in GHs were…special = B (everything seems to point that way, but…)
4. Chaco was a stratified class society = B+ (a rock-hard verity, if #2 and #3 are true)
5. Outlier GHs are real and define Chaco's region = B+ (still a few NIMBYs out there)
6. Road networks and line-of-site communication: Chaco's region was a system = B– (both are documented for a fragment of the region, but only inferred for the rest)
7. Chaco's region encompassed 60,000 people, and perhaps as many as 100,000 people
   60,000 = B (independent analyses hover around that number)
   100,000 = C (possible but perhaps overly enthusiastic)
8. Chaco had bulk and prestige economies
   Bulk = A– (rock-hard verity for beams, pots, rocks, meat; maize depends on #9)
   Prestige = B– (rare things are hard to generalize about)
9. Chaco was not a great place to grow corn = C (conflicting science)
10. Chaco was cosmopolitan = C+ (compared to Mesa Verde, yes; compared to Tula, not so much)

This might seem like a joke, but I'm not joking. We usually take care of this sort of thing by putting "possibly" or "very likely" or some other bet-hedging modifier near the front of every sentence or paragraph. Everything is conditional. But we know that some of our facts are more factual than others. Much like our implicit narratives, our implicit certainties would be more useful if they were out in the open, cards laid on the table. Maybe not graded like term papers, but some version of self-reflective critical analysis. Climate science grades its facts; we should too.

That's evidence, the facts in the case. How about argument? Adjourning briefly from the courtroom and moving back to science or at least to scholarship, many would vote for arguments by abduction. The "best" explanation is, operationally, "true." Abduction has been called "the inference that makes science" (attrib. Ernan McMullin).

What makes an explanation "best"? "Best" how? Lars Fogelin, an archaeological advocate of abduction: "Explanations that are empirically broad, general, modest, conservative, simple, testable, and address many perspectives are better than explanations that are not" (Fogelin 2007:603). Maybe for science but, I think, not for history. Historical events are narrow, specific, outrageous, immoderate, complex, and usually untestable. Beware (for example) the Ides of March: Stabbing Caesar was specific to a time and a place, to a cause and to a crew. Flagrant, revolutionary, complicated, with a narrow (knife-edge) perspective of Roman politics. The assassination was unique and historically unpredictable. But Brutus and the boys' interest in Julius's internal economy is the "best" historical explanation of early Imperial Roman political history. Abduction? *Abuctio ad absurdum*?

Historical arguments are complicated and thick; good arguments will have layers and layers of subarguments—the stuff that footnotes are made of (as Sam Spade, riffing on Prospero, might put it). "Ten Fun Facts about Chaco," presented in chapter 3 as simple statements, averaged under nine words each. Then they required short explanatory paragraphs; which in turn required pages of footnotes, each with references and citations to books, articles, and other arguments developed at length elsewhere. Wow, what a setup for hypertext! And that's where we are going in the next section.

History as Hypertext: The End of History and the Last Book?

It may be possible, in this brave new world, to build judgment and evaluation into the construction of narratives. With hypertext, key phrases or interpretations can be documented, explained, and tagged with the author's estimates of confidence or uncertainty; with (moderated) wiki features, a narrative could be challenged, defended, modified, and so forth in dynamic collaborations not possible in print—and not possible in current models of academic or CRM archaeology.

Consider this excerpt from a condensed, unfootnoted version of *A History of the Ancient Southwest*:

> Chaco Canyon itself was decidedly top-heavy—a city of palaces—but the tip of the social pyramid was in fact rather small: perhaps a thousand or fifteen hundred elites. And the pyramid had a broad base: tens of thousands of commoners across the wide Plateau. At a guess, commoners numbered perhaps 40- or 50,000, about the same size as a Mesoamerican city-state, but spread over a much larger region.[135]

Some readers (I'm told) reject such statements as baseless assertions. But phrases like "top-heavy," "across the wide Plateau," "Mesoamerican city-state" are the products/conclusions of research (by me and many others) spanning many decades. To support "top-heavy Chaco" would require (like "Ten Fun Facts") footnotes to footnotes to footnotes back to references and beyond them to data: The thirty-year-old kiva argument, its twenty-five-year-old implications for population estimates, and those estimates buffed up for a new century— not Bayes-onetted or momentary-ized, but still useful numbers for comparing Chaco (the top-heavy tip) to its region (a sturdy broad-based pyramid). Each of those ranks of footnotes would, moreover, require parenthetical or ancillary discussions of challenges (defeated) and corrections (sustained) over lo those many years. "Top-heavy Chaco's" seventy-odd-word argument, if fully presented in layered, ramified, minutiaed detail, would need a hundred times that many words; say, thirty-odd pages of text. Probably more. And that exegesis would still refer readers to other sources.

Consequently, my writing has devolved into a fiesta of footnotes, increasingly bottom-heavy.[136] (There were about as many words in the footnotes to *A History of the Ancient Southwest* as there were words in the text; I expect this book is even worse.) If you actually read the footnotes—thank you!—you will note an alarming tendency towards footnotes-within-footnotes: parenthetical asides, tangents, alternate readings, references to other works, etc.

We hacked our way through a thicket of such convolutions in "Ten Fun Facts"—threads of argument spliced and spun into rough twine, wrapped round and round a tiny solid core to create the Guinness World Record's Largest Hermeneutic Ball.[137]

So where does this leave narrative? To stretch the tensile metaphor: Narrative—if it is *not* historical fiction—flounders under the heavy chains of scholarly apparatus, a book with more footnotes than text. I've written such books.

Or…hypertext! Beam us up, Scotty, away from this weary world of texts and footnotes and convoluted citations. Do this online! At the least interesting level, it would be possible to replace footnotes with links to the cited source, perhaps presented en bloc as PDFs: Damn the copyrights, full speed ahead. Something like the "supporting information" or "supplemental materials" of science journals, although those are typically DOI documents. But that's simply a convenience for the reader, not a solution to the methodological problem. It would be possible to code each sentence, each phrase with an estimate of certainty. What's rock solid, what's a wild guess? But beyond those fairly mechanical things, I think hypertext and other online capabilities could allow construction of robust narratives:[138] Multiple histories online, cross- and self-correcting! Not a single-authored narrative, but a crowd-sourced web of arguments—from a select crowd, carefully moderated. Of which, more below.

Web work is far beyond my diminishing capabilities and above my plummeting paygrade, but some bright youngster, or a crew of bright youngsters, could pull this off.[139] Here's what I have in mind:

1. A straight-ahead linear narrative text. Old school: Subjects, verbs, sentences; maps—good maps!—graphs, and charts; and so forth. Modeled perhaps on Meinig (see note 71). Making a narrative argument: This caused that, which then caused the other, while this thing off to the side had no effect, etc. Of course, online you can do things you can't do in print—LOTS more figures and illustrations!—but the base model is, well, basic and familiar.

2. HTML (or whatever markup language emerges) for certainty: Clicking on a phrase, a number, an interpretation will link or simply reveal the author's level of certainty along the lines discussed above. Color code the texts? When clicked, cold hard facts remain solid black and shift to a biblical typeface like Old English Text. Wild guesses become a slithery script—Brush perhaps—and turn red with shame. And so forth. Whether this happens sentence by sentence when queried or for the full text at a click could be an option.

3. Another layer in, HTML link to sources, references, citations.

4. Another layer in, HTML or DOI link to the actual cited text—in whole or in part—with the relevant portions highlighted, and exegesis if necessary.

5. And so on and so on, as the philosopher says.

With the exception of (2) "certainty," all this does is hide the scholarly apparatus and, perhaps, make it easier to follow chains of evidence and inference. That's not an enormous gain over conventional print. I identify the weak links in the chain in footnotes—but that means you have to read the footnotes, and that's inconvenient in conventional print. Coding "certainty," if honestly and consistently applied, would at least alert the reader to the more problematic parts of argument, without requiring a dumpster dive into the endnotes. That's a good thing, I think; I know which parts of my argument are dicey, and you should know that I know that, too.

But here's where online media might move narrative prehistory from one man's fancy to a quasi-rigorous archaeological product: A moderated wiki function for contesting, correcting, supporting, and editing both the facts in the case and the case being made, the narrative argument. Building not by consensus but by critical collaboration a solid narrative prehistory of the ancient Southwest.

Having once swum the waters of Wikipedia, I know wikis can be nasty. Dogs eat dogs, trolls eat trolls—that sort of thing. (Nothing new there for archaeology.) It would be essential for wiki history not simply to knock down, but to build up. Perhaps a Southwest narrative history wiki would be members-only or otherwise moderated.[140] The best sort of ad hominem: Only positive people. Leaves me out.

But if you build it, will they come? Based on my experiences in academia and CRM, probably not. We were raised in a single-scholar, principal-investigator universe that does not encourage teamwork but rather rewards individual effort.[141] That creates an oddly static model of learning and knowledge growth. Write something (say, a book or a report). By the time it's out and reviewed, you are on to the next thing, or even the thing after that—and your peers complain that "now that garbage is in the literature and we'll have to muck it out." Very few archaeological books are revised or have second editions, showing growth of knowledge—except, of course, textbooks, where new editions mean new income.

I should rewrite *A History of the Ancient Southwest* every five or ten years, changing the narrative to accommodate new data and ideas. That's not going to happen. But someone should rewrite it, or a committee should rewrite it. Something nimbler than print: That would be the web.

For those of us set in our ways, all that coding and HTML work might well be a waste of time and effort. But the good news is, the Old Guard retreats and the world turns upside down: The Boomers retire.

I hope that younger archaeologists will reinvent archaeological practice, methods, and theory.[142] Not a linguistic turn, or an Ontological Turn, but a cyber turn. With a goal of narrative pre-history.

Getting Our Swagger Back

Many years ago, an International Man of Mystery lost his mojo. Chaos ensued, and the nation's capital only narrowly escaped destruction from a giant "laser beam." Southwestern archaeology faces an existential crisis not unlike his. Well, not "crisis" exactly, but certainly an interesting puzzle: How to push forward when (to simplify a bit) our movements are confined by Pueblo Space, our logic undercut by théorie, our work dismissed as mere speculation, and our legitimacy (indeed, our morality) questioned by Native Americans. As Lou Brown told his team: We'd save everybody a lot of time and trouble if we just went out and shot ourselves.

Southwestern archaeology remains bound in and biased by Pueblo Space; we can escape. Théorie tells us there's no way to know the past, so archaeology must be about the present; I disagree. We live in postfactual times, and what we present to the public holds no more currency than Fake News; we can turn that around. Indians do not care for archaeology (why should they?) and consign it to the dustbin of postcolonial rubbish; that one's hard to argue with.

But I'll try: Archaeology is not inherently colonial. It is (or was) undeniably of the European Enlightenment, but its original focus was not colonial but inward: The Classical past, the pre-Classical Mediterranean Basin, and ultimately the prehistory of European nations. The archaeology of us. When archaeology was applied in colonies, it came as part of the imperial apparatus; but the discipline itself was no more colonial than geology, medicine, engineering, and so forth. (The shrill will insist that those, too, are colonial; they are wrong.) American Anthropology added the nasty colonial biases: The racism of Morgan and his peers. Those biases—now deracinated—carry over in the Glass Ceiling, the Iron Curtain, and Pueblo Space. Those are the problem. If you want to decolonize archaeology, decolonize your head. Identify and control old colonial biases and colonial content. That way lies new knowledge about the past.

But, it's complicated…

Before NAGRPA, before Indigenous Archaeology, before decolonization, before the Ontological Turn, I worked at the Museum of New Mexico with Rina Swentzell from Santa Clara Pueblo. Rina reviewed a "popular" book about archaeological excavations at the Yellow Jacket site. (Enormous collections from the Yellow Jacket project gather dust at my current gig, the Museum of Natural History at the University of Colorado.) In her review (Swentzell 1992), she quoted the book's conclusion: "The most striking impression one acquires of the Yellow Jacket area is the extreme complexity of the prehistoric remains, brought about by repeated rebuilding on the same sites for many centuries. *The Anasazi must have felt very at home here!*" [emphasis hers]. She then asked: "Why did the land, the place, the spirit of the people have to be subjected to the destruction of digging and disturbance to arrive at such a meaningless conclusion?" (Swentzell 1992:278).[143]

Indeed: "They felt at home here"? A platitude straight outta Pueblo Space! Would any disinterested intelligent reader, or any scholar from another field, or any Indian conclude that archaeology was worth doing?

Peruse the pages of *Kiva* and *American Antiquity*. Audit the abstracts from SAA's annual meetings. Canvass the conclusions of *Science* stories. For the most part: Bloodless, technical, interesting only to specialists. Which, to some extent, is as it should be: That's how scholarship progresses. But there was gripping history in the Southwest, at Chaco and Paquimé and Hohokam, for example. Those bright stars are not alone in the firmament, but (I can attest) their histories most directly engage the larger reading public and, perhaps, *justify all the hard, tedious, less-engaging research which underwrites those histories.*

Break out of Pueblo Space! What if archaeology said Yellow Jacket was not only a place where people felt at home but, historically, a local capital for an extensive, expansive polity? Yellow Jacket was a political "outlier" first of Chaco Canyon and later of Aztec Ruins. As the biggest and most elaborate site in the Mesa Verde area, Yellow Jacket was itself a regional center, an intermediate political level between Chaco and Aztec and dozens of smaller Great House communities. It was part of a larger, sweeping history—and we know that history because of technical, tedious archaeological research. That's a much better story: Would it justify the digging and disturbance?

Maybe not. Rina Swentzell is gone, so we can't ask her. But recall the Indian woman in the Aztec Ruins video: We don't need your revisionist history. I don't think any histories we can write will justify archaeology for Native America. They know their heritage: Indians are not our audience. But for archaeologists still engaged with the global project of prehistory, the questions must be answered: History or heritage? Who is our audience? Who are our constituencies? Answer me those questions three, ere the other side you see.

Somewhere over that rainbow lies our lost mojo. Break out of Pueblo Space and work for the world: International solvers of mysteries. To quote Ian Hodder, wildly out of context: In this postcolonial era, "we cannot assume an authority, we have to argue for it" (Hodder 2003a:47).

CHAPTER 7

The End

In the long run, we will all be dead and we will all be wrong.
—attrib. Marshall Sahlins (emending a quote attrib. to J. M. Keynes [again?])

Here's What I Want You to Do

"What do you want us to do?" asked the ASU grad student.

Decolonize your head. Recognize the biases you inherited from American Anthropological Archaeology's early days: Glass Ceiling, Iron Curtain. When a senior Southwesternist panders out platitudes like "intermediate" or "parsimony" or "appropriate scale" or "best explained by" some minimizing bromide, you should wonder: Why are they saying that? Why keep everything simple? But have pity: They say this because their professors said it; their professors said it because their professors…and so on and so on. *"Visiting the iniquity of the fathers upon the children unto the third and fourth generation,"* Moses warned us. Biases so old, they are the air we breathe. Look for biases in received wisdom and current events. Root 'em out!

Read global history. (I gave you a list in chapter 4.) See how they did things in the rest of the world and wonder: Why not in societies north of Mexico? Think locally, globally. To be a good Mesa Verde archaeologist, or a good Hohokam archaeologist, or a good Rio Grande archaeologist, you must be a good Southwestern archaeologist: Learn a lot about areas outside your own. And the Great Basin, and the Plains, and the Mississippi Valley, and the northern half of Mexico. Everybody knew everything—and you should too. *"Broad views of things cannot be acquired by vegetating in one little corner of the earth,"* penned *Samuel Clemens under his* nom de plume. Let your mind wander: Think big!

Think pre-historiographically. (Use *that* in your next game of Scrabble!) We need pre-historiography but it does not exist in American Anthropological Archaeology. Consider every archaeological situation as a narrative. Write it down, with your rationales for plot points and narrative choices, alongside your conventional archaeology. *"A prehistorian, like any other historian!"* insisted *Gordon Childe, a fortnight before he stepped off a cliff.* The Southwest is rich with archaeologies that tell stories, or would if we knew how to write stories. I used Chaco, because it was dramatic and well known and easy to read. But Mimbres-Casas, Hohokam, teapot tempests of Sinagua, the rise of the Rio Grande, Plains-Pueblo—all these are begging for narrative pre-histories. Write 'em—if you dare!

Steady on with science! But base "neo-processual" studies on better history. Bad history = crap science. *"Science is the driving force of civilization!"—a cheer mis-attributed to James Burke of "Connections."* My ragtag shotgun blast of science essays in chapter 4 covered a lot of territory—but there's so much more to do! Pay particular attention to secondary states: With Chaco and Cahokia, that's an area where American Anthropological Archaeology could make a real contribution to the global project. I can't recommend any relevant literature from North America because it doesn't exist. You'll have to write it!

Back off théorie. "Theory is dead" for many literary critics, which does not discourage them from writing long, difficult books about theory's demise. Other social science and humanities disciplines have passed it by. Bizarrely, archaeology makes it a fetish: Theoretical Archaeology. Why would anyone want to do that? *"I would prefer not to," Žižek quips, channeling Bartleby the Scrivener.* Théorie had thirty years and didn't produce. Give us something new!

Shun parsimony as you would shun sin. (OK, for younger readers who might not be ready, quite yet, to shun sin: As you would shun plague.) *"In science we always look for the simplest explanation," deadpanned a Ghostbuster.* But not in history, where simpler is seldom better. Staying close to the data moves us far from the truth. The past, almost certainly, was bigger, brighter, and more complicated than we'd think, looking at bags of sherds!

Think outside Pueblo Space. I'm sure many readers are thinking that what happens in Santa Fe stays in Santa Fe, but that's not true. Pueblo Space pervades our work as archaeologists, even in areas not officially "Pueblo." *"What's past is prologue," writes the Bard; "But," Bacon butts in, "if a man begins with certainties, he ends in doubts!"—were both bits Bacon's?* Pueblo Space makes past prologue for Pueblos, and of that we're certain. I doubt it: The past was different, the past was bigger than Pueblo Space. Escape the Space!

The Good

Signs of hope: On a cheerful note, the magnificent *Oxford Handbook of Southwest Archaeology*, assembled and edited by Barbara Mills and Severin Fowles (2017), is all about history. The introduction by Fowles and Mills is titled "On History in Southwest Archaeology"—great stuff! And the first nine chapters are historiography, nine different methodological perspectives! The Chaco chapter (Plog et al. 2017) arrived too late to join the *cru* of chapter 2. But early tastings from *Oxford Handbook of Southwest Archaeology* suggest hints of historicity floating over subtle subversions of Pueblo Space. A promising start: We shall see how the program matures. Didn't Will Rogers joke, *"You've got to go out on a limb because that's where the fruit is"*?

It remains for the next generations to write the narrative histories we need. But that may be difficult, because…

The Bad

Not "bad" really, but problematic. I've argued, unfashionably, that archaeological pre-history and Indian heritage are two separate, parallel discourses, with different goals, methods, and audiences. But an active segment of archaeology (and many public interpreters) want very badly to mix 'em together. A brew that would please no one. Indians don't need anything from archaeology, except perhaps cease-and-desist. Archaeology would like to use Indian traditional histories but, as discussed in chapter 6, Indians are understandably disinclined to make their heritage public. And if they did, archaeology might not treat them properly: *"We cannot take mythology at face value,"* said Dr. Jones. That annoys Indians, understandably.

An impasse. As a kind of default gesture, many Southwestern archaeologists seem to think that Pueblo Space somehow respects Native heritage: Keep our interpretations in Pueblo Space. Maybe so; but in my conversations with Indians, it's clear that the most respectful thing an archaeologist could do is find another line of work. If we choose to continue in Southwestern archaeology, we must also respect the past, respect the history we study; and that past was not confined to Pueblo Space. *As von Ranke wrote, "It is not for the past as part of the present, but for the past as the past, that the historian is properly concerned."* A conundrum.

So: Respect, diplomacy, clear boundaries.

The Ugly

Chapter 1 took Chaco from Time Immemorial through James K. Polk and Teddy Roosevelt to George H. W. Bush, 1845 to 2000. Chapter 2 took Chaco from Bill Clinton to George W. Bush to Barrack Obama, 2000 to 2015. How will Chaco fare under Donald Trump? Not well, I fear; or far too well: Too many wells. The San Juan Basin (northwestern New Mexico, surrounding Chaco) has been and is being leased for drilling and fracking. *"Drill, baby, drill!" Palin piqued Biden.* Maps of leased and soon-to-be-leased plots are astonishing, appalling. I am currently working (as a junior partner with Ruth Van Dyke and Carrie Heitman) on a project sponsored by the National Park Service, considering the nature and nurture of Chaco landscapes: What do they look like and how do we "manage" them in the face of fracking?

Conventional Chacoan sites we know reasonably well: 150+ "outlier" Great Houses and communities. But we do not know the extent of Chaco's roads. The big road projects took place in the 1980s—three decades ago (Kincaid 1983; Nials et al. 1987). Since then, no one has thrown comparable funding or technology at roads. We know there are more roads to find, probably many more roads: On smaller projects, everywhere we looked we found road segments. There is no regional road map; there are only maps of the few roads we know well and scores of short segments. Policy-makers use those maps. They seem to think that the preservation of roads is perfect and our knowledge of them is complete. Neither is remotely true. When the drilling starts (right now), existing laws and regulations will deal with "outlier" Great Houses and their communities, but the laws and regulations, I fear, will fail the roads. *David Byrne sang, "We're on a road to nowhere."*

This is tragic because, with Chaco, we have a regional archaeology of remarkable clarity. A great proportion—surely, over 90 percent—of its region was never farmed or otherwise disturbed, beyond overgrazing. Sites are out there, visible on the land's surface. We know most of the conventional sites comprising the system, and—potentially—we have actual landscape features that could show us how the system worked: Roads. We can analyze networks with sherds and lithics, but nothing approaches the clarity of a road linking site *A* to site *B* but not to site *C*. Chaco's roads are an amazing gift from the archaeology gods, but WE DO NOT HAVE A MAP. *"It is not down on any map; true places never are"—Ishmael, on Queequeg's origin story.* We will lose Chaco's roads in a welter of well pads, pipelines, and access roads. Look at aerial photographs of fracked landscapes in the American West: That's ugly.

And So, Farewell…

Am I too gloomy, too pessimistic? Maybe; but after almost fifty years in Southwestern archaeology, this is what I see. Unlike young Walter Taylor, whom we met in chapter 1, I'm not making a splash to start a career. I'm wrapping mine up: Drop some knowledge, drop the mic, and drop outta sight.

Goodbye and good luck. Always remember a refrain never sung by the Fab Four: *"And in the end / the gains you make / are equal to / the risks you take."*

Indigenous Chaco

Where were Indians in the long, strange story of archaeology at Chaco? From the very earliest days they were present and accounted for—but not in leading roles. Hundreds of Indians worked in archaeology at Chaco, Awatovi, Hawikku, Snaketown, and many sites on the Rio Grande. Many Indians worked at digs as wage labor—sometimes paid by the piece or find. Jobs were needed, but communities often split on the propriety of participation of tribal members in excavations. A good, short account of those engagements comes in chapter 3 in Chip Colwell's (2010:67–82) *Living Histories*.

Indians were also engaged in the interpretation of the archaeology. Fewkes, Hewett, Judd, Ellis, and others in the first and second generations of Southwestern archaeologists routinely asked Indian informants to interpret finds, large and small. Often those interactions were acknowledged—I have a photo of smiling Neil Judd side by side with Santiago Naranjo, a patriarch of that remarkable Santa Clara family. More often, I'm sure, Indian information was appropriated without formal recognition. Did Indians play the same trickster games on nosy archaeologists that they sometimes played on nosy ethnologists? Probably; who knows?

I do not pretend to present every Native account of Chaco. Rather, I offer accounts that (1) were intended to be public, and (2) have impacted my thinking about Chaco. I have had conversations about Chaco—mostly long and variously detailed—both formal (official) and informal (unofficial) with knowledgeable people from Hopi, Zuni, Acoma, Zia, and Navajo Nation. Many of these conversations took place at or near Chaco. As noted in the text, I've had shorter conversations with individuals from several Rio Grande Pueblos, all unofficial. I've benefited from video clips of people from several Pueblos speaking on the record about Chaco (e.g., Sofaer 1999). And I've presented Chaco's archaeology to the Park's Native American Advisory Council, and benefited from their comments. For all these: My sincere thanks to those who shared their knowledge.

So, what about Chaco? To the many attributed and apocryphal and otherwise uncertain quotes scattered through this book, I'll add yet another, which I swear I saw in an old popular article by Neil Judd but which I've never been able to find again. Judd brought Zuni workmen to Chaco, and they said something like this: White men built these walls. Those Zunis, at least, had never seen Chaco and knew very little about it. If you, gentle reader, find Judd's article, I will be grateful indeed.

Moving from known unknowns to known knowns—as Donald Rumsfeld is said to have said—the rest of this appendix presents one unpublished and several published Native accounts of Chaco. The classic Pueblo ethnographies have little to say, directly, about the place. "Specific stories that refer to Chaco in a recognizable manner are not apparent in the oral histories of most Pueblos" (Reed 2004:10).

I have elsewhere (Lekson 2009a:200) made fast and loose with "White House" from the "Acoma Origin Myths" (introduced in chapter 5). I blush to admit I've appropriated and paraphrased those stories and mixed in elements from other Pueblo accounts to produce a narrative, along the lines that follow: Pueblo traditions tell of a Chaco where "people got power over people"[1] and lived lives and created societies incorrect or inappropriate for Pueblo philosophies today—"men who embraced social-political-religious hierarchy and envisioned control and power over places, resources, and people" (Swentzell 2004: 50; an account we revisit, below). The place, known as White House, was grand and glorious, but became corrupt and ripe for correction. Rather than Old Testament–style destruction, the people—following advice from their spiritual counselors—voted with their feet, left rulers and bad guys behind, and moved on to newer places and better behaviors. They rejected the hierarchical social structures of White House (some accounts tell of a Ceremony of Forgetting; chapter 6) and reinvented themselves as Pueblos.

Or, at least, that's my version. What do Indians say? Most publically available Pueblo accounts of Chaco conform to (and help shape) Pueblo Space: Clan migrations, unspecified ceremonies, and so forth. For example, "Yupköyvi: The Hopi Story of Chaco Canyon" by Leigh Kuwanwisiwma (longtime director of the Hopi Cultural Preservation Office) is widely cited[2] and not atypical:

> Yupköyvi became a gathering place for clans from local areas as well as clans who had stopped at what might be described as "staging areas" some distance away.... Initial settlers became ruling clans, which established order for the religious cycle as well as social responsibilities.... So each clan was allowed to establish itself at Yupköyvi. Each clan chose a matriarch and a patriarch to lead it. The group collected its clan knowledge and incorporated it into its own ceremony. Then the clans announced that they would share their ceremonies publically. Some clans were allowed to construct ceremonial kivas, where the elders guided their followers.... Finally, clan members performed their ceremonies.

Some were elaborate, others simpler. All were performed and witnessed with the highest reverence. All ceremonies were for the good of the people—for good harvests, rain, and the perpetuation of life. This went on for many years as more clans arrived.... Thus was life at Yupköyvi, until slowly the clans left for different places. The Hopi mesas were one destination. Other clans went to Halona, today's Zuni. Still others went to Zia, Acoma and Laguna. Some chose to stay for a while longer until they, too, left. Yupköyvi had served its purpose, and now it was proper to lay it to rest. (Kuwanwisiwma 2004:45–47)

Navajo people, whose clans live in and around Chaco Canyon, go into greater, grimmer detail: A central oppressive ruler, Nááhwíiłbįįhí, the "winner of people" (who was not a local, neither Pueblo nor Navajo) enslaved everyone (both Pueblo and Navajo) and demanded that they build him a magnificent house (Pueblo Alto) and houses for his cronies and kin (the other Great Houses); after a period of oppressive rule, the people rose up in revolt and dispatched him, either by death or by shooting him straight up to the skies or straight south back to Mexico (where he came from). This summary combines several published sources,[3] the best and most recent of which is surely Richard Begay's 2004 account: "For these reasons, the development of a place like Chaco Canyon must not happen again" (Begay 2004:56).

Four other personal accounts from Rina Swenzell (Santa Clara), Simon Ortiz (Acoma), Michael Kabotie (Hopi), and Victor Masayesva Jr. (Hopi):

The late Rina Swentzell (Santa Clara), with whom I worked at MIAC, presented her personal observations, not a traditional history. While accepting with certainty that Chaco was (and remains) a Pueblo place:

My response to the canyon was that some sensibility other than my Pueblo ancestors had worked on the Chaco great houses. There were the familiar elements such as the *nansipu* (the symbolic opening into the underworlds), kivas, plazas, and earth materials, but they were overlain by a strictness and precision of design and execution that was unfamiliar, not just to me but in other sites in the Southwest. It was clear that the purpose of these great villages was not to restate their oneness with the earth but to show the power and specialness of humans. For me, they represented a desire to control human and natural resources.... I concluded that the structures had been built by men in the prime of life with a vision of something beyond daily life and the present moment. These were men who embraced social-political-religious hierarchy and envisioned control and power over places, resources, and people. (Swentzell 2004:50)

Acoma poet Simon Ortiz (1994) says that Chaco was White House ("kash" means white):

> Kashkahtruutih was a beautiful, serene place where everything was pro-
> vided by the spirit-helpers as long as the people respected the sacred
> powers of creation. After a time of this ideal life at Kashkahtruutih, the
> people became dissatisfied and greedy. They wanted more, although they
> had everything they needed, and they became demanding.... Eventually,
> their demands, arrogance, and disrespect resulted in a battle with the
> sacred powers.... All the people had to leave Kashkahtruutih and there-
> after were required to make their own way. They were made to give up the
> one common language they understood and spoke and henceforth had
> to find their own way of speaking.... I've never heard the elder explicitly
> say that the Acoma people and their culture came from Chaco Canyon,
> Mesa Verde or any of the other sites found throughout the Southwest.
> However, traditional oral stories speak about Kashkahtruutih as being
> located to the north-north west.... And at Chaco Canyon, I have realized
> that there is no past and no present, although some people insist that an
> "ancient civilization" achieved the construction of Pueblo Bonito, Chetro
> Ketl, and Casa Rinconada and that this civilization vanished in the thir-
> teenth century. To the Acoma people and other Native Americans, time
> and place are linked, a sacred continuum in which human consciousness
> is interdependent with creation and its process. And Chaco Canyon and
> its marvelous prehistoric communities attest to the undeniable truth of
> the existence of Native Americans a thousand years ago and more, very
> much as they exist today. (Ortiz 1994:72)

The late Michael Kabotie (Hopi) told me this story about Chaco. In 2006, Michael designed a one-off Crow Canyon field trip ("Cultural Exploration") and specifically requested me as a coleader. I did not know him very well, and I wondered: Why me? Toward the end of the trip, he told me a long formal tale about Chaco—his decision, I hadn't asked. Twice: Once privately in a hotel room in Gallup, and again the next day at Chaco, sitting around the walls of a room in the east wing of Pueblo Bonito, with all the Crow Canyon participants and a random pair of tourists who wandered in. Both times, the recitation took about an hour, and I was struck with how closely the version I heard at Pueblo Bonito repeated the version I'd heard privately the night before: Phrases, sen-tences, and of course content. In retrospect, it seems clear that Kabotie wanted me to hear his version of Chaco, which he couched as a traditional tale (every-thing took four tries, etc.). Knowing now the coyote-ness of Michael (and my-self, I guess) I have wondered if he was being a bit tricky, but however much we kidded each other at meals, etc., he seemed very serious when he told his tale—far more serious than he was the rest of that trip, which was a lot of fun.

I paraphrase and compress, of course (I made no recording at the time, but there were twenty witnesses to the Pueblo Bonito telling). It's presented here like a quote, but it's not; it's as faithful a rendering as I can manage:

> Things were going awry at Hopi, and the leaders sought outside help. They sent, four times, to the Kachina City at Chaco. The first time, their emissaries offered the Kachina leaders wealth from Hopi, and were refused. The Hopi returned a second time and offered the best farming lands at Hopi, and were refused. A third time, they offered high offices and positions at Hopi, and again were refused. The fourth time, the Hopi emissaries offered their prayers. The Kachina leaders said: good, that's we were waiting for—but we will take all the other things you offered, too. The Hopi leaders awaited the help promised by the Kachina leaders, but it did not come. Things continued to worsen at Hopi. When the Hopi leaders had all but given up hope, they woke up to massed battalions of Kachinas surrounding their villages. They were the stern Kachinas: Ogres, Whippers, and so forth. To restore order at Hopi, they marched on the villages and meted out justice and correction. There was violence and many Hopi people fought back. There were losses on both sides, but in the end the Kachina armies prevailed, and instituted a reign of very strict control. This was not what the Hopi leaders hoped for, and they sent emissaries (again, four times) to the Kachina City to request that the stern Kachinas be withdrawn, and replaced by kinder Kachinas. The Kachina leaders were persuaded, and replaced the Ogres and Whippers with gentler Kachinas—but left many Ogres and Whippers in case things again went awry.

Kabotie was very specific that Chaco was the Kachina City—which I capitalize because he enunciated the term with initial emphasis on each word—and also about the military aspect of these events, although I do not believe he used the word "battalion." He named more Kachinas for both the initial and the second events, but sadly I am not sufficiently familiar with Hopi Kachinas for the names to have registered. I was, I am ashamed to admit, a poor student: It took me months after the fact to realize that I was, in fact, being instructed. But Michael Kabotie's tellings—both alone and with an audience—were compelling and memorable.

Photographer Victor Masayesva Jr. (Hopi) offers some insights on Chaco—then and now—in text accompanying his striking images:

> It is time to share stories and in the telling stretch the truth, alter the present, definitely ignore the grammatical anticipation of past-present-future. The snake has gone to sleep, and the bear yawns. *Hair matted with blood clots, scorching baby fetuses, they hold their feasts in dark caves*

close by. Someone let me know why imagined stories cannot be told in the presence of snakes, of bears. Is it that they are particularly keen to smell our *powakas*—sorcerers—and perceptive regarding the sorcerers from Chaco Canyon, the ones who were convoluting nature, making the timeless cloud people *duskyapti*, crazy, and cursing the people to forgetfulness so they could not remember the mistakes they had made?...This is why the good-hearted people left Chaco, leaving the *powakas* to their devices. The scientists harnessed time for their purposes, creating velocity. Then they tried the wind. The wind was eager. Then they seduced the clouds. Can we leave again? To where? (Masayesva 2006:61–65; original emphasis)

Notes

Preface

1. Albert Spaulding railed against the notion that "the only purpose of archaeology is to make archaeologists happy...a philosophical position which cannot be tolerated in a scientific context" (Spaulding 1953:590). I agree: Just because you call yourself an archaeologist does not mean you get to define "archaeology" any way you want. That's why they call it a discipline.

2. I am aware of objections to the term "prehistory," taken to mean that nonliterate societies have no history before some Euro-American writes one for them. And, yes, I am talking about "history" in the narrow, conventional academic sense. But I do not mean that tribes had no history in the general sense of the term. More than anything else, this book argues (again and again) that the ancient Southwest had a vibrant, dynamic past, which archaeology has failed to capture. The way archaeology might capture that past is to write a narrative, a "history" in the academic term. And that is what I mean by *pre-history*: a history accessed archaeologically, sans documents required by academic history. Much more on this later, especially in chapters 5 and 6.

3. I wrote a Master's thesis in 1978 (on Mimbres, not Chaco) with a chapter challenging the ahistoricity of (then) New Archaeology. My committee expunged it: They thought it would hurt me, professionally. Walter Taylor's name came up, as I recall.

4. See Joan Mathien's Chaco bibliography at http://www.chacoarchive.org/cra/chaco -resources/bibliography/.

5. I am weary unto death of Chaco and its intrigues. I could have used Mimbres–Casas Grandes, or Sinagua, or Hohokam, or other eventful episodes in the Southwest. All have vivid pre-histories that have suffocated under the strictures of American Anthropological Archaeology. But (unfairly) none of them have the widespread name recognition of Chaco. In chapter 7, I urge others to apply the argument and methods discussed in this book to the Southwest's other historical highlights and they are many. Someone other than me should do that.

6. Young Walter Taylor, all those many years ago in *A Study of Archeology*, asked the right question: "Archeology: History or Anthropology?" (Taylor 1948:25), coming down in favor of the latter. As the Grail Knight told Dr. Jones: "He chose poorly."

7. "Sometimes you have to slap them in the face just to get their attention," as the Ghost of Christmas Present explained to Frank Cross, just before she hit him with a toaster. I quote the great classicist Moses Finley: "This essay has a pervasively critical tone, which is neither accidental nor 'unconscious'...it is concerned with the way ancient historians go about their work, what they say or do not say, what they assume or overlook" (Finley 1990:60). On another tack, our better angel of style Steven Pinker admits to a "deliberately impolite tone" in his articles about obtuse academic writing—which comes in for some grief from me in chapter 5. A sharp poke works better than a gentle nudge, if you are in a hurry. And I am.

8. Anna O. Shepard was not the first or the last to confront this conundrum; but, in her no-nonsense way, she faced it forthrightly: "Can the common human tendency to resent criticism and the resultant fear of offending be corrected by reason? We would like to think that all anthropologists maintain an impersonal attitude toward their work, and that they welcome criticism as a valuable aid. But if we have not yet attained this level, must we not admit it and reckon with the facts?" (Shepard 1937:182).

9. For example, "state." If we'd gotten Chaco into that Old Boys Club back in the 1980s, when the term "state" was common parlance, much of this book would have been unnecessary. Now "state" has been theorized and problematized into a paste; people wrinkle their brows when you say the word. But Chaco belongs in the space-that-was-formerly-state, and to get it there we have to go back to the future, and make our case the old-fashioned way. Should have happened forty years ago. The late 1980s—post–Chaco Project, pre-NAGPRA—was a strategic moment missed because of Pueblo Space: "State" was then (and now) deemed unseemly for any society in the Southwest.

10. I've heard of people reading two copies of *History of the Ancient Southwest* simultaneously, one for text and the other for footnotes. Notes are online both for ease of use and to support a point I will make in chapter 6. The structure of this book is part of my argument.

Chapter 1: Chaco in the Twentieth Century

1. And what about my biases? As the American philosopher Harry Callahan said: A man's got to know his limitations. In my declining years I know some (maybe most?) of my peccadillos, my dispositions, my prejudices, my mistakes (all three of 'em!).

I'm an old White male, agnostic and cynical, wheezing my way up the down escalator toward that Great Seminar Room in the Sky. I have been told many times I have the sense of humor of a fourth-grader, and I cannot argue with that; but at least I have a sense of humor.

I hoped to study Classical Archaeology but my freshman advisor, finding I had no Greek or Latin, shunted me off to Anthropology's archaeology—which (he must have thought) any idiot could do. At the time, I had no idea what Anthropology was. (I'm still wondering.) So, I majored in Anthropology, but my real interest was History. My doctoral training was in close proximity to Lewis Binford, but not directly "under" him (as they say; a terrifying thought). New Archaeology was energized and interesting, but early and often I questioned New Archaeology's and Processual Archaeology's ahistoricism, throwing history on the dust bin of…history. That got me in trouble.

I read a lot of theory, and find some of it useful. I subscribe or identify with no particular school of archaeology (if such still exist) save this: Archaeology is history or it is nothing. But I'd like to use that history in scientific ways: Generalizing, finding patterns and processes. I think the truth is out there: I'm a closet positivist. Binford was a strong persuader.

Three years of fundraising for Crow Canyon sowed seeds of doubt. Asked why a potential patron should write a check for archaeology rather than the Children's Hospital, I could not find answers that satisfied me. Those early doubts redoubled and redoubled again during ten years of NAGPRA (Lekson 2010b) which shook my faith in archaeology; I almost quit the field.

I was asked, over and over, first by *ricos* and then by Indians, why archaeologists do what they do, what good accrues. With *ricos*, I must have answered satisfactorily; we raised lots of money. But with Indians…no, I could not justify archaeology in the face of their outrage. I could not defend Southwestern archaeology to Indians and, ultimately, to myself. Maybe the Indians were right: We should pull the plug. This book is, in part, an argument with myself against that conclusion. Revising the text for a final time, October 8, 2017 (in Bratislava, of all places), I'm not sure I've convinced myself: Southwestern archaeology's small triumphs seem hollow in the face of Native anger. In any event, we revisit this topic in chapter 5. Perhaps by the time I'm revising chapter 5, I'll make up my mind…

2. And which Gustavo Verdesio (2010), nodding to Foucault, calls "regimes of visibility"—the archaeology we CAN see given our colonial lenses, blinders, expectations (my words, not his).

3. The paraphrased quote: "And this is important, because if the entire hominid fossil record were to be rediscovered tomorrow and analyzed by paleontologists with no horses already in the race, it is pretty certain that we would emerge with a picture of human evolution very different from the one we inherited" (Tattersall 2015:213). Tattersall insists that history matters more in his discipline—paleoanthropology—than in other branches of paleontology because of the subject matter: Humans. "In this field, more than most, what we think today continues to be very intensely influenced by what we thought yesterday—and the day before that" (Tattersall 2015:xii); that should go double for archaeology, because we deal with anatomically modern humans, critters much like ourselves.

4. A tactic used throughout this book: Featuring one or a few people to represent broad movements or ideas. For example, Vine Deloria Jr. might represent Indian annoyance with archaeology—he's pretty good at that—but there are legions of Indians who are pissed off about archaeology (and not all of them are fond of Deloria). That tactic—focusing on one or a few persons or one or a few publications—leaves me open to critique of personal attack, but it also got this particular job/book done. You will notice that this book covers a lot of territory, and (as explained elsewhere) hopefully with accuracy if not precision. If I wanted both accuracy AND precision, the effort would expand to encyclopedia length. I don't want that, you don't want that…

5. Gender balance tilted strongly male, but strong women were there too: Bishop and Lange 2001; Davis 1995; Lamphere 1992; Parezo 1993; D. Smith 2005.

6. Excellent histories of Southwestern archaeology can be found in Richard Woodbury's (1993) *60 Years of Southwestern Archaeology: A History of the Pecos Conference*; Don Fowler's (2000) *A Laboratory for Anthropology: Science and Romanticism in the American Southwest, 1846–1930*; James Snead's (2001) *Ruins and Rivals: The Making of Southwest Archaeology*; David Wilcox and Don Fowler's (2002) "The Beginnings of Anthropological Archaeology in the North American Southwest: From Thomas Jefferson to the Pecos Conference"; and chapters in Linda Cordell and Don Fowler's (2005) *Southwest Archaeology in the Twentieth Century*—from which I take my chapter title. A somewhat crankier history of the field runs through *A History of the Ancient Southwest* (Lekson 2009a). For broader contexts, see Hinsley (e.g., 1981, 1986, 1989, 1990); Hinsley and Wilcox (1996); Bieder (1986); Conn (2004); Stocking (1982, 1989).

7. The literature on Europe's reaction to the New World is vast and vastly interesting. Four accounts I have found very useful are Lee Eldridge Huddleston's (1967) *Origins of the American Indians: European Concepts, 1492–1729*; George Kubler's (1991) *Esthetic Recognition of Ancient Amerindian Art*; Benjamin Keen's (1971) *The Aztec Image in Western Thought*; and Stephen Greenblatt's (1991) *Marvelous Possessions: The Wonder of the New World*. Keen and Kubler, in particular, should be read by every practicing North American archaeologist. I am not aware of comparable reviews of

Asia's reaction to the New World. Of course, Gavin Menzies (2003) insists that China explored the New World in 1421 (and the Mediterranean a decade later). So maybe they were not surprised by Columbus's news.

8. Rousseau and, much later, Hegel dismissed Native America as essentially history-less—a conclusion convenient for colonialism.

9. Al Schroeder (1979) provides a catalog of the devastation. Farming peoples in southern Arizona suffered much the same histories of colonization as the Pueblos, and like the Pueblos remain on or near their ancestral lands. As did many of the less settled, hunter-gatherer tribes. Although their histories are fraught with displacement and suppression, the Navajo Nation and most Apache groups remain today more or less on their Native lands. In New Mexico, a particular exception was the Chiricahua Apache, the last "wild" tribe to be reduced. When Geronimo came in the last time, in 1886, all the Chiricahua were declared prisoners of war and sent to prison first in Florida, then to coastal Alabama, and finally in Oklahoma. They were freed in 1912, but their homelands in New Mexico and Arizona were gone, settled by Whites. Most returned to join the Mescalero Apache in their reservation; many stayed on in Oklahoma.

10. Once the pyramids of the Mississippi Valley and the vast geometric monuments of Ohio had been demoted to "mounds" and naturalized as Native, there was no evidence for civilizations—Indian or Lost Race—east of the Great Plains. There are many accounts of early American investigations of eastern woodlands prehistory; one of the most engaging is Roger Kennedy's (1994) *Hidden Cities: The Discovery and Loss of Ancient North American Civilization*, which emphasizes the impact of Native prehistory on early American thought. Another "must read."

11. Albert Gallatin, one of the last real (if late) Enlightenment figures in American intellectual life (he died in 1849, deploring the Mexican War). Gallatin singled out the Pueblos among the many Native societies of North America—one of the first advocates of Pueblo exceptionalism—vis-à-vis "warlike" Navajos and Apaches. His research on the American Indian was largely an armchair affair, reading reports and corresponding with explorers. Compiling information on scores of tribes, he fastened on the Pueblos, approvingly: "If I have dwelt longer on the history these people [the Pueblos] than consistent with the limits of this essay, it is because it has been almost the only refreshing episode in the course of my researches" (Gallatin 1848:xcvii; see also Bieder 1986:50). Gallatin recognized that the Pueblos more closely resembled the settled villagers of Mesoamerica than any other North American tribe. He considered migration north out of Mexico, but settled on selective borrowing; in any event, he concluded that "this singular phenomenon deserves particular attention" (Gallatin 1848:liv). Gallatin may have been the first major American intellectual to declare the Pueblos exceptional. He certainly was not the last.

12. From the start, American Anthropology was Indianology. Steven Conn makes this point about "American anthropologists in the late nineteenth century":

> Whatever their methodological differences, whatever the differences in the materials they studied, archaeologists, linguists, ethnographers, and physical anthropologists in this county all shared the same subject: Native Americans. In the United States at the turn of the twentieth century, Native Americans served as the glue that held together the incipient, almost inchoate anthropology. Conversely, anthropology became the sole disciplinary home for the study of Native Americans. By the end of the nineteenth century, there could have been no American anthropology without Indians to give it some semblance of disciplinary coherence, and there was virtually no serious study of

Indians that was not anthropological. At a disciplinary level, the two were bound together inextricably. (Conn 2002:155)

13. Morgan and Bandelier together laid the foundations of Southwestern archaeology. Morgan shuffled off to his Reward before Boas got off the boat. To be sure, Boas did major foundational work too (Stocking 1960); but Morgan had already established the field as a valid scientific endeavor. In my opinion, Boas himself was less influential than Morgan on the ultimate course of archaeology of North America (although many of Boas's students went on to dabble in the dirt and discover wonderful things). In Stocking's (1974) *Franz Boas Reader*, the word "archaeology" merits only a half-dozen index references, and those mostly point to the work of others. Boas gets only a few mentions in Bruce Trigger's (2006) *History of Archaeological Thought*, mostly through his students or as a generalized "Boasian anthropology." Boas was too busy salvaging ethnology to worry much about archaeological pots and rocks. In his essay on "The History of Anthropology," Boas credits archaeology as essentially the "evolution of culture." "Of course, in many cases the chronological question cannot be answered, and then the archaeological observations simply rank with ethnological observations of primitive people" (Boas in Stocking 1974:23–36).

14. Morgan was president of that organization in 1880.

15. E.g., Bahn 2014; Dyson 2013; Trigger 2006. We make students read these histories, but I'm not sure students understand why they matter. The importance of the difference between American Archaeology (science) and European archaeology (history) cannot be overstressed. To 99 percent of the world, it's academic; but to understand American Archaeology, you must realize that it emerged in a very different intellectual context than almost any other archaeology of its time.

    The difference continues to confound us. Matthew Johnson, a leading British theorist, stated: "For many in North America, archaeology is seen as a subfield of anthropology, or at the very least the two disciplines are seen as closely linked. In Europe, a straw poll of the views of most archaeologists would suggest that the sister discipline of archaeology is history" (Johnson 2010:185).

16. Morgan, arguably, made more of a mark on modern times than almost any other American Anthropologist. Here's my pitch: Karl Marx and, more importantly, Friedrich Engels enthused about Morgan's work, and cited Morgan to support their theories of social evolution which eventually gave us Communism. Communism and various unpleasant reactions to it shaped much (most?) of twentieth-century history. Morgan, of course, did not directly cause the Soviet Union or the People's Republic of China, but his works in translation were part of the Marxist canon, and required reading for academically inclined Marxist theoreticians. I suspect they weren't reading Margaret Mead.

    In *Houses and House-life* (Morgan 1881, which Engels read very carefully), Morgan argued that all New World societies were communal; and (hot dog!!!) communalism *began in the Four Corners* and diffused outward throughout the New World. Since Morgan's view of the Four Corners was heavily Chacoan, one could say that Marxism began with Chaco. It would not be true; but one could say it. *Houses and House-life* was translated into Russian in 1934, when Russia enjoyed a breather between Civil War and Great Patriotic War, as *Doma i domashnyaya zhizn' amerikanskikh tuzemtsev* (Morgan 1934).

17. Southwestern ruins (in models and life-sized mock-ups) and Pueblo Indians (Hopis and Zunis, often in cheesy costumes) were staples at fairs and expositions from 1876 onward: e.g., at Chicago's 1893 Columbian Exposition, St. Louis's 1904 Louisiana

Purchase Exposition, and San Diego's 1915 Panama-California Exposition (Fernlund 2000:239–242; Parezo and Fowler 2007:246–252 and elsewhere; Rinehart 2012; Smith et al. 2011:46–47; Tennert 1987).

18. The "Romantic View" and alternative pre-histories were not only revelations or speculations or academic debates: Some had serious policy implications. The Book of Mormon appeared in 1830, and the State of Deseret (comprising not only Utah but also Nevada, most of Arizona, a large chunk of Colorado, and a bit of New Mexico) was proposed in 1849. The "Mormon War" ran its course in 1857–1858. There were (happily) very few casualties in the Mormon War, but there were in fact casualties: People died over an alternative archaeological ideology. As of course people died in earlier persecutions of Latter-Day Saints, which pushed them into the West.

19. Most famously, not on a Mexican map but on a map compiled in Mexico City by the Prussian polymath Alexander von Humboldt (1806, 1811), which was the basis for many later maps, such as the 1847 Disturnell map which caused the geographic embarrassment redeemed by the Gadsden Purchase.

    I recently saw a Mexican map of 1845 which, at Aztec Ruins location on the Rio Animas, had this text: "Gran des ruinas de los Aztecas" (Garcia 1845)—which was not so indicated on Humboldt's earlier maps. The conventional story has "Aztec Ruins" being the invention of nineteenth-century Anglo settlers; perhaps the new colonists accepted (and anglicized) the judgment of the older colonists? The map also notes "Cheque" at about the place (less certainly than Aztec) where Chaco should be—phonetically close.

20. Forgive the Cold War allusion, but an earlier attempt, "Tortilla Curtain" (Minnis 1984), while funny, did not find favor. This was written before Trump and Trump's Wall; Trump's Wall isn't remotely funny. And I've always liked the drama of Churchill's 1946 quote. The ex-PM turned a fine phrase, although he may not have originated this one. "Iron curtain" had been used before, very early in 1945, by Joseph Goebbels— also in relation to the impending Soviet ascendency in Eastern Europe. And apparently there is an even earlier physical referent: I have seen a real "iron curtain" in the Budapest Opera House, a nineteenth-century thirteen-ton metal monster which could be draped (or, rather, dropped) across the stage to prevent accidental fires in the scenery from cooking customers in orchestra seats. I suppose it could also be used to shield subpar sopranos from rotten vegetables and stale kaiser rolls. "Iron Curtain" is the exact translation of its Hungarian name, and I understand the safety feature was widely adopted across Europe in the days of gaslights.

21. I focus here on Anthropology's hijack/appropriation of America's ancient past, working mainly from histories of science, such as Robert Bieder's (1986) classic *Science Encounters the Indian*. American Anthropological Archaeology in effect said, we—not History—will take care of ancient Native America (if any). Steven Conn (2004), a historian at Ohio State University, has given us an excellent account of the same events, from History's side: *History's Shadow: Native Americans and Historical Consciousness in the Nineteenth Century*. American intellectual life in the nineteenth century was a small pond, so many of its denizens appear in both Bieder and Conn. But Conn's perspective as a historian is essential to understanding how Anthropology got away with the Great History Heist. A few of the early historians (most importantly for the Southwest, Prescott and Bancroft) footnoted speculations about American prehistory, but as History professionalized, that turf was ceded to Archaeology. Conn concludes his book with a quote from late-nineteenth-century antiquarian Stephen Peet, who wondered why American History begins with Columbus: "The question is whether this shall continue to be so." And Conn replies: "That question remains."

Conn's (1998) *Museums and American Intellectual Life, 1876–1926* is also essential reading, exploring the Anthropology-History semifracas in the context of museums and museology.

22. Morgan subdivided each stage: Lower, middle, higher; and he thought Indians stalled out somewhere around Middle Barbarism.

23. Morgan (1876) *Montezuma's Dinner.* For the Southwest, Morgan was preceded by and indebted to Albert Gallatin (1761–1849), a polymath politician (we met above) whose documentary research before the Mexican War convinced him "that the southwestern tribes had no kings or nobility and thus no 'serf of degraded cast'; no clique comprised of despot, favored cast, and priests...but rather a government in the hands of a council of old men," from Gallatin's (1848) introduction to "Hale's Indians of North-west America." Gallatin's remarkable and remarkably long essay—a book-length introduction to a book—is worth reading.

24. Hewett was a confirmed Morganite. Writing about a "New World Culture Type" which encompassed and characterized all Native societies of both North and South America, he declared them all communal and essentially egalitarian:

> It is the glory of the American Indian race that it developed a type of government entirely different from that of the European and more effective. The welfare of the people was the supreme end of government. If individuals became prominent, they were never personally glorified. In America the idea of monarchy had no place. The European, and in this I include the American of today, relinquishes painfully his preconceived ideas. "Empires of the Montezumas" seem necessary for his intellectual satisfaction. May we now drop these childish classifications and see the Indian in the light of his finer achievement in government: that is, a type free from monarchical authority? The typical government throughout the Americas was republican. (Hewett 1930:42)

—by "republican" he meant an "elected" council of elders.

25. Most histories of Southwestern archaeology start the clock somewhere in the nineteenth century, perhaps as early as Lieutenant Simpson's reports on Chaco Canyon in 1849 (Simpson 1964). But the ball really started to roll much later, with Adolph Bandelier's remarkable surveys of 1880–1892. Lieutenant Simpson's observations (like most of the early accounts) were incidental to his real job, which was chasing Navajos. Bandelier was employed by the Archaeological Institute of America to do archaeology and nothing else—the Southwest's first professional archaeologist! Since then, thousands of Southwestern archaeologists (yours truly included) elbowed our way for a place at the trough, making our livings on someone else's past. Thanks, Adolph!

26. Bandelier is not shy about his opinions, which owed much to Morgan. For example: "The usual supposition is that Casas Grandes was the 'capital' of a certain range or district, and that the smaller ruins are those of minor villages.... But I doubt whether there was any governmental tie uniting the villages on the Rio de Casas Grandes between the Boquilla and Corralitos with those near Janos or those near Ascension, even if all these groups were contemporaneously occupied. *It is inconsistent with the nature of Indian institutions that clusters geographically separated should be politically connected.*" (Bandelier 1892:570, emphasis added). That attitude about "the nature of Indian institutions" carried over far into the twentieth century, with turf-based objections to Chaco, its "outliers," and its region. We simply *know* that Indians didn't do stuff like that: Inconsistent with the nature of Indian institutions. But, they did.

27. Also the conclusion of William Henry Jackson in his influential 1878 "Report on Ancient Ruins" cited in Reed 2004:17.

28. Bandelier 1892:592. Actually, he was quoting himself from an earlier report, with his opinion unchanged. His conclusions to his 1892 *Final Report* are worth quoting at length:

> Thus the tales of slow wanderings, or rather shiftings, of Indian clusters from colder to warmer climes across the Southwest, become by no means improbable; but such movements must not be imagined to have been on the same scale as the irruption of vast hordes, such as Europe witnessed in the early part of our era, and which early writers upon Spanish America have conceived to have occurred in Mexico in prehistoric times. [that is: Aztec migrations from a southwestern Aztlan] I say this not in order to censure deserving men who centuries ago took pains to record the fading traditions of tribes then first becoming known to Europeans. At their time ethnology was not yet a science, and they wrote according to the prevailing state of knowledge, and according to the points afforded them for comparison. Hence arose misconceptions and honest exaggerations, which have become deeply engrafted upon ethnological thought, and have cast a veil over ethnological facts. The movements of tribes have been slow and disconnected; there has been, it seems, a general tendency to drift towards the tropics, but never in a continuous stream....
>
> This is a picture of the prehistoric past of the Southwest, somewhat different from that which, modelled upon the ancient history of Europe, has often been presented. On a previous occasion I thus wrote to the Institute on the subject: "The picture which can be dimly traced of this past is a very modest and unpretending one. No great cataclysms of nature, no waves of destruction on a large sale, either natural or human, appear to have interrupted the slow and tedious development of the people before the Spaniard came. One portion rose while another fell; sedentary tribes disappeared or moved off, and wild tribes roamed over the ruins of their former abodes" [quoting himself in Fifth Annual Report to AIA, p. 85]...
>
> Further than what I have intimated in these pages, I do not venture to go for the present. The time has not yet come when positive conclusions in regard to the history of the Southwest can be formulated. In the course of the past ten years new methods of research have been developed in ethnology, as well as in archaeology, and at some future day these may lead to the solution of questions which at present are perhaps not even clearly defined.
>
> Santa Fe, New Mexico
> April 20, 1891

29. Cushing's "My Adventures in Zuni" were published in *Century* magazine 1882–1883. "Cushing's sympathetic view of Pueblo life was published at the same time as racist articles depicting Plains Indians unfavorably during the High Plains Wars. His report demonstrated the basic humanity of the Zunis to readers accustomed only to negative stereotypes and inflammatory depictions of Indian warriors" (Traugott 2012:86).

Cushing's work was criticized by his time's establishment, perhaps unfairly. He was considered a showman and not a serious scholar. David Wilcox wrote an essay—"Restoring Authenticity: Judging Frank Hamilton Cushing's Veracity" (Wilcox 2003) looking at Cushing's critics; he concluded thus about two of his most famous detractors, Frederick Webb Hodge and Jesse Walter Fewkes: "Both rose to fame by trampling on the reputation and discrediting the ideas of the 'Sun' of a previous era, Frank Hamilton Cushing. Were they liars? Let us say that they may have been unscrupulous in pursuit of their ambitions for fame and power" (Wilcox 2003:201–203).

Cushing is remembered at Zuni, but not fondly (e.g., Phil Hughte 1994, *A Zuni Artist Looks at Frank Hamilton Cushing*)—the first of many obnoxious, invasive anthropologists. There's an old Zuni joke—and it's a bitter joke—that goes something like this: A Zuni family consists of a mother, a father, their children, and an anthropologist.

30. Bandelier, Powell, and Hewett were more significant to the Southwest, a place in which Boas conducted little research. Some of Boas's students did important work in the region: Elsie Clews Parsons, A. L. Kroeber, Leslie Spier, and Ruth Bunzell were all to various degrees associated with Boas. And of course Ruth Benedict. "But if there was a disciplinary dynamic that drew Boasians to the area, it seems also clear that some of them—sharing to a considerable extent the backgrounds, motives, sensibilities, experiences, and impressions of nonanthropologist intellectuals—also felt the pull of [D. H.] Lawrence's 'invisible threads of consciousness'" (Stocking 1989:220).

31. Timothy Pauketat, speaking of the (my words) Glass Ceiling over Cahokia, noted that "it was based on the common sense of the nineteenth and early twentieth centuries—that American Indian nations could not have accomplished anything worthy of note. Today some worry that this national legacy can still be seen in contemporary archaeological theorizing: consider the dehistoricizing of evolutionist constructs, such as the chiefdom, or the out-of-hand dismissal of historical complexity via Occam's Razor. And the issue has come to a head over Cahokia, a place Alice Kehoe has noted is 'hidden in plain sight' because of the cumulative biases of our intellectual heritage" (Pauketat 2007:135).

32. The triangle formed by Taos in the north, Milligan Gulch (a large Piro Pueblo) in the south, and Hopi in the west. The hinterlands and resource areas of the many Pueblos reached far beyond the geometric construct. A comparable area in Europe might span Brussels to Paris to Stuttgart, encompassing considerable ethnic, linguistic, and national diversity, among and between populations more densely connected than the "Pueblos."

33. An intermediate category, *rancheria*, designated settlements less permanent than Pueblos but more stable (and predictable) than the Indios Barbaros. In the Southwest, the best-known application was to southern Arizona's O'Odham peoples, who graded from "No Village" hunter-gatherers, to "Two Village" seasonal-round-with-agriculture, to "One Village" settled farmers.

34. The Spanish used the term *pueblo* for the Nahua *altepetl*, a small polity comprising a town and its hinterlands (which we meet again in chapter 3); contra Charles Gibson, *The Aztec under Spanish Rule* (1964), who translated the colonial category "pueblo" simply as "town." An early eighteenth-century dictionary of Castilian Spanish produced by the Royal Academy had this to say about "pueblo":

> Pueblo: El Lugar ó Ciudád que está poblado de gente. Pueblo tanto quiere decir como ayuntamiento de gentes de todas maneras, de aquella tierra dó se llegan.... Se toma también por el conjunto de gentes que habitan el lugar. (Real Academia Española 1726; ellipsis of citations, cross-references)

The first definition of *pueblo* is, of course, "town." But the second definition indicates that *pueblo* was also a political unit, centered on a town and including its territory. Of course there were still other meanings of *pueblo* in the early eighteenth century, one of which is "la gente común y ordinaria de alguna Ciudad ó poblacion, à distincion de los Nobles." Indeed, it is possible to speak of "Pueblos within Pueblos" (Johnson 2017) for political subdivisions within a polity.

35. In central Mexico, *Pueblo de Indios* was one term used for the Native political form we will encounter later in this book as "altepetl"; and also for towns created by colonial policy. It was a colonial policy (encouraged by royal decree in 1545) to "reduce" and aggregate Natives into towns, many of which persist today; but the forms taken by those towns probably mirrored pre-Columbian patterns (e.g., Gutiérrez Mendoza 2012; Ouweneel 1999).

36. E.g., Jorgensen's (1980) analysis of 172 tribes north of Mexico. Clustering programs do exactly that: Given an array of cases, such programs will move more similar together, less similar apart, based on whatever measures and statistics are employed; many programs decide for themselves what's important and what's trivial to a comparison. Caveat emptor. But, what if Jorgensen's sample stretched south of the border? With whom, then, would Pueblos cluster? Someone—not me—should redo Jorgensen, extending the sample to the south.

37. The various groups we call "Pueblo" did not, to my knowledge, get a vote on this terminological assemblage. I suspect they accept it today because they have no choice. Just as they are, legally, all "Indians," they are, legally, all "Pueblo." Roger Echo-Hawk (2010 and elsewhere) has written eloquently on the absurdity of "Indian" as a category or a race; he insists that he is not Indian, he is Pawnee. Are Pueblo people content to be "Pueblo"? I don't know.

38. Murdock's (1981) *Atlas of World Cultures*, the last edition of a compendium initially published in the late 1960s. The notion of Pueblo Culture, of course, goes much further back in American Anthropology: In A. L. Kroeber's 1939 *Cultural and Natural Areas of Native North America*, the "Pueblo Subculture Type" was described (or not) thus: "The true Pueblo culture is so distinctive, and so well known both ethnographically and archaeologically, that its detailed discussion here is unnecessary.... It constituted a localized and self-contained culmination" (Kroeber 1939:34–35).

39. Kohler 2012:213. This is a very useful paper, and one of the few recent analyses that tackles the problem of pan-Pueblo similarities. "Sprachbund" is a speech community of different groups who share many loan-words, perhaps lingua franca(s), and with many multilingual members. See also Mills 2008. There is, alas, little interest in such things today. NAGPRA and postmodern particularity reinforce a long-held, nearly universal belief among Southwesternists that "my valley's different"—emphasizing difference over similarity, local over regional.

40. In my opinion, then, the principal factor generating the great degree of cultural continuity across the Pueblo Southwest during these 700 years [600–1300] was the frequent population movement among its subregions.... These movements not only helped create a Sprachbund; they also helped synchronize (albeit imperfectly) culture change across this region through time. The mixing provided by such large-scale movements would have been reinforced by mobility at smaller scales. Since most communities within these regions would have been too small to be successfully endogamous especially prior to 1300, regular local movement of women (or men) across social group boundaries can also be anticipated and undoubtedly reinforced the effects of the larger inter-regional movements. (Kohler 2013:222–225)

41. Kohler acknowledges the "operation" of Chaco/Aztec: "The political and religious system centered on Chaco Canyon influenced most of the Pueblo world during

the Pueblo II (PII) period (ca. 900–1140) and…would have encompassed different language groups. Remnants of this system continued to influence much of the Northern San Juan region for at least a century thereafter. I do not emphasize these influences below—because I suspect they built on and were made possible by existing similarities largely produced by other mechanisms—but I do not deny their operation" (Kohler 2013:215). He introduces the concept of a "hierarchical society transition" or HST, to complement the Neolithic Demographic Transition; intriguing! I look forward to the further adventures of HST!

42. Southwestern archaeology needs something like Cathy Gere's (2009) fascinating *Knossos and the Prophets of Modernism*. I had hoped to write such a book someday, but this chapter is probably as far along that path as I'll go. Sifting through a hundred years of archaeological writing, finding and noting thousands of knee-jerk, throwaway references to ancient communalism and spirituality…it's more than I can handle. It's a project waiting for the right doctoral student: smart, cynical, with a high tolerance for hooey.

43. Pueblo Mystique and Pueblo Space operate much like the Maya Mystique, pervasive but mistaken ideas of Maya civilization that controlled archaeology in the Maya region through the 1950s. According to David Webster (2006), the key elements of the Maya Mystique were: Unique and exceptionally gifted people; egalitarian ("priests & people"); centers as vacant ceremonial constructs; inscriptions related to esoteric astronomy, calendrical and ritual; and peaceful. Like Pueblo Space, there was powerful "popular" buy-in for this, which in turn influenced archaeology (Webster 2006:130–133). The parallel is risibly close, except for "inscriptions." Ironically, "what finally put paid to the mystique was…the inscriptions. Ultimately it is the epigraphic messages left by the Maya themselves that convinced Mayanists of the existence of kings and nobles, their impressive households, their wars, and many other unexpected things. The irony is that these unique messages were required to open up our minds that the Maya were not so unique after all" (Webster 2006:151).

Webster notes, ruefully, that it was almost impossible to recognize the Mystique when one was in it, working under that umbrella. It pervaded Maya archaeology for decades, and it took exceptional discoveries to break the spell: For example, the discovery of a clearly royal tomb at Palenque and, above all, the decipherment of the inscriptions. And then Maya made sense (Webster 2006:149–150). Much the same could be said for Pueblo Mystique and Pueblo Space—except we have no inscriptions, only the archaeological facts of Chaco, and other anomalies.

44. I'm not making this up: This stuff happens and you can get in trouble pointing it out. As doubtless I will. Here's an account by Charles Briggs of the trouble Sam Gill got into with his deconstruction of "Mother Earth":

> Historian of religion Sam Gill argues that "the notion of Mother Earth as a Native American goddess has been created to meet various needs of Americans of European ancestry" (1987:106). He suggests that it is a story fashioned by white scholars "that supports a range of social, economic, and political relation-ships, very likely oppressive" (1987:128). Lacking a basis in Native American spirituality, the Mother Earth-as-goddess concept helped shape European Americans' self-definitions and bolstered their political-economic ascendancy. Gill claims that the power of this hegemonic image is so strong that Native Americans have internalized the concept of Mother Earth during the past 100 years, thus transforming a white fiction into Native American social reality. One of the foci of his book is the use of these conceptions by

Native American activists in countering threats to land loss and in building a pan-Indian identity (1987:145–146).… Rather than thanking Gill for clearing away white false consciousness, however, a number of Native American writers responded in a highly critical fashion [accusing him of cultural imperialism]. (Briggs 1996:436)

45. The "eternal and unchanging" bit was an obvious draw for weary moderns: Something fixed and permanent in a chaotic world. "In their constructions of the prehistoric and living peoples of the Southwest, Anglo imaginations claimed to see, sought to share, and ultimately brought to market an ethnographic present that remained somehow unchanged over centuries, while clearly having been surrounded by momentous events" (Hinsley 1990:469). Elsewhere, Hinsley (1996:196) called this "stasis as aesthetic therapy."

But "eternal and unchanging" makes things difficult for archaeology, which is all about change.

46. If a higher authority is needed, I offer Peter Whiteley: "Some presumptions I attributed…to New Agers derive in part from [university] classroom inventions of Native Americans: timeless, history-less spiritualists at harmony with one another and in tune with nature—and this is the story many students continue to want to hear" (Whiteley 1993:143).

47. Some representative works in this genre (certainly NOT an exhaustive list): Auerbach 2006; Babcock 1990; Dauber 1990; Dilworth 1996; Ellis 1997; Fowler 1992, 2000; Francaviglia and Narrett 1994; Gibson 1983; Goodman 2002; Gutierrez 1991; Herring 2005; Hinsley 1981, 1989, 1990; Hinsley and Wilcox 1996; Markovich et al. 1990; Mather and Woods 1986; McFeely 2001; Mills 2008a; Morrow et al. 1997; Pacheco 2016; Parezo 1993; Parezo and Fowler 2007; Rothman 2003; Scully 1989; Snead 2001, 2002; Weigle 1989, 1990; Weigle and Babcock 1996; Weixelman 2005; Wilcox 2003; A. Wilson 1997; and Wilson 2014. I've assumed that the reader is familiar with Santa Fe, the City Different; for a good general history, see Noble 1989.

48. "Together, the anthropologists, archaeologists, writers, artists, railroad owners, concessionaires and traders created a view of the American Southwest that appealed to persons of the East and brought money to the Southwest in the form of tourists, land developers and philanthropists" (Thomas 1999:126). It was not entirely a home-grown enchantment: Frank Cushing—part ethnologist, part showman—pitched Zuni in person to Boston society in the 1880s: "Cushing brought rich travelling theater [of Zuni men] eastward in 1882, a year before William F. Cody first took his Wild West show on tour" (Hinsley 1989:180). This made a deep impression on the Brahmins and Gilded Age journalists such as Sylvester Baxter: "The Zunis became the special property of artists and poets, and their pueblo has served as the playground for mimetic anthropologists from Cushing to Dennis Tedlock.… Not surprisingly, Baxter was one of the first to formulate this view of a conflict-free, communal order" (Hinsley 1989: 203); "As the mythicization of an Apollonian Southwest began to take hold in cosmopolitan circles of the east, Zuni society was falling apart through drunkenness, disease, dissension and death" (Hinsley 1989:202). See also Hinsley and Wilcox 1996, McFeely 2001.

49. Pueblo Mystique was partly real and mostly fiction, but it was not ethically "wrong"— in its time. At the turn of the last century, inventing traditions was all the rage. All over Europe, boosters and taste-makers were creating mythical pasts that make the Pueblo Mystique look tame. Think Druids or Celts; or earlier the fantasy worlds of Walter Scott and Richard Wagner. These may have begun as innocent diversions or

amusements, but they too often became propaganda (Cantor 1991; Hobsbawm 1983; Lowenthal 1998). In Hobsbawm's view, "invention of tradition" typically involves a group or society inventing a tradition for themselves—often a nation-state reinventing itself, along faux "traditional" lines with some claim to historicity. Europe was "Mass-Producing Traditions: Europe 1870–1914" (Hobsbawm 1983) at much the same time Santa Fe was inventing the Pueblo Mystique and Buffalo Bill was inventing the Wild West.

And, intriguingly, about that same time Mexico nationalized its prehistory, creating a national identity centered on Aztecs (at least in central Mexico; e.g., Brading 2001; see also Powell 1968). Santa Fe's shenanigans pale in comparison. After the dust settled from the Revolution of 1910, Aztec identity became government policy. The influential Porfiriato Minister of Public Education, José Vasconcelos, strongly promoted Aztec national identity in the 1920s through mural art, museums, and—of course—public education. His philosophy of a "mixed race," *raza cósmica* (Vasconcelos 1997[1925]), remains potent today both in Mexico, and in the United States as La Raza.

This is not to disparage Mexico's Aztec heritage or the reality of La Raza; rather to emphasize that things like this were happening during the creation of the Pueblo Mystique (and Pueblo Space) both here and abroad. What happened in Santa Fe wasn't unusual; except within the United States, where it was indeed unusual. Exceptional, by design.

50. Not alone, of course. The Chamber of Commerce pitched in; and Hewett and the Chamber had epic battles over who controlled the brand (Chauvenet 1983:109–120). And don't forget the artists! Beginning in the 1910s and 1920s and continuing today, artists and writers fell under the Pueblo Mystique and took it in many new directions. "Artists and writers in the Taos and Santa Fe colonies challenged this federal policy of suppressing aboriginal culture. They had come to cherish their Pueblo neighbors; they found them charming, useful, and instructive; useful to painters as models, to writers as source of inspiration for verse, and substance for fiction and nonfiction composition" (Gibson 1981:286). For the literary scene, see Weigle and Fiore (1982). Art historian Jana Perkovik gives most of the credit to art:

> The artists were the first to revolt…. Santa Fe's city leaders took the opportunity to re-imagine the city's traditional architecture and rich cultural history. They engaged the artist community to restore and preserve Santa Fe's old buildings. To ensure it was clear that they were rebuilding something distinct, something local, they called it the "City Different." Now that was something the tourists would take to…. As Umberto Eco would say, it was more representative of reality than reality itself. (Perkovik 2015)

Archaeologists often crossed disciplinary divides between art and archaeology (for example, Ken Chapman: Chapman and Barrie 2008, Munson 2008; and even Edgar Hewett: Chauvenet 1983:135–138). Hewett, after initially assisting its formation (Nelson 2016; Villela 2005), famously feuded with the Santa Fe Art Colony. Those bright young things viewed Hewett as a dotarding relic, as the Supreme Leader might say. (It does not pay to get old.) The Taos art colony (firmly separate from Santa Fe, as the Taos Society of Artists) was all wrapped up in Taos Pueblo—and a few other Pueblos: San Juan, San Ildefonso, Laguna. Their mystical fascinations eclipsed Hewett's scholarly approach. For example, writer Mary Austin (AKA "God's Mother-in-law"): "Regarding herself as something of a prophet, [Austin] envisioned an American acculturation that she termed 'Amerindian' in which an evolving American culture combined with Native American and Hispano rootedness to produce a new cultural synthesis" (Tobias and Woodhouse 2001:97). "She was especially interested in anything that might throw light on the [Pueblo] 'psychology of communism'…in equating the practice of communal landholding among Pueblos with something she might describe as 'communism'" (Chauvenet 1983:140). D.H. Lawrence, a somewhat reluctant member of the Taos circle, loved the Southwest but not so much the Pueblo Mystique: "The Indian bunk is not the Indian's invention. It is ours" (quoted in Scott 2015:188). See also Traugott 2012:Chapter 5; and Scott 2015; for a concentrated dose, Wood 1997; Mather and Woods 1986.

The Indian Market symbolizes the shift of Santa Fe style to Pueblo style. The first market—the Indian Fair—opened under the overall direction of Hewett in 1922 as an adjunct to the increasingly Puebloan Santa Fe Fiesta. At first a sideshow, today Indian Market (as the Fair became) vastly overshadows the older Fiesta. Hewett bowed out, or was forced out in 1927—"his role as culture and art arbiter in Santa Fe was being usurped by a lively and growing Anglo artistic community" (Bernstein 2012:75).

51. "Hewett's work on the 1906 Antiquities Act and its subsequent passage by the U.S. Congress set the stage for the creation of the Southwest. Hewett recognized early that the antiquities of the Southwest were unique and deserved preservation and study by professionals" (Thomas 1999:132).

52. Hewett is under-biographed. One book-length study, Chauvenet 1983, veers close to hagiography. Hewett's personal papers disappeared—rumor has it, burned at his request—but he appears, sometimes obliquely, sometimes acutely, in contemporary media and in the memoirs of his contemporaries; e.g., his lieutenant Ken Chapman (Munson 2008). He had as many detractors as admirers. In those polite Victorian times, if one had nothing nice to say, one said nothing; so Hewett is also curiously absent from or distant in many published reminiscences. But unquestionably Hewett was the central figure in the archaeological tilt of Santa Fe and Santa Fe Style, which begat Pueblo Style.

Hewett's centrality in the invention of the Southwest and Santa Fe was the subject of several articles—my favorites, Richard Frost's (1980) "The Romantic Inflation of Pueblo Culture" and George Stocking's (1982) "The Santa Fe Style in American Anthropology"; and even a dissertation, Jeffrey Thomas's (1999) dissertation, "Promoting the Southwest: Edgar L. Hewett, Anthropology, Archaeology and the Santa Fe Style"; here, a sample:

> Hewett's work, and the work of others in the Southwest, transformed the region into a place of imagination, a colony for artists, a place where Native Americans and Hispanics lived according to cultural norms that pre-dated the United States. Research has seldom been used so effectively to influence culture. (Thomas 1999:2)

53.   One of the biggest factors in Hewett's disagreements with the northeastern establishment was his status as a booster of the region. Hewett used the archaeology of the region to publicize it as an area of considerable interest to tourists and tourist-centered enterprises. Chief among these booster activities was the development of the "Santa Fe Style."…Hewett therefore used the science [of archaeology] as a method of promoting Santa Fe and the American Southwest. (Thomas 1999:48)

54. Since Santa Fe's reinvention in the 1920s, "City Different" has been its official nickname. I've heard Santa Fe called other things: "The place where old archaeologists go

to die"—an anonymous quote from a retired archaeologist who is today alive and well in the City Different. And "a geriatric theme-park"—another anonymous quote, because I never met the hipster who wrote angrily to the *Santa Fe New Mexican* after an octogenarian's Escalade crunched his bicycle. (The bicycle was parked and riderless.) Santa Fe is like other invented places: Beale Street or the French Quarter. But Santa Fe is older and richer and sober. NOT a party town like Beale or Bourbon or Duval.

55. An index of disdain: New Mexico (along with Arizona) was the very last state admitted in 1912 into the Lower 48. North Dakota and Idaho—not exactly hubs of civilization—reached statehood two decades before; even the Indian Territories in Oklahoma became a state five years before New Mexico was finally, grudgingly allowed to join the club.

56. Bishop Lamy's church. Bishops, like university chancellors, build things. The fine fictional account: Willa Cather's (1927) *Death Comes for the Archbishop.*

57. Hard times for the City Different: "In 1912, the city may have seemed at the ebb of its fortunes.... [T]he city no longer enjoyed the preeminent stature it once held. Santa Fe lost much of its commercial hegemony when the Atchison Topeka and Santa Fe Railroad bypassed the city for Albuquerque in the 1880s, and Fort Marcy's military reservation closed in the 1890s.... [T]he city had not prospered. The population had been dwindling since a peak in 1880, and by 1910, the United States census count indicated the city had just over 5,000 people" (Moul and Tigges 1996:138).

58. Albuquerque got the university, Santa Fe got the penitentiary. In 1908, the University in Albuquerque flirted with Pueblo Revival style, lathering mud-brown stucco over Victorian Hodgin Hall—to the horror of Albuquerque's civic leaders, who rose up and brought down the university president, William Tight, deemed responsible for unacceptable primitivism in modernizing Albuquerque. President Tight's Pueblo Revival at the university was a flash in the pan: wrong time, wrong place. John Gaw Meem later, in the 1930s, Pueblo'ed up the place, and won awards for his work.

59. Santa Fe's reinvention as a cultural and historical center began before Hewett, with the creation of a historical society which really came into prominence in 1880, with archaeology in its portfolio: "to snatch from oblivion the wonderful evidences of the prehistoric peoples of the Southwest" (Tobias and Woodhouse 2001:50, quoting the inaugural address of the historical society on February 21, 1881).

60. If not Anglo history, then maybe Anglo art? In the 1910s and 1920s (long after the Santa Fe Ring), northern New Mexico became famous/notorious for its artists' colonies, which grew like weeds (planted by Hewett; Nelson 2016, Viella 2005) in Santa Fe and Taos (e.g., Scott 2015; Traugott 2012). The air was thick with artistic temperament: Bohemian, unruly, avant-garde—and not to most peoples' taste, until they were romanticized (and collected) decades later. Polite readers back east might enjoy being titillated by artists' escapades—think: Mabel Dodge Luhan and Georgia O'Keefe—but artsy scandals did not fill trains, hotels, and restaurants.

61. Stensvaag (1980) recounts how the Historical Society of New Mexico began as a pioneer booster club and then graduated to the old Spanish families, before Hewett stocked its board with his creatures and folded it into his vision of early Colonial and then Indian heritage.

62. For an excellent architectural review, see Chris Wilson's (1997) *The Myth of Santa Fe: Creating a Modern Regional Tradition.* And for proceedings of conferences which brought Southwestern archaeologists and architects together: Markovich, Preiser and Strum 1990; Morrow and Price 1997; and Price and Morrow 2006. Today of course Santa Fe has strict guidelines for architecture in its historic core; preservation has become a mantra if not a mania "The preservationist/conservationist is emerging as

one of the region's heroes, and his or her identity represents a continuing romanticism of the Native American ethos" (Francaviglia 1994:35–36).

It worked: *Santa Fe Style* is the name of a twice-yearly magazine published by Sotheby's International Realty; each issue a glossy 100-plus page catalog of three-million-dollar mud-brick homes. Once, when we were fortunate to occupy the Jack Lambert House at the School of American/Advanced Research, a colleague from cosmopolitan Mexico City visited. We showed him our (temporary) house, proudly pointing out the exposed vigas, the corner fireplace, the Saltillo tiles. This, we bragged, is how ricos live in Santa Fe! Ah, said he, searching from something nice to say: "*rustico, rustico*—many houses in Mexico now reuse old church doors and woodwork."

People in Santa Fe spend enormous amounts of money to live in peasant houses—amenitized and wine-cellared, but still the architecture of *campesinos* and *labradores*.

63. Hewett was the director of archaeology and anthropology exhibits at the San Diego Panama–California Exposition. "The Santa Fe railway spent a quarter of a million dollars at the San Diego fair creating an entire Pueblo apartment house 'as seen at Taos and Zuni' complete with Indians making pottery" (Frost 1980:58).

64. History—faux and real—won out over modernism, or at least a brand of early urban renewal then called "City Beautiful" (Moul and Tigges 1996). With only a few nods to City Beautiful, Santa Fe chose City Adobe.

65. For the new version, Hispanics dressed as conquistadors and hidalgas. "The revived Fiesta celebration of 1919 was a turning point for the festival. The Fiesta was moved from its Fourth of July date to September. The Museum of New Mexico and School of American Research, made up of eastern-educated Anglos, organized the event. The Fiesta focused on the three dominant cultures of Santa Fe with a day devoted to each. Although the Fiesta was incorporated into the Museum of New Mexico's cultural revival effort, Hispanic participation dropped sharply" (Lovato 2004:49). By the late 1920s, many events were limited by fees and tickets, and "the infamous Zozobra" (Lovato 2004:49), a gigantic puppet invented by the anti-Hewett art community, as part of "Pasatiempo," a counterculture counter-Fiesta. With the passing years, Zozobra's climactic demise (he goes up in flames) came to dominate the proceedings. The Indian Market—now a huge event in Santa Fe—began as a small side show to Fiesta in 1922, selling curios; "overshadowed by mariachi music and the Mexican flavor of Santa Fe Fiesta, in 1962 the Indian Market finally moved to its own August weekend" (Bernstein 2012:108). By the final decades of the twentieth century, Indian leaders began to question any Pueblo involvement in a celebration of *la reconquista*. The Fiesta has, in large part, gone back to the local Hispanic community. See C. Wilson 1997:181–231 and—for more recent takes—Bernstein 2012 and Horton 2010.

66. We'd just fought a war with Spain, and we were busily governing colonies we'd judged Spain unfit to govern. For the generation that came through and immediately after the Splendid Little War, the Black Legend was real and contemporary, stoked by yellow journalism's run-up to war. Outside New Mexico, the southwestern Spanish were belittled as semicivilized (consider Lummis's sensational accounts of the Penitente brotherhoods) while Indians—Pueblo Indians in particular—were promoted to Noble Savage (a formulation I owe to Severin Fowles).

67. There were other tribes in New Mexico, but the Navajos and Apaches had very recently been our enemies. Geronimo, whom we met above, kept half of the US Army busy until 1886. His sins, real or imagined, stained "Apache" generally. He became an attraction at fairs and exhibitions—and for his notorious past, "the worst Indian that ever lived." Quite a contrast to the Pueblos. While it would be wrong to call the Pueblos docile—there were many times in the history of each Pueblo when they

demonstrated very practical politics—Pueblos were "tame" (not civilized, but tame) compared to the "savage" Apaches and Navajos. Or so the logic went, and thus they were displayed at fairs and expositions: The fierce old Apache warrior and the industrious, peaceful Pueblos, side-by-side for your consideration.

68.   Hewett's elaborate displays of Indians at the Santa Fe Fiesta and the Southwest Indian Fair tended to reinforce their separate, highly romanticized image in spite of his belief that the events were helping to carve a place in American society for Indians. That these were commercial ventures, in spite of their assertions to the contrary, cannot be denied. Indian cultures were put on sale as a means of educating the public, and ultimately reforming an ethnocentric Indian policy determined to destroy Indianness as a precondition for assimilation. The aim of the new policy initiative was self-determination for the Indians, but the selling of their cultures by well-meaning white patrons like [Mary] Austin and Hewett seems to have compromised this intention.… The abundant paternalism of the movement was matched only by the competition and egotism of those involved. While Austin and Hewett professed to have the Indians' best intentions at heart, their constant assertions that they were the only ones who really knew the Indians and that their organizations were the only legitimate ones dedicated to saving Pueblo cultures undercut the thrust of their work and brought confusion to the reform campaign. Had Austin and Hewett been able to set aside their egos and focus on their common interests, they may have garnered more influence on federal policy. (Meyer 2001:206–207)

69. Archaeology's prominence in this round of myth-making is highlighted in a chapter of a standard history of Santa Fe: "The Search for a New Direction: Archaeology, Health and Civic Organization," chapter 4 in Tobias and Woodhouse 2001:49–67. "By the middle of the first decade of the twentieth century, local attractions [old Hispanic administrative buildings, churches, etc.] crystallized into a more comprehensive picture. By then archaeology had moved to the foreground" and "archaeology loomed as a major path for Santa Fe's cultural development" (Tobias and Woodhouse 2001: 70–71).

70. "The central players in the partnership involved in building the museum included four prominent Santa Feans: lawyer and rancher Frank Springer, who was president of the Maxwell Land Grant and who did legal work for the Santa Fe railway; journalist turned banker Paul A. F. Walter; archaeologist and culture promoter Edgar Lee Hewett; and Hewett's able assistant, commercial artist Kenneth Chapman. Their alliance brought together financial, legislative, cultural and artistic interests" (Traugott 2012:96)—as well as unexplored connections to journalism and the AT&SF!

71. Later the School of American Research, and even later the School for Advanced Research. Santa Fe beat out Mexico City, Los Angeles, Albuquerque, and even Boulder, Colorado (!) for the site of the new School of American Archaeology. Hewett was quite a salesman.

72. In 1905, the AIA named Hewett its second "Fellow in American Archaeology," following literally in the steps of Adolph Bandelier (Thompson 2000:308). The School of American Archaeology was initially sponsored by the Archaeological Institute of America, which wanted Hewett to found the institution in Mexico City. AIA soon cut their ties with Hewett and Santa Fe.

73. "Hewett and Lummis became collaborators in the development of the image of the Southwest, a task that both undertook with zeal" (Thomas 1999:129–30). Lummis was not as bedazzled by the Pueblos as Hewett and others; Lummis "did not create the

latter-day sentimental adulation of the Pueblo Indians, but he drew American attention to these enticingly different people.... The influence of his writing was immense" (Frost 1980:56–57).

74. Santa Fe didn't pretend to BE a Pueblo, of course. It began as one, when the Spanish capitol was relocated atop a Native town. But real Pueblos surrounded the town, and were easily accessed in situ. The AT&SF ran right through three of them.

75. There were also immediate frictions with the existing historical society, which Hewett did not run; "The major focus of the society had been New Mexico history [that is, Spanish and Anglo]; that of the archaeologist was Native Americans. The shift of emphasis may have fostered concern among Hispano intellectuals that their heritage was being slighted" (Tobias and Woodhouse 2001:57).

76. "The infusion of Pueblo forms in the mid-teens added compositional irregularity and, for Anglo-Americans, a more fascinating, non-European form of the exotic" (C. Wilson 1997:145). Pueblo style was taken to caricature: A new state capitol proposed in the 1960s to replace the old Victorian (that had supplanted the Palace); it was round, inspired by Pueblo kivas translated into modern materials. When its design ran into opposition, its roundness was justified by its architect as "very old in the history of New Mexico, having its origin in the pueblo Kivas," and the thing was built: Round like a kiva, but with a nice Territorial trim. Consider Santa Fe's Inn of Loretto: The form is explosively Pueblo—even more Taos than Taos—but its name is conventual. And its stairway miraculous, unlike the omnipresent "kiva ladders," second only to silhouetted coyotes as a Santa Fe cliché.

77. So Manitou Cliff Dwellings (at Colorado Springs) and NaTeSo Pueblo (in Indian Hills) imported Indians from various Pueblos—in the case of Manitou, forging relationships and bonds that have lasted for decades. I'm told there are/were Pueblo families living in Colorado Springs who moved there for Manitou.

Hewett was an unofficial sponsor, or at least supporter, of Manitou Cliff Dwellings—perhaps a measure of his ambivalence towards Mesa Verde (discussed elsewhere in this chapter). Mesa Verde was hard to reach. Manitou was easy: At the end of the streetcar line in Colorado Springs, itself linked by rail to all points east. Why wreck your lower back on a buckboard bouncing into Mesa Verde, when you could see it all at Manitou for a nickel and sleep in a decent hotel? Someone should write a history of Manitou; for now, see Lekson 2009b and Lovato 2007.

78. Writing about a "New World Culture Type" which encompassed and characterized all Native societies of both North and South America, Hewett declared them all communal and essentially egalitarian:

> It is the glory of the American Indian race that it developed a type of government entirely different from that of the European and more effective. The welfare of the people was the supreme end of government. If individuals became prominent, they were never personally glorified. In America the idea of monarchy had no place.... We can truthfully say that these surviving Pueblo communities constitute the oldest existing republics.... The people managed their affairs through chosen representatives.... The Pueblos exemplify...the community type of social structure as distinct from the state or national type. (Hewett 1930:42, 72)

Neil Judd said much the same about Pueblo Bonito, in a 1925 *National Geographic* article: "an experiment in democracy—an experiment which ripened into full bloom and then withered—a full half-millennium before our Pilgrim Fathers dared as similar venture on the bleak coast of New England" (Judd 1925:262).

79. Richard Frost (1980:5) continues: "Their [Pueblos'] positive qualities had grown larger than life. They were admired as ceremonialists and artists. Their pottery was sought by discriminating connoisseurs and curio-hunters. The beauty of their villages was interpreted in oil paintings displayed in prestigious eastern art galleries. Books and magazines sympathetically portrayed Pueblo life, and the style of their architecture inspired the remodeling of the capital city of New Mexico. The Pueblo Indian romance, a generation in the making, was fully ripe."

80. *Art and Archaeology* 9(1) (1920) contains a half-dozen articles assembled by Hewett which show the early marketing of Pueblo aesthetics, the Santa Fe Fiesta, the Santa Fe/Taos art scene, and so forth.

81. Fred Harvey (who deserves a chapter here, but won't get it) and his Indian Detours (Dilworth 2001; Dilworth and Babcock 1989; McLuhan 1985; Weigle 1989). For more on AT&SF's role in creating the Pueblo Mystique, see Weigle and White 1988:52–65, and chapters in Weigle and Babcock 1996.

82. See, for example, Dorsey 1903. George Dorsey was the Curator of Anthropology at Chicago's Field Museum. The AT&SF commissioned and published a popular book, "Indians of the Southwest," a guidebook along the AT&SF route. After steaming through a few Plains tribes, the tour begins—where else?—in Santa Fe. All of the Pueblos are described, and advice offered for how and when to visit. "For several of the more important groups of ruins of the Southwest, Santa Fe forms a convenient starting-point" (Dorsey 1903:53). The book contains useful names and references (hotels, trading posts, etc.) for reaching distant Mesa Verde and Chaco. After many chapters on Hopi, and shorter considerations of Navajo, Apache, and Piman peoples, the train rolls into southern California and those tribes get a closing chapter. All aboard!

83. Hewett's tireless promotion of New Mexico's ancient ruins annoyed some of his contemporaries, who wanted to promote New Mexico's and Santa Fe's other charms and enchantments (Thompson 2000:280)—which, beyond dry air for invalids, were few in the early decades of the twentieth century.

84. A campaign started by Alice Fletcher Cunningham and Matilda Cox Stevenson; Hewett soon took over as the Pajarito Park's most ardent and steadfast promoter. Thompson 2000:275–284. See also Altherr 1985.

85. Bandelier National Monument, thanks in part to the advancement of Mesa Verde to a National Park in 1906, had a long, slow path to national recognition. Altherr 1985; Rothman 1988.

86.   The use of the Native American past as a source of Anglo American identity, however, meant that a specific rationale for the value of Southwestern antiquity to the modern inheritors of the land had to be created. The "archaeology" that emerged from this debate, manifest in the activities of author Charles Lummis, archaeologist and educator Edgar Lee Hewett, politician-scientist Frank Springer, and their contemporaries, disavowed the exclusively scientific agendas of professional anthropologists in favor of one that combined science, education, and regional pride. Largely ignored by modern scholars, the idea of archaeology as [regional] heritage spread widely through the region between 1900 and 1920 and played a central role in the construction of a new identity for the Southwest. (Snead 2002:19)

87. The Mystique affected a range of American intellectual and artistic life, in small but important ways. Leah Dilworth, for example, in her 1996 *Imagining Indians in the Southwest: Persistent Visions of a Primitive Past*, recounts the impacts of the Mystique

(not her word) on modern art and poetry. Chris Wilson chronicled the architectural history in *The Myth of Santa Fe: Creating a Modern Regional Tradition* in 1997. Eliza McFeely in 2001 traced *Zuni and the American Imagination* in literature and letters. Jerold Auerbach, in 2006's *Explorers in Eden: Pueblo Indians and the Promised Land*, traced how the nineteenth-century writers rendered Pueblos in Biblical terms, with a recursive conflation of Pueblos with the ancient Holy Land. More recently, Sascha Scott viewed the matter through the fine arts, in a remarkable 2015 study, *A Strange Mixture: the Art and Politics of Painting Pueblo Indians.* I list these titles not to dress windows, but to make this point: Most graduate students training to work in the Southwest have never read them; instead, we insist that they be familiar with the works of French social philosophers (whom we meet, unavoidably, in chapter 6).

88. A famous public intellectual, like her friend Margaret Mead. Mead wrote Benedict's biography in 1974; among many others, thereafter: Caffrey 1989; Modell 1983; and Young 2005.

89. From *Patterns of Culture*:

> The Zuñi are a ceremonious people, a people who value sobriety and inoffensiveness above all other virtues. Their interest is centered upon their rich and complex ceremonial life…. Their prayers also are formulas, the effectiveness of which comes from their faithful rendition. The amount of traditional prayer forms of this sort in Zuñi can hardly be exaggerated…. The heads of the major priesthoods, with the chief priest of the sun cult and the two chief priests of the war cult, constitute the ruling body, the council, of Zuñi. Zuñi is a theocracy to the last implication. Since priests are holy men and must never during the prosecution of their duties feel anger, nothing is brought before them about which there will not be unanimous agreement…. Personal authority is perhaps the most vigorously disparaged trait in Zuñi. A man who thirsts for power or knowledge, who wishes to be as they scornfully phrase it "a leader of his people" receives nothing but censure and will very likely be persecuted for sorcery…. He avoids office. He may have it thrust upon him, but he does not seek it…. The lack of opportunities for the exercise of authority, both in religious and in domestic situations, is knit up with another fundamental trait: the insistence upon sinking the individual in the group. In Zuñi, responsibility and power are always distributed and the group is made the functioning unit…. Just as according to the Zuñi ideal a man sinks his activities in those of the group and claims no personal authority, so also he is never violent. (Benedict 1934[1989]:59, 61, 67, 98–99, 103, 106)

Benedict's Zuni had a tilde over the "n"; for consistency in this book, I've de-tilded her Zuni. Denver has a major street that traffic reporters pronounce zoon-AYE. And another that's AY-coma, the latter half like the medical condition. No kidding.

90. By 1974 1.6 million copies had sold (Mead 1974) and new editions appeared every few years thereafter. It's never been out of print, and currently (March 2018) ranks no. 148 among all anthropology books on Amazon—eighty years after it was first published!

91. While Benedict's anthropology has fallen out of favor among professionals, in the words of one biographer, "*Patterns of Culture* would be named a classic by most anthropologists" (Young 2005:1). Several lengthy biographies are academic books, an indication of her importance within the discipline, and there can be no question of her impact on the broader audience. I make this declaration because my focus on Benedict has been questioned by anthropologists who blow her off as a poor ethnologist and a failed theorist. She may have been both, but she carried much clout.

92. Consider Hopi: Peter Whiteley (1998:12) summarizes the vast "para-ethnography on Hopi—often garnering a wider audience than the writings of anthropologists—has proliferated since the late nineteenth century" in "a variety of genres." For example: "Popular art films (Godfrey Reggio's *Koyaanisqatsi* and *Powaqqatsi*) relocate simulated Hopi representations in a truly postmodern play of extraterritorial transmutations. The immediate antecedent for the latter is [Frank] Water's *Book of the Hopi*, probably the most widely selling book on Hopi culture, despite its notorious confabulation of fact and imagination.... At present (summer 1997) controversies—especially at Third Mesa over the publications of New Age savagist Thomas Mails (1996)—reproduce long-standing dislike for Water's work in particular. The formal ethnographies, with their guild jargons, at least have the virtue of being less squarely in the public eye."

93. Stocking (1989:222) quoting Margaret Mead: "After armistice brought an end to 'this tornado of world-horror,' when it had 'seemed useless to attempt anything but a steady day-by-day living,' Benedict searched once more for expedients to 'get through these days.' Although she rejected the advice of a friend to 'move to the [Greenwich] village and have a good time, and several love affairs,'" Benedict instead turned to the consolations of Anthropology and, eventually, Zuni. She was enthralled by Zuni. One of Benedict's several biographers described the impression Zuni made on Benedict, who was at that time also a published poet: "Her poetry hinted at the extent to which Ruth had succumbed to the Southwest, as had others before her—ethnographers, travelers, poets, and artists. In poems inspired by the Southwest, Ruth as last 'loosened' the 'psychic machinery,' a change she acknowledged in prose on her second fieldtrip" (Modell 1983:172). "The Pueblo setting filled Ruth Benedict with close to a religious feeling.... She said, 'When I'm God I'm going to build my city there'" (Modell 1983:173). Hook, line, and sinker: Pueblo Mystique.

94. The influence of Indian policy on the creation of the Pueblo Mystique would need another book, yet to be written. Sascha Scott (2015:90–94) makes the case that the tensions between government assimilationist policies and preservationist philosophies among the White supporters of the Pueblos contributed substantially to the now-legendary Pueblo conservatism; that is, the Pueblo Mystique of extraordinary conservatism came at least in part from politicking and lobbying for the preservation of Pueblo culture. The anti-Dance policies of US government assimilationist policies in the 1920s drove Pueblo ceremonialism literally underground, a repeat of Spanish colonial repression. See Scott 2015:132–137. Note, this was in the 1920s—relatively recent times.

95. "Collier and other advocates for Pueblo culture explicitly tied Indian salvation to white salvation, seeing Pueblo culture as a positive counterexample to American society's materialism and spiritual corruptness" (Scott 2015:99).

96. Collier's *The Indians of North America* in 1947 and *Patterns and Ceremonials of the Indians of the Southwest* in 1949. I was flabbergasted to see Collier as the prime example listed on Wikipedia of "Postmodernist Anthropology." (Geertz and Margery Wolf get tangential nods; accessed Sept. 23, 2017.) You should be flabbergasted that I consult Wikipedia.

97. From Collier (1949[1962]:33):

> What these seekers from all over the world pursue, and find, is various, and includes all that North Americans seek and find. It includes archaeology, and the "living archaeology" of tribes whose dynamic past is moving them today; crafts and arts, and the organizational techniques of developing ancient crafts

and arts to modern use while conserving, even increasing, their traditional inspirations.... the saving of the land from water and wind erosion, a "number one" problem of our whole planet, in whose solution a number of the Southwestern tribes are leading the world; and such vistas of psychology and metapsychology as drew Carl Jung from Zurich to Taos Pueblo.

98. "Not strong central authority, but that social genius of pluralistic holism, which Cushing described at Zuni, has kept the Pueblos undissolved while ages of time, and wars, famines and forced migrations have rolled over them. Forcibly dominating central authority is contrary to that particular kind of social genius, a genius of freedom within complex and reciprocal structure, which has enabled the Pueblos to outlast all else besides. And their great political-social significance today is their achievement of freedom within order, order within freedom, and pluralistic unity" (Collier 1962:155).

99. Richard Frost (1980:59) summarized Collier's vision of the Pueblos:

> They embodied the ancient wisdom of tribal man, whose strength lay in the submergence of ego-identity to communal identity, in social reciprocity, artistic creativity, and aesthetic intercourse with the cosmic powers, because they believed the universe was a "living being" that required the sustained will of man for survival. Education, personality, and social institutions were all shaped towards these ceremonial, cosmic ends; the effect upon the individual was not confining but liberating. This "spiritual culture," according to Collier, was as old as Paleolithic man. In its antiquity, the Indian sense of time transcended the past and future alike; the "enduring past and enduring future" were conjoined, eliminating "linear, chronological" time.... The Indians were one with the land, not exploiters but "co-workers with it; they believed they were eternal as it was eternal." Organizationally, the Pueblos were sophisticated, self-governing bodies, deeply democratic and self-disciplined, free of commercial motives, class subjugation, and the subservience of women. Thus they were morally superior to Greek city-states. Their lives were constantly expressed through symbolic art—through ceremonies, dances, songs, myths, masks, pottery, weaving, and painting.

100. The Hopi literature is vast. Laird's (1977) *Hopi Bibliography* lists almost three thousand entries—and that was forty years ago!

101. Heralded by its fans as (for example) "distilled wisdom of Hopi elders." Vine Deloria Jr. (quoted in McLeod 1994:3) was less enthusiastic: "*Book of the Hopi* is regarded by the broad majority of Hopi as a work of fiction." For debunking of Waters's book, see Geertz 1983, 1990.

102. "If the San Francisco–based hippies had a favorite tribe, it was the Hopi—likely reflecting that a few of them had read Frank Waters' *Book of the Hopi* and that some Hopi people willingly, at least initially, interacted with the Anglo-seekers" (S. Smith 2012:65).

103. Waters himself is a field of study; e.g., McLeod 1994. There once was a Frank Waters Society and there still is a Frank Waters Foundation. http://www.frankwaters.org/.

104. Connections between Haight-Ashbury and Hopi generated a (small) scholarly literature; for example: Geertz 1994; McLeod 1994; McCaffery 2005; S. Smith 2012.

105. "Chachunga [Hopi leader] was gracious but urged the hippie assemblage to go back to their homes and be careful on the highway. He was old, needed his rest, and was going home himself.... But the critics could not kill the sentiments at the heart

of the project. The cultural appeal of Indianness was just getting started" (S. Smith 2012:74.

106. "…be Happy" attrib. to Meher Baba, Guru to the Stars. "…be Hopi" attrib. to Janice Day, the gracious proprietress of the Tsakurshovi Trading Post.

107. "In the present literary canon of the New Age, *Book of the Hopi…* has acquired widespread distinction as a sacred text, a foundational document which affirms non-Native rights of access to Native American religious cultural property" (McLeod 1994:301).

108. "In the proliferating literature the New Age, the works of Thomas E. Mails, a non-Native member of the Lutheran ministry, are singular for their advocacy of non-Native appropriation of Native American religious performance traditions…. [He] offers a do-it-yourself *paho*-making ceremony and kachina dance for non-Native readers and, elsewhere in the text, a mail order form for make-your-own *paho* kits" (McLeod 1994:301).

109. Keith Basso in *The Handbook of North American Indians* (1979):

> In keeping with nineteenth-century theories of cultural evolution, it was assumed that knowledge acquired about extant Southwestern societies could be "reversed," so to speak, and used to interpret archaeological materials. In this way—working from the known to the unknown, from the living to the dead by means of analogy—prehistoric cultures could be identified and connected with their surviving descendants. Ethnology and archaeology were opposites sides of the same coin. Concentrating mainly on Puebloan groups, early ethnologists seized upon information contained in myths and so-called migration legends to construct elaborate hypotheses about the origins of basic forms of social organization [citing Cushing, Bandelier, Fewkes, and the two Mindeleffs]. Although most of these hypotheses were subsequently rejected as untestable and unduly speculative…a few workers, following Cushing's lead, combined excursions into conjectural history with lengthy descriptions of ongoing cultures. (Basso 1979:15)

110. A. V. Kidder, in his seminal *Study of Southwestern Archaeology*:

> A review of the subject matter of Southwestern archaeology must necessarily begin with a consideration of the still inhabited pueblos of New Mexico and Arizona. These fascinating communities preserve the ancient culture of the Southwest almost in its aboriginal purity; even the most sophisticated of them are little more than veneered by European civilization, and we can still, as Lummis has so aptly phrased it, "catch our archaeology alive." (Kidder 1924[1962]:142–144)

111. The canonical Classic Ethnographies: Are they accurate? Hang around Pueblos long enough and you will hear tales about anthropologists, from Cushing to White, and how their informants fed them…rubbish. These tales may or may not be true, but one anthropologist's compressed experiences at a particular Pueblo at a particular time seem like a shaky framework upon which to build pre-history. This is not to devalue the Classic Ethnologies, but to insist that we cannot treat them as gospel. Recall the unpleasantness between Goldfrank and Benedict, two ethnologists in the Golden Age who saw very different things in the Pueblos (Bennett 1946). And see Young 2005.

112. "Standard texts from ethnology's Golden Age were cited to prove or support very contradictory accounts of the ancient past—a scholastic enterprise which, consequently, most archaeologists avoided" (Spielmann 2005).

113. I offer no citations, nor need I. I myself am of a certain age and (as we said back then) I watched it all go down.

114. For a history of Southwestern ethnology to about 1975, see Basso (1979). And for balance: Babcock and Parezo (1989), and of course, Fowler 2000.

115. Whiteley 1998:7: "If Hopi ethnography has come to a sort of end, the trajectory of its demise may be of more than ordinary interest, since anthropology practically begins at Hopi and Hopi is substantially represented, both descriptively and analytically, in virtually every theoretical paradigm since Morgan's evolutionism.... Since then, a partial list of those who have conducted at least some ethnographic work at Hopi reads like a metonymic who's who of the earlier disciplinary history within the United States."

116. Cushing was among the first of a long, long line of anthropologists who felt their curiosity was more important than Zuni's privacy; Pandy 1972.

117. Regarding the Direct Historic Approach, its most famous proponent, Julian Steward, had this to say about the Southwest:

> It is, in fact, a striking commentary on the divergent interests of archaeology and ethnology that in the Southwest the gap represented by the four hundred years of the historic period remained largely unfilled, while archaeology devoted itself mainly to prehistoric periods, and ethnology, to the ceremonialism and social organization of the modern Pueblo. And yet it was during this four hundred years that the Pueblo had contacts with one another, with the nomadic and seminomadic tribes, and with the Spaniards, *that account for much of their present culture.*" (Steward 1942:338; emphasis added)

118. "He was not an ethnologist—in fact, the distinguished anthropologist A. L. Kroeber considered Hewett's weakness in ethnology a serious flaw in his archaeological skills—but he learned over the years from the Indians" (Frost 1980:58). "From Hewett's perspective, archaeology was augmented by ethnology, not vice versa" (Snead 2005:30).

119. Lummis (1905) used "catch our archaeology alive" in reference to California folk music. "Archaeology" was elastic, back then; and, as today, susceptible to a well-turned catchphrase (as it were).

120. In his 1929 essay "The Present Status of Archaeology in the United States," Judd observes, "Although we have come to think of them as separate fields for investigation, it is impossible absolutely to divorce archaeology and ethnology" (Judd 1929:410), but he goes on to chide ethnology for ignoring material culture: "In our ethnological researches, study of material culture has rather gone out of fashion during the last quarter century; emphasis has been placed on fast-disappearing languages, ceremonies, and social organizations" (Judd 1929:404). Indeed, for Judd (trained in Classics, not ethnology):

> As we interpret it in this country, archaeology has to do with prehistory. Where written history begins there archaeology ends. Archaeology seeks to supply the text for those chapters that obviously preceded historical beginnings. Archaeology is the backward extension of recorded history!" (Judd 1929:401)

121. Ethnology was OK with that: Archaeologists might be half-baked ethnologists, but if they pasted Pueblos back on the past, they probably would do no harm. Pueblo ethnographer Edward Dozier, himself Tewa with a PhD from UCLA, summed it up: "All of the structures now found in the Pueblos existed in prehistoric times" (Dozier 1970:209).

122. Maybe the second Golden Age. It could be argued that the late nineteenth-century pioneer period—Cushing, Fewkes, Stephens, Bourke et alia—was Golden; but was it ethnology? Not the way the ethnologists went at it in the 1930s and 1940s, with anthropology up and running and fully stocked with methods, jargon, and attitude.

123. Barbara Babcock (1990), in the introduction to a collection of essays titled *Inventing the Southwest* addresses the ethnological bias: "I know that Ruth Benedict was not alone in her characterization of the Pueblo, that there is a romantic, nostalgic attitude on the part of anthropologists as well as artists which sees the organic character of preliterate life as preferable to the heterogeneity of modern life."

   "In the case of Southwestern ethnology," John Bennett pointed out (in his contribution to *Inventing the Southwest*), "these tendencies may often assume a special form conditioned by the pervading sense of mystery and glamour of the country itself. A good deal of ethnology and archaeology in the Southwest has been done with a kind of eager reverence for turquoise, concho belts, Snake Dances, and distant desert vistas" (1946:364–65). Bennett's article in *Southwestern Journal of Anthropology* is well worth reading for ethnology at mid-twentieth-century: He noted two distinct ethnological visions of the Pueblos, the dominant being Benedict's happy-peaceful-etc. idealization, the other Esther Goldfrank's (1945) grittier, sharper, less pleasant (for us) view of Pueblo culture: "These two interpretations have appeared not entirely as explicit, formal, theoretical positions, but more as implicit viewpoints" (p. 362). "Implicit viewpoints": The Pueblo Mystique in ethnology? Bennett continues: "What is perhaps most interesting—and not a little amusing—is that these controversies, so plainly a matter of value and preference, endure as long as they do without some objective attempt to sit down and realistically arbitrate the matter. The Puebloists have been firing their respective interpretations back and forth for a decade, yet none have seen fit to dig into the real issues—at least in print. It is not, perhaps, an easy thing to do, since it requires a good deal of self-objectivity and humility." Benedict won the "debate" with Goldfrank—but there was a lot of *ad hominem* in the outcome.

124. Spielmann 2005:194–195. "After the ethnological immersion of archaeologists like Fewkes at the turn of the century, southwestern archaeology developed remarkably independent from southwestern ethnology, and often in ignorance of what the ethnographic record entailed" (Spielmann 2005:197). The idea of "Pueblo" was ever-present in the archaeological imagination, but it was an ideal idea, uninformed by the actual nitty-gritty of ethnological research—which, by midcentury, had begun to poke holes in the Pueblo Mystique (e.g., Brandt 1994).

125. Two bombshells burst in the early 1970s: Charles Di Peso's (1974) *Casas Grandes* and Emil Haury's (1976) *Hohokam*—Fat Man and Little Boy (the books, not their authors). Di Peso's eight-volume magnum opus described an astonishing cosmopolitan city just south of our border. Haury's massive single-volume book described—for the first time, for many readers—the wonders of Hohokam, with startling canal systems, dense populations, ball courts, remarkable art. After those two explosions, the Southwest was no longer mainly or even principally Pueblo—but don't tell that to Santa Fe! Despite the fact that neither of these fabulous ancient events were Pueblo, the Pueblo Mystique survived and even found application in those strange new worlds: Casas Grandes is called a "pueblo" and Hohokam struggles to be anything but egalitarian— because the Southwest (we know) was intermediate and egalitarian.

126. Prying anthropologists have been replaced by prying artists, prying linguists, prying New Agers, prying environmentalists, and prying tourists. No rest for the Zuni, no peace for the Pueblos. In an old *New Yorker* cartoon, taped to my file cabinet, a nicely dressed matron in hat and gloves and purse wanders into a Pueblo room where a

family sits at breakfast, over their Wheaties. "Oh I *beg* your pardon," she apologizes, "I thought you were extinct."

127. But here's a sample, anyway:

> Some…anthropologists have continued to suggest that the conservatism and tenacity of Pueblo social, political, and religious organizations were relatively unaffected by the pressures of the wider cultural milieu. I suggest exactly the opposite is true…. [I]t is undeniably naïve to suggest that the core of Puebloan organization has remained relatively unaffected by changes that occurred even during the "ethnographic present," let alone during the periods prior to 1880…. The prominent role of religious ceremonial, the so-called "egalitarian" character of political and economic affairs, the absence of individual wealth, are all fundamentally related to changes induced during the contact period. (Upham 1987:267–268, 272)

128. Gregory Johnson (1989:373) acknowledged the shark-tankiness of Southwestern debates: "Commenting on Puebloan political organization seems to be one of life's 'no win' pursuits. Opinions on the same cases expressed during the [1983] seminar ranged from Apollonian egalitarianism to centrally administered and socially stratified social formations. Whatever you say, some large number of folk will be in vigorous disagreement with you."

129. See, for example, Cordell 1997, Reid and Whittlesey 1997, and (somewhat later) Kantner 2004; the better angels of ethnology hover over these fine textbooks.

130. One of several Great Divides, really. Just in the later pre-history, 1300, 1450, and 1600 mark the approximate dates of major historical deflections: 1300, the end of Chaco-Aztec; 1450, the end of Casas Grandes and Hohokam; 1600, the arrival of Spanish colonizers. Surely there were others before 1300. I focus here on 1300 but the other hinge points were just as important, historically.

131. There were earlier hints and allegations of un-Pueblo social difference and complexity at Chaco (Altschul 1978; Grebinger 1973; Martin and Plog 1973:270–271). By the early 1980s, your author had convinced himself (Lekson 1984) and maybe a few others that Chaco was a class-stratified society—based on the very obvious differences between contemporary Great Houses and Unit Pueblos (a difference noted with alarm in the 1930s; e.g., Hawley 1934). Similar conclusions were reached, independently, by John Schelberg (1984, 1992) and David Wilcox (1993). Boomers all, with the obvious exception of Paul S. Martin.

132. I arrived in 1950, but a couple of decades passed before I was functional. This section is notably un-footnoted and under-referenced, because I was there. This is my personal version of what happened in Southwestern archaeology during my so-called career. If you don't like it, write your own.

133. It's worth noting that these laws were not written by archaeologists; they were written by historians and architectural historians. The four criteria for inclusion in the National Register are: (1) associations with historic events; (2) associations with historic people; (3) archetype of a master architect; and, as a special dispensation for archaeology, (4) sites "that have yielded or may be likely to yield, information important in history or prehistory." Kind of a catch-all, and it caught all. People nominated lithic scatters to the National Register, until cooler heads prevailed.

134. CRM began at museums and universities; but the magic of the marketplace soon moved CRM to stand-alone for-profit firms or into much larger engineering or environmental businesses. E.g., Doelle and Phillips 2005; Roberts, Ahlstrom, and Roth 2004.

135. That's nationally. I'd guess the ratio is higher in the Southwest (with huge tracts of federal and tribal lands), perhaps as high as five to one. My data are rag-tag, from various sources with various dates and various degrees of certainty: AAA guides to departments; blogs like "Doug's Archaeology" (Rocks-Macqueen 2014); dated SAA surveys (Zeder 1997; Association Research Inc. 2011); and correspondence with ACRA and several colleagues, nameless and blameless. I claim no particular precision for these numbers but, I think, some accuracy in the ratios. For what they're worth, my back-of-the-envelope numbers (and dates of data): Academic, 1,630+ (2012); Federal agencies, 1,550 (2013); State agencies, 850 (2008); CRM, 7,000 (2008); for a total of about 11,030 archaeologists working in the USA. Except for the federal archaeologists and my personal count of academics (which excludes archaeologists working primarily outside the USA) these estimates all occurred pre-2008 crash, which of course impacted CRM.

136. The scale of the natural laboratory was, at most, a small river valley—the right-sized research for a dissertation. And it was generally assumed that everything was local: What happened in your natural laboratory stayed in your natural laboratory. Outside, uncontrolled inputs would scotch the experiment. Small scales—for a river valley is small—may have respected Pueblo Space (small, local, independent) or it may have reflected research budgets. The latter, more likely. The scale of natural laboratories was shattered first by "regional systems" such as Chaco and Hohokam (ably mapped as macroregions by David Wilcox, e.g., 1999; see also Crown and Judge 1991) and then by a renewed interest in migrations, Kayenta to southeastern Arizona and Mesa Verde to Rio Grande (e.g., Bernardini 2005; Cameron 1995; Clark 2001; Ortman 2012).

137. Garland Press, in the 1970s, published about two hundred volumes of Land Claims documents. Among many others, Florence Hawley Ellis wrote on behalf of several Rio Grande Pueblos; her student Alfred Dittert worked closely with Acoma (and is well remembered there).

138. Iowa's burial protection law passed in 1976—a clear precursor to the later federal legislation. The Slack Farm fiasco came in 1987, and Indian protestors picketed Dickson Mounds around the same time. Archaeologists knew that things were going to change.

139. Other laws important to CRM and "discretionary" field research were also amended in the late twentieth century to include, prominently, consultations with Indian tribes. The key Section 106 of the National Historic Preservation Act requires federal agencies to consult with tribes for projects on and off tribal lands—that is, any project that is subject to Section 106 now involves Indians. The Archaeological Resources Protection Act—under which federal archaeology permits are issued—also requires consultation with tribes as part of the permitting process. NAGPRA, NHPA, and ARPA gave Indians a major role in the regulation of fieldwork on federal lands, or (in most cases) with federal money—in some cases amounting to veto power.

140. And of course all those many individuals may not agree. My university museum was part of a consultation on "Fremont," jointly with a federal agency; when we arrived in the conference room, it became clear that the federal agency had invited one set of tribes, the university another. Whoops.

141. My well-thumbed copy of Elsie Clews Parsons's (1996[1939]) *Pueblo Indian Religion* is an edition of 1,200 pages in two hefty volumes.

142. Fowles persuasively argues that "doings" is not another word for religion, but may more accurately represents a pervasive system of politics or, rather, a tangle of both. This novel argument may be lost on readers who come to his work with an interest

in Pueblo "religion"—which in this ritually beglamoured age includes, perhaps, most Southwestern archaeologists. (All three back-cover blurbs situate his book as or in relation to the study of "religion".) Fowles insists that "the analytical divide between religion and politics…[is] entirely untenable for the precolonial period" (Fowles 2013:240–241). I agree…and disagree. Operations and behaviors and institutions we, today, would call "religious" and "political" were almost certainly intertwined, then. But the analytical categories, now, are still useful for us—if we today study "religion" and/or "politics."

143. I am struck by how archaeologists, who clearly respect Pueblos, insist on our right and ability to chart the course of Pueblo religious beliefs. These are precisely the things Indians tell us are NOT our business, and also things among the most difficult to see, with any certainty, in the archaeological record. But we press on, making remarkable pronouncements about the cosmology, ideology, and rituals of Pueblo ancestors.

144. The model was David Freidel's (1981). Judge's application was not precise; for example, Freidel's model does not involve a central ritual place analogous to Chaco Canyon in Judge's model (Judge 1989:242). The main parallel between the Maya and Chaco models is that both were ritually driven; that was something new for Chaco. Judge's model has been dismissed (unfairly, I think); Freidel's model is still widely if not universally accepted among Mayanists.

　　Judge was also strongly influenced by Kim Malville (my colleague at the University of Colorado), who studied pilgrimage in India, where pilgrimage centers attract staggering numbers of people (millions!); see Malville and Malville 2001. Few Chaco-pilgrimage adherents today realize that the first and most vocal proponent of Chaco-as-Pilgrimage-Center was a brilliant astrophysicist-cum-archaeoastronomer, importing models from the Subcontinent.

145. Nor in Native Mesoamerica. Joel Palka (2012:54–99) provides a review of Mesoamerican pilgrimage in chapter 2 of *Maya Pilgrimage to Ritual Landscapes*. Palka 2012:13: "Maya and Mesoamerican pilgrimage, in comparison to pilgrimage traditions elsewhere, does not focus on a few primary ritual sites. A potentially infinite number of sites exist in the Mesoamerican landscape where people communicate with spiritual beings"—much like the Pueblos, as I understand things. Mesoamerican pilgrimages were—like Pueblo pilgrimages—typically small groups going to landscape features (mountains, caves, springs) or to shrines. However, there are ethnographic accounts that "several hundred to several thousand people have participated in single pilgrimages" (Palka 2012:58; famously, the Huichol). A few cities—most famously Cholula— were ancient, authentic pilgrimage centers; again, mostly for small groups at varied times, not mass pilgrimages on the Chaco model. And, notably: Cholula was a city, a great big bustling settlement, not an empty ceremonial center. Freidel's model of pilgrimage fairs (mentioned above, for Chaco) is central to Palka's (2012:55ff) review. The Maya pilgrimage fair model does indeed move large numbers of people around on a calendar. Palka (and Freidel) note that such an organized regional system with urban pilgrimage centers presupposes a "universalizing religion" (Palka 2012:55), which unites individuals and attracts them to ceremonies and trade fairs. (As noted above, Judge nodded to this requirement by suggesting a "widely shared religion" in Chaco's era.) Universalizing religions are generally associated with fairly high-level sociopolitical entities (state, empires, and so forth); NOT in the Pueblo Space, at least until the friars arrived. I'll give the pro-pilgrimage people their pilgrimage center, if they give me a Chaco state, with a state religion!

　　An interesting and perhaps important aspect of pilgrimage: Palka's (2012:60–61) review of the differences between the Old and New World includes Kubler's (1984) observation that pilgrimage in the Old World benefits the individual pilgrim (think: Hajj or Camino de Santiago); Kubler and others maintain that while the Mesoamerican individual benefits from pilgrimage, there is also a very strong communal function that is a benefit to the community. So too Pueblo pilgrimages—at least some I've been told about. At the same time, "Elites organized pilgrimages and processions, and they were undertaken to affirm community members' different social ranks and status." See also Kantner 1996; Wells and Nelson 2007.

146. Pilgrimage penetrated both popular and secondary scholarly literatures; see Fox 1994 for an early example and Brooks 2013 for a more recent example, among many others.

147. Most famously with the work of Anna Sofaer and her colleagues on the Solstice Project, summarized in Sofaer 2008. See also: http://www.solsticeproject.org/about solstice.html

148. Certainly, it's ritual. Although for farmers, having a calendar is also an economic necessity. The two—ritual and economy—were OF COURSE intertwined. Who would doubt that, when even in twenty-first-century America, our coinage tells us "In God We Trust"? (God may or may not trust American currency: Didn't Jesus chase money changers from the temple?)

149. I do not agree, of course. There were earlier exceptions. Lynne Sebastian's (1992) *Chaco Anasazi: Sociopolitical Evolution in the Pueblo Southwest* focused on power I would call political, but still respects Pueblo Space, coming down on the side of the angels: "very active leadership…by means of religious monopoly [and] the metaphor of ritual"—Chaco, in the end, was ritual (Sebastian 1992:121–123). John Kantner's (1996) prescient "Political Competition among the Chaco Anasazi of the American Southwest" argued that political forces played a major role in the creation of Chaco. Kantner later merged politics with pilgrimage (Kantner and Vaughn 2012). Both Sebastian's and Kantner's early arguments seem to have been swept away by the rising tide of ritual. Jeffrey H. Altschul (1978) also edged towards the political.

150. Drennan 1999; and more famously in Yoffee, Fish, and Milner 1999:266:

> To describe the supposedly non-townish and not really political nature of Chaco, Dick Drennan proposed the term "rituality" to refer to its "ritual boomtown" nature. This neologism is attractive to us, since it is not borrowed from the extensive Western literature on urban geography, and it must be unpacked and explained in its own terms.

What did Drennan have in mind? Something very much like Yoffee's use—there was no distortion there—but it is worth examining the rather difficult context in which Drennan, as an outside arbiter, found himself. He contrasted Mississippian and Southwest—but two Southwests, Chaco and Hohokam, were merged into one. I have argued elsewhere (Lekson 2009) that Hohokam is truly remarkable for its vast public infrastructure in the absence of any easily identified central authority; Chaco, in contrast, is a garden-variety polity, like Dorothy small and meek. But because, at the SW-SE conference, Hohokam was enthusiastically declared a nonstate community (or "communidad") and Mississippian Cahokia was happily truncated at the "chiefdom" level, so Chaco must be something similar or lesser:

> Whether Hohokam or Anasazi groups can be classified as egalitarian or not, elite personages played a far less central social role than they did in Mississippian societies…. [On the regional scale] [i]t is easier to attach the label polity to this scale of integration for Mississippian, because politics seems

to be the arena in which the leaders who integrated these entities emerged. Politics, in the broadest sense at least, are probably not entirely absent from any human society, but they seem remarkably undeveloped in Hohokam and Anasazi societies. It is tempting to call Hohokam and Anasazi entities at the scale *ritualities* or *communalities* (to exaggerate [Suzanne] Fish's use of *communities* for Hohokam regional societies), thereby emphasizing the ritual, communal, group solidarity on which these entities were founded. (Drennan 1999:256–257, emphasis original)

151. The effort's shortcomings certainly were not structural, but rather personnel or personal—proclivities participants brought to the conference table (all nice bright people and fine company!). Among the Southeasternists were several notable "minimizers" (as they called themselves in seminar conversations and later in print) while among the Southwesternists were a few upstart "maximizers" (including your author) who saw the Southwest as more complex than then currently acceptable.

     Today there can be no reasonable doubt that many Mississippian polities of the Southeast were very-nearly-states and Cahokia clearly belongs in that exclusive Old Boys Club. But, in 1999, voting ran strong against that conclusion; and, if Cahokia was a simple chiefdom, what hope for the Southwest, with its few examples (like Chaco) of maybe-possibly-sorta-kinda-state-like? None: In the end Mississippian polities were planed off at the level of "chiefdom" (in the terms of the time) while Southwestern pretenders—so clearly inferior to Cahokia—were dismissed as something far-less-than-a-chiefdom: "communidades" and "ritualities" (Drennan 1999; Yoffee et al. 1999).

152. Yoffee disliked Neo-Evolutionary schemes. Revisiting "rituality" a few years later:

     I used the term "rituality" (adopting the term from R. Drennan; see Yoffee, Fish and Milner 1999) because it seemed to me that Chacoan "complexity" cannot be fit tidily into neo-evolutionary social organization types, such as tribes, complex tribe, big-man systems, chiefdoms (simple and complex), segmentary states, or just plain states, all of which have been employed to characterize the same material evidence at Chaco.... The neologism "rituality" is attractive to me since it must be unpacked and explained in its own context, namely a series of constructions whose place and purpose were concerned with matters of belief and ceremony. (Yoffee 2001:64)

153. The truth will out? Complexity coming in on ritual's coattails: Whitehouse, François, and Turchin (2015) explore "The Role of Ritual in the Evolution of Social Complexity."

154. The Harmonic Convergence was a syzygy of celestial bodies, predicted to be transformative. Perhaps it was. That was the year of "the drive," when John Elway took the Denver Broncos ninety-eight yards to beat the Cleveland Browns and go to the Super Bowl, so maybe the Harmonic Convergence worked. But the Broncos lost the Super Bowl, so maybe it didn't. But in any event, you have learned a new Scrabble word: syzygy.

155. First in articles such as "Ritual Control and Transformation in Middle Range Societies: An Example from the Southwest" (Schachner 2001), about Pueblo I; "Ritual, Power, and Social Differentiation in Small-Scale Societies" (Potter 2000), about Pueblo IV; and—after interest and enthusiasm built up—in edited volumes such as *Religion in the Prehispanic Southwest* (VanPool et al. 2006) and *Religious Transformation in the Late Pre-Hispanic Pueblo World* (Glowacki and Van Keuren 2011).

156. Paul Reed summarized the consensus at about 2000:

> In contrast to models that view Chacoan society as driven by competition and hierarchy, another new approach to social organization envisions a unified but cooperative endeavor. Chacoan society is seen as the result of an integrated, cooperative, and largely egalitarian effort without significant competition or social hierarchy. In this view, ritual and ceremony are paramount concerns, and ritual specialists or priests are the leaders.... Many Chacoan archaeologists have proposed hypotheses regarding social organization that fall into this general view. This view seems to represent a consensus or, at least, a majority opinion of the scholars gathered for the Chaco Synthesis Conferences. (Reed 2004:50–51 and note 17)

Chapter 2: Chaco in the Twenty-First Century

1. My original intent was to review everything Chaco since 2000. Boy! Is there a lot of Chaco since 2000! This chapter was originally much, much longer—far too long. So I selected only a few books and articles that illustrate particular points, and moved the rest online (https://stevelekson.com/), where my comments and appreciations will continue to appear. That division does not reflect on the quality and importance of publications absent from this chapter, but rather reflects the narrow structure and greedy needs of my argument.

2. Mid-twentieth century, Chaco Park archaeologist Gordon R. Vivian raised this awkward issue in a report on the excavation of Kin Kletso (Vivian and Mathews 1964). Vivian concluded that Chaco was escaping Pueblo Space: Chaco was "not in the direct line of the Northern [Rio Grande] Pueblo continuum...the continuation of the direction taken by the Chaco group would have carried it even farther out of the stream of development that culminated in the Rio Grande [Pueblos]" (Vivian and Mathews 1964:115). Vivian's remarkable insight, as far as I can tell, has been all but ignored in the subsequent Chacoan literature. Why? I know the answer: We want Chaco to stay in Pueblo Space.

3. The initial products of which were just beginning to appear in 2000, and rated a mention in Mills 2002. "Chaco Synthesis" was the uninspired name of a long, complicated project supported by the National Park Service in collaboration with the University of Colorado, which spanned the millennial divide. The goal was to pull together the work of the NPS Chaco Project (1969–1986)—a huge field project which did great things and published wonderful technical reports, but failed to conclude, failed to launch. The Chaco Synthesis (under the direction of yrs trly) staged a half-dozen working meetings at various universities and museums, involving over one hundred archaeologists from 1999 to 2004. Those meetings produced a series of books and thematic journal issues, culminating with a volume of twelve thematic chapters by twenty authors, *The Archaeology of Chaco Canyon* (Lekson, editor 2006), and complementing Joan Mathien's 2005 excellent summary of Chaco archaeology and Chaco Project fieldwork *Culture and Ecology of Chaco Canyon*.

4. The Chaco Research Archive was created in 2002 by Stephen Plog and Carrie Heitman, with the assistance of a stellar board of advisors. The Archive is "an online archive and analytical database that integrates much of the widely dispersed archaeological data collected from Chaco Canyon from the late 1890s through the first half of the 20th century"—but it now includes later materials, too, such as the "gray literature" reports of the Chaco Project, including a few by yrs trly. It's a phenomenal resource. www.chacoarchive.org

5. The Salmon Ruins Initiative was an NSF-supported 2001–2014 project sponsored by Archaeology Southwest to complete analysis and reports on Salmon Ruins, a major Chaco Great House near Bloomfield, New Mexico—70 km north of Chaco Canyon. Salmon Ruins had been excavated from 1970–1978 by Cynthia Irwin-Williams (with a cast of hundreds, including yrs trly in a minor role). A preliminary report had been prepared in 1980 but never published. The Salmon Ruins Initiative, led by Paul Reed, compiled the old report and added much new analysis in a three-volume 2006 publication, *Thirty-Five Years of Archaeological Research at Salmon Ruins, New Mexico*, and a 2008 volume of papers edited by Reed, *Chaco's Northern Prodigies: Salmon, Aztec and the Ascendency of the Middle San Juan Region after AD 1100*, and a thematic issue of *Kiva* guest-edited by Reed.

6. The University of New Mexico's Chaco Stratigraphy Project, which began in 2006 with the re-excavations of Neil Judd's 1920s trenches at Pueblo Bonito. The Project is directed by Chip Wills and Patty Crown, and is ongoing. As part of this project, Dr. Crown documented cacao in Chaco cylinder jars—a jaw-dropping side-project. The first major publication from the larger project is Crown's 2016 volume on the artifacts, *The Mounds of Pueblo Bonito, Chaco Canyon: Material Culture and Fauna*. Crown and Wills's Chaco work has expanded to re-excavations in the central core rooms of "Old Bonito"—the ninth-century core of the building.

7. Among others: University of Colorado excavations at the Bluff Great House (Catherine Cameron and yrs trly) and Chimney Rock (Brenda Todd and yrs trly); Crow Canyon Archaeological Center's investigations at several northern San Juan Great Houses (most recently, led by Susan Ryan); and many others. See https://stevelekson.com/

8. Citing Plog and Watson 2012; Wills 2012. But pilgrimage isn't going away: See Wells and Nelson 2007 for a revival of prehispanic mass pilgrimage south of the border that may well immigrate north, in search of a job to do.

9. This might remind readers of Ben Nelson's (1995) comparative study of Chaco and La Quemada. Measure after measure, Chaco came out ahead of La Quemada; but, ultimately, Pueblo Space kept it in its place. "Not if they are complex, but how they are complex"—opening the door for "alternative leadership" and that sort of nonhierarchical stuff. Which may be fine for Pueblos, but almost certainly not for Chaco.

10. Drennan and his colleagues (2010) in their own words: Regarding the burials of Pueblo Bonito, "In any context other than the US Southwest, the presence of such burials would immediately be taken to indicate substantial social inequality" (p. 48). And again, "Burials 13 and 14 at Pueblo Bonito would superficially, at least, suggest strongly individualizing organization, persistent efforts to label it 'corporate' notwithstanding" (p. 71).

    And regarding labor in monuments and public works: "While the nature and purposes of monumental construction in Chaco Canyon were rather different from either Moundville or La Venta, the magnitude of the labor invested clearly puts this case in the top ranks of this set of nine. The tax rate required for such construction in Chaco Canyon was probably also several times higher" (p. 68).

11. I considered quantifying this, taking a longitudinal random sample of Southwestern papers and coding the Pueblo Space buzz words and catch phrases and red flags. A chore too depressing to contemplate. And to what purpose? The results are obvious. If you doubt this, you are welcome to review the Southwestern literature for the past hundred-plus years, and good luck to you.

12. For example, Schelberg 1983:18. In my reading of Schelberg, John made as much sense as anyone on the subject:

> Unfortunately classificatory labels frequently evoke passioned [*sic*] response rather than reasoned debate.... Suggestions of incipient urbanism, stratification or a complex chiefdom are not simple attempts to over-extol the virtues of Chaco or to make the development comparable in grandeur to other areas of the world. It is an attempt, however, to indicate that certain processes had occurred.... Arguments concerning classificatory labels such as "complex chiefdom" (which I believe the Chacoans to have been) or "simple state" obscure the more important questions concerning the conditions that select for stratification. Stratified societies have evolved in many areas of the world and there is no reason to assume a single causality. (Schelberg 1983:17–18)

13. Turner and Turner's 1999 cannibalism study had been preceded by Tim White's 1992 *Prehistoric Cannibalism at Mancos 5MTUMR-2346*—a solid argument in a weighty tome from Princeton University Press with an approving back-cover blurb from Binford himself; which was initially ignored and then speedily forgotten. Its ugly, unwanted message was emphatically expanded by Turner and Turner, and their work was picked up by the press, most notably by Douglas Preston's (1998) provocative article "Cannibals of the Canyon" in *New Yorker* magazine. With the cascade of newspaper stories that followed, the fan was fully and roundly hit.

14. The then-head of Hopi denounced *Man Corn* from his office on TV, pointing to books on his shelf that proved the Hopi were peaceful people (which, of course, they are). Several months later, I was scheduled to meet with Hopi's Cultural Preservation office. As I walked in, I was met (uncharacteristically) with a preemptive question before I could even say hello: If you're here about that cannibalism business, we know all about it and it wasn't us. Like a fool, I did not follow up; I said that my present business concerned proposed excavations at a Great House (as I recall; I remember their opening shot far better than the meeting that followed, which was about something other than cannibalism).

15. I'm not a big fan of Turner's take on Chaco, but for those that reject his thuggish view or Mesoamerican interlopers: Aztec accounts of their arrival in the Basin of Mexico, and their initial attempts to win friends and influence people, were pretty darn thuggish. Real nasty. And those accounts were official court histories of the Aztec emperors.

16. Patricia Lambert, in a 2002 review of "The Archaeology of War: A North American Perspective," notes that "the American Southwest has been a primary focus of archaeological research on warfare in the last decade, and several major synthetic works have recently appeared. However, despite abundant archaeological and ethnohistoric evidence of its presence, the identification and interpretation of warfare in this region remains a contentious subject, at least in part due to perceptions based on modern Puebloan culture" (Lambert 2002:219, internal citations omitted). People outside our field looking in have no difficulty perceiving our peculiar institution, Pueblo Space: "Perceptions based on modern Puebloan culture."

17. Apparently I coined the faux-Latin "Pax Chaco" to reflect the evident absence of widespread warfare during Chaco's time, in a conference paper in 1992—which means I must have been looking at evidence other than bones (Turners' and LeBlanc's books came out in 1999). Certainly settlement patterns before, during, and after Chaco.

Before and after, they circled the wagons and aggregated and eventually retreated up into cliff overhangs; during Chaco, farmsteads dotted the landscape, spaced at distances that suggests an absence of fear. I explored this topic in my one and only *American Antiquity* article (Lekson 2002). My interpretation has been challenged (Cole 2007; Kohler, Cole, and Ciupe 2009), but—right or wrong—it gave aid and comfort to the metaphorical enemy, because Pax Chaco pushed Chaco back into peaceful Pueblo Space. That was not my intent. Given the pervasiveness of warfare before and after Chaco, its absence during Chaco (if real) suggests a strong central authority keeping the peace. In my reading, by the threat of seldom-used force; by more popular readings, by ritual.

18. Anderson's (1983, 1999) "imagined communities" had mainly to do with the printing press, literacy, and ultimately control or influence of the media by the national government. Anderson's highly influential argument is, of course, far more complex than the precis. Tropes of patriotism and racism—and, interestingly, heritage through media and museums—run through Anderson's "imagined communities."

19. And, far less theoretical, nationalist agendas: In the second edition Anderson details his book's many translations, and his fears that "imagined communities" became Bible for nationalism while at the same time being diluted from a top-down invention of tradition or imposition to a kind of cheery *Gemeinschaft.*

20. Which of course she acknowledges; Mills (2004a:241): "The definition of cultural patrimony as prime examples of collectively owned, inalienable objects." That NAGPRA definition is:

> Object of Cultural Patrimony: An object having ongoing historical, traditional, or cultural importance central to the Native American group or culture itself, rather than property owned by an individual Native American, and which, therefore, cannot be alienated, appropriated, or conveyed by any individual regardless of whether or not the individual is a member of the Indian tribe or Native Hawaiian organization and such object shall have been considered inalienable by such Native American group at the time the object was separated from such group. (25 USC 3001(3)(D))

21. I do not doubt that these objects were used in ritual, but what sort of ritual? Rather than ethnographic Zuni, perhaps we can look at Chaco's contemporary world: Mimbres and Hohokam. Mimbres pottery images, contemporary with Chaco, show objects much like suggested Chaco "altars" (Vivian, Dodge, and Hartman 1978) in use, not as altars but as emblems or totems—birds, fish, other animals—mounted on poles carried by bearers, clearly for public display (e.g., Brody, Scott, and LeBlanc 1983:Figure 72). Elements of such a display, found in a Mimbres cave, are curated by the Northwest Museum of Arts and Culture, Spokane, Washington. (They've never been published.) Mimbres pottery also shows knobbed staffs similar to those from Chaco. The Mimbres images show staffs carried by individuals, in one case an elder on a stool/throne (similar to those made later at Paquimé; DiPeso 1974:Figure 367-2), and to my mind suggest that staffs were regalia of authority (Rodeck 1956; Brody 2004:Figures 23, 27). Staffs depicted in contemporary Hohokam art seem to indicate a role as a burden bearer, perhaps a trader (Haury 1976:237–239). Or, as suggested in note 31, political authority. Staffs may mean one thing in modern Pueblos, and perhaps something else in the eleventh century. Our job is to determine what they meant in the eleventh century, and then figure out how that shifted to its current meaning.

22. Annette Weiner's (1992) book: *Inalienable Possessions: The Paradox of Keeping-While-*

Giving. "The Defeat of Hierarchy" is the title of a chapter in that book. (See also Weiner 1985.) The book is about challenging the anthropological faith in *reciprocity*: "It is the tenacious anthropological belief in the inherent nature of the norm of reciprocity that impedes the examination of the particular cultural conditions that empower the owners of inalienable possessions with hegemonic dominance over others. It is, then, not the hoary idea of a return gift that generates the thrust of exchange, but the radiating power of keeping inalienable objects out of exchange" (Weiner 1992:149–150). Hoarding? That could be the case for Bonito, and it's been suggested for Paquimé. Inalienable objects are indeed circulated but not through trade or exchange; and the most prestigious are retained within the noble "house."

23. "The significance of [Weiner's] work is that it points us in new directions, both within and outside of the sphere of exchangeability, for looking at the way that social valuables are produced and used. In this way, Weiner's work recently has become an important influence on the anthropology of materiality" (Mills 2004a:239).

24. "Inalienable wealth takes on important priorities in societies where ranking occurs. Persons and groups need to demonstrate continually who they are in relation to others, and their identities must be attached to those ancestral connections that figure significantly in their statuses, ranks, or titles" (Weiner 1985:210).

25. Weiner (1992:103) does indeed say that European colonization often turns a possession of immense political power into an art object for a foreign museum, or even a tourist trinket. The other ways an "inalienable possession" loses power are physical: Destruction and deterioration.

26. Weiner 1992:98, chapter 4: "Defeat of Hierarchy":

> The central themes of this chapter: first to locate the sources of authentication for inalienable possessions…second, to evaluate the limitations and potentials for keeping inalienable out of exchange, given the necessity to exchange; and third, to see how these problems and their solutions politically impinge on or are affected by the relationships of siblings and spouses. These are the elements that reveal under what circumstances hierarchy is established or defeated. Although gender and kinship are central to the dilemmas of keeping-while-giving, inalienable possessions are the hub around which social identities are displayed, fabricated, exaggerated, modified, or diminished. What is most essential about the trajectories of inalienable possessions, however, is not their individual ownerships but their authentication. The Polynesian cases reveal that shifting the ownership of an inalienable possession from one person to another does not reduce the possession's power as long as beliefs in its sacred authentication continued. (Weiner 1992:99–100)

27. Attributed to Jean-Baptiste Alphonse Karr, nineteenth-century novelist and epigramist. These are tough times for American graduate students: Taught Bourdieu and Foucault and French poststructuralists in all their annoying ambiguity, and now dragged back to Lévi-Strauss's *ancien régime* of binary oppositions and rigid structures.

28. Lévi-Strauss published his essay on "house societies" in 1975. An English translation was published in 1982, and by 1990 American cultural anthropologists finally noticed *Way of the Masks* (e.g., Carsten and Hugh-Jones 1995). Shortly thereafter, archaeologists noticed it too, most importantly in Rosemary Joyce and Susan Gillespie's (2000) edited volume *Beyond Kinship: Social and Material Reproduction in House Societies*, and seven years later in Robin Beck's (2007) *The Durable House: House Society Models in Archaeology.*

29. American Anthropological Archaeology jettisoned Claude's original notion of the noble house and honed in on Lévi-Strauss's more ethereal, conceptual baggage; in particular, a house as "moral being" or "moral person" (*Personne Morale*)—a Straussian notion as unlikely as a "corporate personhood" (Citizens United vs. Federal Election Commission, No. 08-205, 558 U.S. 310, 2010).

30. Susan Gillespie (2000) thinks Lévi-Strauss's house needs repairs:

> Despite his intention to clarify studies of kinship practices, Lévi-Strauss instead garnered a great deal of criticism on virtually every point. His definition of the house has been ignored or rewritten. His characterization of the house as fetishization of marriage alliance has been considered inappropriate or simplistic, although the fetishistic or representational aspect of the house has been carried even further. He has been reprimanded for having ignored what should have been a major object of inquiry—the physical house itself—and rebuked for treating the house as a classificatory type with an outmoded evolutionary trajectory. Finally, has been criticized for failing to rise above the naïve conceptions of kinship that he himself argued against. [However] there is still much to be gained from the original version of the house of Lévi-Strauss. (Gillespie 2000:23–24)

Not much left standing. By 2000, kinship studies were very much on the wane in cultural anthropology; and all but invisible in archaeology (but see Ware 2014). Why does Lévi-Strauss's "house" appeal so strongly to archaeologists? The answer, of course, is that archaeologists leveled Lévi-Strauss's house and rebuilt their own, to a new design—while keeping the Lévi-Strauss brand. We de-constructed his house—blew it to pieces, really—and salvaged the ornamental bits we find attractive, to decorate a whole new edifice. Cultural anthropologists, too:

> the real value of Lévi-Strauss's idea lies not so much in the creation of a new, unwieldly social type to complement or nuance already threadbare categories of traditional kinship theory but rather in providing a jumping-off point allowing a move beyond them towards a more holistic anthropology of architecture which might take its theoretical place alongside the anthropology of the body. (Carsten and Hugh-Jones 1995:2)

But *l'ancien* apparently was having none of this Anglophone meddling. In his last word on the subject (at least in English; Lévi-Strauss 1992) he stuck by his guns, repeating the arguments and analogies of "*Nobles Sauvages*." House Societies were ranked, hierarchical precursors to full-blown states.

31. The Lincoln canes were preceded by Spanish canes of authority. I suspect that whoever advised Old Abe that canes were just the thing (rather than Pendleton blankets, or Peace Medals, or other trinkets) knew of the historical importance of canes of authority in Pueblos. Many Pueblo governors (or rather, their offices) have three or four such canes, some dating back to early colonial times. Canes of this type were, in early colonial times, a symbol of Spanish gentility, a sort of peaceful sword; beyond their meaning in Spanish society, might the Governors' canes have tapped into a much older indigenous tradition of staffs/canes of authority? Both caballeros and caciques knew what canes meant. Bonito's staffs might well prefigure Pueblo governor's canes. Canes are symbols of authority and power from Spanish times on, and perhaps before. Could 300 staffs represent 150+ "outliers" plus the Canyon's noble families, retired when the capital shifted to Aztec? For an excellent description of Pueblo canes

and their history and possible pre-history, see *Canes of Power* (Silver Bullet Productions 2012).

32. EM seems peculiar to the West: Southwest, California, Northwest Coast. It began with Morgan in the Northeast, but is today conspicuous by its absence from (for example) the Mississippi Valley. If it were possible to EM Cahokia, which seems unlikely, could we push beyond that back to Hopewell and Poverty Point? No, of course not. There's something about the Southwest that makes things seem reasonable which are patently absurd elsewhere. And that is Pueblo Space.

33. *Chaco Revisited* boasts three EM enthusiasts: Cultural anthropologist Peter Whiteley in one chapter and archaeologists Kelley Hays-Gilpin and John Ware in another.

Whiteley's theme is "Chacoan kinship." His reference, of course, is Pueblos: "The modern Pueblos are in important respects homologous continuations from Chaco, not analogous metaphors lacking in common derivation. Correlating historic and contemporary Pueblo models with prehistoric Pueblo societies should thus be reconceived for what it is: not ethnographic analogy, but *ethnological homology*." (Whiteley 2015:295, emphasis original) "There is every reason to assume—*since they were not states*—that Ancestral Pueblo social systems, including the most highly developed versions at Chaco Canyon, were articulated through principles and rules of kinship" (Whiteley 2015:298, emphasis added). But…what if they *were* states?

Whiteley's chapter carries on at length, talking Pueblo to Chaco. I'm sure it's a masterful analysis, but with several fundamentally false assumptions, I cannot read it with enthusiasm. Chaco was not a Pueblo (it was a state; chapter 3), Chaco's kivas were not kivas (they were houses; Lekson 1988), and so on and so on. Projecting Pueblo analogies, much less homologies, back onto Chaco is a deeply doubtful enterprise.

But the times favor it, and so do Kelley Hayes-Gilpin and John Ware, whose chapter is titled "The View from Downstream"—a play on "up-streaming": Moving interpretively from the present to the past. Hayes-Gilpin represents Hopi and Ware the Rio Grande. They are more temperate than Whiteley, acknowledging that "whatever Chaco was, it was different than the historic pueblos. Nevertheless, Chacoans were among the ancestors of contemporary Pueblo people, and we can productively use the historic pueblos as 'end points' in our reconstruction of past trajectories of culture change" (Hayes-Gilpin and Ware 2015:322). The rest of the chapter is a festival of homologies. But they end on what I see as a hopeful note: At Chaco's end, "some [Chacoans] reorganized into smaller communities—some of which apparently kept some Chacoan legacies and *some of which rejected all things Chaco*" (Hayes-Gilpin and Ware 2015:344, emphasis added).

34. Ware denies this is teleological: "We do not look at ethnographic variation and deduce that the course of Pueblo social history had to be so-and-so," but how can a ballistic reconstruction be anything but teleological? I absolutely agree with Ware (2014:11): "Historical reconstruction is the essential preliminary to all socio-cultural explanation. We need to know what happened and when, and often in considerable detail, before we can know why things happened the way they did." He thinks EM will get him that history, but his method steamrolls the evidence—Chaco, most particularly—as discussed below. Not a steamroller, perhaps; rather, one of those car-crushing machines that compresses a Buick into a very, very heavy, breadbox-sized cube—sort of like Pueblo Space.

35. That history is not hidden; I wrote one version in *History of the Ancient Southwest* (Lekson 2009a). And see also Scott Rushforth and Steadman Upham's (1992) *A Hopi Social History*. Rushforth is a sociologist, Upham an archaeologist; their book at-

tempted to bridge prehistory/history. Ware does not like this book, because Rush-forth and Upham "argued that the 'horizontal' structures of the Hopis were not fully in place until the 1800s and were the direct result of historic depopulation and organizational simplification" (Ware 2014:58)—formation, that late, of Pueblo social structures is anathema in Ware's world, with Ware's method.

36. Ware believes that EM will move Southwestern archaeology forward. I'm doubtful: Ware "decided to 'revivify old research agendas' [citing Jerrold Levy] and take up questions and issues that fascinated an earlier generation of Pueblo ethnographers" (Ware 2014:xxii). It's a return to the 1920s, maybe even the 1880s; but like Marty McFly, Ware will send us back to the future.

37. Severin Fowles riffs on this theme:

> There is a sense, then, in which Taos and the other [Eastern] pueblos conformed to a traditional model of a stratified society. One can legitimately speak of elites and non-elites. One can speak of hierarchy. One can speak of power. Status was not solely based on achievement; rather, ascription played a heavy hand. This much has been obvious to nearly all serious students of Southwestern ethnography, giving rise to the common assertion that the pueblos were theocracies.... The term "theocracy" invites comparison with much larger-scale phenomena: African polities governed by principles of divine kingship, royal monarchies of medieval Europe, pharaonic Egypt, and the like. Such comparisons are slippery exercises and, when taken too far, draw attention away from a key difference: however "elite" the priests were within the overall moral hierarchy of Pueblos, they nevertheless had no special—let alone kingly—privilege in any significant economic sense, or at least in any sense that we would immediately recognize as economic. Theirs was an elitism without grander residences, larger storehouses, or more wives. With few exceptions, the priests did not partake of privileged cuisine, nor did they wear fancy baubles signifying their status. Priests were even without exemption from hard labor. (Fowles 2013:60)

38. Ware (2014:22–23) dictates the question:

> This book stands or falls on two arguments. The first is that the Pueblo ethnographies are more than a source of speculative analogies. The ethnographic Pueblos are end points on trajectories that preserve important information about the contingent histories of Pueblo social practices and institutions. Archaeologists and other historical scholars need to put aside their biases and become, again, serious students of historical ethnographies.
>
> ...My second argument is that if we are to understand social practices in Pueblo prehistory, we need to combine our study of the historical Pueblo ethnographies with a better grasp of kinship theory in general. Unfortunately, Southwestern archaeologists have gone the other way: they have convinced themselves that answers to kinship questions cannot be derived from material data of deep prehistory.

I'd say those Southwestern archaeologists are quite right: We cannot reconstruct kinship in deep prehistory. Moreover, I'd say that Ware's book stands or falls on quite a very different argument: His method. If his method is not sound, his "two arguments" are irrelevant.

39. Ware: "Skeptics will point out that we can never know precisely what kinship patterns existed long before written history.... Even with living groups, there is often

disagreement among both scholars and Native people about those patterns and how they came to be," [but] "it is important to infer what we can—especially in a book on the social history of tribal societies" (Ware 2014:23–24). This seems a tad circular: It's damn near impossible to do it, but it's OK to do it here, because that's what the book is supposed to do.

40. There's a reason cultural anthropologists abandoned kinship two decades ago; Ware notes this, with dismayed denial. And there's a reason Southwestern archaeology gave up on kinship after a few attempts at "Archaeology as Anthropology" (e.g., Hill 1970; Longacre 1970; and not many thereafter): It's nearly impossible to see kinship in the dirt. You can only project kinship through the calculus of EM, pushing what we think we know about an ethnographic present back into the past—where it does not belong.

41. Ware argues that the variation among and between Pueblos documented in ethnographies proves that Pueblo institutions survived colonization; that is, they were not entirely homogenized through assimilation. He concludes with a rallying cry for EM: "Ethnographic variation is not epiphenomenal! It is real, it is deep, and it matters!" (Ware 2014:183). Nice slogans, but the failure of colonial policies to totally assimilate Pueblos to Spanish/Mexican/American models does not mean that Spanish/Mexican/American policies and actions did not impact, deeply and profoundly, Pueblo histories.

42. Ware seems to think the demographic collapse didn't happen, and has waved at the 2015 book *Beyond Germs* as a warranting text (Cameron et al. 2015). It's not. Ware's demographic quarrel is with Henry Dobyns (1966, 1983); his methodological gripe is with Robert Dunnell (1991).

   In the Southwest, drastic demographic collapse, east and west, began as early as 1300–1400, long before European contact (e.g., Hill et al. 2004). This raises questions about Dobyns's and others' timing of the collapse; but does not *question collapse.*

   Beyond Germs does not argue that population loss was not "precipitous" or "devastating" (Kelton, Swedlund, and Cameron's terms), rather that additional colonial effects exacerbated decline, and then prevented population rebound. "If epidemics had been the only factor involved, Native populations would have recovered within a few generations" but they didn't (Kelton, Swedlund, and Cameron 2015:8). Dunnell's argument, for me at least, remains intact.

   Other studies, like Ann F. Ramenofsky and Jeremy Kulischeck (2013), refine the chronology and causes of the population collapse and question Dobyns's and other's high numbers; but no one denies that the loss was huge and devastating. Devastating to Pueblo societies and to the Ethnological Method.

43. Ramón Gutiérrez (1991), *When Jesus Came, the Corn Mothers Went Away*—a book Ware (2014:181–182) does not like.

44. Ware (2014:152) waves away the Great Divide at 1300: "In my judgement, Pueblo III and at least the early part of Pueblo IV are not primarily about social and political reorganization; they are about drought, arroyo entrenchment, and a scrambling of the monsoonal rainfall systems, resulting in range contraction, social balkanization, and conflict." I suggest that several items on that litany of disasters would probably impact the validity of EM back beyond 1300—and of course there's abundant evidence (noted in the text) for change in cosmology and religion, and to me very clear evidence of political collapse (again, noted in the text).

45. "If Chaco was organized on an eastern Pueblo model, why does Chaco not look more like an eastern Pueblo, and vice versa? Why do eastern pueblos not have great houses and roads? Where are the elites among the Eastern Pueblos, the modern equivalents of the individuals buried in Old Bonito?" (Ware 2014:126–127, original

capitalizations). Very good questions, all of 'em, which Ware (2014:127–131) does not answer in five pages of speculations on kinship versus bureaucracy which follow—a discussion which is actually pretty interesting! Ware devotes a section to "Kinship and Bureaucracy: A Fundamental Tension"; he argues that sodalities detached from kinship and became protobureaucracies (Ware 2014:126–130). Now we're getting somewhere! Norman Yoffee, the arbiter of statehood: "I suggest…that the most important necessary and sufficient condition that separates states from non-states is the emergence of certain socioeconomic and governmental roles that are emancipated from real or fictive kinship" (Yoffee 1993:69). Sodalities, emancipated from kinship?

In a stunning display of ahistorical up-streaming, Ware argues that since modern Pueblos don't have kings, Chaco could never have had kings: "Despite the fact that no modern Pueblo community has a political hierarchy capped by a powerful individual, some archaeologists have argued that self-aggrandizing individuals may have played a prominent role during the Puebloan past in places like Chaco Canyon. I understand the temptation; monumental architecture and exotic trade goods whisper suggestively of the rise of powerful political agents. Of course, if big men, chiefs, or similar self-aggrandizers figured prominently in early Pueblo communities such as Chaco, archaeologists are challenged to explain why such powerful individuals had disappeared by the time Spanish explorers showed up" (Ware 2014:40). The answer is simple: Chaco had kings and the Pueblos got rid of 'em; Pueblos are a reaction AGAINST Chacoan political systems, not a development FROM Chaco (see chapter 3). That's how history works: Shit happens.

46. Save Aztec, Chaco's successor, which should be considered as a package: The Chaco-Aztec polity (Lekson 2009a, 2015a).

47. As I write, Eric Blinman (a well-known Santa Fe archaeologist) has hopped on the bandwagon and delivered a public lecture on "A Revisionist View of Chaco Canyon: Is It Simpler than We Think?" I wasn't in the City Different to hear that lecture, alas.

48. That "someone" would be Cynthia Irwin-Williams, a remarkably astute, intelligent archaeologist. She came to Chaco from hunter-gatherer archaeology, and thus avoided much of the bias and baggage of Pueblo Space. We need more like her.

49. From Ware's *A Pueblo Social History*:

> Consider Upham's (1982) suggestion that late prehistoric communities in the Little Colorado valley of northeastern Arizona were politically linked by intervillage mating networks among elites. It is true that alliances based on inter-marriage are found in every region of every inhabited continent, but all ethnographic Pueblos are endogamous. As Jerry Levy (1994a:239) points out in his critique of Upham's alliance model, "if intervillage alliances were cemented by marriage among elite families, the decline of such a system would have resulted in agomous communities rather than the strict endogamy that we find even among bilateral Tanoans." Levy's critique reminds us that comparative research, no matter how systematic, complements but can never replace historical [i.e., ethnographic] analysis. (Ware 2014:10)

This argument is questionable on several counts, not the least that Levy's insistence that marriage between elites contrary to Pueblo "rules" in the fifteenth century would result in a lack of marriage rules among Pueblo nonelites in the nineteenth century. That's classic Ethnographic Method. Likewise Ware's dismissal of an interpretation of a fifteenth-century situation with the trump card of ethnology: In the idealized ethnographic present, "pueblos are endogamous," therefore no other situation was possible in the past.

50. Well, there are still a few people who want it both ways: Their outlier was vaguely connected to Chaco ("trade," "ritual," "social interactions"), but really it was autonomous and local. I summarize, harshly but fairly I think, a few arguments that are out there right now on the web and in conference papers: A particular outlier was built with local stone, therefore it's local. A particular outlier does not look exactly like Pueblo Bonito, therefore it's local. A particular outlier had local ceramics, therefore it's local. I thought we had hashed all this out decades ago—in fact, we did hash this out, but some people apparently didn't get the memo. A particular outlier (and each and every outlier) is different, therefore it's local. This latter argument gets drawn like a gun to prove Chaco's region was no region.

    Of course buildings are built of local stone; no one is going to haul Cliff House sandstone 150 km to build a "real" Chaco building. Of course they don't look like Pueblo Bonito; there are more than a few parts of Pueblo Bonito that don't look like Pueblo Bonito (the range of variation in a single building at Chaco approximates the range of variation in outliers—controlling for local materials). Of course they used local ceramics; Chaco Canyon didn't make much of its own pottery, they used "local" ceramics from everywhere else. And of course every outlier is different; every great house at Chaco Canyon is different. Still, outliers constitute an easily recognizable class or category. It's a gift from the archaeology gods, which some of us still try to make go away.

    Local is somehow seen as logically better, methodologically preferable, even when Chaco's region is one of the best documented archaeological (big) facts in Southwestern archaeology. There's 150 of these things and you want them all to be somehow autonomous and local? 150 cases of simultaneous equifinality? Gimme a break.

51. I cannot resist pointing out that the two decades of research on Black Mesa was almost entirely working in advance of massive coal-mining machines—great research, but contractually limited in scope. Black Mesa is enormous, and Mr. Peabody's coal trains hauled away only a bit of it. Proportionately, a very small bit. The vast majority of Black Mesa remains unknown to (archaeological) science, and prime country for Great House–hunting. Cedar Mesa (north in Utah) provides a useful lesson: A well-designed, well-executed, systematic sampling of the vast top of Cedar Mesa (the whole thing, not limited to a mine area) missed its two Great Houses—both with Kayenta pottery (Matson and Lipe 2011). That's the nature of rare or singular things: You have to look for them. We did, back in the 1980s and 1990s, and found them nearly everywhere.

52. Scores of very good archaeologists—perhaps hundreds—labored as individuals and as groups for several decades to discover and document the Chaco region. The regional structure is as close to a fact as we will ever get in Southwestern archaeology (at least, regarding anything interesting). It is not an interpretation, it is an empirical pattern, with a great big Chaco in the center and 150+ Great Houses in a repeated, robust contextual pattern scattered around it, over 60,000 sq mi. One may (and should) niggle about details. But at this point, we should be highly suspicious of arguments that wave it off or ignore it. Chaco's regional structure is as much a fact as Chaco's corn agriculture (but wait for chapter 3: There's nothing sure save death and taxes—not even farming).

53. Fowles argues that Taos was beyond Chaco's reach and so too the whole Rio Grande: "Perhaps because the Rio Grande populations wanted it that way.... We might reinterpret the absence of Chaconess as the presence of anti-Chaconess.... In the absence of Great Houses we might find evidence of a refuge from Chacoan orthodoxy" (Fowles 2013:86). But Taos history was not in "developmental isolation and provincialism"

(Fowles 2013:91). They were entangled with Chaco at its northeasternmost outlier, Chimney Rock, if not elsewhere. He suggests that migrants into the Taos area—who eventually became part of Taos—were "refugees, dissidents who fled an expanding regional system...or more provocatively: to what extent might we view the Winter People [a moiety at Taos] as a counterculture that opted out of Chacoan orthodoxy" (Fowles 2013:92). He extends this to the whole Rio Grande Valley: "It is unlikely that all eleventh-century communities in the northern Southwest would-have-if-they-could-have become Chacoan. Many may have purposefully avoided such a fate, viewing social simplicity as more progressive, more enlightened, more evolved than complexity" (Fowles 2013:93). In a word, Taos and the Rio Grande Valley *rejected* Chaco. (Works for me!) There follows a rich history related by Fowles to arrive at modern Taos (of which the Winter People were but one important element). But we can leave Taos's story here. Taos and the Rio Grande Valley rejected Chaco, broke with Chaco, charted their course away from Chaco and its customs.

"Let us assume that there was something to oppose and struggle against, a rotten seed in Chaco's evolving gestalt that populations eventually left behind. The Pueblos themselves frequently imply as much"—Fowles alludes to Pueblo accounts of "past worlds (Chacoan and other) gone corrupt and abandoned in favor of newer worlds, truer center places" (Fowles 2013:83–84). He uses ethnography not so much as a catalogue for objects and conventions to project back into the past, but as a source for real history.

54. Scott Ortman, whose study analyzes migration from the Mesa Verde region to the Tewa Pueblo area around Santa Fe, takes a similar position. Tewa-speakers from the Mesa Verde area without question were impacted by Chaco (or Chaco/Aztec), but left all that behind when they moved to the Rio Grande. The merging of Tewa peoples into existing Rio Grande populations was marked by the renunciation or repudiation by the migrants of many characteristic Mesa Verde and Chaco features (see also Lipe 2006). Ortman sees these deliberate acts as "an overt, negative commentary on the recent past...[part of a] discourse of erasing, or undoing, the recent past" (Ortman 2012:348–349). And again "'wiping out' emblematic features of the recent past and returning to a previous [pre-Chaco] way of life—in this case an earlier period of Mesa Verde culture history" (Ortman 2012:350) transposed or preserved in the Rio Grande Valley. Which, as Fowles argued (above), largely avoided direct Chaco entanglements.

Intriguingly, Keres has been suggested as the probable "prestige language" or "prestige code" of Chaco (Shaul 2014:141–147): "The presence of an elite means an elite way of talking, a prestige code, which was used in rituals and by the elite in general, and by others communicating with the elite" (p. 142).

55. *Pasiwvi*, Hopi for "place of deliberations," was focused on Wupatki and the San Francisco Peaks, but also encompassed a larger part of northeastern Arizona from the Grand Canyon to the Mogollon rim. Wupatki rose as Chaco fell, and represented something of a "rival" to Aztec (Lekson 2009a:156–158). Aztec was huge, a city; Wupatki was much smaller but remarkably eclectic: A Great House, a Great Kiva, and a Hohokam ball court! While Aztec is famous for the near-absence of exotics, Wupatki had more macaws (and other high-end baubles) than Pueblo Bonito. Aztec severed its southern ties; Wupatki kept the lines open. As *pasiwvi*, Wupatki may have been the place where Hopi leaders reinvented their societies as something new, something other than / different from Chaco-Aztec. The quote continues: "This new life plan would be distinct from the complex religious ways that had until then held sway. This Hopi life encompassed the principles of Hopi life today: Cooperation, sharing, respect, compassion, earth stewardship and, most of all, humility" (Kuwanwisiwma

et al. 2012:9). Does this suggest that the "ways that had until then held sway" may NOT have included cooperation, sharing, humility? Only the Hopi know. In any event: Another potentially major historical discontinuity, pinned perhaps to twelfth-century Wupatki.

56. "If Chaco fit neatly into some straight-forward organizational 'box'…we would have found that box by now. This does not mean it was some unique specimen we haven't seen before or since in the world; that is theoretically possible but statistically unlikely. What is more likely…is that we haven't looked at enough boxes yet" (Sebastian 2006: 411, quoting Sebastian 2004).

57. Call Chaco a "kingdom," and you get a big smackdown or the silent treatment. Call the Comanches an "empire," and you win the Bancroft Prize or (almost) the Pulitzer. I refer to Pekka Hämäläinen's (2008) *The Comanche Empire* and S.C. Gwynne's (2011) *Empire of the Summer Moon*. Gwynne's "empire" was figurative and literary, but Hämäläinen's "empire" was literal and strategic: Hämäläinen wanted to jolt historians and anthropologists out of their conventional view that Comanches were a "band-level" society. Hämäläinen argued that the facts strongly suggested otherwise (he's right, read the book). In my words, not his: American Anthropology's biases did injustice to Comanche history. What's true on the Southern Plains is truer in the San Juan Basin. The facts strongly suggest that Chaco was a kingdom (or altepetl)—terms I, like Hämäläinen, used to jolt my colleagues out of Pueblo Space. That word-strategy worked for Comanche, but not for Chaco.

One big difference in the contrary receptions of these historical revisions is the flattening effects of the Pueblo Space versus the Plains' Chiefs-and-Battles mythology. I will not go into the popular imagination of Plains warrior societies—Indian Wars via Hollywood. Suffice it to say that our image of the Plains accepts a horse empire. Pueblo Space does not admit a kingdom.

58. While writing these paragraphs, which took a few days, the Santa Fe newspaper published an oversized magazine-style article, "The Center Holds: Enigmas Endure at Chaco Canyon" (Weideman 2017); and *Science News* magazine displayed on its cover "Mysteries of Chaco Canyon" (Bower 2017; although that was not the title of the article). I don't keep count, but I'd guess that articles and posts touting Chaco's mysteries appear every two or three months, and have for as long as I've been paying attention, which is a long time. No kidding.

59. "No one really knows why this ancient site was built here or what the main purpose or function of the site was. The mystery and beauty of Chaco Canyon has enthralled visitors and researchers for many years. May it continue to do so." An excerpt from a brief report of a field trip to Chaco by the School for Advanced Research in Santa Fe, and sent out to their constituency on "SAR November E-News" of November 1, 2016. This specimen fell into my lap (or rather, popped up on my screen) as I wrote this section; kismet dictates that I share it here. It is a perfectly fair example of all the Chaco-as-mystery out there in Pueblo Space.

60. Stephen Plog introduced the recent volume *Chaco Revisited* with an essay, "Understanding Chaco" (Plog 2015:3–29). Regarding understanding Chaco, Plog says: We don't. Our lack of understanding is not for want of data ("copious amounts of data"). Then why? Plog suggests several "important reasons why key questions about Chaco remain unanswered." First, "the remarkable spatial scale of the Chaco social network"; second, "the complexity of the archaeological record in the canyon"; and third, "there has been too little effort to intensively and rigorously evaluate those [competing] models" of Chaco. To reinforce this last point, he quotes and paraphrases Gwinn Vivian: "There are too 'many "as it was" scenarios developed in attempting

to "explain" the archaeological record' of Chaco and not enough studies that 'use the record as a source of data to confirm or refute testable hypotheses,' models, or propositions" (Plog 2015:12).

Let's consider these dilemmas, which seem to derail our understanding of Chaco. Is the spatial scale of Chaco remarkable? Not really. Chaco's about the same size as Hohokam in the Southwest and pales in comparison to Hopewell and Mississippian in the East. Yet there is not nearly the mystification and hoopla about those three archaeological entities—despite the fact that Hopewell really IS mysterious and weird. Chaco's spatial scale is remarkable only when one's frame of reference is Pueblo Space. While historic Pueblos used impressive expanses of land for wild resources, the Pueblos of Pueblo Space were tidy, self-contained farming villages. If you are expecting a Pueblo, then Chaco's regional scale may come as a surprise. But...why would you expect a Pueblo?

Is the archaeology inside the canyon unusually or even prohibitively complex? Again, no. Chaco archaeology, in fact, is emphatically easy: Unsubtle sites, superb preservation, thousands of tree-ring dates, a century of (comparatively) generous funding, and a broad spectrum of excellent environmental studies—what's to gripe about? Chaco certainly is less challenging than Hohokam, whose far less substantial remains of far more complicated settlements lie under Arizona's capital city. Nobody built a city on top of Chaco. Hohokam archaeologists look at strip malls and wonder what's underneath. Chaco archaeologists stroll through the standing walls of Pueblo Bonito. Chaco's archaeology is more complicated than a hamlet on Black Mesa or a village on Mesa Verde, because Chaco was not those: Chaco was a small regional capital. Of course—of course!!!—its archaeology is more complicated than smaller sites in the northern Southwest—that complication is an index, "data" if you will, telling us Chaco was not farmsteads and Pueblos. But Chaco's archaeology is not alarmingly complex compared to other small regional capitals (think Cahokia) or centers (think Phoenix). Unless one expects the simplicity of Pueblo Space: If so, then Chaco's archaeology might seem a bit intimidating.

Too much speculation and not enough hypothesis testing? Here I agree and disagree. Certainly some of our speculations can hardly be evaluated much less tested. How to test for ceremonial center or rituality? Beats me. But this misses the point. The most useful models of Chaco are not trying to *explain* the archaeological record, they are trying to describe it. What profits us to "test hypotheses explaining" Chaco if we don't first understand what Chaco actually *was*? What good to evaluate an explanation without first correctly defining the explicandum? When I say Chaco was a low-wattage state (or, to anticipate a bit, something like an altepetl), I have explained nothing. But I'm not trying to explain anything; I am describing *what is to be explained.* Plog, and Vivian (2001) before him, seem to miss that point; in large part, I think, because of residual scientism. They appear to want write history through science, narratives through hypothesis testing. That won't work (see chapter 6). It should be possible, of course, to evaluate (NOT test) competing interpretations of Chaco-as-explicandum—but probably not within the framework of science. I'll return to this problem, below and at length in chapter 6.

The single most important reason why key questions about Chaco remain unanswered is simply this: Pueblo Space. That bias makes us expect small scales and simple archaeologies of Pueblos when, at Chaco, we are in fact confronting a small regional capital. Raise your sights! And learn about the archaeology of small regional capitals; most are far more complicated than Chaco, but archaeologists around the globe, working with far less copious and less precise data than Chaco's, somehow make sense of them.

61. Ortman (2016a) review of *Chaco Revisited*. "Enigma" was simply a nicely turned phrase, of course; but it's also the latest of many archaeological allusions to Chaco's mystery.

62. A sampling from the 'teens: Historian Daniel Richter, trying to make sense of Chaco, complained that "the surviving physical evidence leads archaeologists to wildly different conclusions," most particularly "about the degree to which Chaco Canyon was politically stratified" (Richter 2011:17). (Happily, Richter chooses wisely, and gets Chaco right.)

Archaeologist Severin Fowles (2010:195) concurs: "There is little agreement on the nature of Chacoan leadership. Chaco polarizes contemporary scholarship." And a few years later, despaired of Chaco scholarship: "a thing of cults and religious fanaticism"—referring to the current state of its archaeology, not Chaco's spiritual life in the past" (Fowles 2013:75).

In 2010, Stephen Plog's "Reflections on the State of Chacoan Research" concludes: "Despite the profusion of publications we have not made significant progress in understanding key aspects of Chaco" (p. 378). And again: "To paraphrase [David] Phillips (2002:12), we lack a conceptual framework for Chaco that attempts to explain all of the variation we observe, that carefully examines the dynamic nature of social groups and accounts for relationships among those groups" (p. 390). Plog and Phillips might not have a conceptual framework that "explains" Chaco to their liking but I do, we do. Plog and Phillips just don't like where that conceptual framework takes us: Away from Pueblo Space into dangerous territory.

Chapter 3: A History of the Ancient Southwest

1. Great Houses are real, and really different. The stark differences between Pueblo II Great Houses and normal Pueblo II architecture (e.g., the Bc sites) were noted early and often (e.g., Hawley 1934; Kluckhohn 1939). The owners/residents built and maintained the Bc sites; They were domestic, vernacular buildings. Great Houses required labor forces far larger than the number of residents (below) and can quite properly be called monumental architecture. Even Architecture with a capital A.

   The differences between Great Houses and "small sites" has been a central question in Chaco archaeology, from Florence Hawley's realization that Great Houses and Bc sites were in fact contemporary (Hawley 1934); to Gordon Vivian's tricultural systematics (Vivian and Mathews 1965); and the Kluckhohn-Gwinn-Vivian biethnic Chaco ("as an egalitarian enterprise"; Vivian 1989, 1990). "Towns" versus "villages": Those differences have troubled archaeologists for almost a century. The solution seems obvious—nobles and commoners—but that's forbidden in Pueblo Space.

2. Great Houses were *houses*, but not many people lived in them. Great Houses were *houses*, not temples or empty monuments or machines for ritual. Three independent analyses have reached the same conclusion: People lived in Great Houses, but far fewer people than would be suggested by their hundreds of storage rooms (see note 18; see Lekson 1984; Windes 1984; Bernardini 1999).

3. People living in Great Houses were…special. Pueblo Bonito was the only Chaco Canyon Great House where numerous burials were found. Nancy Akins reported that the Bonito burials were bigger and healthier than their contemporaries (Akins 2001, 2003; contra Palkovich 1984); that they were a closely related group (confirmed by Kennett et al. 2017); and that the burials suggest "Chaco Canyon's residents were hierarchically

organized" and "status in the upper levels was ascribed" (Akins 2003:105). Recent analysis of the two main male burials in Bonito's central tomb note that they were "among the most remarkable in the prehispanic Southwest" presenting clear evidence of "hierarchy and social inequality" (Plog and Heitman 2010). In an earlier report, Akins (1986) noted that women of Bonito generally lacked the "squatting facets" that mark the bones of young women presumably tasked with corn grinding, which requires extended daily periods of squatting. Recent genetic research concludes that the Bonito burials in Room 33 (a high-status crypt with 300+ years of burials; Plog and Heitman 2010) were a "matrilineal dynasty" (Kennett et al. 2017).

4. Chaco was a class-stratified society. The differences between Great Houses and Bc sites once was interpreted as two different ethnicities simultaneously sharing Chaco Canyon (e.g., Vivian 1990). Given other lines of evidence—the monumentality of Great Houses (above), bioarchaeology (above), disparities in "high-end" material culture (below), Chaco's regional system (below)—it seems far more likely that, as a pre-PhD punk once suggested, "stratification in housing presumably reflected social distinctions in the population" (Lekson 1984:271). Great Houses were palaces— monumental residences for elite, presumably ruling classes, which incorporated a great deal of nondomestic storage space, specialized ceremonial structures, and probably "offices" for an evolving protobureaucracy (Lekson 2006). Claims that Chaco's Great Houses were purely (or even mostly) ritual or simply farming villages require us to ignore a great deal of robust, fairly unambiguous evidence. Wishful thinking, sending Great House back into Pueblo Space.

5. Outlier Great Houses define Chaco's region. The geographic extent of Great Houses was established by several independent, collaborating projects (Fowler et al. 1987; Kincaid 1983; Marshall et al. 1979; Nials et al. 1987; Powers et al. 1983). Several "outlier" inventories listed the same sites, consistently. Among those who visited "outlier" Great Houses in the four quarters of the Chacoan world, there was little doubt that small "outlier" Great House sites in the north represented the same architectural expressions as small Great Houses in the south. Beyond the massive reality of the Great House itself there was a bundle or package of more subtle landscape features that were consistently but not ubiquitous at "outliers." Southwestern archaeology in the 1980s had not yet come to grips with landscapes; our observational language was insufficient to the task of describing outlier Great Houses while recognizing their variability. The observational language developed or perhaps devolved to "Big Bump" surrounded by a "community" of smaller sites, berms, depressions, etc. (Lekson 1991). For a less enthusiastic view, see Kantner and Kintigh (2006).

6. Road networks: Chaco's region was a system. Road segments have been unequivocally defined in every direction from Chaco except northeast—an area largely devoid of Great Houses. But only a small fraction of the projected road network has received adequate attention. A half-dozen major roads radiate out from Chaco (Kincaid 1983; Nials et al. 1987); local networks of roads appear to link outlier Great Houses and significant natural features (e.g., Hurst and Till 2009).

    Roads unquestionably carried foot traffic (they have elaborate stairs and ramps at topographic breaks) but they also carried symbolism as earthen monuments connecting places in Chaco's region. One valence of symbolism was historical: Later point A was connected to earlier point B, memorialized in a road-monument between noncontemporary places (Fowler et al. 1987; Stein and Fowler 1992; Lekson 1999)—or between a Great House and an important natural feature. Roads surely had meanings beyond the pedestrian. In the rush to ritual, the North Road connecting Chaco to

Salmon and Aztec Ruins was declared a 100 percent symbolic road to nowhere (Marshall 1997), but that interpretation falls before the evidence (Lekson 2015a; Carlson 1966). The roads we know are the ones that are (comparatively) easy to see. We probably know most (nearly all?) outlier Great Houses; we know only a small fraction of roads.

The design, construction and long-term maintenance of roads required as-yet-uncalculated but surely substantial amounts of organized labor. While it is possible that road features have a deeper history in the Southwest, the association of roads with Chacoan Great Houses is clear throughout Chaco's region. Roads are not a series of repeated independent inventions: They reflect Chacoan engineering, transportation, and ideological canons; and in fact, major roads lead ultimately into and out of Chaco Canyon. And their extent appears to correspond to the region defined by outlier Great Houses.

7. Line-of-sight communication: Chaco's region was a system. The existence of line-of-sight communications from Chaco to outliers and among outliers is certain, but its extent is even less documented than roads (Hayes and Windes 1975; Heilen and Leckman 2014; Van Dyke et al. 2016). This system demonstrably spanned 130 mi (200 km) from Chimney Rock to the southern Chuska Valley, and it seems highly likely that it continued out to the edges of Chaco's region. It in part paralleled and in part operated separately from the road network.

Recent studies highlight the importance of "repeater stations"—isolated "shrines" away from residential sites that were positioned to relay information from one Great House to another. The classic case for "repeater stations" was Katherine Freeman's demonstration that Huerfano Butte served as "repeater" between Chimney Rock Great House in southwestern Colorado and Pueblo Alto at Chaco Canyon—a total distance of about 80 mi (130 km) (Freeman et al. 1996). There are no Great Houses or, indeed, residential sites on or near Huerfano Butte. Someone would have to be stationed there to operate the line-of-site system, relaying information to and from Chaco and Chimney Rock. Perhaps constantly, perhaps on some prearranged schedule; but the persons assigned that task were in fact *personnel* in a true technological "system" of communication.

8. Chaco's population. My unimpeachable source: Lekson 1984:272. I like my early estimate because it was based not on hearths (which may be missed on now-vanished upper floors) but on features that are almost impossible to miss: "kivas." My estimate combined Alden Hayes's numbers for small-site populations, based on his survey of the canyon (Hayes 1981), which seemed to me solid and technically standard for Southwestern archaeology at that time. The problem was Great Houses. Pueblo Bonito had 500 rooms (or whatever the number was; I forget). What did those rooms mean for population? For Great Houses—the thorny question, then and now—I developed a method based on the number of "kivas," with one kiva equaling one household. And then multiplied the number of "kivas" by a notional family size. This assumed, of course, that "kivas" were domestic, not ritual (Lekson 1988).

The round rooms reverently presented to the public as "kivas" at Chaco and Mesa Verde were not the ceremonial structures we see today in Pueblos, they were gussied-up pit houses. That was true of so-called "kivas" at Unit Pueblos (five rooms and a "kiva") before, during, and after Chaco, right through Pueblo III. (Note that I'm not including Great Kivas in this discussion; they may have been more like the Pueblo kivas; more on Great Kivas, below.) When first proposed (Lekson 1984:50–51, 1988), this interpretation met stiff resistance (e.g., Plog 1989:147–148); today it's SOP in Mesa

Verde archaeology. "Today, archaeologists typically count households by counting pit structures [pit houses and kivas]…in pre-Pueblo IV sites" (Kohler and Higgins 2016:692). But not in the public imagination, or in NPS interpretation, or in archaeology outside the Four Corners (including Chaco, alas) where every Pueblo II or III pit structure remains a kiva (e.g., Crown and Wills 2003). You just can't make Chaco "kivas" go away, can't chase them out of Pueblo Space: Ritual über alles.

Recognizing that "kivas" were actually pit houses, and equating both with a household is fairly straightforward. But…how big was a household? Based on archaeological conventions of the time, I fixed on 6.4 people—somewhere at the lower end of the continuum between a "nuclear" family (not atomic: parents, a few kids, and a stray aunt or uncle) and an "extended" family (not racked and stretched: founder parents, a couple of nuclear families, and a few other odds and sods). 6.4 was a number I took from archaeological studies of the time—conventions based on nothing much beyond a firm faith that simple people had simple ("nuclear") families. Extended families are, of course, larger, and (as it turns out) far more common: From many societies across the globe, extended families range from 10 to 20 people—about two or three times larger than my 6.4 convention. So my 1984 estimate of 2,100 to 2,700 people at Chaco may be a minimum; Chaco's population was probably more than that, with even more nobles. If I live long enough and can recover from Chaco-fatigue, I may revisit this problem—and the number will surely go up.

9. Chaco's region…60,000 to as many as 100,000 people. The population of the San Juan Basin has been estimated, at Chaco's height, to be around 55,000 (Dean et al. 1994)—an estimate supported by more recent work (Heilen and Leckman 2014:380).

There was a lot more to Chaco's region outside the San Juan Basin. Consider the northern San Juan, which overlaps only slightly with the San Juan Basin. For the Village Ecodynamics Project (VEP) area—a limited portion of the "Central Mesa Verde" subdistrict—a recent estimate of momentary population at 1100 was about 1,000 households; at 5–9 people, that's another 5,000 to 9,000 people (Varien and Potter 2008). It seems safe (to me) to double VEP for the rest of the Central Mesa Verde area, in size much larger than VEP: Mesa Verde itself, southeastern Utah, etc. Say: 10,000 to 20,000 people total (maybe more) in the northern San Juan. That takes us to 60,000 plus. As far as I know, no one has ever attempted population estimates for Chaco's considerable region in northeast Arizona or, to the south, the densely settled Zuni/Cibola region. Archaeology is thick on the ground in both. If only 10,000 each (a modest guess), that gets us to 80,000; but I think Zuni/Cibola was almost certainly more densely occupied. And Chaco's region incorporates other, less densely settled areas. Another 20,000?

Sixty thousand seems solid and certain; 100,000 is an educated guess, but not unlikely.

10. Chaco had bulk and prestige economies. By "economy" I mean: The organization or structure of production and distribution of goods and services. For the first analysis in two decades of a major collection of Chacoan bulk goods, see chapters in Crown (2016).

Economy is one of several aspects of Chaco that has been swept under the prayer rug of ritual. Faith might move mountains, but a quarter-million pine beams came to Chaco from distant forests on peoples' backs (Betancourt et al. 1986; Guiterman et al. 2014). Not to mention tons of crockery (Toll and McKenna 1997; but see Arakawa et al. 2016), rocks (Cameron 1997; Duff et al. 2012), meat (Grimstead et al. 2016), and quite possibly vegetables (Benson et al. 2003; Benson et al. 2008; Benson et al. 2009; Benson 2010; but see cautions in Benson et al. 2010). Tumpline economies operate fairly efficiently over distances up to 150 km (Malville 2001; discussed in Lekson 2009a:132–133), a radius around Chaco which encompasses the sources of these bulk goods. And of course there is no requirement that Chaco's economy was efficient; were that a consideration, they would have built Chaco in the Chuska Valley or on the Animas River. The economy answered to Chaco, not Chaco to the economy.

A brief consideration of prestige goods: Chaco had lots of bling (Matson 2016), and the honored dead of Pueblo Bonito had way more than most. Much was shell, much was shale, much was other materials, but the biggest baddest bling was turquoise. Turquoise came into Chaco from central Nevada, southern Nevada, southern Colorado, northern New Mexico, and southern New Mexico (Hull et al. 2016). At Chaco, commoners in Unit Pueblos crafted beads and tesserae—workshops were found in "small sites" and Great Houses (my interpretation of data in Mathien 1997, Matson 2016; biased by my recollections of excavating a large storage pit at a small site, with hundreds of thousands of bits of turquoise bead–production debris). A lot of that turquoise dandified Chaco's nobles.

We have known for over a century that many Mesoamerican (sensu Kirchhoff) high-status objects found their way to Chaco: Scarlet macaws, copper bells, and so forth (Nelson 2006). Recently we learn that Chaco had cacao from southern Mesoamerica and Black Drink from the Southeast Gulf Coast (Crown and Hurst 2009; Crown et al. 2015).

Chaco may not have been a total black hole, sucking in prestige goods and emitting nothing. I argue elsewhere that Chaco crafted regalia of office from macaw feathers and sent these, and probably turquoise, out to elites at outlier Great Houses (Lekson 2015a:30–34; see also Borson et al. 1998). This can only be a suggestion: While it is easy to see bulk and prestige goods imported into Chaco, it is much harder to demonstrate goods emerging from Chaco—a source for nothing but sandstone— propping up the local gentry and oiling the prestige economy.

11. Chaco was not a great place to grow corn. Currently, one group of archaeologists claims Chaco was an agricultural oasis (Vivian 1990; Vivian et al. 2006; Wills 2017; Wills and Dorshow 2012; Dorshow 2012; Tankersley et al. 2016). Another group, led by USGS geologist Larry Benson, insist Chaco was a lousy place to farm (Benson 2011a, 2011b; Benson et al. 2006; Benson 2016)—which was also the opinion of a number of earlier analyses by both archaeologists and soil scientists (for example, Loose 1979; other early, uniformly pessimistic studies are summarized by Mathien 2005:36–37).

What's a practical prehistorian to do? These disagreements involve experts and expertise beyond the tool kit of most of us (certainly of your author), which appear to disagree on a rather fundamental issue: Chaco's prehistoric productivity. This does not appear to be a compromise situation; these two camps are polemically opposed: One says yes, one says no. It's not that we can average everything out and say that Chaco was 50 percent farmable.

Maybe we could look at a third party: Navajos, who actually tried to raise crops in Chaco Canyon. Navajos were canny farmers; and Chaco's only edible resource, pinyon nuts, was chancy at best. How many Navajos lived at Chaco?

The Chaco Project survey of Chaco Canyon located 43 hogans (Navajo houses) which could be dated to 1750–1820, and 53 which could be dated to 1880–1945 (Brugge 1981:98). A few other hogans could not be assigned to these intervals. That averages out to about 6 to 8 hogans per decade—a crude statistic, but indicative of fairly low population levels during Navajo times. David Brugge (1980) notes that hogans were conspicuous by their absence in early Spanish accounts—accounts which detailed hogans encountered elsewhere. When I asked David Brugge the maximum number of Navajos who lived in and near Chaco Canyon at any one time, he guessed no more than a few hundred people total—and many of those families had farms elsewhere (Brugge 1980; Brugge personal communication 1985). A few hundred Navajos were probably more than Chaco could feed. At its height in the eleventh century, Chaco had 2,500+ mouths to feed.

Given the well-attested bulk importation of wood, pottery, meat, etc., and the very low numbers of actual Navajo farmers which, historically, the canyon could support, I am very much inclined to accept the naysayers and to suggest that corn was a bulk import into Chaco Canyon—a conclusion supported by an initial "sourcing" study of a small sample of Chaco corn cobs, all of which were grown elsewhere (Benson 2010). Chaco might have been better for farming than its immediate surroundings, but that is faint praise indeed. Chaco paled in comparison to the Chuska Valley, the San Juan River valley, and the other agriculturally favorable areas around the outer edges of the San Juan Basin.

12. Chaco was cosmopolitan. Given the size of Chaco's region and the size of its population, it seems likely that more than one language was involved, and more than one ethnicity—insofar as such distinctions were recognized in the eleventh century. (It has been suggested that Keres was Chaco's lingua franca; Shaul 2014.)

Note 10 hinted at the exotic items that reached Chaco from distant lands, Mesoamerica and the Mississippi Valley/Gulf Coast. From a little closer to home, Chaco had a Hohokam shirt: "one of the more important archaeological textiles at the Maxwell Museum" (https://hands.unm.edu/63-50-123.html). The webpage goes on to remind us: "This surviving shirt fragment is a reminder that exchanges between the two cultural centers may have involved a few specific things (including rarities) that usually do not survive in archaeological sites."

At risk of repeating some material from an earlier note, we've known for a century that Chaco had items from and interests in various parts of Mesoamerica (Nelson 2006): Copper objects from Michoacán maybe, macaws and cacao from Veracruz or Mexico's West Coast (Aztatlan or even Oaxaca), Black Drink from the Mississippian region (perhaps from Cahokia itself), and other rare and precious objects from faraway places with strange-sounding names. And Chaco things moved out over equally long distances. Turquoise, for example: John Pohl (2001) recounts how Southwestern turquoise reached Tututepec in coastal Oaxaca by boat, and from thence to Mixtec artisans who created the turquoise-encrusted objects we marvel at in Mexican museums.

"Cosmopolitan," in my dictionary: "Composed of people, constituents, or elements from many different places or levels." Chaco was that. Yes: Chaco was a worldly, cosmopolitan place—the dictionary definition of "cosmopolitan," not the one-world aspirations of Cosmopolitan Archaeologists.

13. Under threat of legal action, Papa substituted "Julian" for his on-again off-again pal, Scott Fitzgerald.

14. Gini coefficients—the current tool of choice for inequality in American Anthropological Archaeology (Kohler and Smith 2018)—may not get the job done because they measure wealth, not class. That distinction is important! The wealth difference between a petty king and a prosperous commoner might not be great. But a king is still a king and a commoner is still a commoner.

15. We would do well to learn about Mesoamerican elites and kings, alongside the Classic Pueblo Ethnographies—a little extra reading. For example, Chase and Chase 1992 and Kurnick and Baron 2016.

16. I won't apologize for saying this in different places in this book, it's really important: Bedrock, bottom-up populism colors our attitudes toward the idea of social differentiation in the Southwest. The default assumption is that agrarian Southwestern (and North American) societies were stateless, classless, and egalitarian. Deviations from that happy state are ascribed to grasping aggrandizers (like everyone else, but with diseased ambition); or minimized by appeals to the holy: Would-be leaders are cloaked in sanctity and (from Voltaire) "live without working, at the expense of rascals who work to live." Not a different class but a different role, rising (up?) from the masses. But in a world of kings and commoners, nobility is a status, not a scam.

17. The last 10–15 years have seen a remarkable explosion of Chaco studies. I note only a few of these intriguing studies here, and many of the rest at https://stevelekson.com/. Most of this new information, considered from beyond Pueblo Space, supports (or does not contradict) the model of Chaco presented in this chapter and in Lekson 2009a and 2015a. Of course these remarkable new data change the narrative: History must accommodate new information. The reviled post hoc accommodative argument: That's exactly how history works (as discussed in chapter 6). It turns out, for example, that Chaco starts earlier than I/we thought (e.g., Plog and Heitman 2010). As I say in chapter 6, my *History of the Ancient Southwest* should have a new edition every five years or so. I'm not going to do that, but I hope some younger, more energetic person(s) will take on that challenge, perhaps in nonpaper media (also discussed in chapter 6).

18. Save, perhaps, one: Great Houses were accommodations or hostels, temporary housing for the influx of thousands of pilgrims. That's a very interesting idea, surely worth consideration.

I think "temporary housing" may be true for elites/nobles visiting the canyon from the countryside, who settled into their not-a-kivas as temporary/seasonal/occasional residences—like a European king's summer palace, but humbler. But what about all those hundreds of other empty rooms? Rooms to let? Probably not: All those famously empty rooms at Pueblo Bonito and Chetro Ketl are securely identified as storage rooms (that is, not residences/living space) by their distinctive small doors with secondary jambs. This type of door—for it is a type—is familiar from small, stand-alone granaries (which can be nothing but storage) throughout the Four Corners. The same type of doors penetrate the walls of Chaco's troublesome empty rooms (Lekson 1984:25–28, 266). From the evidence, all those empty rooms at Chaco Great Houses were built to store stuff, not to house people. Or, moving a step away from the evidence, perhaps to *appear* to store stuff: Conspicuous warehouses proclaiming their proprietors' (potential) wealth. From outside, you can't tell if the storerooms are full or empty.

19. Moreover, "there are no monuments to rulers"—holding Chaco up to Maya standards, or to definitions of "state" taken from the half-dozen primary states (China, Mesopotamia, and the rest of that Old Boys Club). Do we need stelae? Archaeology knows of many stratified societies and states that did not celebrate its rulers Maya-fashion. Indeed, the Maya were anomalous in Mesoamerica for making such a big deal of their kings. Aztecs had emperors (who were buried with pomp and circumstance) but few monumental images remain, no towering statues, no stelae.

20. The latter, in particular, annoyed Southwesternists, many of whom visibly wince; to quote me, talking to myself: "*King* is so loaded, it's so European, ugh. I appeal to authority: Graeber and Sahlins's (2017) encyclopedic *On Kings*. Should I use another word, perhaps a Native or near-Native word? *Cacique*? *Almehnob*? *Cazonci*? *Gobernantes* (the latter hardly Native)? I think not—those terms imply a cut-and-paste

transfer of office, and I'd rather let Southwestern kings define themselves" (Lekson 2009a:303n199). I use "king" because I speak English, and you are reading English, and "king" is a very flexible term. It does not mean only Louis XIV, but also Irish legend King Cormac, who, if he ever really ruled, ruled a kingdom of surpassing smallness. In American Anthropological Archaeology's old neo-evolutionary terms, a king like Cormac would be lucky to be a chief.

21. Bonito may get pride of place, but we haven't excavated Peñasco Blanco, as old and for much of Chaco's history as big as Bonito; Chetro Ketl was as large, if not as old; and the Navajos say the king actually lived in Pueblo Alto.

22. Dr. Gutierrez has my sincere thanks for directing me away from Tarascans and towards Nahuas; but he is in no way responsible for my use or misuse of Nahua ethnohistories.

23. And other Mesoamerican peoples, too. The basic model of multiple noble families sharing governance, commoners obliged to particular nobles, and so forth has been applied to non-Nahuas. Some archaeologists project the altepetl back into the Epiclassic and Early Postclassic (Hirth 2000, 2003, 2008); others say tut-tut, not so fast (Smith 2008a). Models of shared or distributed governance have recently been suggested for late Olmec (by Christopher Pool, reported in Wade 2017a) and Postclassic Tlaxcala (by Lane Fargher and Richard Blanson, reported in Wade 2017b). For Olmec, apparently, that form followed centuries of conventional kingly hierarchy. Chaco's political structure may derive from a Postclassic Mesoamerican model; or Chaco may have coevolved with Mesoamerican developments; or Chaco itself may have developed key features later seen in the Nahua altepetl. These alternatives are not problems for the application of the model to Chaco; they are research questions which might actually be important.

24. Please: Before you blow this off, get your head out of Pueblo Space and read the longer, extensively referenced version in Lekson 2015a:Appendix A. For the record here, my principal sources: Bernal García and García Zambrano (2006), Gutiérrez (2003, 2011), Hirth (2000, 2003, 2008), Hodge (1997), Lockhart (1992), Ouweneel (1999), and Smith (2008a)—Smith is not fond of my (or others') use of *altepetl*, but his works are invaluable references on scale of Nahua city-states, providing many of the numbers offered here (and in chapter 4).

25. Technically, "modulus of elasticity," but "modulus of rupture" allows me to use, in a nasty way, one of the most annoying Social Theory words, "rupture." Oh rapture: rupture!

Chapter 4: A Science of the Ancient Southwest

1. Much of this chapter was written in 2010–2011 at the School for Advanced Research in Santa Fe, and posted in various versions on the page "Southwest in the World" (https://stevelekson.com/). My interest in several of these topics is even more ancient: Parts of this chapter revisit bits of my unpublished, unlamented 1988 dissertation! For this book, I have brushed up the SAR essays but I cannot claim to have brought them comprehensively up-to-date. Happily there is much new Southwestern work on some of these topics (e.g., scalar matters and networks/diffusion); unhappily, not much on others (e.g., secondary states).

2. A few of Arizona State University's many intriguing projects, from their website: Complexities of Ecological and Social Diversity: A Long-Term Perspective; Change Is Hard: The Challenges of Path Dependence; Archaeology of the Human Experience;

and Long-Term Coupled Socioecological Change in the American Southwest and Northern Mexico.

3. Dr. Venkman DID say that. And, to paraphrase Capt. Hector Barbossa: You'd best start believing in science books, missy; you're in one. But if you're a kid and don't know what a slide rule is for: Look at the pictures and just turn the pages. Did Sam Cooke sing that?

4. "Cross-cultural analysis" was the foundation of nineteenth-century anthropology and a staple of twentieth-century anthropology. Today, not so much. A pity. There were (and are) vast databases of cultural information on thousands of societies around the world. (See, for example: http://hraf.yale.edu/.)

5. For a critical review, see philosopher Benoit Dubreuil's (2010) *Human Evolution and the Origins of Hierarchies.*

6. Not everyone disdains "magic numbers." Robert Kelly in his recent compendium of hunter-gatherer ethnoarchaeology devoted several pages to group sizes (Kelly 2013: 168ff), in particular the "magic numbers" of 500 for "bands" and 25 for "local groups" from *Man the Hunter* (Lee and Devore 1968). Martin Wobst (1974) said 475 was likely "minimum breeding population"—a band? And the local group size of 25: Kelly notes that most hunter-gatherer groups were smaller, but

> Marcus Hamilton and his colleagues (2007a) lend some support to both "magic" numbers.... They found a remarkable cross-cultural regularity: starting with a single individual, groups seem to increase by a factor of about 4: families consist of 4–5 people, a residential group of about 14–17 people; social aggregations (e.g., at winter camps) of 50–60 people; periodic aggregations of 150–80 people, and an entire ethnic population of 730–950 people. This regularity holds true even for different environments. (Kelly 2013:172)

Severin Fowles devotes a gratifying number of pages (2013:142–148) to "magic numbers" in his excellent *Archaeology of Doings.* He does not much care for them: "A strange species of Malthusian argument results, one in which scale becomes a kind of agent or invisible hand that makes its own demands upon society" (Fowles 2013:142). Yup, that pretty much sums up my argument—but Fowles is not buying it: "Rarely is it acknowledged that the causal arrow might just as well be reversed. Rarely is it seriously considered that aspiring leaders, prophets, or even new ideologies of human and cosmic order may have themselves been demanding larger communities" (Fowles 2013:142). That works for me too! Once things get going (aspiring leaders with new ideologies) then they take on a life of their own. Like rust or crab grass.

See also the short but excellent discussion of scales and numbers in Dark 1998: 127–133.

7. I use the terms "settlement" and "community" interchangeably. Note that I do NOT define "community" as the minimum unit for social and biological reproduction (Kolb and Snead 1997). For useful reviews, see Kolb and Snead 1997, and N. Mahoney 2000. Also, please note that my use of "scale" and "scalar" differs significantly from recent, exciting research on "urban scaling"—which is commendably cross-cultural (e.g., Ortman and Coffey 2017).

8. Kosse's and my analyses converged and agreed, independently. We did this work at the same time and place: The University of New Mexico in the mid-1980s. Thanks to Lewis Binford, UNM was a hotbed for this kind of research. Kosse and I were both peripheral to Binford's department, she in Maxwell Museum, me in the National

Park Service. We were ignorant of each other's research until a third party introduced us. Thus, our work was independent, and—happily—reached the same conclusions, which makes me think it might be real.

I published first, but Kosse published better. My work appeared in a student journal (Lekson 1985), in an unpublished dissertation (Lekson 1988), and in a chapter in an obscure volume on vernacular architecture (Lekson 1990—material developed in the early 1980s). Kosse's work was more broadly published (Kosse 1990, 1994, 1996, 2000)—appropriately, I think, because her methods were more rigorous and her goals were broader than mine. Sadly, Kosse died in 1995 and we lost a very talented, very smart archaeologist.

9. In many parts of the world, 2,500 isn't a city or a government; it's just a big village. It is quite possible for a peasant village to exceed 2,500 and lack an obvious mayor or king; but in that case, there's almost always a ruler somewhere else, a king over the hill. That is, the peasant village is part of a larger polity. So the rule holds: 2,500 indicates governance, but governance can be internal or external: A mayor running the town itself, or a king in another city providing rules and controls. That's handy, because in archaeology we can't always tell if a settlement is independent or part of a polity. For the 2,500 threshold *as a diagnostic*, it apparently does not matter.

Are there real-world examples of communities bypassing the K-rule? A key question, which will resurface in the discussion of Roland Fletcher's (1995) C- and T-limits in urbanism, and critical to Fletcher's analysis of low-density urbanism (Fletcher 2009). I discuss possible southwestern K-rule scofflaws below, and there are anecdotal exceptions to the K-rule: Permanent, (presumably) independent settlements of more than 2,500 that "bypass" the K-rule by internal subdivision—fissioning in place, as it were. Bypass is usually accomplished by segmentation into clearly defined neighborhoods, barrios, or wards (Smith 2010b).

10. Kosse and I were far from the first to explore the relationship of community/settlement size and sociopolitical complexity. In various versions, that correlation is a (minor) theme in social sciences almost from the beginnings; in its current thread, at least as far back as Naroll (1956), Ember (1963), and Carneiro (1967). Interest within Processual archaeology can be traced from Flannery (1972:423) through Wright (1977), Johnson (1978, 1982; Wright and Johnson 1975), Feinman (1998), Adler (1990), and Kintigh (1994), among others, and of course Kosse and Lekson. And more recently: Binford (2001) and Feinman (2011).

It's not exclusively on this side of the pond. Clive Gamble (1998:436) noted that "interestingly, Bernard and Killworth's sociometric study (1973:183) produced a figure of 2,460 as the maximum group size which has some stability without a formalized hierarchy governing interaction." Bernard and Killworth (1973) reached that figure (2,460) by beginning with the Rule of Six—or, in their case, seven—and building a complex network analysis. Their article, "On the Social Structure of an Ocean-Going Research Vessel and Other Important Things," is an amusing read (at least until they get statistical) and probably useful for current network analyses in the Southwest.

11. Southwestern archaeology is violently allergic to rulers or kings, and will dose down almost any nostrum which soothes the irritation. One of the best-selling palliatives is "sequential" (versus "simultaneous") hierarchies: Gregory A. Johnson (1982:396), thinking about the Southwest, suggested that "simultaneous" hierarchies (that is, conventional hierarchy) might not be the only solution to threshold problems, and he offered "sequential hierarchies: an egalitarian alternative." Sequential hierarchy (aka "heterarchy") is, he admitted, "difficult...to characterize" (Johnson 1982:403), but

they appear to involve consensus decisions on several levels (nuclear family, extended family, group). "Sequential hierarchy is unlikely to be the only social mechanism allowing large aggregations among egalitarian groups. Ceremony, ritual, or what might be called 'generalized feather-waving' is probably another" (Johnson 1982:405). For an attempt to find "sequential hierarchies" in Southwestern prehistory, see Bernardini (1996).

Please note that sequential hierarchies are rare. Johnson notes (1989:386): "We have garden-variety 'chiefdoms' and 'early states' stacked ten deep under the lab table, but elaborate sequential hierarchies may have been a rare phenomenon." For this and other *rara avis* "corporate hierarchy" and "heterarchy" and a posse of "alternative leadership" models, the Southwest's remarkable (and remarkably stereotyped) Pueblos are the constant, overworked reference—a tribute to Southwestern exceptionalism and Pueblo Space. The rarity of sequential hierarchies seems, to me, a very good reason for considering more common conventional hierarchies first; if those fit, fine: Mission accomplished, as one of our less successful commanders-in-chief said.

Bruce Trigger, in an essay on "Cross-Cultural Comparison and Archaeological Theory" (following his seminal 2003 *Understanding Early Civilizations*), is unenthusiastic about "sequential hierarchies" and "heterarchies" and "acephalous states":

> Some relativists believe that social inequality and states are optional, rather than inevitable, consequences of increasing social scale, leaving open the possibility that these are only accidental features of modern industrial societies.... Yet so little is known about the archaeological cultures that are cited as possible examples of stateless early civilizations that these conclusions are no more objective than are interpretations of ink blots. (Trigger 2004:53)

Çatalhöyük comes to mind: Declared elite-free (and therefore Pueblo-like) based on a remarkably tiny sample of the site (Hodder 2011).

12. Hard-wiring leading to emergent properties across different social histories is not as bizarre as you may think, gentle reader. I was gladdened to run across the following quote from Bruce Trigger, an archaeologist I have always greatly admired; and saddened because he is no longer with us. In his essay "Retrospection" (Trigger 2006:252), he refers to his last major work, *Understanding Early Civilization* (2003:252):

> I concluded that many of these similarities resulted from specific aspects of human intelligence operating under similar conditions and hence were constrained by modes of thinking and emotional reactions hard-wired into human beings over long periods of biological evolution.... This is an idea I would have been unwilling to entertain twenty years previously.... While these findings have cast doubt on beliefs I have held all my life, I regard this not as an intellectual defeat but as a welcome challenge. Cherished ideas should not be abandoned lightly, but they also should not go unexamined.

13. Kauffman 1991, 1993, 1995. Also Ilya Prigogene 1984 and Per Bak 1999. Binford (2001: 435), too, was inclined this way: "I strongly suspect that the packing threshold identifies what has been called a point of 'self-organized criticality' (Bak 1969)."

14. Kosse (2000) "Some Regularities in Human Group Formation and the Evolution of Societal Complexity" in the Santa Fe Institute's journal *Complexity*. The article was published posthumously (edited and introduced by Linda Cordell). For anyone intrigued by the subject of this section, Kosse's article is well worth reading—it hints at directions more rigorous than my simplified treatment here.

15. Dunbar (2010:27): "For the twenty-odd tribal societies where census data are available, these clan groups turn out to have a mean size of 153. The sizes of all but one of the villages—and clan-like groupings for these societies—fall between one hundred and 230, which is within the range of variation that, statistically, we would expect from the prediction of 150" (Dunbar 2010:25–26). "In traditional societies, village size seems to approximate this, too. Neolithic villages from the Middle East around 6000 BC typically seem to have contained 120 to 150 people, judging from the number of dwellings. And the estimated size of English villages recorded by William the Conqueror's henchmen in the Domesday Book in 1086 also seems to have been about 150. Similarly, during the eighteenth century the average number of people in a village in every English county except Kent was around 160. (In Kent, it was a hundred)."

16. "Classifications and social conventions allow us to broaden the network of social relationships by making networks of networks, and this in turn allows us to create very large groups indeed. Of course, the level of the relationship is necessarily rather crude but at least it allows us to avoid major social faux pas at the more superficial levels of interaction when we first meet someone we don't know personally" (Dunbar 2010:80).

17. Van Dyke (2007b:119) estimates a lower number: "A more realistic estimate is derived by imagining a row of spectators shoulder to shoulder every 75 cm around the circumference. In this scenario, approximately 75 people could stand around the 56 m circumference of an 18 m great kiva." I'm a big guy, and my shoulders are 45–50 cm across (depending on the kind of day I'm having). The ancient people were smaller than us; and Pueblo proxemics are not ours. Van Dyke's estimate may be overly generous with space: Her movie theater to my bleachers? But her assumptions are more humane and more pleasant to contemplate.

18. The Rule of Six (or Seven) began as an industrial observation. Frederick Taylor (1911) noted that the ratio of producers to nonproducers (i.e., managers) in his factory studies was 6 or 7 to 1. Vytautas A. Graičiūnas (1937 [1933]) first modeled this observation mathematically, demonstrating that while size of an organization increases arithmetically, the potential interactions increase geometrically; Graičiūnas (1937:186) concluded that "no supervisor can supervise directly the work of more than five or at most six subordinates." That is, there exists an observable threshold at 6 (or 7) beyond which management efficiencies rapidly decay.

19. Gregory Johnson (1978) cited sources as far back as midcentury, Stanley Udy (1958, 1970): "The maximum number of items to which an individual can give simultaneous attention ranges between three and seven with a mode at five.... Udy's (1970:50) own data suggest that in activity coordination, this number is probably four" (Johnson 1978:105). Johnson considered cost-benefit analysis of information sources and hierarchies, and concluded: "Across the whole organizational range considered, however, the mean number of organizational units integrated by an immediate superior unit in administrative hierarchy generated on an assumption of efficiency maximization is 3.66, with a range of 2.33 to 6.00. This mean of 3.66 is a reasonable approximation of Udy's figure of 4.0, and the range of 2.33 to 6.00 is remarkably close to that of 3.0 to 7.0 reported in the psychological literature" (1978:105).

In a later paper looking at small-group studies, Gregory Johnson (1982:392–393) applied this "rule of thumb" to specific cases, and noted an evident "organizational threshold" at six or seven individuals. Johnson cites studies of "capacity of an individual to monitor and process information" that suggest that "span of absolute judgment of unidimensional stimuli" and "span of immediate memory...simultaneously retained" are "fairly narrow, and average about 7" (1982:393–394). "If hierarchy development is related to some kind of scalar stress, why should it occur at around group size 6? Unfortunately this question is much more easily asked than answered" (1982:393).

"There appear, then, to be rather severe limits on the maximum size of task-oriented groups that are organized horizontally (nonhierarchically), and these limits may be related to individual information-processing capacity" (Johnson 1982:394; see also Johnson 1982:410–413). These limits caused "scalar stress" (Johnson 1982)—cognitive limits on human information processing. Johnson defined "scalar stress" as cognitive limits on human information processing. "'Scalar stress' measures the number of potential or real face-to-face interactions among decision makers in group of n people, expressed mathematically by the formula $(n^2 - n)/2$" (Johnson 1982:394).

20. "Cross-cultural organizational regularities were argued to be grounded in cognitive constraints, shared by all humans, that limit the number of pieces or channels of information that can be simultaneously processed by the human brain" (Bernardini 1996:372). Citing the usual suspects, Bernardini accepted that "the maximum information processing workload for an individual is exceeded at group sizes of greater than about six people. That is, for consensual group decisions, each person can maximally consider the views of about five other people, plus his own, to arrive at a choice" (Bernardini 1996:374–375).

21. Bernard and Killworth's (1973) analysis began with a factor of seven and reached a maximum hierarchy-free size of 2,460. How 'bout that?

22. Carniero, Yoffee, and Trigger may seem an unlike series of citations but I see them as theoretically sequential: Carniero 1981 → Trigger 2003 → Yoffee 2005. All theory is local.

23. Hewett's identification of Rio Grande Pueblos with Greek city-state democracies was a scam for the Pueblo Mystique, I think. Hewett had to know better—some key administrative institutions in eastern Pueblos can be downright dictatorial. A fact John Ware (2014) makes, but sort of which misses the point: The dictating is hidden, behind the scenes, and not through institutions of rulership and noble-commoner class structures.

24. We have remarkable geographic information—atlases, really—for all of the Pecos periods: Pithouse/Pueblo I (Young and Herr 2012; Reed 2000; Wilshusen et al. 2012); Pueblo II (sensu Chaco: Marshall et al. 1979; Powers et al. 1983; Fowler and Stein 1992; and most recently, Heitman et al. 2016), Pueblo III (Adler, ed., 1996), Pueblo IV (Adams and Duff 2004); and wonderful longitudinal GIS projects: The Coalescent Communities project (Hill et al. 2004; Wilcox 1999; Wilcox et al. 2007) which evolved into the Southwest Social Networks Project (Mills, Clark, et al. 2013; Mills, Roberts, et al. 2013; Mills et al. 2015); and State CRM GIS databases; and more, of course.

Since this is officially my Last Book, I cannot refrain from noting that I (and Bill Lipe) designed the conference that produced the Pueblo III volume (ably brought to print by Michael Adler in 1996), a format followed by subsequent Pithouse/Pueblo I and Pueblo IV volumes—all published by the University of Arizona Press. And of course I had something to do with the Pueblo II work. Making maps is fun!

25. Nancy Mahoney's (2000:Table 2.1) estimates of "maximum momentary population" for several Chacoan "outlier" communities ranged from about 200 to about 970 people. Beyond Chaco Canyon, the largest eleventh-century Pueblo towns were in the Mimbres area. Mimbres towns were at most only a few hundred people: Anyon and LeBlanc (1984:192) estimated "a maximal Galaz village size of 300 people." That

figure agrees reasonably well with the scale proposed by Shafer (2003:133) for NAN Ranch Ruin: "24-plus" "extended family households" or perhaps 250–300 people (my estimate, not Shafer's).

For Pueblo III (twelfth–thirteenth centuries), Michael Adler (1996:97) says the largest Mesa Verde settlements were about 1,500 people. Adler (1996:105), using "momentary population" estimates, notes "empirical support for a demographic size limit of between 1,000 and 1,500 people in Anasazi communities of the Mesa Verde region." Thus, "we are stuck in that grey area described by Kosse (1990) and Lekson (1988), in which community size can be used to argue for either emergent sociopolitical complexity or the lack of complexity" (Adler 1996:105).

Yellow Jacket was the very largest Mesa Verde town in the thirteenth century. Kristin Kuckelman estimates Yellow Jacket's maximum population at between 850 to 1,360 people. See: http://www.crowcanyon.org/publications/yellow_jacket_pueblo.asp

Scott Ortman (2009:Appendix A) studied the population of the largest northern Rio Grande towns in detail; for Sapawe (the largest northern Rio Grande town), Ortman estimates a maximum population of just over 2,300. Very close! But no cigar: Sapawe was occupied for a maximum of 150 years, probably less; apparently, after a few generations, fragmenting into multiple daughter communities. See also Duwe and others 2016.

26. To quote a sometimes reliable source: "The ten most populous Rio Grande Pueblos averaged about 400 residents each during the eighteenth and nineteenth centuries; the western New Mexico Pueblos averaged about 1000 residents during the same period (Simmons 1979:Table 1; Zubrow 1974:Table 2). After the Revolt of 1680, no Pueblo was ever larger than about 1500, except Zuni which occasionally peaked at about 2500 (but which averaged about 1500)" (Lekson 1984:272).

Schroeder (1979:246) suggests that Acoma had 6,000 people at the time of Coronado, but surely this is incorrect. The estimate is based on a Spanish estimate of 500 houses atop Acoma's mesa; currently there are fewer than 100 houses (mostly unoccupied, or occupied only on special occasions) and the mesa top is pretty crowded. The Spanish account was probably…enthusiastic.

Pecos was reputed to be the largest Rio Grande Pueblo when the Spanish arrived; their accounts say 2,000 people. The archaeological data support only half that size. See: http://www.cr.nps.gov/history/online_books/pecos/cris/chap7.htm.

27. Whalen and others 2010. As had David Wilcox before them (in a conference paper), provoking a response from yours truly (Lekson 1999b). All of us are working with precisely the same data—early accounts, etc. My argument was that Di Peso knew the site better than anyone else, having actually worked at Paquimé—which none of us have. David Phillips and David Wilcox walked over the supposed "east wing" and found only limited evidence for archaeological architecture; both of these gentlemen are excellent field archaeologists, so I suspect Whalen and colleagues (2010) are probably correct about the east wing; that is, there isn't an east wing, an area in which Di Peso was not able to excavate. I am disturbed, however, at the seemingly gleeful reduction of number of stories, numbers of rooms, and so forth in west and north wings and other areas where Di Peso actually excavated. And although Whalen and Minnis 2001 (and others) seem intent on whittling it down, the Casas Grandes region was pretty darn big; all this is discussed at even more length in Lekson 2009a:212–214.

28. Kosse (1996:90), looking at a "nonrandom sample of 103 societies" notes that 500 is a threshold for "CAN be" complex; 2,500 is a threshold for "MUST BE" complex. Note that she is referring to the total population of a single settlement polity. "With

so much ambiguity and variability of behavior [between 500 and 2,500] it is not surprising that the material evidence for middle-range societies is less than clear-cut" (Kosse 1996:90). John Bodley, in "The Power of Scale," is big on 500 as a complexity threshold (Bodley 2003:87–89) but it's not quite clear where he gets this figure.

29. Yet curiously absent or muted in early textbooks. Kidder's (1924) *Introduction to the Study of Southwestern Archaeology* mentions the introduction of maize, but that's it. Hewett's 1930 *Ancient Life* even seems to discount maize: "No one carried agriculture to other people and taught it to them" (p. 35), after which Mesoamerica is absent—although Hewett later in the book suggests that Casas Grandes was Aztlán (p. 373)! The first edition of McGregor's *Southwestern Archaeology* (1941) had four index entries for "Mexican influence" and "Mexican traits." All were for Hohokam. His second edition (1965) upped the ante to nine, again all for Hohokam. Gladwin's (1957) *A History of the Ancient Southwest* has nothing; nor does Martin and Plog (1973) *Archaeology of Arizona*—beyond the obligatory nod to maize. It is only with Cordell's several editions of *Prehistory of the Southwest* (which appeared in 1984, 1997, and 2016) that textbooks took Mesoamerica seriously.

30. V. Gordon Childe—probably the most significant mid-twentieth-century archaeologist—published *What Happened in History* (1942), a very influential book about diffusion of early civilizations from the Near East into western Europe.

31. Carl Sauer and his crew more or less invented "cultural landscapes," but they were big on diffusion too; two New World examples: Sauer 1932, 1952. Kroeber 1940 defined Stimulus Diffusion: "the birth of a pattern new to the culture in which it develops, though not completely new in human culture. There is historical connection and dependence, but there is also originality.... Stimulus diffusion might be defined as new pattern growth initiated by precedent in a foreign culture" (Kroeber 1940:20). Stimulus diffusion

> is the idea of the complex or system which is accepted, but it remains for the receiving culture to develop a new content.... Obviously this process is one which will ordinarily leave a minimum of historical evidence.... [M]uch diffusion takes place below the surface of historical record.... [W]hile systems or complexes in two or more cultures may correspond in functional effect, the specific items of cultural content, upon which historians ordinarily rely in proving connection, are likely to be few or even wholly absent. Positive proofs of the operation of idea-diffusion are therefore, in the nature of the case, difficult to secure long after the act, or wherever the historical record is not quite full. (Kroeber 1940:1–2)

Thinking like an anthropologist, and not like a historian, Kroeber looks at parallels between Greek and Hindu theater: "One inference may be drawn from this example: that contacts did occur and that they did have influence far beyond what we could directly infer from the preserved documentary literature. In other words the absence of direct historical records as to connections between Greece and India is no proof that there was no connection" (Kroeber 1940:12). Historians might have a problem with that assertion. Archaeologists should not.

32. Ford died before his remarkable work was published, and his book was seldom cited; but see Clark and Knoll 2005. Di Peso lived to promote his ideas—which resonated with some Southwesterners—and inspired a whole shelf of Di Peso–inspired collected papers: Woosley and Ravesloot 1993; Reyman 1995; Schaafsma and Riley 1999; most recently Minnis and Whalen 2015; and others. But Di Peso's notions were out of

temper with the times: New and Processual archaeology strongly favored local over distant at Paquimé (e.g., Whalen and Minnis 2003).

33. Kristian Kristiansen and Thomas B. Larsson, 2005, *The Rise of Bronze Age Society: Travels, Transmissions and Transformations.* As noted, Kristiansen and Larsson (2005) avoided the word "diffusion"; but it's not the word so much as the legitimacy and importance of long-distance interactions that matter. Kristiansen elsewhere notes that in Europe

> we have witnessed the silent collapse of the dominant post-processual framework, as it did not account for the kinds of evidence we have seen emerge during the last ten years. And neither did the processual framework. In short: we are in a period of theoretical and methodological experimentation and re-orientations, where everything that was "forbidden" research 10–15 years ago are now among the hottest themes: mobility, migration, warfare, comparative analysis, evolution, and the return of grand narratives. (Kristiansen 2014:14)

34. Migration never really vanished in Arizona, thanks to Emil Haury, Lex Lindsay, and Jeff Reid; but interest was muted during the heyday of New Archaeology; e.g., Haury 1958, Lindsay 1987, Reid 1997.

35. And an explosion of new migration studies: Cameron 1995; Clark 2001; Kohler et al. 2010; Lekson et al. 2002; Ortman 2012; among many others. See also: https://www.archaeologysouthwest.org/what-we-do/investigations/salado/.

36. The editors of a recent volume on trade and exchange lament that "archaeological interest in trade and exchange…has declined in recent decades" (Agbe-Davies and Bauer 2010:13) as archaeological attention turned away from global or metanarratives to microhistories.

37. World History overlaps with and could be confused with "Big History," a less-useful current enthusiasm. Big History tries to write global histories starting with the Big Bang. I'm not sure I see the need, or the point.

38. Some notable New World exceptions: For example, Chase-Dunn 2011; Chase-Dunn and Hall 1998; Peregrine 1996; Smith and Berdan 2003. For a recent review of World Systems' sometimes rocky relationship with archaeology, see Hall et al. 2011.

39. Smith and Berdan 2003; Townsend 1998; Dávíla Cabrera 2005, Zaragoza Ocana 2005, and Faust and Richter 2015; Schortman and Urban 2015.

40. "Mound" is a strange, belittling word for the largest pyramid north of Mexico, larger in base area than the pyramids of Giza. North of Mexico, every boat is a canoe, every pyramid a mound, and every king a chief.

41. For an excellent recent account of Mesoamerica in the Eastern US, see Pauketat 2009a:136–145. Discussion of the Mississippi Valley/Southeast and Mesoamerica was not uncommon up to midcentury, but was almost completely foreclosed thereafter. See also chapters in White 2005.

In a 2012 book-length review of *Recent Developments in Southeastern Archaeology*, David Anderson and Kenneth Sassaman (forward thinkers, both!) devote one paragraph to the topic. Their enthusiasm is guarded at best, concluding,

> Some scholars see these interregional connections [between the Southeast and Mesoamerica] as more significant and enduring throughout prehistory than currently assumed, and argue that the comparative study of the large-scale processes common to and possibly shared between these regions is worthy of far more research than they receive at present (e.g., Lekson and

Peregrine 2004; Neitzel 1999; Peregrine and Lekson 2006, 2012). (Anderson and Sassaman 2012:178)

42. Engraved and carved shell pectorals that indicate interaction between the Huasteca and Mississippian are, in fact, earlier in the north. "Engraved shells in the southeastern United States date to a later era [than Classic-period Maya examples], predating those from the Huasteca. The majority of engraved shells were found at the archaeological site of Spiro, Oklahoma. Whereas the apogee of Spiro dates to the Harlan Phase (AD 950–1200), those from the Huasteca emerged between the thirteenth and fifteenth centuries" (Dávila Cabrera 2015:146).

43. Cahokia's map provides powerful data: The place *looks like* a major Mesoamerican city, while Chaco does not. It is not clear to me why trinkets trump monuments.

44. It would be interesting to do the metallurgy on Huastec copper artifacts; where did the metal come from? From West Mexico or the Upper Peninsula?

45. We might also consult with Political Scientists of the International Relations bent, who have whole typologies for cultural connections on the state level—which is the level we are on; see for example Dark 1998:133–137.

46. This would be something like the "comparative archaeology" I (and others: Cordell et al. 1994:175–178 for my bit) envisioned twenty-five years ago.

47. I've had a few successes, lifting the Glass Ceiling: I was asked to contribute a chapter on Chaco to a volume on palaces (Lekson 2006a in Christie and Sarro 2006); another to a volume in the *Cambridge History of the World* on "A World with States, Empires, and Networks" (Lekson 2015b in Benjamin 2015); and a third to a volume on "Ritual in Archaic States" (Lekson 2016 in Murphy 2016). Those editors sought me out, not vice versa. I explained to them that most Southwesternists would shudder to see Chaco in such exalted company, crashing those toney parties. They insisted. I'm sure some readers are quoting to themselves A. Lincoln (attrib.) on fooling some of the people all of the time. I'd prefer to think that you can't fool all of the people all of the time. That is, right-thinking archaeologists unencumbered by Southwestern biases see Chaco for what it was. Anyway, it's a start.

48. I've read *Societies against the State* (Clastres 1989) and *Hierarchy in the Forest* (Boehm 2001). I found the latter unconvincing because Boehm seems to assume that all hunter-gatherers were egalitarian; that's not so. Yes, there are ways to live that avoid "states" as I define that term here; Pueblos do that. But so many complicated agricultural societies go the route of state/king (maybe all? Trigger 2003) that we should question the special pleading of Pueblo Space which keeps Chaco out of that very, very common condition.

49. So did David Wilcox (1993). Neither of us had much luck.

50. Actually, Chaco was recognized by the UN (UNESCO) as a World Heritage site, and they got it right: "Chaco Canyon, a major centre of ancestral Pueblo culture between 850 and 1250, was a focus for ceremonials, trade and political activity for the prehistoric Four Corners area. Chaco is remarkable for its monumental public and ceremonial buildings and its distinctive architecture—it has an ancient urban ceremonial centre that is unlike anything constructed before or since."—this from UNESCO's World Heritage website. Ritual, mysteries, and spirituality dialed down, not a hint of pilgrimage, and the political, economic, and ceremonial dialed up. Of course it's dated, but I like it. (And, no, I didn't write it.)

51. A formulation that owes much to Severin Fowles's careful reading of an early version of this chapter—but for which he bears no blame, only my thanks for extracting

and clarifying my embedded arguments. Still, this may seem a low bar for archaeologists accustomed to old checklist definitions of states: "Writing," "Weights and measures," "standing armies," "craft guilds," and so forth. Those lists reflect Victorian-era thinking, with the British Empire as the obvious peak of progress. Britain had those things, plus pomp and glory. Ancient state candidates were required to satisfy the list. "State" became a sort of Old Boy's Club of approved civilizations—those meeting the Committee's criteria. Many archaeologists research statelike polities, and there is growing interest in comparisons, contrasts, and continuities rather than exclusionary categories. Ben Nelson said it well: "not if they were complex, but how they were complex"—although elsewhere I quibble with this quote, a bit. If our field of view is confined by Pueblo Space, we can't address that challenge effectively. Can't say it too often: We have to recognize that Chaco was a something like a state just to ask the right questions.

52. "Secondary state" has other meanings. In International Relations, "secondary state" means a minor state which chooses to be unaligned with the great powers. It's like "primate center," archaeology jargon sometimes encountered in the state business. "Primate center," for most civilians, means "monkey house."

53. The word "state" appears only twice in *Recent Developments in Southeastern Archaeology*, and then only as counterexamples; for example, "Whether most tributary economies [in Mississippian chiefdoms] were anywhere near as formal as those in state-level societies is highly debatable" (Anderson and Sassaman 2012:168).

54. Patricia O'Brien (1989, 1991) proposed the "Ramey State," but failed to persuade her conservative colleagues. Alice Kehoe (1998:150–171) argued eloquently that Cahokia was a state "hidden in plain sight."

55. This comes from a 1998 Smithsonian Institution Press book, *The Cahokia Chiefdom*, by George R. Milner (republished by the University of Florida Press in 2006). *The Cahokia Chiefdom* was hailed in an *American Antiquity* review as "a tonic against earlier hasty overestimations of Cahokia's size and complexity." What they saw as wisdom I see as bias, Glass Ceiling, and misplaced parsimony:

> Only when the simpler sociopolitical model can be shown to be inconsistent with the archaeological data can scholars convincingly argue that Cahokia was something other than an unusually large version of the Mississippian chiefdoms that developed elsewhere in eastern North America. (Milner 1998:176)

56. Rereading *Chiefdoms and Other Archaeological Delusions* for writing this book, I am struck by the parallel themes and thinking between Pauketat's and my work—not to drag Tim down into my swamp. We know each other, we cite each other, and we have participated in several seminars and field conferences. But we came to our views independently, probably by very different paths. Much like the parallel but independent research by Kris Kosse and me on population thresholds, I am greatly heartened by similarities between Pauketat's work and mine. As Tim might agree, it's lonely work and not much fun. Pauketat may or may not welcome my claim for similarities, but I have found his work both inspirational and comforting—in a confirmatory way. But don't hold that against him, please.

57. The equation of Pauketat's "civilization" and my notion of "governance" seems, to me, appropriate; see Pauketat 2007:17. But he, of course, means much more than political hierarchy and structures—those are already allowed (as chiefdoms) in the

Mississippi Valley. "I need a word, and *civilization* is awaiting reclamation from the ethnocentrism and racism of an earlier anthropology. Civilization as I use it isn't a qualitative transformation, a dawning of high culture in some ancient world. And it isn't an advanced type of social system. It didn't just happen once on each island or continental land mass. No. *Civilization is an ongoing historical process, not an evolutionary phenomenon*" (Pauketat 2007:17–18; original emphasis).

58. There were consequences. It's one thing to damn the torpedoes, another to take one amidships. There's a dismissive passage in Flannery and Marcus's (2012:157) *Creation of Inequality*, which seems to be aimed at Chaco and at me (perhaps I just flatter myself): "To some archaeologists, familiar mainly with sites in the Southwest, Pueblo Bonito seems as spectacular as the ancient cities of Mexico." If that was a shot across my bow, I must note that I'm reasonably familiar with the ancient cities of Mexico.

   I am aware that some people think my fussing over Chaco is parvenu pretension, crowing on the dunghill. I don't even like the place: It's a black hole for archaeology, a drain on cheer and energy, and I'm really tired of writing about it. (So too may you be, dear reader.) But it's important to get Chaco right; just doing my job, trying to get it right.

59. The contributors to the landmark *Archaic States* asked two questions:

   > How do third- and fourth-generation states differ from first- and second-generation states?…and what to call the polities on the periphery of states when they acquire some of the trappings of that state but are never really incorporated into it? (Marcus and Feinman 1998:6)

   Norman Yoffee's 2005 response, *Myths of the Archaic State*, was largely critical; but he too was much intrigued by secondary states:

   > The rise of secondary states is not separable from regional trends and the impingement of prior states…. While archaeological research must perforce be focused on sites and in local regions, explanations for social and political change must often seek larger historical contexts, as comparisons with other ancient states suggest. (Yoffee 2005:192)

60. A few examples from a range of post-2000 studies: Shelach and Pines (2006), "Secondary State Formation and the Development of Local Identity"; Joffe (2002), "The Rise of Secondary States in the Iron Age Levant"; Carter (2010), *Rethinking Secondary State Formation in Medieval Iceland*; Thurston (2002), *Landscapes of Power, Landscapes of Conflict* (a "third generation processual analysis," according to Timothy Earle's forward); Barnes (2007), *State Formation in Japan*. More recently, Earle reconsiders the differences between primary and secondary states:

   > The typological distinction [between primary and secondary states] should be rethought in terms of processes of state formation based on how emerging state institutions were financed either internally [primary] or externally [secondary]. Institutions that constitute states "are not exportable" (Price 1987:182). States should not be considered as a trait that can diffuse; they developed both in isolation and equally in association with other states. All chiefly leaders wish to be kings, and the origin of states depended on whether would-be sovereigns could develop systems of finance to support state institutions and to exclude rights of the common horde." (Earle 2016:302)

He concludes: "I question whether the distinction between primary and second-ary states has real analytical value.... Processes of finance were the drivers here, not the borrowing of ideas (Earle 2016:306).

I wonder: Why not borrow ideas? Chiefs want to become kings; they do not in-vent kingship. Earle puts the economic cart before the aggrandizing horse. His point, which seems reasonable, is that if someone wants to be king, they have to pay for it. But that's another problem—and an American question.

61. The Aztecs established an empire over many squabbling *altepetl*, in the "fifth [and final] generation state."

62. In too many conversations about "kings" in the Southwest, my colleagues dropped the "D" word: Despot. A strong theme in American bias against royalty is the notion that all kings are nasty. Read Plato, read Voltaire: Kings can be benign despots or enlight-ened absolutists or philosopher kings. Theoretically, anyway.

63. The full quote from Carl Sauer's (1954) comments on Paul Kirchhoff's "Gatherers and Farmers in the Greater Southwest" in *American Anthropologist*:

> The notion of *Apartheid* of a Southwest Culture would not have arisen, it seems to me, if Mexico had been the center from which anthropological studies spread through North America. Kirchhoff has approached the matter from the south; our students, coming into the Southwest from the north, saw that they were getting into something strongly different, but stopped at the international border and failed to see how much of the complex lay beyond. Moreover, the notions about the Southwest Culture originated in the years when it was considered proper to infer endemism as dominant in culture, to maximize development *in situ* and to minimize the significance of dispersal and diffusion. A familiar example is the postulated succession of stages from Basketmaker I to Pueblo V, construed mainly as autochthonous "evolution." (Sauer 1954:553, italics original)

In the past I used a version of this quote from Sauer's *Selected Essays 1963–1975*, edited by Robert Callahan (1981). I underestimated Callahan's note that he had "edited and abridged" Sauer's original, for example replacing "*Apartheid*" with "indepen-dence and isolation" (Callahan 1981:159). *Apartheid* literally means "separateness"; it became South African policy in 1948, shortly before Sauer's essay was written—but probably not the word we'd use today. Callahan's editing did no violence to Sauer's original essay, but I apologize for presenting an altered anthologized version and not the original text from *American Anthropologist*.

64. Early kings presumably had divine right, or a mandate of heaven, or some other celes-tial blessing and backing. Many were themselves divine (Trigger 2003). Divine king-ship worked until it ran smack into the Enlightenment, which was sour on religion and skeptical about divinity of kings—but not initially antiroyal. It's not necessarily bad to have a king. The English king gave up his divine right as late as 1689, but not (ultimately) his office. Divine or not, it's important to realize that kings and royalty remained qualitatively different: They did not cease to be kings in exile, in defeat, or in a basement in the Urals.

65. I use the word "populist" in its original, benign meaning; in my desk dictionary "a be-liever in or advocate of the rights, wisdom, or virtues of the common people." During review and revision of this book, "populist" got hijacked by crazies.

66. And a Canadian, Bruce Trigger (2003:142): "In early civilizations and complex pre-industrial societies, inequality was regarded as a normal condition...rather than a social evil.... If egalitarian social organization was known to people in early civiliza-

tions, it was as a feature of small-scale and usually despised societies beyond the pale." Of course, Trigger was a Marxist.

67. The American view underwrites Collective Action accounts, such as Blanton and Fargher's (2008) remarkable *Collective Action in the Formation of Pre-Modern States* (see also Fargher 2016). What's in it for the working stiff? Eric Wolf (1999) shows us a state can be an ideology in *Envisioning Power: Ideologies of Dominance and Crisis.* We do it this way because we do it this way, not because of cost-benefit ratios.

68. How much agency does an individual in a small, traditional society have? Some, to be sure; but exercise too much agency in a Pueblo (for example) and you'll get stern instructions on your proper limits, how to behave. Exercise a little more agency and they'll escort you to the edge of town, which is sometimes coterminous with the edge of a mesa.

69. It's a lot cheaper to dig households than pyramids. Just pointing that out. I'm sure that had no bearing on the shift in anthropological interests from kings to commoners.

70. Kent Flannery (1999) examined this process in an article titled "Process and Agency in Early State Formation." (See also "How to Create a Kingdom" in Flannery and Marcus 2012:341–366—less useful for my argument here.) Since all his examples are historic and well documented, they are all secondary states—"early" for their various areas, but still secondary. And all the examples involved aggressive "alpha males" who used military conquest and expansion to consolidate their power—"the subjugation of rival polities" (Flannery 1999:16). Since Chaco lacked rival polities (with the possible exception of Hohokam, which Chaco clearly did NOT subjugate) I doubt that was the process at Chaco—although David Wilcox (1993) long ago suggested Chaco was empire-like within the Four Corners region (his later interpretations were less martial, e.g., Wilcox 1999). Some of Flannery's processes may apply: His early states "each made use of role models" (Flannery 1999:14; that is, they copied and modified familiar sociopolitical structures); after taking charge, "all state founders, however autocratic, need support; they get it by making a least a pretense of power-sharing" with councils and similar bodies (p. 15); and they all change the existing ideologies "to one more appropriate for a state...this is usually not through revolutionary moves to promote wholesale overthrow of the system, but through self-interested change in the meaning of existing relations" (p. 15), "this transformation of ideology is a universal in state formation" (p. 17). Those things probably happened at Chaco: Role models from Mesoamerica, power sharing through Great Kiva assemblies, ideological change suggested by things like the dramatic stylistic shifts from Basketmaker III–Pueblo I to Pueblo II–III rock art and the sudden and broad adoption of Dogoszhi-style pottery design (Neitzel et al. 2002).

71. Political Science does; but Political Science generally only goes back as far as Aristotle. For most of human experience, it's up to archaeologists. And we are on it: Comparing "complex societies" has become a genre in our field and a productive one indeed; e.g., chapters in Feinman and Marcus 1998; chapters in Smith 2012.

72. Tim Pauketat (2007) used Morton Fried's (1967, 1978) ideas about secondary states to explain the proliferation of post-Cahokia chiefdoms in the Southeast (citing Anderson's map [1999:Figure 15.5]; Pauketat's Figure 4.2). "Secondary polities" broke the rules because they skipped evolutionary steps, and required external drivers—which didn't sit well with neo-evolutionists:

> However, a lot of water has passed under the definitional bridge since Wright and Johnson codified their thoughts on hierarchy. And while there still exists a shoot-from-the-hip I-know-a-state-when-I-see-one attitude among some

[Yoffee's Rule], there is also a growing recognition that many presumed states in many places can't be defined using a single standard or checklist of traits. (Pauketat 2007:144)

73. An excellent short summary by Marcus and Sabloff (2008:4–12). Comparative studies are not fashionable in an era of "social construction" of this and that. As Roland Fletcher notes, "Sociality must properly be understood in local terms.... But very soon we will have to confront cross-comparability because it actually matters" (Fletcher 2010). And he argues for the physical, material aspects of urbanism (population, area, etc.).

74. Price (1978:170–175) offers, for example, Teotihuacan's expansion into Guatemala. She notes that Teotihuacan was highly urbanized (that is, big and dense), but Maya cities were not (Price 1978:175). This does not bother her. "This lack of true cities may be taken as a strong suggestion of secondary status…because known pristine sequences tend strongly to develop cities, and to do so in a homotaxially early phase of their evolution, the lack of urban settlements may be taken with some confidence to indicate secondary status" (Price 1978:175–176). That is, secondary states should NOT have big and dense, Western-style cities.

75. Cities without the state: Norman Yoffee, in *Myths of the Archaic State*, suggests that the city defines the state: "Whereas neo-evolutionists seem to have regarded cities as place-holders at the top of settlement hierarchies they called states, I argue that cities were the transformative social environments in which states were themselves created" (Yoffee: 2005:45).

Several people whose work I admire argue that it's cities that create civilization, not the reverse. Norman Yoffee (2005:42–90; see also Yoffee and Terrenato 2015) and Geoffrey West (2017:295) put cities first: West's discussion is subtitled "Cities as the Great Social Incubator."

76. Amos Rapoport's (1993:32) definition of city: "The culturally neutral, cross-culturally valid definition of a city is also as an instrument for the organization of surrounding territory, making it dependent, integrating regions, and generating effective space."

77. Rapoport (1969, 1976, 1982), in my opinion, was to vernacular architecture what Binford was to hunter-gatherers. His work, though old, weathered well: It is systematic, logical, and factually based—and the facts haven't changed (much). And his books are still cited, particularly by those working comparative approaches (e.g., Blanton 1994; Smith 2008a; Fletcher 1995). There has been much useful scholarship along the same lines since Rapoport's. To find it, the field of "vernacular architecture" is a very good place to start (e.g., Oliver 1998; Vellinga et al. 2008).

78. Alas, there is no succinct quote where Rapoport says: Chaco was a capital. If there was, when I am dead and chested you would find it written on my heart. He simply lists Chaco among his early or preindustrial capitals—which, in a way, is even cooler. For example, in discussions of centrality and roads: "Centrality is reinforced by an emphasis on meaning and symbolism, which can be achieved in various ways. One is by assemblies at the capital of chiefs and subordinate kings, another through the residence there of conquered kings or through pilgrimage" (Rapoport 1993:34). These capitals were the center of road networks, and again he cites Chaco among his examples.

And on labor investment: "Capitals, and especially their cores, are front regions par excellence, that is, they communicate the desired meanings. This is why so many resources are devoted to them. The construction of monumental and ceremonial complexes demands much effort and planning, and astonishing amounts of labour," and here he cites Chaco and Cahokia, alongside Peru and Maya (Rapoport 1993: 35–36).

79. Mesoamerican capitals were also reinforcement of political power. Mesoamerican capitals were designed as much for polity as ritual:

> For Mesoamerican archaeologists a focus on political authority resonates well with indigenous views known from pre-Hispanic and early Colonial-period documents. As noted by many scholars, indigenous terms that accord most closely with our notion of cities refer to the seats of power of ruling dynasties that extend beyond particular settlements to the broader territory claimed by the ruler…consistent with the trend in archaeological theory towards a more relational view of urbanism." (Joyce 2010:189–190)

> George Cowgill (2004:535) noted that many early cities were, in fact, creations: "Many of the first cities (some would say all) may have been intentionally created in their entirety to serve the interests of powerful individuals or groups. In theoretical terms, the idea of cities as inventions is appealing, but much remains to be done to develop this notion." The cities of the Chaco Meridian may well have been inventions of the elites.

80. Much of this may sound familiar today; but recall that Rapoport published this in 1993. Wendy Ashmore's "Site Planning Principles and Concepts of Directionality among the Ancient Maya" was published in 1991. "Anasazi ritual landscapes" hit the limelight one year later (Stein and Lekson 1992). The British invasion of "phenomenological" landscape studies mostly postdates 1993 (reviewed in Lekson 1996) and did not really penetrate American Archaeology for several (many?) years thereafter. Rapo was pomo before mo went po.

81. His data include more than 300 "hunter-gatherer communities, small scale agricultural settlements, agrarian-based urban communities, and industrial urban communities" (Fletcher 1997:Fig. 4.3). One could, of course, quibble with the size and nature of the sample—"a world-wide grab sample" (Fletcher 1995:75; see also his note 6 on page 235). But I am not aware of any comparable data set that ranges from mobile hunter-gatherers to modern cities.

82. There are compendia of cities, databases and so forth, but they are (to my knowledge) largely limited to historic periods. Combining pre-history with history is a challenge. Constantinos Doxiadis took a stab at it, with (for example) his interesting 1968 book *Ekistics*. It's my impression that Ekistics faded; Googling the Athens Center of Ekistics brings no recent returns.

83. To fully explicate how this matters to Fletcher's theories is beyond the scope of this short section. Easier (and better) to read Fletcher's book (paying particular attention to his Figure 4.16).

84. Marcus and Sabloff (2008:13) listed seven "elements often invoked in definitions of the city":

1. Heterogeneous people, occupations, crafts, classes, and statuses.
2. Diverse political, social, religious, economic, and administrative buildings, institutions, wards, neighborhoods and associated personnel.
3. Dense packing or crowding of residential and nonresidential structures.
4. A monumental core of unique buildings (for example, a cathedral or temple, a library, a palace, a central market, a courthouse, or a set of administrative buildings).

5. A skyline or "city profile" that shows maximum building height at the center of the city and less and less height as one moves away from the city center.

6. A central focus—sometimes a sacred center, whose access was restricted and where temples predominated, and sometimes an administrative center where governmental buildings were concentrated.

7. Special organizational features, such as grid-like modules like city blocks, streets, city walls, ward or barrio walls, canals, sewers, aqueducts, parks, and public squares.

85. "In Mesoamerica alone, most ancient cities fall into the [i.e., Fletcher's] low-density group. Many of the early cities in South America, Africa, and Southeast Asia can also be characterized as low-density cities. Archaeologists and historians working in these areas have generated considerable information on this ancient urban form, but comparative analysis has only recently begun" (Isendahl and Smith 2013:133).

86. A huge literature on Teotihuacan, of course; I rely on Cowgill 2008. The Aztecs jammed their capital onto a small island, the only land they could get (or build). Perhaps that's why Tenochtitlan had European urban densities.

87. But Pueblo IV villages were not cities. They did not service or transform regions. And they were not capitals.

88. Kenneth Hirth (2008) suggests that the centers Smith calls cities were at most "incidental urbanism"—the altepetl itself was the operative social and political unit, and the cluster of palaces and temples near its conceptual center (which the Spanish called capitals) were simply clusters of palaces and temples. You say paTAYto, I say pohTAHto; let's call the whole thing off.

89. "It appears that farming in urban contexts was quite widespread around the world through history and prehistory (although systematic comparative research has yet to be done)" (Isendahl and Smith 2013:142).

90. Much like the problem we saw with "states"—because Pueblo Space denies states, the referents for Southwestern archaeology are often out of date or inappropriate. So, too, for "city."

91. In 2008 at the Southwest Symposium at Tempe, Arizona, Smith (2008b) presented a poster "Urbanism in the Southwest? A New Perspective," available on his web page: http://www.public.asu.edu/~mesmith9/1-CompleteSet/MES-08-Urbanism%20 in%20the%20Southwest.pdf.

In the poster, he applied the regional definition of city to Southwest cases, noted that urbanism is possible absent the state, and evaluated my claims (Lekson et al. 2006) that Chaco was a city. Working with the regional definition, he concluded that Chaco was not a city, but Phoenix Basin Hohokam might have been. It was a good poster and I liked it, although of course I differed in the assessment of Chaco. After a series of emails arguing that Chaco was indeed the center of and central to a region, Dr. Smith revised his view in a gracious email with the subject line: "OK, you win. City." (Michael Smith, personal communication, January 12, 2011). He was, however, entirely unconvinced by my subsequent suggestion that Chaco was an altepetl.

92. In the index to Whalen and Minnis (2001): "Paquimé. See Casas Grandes." But the old name returns in Minnis and Whalen's (2016) excellent "popular" volume, Discovering Paquimé.

93. The words "city" and "urban" are all but absent from Whalen and Minnis 2001 and 2009; and Whalen et al. 2010. Whalen and Minnis (2001, 2009) were convinced that Casas Grandes was an "intermediate society," and those don't have cities. Not allowed.

94. Subsequent work by Crow Canyon Archaeological Center reduced that figure to a range from 850 to 1,360 people (Kuckelman 2003).

95. "Ceremonial center" was a mistake typical of its times. Lots of kivas do not indicate phenomenal religiosity. "Kivas" were, instead, indicative of homes and households. See note 8 in chapter 3.

96. Those canals are really important; most places in the world, canals running through a string of separate settlements demand central administration, to avoid water wars; Hohokam archaeologists have scoured the earth to find a comparable system that apparently does not have a Chief of Canals or a Bureau of Canals (Hunt et al. 2005).

97. Suggestions for marketplaces forming a truly regional economy are made almost apologetically; markets smack of cities and states (Abbott et al. 2007).

98. I unkindly called these "fungus" (rainfall) and "flushing" (stream flow) models; Lekson 2009a:143–150. Blame the climate: Benson and Berry 2009; Benson et al. 2009; Weiss and Bradley 2001, among many, many others—see for example reviews in Tainter 2008. Climate is king in Southwestern archaeology, of course, but there was more to life than variance around mean precipitation. Around the turn of the Millennium, a role for "social strife" rose among Four Corners archaeologists (reported by George Johnson in the *New York Times*, August 20, 1996). In part, to accommodate the apparent fact that people bailed out of the Four Corners long before the droughts hit. They started leaving during a time of good climate and bad vibes.

99. Linda Cordell and Maxine McBrinn, in the standard textbook: "This term is inappropriate for two reasons. First, it is offensive to the descendants of the people who once lived in these places.... Second, the term abandonment was used in ways that conflated a variety of processes that are very different from one another" (Cordell and McBrinn 2012:223).

    I have no quarrel with reason #1. If Pueblos find "abandonment" offensive, it should go. Reason #2 tells us "it's complicated" and of course it is, but the end result was the same—several dramatic depopulations—worth searching for regularities.

100. Resilience theory seems not so much a theory but rather a sophisticated observational language, like *Annaliste* history. (That's not necessarily a bad thing.) An intriguing article by Charles Redman and Ann Kinzig (2003) suggests that resilience theory is pretty resilient: Whatever you throw at it, the terms can handle it. That seems, to me, more a (useful) set of terms rather than an actual theory about how the world works, not really capital-"T" Theory as I define that in chapter 6.

101. Cycles have a history within history, and it's choppy. Historians rejected the cycles of Oswald Spengler's (1922–1923) *Decline of the West*, published between the Wars, as ill-informed mysticism. Arnold Toynbee's (1934–1961) *Study of History*—also cyclic—published after World War II, fared no better. Yet both were influential bestsellers: Themes of cyclic rises and falls fit their times.

102. Archaeologist K. R. Dark's remarkable *The Waves of Time* (1998) has had more influence in Political Science than in its home discipline. Dark had this to say about cycles in Mesoamerica, for example:

    > It is interesting to note that Mesoamerica, unlike the "Old World" and China, does not exhibit what seems to be a cyclic pattern of growth and decline.... Consequently, as we can see, a successive sequence of states is evidenced in Mesoamerica. [But Mesoamerica was not] unified under a single polity, even if the Toltec and Aztec kingdoms were both expansive and hegemonic. (Dark 1998:210)

Dark's "Waves of Time" end up with modern nation-states and links them back to their ancient precursors. A Political Scientist I used to pal around with was flabbergasted that I (and, I think, many other archaeologists) did not know Dark's work. Dark is an archaeologist, after all.

    Joyce Marcus's (1998) "dynamic model" of Mesoamerican (and other) early states, proposes a cycle of "consolidation, expansion, and dissolution." States began as a large territorial state—"consolidation" in Marcus's words—which arcs through a dynamic history of militaristic "expansion," eventually falling, followed by "dissolution" into many smaller secondary and successor states (Marcus 1998:60).

103. Cycles formed a minor but important theme in early Sociology, through the work of founding fathers Vilfredo Pareto and Pitirim Sorokin.

104. Nikolai Kondratieff was a Soviet economist who was influential in the West until he was eclipsed by Keynes, and in the East until he was shot by Stalin. Years later, after the collapse of the Soviet Union, his work was rehabilitated by the Russian Academy of Sciences: A cycle of sorts.

105. Khaldun's career was even more eventful than Kondratieff's, with intrigues and exiles and adventures that could fill a book—and have: Fromherz (2010).

106. Upham's "adaptive diversity" got some play at the time, but is seldom cited today. David Stuart's ideas surfaced first in Stuart and Gauthier 1981, recycled in Stuart's (2014) *Anasazi America: Seventeen Centuries on the Road from Center Place*. That's the second edition; it was first published in 2000. To my mind, sadly overlooked, and seldom cited in the current Chaco literature. Stuart, when recently (2014) asked, "Has your power and efficiency model caught on with other archaeologists as a research paradigm?" replied:

> Not really, most archaeologists are still invested in very particularistic explanations focusing on material culture, architecture and regional dynamics. Though many are extraordinarily talented at such analyses, few have studied ecology, agronomy, demography and climate in enough detail to put their better regional studies into modern analytical perspectives. So, as wonderful to read as many archaeological works are, few practitioners are interested in the level of analysis I champion. It's another story, though, among a number of general anthropologists/ethnologists (some of whom refer to themselves as specializing in "cultural energetics") and those from other fields in the natural sciences. Thus, the first edition of *Anasazi America* was reviewed in the journal *Science* before it attracted much attention in archaeology.

See more at: http://newmexicomercury.com/blog/comments/five_questions_with _new_mexico_authors_david_e._stuart#sthash.PY410Mal.dpuf.

107. Turchin attributes the cyclic successes (the rises and upticks) of polities to a quality he calls *asabiyah* (following Ibn Khaldun): The cohesiveness and solidarity of a group, and hence its ability to succeed in collective actions. *Asabiyah* is a positive property of metaethnic identity (kind of like "imagined communities" in their original sense; see chapter 2), which often develops on frontiers:

> It is hard to imagine how large groups arise and maintain themselves in a homogeneous environment populated by many small groups, with an ethnic distance separating each pair of groups of roughly the same order of magnitude. But what if there is a major ethnic boundary? . . . A small group near such a boundary will be confronted with very different others, dwarfing in their

"otherness" neighboring groups that are on the same side of the meta-ethnic line.... This should lead to enhanced alliance formation among groups on the same side of the boundary. (Turchin 2003:53)

Thus formed, political units (polities) thereafter follow formal, predictable, secular cycles. Turchin's penchant for neologisms and borrowed argot—*asabiyah*?—make it possible to dismiss his work as pop–political science. But his ideas, logic, and data, to me seem sound.

108. Ditto for Paquimé (Casas Grandes). The literature on Paquimé's rise is rich and (like Chaco's) contentious. There is comparatively little written on its fall: Di Peso 1974: 316–327; Lekson 2009a:215–216; Phillips and Gamboa 2015; Whalen and Minnis 2012.

109. Among the many places where Tainter's *Collapse of Complex Societies* does not appear are Vivian and Hilpert's (2012) *Chaco Handbook: An Encyclopedic Guide*; the many chapters in *The Archaeology of Chaco Canyon* (Lekson, ed. 2006; although it appears in Lekson 2009a!); the several chapters in *Chaco Revisited* (Heitman and Plog 2015); as far as I can tell, in any of the slew of recent articles about Chacoan agriculture; and many other recent articles and chapters and theses. I am happy to report that "Tainter 1988" is listed in Joan Mathien's Chaco Bibliography, on the online Chaco Research Archive http://www.chacoarchive.org/cra/chaco-resources/bibliography/#t.

110. Diamond obviously is not an archaeologist; he's a scientist but hard to pin down, bit of a polymath. His website says: "Professor of geography...he began his scientific career in physiology and expanded into evolutionary biology and biogeography." He's in the National Academy of Sciences, he's won the National Medal of Science, and a MacArthur genius grant—among other laurels. So he's the real deal, not a popular science writer/journalist. Nothing wrong with popular sciences writers/journalists (some of my best friends are popular science writers), I'm just establishing Diamond's credentials.

111. A few Anthropological criticisms painted Diamond's arguments as racist. I think those criticisms were wrong and unhelpful.

112. In *Third Chimpanzee* (1992), Diamond explores archaeological cases and concludes,

Archaeology is often viewed as a socially irrelevant academic discipline that becomes a prime target for budget cuts whenever money gets tight. In fact, archaeological research is one of the best bargains available to government planners. All over the world, we're launching developments that have great potential for doing irreversible damage, and that are really just more powerful versions of ideas put into operation by past societies. We can't afford the experiment of developing five countries in five different ways and seeing which four countries get ruined. Instead, it will cost us less in the long run if we hire archaeologists to find what happened the last time than if we go making the same mistakes again. (Diamond 1992:336)

113. My best (and only) contact inside the Beltway (a brother who, after a State Department career, became a senior VP at the Institute for Peace) thinks *Guns, Germs and Steel* was a fine—but not flawless—book; and he assures me that most of his policy-wonk pals shared that assessment.

114. Not everyone joined the lynch mob. George Cowgill, as always, exhibited wisdom:

Jared Diamond (2005) has provoked very mixed reactions among archaeologists but the issues he raises must be addressed—especially the extent to

which a research emphasis on interactions between humans and physical environments neglects or oversimplifies relations of humans with one another.
(Cowgill 2008:971)

For a range of views, some positive, see deMenocal et al. 2005 and Faulseit 2016. And
for a thoughtful analysis, Fowles 2016b.

115. Yoffee had collapse credentials, collapse cred: He edited *The Collapse of Ancient States
and Civilizations*, with George Cowgill, way back in 1988.

116. Times were tough all over. In the Mississippi Valley, everyone left Cahokia and created
the famous "Vacant Quarter." Archaeology in the eastern Woodlands must confront
precolumbian collapse.

117. As with most things Di Peso, later analyses challenged his interpretation. David
Phillips and Eduardo Gamboa (2015:166), on "the fall of Paquimé"—their analysis
is mostly chronological and supports an end date of 1450. Gamboa suggests "internal
violence and collapse, without an external cause." See also Whalen and Minnis 2012,
who contend that relic populations persisted after 1450 in the old Casas Grandes region; but still, the great city was *gone*.

118. Actually, he (or his fate) stood on Zeus's golden scale. Achilles on one side, Hector on
the other. Hector's pan dipped toward Hades, where that hero shortly followed. The
Homer of this quote, of course, is Bart's father and not the Bard. And to anticipate the
next line: The poet came not from Ionia, but from Texas.

119. The idea and ideal of the city-state—the *polis*—come from Aristotle's *Politics*. The
basic form—an autonomous and largely self-sufficient small state with a single city-
center/capital—was not unique to or invented by the Greeks, whose *poleis* were preceded by city-states of Mesopotamia, and the more proximate Phoenicians, among
others. Two modern, influential archaeological definitions of city-states:

First, Mogens Herman Hansen (2006:9), distilling many years of cross-cultural
city-state research with his Polis Centre: "City formation and state formation go hand
in hand; but the relations between them vary.... There is a set of examples...in which
each city is the centre of a small state consisting of town plus hinterland and, looked
at the other way round, each state is relatively small and has, typically, one single city
as the centre of society. And that is what we call a city-state."

Second, Deborah Nichols and Thomas Charlton (1997:1), addressing mainly
Mesoamerican cases: "In general we understand city-states to be small, territorially
based, politically independent state systems, characterized by a capital city or town,
with an economically and socially adjacent hinterland. The whole unit, city plus
hinterlands, is relatively self-sufficient economically and perceived as being ethnically
distinct from other similar state systems. City-states frequently, but not inevitably,
occur in groups of fairly evenly spaced units of approximately equal size.... These
small polities and small states in the Basin [of Mexico] and elsewhere in Mesoamerica
have been referred to variously as *altepetl*, *señorios*, *cacicazgos*, kingdoms, petty kingdoms, principalities, and city-states, terms often used interchangeably."

120. I have found particularly useful: Griffeth and Thomas 1981; Hansen 2000, 2002, 2006;
Hansen and Nielsen 2005; Nichols and Charlton 1997; Martines 1988; Parker 2004;
Scott 2012; Smith 2008a; Trigger 2003:Chapter 6; Yoffee 1997. Martines 1988 was one
of the sources I enjoyed reading when I was looking at northern Italian Renaissance
cities for ideas about Chaco.

121. Their argument is a bit of bait-and-switch, insisting that "city-state" must equal Aristotle's *polis* and then gigging people for using "city-state" to describe things that were

not exactly *polies*. No non-Greek city-state enthusiast I've read was suggesting their "city-states" were exactly Aristotle's *polis*, which was a philosophical ideal. This seems a bit (but not entirely) circular:

> A term which many participants would like to see phased out is "city-state." This term came into widespread use as a kind of English synonym for the Greek *polis*. There are two problems with its use: (1) many Aegean specialists do not believe the *polis* was a state at all, and (2) many of the polities all over the world to which the term has been applied do not resemble the Greek *polis*. The *polis* has been defined as a democratic and self-sufficient polity in which the majority of towns and villages had a high degree of autonomy and very little economic control over their citizens. Almost no society to which this term has been applied in Mesoamerica (for example) fits this definition. (Marcus and Feinman 1998:8)

122. Trigger's take: "City-states were relatively small polities, consisting of an urban core surrounded by farmland containing smaller units of settlement. In territorial states a ruler governed a larger region through a multilevel hierarchy of provincial and local administrators in a corresponding hierarchy of administrative centers" (Trigger 2003:92). The question is: Are they a distinct class or an evolutionary step? He favors the former, but guardedly.

123. Of course, with Yoffee, it's…complicated:

> The term *city-state* is inherently and intentionally flexible, allowing for, even expecting, important differences in major political and socioeconomic institutions, and it requires that variability be delineated and explained. In some cases, however, the variability itself is illusory since *narratives of uniqueness can also result from failures of cross-cultural imagination*. Use of the comparative method (which is mandated by the term *city-state*) is thus, paradoxically, the only way in which attributions of uniqueness can gain plausibility. (Yoffee 1997:263; emphasis added)

124. For example, Marcus (1998; in Feinman and Marcus 1998, "Peaks and Valleys") basically argues that city-states were remnants of older, larger territorial states which fragmented. That might account for some city-states but not for Cahokia or Chaco; which were in their regions sui generis, more or less. Which is why Cahokia and Chaco should have seats at the State Dinner.

125. "How to Make a Polity (in the Central Mesa Verde Region)," a recent *American Antiquity* article by Stefani Crabtree, Kyle Bocinsky, Paul Hooper, Susan Ryan, and Tim Kohler (2017), lifts my spirits even more than the Notable Archaeologist's "Yes, but it's complicated…" This, my friends, is how to do it.

Chapter 5: An Appraisal of the Ancient Southwest

1. "Indian" is of course false and wrong, the first of many European errors. Columbus wanted the Subcontinent, he got a New World. It's all marketing, so Columbus called them "Indians." Roger Echo-Hawk (2010) makes a convincing argument against the brand. He insists he is Pawnee, not Indian. Navajos are not Hopis; Zuni is not Taos. Each tribe stands alone, each a sovereign nation. But modern "tribes"—today, sovereign nations—were, to varying degrees, colonial constructs. A score of separate Hopi villages, for example, became a unified "tribe" only when Washington drew a rectangle around all those villages and announced: You're the Hopi Tribe now. Apache

and Navajo local groups were forced into unwanted aggregates for the convenience of American administrators. In Indian law, heritage, and to a very great extent anthropology we practice what Tom Sheridan (2005) calls "strategic essentialism": We know tribes are constructs but we treat them as entities. Because they are.

2. I do not refer here to the deeper depths of archaeological theory; those are a problem too, reserved for chapter 6. By "Postmodernity" I mean the general erosion of reason in the latter part of the twentieth century which gave us constructivism in public education and undermined rationalism across a wide range of authorities.

3. A brief recapitulation: Beginning way back in the 1970s, for a half-dozen years I worked side by side with Indians (work = picks and shovels, wheelbarrows, stadia rods, etc.). Then for four or five years I collaborated with Indian artists, writers, intellectuals, and political leaders first at the Museum of Indian Arts and Culture (a thematic precursor to NMAI) and at Crow Canyon (recruiting, with Rich Wilshusen and other Crow Canyon staff, their initial Native American Advisory Board). Then several years teaching (and doing) Indian and Indigenous issues in a Museum Studies graduate program at a university museum. And finally, over six years, I consulted with 80+ tribes (mostly face to face, home and away) for NAGPRA. We got it done: The University of Colorado Museum of Natural History is one of the few big museums to have completed repatriation (and assist with reburial) of our entire holdings, 600+ human remains and associated funerary objects. Very much a team effort with Debbie Confer, Christie Cain, and Jan Bernstein. Those were the big-ticket items; along the way, scores of collaborations with individual Indians (tours, panels, symposia, exhibits, and so forth); a dozen appearances before NPS and other Native American advisory groups; on-site consultations with tribes at various excavations; and more than a few lasting friendships.

4. From Aristotle to Žižek, Bacon to (E. O.) Wilson, I've read widely, and without apology—as Joyce Carol Oates supposedly advised aspiring writers.

5. Europeans are easy with the idea of "heritage" as the past used socially and politically in the present (see chapters in Fairclough and others 2008), but many American archaeologists seem to think that heritage and history mean essentially the same thing—at least as far as Native American history/heritage. The National Park Service muddied these waters when, with NAGPRA hovering in the wings, they changed the names and aims of CRM to "heritage management"—a shift that took place, I think, throughout federal agencies. Park Service journals such as *CRM: Journal of Heritage Stewardship* (2003–2011) in parallel with the hopefully titled *Common Ground* (1994–2011) replaced the earlier, prosaic *CRM Bulletin* (1978–1990) and *CRM* (1991–2002). At least this is my impression: I decline to research the issue further for this book (this madness must stop somewhere). I mention it as a possibly fruitful topic for others: When did history become heritage in our national archaeological program? And why?

6. The book also appeared with the title *Possessed by the Past*. Lowenthal's (1985, 1999, 2015) *The Past Is a Foreign Country* is the other book, the one archaeologists read.

7. Heritage can also be a tool for control, can cut off discussion. Steven Conn (also following Lowenthal) notes that with heritage narratives "there is little room for the argument, debate and polyphony that is the very essence of history" (Conn 2010:48). Speaking of European situations, Geoffrey Scarre and Robin Coningham: "Accusations of 'cultural appropriation' and claims that others have taken what is rightfully ours are often employed more with the aim of guillotining reasonable debate than of advancing it. Once you identify something of your heritage, then anyone else's

claims to or concern with it can be rejected as irrelevant and intrusive, a threat to your own rightful possession or even an assault on your identity" (Scarre and Coningham 2012:2). Although it's hovering overhead, that exclusionary use of heritage has not been a major problem in the Southwest—so far.

8. Chaco—under US administration—began as a National Monument, "an object of historic or scientific interest"; graduated to National Historical Park "for the enjoyment of future generations"; and later was elevated to a World Heritage Site, for its "outstanding universal value" under Criterion iii: "A unique or at least exceptional testimony to a cultural tradition or to a civilization which is living or which has disappeared."

9. The Natives are not shy about making claims. For example: Hopi heritage tells of the Red City, Palatkwapi, to the south, but accounts are vague on its actual location. With the CRM explosion in Hohokam, Palatkwapi was said to be in southern Arizona. And with expanding knowledge of Paquimé, that became a favored locus. "It is tempting to view the successively southern claims for Palatkwapi's location as an ever-widening land claim fueled by Hopi access to archaeological accounts. This is undoubtedly the case, but there is more to it. The stories and their recent elaborations are plausible if only on a small scale, and should not be dismissed out of hand" (Hays-Gilpin 2008).

10. For lowercase-"h" "history" I considered awkward replacement terms like "actual-ancient-events," or "history-as-it-happened" (versus "History-as-written"), but in the end, I could find no solution that wasn't cumbersome and ugly. So for stylistic reasons I accept a degree of sloppiness. Mea culpa.

11. For example, Jeremy Sabloff's (2008) *Archaeology Matters*; Randall McGuire's (2008) *Archaeology as Political Action*; and Scott Ortman's (2016b) "What Difference Does Archaeology Make?" among many others. Calls for "action archaeology" (Sabloff) or for "emancipatory praxis" (McGuire) or for archaeology to be more about the present "and less about the past" (Ortman) are, of course, all tied up with théorie (chapter 6) and Indigenous Archaeology, but they are broader and more programmatic in calling for archaeology as an agent or promoter of social change across a wide range of issues. I wonder: If you want to cure the world's ills (a fine and proper thing to do!), is archaeology an efficient platform? It seems an odd pulpit from which to preach. If changing the world is your goal, would it not make more sense to work for an NGO or a political party? Which, indeed, some of my colleagues have done, God bless 'em.

In pondering this matter, I considered revisionist historians: Their products might change society. I write revisionist pre-history and I'm not sure my work would have the desired effect. That could reflect the local politics of my region, the Southwest.

12. That slap upside the head got Anthropology's attention and launched hand-wringing conference sessions and edited volumes such as *Indians and Anthropologists: Vine Deloria Jr. and the Critique of Anthropology* (Biolsi and Zimmerman 1997). It was at least partly responsible for the end of cultural anthropology/ethnology in the Native Southwest.

Joe Watkins (2000:3) dates the open, active, confrontational opposition of Indians to anthropology and archaeology, after many decades of "uneasy truce," to around 1969—the year, he points out, *Playboy* magazine published excerpts from Deloria's *Custer Died for Your Sins*. Deloria's books were required reading for Indian intellectuals, but *Playboy* brought it to the masses—or at least to horny guys, of which there were many, some of whom apparently were policy-makers.

13. They quote cultural anthropologist Elizabeth Brandt: "'Throughout the late 1960s and early 1970s most researchers of my generation were influenced by the concerns

and critiques of anthropology by Indian people,' continues Brandt, citing Deloria's work in particular. 'There has been little ethnographic work since.... Many anthropologists discouraged with the prospects for research and publication in the Southwest in light of the new circumstances [that is, the new politics of representation] changed their emphases and began to work in other areas of the world'" (Brandt 2002:116, 118). Fowles and Mills note: "There are notable exceptions.... [B]y and large, however, ethnographers packed their bags and left, effectively leaving archaeology as the sole face of anthropology in the Southwest" (Fowles and Mills 2017:41).

14. Remarkable exceptions of great importance to Chaco are recent 14C, DNA, and other sourcing studies carried out on human remains from Chaco and Aztec (e.g., Plog and Heitman 2010; Price et al. 2017), mainly using AMNH collections. These studies seem to be flying under the regulatory or tribal radars; they show how much archaeology is lost with the diminishment of bioarchaeology in the Southwest.

15. Indians ask: Who gave you the right to tell other peoples' histories? If we are only concerned with local history or local heritage, that's a very good question. But if we globalize matters, I have an answer: That would be our mutual African grand-grand-grand-grand[Nth]-mother, who encouraged her child's inquisitiveness to know the world—an australopithecine with a bump of curiosity. Ever since, humans wanted to know about and to make sense of their world; different cultures handle that curiosity differently. And of course all cultures set limits: Curiosity can be bridled.

But maybe that's not the right answer to give, or the right question to ask. I happen to make sense of my world through the natural, material, scientific notions of the European Enlightenment—and so does archaeology and archaeology's main audiences. Maybe turn the question on its head? Here's what Enlightenment thinkers asked of priests and bishops, nobles and kings: We want to know how our world works; who gave you the right to stop us? Priests and princes had powerful answers to that impertinence, and things sometimes got nasty; but thus began what we might euphemistically call the conversation between reason and religion—within Europe.

I do not suggest a parallel with Indians and archaeology in the New World; those relations are complicated by colonialism, conquest, and genocide. I suspect that Indians would find my answer about our australopithecine grandmothers unsatisfactory too, on several counts. But that's my answer, to myself. I do archaeology because archaeology gives us an account of the human past we can use to understand how the world works. To anticipate chapter 6: Capital-"T" Theory, scientific theory. Globally, archaeology needs no apology; locally, it needs respectful diplomacy with tribes.

16. I've been caught in the middle (literally) of that argument. See, if you wish, the account in Lekson 2010a. At one meeting addressing these issues, a tribal representative angrily complained that NAGPRA was just another White law aimed at dividing Indians, setting tribe against tribe. I had never thought of NAGPRA that way...

17. Loris Ann Taylor (Hopi). It's an excellent video, by the way, and she's an eloquent voice in it, representing her views; the video includes several archaeological voices saying archaeological things.

18. It seems slightly ironic that Chaco today is managed for "wilderness values" when, in the eleventh century, Chaco was the opposite of wilderness. And until mid-twentieth century, Chaco was home to many Navajo families, not wilderness. Simon Schama (1995) reminds us that "wilderness values" have, like "heritage," European backstories. I know and you know what we mean by "wilderness"; we value the loneliness and emptiness of Chaco, compared to our noisy, cluttered urban homelands. Archaeology tells us that Chaco was not wilderness, long ago; and that's a strong demonstration

that archaeology is NOT heritage. Archaeology tells us what happened then, not what we want to happen now.

19. Hewett also reclaimed Chaco for New Mexico from New York's American Museum of Natural History by foreclosing on AMNH's operations at Pueblo Bonito. Now that's a heritage claim!

20. Demonstrated, as I write, by the range of opponents to proposed fracking around Chaco: Historic preservationists, wilderness advocates, Dark Sky enthusiasts, archaeologists, tribes, and more. A sad subject we will revisit in chapter 7.

21. The Great Kiva of Casa Rinconada is today closed to the public because New Age shenanigans offended the Pueblos (and most everyone else). I was in Chaco at the time, and know most of the subsequent story, and it's bizarre. Buy me a beer sometime and I'll tell ya all 'bout it.

22. The aesthetics of ruins are seldom considered by archaeologists, but for a significant element of our constituency, those values are paramount. Lowenthal (1999) riffs on this, and the literature is large: classics like Rose Macaulay's (1953) *Pleasure of Ruins* and J. B. Jackson's (1980) *Necessity for Ruins*; more recently a dense academic analysis by philosopher Robert Ginsberg (2004); breezier art criticism in Brian Dillon's (2014) *Ruin Lust*; and Classicist Christopher Woodward's (2003) *In Ruins*. And of course Michael Shanks's oeuvre. Ancient ruins in the Southwest are seldom managed for aesthetics, witness the remarkable tin roof over Casa Grande. That roof is a personal favorite; hard to be more hegemonic than that: Casa Grande wants to melt away, but we won't let it.

23. As Kelley Hays-Gilpin points out: "Ultimately, 'preserving' Pueblo religion is the responsibility of the Pueblo communities and not of anthropologists who, at best, can offer assistance if invited" (Hays-Gilpin 2011:613).

24. There are of course non-Western historiographic traditions which are not heritage. A useful survey (written, of course, in the Western analytical tradition): George Iggers and Edward Wang's (2008) *A Global History of Modern Historiography*.

25. Maybe not truth; that's too much to ask. David Lowenthal, no fan of Post-modernity, notes that we painted ourselves into a post-truth era (long before Trump): "Historians still strive for unbiased consensual understanding…. But 'truth' in the old sense—a veridical account of the past based on consensually agreed evidence—has become passé" (Lowenthal 2015:14).

26. "Myth" is considered pejorative when applied to Native or Indigenous accounts, but it needn't be: We honor myths as the foundation of Western literature and thought. Where would we be without Zeus and Athena, or the equally mythical Honest Broker and Scientific Certainty?

27. This essay was greatly expanded into a book, *A Forest of Time: American Indian Ways of History* (Nabokov 2002). Nabokov is not currently a name to conjure with in Indian Country, as discussed elsewhere in this chapter. But that does not diminish the value of his considerable scholarship.

28. Hunt had a checkered career (Nabokov 2015): He left (or was expelled from) Acoma and traveled as a demonstrator of American Indian culture—a "show Indian" with the circus. He was paid by the Bureau of American Ethnology to tell his version of the Acoma origin story, the edition originally published by Matthew Stirling in 1946.

29. According to one news account in *Indian Country Today*:

> Theresa Pasqual as director of Acoma's Historic Preservation Office, said that the Pueblo has its own protocol of how information is passed down generationally and, "Once that information becomes widely available the Pueblo

loses that ability. The traditional religious leadership has always expressed that this information gives us the basis for who we are." (Jacobs 2016)

And another report, in the *Santa Fe Reporter*:

Brian Vallo, the director of the Indian Arts Research Center at the School for Advanced Research, talked about the unique set of stories that explain how each clan came to be part of Acoma. "Those stories are life guides: They are very sacred. Different clan groups and societies have their own version, so the stories differ as a result. So, you know…you don't share that information with anyone else. Even internally some things are secret until you reach a certain age." (Iberico Lozada 2016)

30. Barbara Mills, in her influential chapter on "Remembering While Forgetting," drives home the depth and reliability of Pueblo histories, while noting their selective remembrance and selective forgetting:

The memory of Chaco also resides in the historical narratives of contemporary Native Americans in the Southwest. As Leigh Kuwanwisiwma (2004) recounts, Chaco Canyon is the place called Yupköyvi to the Hopi. Not all clans trace their migration pathways from or through Chaco. Of those that do, there is a history of clan order and particularly memorable places where ceremonies were performed. This history, recounted over 800 years later, demonstrates the efficacy of Pueblo ways of remembering while forgetting, and how the Chacoan past became the present. (Mills 2008:107–108)

31. "Shaping a field that is fundamentally geared toward establishing more inclusive, democratic, and reciprocal relationships with descendant communities" (Colwell-Chanthaphonh and Ferguson 2008:3). Full collaboration requires "goals develop[ed] jointly," "full voice for [all] stakeholders," and "needs of all parties realized"—consensus which seems unlikely if we are after historical facts. Facts all come with points of view, as the poet said.

32. Very, very few archaeologists are Native/Indigenous. Dorothy Lippert (2008) said, in 2006, only about a dozen. Today, happily there are more, including excellent, articulate advocates such as Joe Watkins, Michael Wilcox, Joseph "Woody" Aguilar, and Sonya Atalay, among others. More young Native people are engaging in CRM archaeology, mostly through tribal heritage programs. All this is very good indeed; but, as explained below, I doubt that archaeology as pre-history is an Indigenous interest. Rather, archaeology can be an instrument of heritage. (Please be clear: heritage is not bad or inferior, but heritage is not pre-history.) I once heard a very smart, well-educated Indian announce that she would become an archaeologist and "subvert it from within." She said it with a smile, but…

33. See, for an example of collaborative history, Benally and Iverson 2005. But Miller and Riding In argue for a purely Indigenous History that

privileges and upholds works by other Indigenous scholars, relegating non-Indigenous works to a secondary status. Some readers may be put off by that tactic, but it is common in the development of disciplinary literatures, and historians use it habitually, referring primarily to the works of other historians instead of otherwise relevant works by writers in other disciplines. (Miller and Riding In 2011:4)

34. I read broadly, and I chatted up a few of the central figures. To reassure Indigenous Archaeologists that I've done my homework: In addition to those cited, others from which my extracts and notes did not make the cut for this chapter include books and edited volumes such as Bruchac et al. 2010; Colwell-Chanthaphonh 2012; Colwell-Chanthaphonh and Ferguson 2008; Liebmann and Rizvi 2008; Lydon and Rizvi 2010; McGuire 2008; McNiven and Russell 2005; McNiven 2016; Nicholas 2010; Silliman 2008; Smith and Wobst 2005; and Stottman 2010, among others. I gave them a fair read because it seemed to me with so much smoke, there must be fire. And fire there is: Ardent and commendable enthusiasm for social and political programs. For slightly less polemical perspectives, I very much appreciate the thoughtful analyses of Joe Watkins (e.g., 2000, 2003), and Sonya Atalay (2006, 2008, 2012). I hope I haven't damned them with my (sincere) praise.

35. Colwell and others (2010:Table 1) list eight salient but rather disparate characteristics, seven of which are unabashed social or political agendas, while the eighth is a general appeal to "theory." See also Nicholas (2008:1660).

36. "Reversing scientific colonialism may well be the primary ethical challenge facing archaeology" (Nicholas and Hollowell 2007:62). Indigenous Archaeology is a movement: Madonna Moss correctly notes that in "feminist, Marxist, and postcolonial [Indigenous] archaeologies…their practitioners aspire to contribute to social change beyond the realm of archaeology itself" (Moss 2005:581). And, presented as moral imperatives, all but impervious to analytical criticism.

   It's actually dangerous to question Indigenous Archaeology. For example, George McGhee's (2008) critical *American Antiquity* essay "Aboriginalism and the Problems of Indigenous Archaeology" provoked a flurry (almost a frenzy) of articles by ten authors—a who's who of Indigenous Archaeology—in a later *American Antiquity* issue (Colwell-Chanthaphonh et al. 2010; Croes 2010; Silliman 2010; and Wilcox 2010). McGhee, in my opinion, made a reasonable case, both historically and logically; his critics countered largely with moral claims. Not, for me, persuasive; as McGhee (2010) replied: Strawmen, red herrings, and frustrated expectations.

   While the substantive value of Indigenous Archaeology is not the central theme of this section, I may as well go on record: I agree with George McGhee (2008:239): "Indigenous archaeology is a social project without a demonstrated intellectual foundation." By siding with McGhee I forfeit, of course, what little credibility I might have with the Committee on Archaeological Morality. But…McGhee was mostly right: Indigenous Archaeology requires the sort of essentialism we work hard to avoid. Much the same point was made, eloquently, by Roger Echo-Hawk (2010), who questioned as essentialist (and racial) the terms "Indian" and "Indigenous." Echo-Hawk's argument shook or at least stirred proponents of Indigenous Archaeology (see papers in *SAA Archaeological Record* vol. 10, no. 3 [2010]).

37. "Acceptance of alternative worldviews and histories as valid forms of meaning-making is one of the greatest challenges faced by archaeology and by sciences in general" (Nicholas and Hollowell 2007:63). Indeed. How would we do that, and still have archaeology? Not to mention science? Their claim presages problems of the Ontological Turn in archaeological theory, discussed in chapter 6.

   Take, for example, Ian McNiven's 2016 "Theoretical Challenges of Indigenous Archaeology." He notes, correctly, that Indigenous Archaeology has been mostly a call for collaboration, with theory "minimally articulated beyond praxis" (McNiven 2016:27). He begins by "challenging ontological and epistemological divides and dualisms within mainstream Western archaeology." (Nobody likes nasty dualisms!)

He notes two (but not dual!) theoretical agendas for his brand of Indigenous Archaeology: First, "challenge objectivist tangibility." Second, "challenge secularist archaeologies of a detached past with archaeologies…linked to identity and diachronic explorations of ontology and spiritualism" (McNiven 2016:1). I'll pass on both.

38. Wylie conflates Indigenous Archaeology with the "community archaeology" of her title, but her essay is all about Indigenous Archaeology (see also Atalay 2012).

    In my original manuscript for this book, I riffed at length on the curious provenance of Wylie's essay, which begins with Paul Boghossian's (2006) seminal critique of NAGPRA, follows his thread back to George Johnson's (1996) "Indian creationists," relies on Larry Zimmerman and Roger Anyon quotes in Johnson's article, to speak hopefully for Indigenous Archaeology—while ignoring Vine Deloria, Dorothy Lippert, Susan Harjo, and other Indians with very dark views on archaeology of any stripe. Wylie's essay was thoughtful and logical, of course, but it concludes with two (to me, odd) defenses for replacing Western rationalism in archaeology: (1) archaeology might get new ideas from Indians; and (2) diversity is good. Thin justifications for rejecting the Enlightenment.

39. It's hard to see how that's so: Is Indigenous Archaeology relevant to Ur, or Lascaux, or Olduvai? For Caral? For Göbekli Tepe? No, probably not. Wylie asks: "How can an openness to exploring 'a different kind of science' enrich, rather than fatally compromise, a social science like archaeology?" (Wylie 2014:73). I'd say: It can't; it will indeed fatally compromise archaeology, much less social science. In an article published long after Johnson's *New York Times* article, Zimmerman states that comingling Indian thinking and science is "not possible," and offers this solution: "Ethnocritical archaeology, in which archaeologists and indigenous people share construction of the past" (Zimmerman 2001:178). Parallel narratives, already a workable solution. Zimmerman might not hold those views today; nothing wrong there, we all change our minds.

40. What do I mean by "heritage technicians"? It's not necessarily a bad thing: I mean professionally trained archaeologists who work primarily in the service of tribal heritage. You could, if you wish, say "heritage professionals." Kelley Hays-Gilpin asks: "Can methods and theories developed by archaeologists from outside the Pueblo world assist Pueblo people with writing detailed long-term histories, documenting land claims and use-rights to shrines, plant-gathering areas, and other sacred places, and establishing cultural affiliation for repatriation of human remains, funerary objects, and sacred objects in museums and private collections? Or must Pueblo scholars invent new ways to meet these goals?" (Hays-Gilpin 2011:613).

    More pointedly, Chuck Gibbs in the online journal *Sapiens*: "Over the years, I have reached the conclusion that American archaeology has more to offer Native Americans than it does Euro-Americans. What was once an instrument of oppression now seems to me an instrument of self-determination.… The Hopi call their ancestral sites 'footprints.' Such places document Native American history more effectively than any textbook. I view it as my obligation to make these footprints more accessible and relevant to Native American students" (Riggs 2017:Sapiens online).

    If that's what some people want to do, OK by me. Just don't insist that we all do it, or that it's the only way to do archaeology. I see Indigenous Archaeology as local responses to local situations, local politics. But we should not claim that working in the service of tribes changes archaeology fundamentally as a discipline: Archaeology is still the study of what happened in history. Archaeology is history, not heritage.

41. Here's what Zimmerman (2012:116) wants archaeology to let go; his quotes, abbreviated by me to bullet points, with my exegesis in brackets. Here's what archaeology should lose:

    1. Past as public heritage. [Tribal heritage overrules History.]
    2. Independent agency. [All work *must* be collaborative.]
    3. Academic freedom.
    4. An idea that there is a single past.... [T]he past is multivocal and multi-threaded; positivist views that there is single, knowable past do not work for Indigenous archaeology.
    5. Western views of science. [Like Vine Deloria 1995:15, "much of Western science must go."]
    6. Traditional field and laboratory methods.

    That does not leave very much. Lose all that, and archaeology is no longer archaeology. Which may be what Zimmerman and other enthusiasts want, but I don't. Nor should you. Why would American Anthropological Archaeology fold up shop when archaeologies everywhere else in the world press on with their business, the business of learning about the past?

42. Indian initiatives are present, to be sure! For example, Joe Watkins, a Native American archaeologist: "The development of a truly indigenous archaeology will never happen until indigenous populations control the quality and quantity of archaeology performed within their homelands" (Watkins 2000:177). That's a basis for policy.

43. Read Deloria (1969, 1995, 2002). Read Harjo (e.g., in Preucel 2011). Read Echo-Hawk (2012). Read Riding In (1992, 2012) and Miller and Riding In (2011). Read O'Laughlin (2013). Read Dumont (2013). Read Lippert (2008). And take them seriously: Don't Pollyanna away their very real anger.

44. Pueblos of course have their own ideas of what's proper and useful. Leigh Kuwanwisiwma (2004:43), of the Hopi Cultural Preservation Office, tells us how Hopi uses archaeological data: "Indeed, [Hopi] seriously considers scientific findings and extracts information that corroborates Hopi traditional knowledge or is credible in terms of that knowledge. Although this may seem overselective, Hopis are not surprised that scientific conclusions complement their knowledge and verify cultural continuity between themselves and cultures thousands of years old." Whatever works.

45. These phrases come from several sources; for an overview, see Cajete 2016, or the Worldwide Indigenous Science Network at http://wisn.org/. Indigenous Science includes superb engineering, keenly observed natural history, and thick layerings of spirituality. Not saying that spirituality is a bad thing, just not something we need in archaeology.

46. The rest of the quote, attributed to Aldous Huxley: "What is science? Science is angling in the mud—angling for immortality and for anything else that may happen to turn up."

47. We are lucky to have archaeologists who push archaeology into the marketplace of ideas: Books with broader impacts, beyond local interest. From the Southwest, Steven LeBlanc's (1999; LeBlanc and Register 2004) books on ancient warfare are widely read. Anthropological archaeologists Kent Flannery and Joyce Marcus (2012) and classicist Ian Morris (2010, 2014, 2015) and Bryan Fagan (too many to list! http://www.brianfagan.com/) and more than a few others write thoughtful "general audience" books. Most recently, I was thrilled by Robert Kelly's (2016) *The Fifth Beginning: What Six Million Years of Human History Can Tell Us about Our Future.* The content,

to be sure; but even more the concept, the bold use of American Anthropological Archaeology to address fundamental human questions. It's great when an archaeologist writes a book like that, because not many of us can. I can't.

We may disagree with what they say, but we should laud them to the skies for saying it. As Voltaire is said to have said, I may disapprove of what you say, but I will defend to the death your right to say it. (He didn't say that; those words were put in his mouth by a friendly biographer.)

48. No individual could read all the output of CRM archaeology in the Southwest. Moreover, the distribution of CRM gray literature is often intentionally limited; you can't read it even if you wanted to. Happily, the bigger projects are often published in multivolume reports. Big CRM budgets can do archaeology beyond NSF's wildest dreams; and CRM has the talent to use that money wisely.

49. And sometimes CRM writes for larger audiences, with great success. I'm thinking, in the Southwest, of Archaeology Southwest's long-term commitment to public audiences, which the many titles in their *Archaeology Southwest Magazine* do exceedingly well. And several other CRM organizations do equally great work along these lines. SAR Press (not a CRM firm!) does outstanding work with its "popular archaeology" series, originally "curated" by David Grant Noble.

50. In chapter 1, I estimated about 11,000 archaeologists working in the USA. My guess of 1,500 in the Southwest, assembled from several informal sources, is almost certainly too low. More like 2,000? Who knows? In any event, there are a LOT of Southwestern archaeologists, one or more under every wet rock.

51. A political "constituency" elects its representative. We can be fairly certain that Indians would not elect archaeologists to represent their past. "Constituency" is imprecise, but more melodious than "stakeholder"—which sounds like Professor Van Helsing's assistant.

52. One cause of the happy accident was SFI's Nobel laureate physicist founder Murray Gell-Mann's polymathematical interest in prehistory; later cemented by several years of an outstanding archaeologist, Jerry Sabloff, as SFI's president. The Santa Fe Institute's location in the City Different is another happy accident, of a sort: Its founding owed much to Los Alamos, over the river and through the woods. Most of SFI's founders were nuclear Los Alamos physicists who wanted to do something more elevating than building bombs.

53. The Department of Anthropology at ASU reinvented itself as the School of Human Evolution and Social Change and proudly announced "ground-breaking collaborative social science"—and they made good on that promise, with cross-disciplinary projects escaping the confines of conventional Anthropology. I've listed a few of its many projects elsewhere in this volume. All engage other disciplines with notable results. ASU is not alone, of course, in exporting our products; but they may be the most prolific.

54. It's great today to see many American Archaeologists working to reach the nonspecialist audiences. It wasn't always so. When I got into this business about fifty years ago, archaeology shunned popular audiences and media. This was especially true in the academy, and remains true: Universities actively discourage "popular" writing for a professor's first six or seven years—that is, before tenure; and those rules and habits become ingrained.

It took me a while to figure all this out. My first decade as an archaeologist, I learned my craft through a string of shovel-bum jobs across the Southwest, ending up with the National Park Service's Chaco Project, which kept me busy for ten years. Our offices were at the University of New Mexico, where I got a close look at academic life. With Lew Binford and several other colorful characters, it was not dull. When they got tired of beating up each other, UNM's Department of Anthropology beat up NPS and public archaeology—despite UNM's thriving CRM operation (in a separate building) and Maxwell Museum of Anthropology (right next door). (I'll spare you the details.)

Halfway into my NPS stint, I realized that we nonacademic archaeologists weren't doing much for the public, either. In NPS, that job was done by "interpreters." But NPS (and other) "interpreters" were typically decades behind the times, archaeologically; and (this is important) they never, ever, ever ventured out of Pueblo Space—still a big problem. So in 1987 I wrote my first article for *Archaeology* magazine, and the next year an article in *Scientific American*, followed by more articles in *Archaeology* and *New Mexico* magazine and *El Palacio* and so forth. I was well aware that appearing in those outlets would compromise my scholarship, my academic integrity—and it did. (Again, I'll spare you details.) But I wasn't then (or now, really) interested in being a professor. It needed doing and *no one else was doing it*—with the single, notable exception of David E. Stuart. So I did it. And thereafter, throughout my career, I attended to nonspecialist audiences with trade books, exhibits, lectures (we all do lectures; I do a LOT of lectures). I worked in museums and I tried to run Crow Canyon. Public archaeology was my career, although along the way I managed a bit of research, too.

That was annoying because at heart I'm a research archaeologist; I did the public stuff because it needed to be done. A few years before the Millennium, I realized that the two spheres *need not be separate*. Indeed, as I argue in the text, research would be better if it answered the interests of the public—history—and not American Anthropological theory. I started writing "crossover" books, like *Chaco Meridian* (1999a, 2015a) and *A History of the Ancient Southwest* (2009a): Technical books intended for professional audiences but accessible to public readers willing to work a bit. Did that work? Yes and no: The public read those books and got something new, something outside Pueblo Space. But the professional audience for whom those books (and this book) were intended blew 'em off—in part because they didn't care for my conclusions, but also in part *because they were accessible*—public, popular. (Once again, I'll spare you details.)

I hope this extended note established that I know about this stuff: I've done it and thought about it for decades. Please judge my opinions in that context; thanks. My knowing about this stuff does not mean that my opinions are correct, of course; only that my opinions are informed.

Chapter 6: A Future for the Ancient Southwest

1. For an interesting if ultimately wrong-headed alternative categorization: Gabriel Abend's 2008 article on "The Meaning of 'Theory'" in sociology.

2. Lewis Binford—I paraphrase a personal communication, from sometime in the 1980s. In print: "Theory is a *causal* argument about patterning in nature" (Binford 2001:243). In a footnote to this sentence, "It cannot be stated too often or with too much emphasis that it is not possible to see a cause. A cause is a relational statement developed through argument" (Binford 2001:482n2).

3. Some of my thinking could fall at various places on the critical theory spectrum. But I am only trying to clarify our knowledge of the past, not to advance a political agenda in the present. I have searched my soul and I do not see how identifying state-level societies in the ancient Southwest (the core of my argument) should affect current or future social and political situations—except perhaps to drive a tiny tack into Marxism's

well-nailed coffin, an act which is at this point truly and only academic. Whether this argument has any impacts on Indian people is, as far as I can see, entirely up to Indian people.

4. But not entirely! I originally planned to focus on Slavoj Žižek as my example of theoretical excess—"I am a Hegelian. If you have a good theory, forget about reality!" Žižek has been variously described as the Most Dangerous Philosopher in the West, the Elvis of Culture Theory, and the Ken Dowd of Post-Lacanian Hegelianism. A big target—but not exactly a familiar face at the Southwest Symposium. In the end, I chose as my *exemple par excellence* Laurent Olivier, a French archaeologist we will meet later in this chapter. The trouble, after all, was mostly French; the Brits did some damage, as did Austrian-born American Paul Feyerabend. And Slovenians (like Žižek), none at all, unless perhaps yrs trly.

5. Francois Cusset, professor of American Studies at École normale supérieure de Saint-Cloud, describes théorie in America thus:

> A deep mystery, skillfully maintained, surrounds the term 'theory,' this new transdisciplinary object fashioned by [American] literary scholars from French poststructuralism. This mystery distinguishes it, in any case, from the previous uses of the term, all more or less linked to science [including social science, e.g., Marxism]. Moving against the grain of these more precise definitions, the new theory of which it is everywhere a question for the last thirty years in [American] literature departments, whether it is designated as French or simply as literary, remains mysteriously intransitive, with no other object than its own enigma: It is above all a discourse on itself, and on the conditions of its production—and therefore on the university. For it had to remain itself, without object, since to aim at a more particular or transitive utility it would quickly lose ground in comparison to approaches that were less innovative but otherwise useful outside the campus. (Cusset 2008:99)

We return to Cusset's amusing book—written by a French intellectual for other French intellectuals, *prochainement*.

6. This, from a TAG paper, archived on Shanks's webpage http://humanitieslab.stanford .edu/23/Home.

7. Severn Fowles correctly points out that the Southwest has been largely impervious to the wilder flights of théorie. He notes that things that look like théorie in the Southwest may have alternate histories. Contrasting our standard Processual-Plus and an emerging, more humanistic Southwestern practice hovering around Native American concerns (my words, not his), Fowles continues,

> Superficially, the contrast between these two intellectual moments may look like the old opposition between processual and post-processual archaeology.... By my reading, however, this characterization is quite incorrect, not only because there never was a British Invasion in the Southwest archaeological theory (which goes without saying in the Southwest but is news to some British colleagues) but because such a characterization obscures the profound influence of the Native American Graves Protection and Repatriation Act— and the new world of decolonization it stands for—on the source of American archaeology, particularly in the Southwest. (Fowles 2016a:178)

I agree. But perhaps Fowles gives the Southwest too much/too little credit: Théorie may only now be reaching our region. In my experience, Southwestern archaeology was consistently a decade or so behind developments on our Coasts—which themselves were a decade or so behind developments on the Continent. (Most of "my experience" was pre-web, pre–social media; so these lags may no longer apply.) I review NSF dissertation improvement proposals and I of course work with graduate students at my university and elsewhere. It is (almost) charming to see the labored logics that invoke the philosophies of "old post-processualism." It's like the kids don't really believe it, but they feel compelled to name the names. And as a museum pro and a relentless popularizer of Southwestern archaeology, I see the rot of epistemological relativism, science studies, and the whole baggage of théorie influencing—probably at third or fourth hand—constructivist and antiscience representations of our field, and what we have learned. (I sat on a committee advising a major Southwestern museum on a new archaeology exhibit; the convener opened the proceedings with "Now we all know that science is just another belief system…" and it went downhill from there.) And as a somewhat battered veteran of what is sometimes termed "the consultation community," I see increasingly the language of théorie used to underwrite, philosophically, what is at heart human rights laws and regulations—which need no such justification.

8. For younger readers who may have arrived after the heyday of French Poststructuralism, I recommend Laurent Binet's (2015) *The Seventh Function of Language*—a mystery/police procedural about the demise of Roland Barthes, run down by a laundry van on February 25, 1980 (this is a fact). An accident? Maybe not. *Seventh Function*—which features Foucault, Derrida, Deleuze, Althusser, Eco, and a great deal of literary theory—is not entirely respectful of Binet's elders, but offers an easy, raunchy entrée into their odd world. It includes an epic dust-up at a (fictional) 1980 conference at Cornell with most of the major French linguistic philosophers of that era, the continentals slugging it out with the American analytics including John Searle, Noam Chomsky, and Jonathan Culler; in the end, Derrida is killed by a gigantic hound.

9. Théorie became an end to itself, and undeniably faddish. "Theory has become its own industry, merely trading an old canon for a new one, and retaining the same hierarchies and worshipful groupthink. There is little subversion to putting Judith Butler or Slavoj Žižek on a T-shirt, or to liking them on Facebook" (Balzer 2014:11). Some (how much?) théorie is simply careerist: "Postmodernism may not help us understand the past, but it was a wonderful career advancement tool for its first and loudest advocates" (Shott 2005:3). As was the strident scientism of some New Archaeology.

10. Cusset is intrigued but bemused at French théorie in America, because in the 1980s, "right when the works of Foucault, Deleuze, Lyotard, and Derrida were being put to work on American campuses…those very names were being demonized in France" (Cusset 2008:xviii). In the late 1980s, an SAA panel on "Theory in Archaeology" included one working French archaeologist. She listened to American panelists one-up each other with Foucaultisms and other French zingers, and observed thus: I am impressed that Americans are so comfortable with Foucault, because in France most of us have no idea what he's talking about.

Bruno Latour agreed: "The French, having sold postmodernism to the whole world, are proud of never having partaken of it, a little like cynical pushers who would sell coke, but only drink Coke" (Latour 2007:16). He changes the subject: "The postmodern is an interesting symptom of transition, let's accept it as such, use it to bring about the end of modernism more quickly, and, for goodness sake…let's talk about something else" (Latour 2007:16–17).

In Britain, we are told, enthusiasm for French Poststructuralism peaked in the early 1990s and then waned ("the Death of Theory")—almost before it reached American shores (Pluciennik 2011:35).

11. In an essay titled "Pierre Bourdieu's Argument against Ordinary Language," Michael Billig recounts Pierre's demand that the language of social studies be ornate and obtuse. "If what literary theorists wrote was easy, then it would be common sense. And if it were common sense, then it would be conservative and nonintellectual. So, literary theory has to be difficult" (Billig 2013:90). I can't prevent the French from being French, lamented Charles de Gaulle; impenetrability comes with the territory. It's not limited to French Poststructural prose, of course: as Martin Heidegger (neither French nor Poststructural) is said to have said, "Making itself intelligible is suicide for philosophy."

12. Bruno Latour, one of the last men standing of French théorists of that early group, now laments his eager deconstructions which today underwrite agendas he finds distasteful. He didn't really mean it, he protests; of his partners in "science studies," he insists "several of them, at least, pride themselves on *extending* the scientific outlook to science itself" (Latour 1999:2, emphasis original). Several of that pack, perhaps; but one could question if their notion of "scientific outlook" conforms to something a real scientist might recognize. I find Latour's apologia disingenuous; having overseen the havoc, he now distances himself from the wreckage. But the damage is done:

> While we spent years trying to detect the real prejudices hidden behind the appearance of objective statements, do we now have to reveal the real objective and incontrovertible facts hidden behind the *illusion* of prejudices? And yet entire PhD programs are still running to make sure that good American kids are learning the hard way that facts are made up, that there is no such thing as natural, unmediated, unbiased access to truth, that we are always prisoners of language, that we always speak from a particular standpoint, and so on, while dangerous extremists are using the very same argument of social construction to destroy hard-won evidence that could save our lives. Was I wrong to participate in the invention of this field known as science studies? Is it enough to say that we did not really mean what we said? Why does it burn my tongue to say that global warming is a fact whether you like it or not? Why can't I simply say that the argument is closed for good? (Latour 2004:227)

This is one of the least attractive aspects of théorie: Young Turks staked bold—even outré—claims; held them long enough to benefit professionally; and then backed away: We didn't really mean it, at least not to that extreme. I should note that I found equally distasteful the rhetorical excesses of the Young Scientists of (very old) New Archaeology.

13. Theory-of-the-month club? Would that be Speculative Realism, or the Ontological Turn, or New Materialism? Like Dorothy, head spinning in Munchkinland: "People come and go so quickly here!" New Materialism, for example, surfaced only a few years ago, but according to "New Materialist Cartographies" website there are already twenty-two distinct variations (who knew?), listed alphabetically from "activist materialism" to "vital materialism."

Marshall Sahlins (2002:73–74), not one to suffer foolishness gladly, had this to say about the parade of paradigms (as he called them):

> In the social sciences you couldn't tell a paradigm from a fad.... In the social sciences, the pressure to shift from one theoretical regime to another...does not appear to follow the piling up of anomalies in the waning paradigm, as it

does in natural science.... There is an inflation effect in social science paradigms, which quickly cheapens them. The way that "power" explains everything from Vietnamese second person plural pronouns to Brazilian workers'
architectural bricolage, African Christianity or Japanese Sumo wrestling....
Paradigms change in the social sciences because, their persuasiveness really
being more political than empirical, they become commonplace universals.
People get tired of them. They get bored.

14. "This heterogeneity means that archaeology has no center. No core. There is no
single orthodoxy" (Witmore and Shanks 2013:383). "So how have we arrived at the
current state of affairs?...Fragmentation is also a hyper-defensive strategy implemented in the wake of hypercritical aggression; the fragment is that which is most
resistant to critique.... Critique is a healthy aspect of the discipline" (p. 385). VanPool
and VanPool seem excited by "theoretical plurality" in their "Introduction: Method,
Theory and the Essential Tension" (VanPool and VanPool 2003:1): "In recent years,
archaeological theory appears to have fragmented into 'a thousand archaeologies'
(Schiffer 1988:479).... Needless to say, this is an exciting time for archaeology as a
discipline."

    Is it? Not all of us are charmed by fragmentation, nor do we celebrate its perverse
diversity. John Bintliff is one among many annoyed, and I feel his pain:

> By constantly changing the goalposts, the list of required sacred texts, theory
> teachers have led young scholars to feel intellectually inadequate, since hardly
> have they scoured the pages of Lévi-Strauss so as to parrot Structuralism,
> then they are told this is dropped in favor of Giddens' Agency theory, and so
> on. Keeping up with cultural fashion, rather than bringing students to self-
> evaluation of intellectual approaches places power in the hands of teachers.
> We have found an increasing trend in classes, for students to repeat pages
> of leading theory texts as factual accounts of the world.... If one challenges
> students or young researchers to justify why a particular concept or approach
> has been taken, it is generally the case that the answer is merely that "a leading
> authority wrote this." Citation of sacred texts becomes more and more the
> only authority needed to prove a case-study, rather than matching several
> alternative models to the data. (Bintliff 2011:8)

15. A recent one, Harris and Cipolla 2017 (which I read, cover to cover), is advertised
thus: "Written in a way to maximize its accessibility, in direct contrast to many of
the sources on which it draws, *Archaeological Theory in the New Millennium* is an
essential guide to cutting-edge theory." Not just a *vade mecum* but a (very necessary)
précis/exegesis. Among many theory guides out there, Gibbon 2015 is level-headed
and refreshingly undertheorized.

16. Older théorie almost always ultimately references nineteenth- and twentieth-century
European philosophy. If one is trying to understand ancient societies, modern European philosophy seems like an odd place to shop. But still we turn to the consolations
of philosophy. There are a range of philosophical choices—to be facetious—and by
our choices we shall know us. I cringe when I see appeals to Heidegger; he was not a
very nice man. It's hard to take seriously arguments that reference as seminal thinkers the likes of mad Aby Warburg (Olivier 2011; whom we will meet shortly) or H. P.
Lovecraft (Harman 2012; whom we will not meet). I read Lovecraft when I was a kid;
then I grew up.

17. Ian Hodder: "I think there has been a shift in what the goal or the object has been. The
goal of archaeology used to be the study of the past through material remains, but I

think it has shifted or, rather, ought to shift, to be the process of studying the relationships between people and their material pasts [in the present]" (Hodder 2013:130). For a chorus of well-theorized assent, see Olsen et al. (2012).

Archaeology is not just in the present, but *active* in the present: Lynn Meskell, describing "cosmopolitan archaeology" (théorie-of-the-month, a few months back): "Cosmopolitanism describes a wide variety of important positions in moral and sociopolitical philosophy brought together by the belief that we are all citizens of the world who have responsibilities to others, regardless of political affiliation" (Meskell 2009:1). See also Stottman 2010 and McGuire 2008.

18. The imposition of modern, Western philosophical discourses—and even those that *reject* Western ontologies are framed and argued in Western logics—upon the ancients makes perhaps even less sense than up-streaming Classic Ethnographies onto the denizens of Chaco and Mesa Verde. What would the people of Mesa Verde make of Latour or DeLanda? Probably what modern Indians made of Marx: Just another Old World shell game, foreign and irrelevant (chapters in Churchill 1983).

19. De Certeau's (1988) *The Writing of History* is not much help. Originally published in 1975, it arrived in English translation six years after Wolf's (1982) *Europe and the People without History*, which does the same work, only better.

20. Friendly colleagues closely engaged with théorie warn me that these generalizations may not represent the Ontological Turn of its core thinkers—while admitting that these generalizations of the Ontological Turn do reflect the views of graduate students and professors who engage only the secondary literature. But the problem is, graduate students and their professors are the ones who apply these notions and, perhaps, make policies. What Viveiros de Castro or Latour think may be less important than the Ontological Turn as applied in American Anthropological Archaeology. As we saw in chapter 2, imported concepts mysteriously morph in Pueblo Space. In théorie as in Wonderland, words mean just what you choose them to mean—neither more nor less (attrib. to Humpty Dumpty).

21. One wonders, other than academic gamesmanship, why we need yet another word for culture—first "habitus," now "ontology." A question which has of course been asked: "Debate: Ontology is Just Another Word for Culture" (Venkatesan 2010). "At the end of the discussion, the audience voted on the motion. The motion 'Ontology is just another word for culture' lost with 19 votes in favor, 39 against.... Had the word 'just' not been part of the motion, the outcome may well have been very different" (Venkatesan 2010:199). And thus is knowledge made.

22. I'm not starting at shadows: Two enthusiasts of the Ontological Turn question backward projections of the ontology of the moment: "New animism [for example] seems to unintentionally replicate some of the representational patterns that Said critiqued: taking one instance or moment of radical alterity and embellishing it to create an Other world envisioned by a western academic. It seems like Orientalism in a new guise" (Harris and Cipolla 2017:203). They continue, questioning the seeming universal enthusiasm for animism: "There is no reason to think that animism, per se, has any role to play in the pasts I investigate [in Europe]. It has already proved popular to apply these ideas there, and I find this a little problematic as rather than making the ontologies of the past more varied, it can reduce their complexity" (p. 205). Remember when everything was shamanism? Even Maya kings? It's like that.

23. There are exceptions, e.g., Ortman 2012.

24. Attempts to link modern languages to ancient Chaco are as difficult—and probably futile—as assigning "cultural affiliation" to thousand-years-gone ancient societies. But we do it, because we must.

25. I agree with Severin Fowles:

> I will be frank and admit, first, that as an archaeological anthropologist I am not interested in speculating about multiple realities; I am happy to leave this to physicists and philosophers.... As I see it, the problem with going further and adopting ontological pluralization as an anthropological methodology is that this move ends up being so ironically, tragically, and embarrassingly modern.... There is nothing more profoundly modern than the effort to step outside modernity. (Alberti et al. 2011:906–907)

26. Hodder 2003a. Hodder does not seem to run with the newly turned Ontologists; but flirtations with epistemic relativism in his and other foundational Postprocessual théorie sowed the fields from which we reap this harvest.

27. Do I exaggerate? No. Recall from chapter 5 that of Anthropology's fantastic four sub-disciplines, three have been eclipsed in the Native Southwest. Conventional ethnography and historical linguistics are essentially gone, and bioarchaeology is on the run. Their parent subdisciplines have been largely transformed into applied anthropologies. Archaeology, too: Most of our archaeology is applied CRM. There's nothing wrong with Applied Anthropologies, but I'd hate to see conventional Southwestern archaeology diminish just when it might escape a century's confinement in Pueblo Space, and actually figure a few things out.

28. "We begin to witness archaeologies built within indigenous ontologies or between indigenous and western worlds.... The general idea is that we are trying to move beyond the limitations of a western perspective that sees one world best explained through scientific inquiry" (Harris and Cipolla 2017:180, 181). "This is the crucial move from one world to two or more worlds. It is a move that takes western science off its pedestal and asks: what am I (the western observer) missing?" (p. 184). "Several scholars have raised concerns about the turn to these kinds of alternative or multiple ontologies.... Nonetheless, these ontological critiques are having a noticeable impact on many disciplines including archaeology, and offer very provocative tools to think with. As Bruno Latour has asked, are these kinds of approaches simply another way of looking at the world, or something that explodes our assumptions?" (p. 185).

29. A reviewer of this book manuscript suggested that, instead of Olivier, I consider Ian Hodder's (2012) *Entangled*, a book far more likely to be read by Southwesternists. (I've read it several times.) There are many good bits in *Entangled* and far less pointless théorie. And there's that meet-'em-in-the-elevator thing.

   Hodder's book leads up to what he calls "tanglegrams" which on first blush look remarkably like flowcharts or even (gasp) systems diagrams (a point noted by other readers; e.g., Mills 2013). The fact that the relationship between human and material is, to varying degrees, reciprocal and "entangled" has been an anthropological chestnut since the hoary days of *Man the Tool-Maker* (Oakley 1946). Not just tools; a prominent midcentury British philosopher opined, "We shape our buildings; thereafter they shape us." Hodder maps intriguing entanglements between and among rooms at Çatalhöyük—features, objects, and so forth. A larger entanglement would surely be the architecture itself: What sort of society built that bizarre beehive, and how did its densely packed modularity shape the next generations? (Hodder deals with these questions elsewhere; e.g., Hodder 2006.)

   My marginalia in *Entangled* includes this question: "Re-write this [book] without the word 'archaeology'?" Except for several specifically archaeological examples—which could easily be replaced by nonarchaeological examples—I think the answer would be "yes." Is that a weakness or a strength?

30. Originally published as *Le Sombre abîme du Temps: Mémoire et archéologie*, and re-portedly written at the urging of Sander van der Leeuw, who provided a back-cover blurb along with Michael Shanks. Not to be confused with Paolo Rossi's 1984 *The Dark Abyss of Time*, originally published as "Segni del Tempo" in 1979 (Feltrinelli Edi-tore)—a pioneering "Big History." Olivier is not a flash in the pan; see also his chapter on "Time" in the ponderous *Oxford Handbook of the Archaeology of the Contemporary World*, edited by Paul Graves-Brown and Rodney Harrison (Oxford University Press, 2013).

31. If Warburg's name seems familiar, it might be from his pilgrimage in 1895 to Hopi, to see the "snake dance." He never saw the snake dance but he wrote about it, and published his photos of Hopi kachinas (Warburg 1939, reprinted as Warburg 1995). Google "Warburg image" and you'll find a photo of Warburg wearing a hemis kachina mask. Ouch.

    Darwin's influence on Freud is well known—the key difference being that Dar-win's ideas worked, Freud's did not. (Freud's failures, strangely, do not disqualify him from *théorie*.) Walter Benjamin seems an odd third alongside two architects of modernity—typically, one would draw Marx for three-of-a-kind. Benjamin, of course, was from a later generation. Loosely associated with the Frankfurt school, his eclectic writings on literature and art—today associated with a resurgence of Romanticism—made him something of a cult figure, after his tragic (and Romantic) death fleeing the Nazis. Benjamin's cult is more than matched by Aby Warburg, a German art histo-rian of roughly Benjamin's generation, who left Germany ahead of the Nazis but died before the War. Warburg too has achieved cult status, with institutes and journals devoted to his eclectic and (mildly put) idiosyncratic thought. Benjamin and—more so—Warburg are central to Olivier's argument, to his critique of archaeology.

32. Quo vadis history? In the end, Olivier wants it both ways—and perhaps that makes sense to him. After a book spent decrying historicism and historical senses of time, he insists:

    > This in no way means that we must abandon the basic historicist perspective of archaeology whose aim is to reproduce the material reality of the past.... The point then is not to reject history, but rather to assign it to its true place in archaeology by making the discipline the "science of the past" that it has always sought to be. This is a theoretical matter; archaeology must define its objective: not the past, but what one might call that which is subject to the past. Whereas history seeks to establish what happened to people, archae-ology explains what happened to things.... Archaeology studies how things and beings have "absorbed" past events, both how they came to evolve on the basis of their situation and their inherited past, and how they contributed to these evolutionary processes. (Olivier 2011:189)

33. Olivier chides: "We have never been able to free ourselves from archaeology as cul-ture history, principally because one of the basic hypotheses of the discipline holds that the past that lies outside of recorded history is historically knowable" (Olivier 2011:182–183). His "culture history" is not the American culture history; and his ar-chaeology—for which, prehistory is unknowable—is not American Anthropological Archaeology.

34. The quote continues: "It is a concept which puts archaeology in harmony with its subject, which is to say the material archives of memory of the past, by redirecting the discipline's focus to the study of filiations" (Olivier 2011:xvii).

What are "filiations" and how do we find them? These questions are not explicitly addressed (this is, after all, French théorie); but here Warburg seems relevant. Olivier laments that "we no longer know how to deal with artifacts and ways of organizing them that once seemed so obvious to us; we no longer know what grid to place them in." Warburg had grids—and they were brilliantly aesthetic or completely bonkers or both. Warburg was nuts—not an opinion, a real (and very sad) diagnosis of mental illness; a fact that Olivier acknowledges (Olivier 2011:149). Warburg obsessively collected and collated art images according to his own peculiar methods, creating a gridded *Mnemosyne Atlas*—a catalog of filiations?—"schizophrenic collages." Olivier admires the *Atlas*: there is madness in Warburg's method, and apparently that's attractive: "The temptation has been great to integrate Warburg's reflections into the thoroughly traditional approach of the Academy where, normalized at last, they could take their place. Warburg's ideas have to be seen for what they are: pathological and delirious, to be sure, but extraordinarily perspicacious and fecund" (Olivier 2011:152). Madness, it seems, is the path to filiation.

35. I wish I'd coined that one, but it was Marshall Sahlins in an essay titled "Know Thyself": "There is a certain species of academic whiffle bird that is known to fly in ever-decreasing hermeneutic circles until…" (that's the end of his sentence; Sahlins 2002:76). In the fifth edition of this small book, he completes the sentence, indelicately: "…fly in ever-decreasing hermeneutic circles until it flies up its own backside" (Sahlins 2018:67).

36. This, from a recent edition of the tour leaflet at Mesa Verde's Far View site:

> Archeologists Have As Many Questions As Answers Based On The Results Of Excavations. From Your Visit To Mesa Verde National Park, We Hope You Will Join With Us In Speculating About The Everyday Life Of The Ancient Puebloans. How Were Their Lives Like Ours? How Were They Different From Ours? Each Year, New Archeological Research Provides Us With More Answers And New Questions.

And this, from the NPS brochure for Tusayan Ruin (http://www.nps.gov/grca/plan yourvisit/upload/Tusayan.pdf):

> As you walk around the ruins, remember that the history of these people and their culture exists only through the artifacts found at this and similar sites and through the stories of their descendants. You will notice that many statements in the brochure and on the signs begin with "perhaps," "it seems" or "maybe." There are few definitive answers.

Those refrains float like flute music over every Southwestern site: mysteries, questions, speculations.

37. Southwestern archaeology could institute a "swear jar" convention: Anytime an archaeologist says "I'm only guessing" or any variation of that phrase, it's five bucks in the jar. The funds could be used for deprogramming us from Pueblo Space, and reprogramming us in positive thinking.

38. If this were easy, everyone could do it—a conundrum for Community Archaeology. We say we want everyone to do it, but we do not REALLY want everyone to do it. Archaeology is specialized work, requiring training and experience. It's not the same thing, but would we want Community Brain Surgery?

39. I can offer no hard proof, but anecdotally it seems that many (most?) of my colleagues who use "just-so stories" dismissively are unaware of their august provenance

in Kipling's fables. I suspect those same scholars, if made aware of the first "just-so" author, would be equally dismissive of the old White male imperialist who told us how the camel got his hump and the beginning of the armadillo. This, despite the fact that Kipling's "just-so stories" directly addressed items of real archaeological interest: The origins of domestication and writing, for example. Incorrectly, of course, but amusingly.

40. And to these two articles, I could add a recent and important book, Michael Schiffer's (2017) *Archaeology's Footprints in the Modern World*. Not a compilation of what archaeology needs to do, like "Grand Challenges" and "Key Issues," but a brilliant listing of what archaeology already does for the wider world. He addresses fourteen themes, each with three examples, for a total of forty-two good things about archaeology. Last and presumably not least, his final theme is history: "Revealing our prehistoric past" (p. 281) with three examples "In the Beginning," "From Foragers to Farmers," and "The Urban Revolution." The thirty-nine other themes range from "debunking myths" to cultural tourism to supporting environmental sciences, and so on. It's an exhaustive list, and slightly exhausting: I was reminded, faintly, of lists of "practical applications" issued by NASA to support funding the space program: Tang, Corningware, freeze-dried ice cream, cordless portable vacuums, and so on. But Schiffer's book is a good, hefty exhibit to present when asked: Archaeology, what is it good for?

41. In "Grand Challenges," process trumps history; history did not constitute a Grand Challenge:

> The 25 grand challenges presented here focus on cultural processes and the operation of coupled human and natural systems—not on particular events of the past. While this will not surprise archaeologists, to a nonspecialist there is a notable lack of concern with the earliest, the largest, and the otherwise unique. This focus on the dynamics of culture indicates no lack of regard for prehistory; the facts of the past provide the evidence that is essential for us to confront all of the problems presented here. (Kintigh et al. 2014b:7)

> How is it that we know those "facts of the past"? They are more than a chronological list of events; there are causes and consequences. We need history: The "facts of the past" are events linked through history. It should be noted, in fairness, that "Grand Challenges" was commissioned by the National Science Foundation. NSF does not often fund history; that would be NEH.

42. An incredulity to pre-historiography; but the concluding thoughts on "Key Issues" are commendably broad and well worth quoting:

> If we were to identify an area of concern, we would stress the need for archaeologists working in the SW/NW region to remain engaged with our colleagues working in other areas of the world, to participate in broader discussions of alternative theoretical perspectives, and to continue the development of new research methods. The literature on the SW/NW has become vast and the discipline as a whole has become more specialized, both trends that can have the unfortunate impact of encouraging us to more narrowly focus on our own specific geographical areas and to attempt to understand those areas from limited theoretical perspectives. (Plog et al. 2015:19)

43. Epic fail, in my opinion. I am not the only one to notice, of course. For example, Randall McGuire in a notable (1994) "position paper" on "Historical Processes and Southwestern Prehistory." Having correctly diagnosed the problem, McGuire saw

three kinds of history in anthropology: (1) cultural sources, "Ralph Linton at his breakfast table" analyzing the diffuse origins of bacon, eggs, and coffee; (2) cultural difference, Geertz's notion of historical change as "continuous cultural process with few, if any, sharp breaks"; and (3) material social process. McGuire (1994:200) also noted that "historical processes of change" were present in pre-historic as well as historic times. And he concludes nobly:

> Developmental change [evolution] can only be understood in the context of real historical sequences where nondevelopmental change, digression, and diversity are as important to the understanding of change as the regularities and abstractions that evolutionary studies seek.... History is made by the actions of real people not abstractions. People are not free to make history any way they want. Their actions are conditioned by...circumstances of their existence, even as their actions transform these circumstances. (McGuire 1994:200)

In that same volume, Norman Yoffee (1994:341–342), considering the sad state of historicity in Southwestern archaeology, suggested back in the early 1990s (using that era's trope of the negative), "Perhaps archaeologists, increasingly self-conscious about how they know the past, will soon be teaching courses on 'prehistoriography.' (Not.)"

Alas, as Fowles and Mills (2017) note: "The SFI volume [which included McGuire's position paper and Yoffee's bon mots] had limited impact at the time...but more recent work has revived the debate." (I was at that conference!)

See also Alice Kehoe's extended critique of ahistoricity in American Anthropological Archaeology, *Land of Prehistory* (Kehoe 1998).

History turns some people off. Chip Wills complains: "It is common today for archaeologists to describe inferences about the meaning of their data as 'history' rather than hypothetical reconstructions, a difference that often encourages elegant storytelling about how people got from one temporal point to another in the past, but frequently lacks the historiography that historians utilize to evaluate the knowledge claims made in such narratives" (Wills 2009:284–285). Beyond the remarkable claim that history is "common" in American Archaeology, I agree absolutely that we lack a developed pre-historiography. That should be Job One, and it probably won't involve hypothetical reconstructions.

44. "How do we 'do' history for ancient times?"—I put this question to most of the archaeology faculty at one of our leading universities, very kindly assembled for a lecture I was giving. One of their senior scholars—a wise and thoughtful archaeologist!—replied: We make it up as we go along. Fair enough: That's what I did writing *A History of the Ancient Southwest*, made up methods on the run. It was an experiment, and the outcome was some ideas about pre-historiography.

45. This is very close to the argument of Timothy Pauketat (2001) for "Historical Processualism"—an earlier effort that is curiously uncited by Beck and colleagues (2007). It is cited in passing by Susan Gillespie in her comments. Eventful archaeology has made an impact, which is great; see, for example, Gilmore and O'Donoughue 2015. Events are history!

46. The full quote, from http://peterturchin.com/cliodynamics/:

> Cliodynamics is the new transdisciplinary area of research at the intersection of historical macrosociology, economic history/cliometrics, mathematical modeling of long-term social processes, and the construction and analysis

of historical databases. Mathematical approaches—modeling historical processes with differential equations or agent-based simulations; sophisticated statistical approaches to data analysis—are a key ingredient in the cliodynamic research program. But ultimately the aim is to discover general principles that explain the functioning and dynamics of actual historical societies.

47. Which produced a study of possible relevance in Chaco's ritual/political tug-of-war: See Whitehouse, François, and Turchin's (2015) "Role of Ritual in the Evolution of Social Complexity."

48. Michael Shanks's "An Archaeological Narratology" (in *The Archaeological Imagination*; Shanks 2012:127–144) is humanist théorie actually taking on pre-historiography. (I do not count Michel de Certeau's 1988 *The Writing of History* and others of its ilk— it's *prehistory* I'm after.) Like most of Shanks's stuff, fun to read but of little practical application. He waves at historiographers he finds congenial and offers us a series of diagrams with titles like "Phantasmatic reality," "The Semiotic Square," "The voice against the wind," and so forth. He concludes: "There is no definite end to these diagrams" (p. 144), which I read two ways: No termination or no purpose. "This is another way of pointing out that the archaeological, or antiquarian, imagination is far wider than what is now the discipline of archaeology" (p. 144). He likes that vagueness; I don't.

More usefully: Ian Morris (2000:310): "There is no single, all-best structure for an archaeological narrative. Shanks (1992) and Tilly (1992) suggest that archaeologists might experiment with nonlinear narratives.... But I defended the value of chronologically tight, sequential stories.... I also emphasized the humanistic basis of cultural history, and the centrality of the event as an analytical category.... The principles involved—of how to weave a rich and compelling narrative from the material record— are much the same whether we are looking at Çatalhöyük or Annapolis."

The range of approaches discussed in Van Dyke and Bernbeck (2015) *Subjects and Narratives in Archaeology* encompass a variety of media and genres—creative nonfiction, fiction, theater, docudrama, and more—but strangely (to me) not straight-up historical narrative. If we can do all that other stuff, surely we can do simple straight-up history.

49. Pauketat's (2013) *An Archaeology of the Cosmos: Rethinking Agency and Religion in Ancient America* is a brilliant effort and stands alongside Fowles's (2013) *Archaeology of Doings: Secularism and the Study of Pueblo Religion* as two of the most successful recent studies of ancient religion. Impressive energy and prodigious intellect went into researching some of the least knowable aspects of the ancient past. With good results: They are both great efforts and good reads. If we can do *that*—know religion and cosmology—surely we can do narrative history.

50. A southwestern application appears in the introduction to an edited volume, *Big Histories, Human Lives* (Robb and Pauketat 2013), which "combine[s] interpretive strands to create a multiscalar history...[bringing] together the ideas of history as multiple genealogies of practice and the vision of history as a palimpsest of qualitatively different processes" (Robb and Pauketat 2013:26). For the Southwest, they offer a complex diagram (their Figure 1.1) illustrating "history as multilayered processes." Time runs up the Y-axis, ranging from "a few centuries" to "millennium"; parallel ribbons of multilayered processes are punctuated or delimited by areas of "historical ontology," "ways of doing things," "historical landscapes," "local political histories and cycles," and "tipping points." It's interesting, but it's not narrative. But surely it is

underwritten by silent narratives—silent in that they are (in this presentation) unexamined. Where do the stories woven into the Y-axis come from?

51. But not, of course, all. Pauketat's (2007) *Chiefdoms and Other Archaeological Delusions* cleared the way for his historical approach in the Southeast by slashing and burning through American Anthropological Archaeology's dead wood and detritus. Pauketat's book so roused his readership that a sixty-plus-page "book review forum" was published in *Native South* (Volume 2, 2009), a series of critical essays (not all negative!) by leading Southeasternists, with a response from Pauketat. And another extended discussion in *Social Evolution and History* 9(1), 2010. In his response to his critics in *Native South*, Tim writes,

> My goals involved giving the establishment a slap in the face, not out of malice but because of the clear and present danger to our archaeological heritage.... The stakes, I submit, are high enough to demand a new approach. Why do archaeology at all if we simply recycle old ideas, over and over again? Time to wake up. Time to do things a little differently. (Pauketat 2009b:127–128)

52. According to Sassaman:

> To rewrite Archaic "prehistory" as history is to write about Archaic experiences with migration, encounter, ethnogenesis, coalescence, and fissioning. I believe most Archaic specialists would acknowledge that these sorts of events and processes truly mattered, but I am afraid that few would privilege such factors over the constraints and limitations of "nature." (Sassaman 2010:xvii)

53. It might be objected that my arguments are well and good for the densely dated and data-ed later Southwest, but they cannot apply to earlier hunter-gatherer situations. Sassaman shows that is not so: The Eastern Archaic, once freed from "the conceptual straightjacket which is 'prehistory,'" (his words) requires a historic approach.

54. Attempts to inject *Annaliste* notions into American Archaeology "have not resulted in major advances in understanding time, scale and change in archaeology" (Robb and Pauketat 2013:12).

55. "The role of narrative in explanation has received considerable attention in most of the subdisciplines concerned with questions of historical process.... Archaeologists, however, have been curiously reluctant to consider the proposition that their reconstructions of the past are fundamentally narrative in character" (Ballard 2003:135).

56. Like everything accessible to théorie, "narrative" has been complicated and even made subject of a subdiscipline with its own journals, etc. See, for example, Herman 2007a, 2007b, 2012.

57. "In the past fifteen years, as the 'narrative turn in the humanities' gave way to the narrative turn everywhere (politics, science studies, law, medicine, and last, but not least, cognitive science), few words have enjoyed so much use and suffered so much abuse as narrative and its partial synonym, story" (Marie-Laure Ryan 2007:22).

58. Alex Callinicos (1995) offers a useful analysis of historical narrative in "History as Narrative" (his chapter 2)—in opposition to "History as Theory" (his chapter 3).

59. "Archaeological explanations evidently work, insofar as the discipline is able to proceed with shared understandings of plausibility, but it is not clear that archaeologists necessarily understand how or why their own explanations succeed in convincing their colleagues. What I seek to explore in this paper is the contention that archaeological explanation develops within and through frameworks that are fundamentally narrative in character" (Ballard 2003:135).

60. R. G. Collingwood, an inspiration for British "interpretive archaeology," was a historian turned archaeologist! His *The Idea of History* (Collingwood 1956[1946]) is still essential historiography.

61. In contrast, in Preucel and Mrozowski's (2010) *Contemporary Archaeology in Theory: The New Pragmatism*, only one of thirty-two contributions even mentions history (Timothy Pauketat, with Historical Processualism).

62. Life imitates art, or art imitates life? White asserts that history follows western literary traditions, but what if fictional literary plots mirror trajectories familiar from historical realities?

63. In 2013, historian Robin Fleming was declared a 2013 MacArthur genius for mixing material (archaeology) with documentary sources to write history for early medieval Britain. See Fleming 2011. Other historians who rush in where archaeologists fear to tread include Brooks (2013), Foster (2012), Fraser (1988), and Kelley (2003). As the poet Mac Rebennack said: If we don't do it, somebody else will.

64. They've been thinking about how to do it—more than we have, alas. The introductory essay by (big) historian Daniel Lord Smail and cultural anthropologist Andrew Shryock from a 2013 *American Historical Review* forum, "Investigating the History in Prehistories," is worth an extended quote (since few archaeologists read *American Historical Review*):

> To work in the distant past, we must shift our focus, break a few well-entrenched analytical habits, and familiarize ourselves with new literatures and methods. As difficult as this retooling itself might be, working outside the narrative arc of modernity is an even greater challenge. What would this move entail? First, it would require that we analyze trends and events in ways that do not preconfigure them as moments of origin or points of culmination. Every developmental sequence would have to be connected to preceding conditions that generate an explanatory present, and this cascade of connectivity would reduce our narrative recourse to high contingency (or rupture) and increase the utility of comparison. Second, working outside the arc of modernity would mean that storylines could privilege neither themes of mastery over nature nor a growing capacity for freedom or agency, notions of moral progress, or attempts to associate these trends with increasing social complexity. It would be wrong to dismiss these tropes as misleading ideological commitments—they are often indispensable to social movements and political action—but they should not be treated as essential elements of historical storytelling. (Smail and Shryock 2013:722)

For their *Deep History: The Architecture of Past and Present* (Shryock and Smail 2011), they invited a few archaeologists to the party. History will have to "re-tool," "break a few entrenched habits," "work outside the narrative arc." American Anthropological Archaeology will have to do so, too, and even more.

65. For the Southwest, several narratives bridge (late) pre-history to history. These are mostly the work of nonarchaeologists: Sociologists and historians. For example, Thomas Hall's (1989) *Social Change in the Southwest, 1350–1880*; Scott Rushforth and archaeologist Steadman Upham's (1992) *Hopi Social History*, which spans 1450 to 1990; William Carter's (2009) *Indian Alliances and the Spanish in the Southwest, 750–1750*; James F. Brooks's (June 2013) article in *American Historical Review*, "Women, Men, and Cycles of Evangelism in the Southwest Borderlands, AD 750 to 1750." And of course my *History of the Ancient Southwest* and John Ware's *A Pueblo Social History*.

There are others (and attempts in other regions; e.g., Kehoe 2002). Seek them out, see how they do it. We're all learning here.

66. And later, Ian Morris argues that archaeology fifty years ago was history (at least in Europe) but today it has fragmented into science, social science ("probably anthropology"), or "archaeology is archaeology is archaeology.... Or maybe it is like literary criticism, or even a form of political activism.... But, overall, the one group that archaeologists hardly ever hold up as a model is the tribe of historians, the only other scholars to devote themselves systematically to the human past" (Morris 2010:3).

67. In his book *Archaeology as Cultural History*, Ian Morris (2000:3) proclaims: "Archaeology is cultural history or it is nothing. I hold this truth to be self-evident, but like most such truths, the problems begin when we try to say exactly what it means." He argues cogently that neither Processual nor Postprocessual archaeologies have come to grips with history and historiography—contra Postprocessual noises about the Historical Turn. Here's Morris (2000:24) on Postprocessual's engagement with history:

> Despite postprocessualists' rhetoric, the 1980s historical turn was less serious in archaeology than in other social sciences, largely, I think because it went on within frameworks inherited from 1960s arguments about culture history vs. culture process, and ultimately from late nineteenth-century divisions of academic labor.... To the extent that sociologists and anthropologists talk about history, postprocessualists take over their language. They have been excited by what they have read in Bourdieu, Giddens, and Sahlins, but they have taken history as second-hand from them, feeling little need to engage directly with historians.

Morris (2000:19) notes that "by the 1920s they [in US] had enough evidence to conclude that the natives did have some kind of history before Europeans arrived." He lauds Walter W. Taylor's (1948) insistence on history, but "Taylor's lone voice could not overcome three generations of institutional divisions and anthropological hostility to historicism" (Morris 2000:21).

It is important to note that Morris's "cultural history" is not American Anthropological Archaeology's "culture history." They are very different things. I assume the reader knows the American usage of "culture history"—a nonnarrative time-space matrix showing us who and what was where, when (Lyman, O'Brien, and Dunnell 1997). Morris's "Cultural history" is a trend in academic history which, in brief, imports anthropological sensibilities into conventional history. For a review of cultural history, see Arcangeli 2011.

Peter Burke (2004) surveys that kind of "Cultural History," a disparate and divided approach in History, which arose in the 1970s and by century's end was ascendant in the academy. "The common ground of cultural historians might be described as a concern with the symbolic and its interpretation. Symbols, conscious or unconscious, can be found everywhere, from art to everyday life, but an approach to the past in terms of symbolism is just one approach among others. A cultural history of trousers, for instance, would differ from an economic history of the same subject" (Burke 2004:3). "One of the most distinctive features of the practice of cultural history, from the 1960s to the 1990s, has been the turn to anthropology" (Burke 2004:30). But "New Culture History" is no longer new. "It becomes impossible to avoid the question whether the time has come for a still newer phase...a more radical movement or...a rapprochement with more traditional forms of history" (Burke 2004:100). He cites, with approval, Marshall Sahlins, who showed that "it is possible to write cultural history itself in a narrative form, very different from the relatively static 'portraits of ages' of early cultural history" (Burke 2004:123).

68. Ian Morris (2000:7) again: "The crucial issue is not the presence or absence of writing but the density, quality, and variety of data points." Data points in the Southwest are dense indeed, high quality, and wondrously varied.

69. Hayden flirted with postmodernity (and is hailed as a hero by théorie historians) but he emphatically denies he's a relativist and denounces nihilists like Lyotard: For White, the past actually happened. However, I'm not a huge fan of Hayden's historiography. For more solid stuff, I recommend Ann Curthoys and John Docker's (2005) *Is History Fiction?* American no-nonsense historiography: They dismiss relativism in their review of "Anti-Postmodernism and the Holocaust" (chapter 10); and in "History Wars" (chapter 11) they deflate théorie—referencing Keith Windschuttle's (1996) *Killing of History*. (Windschuttle said things that needed to be said, but he's perhaps not the most useful ally.) For a more measured, academically acceptable product: Jeremy Popkin's (2015) *From Herodotus to H-Net: The Story of Historiography*—quoted from time to time in this book.

70. You needn't be a Positivist, if that's socially awkward. But what's the harm in a little informal Positivism? Not Comte's Positivism, but a rosy upbeat notion of a knowable world. As the poet Mercer wrote and the chanteuse Fitzgerald sang: You've got to accentuate the positive / Eliminate the negative / Latch on to the affirmative / But don't mess with Mister In-between. This is not a throwaway joke; we will return to this theme in the discussion of archaeology's loss of authority—which actually matters.

71. I strongly recommend the historical geography of Donald Meinig, of Syracuse University. His magisterial, four-volume *The Shaping of America: A Geographical Perspective of 500 Years of History* (1986, 1992, 1995, 2004) is unsurpassed. But it is an earlier work to which I direct your attention: His *Southwest: Three Peoples in Geographical Change 1600–1970* (Meinig 1971), a slim volume that profoundly influenced my youthful (and all subsequent) thinking. If I could produce a worthy prequel—"Southwest: Peoples in Geographical Change 500–1600"—I could die happy. (I tried once, in a 1998 SAA poster, "The Spatial Structure of the Ancient Southwest," a series of overly busy map-diagrams; it flopped.)

As noted in chapter 4, note 24, we have Big Site atlases for every Pecos stage from Basketmaker III to Pueblo IV. We have the data. But we do not (yet) have the histories which could turn those data into historical geographies.

We need narratives! Note that Meinig used *other people's histories*—much like Diamond and Turchin (discussed above). It is the synthesis and presentation that was uniquely Meinig's own—and his cartographer's!

72. Big History routinely casts cultures and civilization as agents. Rome did this, Han did that. There is an interesting conversation among historians about scale in *American Historical Review*: "How Size Matters: Questions of Scale in History" (2013, *American Historical Review* 118[5]:1431–1472).

We don't like our taxons used this way: Michael Graves (2010), in his *Choice* review of *History of the Ancient Southwest*, noted with distaste that "cultural units operate at regional scales, with successive geographic florescence followed by diminishment and political leaderships that never seem to get it quite right." Well, right: That's pretty much how the deal went down. That's standard in world history.

73. By focusing on nobles (political agents) I could be accused of ignoring commoners. Surely a complete history would have both? Well, we know a lot about Southwestern commoners: They've been our principal study for a hundred years. Until very re-

cently, we didn't know we had nobles. Alas, many of my Southwestern colleagues still can't see 'em, through the fog of Pueblo Space.

74. This argument, when I've presented it at conferences, etc., is met with annoyance or sometimes even anger because it seems to cut Indians out of the loop. I'm all for having Indians in the loop. My point is almost exactly what théoriciens are saying (and what Lew Binford said, many years ago): We understand the past IN THE PRESENT. Archaeology writes history or pre-history to be understood IN THE PRESENT. We do not write fanciful accounts of how we think "history" might have been told by actors and agents—in this case, by Indians—of ancient times; or (contra some threads of théorie) how those then-current events might have been perceived or understood by Indians of ancient times. How could we even pretend to know those things?

Nor do we write fanciful accounts of how traditional history/heritage might be told by tribal peoples. That is, literally, none of our business.

75. These principles seem solid, safe, and simple when compared to the frankly astonishing assertions we read about spiritual life in the ancient Southwest. Statements about what people thought and believed a thousand years ago have become routine, almost de rigueur; but most are based on nothing more than a wing and a prayer—and Parsons's (1939) *Pueblo Indian Religion*. I can and have justified my axioms and methods. You may not agree with them, but at least their rationale is knowable. Insofar as there has been methodological thought behind ideological up-streaming, it appears to be vague, faith-based assertions that "Pueblos are very conservative about religion." The leaps are amazing.

76. They react to my work, rather than read it. *A History of the Ancient Southwest's* one negative review (honest, there was only one that I know of) came from a distinguished archaeologist who fumed and sputtered about my jokey titles and taglines, and pretty much missed the whole point of the book. Oh well. This happened before, with *Chaco Meridian*, loudly condemned by people who hadn't read it. More than a few people, as it turns out. One such incident is retold by David Roberts (2015:Chapter 4).

77. "A conjunctural scaffolding helps to construct a better house of history" (Braudel 1990:487). Conjuncture: What happened simultaneously. Events or trends in one realm (economics) versus trends in another (demography), etc.

78. I've nagged so often about Thinking Big, my nags would fill a long and tedious tome. Here's another, not from me but from a superb prehistory/history of the Mediterranean:

At its best, a close focus encourages us to look at regional and micro-regional processes…. Without such insights, large-scale history becomes suspiciously smooth, and attempts to understand commonalities and interconnections remain just-so stories…. At its worst, however, the result [of "close focus"] is archaeological and intellectual parochialism, a myopia that misses the linkages and parallels that give structure and explanatory coherence to the whole, that exalts what Freud condemned as the "narcissism of small difference," with each case unique unto itself. Degrees of diversity are hardly a surprise, given that none of us is able to transmit even our genes and ideas with complete fidelity; far more striking are those instances where, despite the inevitability of difference, we find that we can in fact still connect, compare, and generalize to good effect. Archaeology…too easily finds itself in the position of a person at the bottom of a well, who can see a small patch of sky with perfect clarity, but misses the scope and constellations of the heavens. (Broodbank 2013:23)

79. Other archaeologists use the term "triangulation" in other ways. Chapman and Wylie 2015:211: "Multiple Working Hypotheses, Strategies of Elimination, and Triangulation" (the title of Part III of their book). See also Wylie 2002, and Kirch and Green 2001. Martin Bell (2015) summarizes this usage:

> Related approaches in anthropology are interpretations based on cables, comprising multiple strands of evidence, and tacking, a dialectical process between the contrasting perspectives of the anthropologist and the subject. [citations omitted] This is analogous to the process that Wylie (2002) has called "triangulation," whereby an interpretation that may not be entirely convincingly demonstrated from any one source becomes more precisely grounded by triangulation with other sources of varying independence. (Bell 2015:50)

My triangulation is a bit closer to David Hurst Thomas's (1991) "cubist perspective"—looking at things from every angle. If extended outward, triangulation is not far off the historian's technique of "contextualization"—looking back in from one more layer out, concentric contexts: Time, space, history, whatever. It's always worth going two or three layers out, and then, when you think you've gone far enough, go one more.

My triangulation point of temporal peers is, I think, not the same as historian's "side-streaming." Side-streaming is the use of ethnographic information from contemporary tribes and peoples to infill details of a group of interest, for which that type of information is absent (e.g., Richter 1992:5; Hämäläinen 2008:13). This is rather like ethnographic "up-streaming" (discussed elsewhere). Temporal peers may be quite unlike the triangulation target.

80. At least, that was the story in Lekson 2009a. New data—discussed elsewhere in this book—gets Chaco going several decades earlier that we'd thought, with a great deal of input (wood, for example) from the south, rather than the north. These new facts, along with several other recent studies, require us to rewrite our pre-history. That's fine: That's exactly how history works, post hoc accommodative arguments! But not here, in this book. One task at a time.

81. Comparison has been largely abandoned in cultural anthropology; HRAF is conspicuous by its absence in most sociocultural articles in *American Anthropologist*. (Devotees remain, but only a few.) Comparison is also under fire in American Anthropological Archaeology, particularly from théoriciens. Not many of whom work in the Southwest, for now. But Tim Kohler (2012:331), in an approving review of Michael Smith's (2012) *Comparative Archaeology of Complex Societies*, notes with regret that rigorous, systematic comparison is uncommon: "Once the camel's nose of comparison has cracked open archaeology's somewhat claustrophobic tent, who can tell what fresh air might get in?"

82. Not to be confused with counternarratives! This book and my *History of the Ancient Southwest* are counternarratives (not counterfactuals!)—as Norman Yoffee defines them: "By counternarratives, I mean simply those ideas that have challenged prevailing wisdom, examining current 'paradigms' and finding flaws in them, and then producing new ideas and explanations for social behavior and change.... Now, this goal may seem perfectly obvious to archaeologists and world historians, but until recently, one may claim that few studies, especially in archaeology and ancient history, have taken up the challenge" (Yoffee 2016:346).

83. But see Walter Scheidel's (2017:389–401) chapter, "What If? From History to Counterfactuals," in his intriguing *The Great Leveler: Violence and the History of Inequality*.

He develops four counterfactual histories of the twentieth century, and finds it a useful exercise. Another Classicist in the lead!

Most historians are less enthusiastic. Elazar Weinryb's (2008:109) essay on "Historical Counterfactuals" in *A Companion to the Philosophy of History and Historiography* is typical:

> Historiography is replete with counterfactuals.... Notwithstanding the ubiquity of counterfactuals in historiography, traditionally counterfactual thinking has been quite unpopular with historians.... Counterfactuals form a part of our understanding of the past because they play an essential role in explanations of action that try to take the historical agents' point of view.... [Counterfactual] causal ascriptions have an essential role in practical inferences, as possible courses of action are viewed in the light of probable outcomes. (Weinryb 2008:109, 115, 116)

The British philosopher Winston Churchill (who is quoted several times in this book, sometimes accurately) was a prolific popular historian. He contributed to an interesting early volume of counterfactual essays, *If, or History Rewritten* (Squire 1931). Churchill's essay, "If Lee Had Not Won the Battle of Gettysburg" (in Squire 1931:259–284), is a real twister: It starts with the counterfactual of Lee winning, and then spins a counter-counterfactual from that perspective of what things would be like if the North had won. Ties your brain in knots: I do not recommend this procedure.

84. Janet Spector's (1993) use of "fictionalized accounts" in *What This Awl Means* was widely praised, as was Charles Hudson's (2003) *Conversations with the High Priest of Coosa*—both scholarly books delving into fiction. The last time any scholar tried that in the Southwest was Adolph Bandelier's (1890) *Delight Makers*—not counting many books by real novelists: Kathleen and Michael Gear, Louis L'Amour, Douglas Preston, and others.

85. It would probably be useful for archaeologists to study historical fiction or what today is called "nonfiction novel"—if there were courses or analyses or scholarly treatises. Are there? Not that I could find, in a search of the web and the library.

86. The Ontological Turn right down the rabbit hole. For ancient times and prehistory, that goal—knowing how men and women from the past thought about their world—seems as difficult (or more so) as the enthusiasms of not long ago for "the individual in prehistory." Every once in a while we can see an individual, streaking like a subatomic particle across a sensor; but we can't expect to build narratives about individuals, much less their thoughts and motivations. Except for truly exceptional situations, the quest for "individual in prehistory" was doomed before it began. So, too, ancient ontologies. As Henry James said: It's humbug.

87. "Staying close to the data" sounds laudatory. It's not; as a mantra, it's nonsense. Stay really close to the data and you limit them to chipping rocks and breaking pots, occasionally stacking up stones for a house. Staying close to the data for a century gave us a corn-beans-and-squash Southwest, the Southwest of Pueblo Space.

Archaeological data are an uncertain small sample of a tiny fraction of fragmentary detritus representing—very indirectly—a vast, dynamic array of events. Binford and Hodder agreed that everything beyond the measurement of a posthole is interpretation. How "far" from the data can our interpretations go? How long can our chain of inference stretch?

88. For example, Bernardini 2005; Fowles 2013; Liebmann 2012; Ortman 2012; among others. A rich field on the right side of the Great Divide! My sketch of pre-history

(Lekson 2009a) ended formally at 1600, about the time the Spanish arrived; but in reality modern-ish Pueblos emerged about 1450. The era from 1450–1600 was not without incident; historically complex but underresearched. Recall that this late period was indicated for "history" in the list of "Key Issues…in the Archaeology of the American Southwest" (Plog et al. 2015).

89. Ronald Mason's 2006 book-length critique of "Archaeology and North American Indian Oral Traditions" met a rough reception. (The main title: *Inconstant Companions*.) Well worth reading, however, for a hard-nosed analysis of the issue. For a more optimistic (but not uncritical) assessment, see Whiteley 2002.

90. Two recent considerations, the first by Stephen Plog and the second by Michael Schiffer, of traditional histories and heritage in archaeology. Stephen Plog:

> The connection between Navajo oral traditions and Chacoan patterns thus needs to be demonstrated, not asserted. Oral traditions are important sources of information that too often have been neglected by generations of archaeologists. They warrant the increased attention they have received in recent years. However, I agree with [cultural anthropologist Peter] Whiteley (2008: 575) that "a critical question for effective use of oral traditions in archaeological explanations…lies in their transfer to propositional statements subject to canons of testability. I do not agree with the skeptics who argue that no scientific propositions can be generated from oral traditions, but an unquestioning teleological reading from present socially embedded perspectives raises heuristic problems. If there is to be special pleading for some epistemologies, where critical scrutiny is somehow off-limits, this will vitiate their value for scientific explanation." This is not to claim that all people must evaluate oral traditions in this manner. Different people choose different ways of knowing the past. For archaeologists, however, I believe that it is important for the advancement of knowledge that we evaluate propositions and we present the evidence on which those evaluations are based. (Plog 2010:382–383)

And Michael Schiffer:

> People may accept their society's stories without question, but archaeologists—as scientists—are a skeptical lot. We do not take stories at face value but treat them as hypotheses that may be evaluated on the basis of relevant evidence. Sometimes our research validates a story, other times it does not. Archaeological findings can become the focus of controversy, especially if they undermine traditional beliefs. (Schiffer 2017:3)

I applaud Schiffer's (one hopes, intentional) nod to Indiana Jones's dictum, "We cannot take mythology at face value," which I was hoping somehow to use in this section. And now I have, without getting my hands too dirty. Thanks, Mike!

91. Peter Nabokov in his essay "Native Views of History" puts it thus: "The spectrum of American Indian narratives, behaviors, and symbols which carry any information faintly deemed 'historical' actually falls on any number of different points between the idealized poles of chronology (history) and cosmology (mythology)" (Nabokov 1996:9).

92. Traditional histories in the Bible lie at the core of the Western tradition, Western heritage. Credence or criticism given by archaeology to those holy texts famously split biblical and Levantine archaeologies. The former bolsters biblical heritage, the latter

writes history. Serious History treats the Good Book as any other traditional text—judging its parts relevant/irrelevant, right/wrong, etc. Elsewhere in the canon, the great classicist Moses Finley warned us about a seminal Western traditional history: "Homeric heroes recite their genealogies frequently and in detail, and without exception a few steps back take them from human ancestors to gods or goddesses" (Finley 1990:27). Schliemann's attempts to validate Homer by finding Troy or Evan's search for Minos at Knossos are famous examples of European traditional histories (heritage) gone wrong. Viking archaeology conventionally was driven by its traditional histories, the Sagas. That's changing: The actual archaeology is now in the driver's seat, and the Sagas are subject to correction. Richard Hall, then director of the York Viking excavations, on changing archaeological engagement with Sagas:

> Until quite recently the Icelandic sagas and other more learned works written in the twelfth and thirteenth centuries were regarded [by archaeologists] as almost infallible pointers to sites where named individuals built their farmsteads or famous events took place in the Viking Age, 300 or more years before the stories were written down.... Today, these literary masterpieces are treated more carefully by archaeologists.... Subconsciously, or with art and craft, the saga writers were reinforcing the views of their [twelfth- and thirteenth-century] contemporaries. (Hall 2012:155)

And of course there is the classic African work of Jan Vansina (1985)—American Anthropological Archaeology's go-to citation for the reliability/unreliability of oral traditions. There's more out there than his *Oral Tradition as History*, as it turns out.

93. Here are some highlights (Smith 2011b; internal citation omitted):

> Among scholars, four positions on the historical usefulness of Aztec historical accounts can be identified: 1) a highly credulous attitude that assumes that most of the native historical records do indeed record accurate information if we can just find the correct interpretations; 2) the application of explicit historiographic methods coupled with key assumptions leading to the view that the Aztec histories do preserve some valid information on Tula, Tollan and Topiltzin Quetzlcoatl; 3) the application of explicit historiographic methods and a more critical attitude, leading to the view that events of the Early Postclassic period (and certainly the Epiclassic period) are so far removed from the time of production of the surviving accounts that they are outside the realm of credible historical reconstruction; and 4) the assertion that no usable historical information exists in the native histories. The first and fourth views are fringe views that need not concern us further; the important issue is the distinction between the second and third positions. Comparative cases of oral political history indicate that such accounts rarely have great time depth; this finding supports the third position. (Smith 2011b:476)

He notes Joseph Miller's (1980) studies in Africa, Fentress and Wickham's (1992) conclusion that oral history reflects the "groups feelings and beliefs, rather than what the past itself was," and David Henige's (1974) *The Chronology of Oral Tradition*. "Henige (1974:190–191) concludes that in most cases, oral political history does not preserve reliable chronological information for more than a century prior to transcription" (Smith 2011b:477). "Given what we know about the context and production of native histories in Yucatan and central Mexico, and the results of comparative research by

Henige and others, it simply is not tenable to maintain that these traditions can provide historical information on Tula and Chichén Itzá" (p. 478)—sites about as old as Chaco. Worth noting.

94. Tribal traditional histories in the Southwest are, in Nabokov's (2002:239) words, "uniquely American Indian blends of spiritual, documentary, and opportunistic contemplations of the past." They challenge the conventional Western historian, he notes, but certainly the conventional Western historian must accord them evidentiary status. But, he concludes, "instead of cramming them into familiar paradigms, might we not temper the hegemony of Western historiography by interpreting it *into them* every now and then?" (Nabokov 2002:239; emphasis original). That is, instead of cherry picking from recorded "myths" and "stories" to write Western history (as I and many others have done), reverse the flow and offer Western history to the Native historians for their evaluation and interpretation and possible use. This seems a noble (if somewhat unlikely) goal, but fraught: What if the Western history I write is something Native historians do not want to hear? Which appears to be the case with my version of Chaco.

95. Severin Fowles observed: "How different the picture looks if when we seriously investigate the migrations, creolizations, battles, alliance and so forth that fill indigenous histories!" (Fowles 2013:91). Yes indeed; if not all the details, at least the assurance that there was indeed history in the ancient Southwest.

96. For example, Silko 1996 and Swentzell 1991. Here's the Acoma poet Simon Ortiz (1994):

> As a boy, I used to hear elders speaking about…the past, but not as some far-away event; it was as if it was right in the present. That's why it is so important to regard the past: *because it is the present.*… It is all one moment, and I am certain that there is no line, gap, margin or barrier between the natural and the human environment; there is only the power and sacredness of existence of the Pueblo and all Native Americans know it. (Ortiz 1994:69, 71, original emphasis)

> Larry Zimmerman, a strong advocate of Indigenous Archaeology: "Simply put, the past and the present are essentially the same in content and meaning, although details may differ. As a tradition-oriented Native American, if you know the oral history of your people, you need no other mechanisms for 'discovering' your people's past" (Zimmerman 2001:173). Gertrude Stein might have said: There is there there, but no past past.

97. Roger Echo-Hawk is not alone in thinking that Native tales recall the megafauna, extinct after about 13,000 years ago. I worked closely with a professor of American Indian Studies from Isleta Pueblo, who had the same idea.

98. Fred Eggan (1967), a generally sympathetic observer, traced the decay of Hopi accounts of a notable nineteenth-century dust-up between Hopis and Navajos, in two versions recorded forty years apart. The first, close to the actual event, was detailed and specific to the event. The latter, four decades later, was vague on both events and causes, and tended toward general Hopi principles and cultural differences between Hopi and Navajo. Eggan was not discounting oral traditions as sources of history, but he cautioned that much critical analysis would be required to separate the historical from the mythological or programmatic. Of course, traditional versions of relatively recent events can be demonstrably accurate (e.g., Wiget 1982); but are those "traditional" or rather eyewitness memories?

Peter Nabokov (2002:67–76) reviews various estimates of "decay rates" for Native American oral history. Most historians, it appears, assume an outside limit of 100 to 150 years for historical "fact" which then slides first into tradition, then myth. It seems likely that tribes living on or near the places where events happened will have "sharper" and longer historical traditions, that is, more details deeper into the past, linked to landscape features; see also Basso 1996. Another intriguing review of Native American oral history and "myth-history": Snow 2016.

99. Michael Smith (2011b:477) cites various studies which suggest "that in most cases, oral political history does not preserve reliable chronological information for more than a century prior to the transcription of the oral tradition." That's not very encouraging. But on the bright side for the Southwest, Smith cites other studies that suggest "that societies with more open systems of social stratification tend to produce historical traditions that are empirically reliable, whereas societies with more closed social stratification systems almost always produce mythologized official historical accounts" (p. 477). That is, noncomplex societies' traditional histories are truer than complex societies', where history has more work to do, legitimizing kings and so forth. Perhaps court histories of ancient Chaco—for surely they had histories!—twisted the truth like Aztec court histories; perhaps those histories died with Chaco. Pueblo traditional histories after that episode of "closed social stratification" stuck closer to what really happened.

100. Keith Basso famously wrote that *Wisdom Sits in Places*—the title of his 1996 book on Western Apache traditional history. See also Nabokov 2002:Chapter 5, "Anchoring the Past in Place: Geography and History," for a broader North American survey. It is interesting to note that Southwestern tribal traditions refer to specific archaeological sites, while tribal traditions of the East apparently fail to mention any place that could be construed as Cahokia (and many other major sites). Most Southwestern tribes are still on or near their lands; most Southeastern tribes were displaced.

101. Pueblo people left Chaco and Aztec by 1300. Shortly thereafter—some would say even at that time—Navajo people became the sole proprietors and custodians of the old Chacoan polity. Navajo people live in and among its ruins and have names and stories for many key features, natural or built (e.g., Kelley and Francis 1994; Linford 2000). Those stories are often quite specific, in contrast to the poetic generalities of White House. For example, the powerful figure non-Native people call "the Great Gambler," who one knowledgeable Navajo described as "our king" (see Appendix).

Navajos may have seen Chaco's fall. They certainly learned much (shortly after the fall) from Pueblo people, incorporated into Navajo knowledge through capture, marriage, trade, ritual relations—a broad band of channels. Pueblo peoples' traditional histories of Chaco—and the lessons and principles learned there—are central to their heritage; but not perhaps the details. (At least in accounts I've heard.) Navajo people know and share details. Navajo people live on that landscape and encounter the ruins every day, constantly refreshing memories through daily life. Relatively few Pueblo people visited Chaco places, on periodic pilgrimages; thus (I think) the details faded while the key themes and morals remained.

Acoma, Zia, and several other Keres Pueblos have traditional histories of White House, a notable place to the north where wonderful and terrible things happened (see Appendix). At White House, "people got power over people" and, ultimately, that was judged to be wrong for Pueblos. During Florence Hawley Ellis's work for the NPS's Wetherill Mesa Project, she identified White House as Mesa Verde. I have suggested it was Chaco Canyon. Several Keresan Pueblo people have told me that those specific identifications are misguided: White House was the whole Four Corners area—which I would like to interpret as the Chaco/Aztec polity.

102. When the people left White House (see preceding note and Appendix), en route to a new home to be revealed by portents, they stopped to perform a "ceremony of forgetting." Matthew Stirling published an early account: "It is not known how far they went, but finally they stopped at a place where they went through the ceremony of forgetting. It is not known how far they went when they symbolically crossed the four mountains and left their sickness and trouble behind" (1942:75).

   Barbara Mills (2008b) wrote eloquently about "remembering while forgetting" at Chaco—not in reference to this story, specifically. Suppressing powerful historical or ritual knowledge, or confining it to a few who need to know, appears to be common among Pueblos and, of course, many other societies. Including our own. We release information on a need-to-know basis.

   The problematic events at White House (Chaco/Aztec?) were never forgotten, but the ceremony of forgetting probably ensured that the full story is remembered (and recounted) only when needed in the present—the bad example with which to correct improper behaviors.

103. Leigh Kuwanwisiwma (Hopi) writes: "Few researchers have bothered to ask the Hopis who they are. Those who did were treated with suspicion by the Hopis and on some occasions deliberately given misleading information" (2004:43).

104. Leslie Marmon Silko (Laguna) wrote, "The ancient Pueblo people sought a communal truth, not an absolute truth. For them the truth lived somewhere within the web of differing versions, disputes over minor points, and outright contractions tangled with old feuds and village rivalries" (Silko 1996).

105. The Indian Land Claims Commission, established in 1946, used traditional histories in its work: Compensating tribes for lost lands. The Native American Graves Protection and Repatriation Act of 1990 also considers traditional histories in establishing cultural affiliations of cultural items off reservations. Traditional histories can be potent legal tools.

106. When NAGPRA was new, Hopi sent a now-legendary letter making potential claims on just about everything everywhere. Why not? Hopi clans, indeed, have continental provenances, from sea to shining sea. Given the sad history of Indian Lands, going big made a lot more sense than playing small.

107. Consider Michael Katobie and Delbridge Honanie's (Hopi; indeed, *Artists Hopid*) kiva mural at the Museum of Northern Arizona at Flagstaff. It begins with Chaco and ends with the World Wide Web.

108. "Rather than grading different narratives for some form of absolute truth content, we should be asking which alternative we find the most useful relative to the immediate question at hand" (Ballard 2003:144). Different narratives, like different Capital-"T" Theories, may be useful for different parts of the story.

109. Ian Morris rightly insists that we must develop ways to evaluate archaeological narratives: "There are ways to move outside a world of competing representations, and... this is necessary if we want a cultural history of society rather than a bloodless, aestheticized literary exercise" (Morris 2000:16–17).

   Anthropology has been curiously uninterested in systematic evaluations of the kinds presented here. Or perhaps I slept through that lecture. Liebow and colleagues (2013) recently suggested standards "On Evidence and the Public Interest" in Anthropology, with these qualities of evidence: Credible, acceptable, actionable:

By credible, we mean "bias free."...By acceptable, we mean the degree to which the findings of a study or group of studies conform to conventional wisdom derived from local knowledge.... By actionable, we mean the degree to which the findings of a study or multiple studies are feasible to implement in a particular situation. (Liebow et al. 2013:642)

These are not so much standards of proof or levels of certainty, but criteria for forming and implementing policy.

110. The past should not be presented as a matter of belief. To "believe" lowers us to the level of religion: "It's time to ask yourself, Dr. Jones: What do you believe?" (attrib. Walter Donovan).

111. This tag has also been attributed to Bernard Baruch, apparently on the basis of a quote in the January 6, 1950, *Deming Headlight*(!). Stunned by this unlikely Luna County provenance, I have made no effort to confirm or deny the Baruch attribution. If it is not true, I wish it were so.

112. Gwinn Vivian, in particular, took me to task:

Lekson notes his frustration with colleagues who ask for "proof" to support his revised Puebloan history. I am frustrated by his admonition that "we allow ourselves to see" this "extraordinarily visible, knowable example of political continuity across time and tide" using only "circumstantial, anecdotal, (and) juristic" evidence. In 1994 Lekson, Linda Cordell and George Gumerman urged the building of "a comparative archaeology of polities and their residual landscapes" that would include "archaeologically-knowable empirical patterns of architecture, settlement, and region..." In 1999 Lekson observes that such an archaeology does not exist. Why not use the Chaco-Aztec-Paquime data to initiate just such an archaeology? *The Chaco Meridian* presents some of the data; it is time to develop a methodology worthy of testing those data. (Vivian 2001:144, internal references omitted)

I did indeed call for a comparative archaeology, all those many years ago; and by and large, it still does not exist. When I tried to compile compendia of Early State landscapes and so forth, I was hissed away by those studying Early States for my presumption in thinking that Chaco could be usefully compared to that group. They were right: Chaco was not an Early State, it was a secondary state. And those are so varied in structure that I despair of single-handedly making sense of them.

All archaeological evidence is circumstantial, and much is anecdotal. It was the "juristic" form of my argument that, I think, most annoyed my annoyed colleagues. Perhaps that was the wrong term—or, as we shall see, perhaps it was in fact appropriate—certainly I think to make better historical arguments, archaeology might learn more from law than from science.

Oddly enough, it was only upon writing the preceding sentence that I remembered Vine Deloria telling me precisely that, long ago; something like, "Archaeologists don't know how to mount an argument; they should take some training in law"—as he had. So maybe I owe this interest to Deloria.

113. A terrible word, but Roget offers nothing better. "Convincement" is entailed by "I am not convinced"—the kiss of death in the archaeological phrase book.

114. You'd have to really care about Grant to work back to source references, analyze the two arguments, and essentially write your own biography of the man. Most of us don't care that much about Grant, except on a fifty.

115. For the Pueblo III conference, we picked people who had the requisite knowledge and who—importantly—would play well together. The result was a well-structured volume (Adler 1996) that inspired a series of time period pieces, all of which were, in their time, essential. For the Chaco Synthesis, I tried to engage everyone who had any standing on Chaco matters (several declined; but the offer had been made). The result was a volume (Lekson 2009a) that, despite a reasonably logical organization, was all over the map. It has been described as a landmark volume, but also correctly criticized for its many "Chacos." Chaco chaos.

116. History uses peer review, of course. Looking at the *American Historical Review*'s description of peer review, the process seems very much like the exercises with which we are familiar.

117. Editors of scholarly journals are active shapers of content. Each journal has a mission, a style, and a set of parameters for what's appropriate and what's not. Editors have a huge impact: Remember when the Tedlocks took over *American Anthropologist*? That was the beginning of the exodus of archaeologists from AAA. Even today's pay-to-play online journals: Their mission appears to be making money and advancing the careers of entrepreneurial scholars. That's a mission, a style.

118. "Post-publication review" is new (and not yet widely used) but interesting. Publish, review, and, depending on the reviews, list or delist. Online preprints have huge potential: Cheap, quick, and gets out to the audience. But will we read 'em?

119. Lopping off the right quartile: "Perhaps the most widely recognized failure of peer review is its inability to ensure the identification of high-quality work. The list of important scientific papers that were rejected by some peer-reviewed journals goes back at least as far as the editor of *Philosophical Transaction*'s 1796 rejection of Edward Jenner's report of the first vaccination against smallpox" (Michaels 2006:224).

It may be useful to think about this question as "precision" and "accuracy." Working within Pueblo Space limits us to a set of interpretations, which with great regularity we can predict will be made again and again: That is, they have the appearance of "precision," hitting the same spot on the target again and again, the clear central tendency. Without the restrictions of Pueblo Space, our shots might be more scattered, but some will hit the target: "Accuracy." Archaeology outside Pueblo Space: Less precise but more accurate.

120. My bell-curve metaphor is flawed on several counts. Most significantly, reviewers are not random. As a journal editor and sometime reviewer myself, I know that reviewers are picked because of their perceived expertise, and after that first criteria, because they are Good Citizens or they owe the editor a favor. Nonrandom.

121. Variously attributed to Benjamin Disraeli and/or Mark Twain, paraphrasing Disraeli. Among others.

122. The most strident: Carrier 2012. He ventures into an extended promotion of Bayesian history in aid of his quest to prove Jesus didn't exist. One mordant blogger noted: "The Reverend Bayes originally used his theorem to prove the existence of God, while in his next book, Carrier will apparently use the same theorem to disprove the existence of the historical Jesus" (Bond 2013). Not a good book, but an interesting argument.

123. There are good reasons why frequentist (or formal) statisticians locked Bayes in the closet through most of the nineteenth and twentieth centuries. Bayes cooks the books. Bayesian statistics build in "prior knowledge" which can mean "bias," hiding that statistical crime deep in the thousands of iterations involved in reaching Bayesian conclusions. Another good reason why frequentists discounted Bayesian approaches

was the sheer computational power required for Bayesian work; real roll-up-your-sleeves Bayesian statistics were possible only on mainframes before computers arrived on everyone's desk in the 1980s. For an accessible account of the controversy, see McGrayne 2012; for inaccessible accounts, try the web.

124. Appendix D of *Advancing the Science of Climate Change: America's Climate Choices,* Panel on Advancing the Science of Climate Change; Board on Atmospheric Sciences and Climate, Division of Earth and Life Studies; National Research Council of the National Academies, Washington: National Academies Press, http://www.nap.edu /catalog/12782/advancing-the-science-of-climate-change.

125. *Terminology for Describing Confidence About Facts:* Appendix D, http://www.nap.edu /read/12782/chapter/26.

126. Other standards of certainty exist, for example in intelligence/security. These can be life-and-death judgments. How sure are we? Should we send in the drones? Happily, far less hangs on archaeological certainty. An errant account of the past (how would we know?) does little real damage; an incorrect or inadequate predictive model might destroy a few sites; but nobody gets hurt. If the CIA goofs, it's not pretty. For a peek at how spooks think about these things, see: Estimative probability, https:// www.cia.gov/library/center-for-the-study-of-intelligence/csi-publications/books -and-monographs/sherman-kent-and-the-board-of-national-estimates-collected -essays/6words.html.

The CIA did not adopt this terminology. They must have a method, but it's classified. I don't know that for a fact, but I make that statement with High Confidence.

127. It seems that there are British precedents for invoking legal standards in archaeology: "Augustus Pitt-Rivers is often called the 'father of British field-archaeology,' and he introduced the concept that archaeological evidence should be able to stand up in a court of law" (Thurley 2013:107). I have not followed up on this; would current British theoretical archaeology survive Pitt-Rivers's test?

128. For example, Kosso 2008. Discussing "evidence" he contrasts history-science versus history-courtroom trial. History, he says, is much more like a legal argument than scientific hypothesis testing (Kosso 2008:15–16). I agree.

129. For science, the Daubert test from the Supreme Court case Daubert v. Merrell Dow Pharmaceuticals, 509 U.S. 579 (1993):
   1. The theory is testable.
   2. The theory has been peer reviewed.
   3. The theory has defined reliability and error rates.
   4. The theory is generally accepted by the scientific community.

And for history: There are legal standards for what constitutes an "objective historian," which came out of a UK court case over holocaust denial (Irving v. Penguin Books; briefly encountered in chapter 5). These standards were summarized by Wendie Schneider in the *Yale Law Journal.* My paraphrase from Schneider (2001:1535), regarding the (legally) contentious historian:

> (1) She must treat sources with appropriate reservations; (2) she must not dismiss counterevidence without scholarly consideration; (3) she must be evenhanded in her treatment of evidence and eschew "cherry-picking"; (4) she must clearly indicate any speculation; (5) she must not mistranslate documents or mislead by omitting parts of documents; (6) she must weigh the authenticity of all accounts, not merely those that contradict her favored view; and (7) she must take the motives of historical actors into consideration.

Schneider notes (2001:1531): "Historians are not alone among social scientists and other nonscientific experts in confronting an absence of coherent standards."

130. For example: David A. Schum's (2003) "Evidence and Inference about Past Events" summarizes case studies (in the book of that same name), and very usefully presents discussions/summaries of:

    (1) "substance-blind"—"ignore the *substance* of evidence and focus instead on its *inferential properties*" (Schum 2003:15), and provide a chart or spreadsheet for characterizing: on one axis, "tangible, testimonial unequivocal, testimonial equivocal, missing tangibles or testimony, and authoritative records" and on the other axis, a scale of decreasing relevance: direct, circumstantial, and ancillary (my paraphrase of Schum 2003:16, Fig. 1.1).

    (2) chains of reasoning to establish "directly relevant and ancillary evidence" (Schum 2003:21, Fig. 1.2).

    (3) "recurrent combinations of evidence" and their properties: "dissonance: contradictory, divergent, conflicting; harmonious: corroborative, convergent, evidential synergism, inferential redundancy" (Schum 2003:22–25).

    (4) probabilistic arguments, including Bayes, Baconian, and Belief Functions (Schum 2003:25).

    (5) Wigmore analysis [a kind of Harris Matrix of events and certainties]— widely cited (Schum 2003:26–32; see Wigmore 1937).

131. Preponderance of the evidence is the legal standard under NAGPRA for determining cultural affiliation. In practical terms, it establishes "cultural affiliation"; in archaeological terms, social identity. What is preponderance of the evidence? More probable than not; a bit better than 50-50. In practice, it is often (and inconsistently) translated as more classes of NAGPRA evidence than a competing claim, or more than half of the NAGPRA classes. I have seen preponderance of the evidence applied as a check-off: If one claim has evidence (of any kind or quality) for more of NAGPRA's evidence classes than another claim, that is preponderance of the evidence. Hopi could list five of seven classes; Navajo could list only one: Result, it's Hopi. NAGPRA is serious business. Metaphorically it's life and death for tribes, and concretely it's life or death for museum collections. If "preponderance of the evidence" is sufficient to restore patrimony or to empty a museum, I could argue that it should suffice for the far less serious problems of archaeological narrative creation. But I don't make that claim; I'd like to hold archaeology to a higher standard.

132. Weiss (2003) equated "clear and convincing evidence" in law with "*substantially proven*" in science, with a probability of 90–99 percent. That seems impossibly high for archaeology. In his probability allocations, archaeology is more likely to hit "preponderance of the evidence—more probable than not; *more likely true than untrue* [50–67 percent]"; or maybe sometimes "substantial and credible evidence; *probable* [67–80 percent]." But "clear and convincing" in its legal definition, unshackled by statistical probabilities, is my goal.

133. Of course we fuss about evidence: Convoluted 14C, contaminated tests, compromised contexts, etc. But compared to arguments about interpretation, evidence is fairly straightforward. Thank God.

134. Thoreau was called both "Hank" and "Crank" but I am unable to find definitive authority that he was, in his time, called "Hank the Crank." I submit that if he wasn't, he should have been.

135. Slightly updated population estimates from https://stevelekson.com/.

136. John McCarthy (2008:542), considering "interpretive narrative archaeology," concludes (emphasis added):

> This approach cannot become a refuge for those practitioners unable or unwilling to organize and present their data coherently. The data upon which our narratives are based must be available for independent review and reinterpretation by others if only *relegated to fine-print appendices at the back of the report.*

I hope we can rethink and reinvent the notions of appendices and footnotes—relics of print.

137. My imagination wobbles between the Gordian Knot and an exploded baseball. Plutarch meets *The Natural*: "Ya really knocked the cover off that one, Alexander!"

138. Jeremy Popkin in his 2015 historiography welcomes the brave new world of "History in the Internet Era":

> The most significant historiographical developments in the years since 2000 have not been shifts in the balance between the various forms of history, but rather a new awareness of the importance of changes in the ways in which historical knowledge is communicated. No new methodological approach to historical research has had as much impact on history in the past two decades as the development of the Internet. (Popkin 2015:170)

139. I attempted to recast "top-heavy" Chaco along the lines suggested below, but *in print for this book*. It did not work, and you (and the publisher) can thank whatever gods might be that I left it among the shreds and patches on my cutting room floor. It had links within links indicated by brackets within brackets, some of which were so concentrically layered that it reminded me of the old John Barth story, "Menelaiad," in which a half-dozen simultaneous narratives within narratives came together in the single word: """"""NO!"""""" But the structure I'm thinking of is not nested and hierarchical, but relational. So I tried a graph; that, too, was beyond my talents. What I'm thinking of is more than 2-D print can do, which of course is precisely the point. But more than my 2-D mind can do.

140. Opening up a giant economy-sized #10 can of political worms. But if we can issue permits for archaeological fieldwork, if we can trust crusty editors with our cherished prose, surely we can devise a scheme to keep out crazies—without the pitfalls and perils of peer review.

141. An odd relic of archaeology's humanist origins: Sole authorship, lead author, etc.—not the multiple authorship of most scientific disciplines: Twelve authors, twenty authors!

142. For some interesting ideas on how to begin: Copplestone and Dunne (2017).

143. Lange et al. 1986. As published, her review read "the description of digging," but Swentzell assured me it was meant to be "the destruction of digging."

Appendix: Indigenous Chaco

1. A quote from a Pueblo man in a Solstice Project video (Sofaer 1999).

2. See, for example, Ferguson and Koyiyumptewa 2009.

3. E.g., Chapin 1940; Matthews 1889. And see versions presented in Kelley and Francis 1994. I have benefited from long discussions on this matter with Tim Begay and Taft Blackhorse, among other knowledgeable Dine people.

References

Abbott, David R.

2003   The Politics of Decline in Canal System 2. In *Centuries of Decline during the Hohokam Classic Period at Pueblo Grande*, edited by David R. Abbott, pp. 201–227. University of Arizona Press, Tucson.

Abbott, David R., Alexa M. Smith, and Emiliano Gallaga

2007   Ballcourts and Ceramics: The Case for Hohokam Marketplaces in the Arizona Desert. *American Antiquity* 72:461–484.

Abend, Gabriel

2008   The Meaning of "Theory." *Sociological Theory* 26(2):173–199.

Acemoglu, Daron, and James A. Robinson

2012   *Why Nations Fail: The Origins of Power Prosperity and Poverty*. Crown Publishing Group, New York.

Adams, E. Charles

1991   *The Origin and Development of the Pueblo Katsina Cult*. University of Arizona Press, Tucson.

Adams, E. Charles, and Andrew I. Duff (editors)

2004   *The Protohistoric Pueblo World, AD 1275–1600*. University of Arizona Press, Tucson.

Adler, Michael A.

1990   Communities of Soil and Stone: An Archaeological Investigation of Population Aggregation among the Mesa Verde Anasazi, AD 900–1300. Doctoral dissertation, University of Michigan, Ann Arbor. Ann Arbor: University Microfilms.

1996   Fathoming the Scale of Anasazi Communities. In *Interpreting Southwestern Diversity: Underlying Principles and Overarching Patterns*, edited by Paul R. Fish and Jefferson J. Reid, pp. 97–106. Anthropological Research Papers 48. Arizona State University, Tempe.

Adler, Michael A. (editor)

1996   *The Prehistoric Pueblo World, AD 1150–1350*. University of Arizona Press, Tucson.

Agbe-Davies, Anna S., and Alexander A. Bauer

2010   Rethinking Trade as a Social Activity: An Introduction. In *Social Archaeologies of Trade and Exchange: Exploring Relationships among People, Places, and Things*, edited by A. A. Bauer and A. S. Agbe-Davies, pp. 13–28. Left Coast Press, Walnut Creek, California.

Akins, Nancy J.

1986   *A Biocultural Approach to Human Burials from Chaco Canyon, New Mexico*. Reports of the Chaco Center No. 9. Division of Cultural Research, National Park Service, Santa Fe, New Mexico.

2001   Chaco Canyon Mortuary Practices, Archaeological Correlates of Complexity. In *Ancient Burial Practices in the American Southwest*, edited by Douglas R. Mitchell and Judy L. Brunson-Hadley, pp. 167–190. University of New Mexico Press, Albuquerque.

2003   The Burials of Pueblo Bonito. In *Pueblo Bonito: Center of the Chacoan World*, edited by Jill E. Neitzel, pp. 94–106. Smithsonian Books, Washington, DC.

Alberti, Benjamin, Severin Fowles, Martin Holbraad, Yvonne Marshall, and Christopher Witmore

2011   "Worlds Otherwise": Archaeology, Anthropology, and Ontological Difference. *Current Anthropology* 52(6):896–912.

Altherr, Thomas L.

1985   The Pajarito or Cliff Dwellers' National Park Proposal, 1900–1920. *New Mexico Historical Review* 60(3):271–294.

Altschul, Jeffrey H.

1978   The Development of the Chacoan Interaction Sphere. *Journal of Anthropological Research* 34:109–146.

Anderson, Benedict

1983   *Imagined Communities: Reflections on the Origins and Spread of Nationalism.* Verso, New York.

1991   *Imagined Communities: Reflections on the Origins and Spread of Nationalism.* 2nd ed. Verso, New York.

1999   Introduction. In *Tales from Djakarta: Caricatures of Circumstances and Their Human Beings*, edited by Pramoedya Ananta Toer, pp. xi–xviii. Southeast Asia Program Publication, Cornell University, Ithaca, New York.

2006   *Imagined Communities: Reflections on the Origins and Spread of Nationalism.* Revised edition. Verso, New York.

Anderson, David G.

1994   *The Savannah River Chiefdoms: Political Change in the Late Prehistoric Southeast.* University of Alabama Press, Tuscaloosa.

Anderson, David G., and Kenneth E. Sassaman

2012   *Recent Developments in Southeastern Archaeology: From Colonization to Complexity.* SAA Press, Washington, DC.

Anderson, Terence J., and William Twining

2015   Law and Archaeology: Modified Wigmorean Analysis. In *Material Evidence: Learning from Archaeological Practice*, edited by Robert Chapman and Alison Wylie, pp. 271–286. Routledge, London.

Anyon, Roger, and Steven A. LeBlanc

1984   *The Galaz Ruin.* University of New Mexico Press, Albuquerque.

Arakawa, Fumiyasu

2012   Cyclical Cultural Trajectories: A Case Study from the Mesa Verde. *Journal of Anthropological Research* 68:35–69.

Arakawa, Fumiyasu, David Gonzales, Nancy McMillan, and Molly Murphy

2016   Evaluation of Trade and Interaction between Chaco Canyon and Chaco Outlier Sites in the American Southwest by Investigating Trachybasalt Temper in Pottery Sherds. *Journal of Archaeological Science* 6:115–124.

Arcangeli, Alessandro

2011   *Cultural History: A Concise Introduction.* Routledge, London.

Ashmore, Wendy

1991   Site Planning Principles and Concepts of Directionality among the Ancient Maya. *Latin American Antiquity* 2(3):199–226.

Association Research Inc. (ARI)

2011   Report on the 2010 Membership Needs Survey Conducted for the SAA. http://ecommerce.saa.org/saa/staticcontent/staticpages/survey10/executiveSummary.pdf, accessed May 25, 2018.

Atalay, Sonya

2006　Indigenous Archaeology as Decolonizing Practice. *American Indian Quarterly* 30:280–310.

2008　Multivocality and Indigenous Archaeologies. In *Evaluating Multiple Narratives: Beyond Nationalist, Colonialist, and Imperialist Archaeologies*, edited by Junko Habu, Claire Fawcett, and John M. Matsunaga, pp. 29–44. Springer, New York.

2012　*Community-Based Archaeology.* University of California Press, Berkeley.

Auerbach, Jerold

2006　*Explorers in Eden: Pueblo Indians and the Promised Land.* University of New Mexico Press, Albuquerque.

Babcock, Barbara A.

1990　By Way of Introduction. *Journal of the Southwest* 32(4):383–399.

Babcock, Barbara A., and Nancy J. Parezo

1989　*Daughters of the Desert: Women Anthropologists and the Native American Southwest, 1880–1980, an Illustrated Catalogue.* University of New Mexico Press, Albuquerque.

Bahn, Paul (editor)

2014　*History of Archaeology: An Introduction.* Routledge, London.

Bak, Per

1999　*How Nature Works: The Science of Self-Organized Criticality.* Copernicus Center Press, Kraków.

Ballard, Chris

2003　Writing (Pre)history: Narrative and Archaeological Explanation in the New Guinea Highlands. *Archaeology in Oceania* 38:135–148.

Balzer, David

2014　*Curationism: How Curating Took the Art World and Everything Else.* Coach House Books, Toronto.

Bandelier, Adolph F.

1885　*The Romantic School in American Archaeology.* Trow Printing and Bookbinding, New York.

1890　*The Delight Makers.* Dodd, Mead, and Company, New York.

1890–1892　*Final Report of Investigations among the Indians of the Southwestern United States, Carried on Mainly in the Years from 1880 to 1885.* American Series, vols. 3–4. Archaeological Institute of America, Cambridge, Massachusetts.

1892　The "Montezuma" of the Pueblo Indians. *American Anthropologist* 5(4):319–326.

Bandy, Matthew S.

2004　Fissioning, Scalar Stress, and Social Evolution in Early Village Societies. *American Anthropologist* 106(2): 322–333.

Barker, Alex W., Craig E. Skinner, M. Steven Shackley, Michael D. Glascock, and J. Daniel Rogers

2002　Mesoamerican Origin for an Obsidian Scraper from the Precolumbian Southeastern United States. *American Antiquity* 67(1):103–108.

Barnes, Gina L.

2007　*State Formation in Japan: Emergence of a Fourth-Century Ruling Elite.* Routledge, London.

Basso, Keith

1979　History of Ethnological Research. In *Handbook of North American Indians*, Vol. 9, *Southwest*, edited by Alfonso Ortiz, pp. 14–21. Smithsonian Institution, Washington, DC.

1996　*Wisdom Sits in Places: Landscape and Language Among the Western Apache.* University of New Mexico Press, Albuquerque.

Beck, Robin A., Jr. (editor)

2007   *The Durable House: House Society Models in Archaeology.* Occasional Paper 35. Center for Archaeological Investigations, Southern Illinois University, Carbondale.

Beck, Robin A., Jr., Douglas J. Bolender, James A. Brown, and Timothy K. Earle

2007   Eventful Archaeology: The Place of Space in Structural Transformation. *Current Anthropology* 48(6):833–860.

Begay, Richard M.

2004   Tsé Bíyah 'Anii'áhí: Chaco Canyon and Its Place in Navajo History. In *In Search of Chaco: New Approaches to an Archaeological Enigma*, edited by David Grant Noble, pp. 55–60. School of American Research Press, Santa Fe, New Mexico.

Bell, Martin

2015   Experimental Archaeology at the Crossroads: A Contribution to Interpretation or Evidence of "Xeroxing"? In *Material Evidence: Learning from Archaeological Practice*, edited by Robert Chapman and Alison Wylie, pp. 42–58. Routledge, New York.

Benally, AnCita, and Peter Iverson

2005   Finding History. *Western Historical Quarterly* 36(3):353–358.

Benedict, Ruth

1934[1989] *Patterns of Culture.* Houghton Mifflin, Boston.

Benjamin, Craig (editor)

2015   *A World with States, Empires, and Networks.* Volume 4, *Cambridge History of the World.* Cambridge University Press, Cambridge, UK.

Bennett, John W.

1946   The Interpretation of Pueblo Culture: A Question of Values. *Southwestern Journal of Anthropology* 2(4): 361–374.

Benson, Larry V.

2010   Who Provided Maize to Chaco Canyon after the Mid-12th-Century Drought? *Journal of Archaeological Science* 37:621–629.

2011a   Factors Controlling Pre-Columbian and Early Historic Maize Productivity in the American Southwest, Part 1: The Southern Colorado Plateau and Rio Grande Regions. *Journal of Archaeological Method and Theory* 18(1):1–60.

2011b   Factors Controlling Pre-Columbian and Early Historic Maize Productivity in the American Southwest, Part 2: The Chaco Halo, Mesa Verde, Pajarito Plateau/Bandelier, and Zuni Archaeological Regions. *Journal of Archaeological Method and Theory* 18(1):61–109.

2016   The Chuska Slope as an Agricultural Alternative to Chaco Canyon: A Rebuttal of Tankersley et al. *Journal of Archaeological Science: Reports* 16:456–471.

Benson, Larry V., and Michael S. Berry

2009   Climate Change and Cultural Response in the Prehistoric American Southwest. *Kiva* 75:89–119.

Benson, Larry, Linda Cordell, Kirk Vincent, Howard Taylor, John Stein, G. Lang Farmer, and Kiyoto Futa

2003   Ancient Maize from Chacoan Great Houses: Where Was It Grown? *Proceedings of the National Academy of Sciences* 100(22):13111–13115.

Benson, Larry V., John R. Stein, and Howard E. Taylor

2009   Possible Sources of Archaeological Maize Found in Chaco Canyon and Aztec Ruin, New Mexico. *Journal of Archaeological Science* 36: 387–407.

Benson, L., John Stein, Howard Taylor, R. Freidman, and Tomas C. Windes

2006   The Agricultural Productivity of Chaco Canyon and the Source(s) of Pre-Hispanic Maize Found in the Pueblo Bonito Great House. In *Histories of Maize: Multidisci-*

plinary Approaches to the Prehistory, Biogeography, Domestication, and Evolution of Maize. edited by J. E. Staller, R. H. Tykot, and B. F. Benz, pp. 289–314. Academic Press, Burlington, Massachusetts.

Benson, Larry V., Howard E. Taylor, K. A. Peterson, B. D. Shattuck, C. A. Ramotnik, and John R. Stein

2008 Development and Evaluation of Geochemical Methods for the Sourcing of Archaeological Maize. *Journal of Archaeological Science* 35:912–921.

Benson, Larry V., Howard E. Taylor, T. I. Plowman, D. A. Roth, and R. C. Antweiler

2010 The Cleaning of Burned and Contaminated Archaeological Maize Prior to 87Sr/86Sr Analysis. *Journal of Archaeological Science* 37:84–91.

Benson, Larry V., Timothy R. Pauketat, and Edward R. Cook

2009 Cahokia's Boom and Bust in the Context of Climate Change. *American Antiquity* 74(3):467–483.

Bentley, Jerry H.

1993 *Old World Encounters: Cross-cultural Contacts and Exchanges in Pre-Modern Times.* Oxford University Press, New York.

Bernal, Ignacio

1980 *A History of Mexican Archaeology.* Thames and Hudson, London.

Bernal García, M. E., and A. J. García Zambrano

2006 El altepetl colonial y sus antecedents prehispanicos: Contexto teorico-historiografico. In *Territorialidad y paisaje en el altepetl del siglo XVI*, edited by F. Fernandez-Christlieb and A. J. Garcia-Zambrano, pp. 31–113. Fondo de Cultura Economica/Instituto de Geografia, Mexico.

Bernard, H. Russell, and Peter D. Killworth

1973 On the Social Structure of an Ocean-Going Research Vessel and Other Important Things. *Social Science Research* 2:145–184.

Bernardini, Wesley

1996 Transitions in Social Organization: A Predictive Model from Southwestern Archaeology. *Journal of Anthropological Archaeology* 15:372–402.

1999 Reassessing the Scale of Social Action at Pueblo Bonito, Chaco Canyon, New Mexico. *Kiva* 64:447–470.

2005 *Hopi Oral Tradition and the Archaeology of Identity.* University of Arizona Press, Tucson.

Bernstein, Bruce

2012 *Santa Fe Indian Market: A History of Native Arts and the Marketplace.* Museum of New Mexico Press, Santa Fe.

Berry, Michael S.

1984 *Time, Space and Transition in Anasazi Prehistory.* University of Utah Press, Salt Lake City.

Berry, Michael S., and Larry V. Benson

2010 Tree-Ring Dates and Demographic Change in the Southern Colorado Plateau and Rio Grande Regions. In *Leaving Mesa Verde: Peril and Change in the Thirteenth-Century Southwest*, edited by T. A. Kohler, M. D. Varien, and A. M. Wright, pp. 53–74. University of Arizona Press, Tucson.

Betancourt, Julio L., Jeffrey S. Dean, and Herbert M. Hull

1986 Prehistoric Long-Distance Transport of Construction Beams, Chaco Canyon, New Mexico. *American Antiquity* 51:370–375.

Bieder, Robert E.

1986 *Science Encounters the Indian, 1820–1880: The Early Days of American Ethnology.* University of Oklahoma Press, Norman.

Billig, Michael

2013   *Learn to Write Badly: How to Succeed in the Social Sciences.* Cambridge University Press, Cambridge, UK.

Binet, Laurent

2015   *The Seventh Function of Language: A Novel.* Farrar, Straus, and Giroux, New York.

Binford, Lewis

2001   *Constructing Frames of Reference: An Analytical Method for Archaeological Theory Building Using Hunter-Gatherer and Environmental Data Sets.* University of California Press, Berkeley.

Bintliff, John

2008   History and Continental Approaches. In *Handbook of Archaeological Theories,* edited by R. Alexander Bentley, Herbert D. G. Maschner, and Christopher Chippindale, pp. 147–164. AltaMira Press, Lanham, Maryland.

2011   The Death of Archaeological Theory. In *The Death of Archaeological Theory,* edited by John Bintliff and Mark Pearce, pp. 7–22. Oxbow Books, Oxford, UK.

Bintliff, John (editor)

1991   *The Annales School and Archaeology.* New York University Press, New York.

Biolsi, Thomas, and Larry Zimmerman

1997   *Indians and Anthropologists: Vine Deloria Jr. and the Critique of Anthropology.* University of Arizona Press, Tucson.

Bishop, Ferman

1955   Henry James Criticizes *The Tory Lover. American Literature* 27:262–264.

Bishop, Ronald L., and Frederick W. Lange (editors)

1991   *The Ceramic Legacy of Anna O. Shepard.* University Press of Colorado, Niwot.

Blanton, Richard E.

1994   *Houses and Households: A Comparative Study.* Plenum Press, New York.

Blanton, Richard, and Lane Fargher

2008   *Collective Action in the Formation of Pre-Modern States.* Springer, New York.

Blanton, Richard E., Gary M. Feinman, Stephen A. Kowalewski, and Peter N. Peregrine

1996   A Dual-Processual Theory for the Evolution of Mesoamerican Civilizations. *Current Anthropology* 37:1–14.

Bocinsky, R. Kyle, Johnathan Rush, Keith W. Kintigh, and Timothy A. Kohler

2016   Exploration and Exploitation in the Macrohistory of the Pre-Hispanic Pueblo Southwest. *Science Advances* 2:e1501532.

Bodley, John H.

2003   *The Power of Scale: A Global History Approach.* M. E. Sharpe, Armonk, New York.

Boehm, Christopher

2001   *Hierarchy in the Forest: The Evolution of Egalitarian Behavior.* Harvard University Press, Cambridge, Massachusetts.

Boghossian, Paul

2006   *Fear of Knowledge: Against Relativism and Constructivism.* Clarendon Press, Oxford, UK.

Bolender, D. J. (editor)

2010   *Eventful Archaeologies: New Approaches to Social Transformation in the Archaeological Record.* State University of New York Press, Albany.

Bond, Stephen

2013   The Cult of Bayes' Theorem. https://web.archive.org/web/20130224192829/http://plover.net/~bonds/cultofbayes.html, accessed May 25, 2018.

Borson, Nancy, Frances Berdan, Edward Stark, Jake States, and Peter J. Wettstein
1998   Origins of an Anasazi Macaw Feather Artifact. *American Antiquity* 63(1):131–142.
Bostwick, Todd W.
2006   *Byron Cummings: Dean of Southwest Archaeology.* University of Arizona Press, Tucson.
Bower, Bruce
2017   Seeing Chaco in a New Light. *Science News* 191(10):16–21.
Brading, D. A.
2001   Monuments and Nationalism in Modern Mexico. *Nations and Nationalism* 7(4): 521–531.
Brandes, Ray
1960   Archaeological Awareness of the Southwest, as Illustrated in Literature to 1890. *Arizona and the West* 1(2):6–25.
Brandt, Elizabeth A.
1994   Egalitarianism, Hierarchy, and Centralization in the Pueblos. In *The Ancient Southwestern Community*, edited by W. H. Wills and Robert D. Leonard, pp. 9–23. University of New Mexico Press, Albuquerque.
2002   The Climate for Ethnographic/Ethnohistoric Research in the Southwest. In *Traditions, Transitions, and Technologies: Themes in Southwestern Archaeology*, edited by Sarah H. Schlanger, pp. 113–126. University Press of Colorado, Boulder.
Braudel, Fernand
1990 [1986] *The Identity of France. Vol II, People and Production.* Translated by Siân Reynolds. Harper Collins, New York.
Briggs, Charles L.
1996   The Politics of Discursive Authority in Research on the "Invention of Tradition." *Cultural Anthropology* 11(4):435–469.
Brody, J. J.
2004   *Mimbres Painted Pottery*, 2nd ed. School of American Research Press, Santa Fe, New Mexico.
Brody, J. J., Catherine J. Scott, and Steven A. LeBlanc
1983   *Mimbres Pottery: Ancient Art of the American Southwest.* Hudson Hills Press in association with The American Federation of Arts, New York.
Broodbank, Cyprian
2013   *Making of the Middle Sea: A History of the Mediterranean from the Beginning to the Emergence of the Classical World.* Oxford University Press Oxford, UK.
Brooks, James F.
2013   Women, Men, and Cycles of Evangelism in the Southwest Borderlands, AD 750 to 1750. *American Historical Review* 118(3):738–764.
Brose, David S.
2001   Introduction to Eastern North America at the Dawn of European Colonization. In *Societies in Eclipse: Archaeology of the Eastern Woodlands Indians, AD 1400–1700*, edited by David S. Brose, C. Wesley Cowan, and Robert C. Mainfort Jr., pp. 1–7. Smithsonian Institution Press, Washington, DC.
Brown, James
2007   On the Identity of the Birdman within Mississippian Period Art and Iconography. In *Ancient Objects and Sacred Realms: Interpretations of Mississippian Iconography*, edited by F. Kent Reilly III and James F. Garber, pp. 56–106. University of Texas Press, Austin.

Bruchac, Margaret M., Siobhan M. Hart, and H. Martin Wobst (editors)

2010   *Indigenous Archaeologies: A Reader on Decolonization.* Left Coast Press, Walnut Creek, California.

Brugge, David M.

1980   *A History of the Chaco Navajos.* Reports of the Chaco Center No. 4. National Park Service, Albuquerque, New Mexico.

1981   The Historical Archaeology of Chaco Canyon. In *Archaeological Surveys of Chaco Canyon, New Mexico*, edited by Alden C. Hayes, David M. Brugge, and W. James Judge, pp. 69–106. Publications in Archaeology 18A. National Park Service, Washington, DC.

Buck, Caitlin E., and Bo Meson

2015   On Being a Good Bayesian. *World Archaeology* 47(4):567–584.

Burke, Peter

2004   *What Is Cultural History?* Polity Press, Cambridge.

Caffrey, Margaret M.

1989   *Ruth Benedict: Stranger in This Land.* University of Texas Press, Austin.

Cajete, Gregory

2016   *Native Science: Natural Laws of Interdependence.* Clear Light Publishers, Santa Fe, New Mexico.

Callahan, Bob (editor)

1981   *Selected Essays 1963–1975: Caul O. Sauer.* Turtle Island Press, Berkeley.

Callinicos, Alex

1995   *Theories and Narratives: Reflections on the Philosophy of History.* Duke University Press, Durham, North Carolina.

Cameron, Catherine M. (editor)

1995   Migration and the Movement of Southwestern Peoples. *Journal of Anthropological Archaeology* 14(2):104–124.

1997   The Chipped Stone of Chaco Canyon, New Mexico. In *Ceramics, Lithics and Ornaments of Chaco Canyon*, edited by Frances Joan Mathien, pp. 531–658. Publications in Archaeology 18G. National Park Service, Santa Fe, New Mexico.

Cameron, Catherine M., and Andrew I. Duff

2008   History and Process in Village Formation: Contexts and Contrasts from the Northern Southwest. *American Antiquity* 73(1):29–57.

Cameron Catherine M., Paul Kelton, and Alan C. Swedlund (editors)

2015   *Beyond Germs: Native Depopulation in North America.* University of Arizona Press, Tucson.

Cantor, Norman F.

1991   *Inventing the Middle Ages: The Lives, Works, and Ideas of the Great Medievalists of the Twentieth Century.* William Morrow, New York.

Canuto, Marcello-Andrea, and Jason Yaeger (editors)

2000   *Archaeology of Communities: A New World Perspective.* Routledge, Cambridge.

Carlson, Roy L.

1966   Twin Angels Pueblo. *American Antiquity* 31:676–682.

Carneiro, Robert L.

1981   The Chiefdom: Precursor to the State. In *The Transition to Statehood in the New World*, edited by Grant D. Jones and Robert R. Kautz, pp. 37–39. Cambridge University Press, Cambridge.

Carniero, Robert L. (editor)

1967   *The Evolution of Society: Selections from Herbert Spencer's Principles of Sociology.* University of Chicago Press, Chicago.

Carrier, Richard C.
2012   *Proving History: Bayes's Theorem and the Quest for the Historical Jesus.* Prometheus Books, Amherst, New York.

Carsten, Janet, and Stephen Hugh-Jones (editors)
1995   *About the House: Lévi-Strauss and Beyond.* Cambridge University Press, Cambridge, UK.

Carter, Tara D.
2010   Rethinking Secondary State Formation in Medieval Iceland: Trade and Social Connectivity in the Norse Economic Territory. PhD dissertation, University of California, San Diego.

Carter, William B.
2009   *Indian Alliances and the Spanish in the Southwest, 750–1750.* University of Oklahoma Press, Norman.

Cather, Willa
1927   *Death Comes for the Archbishop.* Alfred A. Knopf, New York.

Chanda, Nayan
2007   *Bound Together: How Traders, Preachers, Adventurers, and Warriors Shaped Globalization.* Yale University Press, New Haven, Connecticut.

Chapin, Gretchen
1940   A Navajo Myth from the Chaco Canyon. *New Mexico Anthropologist* 4(4):63–67.

Chapman, Janet, and Karen Barrie
2008   *Kenneth Milton Chapman: A Life Dedicated to Indian Arts and Artists.* University of New Mexico Press, Albuquerque.

Chapman, Robert, and Alison Wylie (editors)
2015   *Material Evidence: Learning from Archaeological Practice.* Routledge, London.

Chase, Diane Z., and Arlen F. Chase (editors)
1992   *Mesoamerican Elites.* University of Oklahoma Press, Norman.

Chase-Dunn, Christopher
2011   Evolution of Nested Networks in the Prehistoric U.S. Southwest: A Comparative World-Systems Approach. In *Evolution: Cosmic, Biological, and Social*, edited by Leonid E. Grinin, Robert L. Carneiro, Andrey V. Korotayev, and Fred Spier, pp. 251–273. 'Uchitel' Publishing House, Volgograd, Russia.

Chase-Dunn, Christopher, and Thomas D. Hall
1998   World-Systems in North America: Networks, Rise and Fall and Pulsations of Trade in Stateless Societies. *American Indian Culture and Research Journal* 22(1):23–72.

Chauvenet, Beatrice
1983   *Hewett and Friends.* Museum of New Mexico Press, Santa Fe.

Chew, Sing C.
2001   *World Ecological Degradation: Accumulation, Urbanization, and Deforestation, 3000 BC–AD 2000.* AltaMira Press, Walnut Creek, California.
2007   *The Recurring Dark Ages: Ecological Stress, Climate Change, and System Transformation.* AltaMira Press, Lanham, Maryland.

Childe, V. Gordon
1942   *What Happened in History.* Penguin Books, London.

Christie, Jessica, and Patricia Sarro (editors)
2006   *Palaces and Power in the Americas.* University of Texas Press, Austin.

Christman, Florence
1985   *The Romance of Balboa Park.* 4th ed. San Diego Historical Society, San Diego.

Churchill, Ward (editor)
1983   *Essays in Marxism and Native Americans.* South End Press, Boston.

Clark, Jeffrey J.

2001   *Tracking Pueblo Migrations.* Anthropological Papers 65. University of Arizona Press, Tucson.

Clark, John E., and Michelle Knoll

2005   The American Formative Revisited. In *Gulf Coast Archaeology*, edited by Nancy Marie White, pp. 281–303. University Press of Florida, Gainesville.

Clastres, Pierre

1989   *Societies against the State.* 2nd ed. Zone Books, New York.

Clayton, Victoria

2015   The Needless Complexity of Academic Writing. *The Atlantic* online, 26 October.

Cobb, Charles R.

2005   Archaeology and the "Savage Slot": Displacement and Emplacement in the Premodern World. *American Anthropologist* 107(4): 563–574.

2014   What I Believe: A Memoir of Processualism to Neohistorical Anthropology. *Southeastern Archaeology* 33(2):214–225.

Collier, John

1947   *Indians of the Americas.* W. W. Norton, New York.

1949   *Patterns and Ceremonials of the Indians of the Southwest.* E. P. Dutton, Boston.

1962   *On the Gleaming Way: Navajos, Eastern Pueblos, Zunis, Hopis, Apaches and Their Land and Their Meanings to the World.* Sage Books, Denver, Colorado.

Collingwood, R. G.

1956   [1946] *The Idea of History.* Oxford University Press, Oxford, UK.

Colwell-Chanthaphonh, Chip

2010   *Living Histories: Native Americans and Southwestern Archaeology.* AltaMira Press, Lanham, Maryland.

2012   Archaeology and Indigenous Collaboration. In *Archaeological Theory Today*, edited by Ian Hodder, pp. 267–291. Polity Press, Cambridge, UK.

Colwell-Chanthaphonh, Chip, and T. J. Ferguson (editors)

2008   *Collaboration in Archaeological Practice: Engaging Descendant Communities.* AltaMira Press, Lanham, Maryland.

Colwell-Chanthaphonh, Chip, T. J. Ferguson, Dorothy Lippert, Randall H. McGuire, George R. Nicholas, Joe E. Watkins, and Larry J. Zimmerman

2010   The Premise and Promise of Indigenous Archaeology. *American Antiquity* 75(2):228–238.

Conn, Steven

1998   *Museums and American Intellectual Life, 1876–1926.* University of Chicago Press, Chicago.

2004   *History's Shadow: Native Americans and Historical Consciousness in the Nineteenth Century.* University of Chicago Press, Chicago.

2010   *Do Museums Still Need Objects?* University of Pennsylvania Press, Philadelphia.

Copplestone, Tara, and Daniel Dunne

2017   Digital Media, Creativity, Narrative Structure and Heritage. *Internet Archaeology* 44. http://intarch.ac.uk/journal/issue44/2/toc.html, accessed May 25, 2018.

Cordell, Linda

1984   *Prehistory of the Southwest.* Academic Press, Orlando, Florida.

1997   *Archaeology of the Southwest.* 2nd ed. Academic Press, San Diego.

Cordell, Linda S., and Don D. Fowler (editors)

2005   *Southwest Archaeology in the Twentieth Century.* University of Utah Press, Salt Lake City.

Cordell, Linda S., Jane H. Kelley, Keith W. Kintigh, Stephen H. Lekson, and Rolf M. Sinclair
1994   Toward Increasing Our Knowledge of the Past: A Discussion. In *Understanding Complexity in the Prehistoric Southwest*, edited by George J. Gumerman and Murray Gell-Mann, pp. 163–191. Santa Fe Institute Studies in the Sciences of Complexity Proceedings 16. Addison Wesley Publishing Group, Reading, Massachusetts.

Cordell, Linda S., and Maxine McBrinn
2012   *Archaeology of the Southwest*. 3rd ed. Routledge, Cambridge, UK.

Cordell, Linda S., and Fred Plog
1979   Escaping the Confines of Normative Thought: A Reevaluation of Puebloan Prehistory. *American Antiquity* 44:405–429.

Courlander, Harold
1971   *Fourth World of the Hopis*. Crown Publishers, New York.

Cowgill, George L.
2004   Origins and Development of Urbanism: Archaeological Perspectives. *Annual Review of Anthropology* 33:525–549.
2008   An Update on Teotihuacan. *Antiquity* 82:962–975.

Cowgill, George L., Michelle Hegmon, and George R. Milner
2002   North America and Mesoamerica. In *Archaeology: The Widening Debate*, edited by Barry Cunliffe, Wendy Davies, and Colin Renfrew, pp. 145–192. Oxford University Press, Oxford.

Crabtree, Stefani A., R. Kyle Bocinsky, Paul L. Hooper, Susan C. Ryan, and Timothy A. Kohler
2017   How to Make a Polity (in the Central Mesa Verde Region). *American Antiquity* 82(1):71–95.

Craig, Benjamin (editor)
2015   *A World with States, Empires, and Networks. Cambridge History of the World*, Vol 4. Cambridge University Press, Cambridge.

Croes, Dale R.
2010   Courage and Thoughtful Scholarship: Indigenous Archaeology Partnerships. *American Antiquity* 75(2):211–221.

Cronon, William
2004   *Getting Ready to Do History*. The Carnegie Foundation for the Advancement of Teaching, Washington, DC.

Crown, Patricia L. (editor)
2016   *The Mounds of Pueblo Bonito, Chaco Canyon: Material Culture and Fauna*. University of New Mexico Press, Albuquerque.

Crown, Patricia L., Jiyan Gu, W. Jeffrey Hurst, Timothy J. Ward, Ardith D. Bravenec, Syed Ali, Laura Kebert, Marlaina Berch, Erin Redman, Patrick D. Lyons, Jamie Merewether, David A. Phillips, Lori S. Reed, and Kyle Woodson
2015   Ritual Drinks in the Pre-Hispanic US Southwest and Mexican Northwest. *Proceedings of the National Academy of Sciences* 112(37):11436–11442.

Crown, Patricia L., and W. Jeffrey Hurst
2009   Evidence of Cacao Use in the Prehispanic American Southwest. *Proceedings of the National Academy of Sciences* 106(7):2110–2113.

Crown, Patricia L., and James W. Judge (editors)
1991   *Chaco and Hohokam: Prehistoric Regional Systems in the American Southwest*. School of American Research Press, Santa Fe, New Mexico.

Crown, Patricia L., and W. H. Wills
2003   Modifying Pottery and Kivas at Chaco: Pentimento, Restoration, or Renewal? *American Antiquity* 68(3):511–532.

Curthoys, Ann, and John Docker
2005   *Is History Fiction?* University of Michigan Press, Ann Arbor.

Cushing, Frank Hamilton
1882–1883 My Adventures in Zuni. *Century Illustrated Magazine* 25: 191–207, 500–511. Facsimile reprint: Filter Press, Palmer Lake CO, 1967.

Cusset, François
2008   *French Theory: How Foucault, Derrida, Deleuze, & Co. Transformed the Intellectual Life of the United States.* University of Minnesota Press, Minneapolis.

Dark, K. R.
1998   *The Waves of Time: Long-Term Change and International Relations.* Continuum, London.

Darling, J. Andrew
2008   Mass Inhumation and the Execution of Witches in the American Southwest. *American Anthropologist* 100(3):732–752.

Dauber, Kenneth
1990   Pueblo Pottery and the Politics of Regional Identity. *Journal of the Southwest* 32(4): 576–596.

David, Paul A.
2007   Path Dependence: A Foundational Concept for Historical Social Science. *Cliometrics* 1:91–114.

Dávila Cabrera, Patricio
2005   Mound Builders along the Coast of Mexico and the Eastern United States. In *Gulf Coast Archaeology*, edited by Nancy M. White, pp. 87–107. University Press of Florida, Gainesville.
2015   Trapezoidal Shell Pectorals from the Huasteca. In *The Huasteca: Culture, History, and Interregional Exchange*, edited by Katherine A. Faust and Kim N. Richter, pp. 128–151. University of Oklahoma Press, Norman.

Davis, Carolyn O'Bagy
1995   *Treasured Earth: Hattie Cosgrove's Mimbres Archaeology in the American Southwest.* Sanpete Publications, Tucson, Arizona.

Dawdy, Shannon Lee
2011   Introduction. In *The Dark Abyss of Time: Archaeology and Memory*, by Laurent Olivier. AltaMira Press, Lanham, Maryland.

Dean, Jeffrey S., William H. Doelle, and Janet D. Orcutt
1994   Adaptive Stress: Environment and Demography. In *Themes in Southwest Prehistory*, edited by George J. Gumerman, pp. 53–86. School of American Research Press, Santa Fe, New Mexico.

de Certeau, Michel
1988   *The Writing of History.* Columbia University Press, New York.

Deloria, Vine, Jr.
1969   *Custer Died for Your Sins: An Indian Manifesto.* Macmillan, New York.
1995   *Red Earth, White Lies: Native Americans and the Myth of Scientific Fact.* Scribner, New York.
2002   *Evolution, Creationism, and Other Modern Myths.* Fulcrum Publishing, Chicago.

deMenocal, Peter B., Edward R. Cook, David Demeritt, Alf Hornborg, Patrick V. Kirch, Richard McElreath, and Joseph A. Tainter
2005   Perspectives on Jared Diamond's Collapse: How Societies Choose to Fail or Succeed. *Current Anthropology* 46 (supplemental materials):S91–S99.

De Ruiter, Jan, Gavin Weston, and Stephen M. Lyons

2014 Dunbar's Number: Group Size and Brain Physiology in Humans Reexamined. *American Anthropologist* 113(4):557–568.

Diamond, Jared

1992 *The Third Chimpanzee: The Evolution and Future of the Human Animal*. Harper Perennial, New York.

1997 *Guns, Germs, and Steel: The Fates of Human Societies*. W. W. Norton, New York.

2005 *Collapse: How Societies Choose to Fail or Succeed*. Penguin Group, New York.

Diamond, Jared, and James A. Robinson (editors)

2011 *Natural Experiments of History*. Belknap Press of Harvard University Press, Cambridge, Massachusetts.

Dillon, Brian

2014 *Ruin Lust: Artists' Fascination with Ruins, from Turner to the Present Day*. Tate Publishing, London.

Dilworth, Leah

1996 *Imagining Indians in the Southwest: Persistent Visions of a Primitive Past*. Smithsonian Institution Press, Washington, DC.

2001 Tourists and Indians in Fred Harvey's Southwest. In *Seeing and Being Seen: Tourism in the American Southwest*, edited by David M. Wrobel and Patrick T. Long, pp. 142–164. University of Kansas Press, Lawrence.

Di Peso, Charles C.

1974 *Casas Grandes: A Fallen Trading Center of the Gran Chichimeca*, vols. 1–3. Amerind Foundation, Dragoon, Arizona.

Dobyns, Henry

1966 Estimating Aboriginal American Population. *Current Anthropology* 7:395–416.

1983 *Their Numbers Become Thinned*. University of Tennessee Press, Knoxville.

Doelle, William H., and David A. Phillips Jr.

2005 From the Academy to the Private Sector: CRM's Rapid Transformation within the Archaeological Profession. In *Southwest Archaeology in the Twentieth Century*, edited by Linda S. Cordell and Don D. Fowler, pp. 97–108. University of Utah Press, Salt Lake City.

Dorshow, Wetherbee Bryan

2012 Modeling Agricultural Potential in Chaco Canyon during the Bonito Phase: A Predictive Geospatial Approach. *Journal of Archaeological Science* 39: 2098–2115.

Doxiadis, Constantinos A.

1968 *Ekistics: An Introduction to the Science of Human Settlements*. Oxford University Press, New York.

Doyel, David E. (editor)

1987 *The Hohokam Village: Site Structure and Organization*. AAAS Publication 87-15. Southwestern and Rocky Mountain Division of the American Association for the Advancement of Science, Glenwood Springs, Colorado.

Doyel, David E., Suzanne K. Fish, and Paul R. Fish (editors)

2000 *The Hohokam Village Revisited*. Southwestern and Rocky Mountain Division of the American Association for the Advancement of Science, Fort Collins, Colorado.

Dozier, Edward P.

1970a Making Inferences from the Present to the Past. In *Reconstructing Prehistoric Pueblo Societies*, edited by William A. Longacre, pp. 202–213. University of New Mexico Press, Albuquerque.

1970b   *The Pueblo Indians of North America.* Holt, Reinhart, and Winston, New York.

Drennan, Robert
1999   Analytical Scales, Building Blocks, and Comparisons. In *Great Towns and Regional Polities,* edited by Jill E. Neitzell, pp. 255–259. University of New Mexico Press, Albuquerque.

Drennan, Robert, Christian Peterson, and Jake Fox
2010   Degrees and Kinds of Inequality. In *Pathways to Power,* edited by T. Douglas Price, pp. 45–76. Springer, New York.

Dubreuil, Benoit
2010   *Human Evolution and the Origins of Hierarchies.* Cambridge University Press, Cambridge, UK.

Duff, Andrew I., Jeremy M. Moss, Thomas C. Windes, John Kantner, and M. Steven Shackley
2012   Patterning in Procurement of Obsidian in Chaco Canyon and in Chaco-Era Communities in New Mexico as Revealed by X-Ray Fluorescence. *Journal of Archaeological Science* 39:2995–3007.

Dumont, Clayton W., Jr.
2013   Navigating a Colonial Quagmire: Affirming Native Lives in the Struggle to Defend Our Dead. *In Accomplishing NAGPRA: Perspectives on the Intent, Impact, and Future of the Native American Graves Protection and Repatriation Act,* edited by Sangita Chari and Jaime M. N. Lavallee, pp. 239–264. Oregon State University Press, Corvallis.

Dunbar, Robin I. M.
1992   Neocortex Size as a Constraint on Group Size in Primates. *Journal of Human Evolution* 22:469–493.

1993   Coevolution of Neocortical Size, Group Size, and Language in Humans. *Behavioral and Brain Science* 16(4):681–735.

1995   The Price of Being at the Top. *Nature* 373(6509):22–23.

1998   The Social Brain Hypothesis. *Evolutionary Anthropology* 6(5):178–190.

2009   The Social Brain Hypothesis and Its Implications for Social Evolution. *Annals of Human Biology* 36(5):562–572.

2010   *How Many Friends Does One Person Need? Dunbar's Number and Other Evolutionary Quirks.* Harvard University Press, Cambridge, Massachusetts.

Dunbar, Robin, Clive Gamble, and John Gowlet (editors)
2010   *Social Brain, Distributed Mind.* Proceedings of the British Academy 158. Oxford University Press, Oxford, UK.

Dunnell, Robert C.
1991   Methodological Impacts of Catastrophic Depopulation on American Archaeology and Ethnology. In *Columbian Consequences,* vol. 3: *The Spanish Borderlands in Pan-American Perspective,* edited by David Hurst Thomas, pp. 561–580. Smithsonian Institution, Washington, DC.

Duwe, Samuel, B. Sunday Eiselt, J. Andrew Darling, Mark D. Willis, and Chester Walker
2016   The Pueblo Decomposition Model: A Method for Quantifying Architectural Rubble to Estimate Population Size. *Journal of Archaeological Science* 65:20–31.

Dyson, Stephen L.
2013   *In Pursuit of Ancient Pasts: A History of Classical Archaeology in the Nineteenth and Twentieth Centuries.* Yale University Press, New Haven, Connecticut.

Eagleton, Terry
2003   *After Theory.* Basic Books, New York.

Earle, Timothy R.
2001   Institutionalization of Chiefdoms: Why Landscapes Are Built. In *Leaders to*

Rulers, edited by J. Haas, pp. 105–124. Kluwer Academic/Plenum Publishers, New York.

2016 Pathways to power: Corporate and network strategies, staple and wealth finance, and primary and secondary states. In *Alternative Pathways to Complexity*, edited by L. Fargher and V. Heredia, pp. 291–308. University Press of Colorado, Boulder.

Echo-Hawk, Roger

2010 *The Magic Children: Racial Identity at the End of the Age of Race*. Routledge, New York.

Echo-Hawk, Walter

2012 Debunking the Top Ten Reasons Given by Scientists to Keep Dead Indians. *Arizona State Law Journal* 44(2):645–648.

Eggan, Fred

1967 From History to Myth: A Hopi Example. In *Studies in Southwestern Ethnolinguistics*, edited by Dell H. Hymes, pp. 33–53. Mouton, The Hague/Paris.

Ellis, Richard

1997 The Changing Image of the Anasazi World in the American Imagination. In *Anasazi Architecture and American Design*, edited by Baker H. Morrow and V. B. Price, pp. 16–23. University of New Mexico Press, Albuquerque.

Ember, Melvin

1963 The Relationship between Economic and Political Development in Nonindustrialized Societies. *Ethnology* 2:228–248.

Engelhardt, Joshua D., and Ivy A. Rieger (editors)

2017 *These "Thin Partitions": Bridging the Growing Divide between Cultural Anthropology and Archaeology*. University Press of Colorado, Boulder.

Fairclough, Graham, Rodney Harrison, John H. Jameson Jr., and John Schofield (editors)

2008 *The Heritage Reader*. Routledge, London.

Fargher, Lane F.

2016 Corporate Power Strategies, Collective Action, and Control of Principals: A Cross-Cultural Perspective. In *Alternate Pathways to Complexity*, edited by Lane F. Fargher and Verenice Y. Heredia Espinoza, pp. 309–326. University Press of Colorado, Boulder.

Faulseit, Ronald K. (editor)

2016 Beyond Collapse: Archaeological Perspectives on Resilience, Revitalization, and Transformation in Complex Societies. Southern Illinois University Press, Carbondale.

Faust, Katherine A., and Kim N. Richter (editors)

2015 *The Huasteca: Culture, History and Interregional Exchange*. University of Oklahoma Press, Norman.

Feinman, Gary M.

1998 Scale and Social Organization: Perspectives on the Archaic State. In *Archaic States*, edited by Gary M. Feinman and Joyce Marcus, pp. 95–133. School of American Research, Santa Fe, New Mexico.

2011 Size, Complexity, and Organizational Variation: A Comparative Approach. *Cross-Cultural Research* 45(1):37–58.

Feinman, Gary M., and Joyce Marcus (editors)

1998 *Archaic States*. School of American Research Press, Santa Fe, New Mexico.

Ferguson, T. J., and Stewart B. Koyiyumptewa

2009 *Footprints and Clouds in a Living Landscape: Notes on Hopi Culture and History Relating to Chaco Canyon, Aztec Ruin, and Mount Taylor*. Hopi Cultural Preservation Office, Kykotsmovi, Arizona.

Ferguson, W. M., and A. H. Rohn

1986   *Anasazi Ruins of the Southwest in Color.* University of New Mexico Press, Albuquerque.

Fernández-Armesto, Felipe

2012   It's Good to Have a King. *Wall Street Journal* 10 May.

Fernlund, Kevin J.

2000   *William Henry Holmes and the Rediscovery of the American West.* University of New Mexico Press, Albuquerque.

Finley, M. I.

1990   *The Use and Abuse of History.* Penguin Books, London.

Fish, Suzanne

1996   Dynamics of Scale in the Southern Deserts. In *Interpreting Southwestern Diversity,* edited by Paul R. Fish and J. Jefferson Reid, pp. 107–114. Anthropological Research Papers 48. Arizona State University, Tempe.

Fish, Suzanne, and Paul R. Fish

2007   The Hohokam Millennium. In *The Hohokam Millennium,* edited by Suzanne Fish and Paul R. Fish, pp. 1–11. School for Advanced Research Press, Santa Fe, New Mexico.

Flannery, Kent V.

1972   The Cultural Evolution of Civilizations. *Annual Review of Ecology and Systematics* 3:399–426.

1999   Process and Agency in Early State Formation. *Cambridge Archaeological Journal* 9(1):3–21.

Flannery, Kent, and Joyce Marcus

2012   *The Creation of Inequality.* Harvard University Press, Cambridge, Massachusetts.

Fleming, Robin

2011   *Britain after Rome: The Fall and Rise, 400 to 1070.* Penguin, London.

Fletcher, Roland

1995   *The Limits of Settlement Growth: A Theoretical Outline.* Cambridge University Press, Cambridge, UK.

2009   Low-Density, Agrarian-Based Urbanism: A Comparative View. *Insights* 2(4):2–19.

2010   Shining Stars and Black Holes: Urbanism, Comparison and Comparability. *Journal of Urban History* 36(2):251–256.

Fogelin, Lars

2007   Inference to the Best Explanation: A Common and Effective Form of Archaeological Reasoning. *American Antiquity* 72(4):603–625.

Ford, James A.

1969   *A Comparison of the Formative Cultures of the Americas: Diffusion or the Psychic Unity of Mankind.* Smithsonian Institution Press, Washington, DC.

Ford, Richard I., A. H. Schroeder, and S. L. Peckham

1972   Three Perspectives on Puebloan Prehistory. In *New Perspectives on the Pueblos,* edited by Alfonso Ortiz, pp. 22–40. University of New Mexico Press, Albuquerque.

Foster, William C.

2012   *Climate and Culture Change in North America AD 900–1600.* University of Texas Press, Austin.

Fowler, Andrew P., and John R. Stein

1992   The Anasazi Great House in Space, Time and Paradigm. In *Anasazi Regional Organization and the Chaco System,* edited by David E. Doyel, pp. 101–122. Anthropological Papers 5. Maxwell Museum of Anthropology, Albuquerque, New Mexico.

Fowler, Andrew P., John R. Stein, and Roger Anyon

1987 *An Archaeological Reconnaissance of West-Central New Mexico: The Anasazi Monuments Project.* Historic Preservation Division, Office of Cultural Affairs, Santa Fe, New Mexico.

Fowler, Don D.

1992 Models of Southwest Prehistory, 1840–1914. In *Reconsidering Our Past: Essays on the History of American Archaeology*, edited by Jonathan E. Reyman, pp. 15–34. Avebury Press, Aldershot, UK.

2000 *A Laboratory for Anthropology: Science and Romanticism in the American Southwest, 1846–1930.* University of Utah Press, Salt Lake City.

Fowles, Severin M.

2010 A People's History of the American Southwest. In *Ancient Complexities: New Perspectives in Pre-Columbian North America*, edited by Susan Alt, pp. 183–204. University of Utah Press, Salt Lake City.

2013 *An Archaeology of Doings: Secularism and the Study of Pueblo Religion.* School for Advanced Research Press, Santa Fe, New Mexico.

2016a The Stress of History: Stories of an Unfinished Kiva. In *Exploring Cause and Explanation*, edited by Cynthia L. Herhahn and Ann F. Ramenofsky, pp. 177–198. University Press of Colorado, Boulder.

2016b Writing Collapse. In *Social Theory in Archaeology and Ancient History: The Present and Future of Counternarratives*, edited by Geoffrey Emberling, pp. 205–230. Cambridge University Press, Cambridge, UK.

Fowles, Severin, and Barbara J. Mills

2017 On History in Southwest Archaeology. In *Oxford Handbook of Southwest Archaeology*, edited by Barbara J. Mills and Severin Fowles, pp. 3–71. Oxford University Press, Oxford.

Fox, Steve

1994 Sacred Pedestrians: The Many Faces of Southwest Pilgrimage. *Journal of the Southwest* 36(1):33–53.

Francaviglia, Richard, and David Narrett (editors)

1994 *Essays on Changing Images of the Southwest.* Texas A&M University Press, College Station.

Frank, Andre Gunder, and Barry K. Gills (editors)

1996 *The World System: Five Hundred Years or Five Thousand?* Routledge, London.

Fraser, George MacDonald

1988 *The Hollywood History of the World.* Penguin, London.

Freeman, Katherine, Robert Bliss, and Jennifer Thompson

1996 Visual Communication between Chimney Rock and Chaco Canyon. Paper presented at Oxford V Conference on Archaeoastronomy, Santa Fe, New Mexico, August 3–13.

Freidel, David A.

1981 The Political Economics of Residential Dispersion among the Lowland Maya. In *Lowland Maya Settlement Patterns*, edited by Wendy Ashmore, pp. 371–382. University of New Mexico Press, Albuquerque.

Fried, Morton H.

1967 *The Evolution of Political Society.* Random House, New York.

Friedman, Richard A., John R. Stein, and Taft Blackhorse Jr.

2003 A Study of a Pre-Columbian Irrigation System at Newcomb, New Mexico. *Journal of GIS in Archaeology* 1:3–10.

Fromherz, Allen James

2010   *Ibn Khaldun: Life and Times*. Edinburgh University Press, Edinburgh.

Frost, Richard H.

1980   The Romantic Inflation of Pueblo Culture. *American West* 17(1):5–9, 56–60.

Gallatin, Albert

1848   Introduction to "Hale's Indians of North-west America." *Transactions of the American Ethnological Society* 2:xxiii–clxxxviii.

Gamble, Clive

1998   Paleolithic Society and the Release from Proximity: A Network Approach to Intimate Relations. *World Archaeology* 29:426–449.

Garcia, Pedro Conde

1845   Carta Geografica General de la Republica Mexicana Formada el Ano de 1845. Seccion de Geografica del Ministerio de la Guerra, Mexico City.

Gavrilets, Sergey, David G. Anderson, and Peter Turchin

2010   Cycling in the Complexity of Early Societies. *Cliodynamics* 1:58–80.

Geertz, Armin W.

1983   Book of the Hopi: The Hopi's Book? *Anthropos* 78:547–556.

1990   Reflections on the Study of Hopi Mythology. In *Religion in Native North America*, edited by Christopher Vecsey, pp. 119–135. University of Idaho Press, Moscow.

1994   *The Invention of Prophecy*. University of California Press, Berkeley.

Gere, Cathy

2009   *Knossos and the Prophets of Modernism*. University of Chicago Press, Chicago.

Gibbon, Guy

2013   *Critically Reading the Theory and Methods of Archaeology: An Introductory Guide*. AltaMira Press, Lanham, Maryland.

Gibson, Arrell Morgan

1981   Native American Muses. *New Mexico Historical Review* 56(3):285–302.

1983   *The Santa Fe and Taos Colonies: Age of the Muses, 1900–1942*. University of Oklahoma Press, Norman.

Gibson, Charles

1964   *The Aztecs under Spanish Rule*. Stanford University Press, Stanford, California.

Gill, Sam

1987   *Mother Earth: An American Story*. University of Chicago Press, Chicago.

Gilman, Patricia A., Marc Thompson, and Kristina C. Wyckoff

2014   Ritual Change and the Distant: Mesoamerican Iconography, Scarlet Macaws, and Great Kivas in the Mimbres Region of Southwestern New Mexico. *American Antiquity* 79(1):90–107.

Gilmore, Zackary I., and Jason M. O'Donoughue (editors)

2015   *The Archaeology of Events: Cultural Change and Continuity in the Pre-Columbian Southeast*. University of Alabama Press, Tuscaloosa.

Ginsberg, Robert

2004   *The Aesthetics of Ruins*. Rodopi, Amsterdam.

Gladwin, Harold Sterling

1957   *A History of the Ancient Southwest*. Bond Wheelright Company, Portland, Oregon.

Glowacki, Donna M., and Scott Van Keuren (editors)

2011   *Religious Transformation in the Late Pre-Hispanic Pueblo World*. University of Arizona Press, Tucson.

Goldfrank, Esther S.

1945   Socialization, Personality, and the Structure of Pueblo Society. *American Anthropologist* 47:516–539.

Goodman, Audrey
2002   *Translating Southwestern Landscapes: The Making of an Anglo Literary Region.* University of Arizona Press, Tucson.

Goodman, Claire Garber, and Anne-Marie E. Cantwell
1984   *Copper Artifacts in Late Eastern Woodlands Prehistory.* Center for American Archeology at Northwestern University, Evanston, Illinois.

Graeber, David, and Marshall Sahlins
2017   *On Kings.* Hau Books, Chicago.

Graičiūnas, Vytautas A.
1937   Relationships in Organization. The Bulletin of the International Management Institute. In *Papers on the Science of Administration*, edited by Luther Gullick and L. Urwick, pp. 181–187. Institute of Public Administration, New York.

Graves, Michael W.
2010   Review of *History of the Ancient Southwest. CHOICE* May 2010.

Gravilets, Sergey, David G. Anderson, and Peter Turchin
2010   Cycling in the Complexity of Early Societies. *Cliodynamics* 1:58–80.

Grebinger, Paul
1973   Prehistoric Social Organization in Chaco Canyon, New Mexico: An Alternative Reconstruction. *Kiva* 39:3–25.

Greenblatt, Stephen
1991   *Marvelous Possessions: The Wonder of the New World.* University of Chicago Press, Chicago.

Gregory, David A., and David R. Wilcox (editors)
2007   *Zuni Origins: Toward a New Synthesis of Southwestern Archaeology.* University of Arizona Press, Tucson.

Griffeth, Robert, and Carol G. Thomas (editors)
1981   *The City-State in Five Cultures.* ABC-CLIO, Santa Barbara, California.

Grimstead, D. N., J. Quade, and M. C. Stiner
2016   Isotopic Evidence for Long-Distance Mammal Procurement, Chaco Canyon, New Mexico, USA. *Geoarchaeology* 31(5):335–354.

Guiterman, Christopher H., Thomas W. Swetnam, and Jeffrey S. Dean
2014   Eleventh-Century Shift in Timber Procurement Areas for the Great Houses of Chaco Canyon. *Proceedings of the National Academy of Sciences* 113(5):1186–1190.

Gumerman, George J., and David A. Phillips Jr.
1978   Archaeology beyond Anthropology. *American Antiquity* 43(2):184–191.

Gutiérrez, Ramón
1991   *When Jesus Came, the Corn Mothers Went Away: Marriage, Sexuality, and Power in New Mexico, 1500–1846.* Stanford University Press, Palo Alto, California.

Gutiérrez Mendoza, Gerardo
2003   Territorial Structure and Urbanism in Mesoamerica: The Huaxtec and Mixtec-Tlapanec-Nahua Cases. In *Urbanism in Mesoamerica*, edited by W. Sanders, G. Mastache, and R. Cobean, pp. 85–118. Pennsylvania State University and Instituto Nacional de Antropología e Historia, University Park.

2012   Hacia un modelo general para entender la estructura político-territorial del Estado nativo mesoamericano *(altepetl).* In *El poder compartido: Ensayos sobre la arqueología de organizaciones políticas segmentarias y oligárquicas*, edited by Annick Daneels and Gerardo Gutiérrez Mendoza, pp. 27–66. Centro de Investigaciones y Estudios Superiores en Antropología Social, Mexico City.

Gwynne, S. C.
2011   *Empire of the Summer Moon.* Scribner, New York.

Hall, Richard
2012   *The World of the Vikings.* Thames & Hudson, New York.
Hall, Thomas D.
1989   *Social Change in the Southwest, 1350–1880.* University Press of Kansas, Lawrence.
2009   Puzzles in the Comparative Study of Frontiers: Problems, Some Solutions, and Methodological Implications. *Journal of World-Systems Research* 15(1):25–47.
Hall, Thomas D., P. Nick Kardulias, and Christopher Chase-Dunn
2011   World-Systems Analysis and Archaeology: Continuing the Dialogue. *Journal of Archaeological Research* 19(3):233–279.
Hall, Thomas D., and Peter Turchin
2007   Lessons from Population Ecology for World-Systems Analyses of Long-Distance Synchrony. In *World System and the Earth System: Global Socioenvironmental Change and Sustainability since the Neolithic,* edited by A. Hornborg and C. Crumley, pp. 74–90. Left Coast Press, Walnut Creek, California.
Hämäläinen, Pekka
2008   *The Comanche Empire.* Yale University Press, New Haven, Connecticut.
Hanegraaff, Wouter J.
1996   *New Age Religion and Western Culture: Esotericism in the Mirror of Secular Thought.* E. J. Brill, Leiden, UK.
Hand, David J.
2014   *The Improbability Principle: Why Coincidences, Miracles, and Rare Events Happen Every Day.* Scientific American/Farrar, Straus and Giroux, New York.
Hansen, Mogens Herman (editor)
2000   *A Comparative Study of Thirty City-State Cultures: An Investigation.* Det Kongelige Danske Videnskabernes Selskab, Copenhagen.
2002   *A Comparative Study of Six City-State Cultures.* Det Kongelige Danske Videnskabernes Selskab, Copenhagen.
Hansen, Mogens Herman
2006   *Polis: An Introduction to the Ancient Greek City-State.* Oxford University Press, Oxford, UK.
Hansen, Mogens Herman, and Thomas Heine Nielsen (editors)
2005   *An Inventory of Archaic and Classical Poleis: An Investigation Conducted by the Copenhagen Polis Centre for the Danish National Research Foundation.* Oxford University Press, Oxford, UK.
Harman, Garman
2012   *Weird Realism: Lovecraft and Philosophy.* Zero Books, Winchester, UK.
Harris, Marvin
1968   *The Rise of Anthropological Theory.* T. Y. Crowell, New York.
Harris, Oliver J. T., and Craig N. Cipolla
2017   *Archaeological Theory in the New Millennium: Introducing Current Perspectives.* Routledge, London.
Hassig, Ross
2001   Counterfactuals and Revisionism in Historical Explanation. *Anthropological Theory* 1(1):57–72.
Haury, Emil W.
1976   *The Hohokam: Desert Farmers and Craftsmen.* University of Arizona Press, Tucson.
1958   Evidence at Point of Pines for a Prehistoric Migration from Northern Arizona. In *Migrations in New World Culture History,* edited by Raymond H. Thompson,

pp. 1–8. University of Arizona Bulletin 29(2), Social Science Bulletin 27. University of Arizona, Tucson.

Hawley, Florence M.

1934   *The Significance of the Dated Prehistory of Chetro Ketl*. University of New Mexico Bulletin 246. University of New Mexico, Albuquerque.

1937   Pueblo Social Organization as a Lead to Pueblo History. *American Anthropologist* 39:504–522.

Hayes, Alden C.

1981   A Survey of Chaco Canyon Archaeology. In *Archaeological Surveys of Chaco Canyon, New Mexico*, edited by Alden C. Hayes, David M. Brugge, and W. James Judge, pp. 1–68. Publications in Archaeology 18A. National Park Service, Washington, DC.

Hayes, Alden C., and Thomas C. Windes

1975   An Anasazi Shrine in Chaco Canyon. In *Collected Papers in Honor of Florence Hawley Ellis*, edited by Theodore R. Frisbie, pp. 143–156. Papers of the Archaeological Society of New Mexico No. 2. University of Oklahoma Press, Norman.

Hayes, Alden C., Jon Nathan Young, and A. H. Warren

1981   *Excavation of Mound 7, Gran Quivira National Monument, New Mexico*. Publications in Archaeology 16. National Park Service, Washington, DC.

Hays-Gilpin, Kelley

2008   All Roads Lead to Hopi. In *Las vías del noroeste, II: propuesta para una perspectiva sistèmica e interdisciplinaria*, edited by Cario Bonfiglioli, Arturo Gutiérrez, Marie-Areti Hers, María Eugenia Olavarría, pp. 65–82. UNAM, Instituto de Investigaciones Antropológicas, México.

2011   North America: Pueblos. In *The Oxford Handbook of the Archaeology of Ritual and Religion*, edited by Timothy Insoll, pp. 600–622. Oxford University Press, Oxford.

Hays-Gilpin, Kelley, and John Ware

2015   Chaco: The View from Downstream. In *Chaco Revisited: New Research on the Prehistory of Chaco Canyon, New Mexico*, edited by Carrie C. Heitman and Stephen Plog, pp. 322–346. University of Arizona Press, Tucson.

Hegmon, Michelle

2003   Setting Theoretical Egos Aside: Issues and Theory in North American Archaeology. *American Antiquity* 68:213–243.

2017   Path Dependency. In *Oxford Handbook of Southwestern Archaeology*, edited by Barbara J. Mills and Severin Fowles, pp. 155–167. Oxford University Press, Oxford, UK.

Hegmon, Michelle, Jerry B. Howard, Michael O'Hara, and Matthew A. Peeples

2016   Path Dependence and the Long-Term Trajectory of Prehistoric Hohokam Irrigation in Arizona. In *Archaeology of Entanglement: Entwinements and Entrapments of the Past*, edited by Lindsay Der and Francesca Fernandini, pp. 173–188. Left Coast Press, Walnut Creek, California.

Heilen, Michael P., and Phillip O. Leckman

2014   Cultural Landscapes of the Chuska Valley from a Distributional, Relational, and Spatial Perspective. In *Bridging the Basin: Land Use and Social History in the Southern Chuska Valley*, Volume 3: *Analysis*, edited by Monica L. Murrell and Bradley J. Vierra, pp. 41–166. Technical Report 14-08. Statistical Research, Inc., Albuquerque, New Mexico.

Heitman, Carrie C.

2015   The House of Our Ancestors: New Research on the Prehistory of Chaco Canyon, New Mexico, AD 800–1200. In *Chaco Revisited: New Research on the Prehistory of*

Chaco Canyon, New Mexico, edited by Stephen Plog and Carrie C. Heitman, pp. 215–248. University of Arizona Press, Tucson.

Heitman, Carrie C., Ruth Van Dyke, Matthew Peebles, and Kyle Boczinsky

2016   *Greater Chaco Landscapes Great House Communities GIS Integration Dataset.* GIS dataset submitted to the National Park Service in partial fulfillment of Rocky Mountain Cooperative Ecosystems Study Unit Task Agreement Number P14AC01703, Project #UCOB-109.

Heitman, Carrie C., and Stephen Plog (editors)

2015   *Chaco Revisited: New Research on the Prehistory of Chaco Canyon, New Mexico.* University of Arizona Press, Tucson.

Helms, Mary W.

1988   *Ulysses' Sail: An Ethnographic Odyssey of Power, Knowledge and Geographical Distance.* Princeton University Press, Princeton, New Jersey.

1992   Long Distance Contacts, Elite Aspirations, and the Age of Discovery in Cosmological Context. In *Resources, Power, and Interregional Interaction*, edited by Edward Schortman and Patricia A. Urban, pp. 157–174. Springer, New York.

Henige, David

1974   *The Chronology of Oral Tradition.* Clarendon Press, Oxford, UK.

Herman, David

2012   *Narrative Theory: Core Concepts and Critical Debates.* Ohio State University Press, Columbus.

Herman, David (editor)

2007a   *The Cambridge Companion to Narrative.* Cambridge University Press, Cambridge, UK.

2007b   *The Routledge Encyclopedia of Narrative Theory.* Routledge, New York.

Herring, George D.

2005   The Peaceful Pueblo Past: Frontier Politics and the Peaceful Pueblo Indian Image in American Ethnology and Archaeology. Unpublished Master's thesis, San Diego State University.

Hewett, Edgar

1930   *Ancient Life in the American Southwest.* Bobbs-Merrill, Indianapolis, Indiana.

Hibben, Frank C.

1975   *Kiva Art of the Anasazi at Pottery Mound.* KC Publications, Las Vegas.

Hill, James

1970   *Broken K Pueblo: Prehistoric Social Organization in the American Southwest.* University of Arizona Press, Tucson.

Hill, Jane H.

2007   The Zuni Language in Southwestern Areal Context. In *Zuni Origins: Toward a New Synthesis of Southwestern Archaeology*, edited by David A. Gregory and David R. Wilcox, pp. 22–38. University of Arizona Press, Tucson.

Hill, J. Brett, Jeffery J. Clark, William H. Doelle, and Patrick D. Lyons

2004   Prehistoric Demography in the Southwest: Migration, Coalescence, and Hohokam Population Decline. *American Antiquity* 69:689–716.

Hill, R. A., and R. I. M. Dunbar

2003   Social Network Size in Humans. *Human Nature* 14(1):53–72.

Hinsley, Curtis M.

1981   *Savages and Scientists: The Smithsonian Institution and the Development of American Anthropology, 1846–1910.* Smithsonian Institution Press, Washington, DC.

1986   Edgar Lee Hewett and the School of American Research in Santa Fe, 1906–1912. In

American Archaeology Past and Future: A Celebration of the Society of American Archaeology, 1935–1985, edited by David J. Meltzer, Don D. Fowler, and Jeremy A. Sabloff, pp. 217–236. Smithsonian Institution Press, Washington, DC.

1989   Zunis and Brahmins: Cultural Ambivalence in the Gilded Age. In *Romantic Motives: Essays on the Anthropological Sensibility*, edited by George W. Stocking Jr., pp. 169–207. History of Anthropology Vol. 6. University of Wisconsin Press, Madison.

1990   Authoring Authenticity. *Journal of the Southwest (Inventing the Southwest)* 32(4): 462–478.

1996   The Promise of the Southwest: A Humanized Landscape. In *The Southwest in the American Imagination: The Writings of Sylvester Baxter, 1881–1889*, edited by Curtis M. Hinsley and David R. Wilcox, pp. 181–206. University of Arizona Press, Tucson.

Hinsley, Curtis M., and David R. Wilcox

1996   *The Southwest in the American Imagination: The Writings of Sylvester Baxter, 1881–1889*. University of Arizona Press, Tucson.

Hirth, Kenneth G.

2000   Ancient Urbanism at Xochicalco: The Evolution and Organization of a Prehispanic Society. In *Archaeological Research at Xochicalco*, Vol. 1. University of Utah Press, Salt Lake City.

2003   The Altepetl and Urban Structure in Prehispanic Mesoamerica. In *Urbanism in Mesoamerica*, Vol. 1, edited by William T. Sanders, Alba Guadelupe Mastache, and Robert H. Cobean, pp. 57–84. Instituto Nacional de Antropología e Historia, Pennsylvania State University, University Park.

2008   Incidental Urbanism: The Structure of the Prehispanic City in Central Mexico. In *The Ancient City: New Perspectives on Urbanism in the Old and New World*, edited by Joyce Marcus and Jeremy A. Sabloff, pp. 273–297. School for Advanced Research Press, Santa Fe, New Mexico.

Hobsbawm, Eric

1983   Mass-Producing Traditions: Europe 1870–1914. In *The Invention of Tradition*, edited by Eric Hobsbawm and Terence Ranger, pp. 263–307. Cambridge University Press, Cambridge, UK.

Hodder, Ian

2003a   *Archaeology beyond Dialogue*. University of Utah Press, Salt Lake City.

2003b   An Archaeology of the Four-Field Approach in Anthropology in the United States. In *Unwrapping the Sacred Bundle: Reflections on the Disciplining of Anthropology*, edited by Daniel A. Segal and Sylvia J. Yanagisako, pp. 126–140. Duke University Press, Durham, North Carolina.

2006   *Çatalhöyük: The Leopard's Tale*. Thames and Hudson, London.

2012   *Entangled: An Archaeology of the Relationships between Humans and Things*. Wiley-Blackwell, Oxford.

2013   Ian Hodder. In *Archaeology in the Making: Conversations through a Discipline*, edited by William L. Rathje, Michael Shanks, and Christopher Witmore, pp. 122–140. Routledge, Abingdon, UK.

Hodge, Mary G.

1997   When Is a City-State? Archaeological Measures of Aztec City-States and Aztec City-State Systems. In *The Archaeology of City-States*, edited by Deborah L. Nichols and Thomas H. Charlton, pp. 209–227. Smithsonian Institution Press, Washington, DC.

Horton, Sarah Bronwen

2010   *The Santa Fe Fiesta, Reinvented: Staking Ethno-Nationalist Claims to a Disappearing Homeland*. School for Advanced Research Press, Santa Fe, New Mexico.

Huddleston, Lee Eldridge

1967   *Origins of the American Indians: European Concepts, 1492–1729*. University of Texas Press, Austin.

Hudson, Charles

2003   *Conversations with the High Priest of Coosa*. 2nd ed. University of North Carolina Press, Chapel Hill.

Hughte, Phil

1994   *A Zuni Artist Looks at Frank Hamilton Cushing*. Zuni A:shiwi Publishing, Zuni, New Mexico.

Hull, Sharon, Frances Joan Mathien, and Mostafa Fayek

2016   Turquoise Trade in the San Juan Basin, AD 900–1280. In *Exploring Cause and Explanation*, edited by Cynthia L. Herhahn and Ann F. Ramenofsky, pp. 213–239. University Press of Colorado, Boulder.

Hunt, Edward Proctor

2015   *The Origin Myth of Acoma Pueblo*. Penguin Classics, New York.

Hunt, Lynn

2014   *Writing History in the Global Era*. W. W. Norton, New York.

Hunt, Robert C., David Guillet, David R. Abbott, James Bayman, Paul Fish, Suzanne Fish, Keith Kintigh, and James A. Neely

2005   Plausible Ethnographic Analogies for the Social Organization of Hohokam Canal Irrigation. *American Antiquity* (70)3:433–456.

Hurst, Winston B., and Jonathan D. Till

2009   A Brief Survey of Great Houses and Related Features in Southeastern Utah. In *Chaco and After in the Northern San Juan*, edited by Catherine M. Cameron, pp. 44–80. University of Arizona Press, Tucson.

Iberico Lozada, Lucas

2016   The Professor and the Pueblo. *Santa Fe Reporter* 26 January.

Iggers, George G., and Q. Edward Wang

2008   *A Global History of Modern Historiography*. Pearson Education Limited, Harlow, England.

Isbell, William H.

2000   What We Should Be Studying: The Imagined Community and the Natural Community. In *The Archaeology of Communities: A New World Perspective*, edited by Marcello A. Canuto and Jason Yeager, pp. 243–266. Routledge, Cambridge.

Isendahl, Christian, and Michael E. Smith

2013   Sustainable Agrarian Urbanism: The Low-Density Cities of the Mayas and Aztecs. *Cities* 31:132–143.

Jackson, J. B.

1980   *Necessity for Ruins*. University of Massachusetts Press, Amherst.

Jacobs, Alex

2016   Don't Buy This Book! Acoma Pueblo vs Peter Nabokov: When the Sacred Is Made Profane. *Indian Country Today* 16 February.

Jennings, Justin

2011   *Globalizations in the Ancient World*. Cambridge University Press, Cambridge, UK.

Joffe, Alexander H.

2002   The Rise of Secondary States in the Iron Age Levant. *Journal of the Economic and Social History of the Orient* 45(4):425–467.

Johnson, Benjamin D.
2017   *Pueblos within Pueblos: Tlaxacalli Communities in Achohuacan, Mexico, ca. 1272–1692.* University Press of Colorado, Boulder.

Johnson, Gregory A.
1978   Information Sources and the Development of Decision-Making Organizations. In *Social Archaeology: Beyond Subsistence and Dating,* edited by Charles E. Redman, pp. 87–112. Academic Press, New York.
1982   Organizational Structure and Scalar Stress. In *Theory and Explanation in Archaeology,* edited by Colin Renfrew, pp. 389–423. Academic Press, New York.
1989   Dynamics of Southwestern Prehistory: Far Outside Looking In. In *Dynamics of Southwest Prehistory,* edited by Linda S. Cordell and George J. Gumerman, pp. 371–389. Smithsonian Institution Press, Washington, DC.

Johnson, George
1996   Indian Tribes' Creationists Thwart Archaeologists. *New York Times,* 22 October.

Johnson, Matthew H.
2010   *Archaeological Theory: An Introduction.* Wiley-Blackwell, Hoboken, New Jersey.
2011   On the Nature of Empiricism in Archaeology. *Journal of the Royal Anthropological Institute* 17: 764–787.

Jorgensen, Joseph G.
1980   *Western Indians: Comparative Environments, Languages, and Cultures of 172 Western American Indian Tribes.* W. H. Freeman, San Francisco.

Joyce, Arthur A.
2010   Theorizing Urbanism in Ancient Mesoamerica. *Ancient Mesoamerica* 20:189–196.

Joyce, Rosemary A., and Susan D. Gillespie (editors)
2000   *Beyond Kinship: Social and Material Reproduction in House Societies.* University of Pennsylvania Press, Philadelphia.

Judd, Neil M.
1925   Everyday Life in Pueblo Bonito as Disclosed by the National Geographic Society's Archaeological Explorations in the Chaco Canyon National Monument. *National Geographic Magazine* 48:227–262.
1929   The Present Status of Archaeology in the United States. *American Anthropologist* 31(3):401–418.

Judge, W. James
1979   The Development of a Complex Cultural Ecosystem in the Chaco Basin, New Mexico. In *Proceedings of the First Conference on Scientific Research in the National Parks,* Vol. 2, edited by R. M. Linn, pp. 901–906. Translation and Proceedings Series 4. National Park Service, Washington, DC.
1989   Chaco Canyon—San Juan Basin. In *Dynamics of Southwest Prehistory,* edited by Linda S. Cordell and George J. Gumerman, pp. 209–261. Smithsonian Institution Press, Washington, DC.

Judge, W. James, and Linda S. Cordell
2006   Society and Polity. In *The Archaeology of Chaco Canyon: An Eleventh Century Pueblo Regional Center,* edited by Stephen H. Lekson, pp. 189–210. School of American Research Press, Santa Fe, New Mexico.

Kantner, John
1996   Political Competition among the Chaco Anasazi of the American Southwest. *Journal of Anthropological Archaeology* 15(1):41–105.
2003   Rethinking Chaco as a System. *Kiva* 69(2):207–227.
2004   *Ancient Puebloan Southwest.* Cambridge University Press, Cambridge.

Kantner, John, and Keith Kintigh

2006   The Chaco World. In *The Archaeology of Chaco Canyon: An Eleventh Century Pueblo Regional Center*, edited by Stephen H. Lekson, pp. 153–188. School of American Research Press, Santa Fe, New Mexico.

Kantner, John, and Kevin J. Vaughn

2012   Pilgrimage as Costly Signal: Religiously Motivated Cooperation in Chaco and Nasca. *Journal of Anthropological Archaeology* 31:66–82.

Kauffman, Stuart A.

1991   Antichaos and Adaptation. *Scientific American* 265:78–84.

1993   *The Origins of Order: Self Organization and Selection in Evolution.* Oxford University Press, New York.

1995   *At Home in the Universe: The Search for the Laws of Self-Organization and Complexity.* Oxford University Press, New York.

Keen, Benjamin

1971   *The Aztec Image in Western Thought.* Rutgers University Press, New Brunswick, New Jersey.

Kehoe, Alice Beck

1998   *The Land of Prehistory: A Critical History of American Archaeology.* Routledge, New York.

2002   *America before the European Invasions.* Longman, Harlow, UK.

Kelley, Donald R.

2003   The Rise of Prehistory. *Journal of World History* 14(1):17–36.

Kelley, Klara Bonsack, and Harris Francis

1994   *Navajo Sacred Places.* Indiana University Press, Bloomington.

Kelly, Robert L.

2013   *The Lifeways of Hunter-Gatherers: The Foraging Spectrum.* 2nd ed. Cambridge University Press, Cambridge, UK.

2016   *The Fifth Beginning: What Six Million Years of Human History Can Tell Us About Our Future.* University of California Press, Berkeley.

Kelton, Paul, Alan C. Swedlund, and Catherine M. Cameron

2015   Introduction. In *Beyond Germs: Native Depopulation in North America*, edited by Catherine M. Cameron, Paul Kelton, and Alan C. Swedlund, pp. 3–15. University of Arizona Press, Tucson.

Kennedy, Roger

1994   *Hidden Cities: The Discovery and Loss of Ancient North American Civilization.* Penguin Books, New York.

Kennett, Douglas J., Stephen Plog, Richard J. George, Brendan J. Culleton, Adam S. Watson, Pontus Skoglund, Nadin Rohland, Swapan Mallick, Kristin Stewardson, Logan Kistler, Steven A. LeBlanc, Peter M. Whiteley, David Reich, and George H. Perry

2017   Archaeogenomic Evidence Reveals Prehistoric Matrilineal Dynasty. *Nature Communications* 8(14115):1–9.

Kidder, Alfred V.

1936   Speculations on New World Prehistory. In *Essays in Anthropology Presented to A. L. Kroeber*, [no editor named], pp. 143–152. University of California Press, Berkeley.

1962 [1924] *Introduction to the Study of Southwestern Archaeology.* Yale University Press, New Haven, Connecticut.

Kincaid, Chris (editor)

1983   *Chaco Roads Project Phase I: A Reappraisal of Prehistoric Roads in the San Juan Basin.* Bureau of Land Management, Albuquerque, New Mexico.

Kintigh, Keith

1994   Chaco, Communal Architecture, and Cibola Aggregation. In *The Ancient South-western Community: Models and Methods for the Study of Prehistoric Social Orga-nization*, edited by W. H. Wills and Robert D. Leonard, pp. 131–140. University of New Mexico Press, Albuquerque.

Kintigh, Keith W., Jeffrey H. Altschul, Mary C. Beaudry, Robert D. Drennan, Ann P. Kinzig, Timothy A. Kohler, W. Fredrick Limp, Herbert D. G. Maschner, William K. Michener, Timothy R. Pauketat, Peter Peregrine, Jeremy A. Sabloff, Tony J. Wilkinson, Henry T. Wright, and Melinda A. Zeder

2014a   Grand Challenges for Archaeology. *Proceedings of the National Academy of Sci-ences* 111(3):879–880.

2014b   Grand Challenges for Archaeology. *American Antiquity* 79(1):5–24.

Kirch, Patrick Vinton, and Roger C. Green

2001   *Hawaiki, Ancestral Polynesia: An Essay in Historical Anthropology*. Cambridge University Press, Cambridge.

Kirchhoff, Paul

1954   Gatherers and Farmers in the Greater Southwest: A Problem in Classification. *American Anthropologist* 56(4):529–550.

Kluckhohn, Clyde

1939   Discussion. In Preliminary Report on the 1937 Excavations, Bc 50–51, Chaco Canyon, New Mexico, edited by Clyde Kluckhohn and Paul Reiter, pp. 151–162. University of New Mexico Bulletin 345, Anthropological Series Vol. 3, No. 2. Uni-versity of New Mexico Press, Albuquerque.

Knapp, A. Bernard

2009   Migration, Hybridisation and Collapse: Bronze Age Cyprus and the Eastern Mediterranean. *Scienze Dell-Antichita: Storia, Archeologia, Antropologia* 15:219–239.

Kohler, Timothy A.

2012   Comparative Archaeology: The Camel's Nose? *Cliodynamics* 3(2):323–332.

2013   How the Pueblos Got Their Sprachbund. *Journal of Archaeological Method and Theory* 20:212–234.

Kohler, Timothy A., and R. Kyle Bocinsky

2017   Crisis as Opportunities for Culture Change. In *Crisis to Collapse: The Archaeology of Social Breakdown*, edited by Tim Cunningham and Jan Dreissen, pp. 263–273. AEGIS 11. Presses Universitaires de Louvain, Louvain-la-Neuve, Belgium.

Kohler, Timothy A., Denton Cockburn, Paul L. Hooper, R. Kyle Bocinsky, and Ziad Kobti

2012   The Co-evolution of Group Size and Leadership: An Agent Based Public Goods Model for Prehispanic Pueblo Societies. *Advances in Complex Systems* 15(1–2): 1150007.

Kohler, Timothy A., Sarah Cole, and Stanca Ciupe

2009   Population and Warfare: A Test of the Turchin Model in Pueblo Societies. In *Pat-tern and Process in Cultural Evolution*, edited by Stephen Shennan, pp. 277–295. University of California Press, Berkeley.

Kohler, Timothy A., and Rebecca Higgins

2016   Quantifying Household Inequality in Early Pueblo Villages. *Current Anthropology* 57(5):690–697.

Kohler, Timothy A., and Michael E. Smith (editors)

2018   *Ten Thousand Years of Inequality: The Archaeology of Wealth Differences*. Univer-sity of Arizona Press, Tucson.

Kohler, Timothy A., Mark D. Varien, and Aaron M. Wright (editors)
2010   *Leaving Mesa Verde: Peril and Change in the Thirteenth-Century Southwest.* University of Arizona Press, Tucson.

Kolb, Michael J., and James E. Snead
1997   It's a Small World after All: Comparative Analyses of Community Organization in Archaeology. *American Antiquity* 62(4):609–628.

Kosse, Krisztina
1990   Group Size and Society Complexity: Thresholds in the Long-Term Memory. *Journal of Anthropological Archaeology* 9:275–303.
1994   The Evolution of Large, Complex Groups: A Hypothesis. *Journal of Anthropological Archaeology* 13:35–50.
1996   Middle-Range Societies from a Scalar Perspective. In *Interpreting Southwestern Diversity: Underlying Principles and Overarching Patterns*, edited by Paul R. Fish and J. Jefferson Reid, pp. 87–96. Archaeological Research Papers 48. Arizona State University, Tempe.
2000   Some Regularities in Human Group Formation and the Evolution of Societal Complexity. *Complexity* 6(1):60–64.

Kosso, Peter
2008   Philosophy of Historiography. In *A Companion to the Philosophy of History and Historiography*, edited by Aviezer Tucker, pp. 7–25. Wiley-Blackwell, Malden, Massachusetts.

Kowalski, Jeff Karl, and Cynthia Kristan-Graham (editors)
2011   *Twin Tollans.* Dumbarton Oaks, Washington, DC.

Krakauer, David C.
2007   The Quest for Patterns in Meta-History. Santa Fe Institute Bulletin 22(1):32–39.

Krech, Shepard, III
2009   *Spirits of the Air: Birds and American Indians in the South.* University of Georgia Press, Athens.

Kristiansen, Kristian
2014   Towards a New Paradigm? The Third Science Revolution and Its Possible Consequences in Archaeology. *Current Swedish Archaeology* 22:11–71.

Kristiansen, Kristian, and Thomas B. Larsson
2005   *The Rise of Bronze Age Society: Travels, Transmissions and Transformations.* Cambridge University Press, Cambridge.

Kroeber, A. L.
1939   *Cultural and Natural Areas of Native North America.* University of California Press, Berkeley.
1940   Stimulus Diffusion. *American Anthropologist* 42(1):1–20.

Kubler, George
1962   *The Shape of Time: Remarks on the History of Things.* Yale University Press, New Haven, Connecticut.
1975   History—or Anthropology—of Art? *Critical Inquiry* 1(4):757–767.
1984   *The Art and Architecture of Ancient America.* 3rd ed. Penguin, New York.
1991   *Esthetic Recognition of Ancient Amerindian Art.* Yale University Press, New Haven, Connecticut.

Kuckelman, Kristin A.
2016   Cycles of Subsistence Stress, Warfare, and Population Movement in the Northern San Juan. In *The Archaeology of Food and Warfare*, edited by A. M. VanDerwarker and G. D. Wilson, pp. 107–132. Springer International Publishing, Switzerland.

Kuckelman, Kristin A. (editor)

2003   *The Archaeology of Yellow Jacket Pueblo (Site 5MT5): Excavations at a Large Community Center in Southwestern Colorado.* Available at http://www.crowcanyon .org/yellowjacket, accessed January 30, 2017.

Kurnick, Sarah, and Joanne Baron (editors)

2016   *Political Strategies in Precolumbian Mesoamerica.* University Press of Colorado, Boulder.

Kuwanwisiwma, Leigh J.

2004   Yupkoyvi: The Hopi Story of Chaco Canyon. In *In Search of Chaco: New Approaches to an Archaeological Enigma,* edited by David Grant Noble, pp. 41–47. School of American Research Press, Santa Fe, New Mexico.

Kuwanwisiwma, Leigh J., Stewart B. Koyiyumptewa, and Anita Poleahla

2012   Pasiwvi: Place of Deliberations. In *Hisat'sinom: Ancient Peoples in a Land Without Water,* edited by Christian E. Downum, pp. 7–9. School for Advanced Research Press, Santa Fe, New Mexico.

Laird, W. David

1977   *Hopi Bibliography.* University of Arizona Press, Tucson.

Lambert, Patricia M.

2002   The Archaeology of War: A North American Perspective. *Journal of Archaeological Research* 10(3):207–241.

Lamphere, Louise (editor)

1992   Women, Anthropology, Tourism and the Southwest. *Frontiers* 12(3):5–12.

Lange, Frederick, Nancy Mahaney, Joe Ben Wheat, and Mark L. Chanault

1986   *Yellow Jacket: A Four Corners Anasazi Ceremonial Center.* Johnson Books, Boulder, Colorado.

La Real Academia Española

1726   *Diccionario de la Lengua Castellana.* La Real Academia Española, Madrid.

Latour, Bruno

1999   *Pandora's Hope: Essays on the Reality of Science Studies.* Harvard University Press, Cambridge, Massachusetts.

2004   Why Has Critique Run Out of Steam? From Matters of Fact to Matters of Concern. *Critical Inquiry* 30(2):225–248.

2007   The Recall of Modernity: Anthropological Approaches. *Cultural Studies Review* 13(1):11–30.

Laurence, Ray

2012   *Roman Archaeology for Historians.* Routledge, London.

LeBlanc, Steven A.

1989   Cibola: Shifting Cultural Boundaries. In *Dynamics of Southwest Prehistory,* edited by Linda S. Cordell and George J. Gumerman, pp. 337–369. Smithsonian Institution Press, Washington, DC.

1999   *Prehistoric Warfare in the American Southwest.* University of Utah Press, Salt Lake City.

LeBlanc, Steven A., and Katherine E. Register

2004   *Constant Battles: Why We Fight.* St. Martin's Griffin, New York.

Lee, Richard B., and Irven Devore (editors)

1968   *Man the Hunter.* Aldine Publishing, Chicago.

Lekson, Stephen H.

1983   Chacoan Architecture in Continental Context. *In Proceedings of the Anasazi Symposium 1981,* compiled by Jack E. Smith, pp. 183–194. Mesa Verde Museum Association, Mesa Verde National Park, Colorado.

1984   *Great Pueblo Architecture of Chaco Canyon, New Mexico.* National Park Service, Santa Fe, New Mexico.

1985   Largest Settlement Size and the Interpretation of Socio-political Complexity at Chaco Canyon, New Mexico. *Haliksa'i: UNM Contributions to Anthropology* 4:68–75.

1988   The Idea of the Kivas in Anasazi Archaeology. *Kiva* 53:213–234.

1990   Cross-cultural Perspectives on the Community. In *On Vernacular Architecture: Paradigms of Environmental Response*, edited by Mete Turan, pp. 122–145. Gower, Avebury, UK.

1991   Settlement Pattern and the Chaco Region. In *Chaco and Hohokam: Prehistoric Regional Systems in the American Southwest*, edited by Patricia L. Crown and W. James Judge, pp. 31–55. School of American Research Press, Santa Fe, New Mexico.

1996   Scale and Process in the Southwest. In *Interpreting Southwestern Diversity: Underlying Principles and Overarching Patterns*, edited by Paul R. Fish and Jefferson J. Reid, pp. 81–86. Anthropological Research Papers 48. Arizona State University, Tempe.

1997   Museums and the Market: Exploring Santa Fe. *Nonrenewable Resources* 6(2): 99–109.

1999a   *The Chaco Meridian: Centers of Political Power in the Ancient Southwest.* AltaMira Press, Walnut Creek, California.

1999b   Was Casas a Pueblo? In *The Casas Grandes World*, edited by Curtis F. Schaafsma and Carroll L. Riley, pp. 84–92. University of Utah Press, Salt Lake City.

2002   War in the Southwest, War in the World. *American Antiquity* 67(4):607–624.

2006   Lords of the Great House. In *Palaces and Power in the Americas: From Peru to the Northwest Coast*, edited by Jessica Christie and Patricia Sarro, pp. 99–114. University of Texas Press, Austin.

2009a   *A History of the Ancient Southwest.* School for Advanced Research Press, Santa Fe, New Mexico.

2009b   Lost Cities, Prairie Castles: Mesa Verde, Manitou Cliff Dwellings, Bent's Old Fort and the Fort Restaurant. In *The Archaeology of Meaningful Places*, edited by Maria Nieves Zedeno and Brenda Bowser, pp. 163–179. University of Utah Press, Salt Lake City.

2010a   Good Gray Intermediate: Why Native Societies of North America Can't Be States. In *Ancient Complexities: New Perspectives in Precolumbian North America*, edited by Susan M. Alt, pp. 117–182. University of Utah Press, Salt Lake City.

2010b   My Adventures in Zuni—and Kykostmovi, and Window Rock, and… *Museum Anthropology* 33(2):180–193.

2012   Continuities and Discontinuities in Southwestern Religions. In *Enduring Motives: The Archaeology of Tradition and Religion in Native America*, edited by Linea Sundstrom and Warren DeBoer, pp. 201–209. University of Alabama Press, Tuscaloosa.

2014   Thinking about Fremont: The Later Prehistory of the Great Basin and the Southwest. In *Archaeology in the Great Basin and Southwest: Papers in Honor of Don D. Fowler*, edited by Nancy J. Parezo and Joel C. Janetski, pp. 109–117. University of Utah Press, Salt Lake City.

2015a   *Chaco Meridian: One Thousand Years of Political and Religious Power in the Ancient Southwest.* 2nd ed. Rowman and Littlefield, Lanham, Maryland.

2015b   Chaco Canyon and the US Southwest. In *A World with States, Empires, and Networks. Cambridge History of the World*, Volume 4, edited by Craig Benjamin, pp. 572–602. Cambridge University Press, Cambridge.

2016   The Architecture of Ritual and Polity at Chaco Canyon. In *Ritual in Archaic States*, edited by Joanne Murphy, pp. 192–219. University Press of Florida, Gainesville.

2017   Narrative Histories. In *Oxford Handbook of Southwestern Archaeology*, edited by Barbara J. Mills and Severn Fowles, pp. 91–107. Oxford University Press, Oxford.

Lekson, Stephen H. (editor)

2006   *The Archaeology of Chaco Canyon: An Eleventh-Century Pueblo Regional Center.* School of American Research Press, Santa Fe, New Mexico.

Lekson, Stephen H., Curtis Nepstad-Thornberry, Brian E. Yunker, David P. Cain, Toni Sudar-Laumbach, and Karl W. Laumbach

2002   Migrations in the Southwest: Pinnacle Ruin, Southwestern New Mexico. *Kiva* 68: 73–101.

Lekson, Stephen H., and Peter N. Peregrine

2004   A Continental Perspective for North American Archaeology. *SAA Archaeological Record* 4(1):15–19.

Lekson, Stephen H., Thomas C. Windes, and Peter J. McKenna

2006   Architecture. *In The Archaeology of Chaco Canyon*, edited by Stephen H. Lekson, pp. 67–116. School for Advanced Research Press, Santa Fe, New Mexico.

Lévi-Strauss, Claude

1975   *La Voie des Masques I.* Genève, Skira.

1979   *La Voie des Masques II.* Plon, Paris.

1982   The Social Organization of the Kwakiutl. In *The Way of the Masks*. Translated by Sylvia Modelski, pp. 163–187. University of Washington Press, Seattle.

1992   Maison. In *Dictionnaire de l'ethnologie et de l'anthropologie*, edited by P. Bonte and M. Izard, pp. 434–436. Presses Universitaires de France, Paris.

Liebmann, Matthew

2012   *Revolt: An Archaeological History of Pueblo Resistance and Revitalization in 17th Century New Mexico.* University of Arizona Press, Tucson.

Liebmann, Matthew, and Uzma Z. Rizvi

2008   *Archaeology and the Postcolonial Critique.* AltaMira Press, Lanham, Maryland.

Liebow, Edward, Virginia R. Dominguez, Peter Neal Peregrine, Teresa L. McCarty, Mark Nichter, Bonnie Nardi, and Jennifer Leeman

2013   On Evidence and the Public Interest. *American Anthropologist* 115(4):642–655.

Lindsay, Alexander

1987   Anasazi Population Movements to Southeastern Arizona. *American Anthropologist* 6:190–198.

Linford, Laurance D.

2000   *Navajo Places: History, Legend, Landscape.* University of Utah Press, Salt Lake City.

Lipe, William

2006   Notes from the North. In *The Archaeology of Chaco Canyon: An Eleventh Century Pueblo Regional Center*, edited by Stephen H. Lekson, pp. 261–313. School of American Research Press, Santa Fe, New Mexico.

Lippert, Dorothy

2008   Not the End, Not the Middle, but the Beginning: Repatriation as a Transformative Mechanism for Archaeologists and Indigenous People. In *Collaboration in*

Archaeological Practice: Engaging Descendant Communities, edited by C. Colwell-Chanthaphonh and T. J. Ferguson, pp. 119–130. AltaMira Press, Lanham, Maryland.

Livingston, Joan

2013   Book of the Hopi 50 Years Later. *Taos News*, 15 October.

Locke, John

1690   *Second Treatise of Civil Government*. Awnsham Churchill, London.

Lockhart, James

1992   *The Nahuas after the Conquest: A Social and Cultural History of the Indians of Central Mexico, Sixteenth Through Eighteenth Centuries*. Stanford University Press, Stanford.

Longacre, William A.

1970   *Archaeology as Anthropology: A Case Study*. University of Arizona Press, Tucson.

Loose, Richard W.

1979   Research Design. In *Anasazi Communities of the San Juan Basin*, edited by Michael P. Marshall, John R. Stein, Richard W. Loose, and Judith E. Novotny, pp. 355–363. Public Service Company of New Mexico, Albuquerque.

Lovato, Andrew Leo

2004   *Santa Fe Hispanic Culture: Preserving Identity in a Tourist Town*. University of New Mexico Press, Albuquerque.

Lovato, Troy R.

2007   *Inauthentic Archaeologies: Public Uses and Abuses of the Past*. Left Coast Press, Walnut Creek, California.

Lowenthal, David E.

1985   *The Past Is a Foreign Country*. Cambridge University Press, Cambridge, UK.

1998   *The Heritage Crusade and the Spoils of History*. Cambridge University Press, Cambridge, UK.

1999   *The Past Is a Foreign Country*. 2nd ed. Cambridge University Press, Cambridge, UK.

2015   *The Past Is a Foreign Country, Revisited*. Cambridge University Press, Cambridge, UK.

Lowie, Robert H.

1915   Oral Traditions and History. *American Anthropologist* 17(3):597–599.

Lummis, Charles

1893   *The Land of Poco Tiempo*. Charles Scribner's Sons, New York.

1905   Catching Our Archaeology Alive. *Out West: A Magazine of the Old Pacific and the New* 22:35–44.

Lydon, Jane, and Uzma Z. Rizvi (editors)

2010   *Handbook of Postcolonial Archaeology*. Left Coast Press, Walnut Creek, California.

Lyman, R. Lee, Michael J. O'Brien, and Robert C. Dunnell

1997   *The Rise and Fall of Culture History*. Springer, New York.

Macaulay, Rose

1953[1984] *Pleasure of Ruins*. Weidenfield and Nicolson, London.

Mahoney, Nancy M.

2000   Redefining the Scale of Chacoan Communities. In *Great House Communities across the Chacoan Landscape*, edited by John Kantner and Nancy M. Mahoney, pp. 19–38. Anthropological Papers of the University of Arizona 64. University of Arizona Press, Tucson.

Mair, Victor H. (editor)

2006   *Contact and Exchange in the Ancient World*. University of Hawaii Press, Honolulu.

Malville, J. M., and Malville, N. J.

2001   Pilgrimage and Periodical Festivals as Processes of Social Integration in Chaco Canyon. *Kiva* 66:327–344.

Malville, Nancy J.

2001   Long-Distance Transport of Bulk Goods in the Pre-Hispanic American Southwest. *Journal of Anthropological Anthropology* 20:230–243.

Manning, Patrick

2003   *Navigating World History: Historians Create a Global Past.* Palgrave Macmillan, New York.

Marcus, Joyce

1998   The Peaks and Valleys of Ancient States: An Extension of the Dynamic Model. In *Archaic States*, edited by Gary M. Feinman and Joyce Marcus, pp. 59–94. School of American Research Press, Santa Fe, New Mexico.

2004   Primary and Secondary State Formation in Southern Mesoamerica. In *Understanding Early Classic Copan*, edited by E. E. Bell, M. A. Canuto, and R. J. Sharer, pp. 357–373. University of Pennsylvania Museum of Archaeology and Anthropology, Philadelphia.

Marcus, Joyce, and Gary M. Feinman

1998   Introduction. In *Archaic States*, edited by Gary M. Feinman and Joyce Marcus, pp. 3–13. School of American Research, Santa Fe, New Mexico.

Marcus, Joyce, and Jeremy A. Sabloff

2008   Introduction. In *The Ancient City: New Perspectives on Urbanism in the Old and New World*, edited by Joyce Marcus and Jeremy A. Sabloff, pp. 3–26. School for Advanced Research Press, Santa Fe, New Mexico.

Markovich, Nicholas C., Wolfgang F. E. Preiser, and Fred G. Sturm (editors)

1990   *Pueblo Style and Regional Design.* Van Nostrand Reinhold, New York.

Marlar, Richard A., Banks L. Leonard, Brian R. Billman, Patricia M. Lambert, and Jennifer E. Marlar

2000   Biochemical Evidence of Cannibalism at a Prehistoric Puebloan Site in Southwestern Colorado. *Nature* 407(6800):74–78.

Marshall, Michael P.

1997   The Chacoan Roads: A Cosmological Interpretation. In *Anasazi Architecture and American Design*, edited by Baker H. Morrow and V. B. Price, pp. 62–74. University of New Mexico Press, Albuquerque.

Marshall, Michael P., John R. Stein, Richard W. Loose, and Judith E. Novotny

1979   *Anasazi Communities of the San Juan Basin.* State Historic Preservation Bureau, Santa Fe, New Mexico.

Martin, Paul S.

1936   *Lowry Ruin in Southwestern Colorado.* Anthropological Series, Field Museum of Natural History 23(1). Field Museum of Natural History, Chicago.

Martin, Paul S., and Fred Plog

1973   *The Archaeology of Arizona: A Study of the Southwest Region.* Doubleday/Natural History Press, Garden City, New Jersey.

Martines, Lauro

1988   *Power and Imagination: City-States in Renaissance Italy.* Johns Hopkins University Press, Baltimore.

Masayesva, Victor, Jr.

2006   *Husks of Time: The Photographs of Victor Masayesva.* University of Arizona Press, Phoenix.

Mason, Ronald J.

2006   *Inconstant Companions: Archaeology and North American Indian Oral Traditions.* University of Alabama Press, Tuscaloosa.

Mather, Christine, and Sharon Woods

1986   *Santa Fe Style.* Rizzoli, New York.

Mathien, Frances Joan

1993   Anthropological Investigations. In *The Pajarito Plateau: A Bibliography.* Southwest Cultural Resources Center. Professional Paper 49, pp. 9–34. National Park Service, Santa Fe, New Mexico.

1997   Ornaments of the Chaco Anasazi. In *Ceramics, Lithics, and Ornaments of Chaco Canyon: Analyses of Artifacts from the Chaco Project 1971–1978.* Vol. III, *Lithics and Ornaments,* edited by Francis Joan Mathien, pp. 1119–1219. Publications in Archaeology 18G. National Park Service, Santa Fe, New Mexico.

2005   *Culture and Ecology of Chaco Canyon and the San Juan Basin.* Studies in Archaeology 18H. National Park Service, Santa Fe, New Mexico.

Matson, Hannah Victoria

2016   Ornaments as Socially Valuable Objects: Jewelry and Identity in the Chaco and Post-Chaco Worlds. *Journal of Anthropological Archaeology* 42: 122–139.

Matthews, Washington

1889   Noqoìlpi, the Gambler: A Navajo Myth. *Journal of American Folklore* 2(5):89–94.

McAnany, Patricia A., and Norman Yoffee (editors)

2010   *Questioning Collapse.* Cambridge University Press, Cambridge.

McCaffery, Nick

2005   *Global Hopi, Local Hippie: An Anthropological Study of Hopi Identity in Relation to the New Age.* Queen's University of Belfast, Belfast, UK.

McCarthy, John P.

2008   More Than Just "Telling the Story": Interpretive Narrative Archaeology. In *The Heritage Reader,* edited by Graham Fairclough, Rodney Harrison, John H. Jameson Jr., and John Schofield, pp. 536–544. Routledge, London.

McLeod, Roxie

1994   Dreams and Rumors: A History of *Book of the Hopi.* Unpublished Master's thesis, University of Colorado, Boulder.

McCullagh, C. Behan

2009   Colligation. In *A Companion to the Philosophy of History and Historiography,* edited by Aviezer Tucker, pp. 152–161. Blackwell, Malden, Massachusetts.

McFeely, Eliza

2001   *Zuni and the American Imagination.* Hill and Wang, New York.

McGhee, George

2008   Aboriginalism and the Problems of Indigenous Archaeology. *American Antiquity* 73:579–597.

2010   Of Strawmen, Herrings, and Frustrated Expectations. *American Antiquity* 75(2): 239–243.

McGrayne, Sharon Bertsch

2012   *The Theory That Would Not Die: How Bayes' Rule Cracked the Enigma Code, Hunted Down Russian Submarines, and Emerged Triumphant from Two Centuries of Controversy.* Yale University Press, New Haven, Connecticut.

McGregor, John C.

1941   *Southwestern Archaeology.* J. Wiley and Sons, New York.

1965 *Southwestern Archaeology*, 2nd ed. University of Illinois Press, Urbana.

McGuire, Randall H.

1994 Historical Processes and Southwestern Prehistory: A Position Paper. In *Understanding Complexity in the Prehistoric Southwest*, edited by George Gumerman and Murray Gell-Mann, pp. 193–202. SFI Studies in the Sciences of Complexity, Proceedings 16. Addison-Wesley, Reading, Massachusetts.

2008 *Archaeology as Political Action*. University of California Press, Berkeley.

McNeill, Robert, and William H. McNeill

2003 *The Human Web: A Bird's-Eye View of World History*. W. W. Norton, New York.

McNiven, Ian J.

2016 Theoretical Challenges of Indigenous Archaeology: Setting an Agenda. *American Antiquity* 81(1):27–41.

McNiven, Ian J., and Lynette Russell

2005 *Appropriated Pasts: Indigenous Peoples and the Colonial Culture of Archaeology*. AltaMira Press, Lanham, Maryland.

Mead, Margaret

1974 *Ruth Benedict*. Columbia University Press, New York.

Mead, Walter Russell

2010 The Crisis of the American Intellectual. *The American Interest* 8 December. https://www.the-american-interest.com/2010/12/08/the-crisis-of-the-american-intellectual/, accessed May 25, 2018.

Meinig, Donald W.

1971 *Southwest: Three Peoples in Geographical Change 1600–1970*. Oxford University Press, New York.

1986, 1993, 1998, 2004 *The Shaping of America: A Geographical Perspective on 500 Years of History*. 4 volumes. Yale University Press, New Haven, Connecticut.

Menzies, Gavin

2003 *1421: The Year China Discovered America*. William Morrow, New York.

Meskell, Lynn (editor)

2009 *Cosmopolitan Archaeologies*. Duke University Press, Durham, North Carolina.

Meyer, Carter Jones

2001 Saving the Pueblos: Commercialism and Indian Reform in the 1920s. In *Selling the Indian: Commercializing and Appropriating American Indian Cultures*, edited by Carter Jones Meyer and Diana Royer, pp. 191–211. University of Arizona Press, Tucson.

Michaels, David

2006 Politicizing Peer Review: Scientific Perspective. In *Rescuing Science from Politics: Regulation and the Distortion of Scientific Research*, edited by Wendy Wagner and Rena Steinzor, pp. 224. Cambridge University Press, Cambridge, UK.

Miller, Susan A.

2011 Native America Writes Back: The Origin of the Indigenous Paradigm in History. In *Native Historians Write Back: Decolonizing American Indian History*, edited by Susan A. Miller and James Riding In, pp. 9–24. Texas Tech Press, Lubbock.

Mills, Barbara J.

2002 Recent Research on Chaco: Changing Views on Economy, Ritual, and Society. *Journal of Archaeological Research* 10(1):65–117.

2004a The Establishment and Defeat of Hierarchy: Inalienable Possessions and the History of Collective Prestige Structures in the Pueblo Southwest. *American Anthropologist* 106(2):238–251.

2004b   Key Debates in Chacoan Archaeology. *In* In Search of Chaco: New Approaches to an Archaeological Enigma. David Grant Noble, ed. pp. 122–30. School of American Research Press, Santa Fe, New Mexico.

2008a   How the Pueblos Became Global: Colonial Appropriations, Resistance, and Diversity in the North American Southwest. *Archaeologies: Journal of the World Archaeological Congress* 4(2):218–231.

2008b   Remembering While Forgetting: Depositional Practices and Social Memory at Chaco. In *Memory Work*, edited by Barbara J. Mills and William H. Walker, pp. 81–108. School for Advanced Research Press, Santa Fe, New Mexico.

2013   Human-Thing Theory [review of Hodder's *Entangled*]. *Current Anthropology* 54(4):515–516.

2015   Unpacking the House: Ritual Practice and Social Networks at Chaco. In *Chaco Revisited*, edited by Carrie Heitman and Stephen Plog, pp. 249–271. Amerind Seminar Series. University of Arizona Press, Tucson.

Mills, Barbara J., Jeffery J. Clark, Matthew Peeples, W. Randall Haas Jr., John M. Roberts Jr., Brett Hill, Deborah L. Huntley, Lewis Borck, Ronald L. Breiger, Aaron Clauset, and M. Steven Shackley

2013   The Transformation of Social Networks in the Late Prehispanic US Southwest. *Proceedings of the National Academy of Sciences* 110(15):5785–5790.

Mills, Barbara J., John M. Roberts Jr., Jeffery C. Clark, W. Randall Haas Jr., Deborah L. Huntley, Matthew Peeples, Meghan Trowbridge, Lewis Borck, and Ronald L. Breiger

2013   Late Prehispanic Social Dynamics in the Southwest US, AD 1200–1500. In *Regional Network Analysis in Archaeology*, edited by Carl Knappett, pp. 181–202. Oxford University Press, Oxford, UK.

Mills, Barbara J., Matthew A. Peeples, William R. Haas Jr., Lewis Borck, Jeffery J. Clark, and John M. Roberts Jr.

2015   Multiscalar Perspectives on Social Networks in the Late Prehispanic Southwest. *American Antiquity* 80(1):3–24.

Mills, Barbara J., and Severin Fowles (editors)

2017   *Oxford Handbook of Southwest Archaeology*. Oxford University Press, Oxford.

Milner, George R.

1998   *The Cahokia Chiefdom: The Archaeology of a Mississippian Society*. Smithsonian Institution Press, Washington, DC.

Minnis, Paul E.

1984   Peeking under the Tortilla Curtain: Regional Interaction and Integration on the Northeastern Periphery of Casas Grandes. *American Archaeology* 4:181–193.

Minnis, Paul E., and Michael E. Whalen

2016   *Discovering Paquimé*. University of Arizona Press, Tucson.

Minnis, Paul E., and Michael E. Whalen (editors)

2015   *Ancient Paquimé and the Casas Grandes World*. University of Arizona Press, Tucson.

Modell, Judith Schachter

1983   *Ruth Benedict: Patterns of a Life*. University of Pennsylvania Press, Philadelphia.

Morgan, Lewis Henry

1876   Montezuma's Dinner. *North American Review* 122:265–308.

1880   *A Study of the Houses of the American Aborigines with a Scheme of Exploration of the Ruins in New Mexico and Elsewhere*. First Annual Report of the Executive Committee, with Accompanying Papers, Archaeological Institute of America, 1879–1880, pp. 29–80. Archaeological Institute of America, Cambridge, Massachusetts.

1965 [1881] *Houses and House-life of the American Aborigines.* University of Chicago Press, Chicago. 01n16

1934 *Doma i domashnyaya zhizn' amerikanskikh tuzemtsev.* Institute of Peoples of the North, Leningrad.

Morris, Ian

2000 *Archaeology as Cultural History: Words and Things in Iron Age Greece.* Blackwell, Malden, Massachusetts.

2010 *Why the West Rules—for Now.* Farrar, Straus, and Giroux, New York.

2014 *War! What Is It Good For? Conflict and the Progress of Civilization from Primates to Robots.* Farrar, Straus, and Giroux, New York.

2015 *Foragers, Farmers, and Fossil Fuels: How Human Values Evolve.* Princeton University Press, Princeton, New Jersey.

Morrow, Baker H., and V. B. Price (editors)

1997 *Anasazi Architecture and American Design.* University of New Mexico Press, Albuquerque.

Moses, Daniel Noah

2009 *The Promise of Progress: The Life and Work of Lewis Henry Morgan.* University of Missouri Press, Columbia.

Moss, Madonna L.

2005 Rifts in the Theoretical Landscape of Archaeology in the United States: A Comment on Hegmon and Watkins. *American Antiquity* 70(3):581–587.

Moul, Harry, and Linda Tigges

1996 The Santa Fe 1912 City Plan: A "City Beautiful" and City Planning Document. *New Mexico Historical Review* 71(2):135–155.

Munson, Marit K. (editor)

2008 *Kenneth Chapman's Santa Fe: Artists and Archaeologists, 1907–1931.* School for Advanced Research Press, Santa Fe, New Mexico.

Murdock, George Peter

1981 *Atlas of World Cultures.* University of Pittsburg Press, Pittsburg.

Murphy, Joanne

2016 *Ritual in Archaic States.* University Press of Florida, Gainesville.

Nabokov, Peter

1996 Native Views of History. In *The Cambridge History of the Native Peoples of the Americas, Vol I, North America, Part 1,* edited by Bruce G. Trigger and Wilcomb E. Washburn, pp. 1–59. Cambridge University Press, Cambridge, UK.

2002 *A Forest of Time: American Indian Ways of History.* Cambridge University Press, Cambridge, UK.

2015 *How the World Moves: The Odyssey of an American Indian Family.* Viking Press, New York.

Naroll, Raoul

1956 A Preliminary Index of Social Development. *American Anthropologist* 56:687–715.

National Research Council of the National Academies

2010 Appendix D. In *Advancing the Science of Climate Change: America's Climate Choices, Panel on Advancing the Science of Climate Change; Board on Atmospheric Sciences and Climate, Division on Earth and Life Studies.* The National Academies Press, Washington, DC.

Neitzel, Jill E. (editor)

1999 *Great Towns and Regional Polities in the Prehistoric American Southwest and Southeast.* University of New Mexico Press, Albuquerque.

2003   *Pueblo Bonito: Center of the Chacoan World.* Smithsonian Books, Washington.

Neitzel, Jill E., H. Neff, M. Glascock, and R. Bishop

2002   Chaco and the Production of Dogoszhi-Style Pottery. In *Ceramic Production and Circulation in the Greater Southwest: Source Determination by INAA and Complementary Mineralogical Investigations*, edited by D. Glowacki and H. Neff, pp. 47–65. The Cotsen Institute of Archaeology, Los Angeles.

Nelson, Ben A.

1995   Complexity, Hierarchy, and Scale: A Controlled Comparison between Chaco Canyon, New Mexico, and La Quemada, Zacatecas. *American Antiquity* 60(4):597–618.

2000   Aggregation, Warfare, and the Spread of the Mesoamerican Tradition. In *The Archaeology of Regional Interaction: Religion, Warfare, and Exchange across the American Southwest and Beyond*, edited by Michelle Hegmon, pp. 317–337. University Press of Colorado, Boulder.

2006   Mesoamerican Objects and Symbols in Chaco Canyon Contexts. In *The Archaeology of Chaco Canyon: An Eleventh-Century Pueblo Regional Center*, edited by Stephen H. Lekson, pp. 339–371. School of American Research Press, Santa Fe, New Mexico.

Nelson, Kate

2016   Finding Their Niche. *El Palacio* 121(4):45–49.

Nelson, Margaret C.

1999   *Mimbres during the 12th Century: Abandonment, Continuity, and Reorganization.* University of Arizona Press, Tucson.

New Materialist Cartographies

2017   *Home—New Materialist Cartographies.* Last modified 28 December 2016. https://newmaterialistscartographies.wikispaces.com, accessed May 25, 2018.

Nials, Fred, John Stein, and John Roney

1987   *Chacoan Roads in the Southern Periphery: Results of Phase II of the BLM Chaco Roads Project.* Cultural Resource Series 1. Bureau of Land Management, Albuquerque, New Mexico.

Nicholas, George P.

2008   Native Peoples and Archaeology. In *Encyclopedia of Archaeology*, Volume 3, edited by Deborah Pearsall, pp. 1660–1669. Academic Press, New York.

Nicholas, George P. (editor)

2010   *Being and Becoming Indigenous Archaeologists.* Left Coast Press, Walnut Creek, California.

Nicholas, George, and Julie Hollowell

2007   Ethical Challenges to a Postcolonial Archaeology: The Legacy of Scientific Colonialism. In *Archaeology and Capitalism: From Ethics to Politics*, edited by Yannis Hamilakis and Philip Duke, pp. 59–82. Left Coast Press, Walnut Creek, California.

Nichols, Deborah L., and Thomas Charlton (editors)

1997   *The Archaeology of City-States: Cross-Cultural Approaches.* Smithsonian Press, Washington, DC.

Nichols, Deborah L., and Thomas Charlton

1997   The City-Sate Concept: Development and Applications. In *The Archaeology of City-States: Cross-Cultural Approaches*, edited by Deborah A. Nichols and Thomas Charlton, pp. 1–14. Smithsonian Press, Washington, DC.

Nimkoff, M. F., and Russell Middleton

1960   Types of Family and Types of Economy. *American Journal of Sociology* 66(3):215–225.

Noble, David Grant (editor)

1989   *Santa Fe: History of an Ancient City.* School of American Research Press, Santa Fe, New Mexico.

2004   *In Search of Chaco: New Approaches to an Archaeological Enigma.* School of American Research Press, Santa Fe, New Mexico.

Novick, Peter

1998   *That Noble Dream: The "Objectivity Question" and the American Historical Profession.* Cambridge University Press, Cambridge.

Oakley, Kenneth P.

1946   *Man the Toolmaker.* British Museum, London.

O'Brien, Patricia J.

1989   Cahokia: The Political Capital of the "Ramey" State? *North American Archaeologist* 10:275–292.

1991   Early State Economics: Cahokia, Capital of the Ramey State. In *Early State Economics*, edited by Henri J. M. Claessen and Pieter van de Velde, pp. 143–175. Transaction Publishers, New Brunswick, New Jersey.

O'Laughlin, Shannon Keller

2013   Moving Forward from the Last Twenty Years: Finding a New Balance. In *Accomplishing NAGPRA: Perspectives on the Intent, Impact, and Future of the Native American Graves Protection and Repatriation Act*, edited by Sangita Chari and Jaime M. N. Lavallee, pp. 223–238. Oregon State University Press, Corvallis.

Oliver, Paul (editor)

1998   *Encyclopedia of Vernacular Architecture of the World.* Cambridge University Press, Cambridge, UK.

Olivier, Laurent

2011   *The Dark Abyss of Time: Archaeology and Memory.* Translated by Arthur Greenspan. AltaMira Press, Lanham, Maryland.

Olsen, Bjørnar, Michael Shanks, Timothy Webmoor, and Christopher Witmore

2012   *Archaeology: the Discipline of Things.* University of California Press, Berkeley.

Ortiz, Simon J.

1994   What We See: A Perspective on Chaco Canyon and Pueblo Ancestry. In *Chaco Canyon: A Center and Its World*, edited by Mary Wachs, pp. 65–72. Museum of New Mexico Press, Santa Fe.

Ortman, Scott G.

2009   Genes, Language and Culture in Tewa Ethnogenesis, AD 1150–1450. PhD dissertation, Arizona State University, Tempe.

2012   *Winds from the North: Tewa Origins and Historical Anthropology.* University of Utah Press, Salt Lake City.

2016a   Review of *Chaco Revisited. American Antiquity* 81(2):393–394.

2016b   Perspective: What Difference Does Archaeology Make? *El Palacio* 121(2):22–23.

Ortman, Scott G., and Grant D. Coffey

2017   Settlement Scaling in Middle-Range Societies. *American Antiquity* 82(4):662–682.

Ortman, Scott G., Mark D. Varien, and T. Lee Gripp

2007   Empirical Bayesian Methods for Archaeological Survey Data: An Application from the Mesa Verde Region. *American Antiquity* 72(2):241–272.

Ouweneel, Arij

1999   Altepeme and Pueblos de Indios: Some Comparative Theoretical Perspectives on the Analysis of the Colonial Indian Communities. In *The Indian Community of Colonial Mexico: Fifteen Essays on Land Tenure, Corporate Organizations, Ideology and Village Politics*, edited by Arij Ouweneel and Simon Miller, pp. 1–37. Centro de Estudios y Documentación Latinoamericanos, Amsterdam.

Pacheco, Ana

2016   *A History of Spirituality in Santa Fe: The City of Holy Faith.* History Press, Charleston, South Carolina.

Padget, Martin

1995   Travel, Exoticism, and the Writing of Region: Charles Fletcher Lummis and the Creation of the Southwest. *Journal of the Southwest* 37(3):421–449.

Palka, Joel W.

2012   *Maya Pilgrimages to Ritual Landscapes: Insights from Archaeology, History and Ethnography.* University of New Mexico Press, Albuquerque.

Palkovich, Ann M.

1984   Disease and Mortality Patterns in the Burial Rooms of Pueblo Bonito: Preliminary Considerations. In *Recent Research on Chaco Prehistory*, edited by W. James Judge and J. D. Schelberg, pp. 103–113. Reports of the Chaco Center No. 8. National Park Service, Albuquerque, New Mexico.

Pandy, Triloki Nath

1972   Anthropologists at Zuni. *Proceedings of the American Philosophical Society* 116(4): 321–337.

Parezo, Nancy J.

1993   *Hidden Scholars: Women Anthropologists and the Native American Southwest.* University of New Mexico Press, Albuquerque.

Parezo, Nancy J., and Don D. Fowler

2007   *Anthropology Goes to the Fair: The 1904 Louisiana Purchase Exposition.* University of Nebraska Press, Lincoln.

Parker, Geoffrey

2004   *Sovereign City: The City-State through History.* Reaktion, London.

Parkinson, William A., and Michael L. Galaty

2007   Secondary States in Perspective: An Integrated Approach to State Formation in the Prehistoric Aegean. *American Anthropologist* 109(1):113–129.

Parkinson, William A., and Michael L. Galaty (editors)

2009   *Archaic State Interaction: The Eastern Mediterranean in the Bronze Age.* School for Advanced Research Press, Santa Fe, New Mexico.

Parsons, Elsie Clews

1996   [1939] *Pueblo Indian Religion*, Volumes 1 and 2. University of Nebraska Press, Lincoln.

Pasternak, Burton, Carole R. Ember, and Melvin Ember

1976   On the Conditions Favoring Extended Family Households. *Journal of Anthropological Research* 32(2):109–123.

Pauketat, Timothy R.

2001   Practice and History in Archaeology. *Anthropological Theory* 1(1):73–98.

2007   *Chiefdoms and Other Archaeological Delusions.* AltaMira Press, Lanham, Maryland.

2009a   *Cahokia: Ancient America's Great City on the Mississippi.* Penguin Books, New York.

2009b   My Delusions. *Native South* 2:126–132.

2013   *An Archaeology of the Cosmos: Rethinking Agency and Religion in Ancient America.* Routledge, Lanham, Maryland.

Peeples, Matthew, Barbara Mills, Jeff Clark, Ben Bellorado, and Tom Windes

2016   Social Networks and the Scale of the Chaco World. Paper presented at the 81st Annual Meeting of the Society for American Archaeology, Orlando, Florida.

Peregrine, Peter N. (editor)

1996   *Pre-Columbian World Systems: Theory, Data, and Debate.* Prehistory Press, Madison, Wisconsin.

Peregrine, Peter N., and Stephen H. Lekson

2006   Southeast, Southwest, Mexico: Continental Perspectives on Mississippian Polities. In *Leadership and Polity in Mississippian Societies,* edited by Brian Butler and Paul Welch, pp. 351–364. Occasional Papers 33. Center for Archaeological Investigations, Carbondale, Illinois.

2012   The North American Oikoumene. In *Oxford Handbook of North American Archaeology,* edited by Timothy R. Pauketat, pp. 64–72. Oxford University Press, New York.

Perkovic, Jana

2015   How Santa Fe Reinvented Itself as the "City Different." http://www.blouinartinfo.com/news/story/1191724/how-santa-fe-reinvented-itself-as-the-city-different, accessed August 3, 2017.

Phillips, David A., Jr.

1996   Rethinking Chaco. In *Debating Complexity: Proceedings of the 26th Annual Chacmool Conference,* edited by D. A. Meyer, P. C. Dawson, and D. T. Hanna, pp. 333–338. The Archaeological Association of the University of Calgary, Calgary.

2002   *Rethinking Chaco.* www.unm.edu/~dap/chaco/chaco.html.

Phillips, David A., Jr., and Eduardo Gamboa

2015   The End of Paquimé and the Casas Grandes Culture. In *Ancient Paquimé and the Casas Grandes World,* edited by Paul E. Minnis and Michael E. Whalen, pp. 148–171. University of Arizona Press, Tucson.

Pinker, Steven

2014   *The Sense of Style: The Thinking Person's Guide to Writing in the 21st Century.* Viking Press, New York.

Plog, Stephen

1989   Ritual, Exchange, and the Development of Regional Systems. In *The Architecture of Social Integration in Prehistoric Pueblos,* edited by William D. Lipe and Michelle Hegmon, pp. 143–154. Occasional Paper 1. Crow Canyon Archaeological Center, Cortez, Colorado.

2010   Reflections on the State of Chacoan Research: A Review. *Kiva* 75:373–391.

2015   Understanding Chaco: Past, Present, and Future. In *Chaco Revisited: New Research on the Prehistory of Chaco Canyon, New Mexico,* edited by Carrie C. Heitman and Stephen Plog, pp. 3–29. University of Arizona Press, Tucson.

Plog, Stephen, and Carrie Heitman

2010   Hierarchy and Social Inequality in the American Southwest, AD 800–1200. *Proceedings of the National Academy of Sciences* 107(46):19619–19626.

Plog, Stephen, and Adam S. Watson

2012   The Chaco Pilgrimage Model: Evaluating the Evidence from Pueblo Alto. *American Antiquity* 77(3):444–477.

Plog, Stephen, Carrie C. Heitman, and Adam S. Watson

2017   Key Dimensions of the Cultural Trajectories of Chaco Canyon. In *Oxford Handbook of Southwest Archaeology,* edited by Barbara Mills and Severin Fowles, pp. 285–305. Oxford University Press, Oxford.

Plog, Stephen, Paul R. Fish, Donna M. Glowacki, and Suzanne K. Fish

2015   Key Issues and Topics in the Archaeology of the American Southwest and Northwestern Mexico. *Kiva* 81(1–2):2–30.

Pluciennik, Mark

1999   Archaeological Narratives and Other Ways of Telling. *Current Anthropology* 40(5): 653–678.

2011   Theory, Fashion, Culture. In *The Death of Archaeological Theory*, edited by John Bintliff and Mark Pearce, pp. 31–47. Oxbow Books, Oxford.

Pohl, John M. D.

2001   Chichimecatlalli: Strategies for Cultural and Commercial Exchange between Mexico and the American Southwest, 1100–1521. In *The Road to Aztlan*, edited by Virginia M. Fields and Victor Zamudio-Taylor, pp. 86–101. Los Angeles County Museum of Art, Los Angeles.

Popkin, Jeremy D.

2015   *From Herodotus to H-Net: The Story of Historiography*. Oxford University Press, New York.

Potter, James M.

2000   Ritual, Power, and Social Differentiation in Small-Scale Societies. In *Hierarchies in Action: Cui Bono?* edited by Michael W. Diehl, pp. 295–316. Center for Archaeological Investigations, Occasional Paper 27. Southern Illinois University, Carbondale.

Powell, T. G.

1968   Mexican Intellectuals and the Indian Question, 1876–1911. *Hispanic American Historical Review* 48(1):19–36.

Powers, Robert P., William B. Gillespie, and Stephen H. Lekson

1983   *The Outlier Survey: A Regional View of Settlement in the San Juan Basin*. Reports of the Chaco Center 3. National Park Service, Albuquerque, New Mexico.

Preucel, Robert W.

2011   An Archaeology of NAGPRA: Conversations with Suzan Shown Harjo. *Journal of Social Archaeology* 11(2):130–143.

Prescott, William

1843   *History of the Conquest of Mexico*. Chatto and Windus, London.

Preston, Douglas

1998   Cannibals of the Canyon. *New Yorker* 30 November:76–89.

Price, Barbara J.

1978   Secondary State Formation: An Explanatory Model. In *Origins of the State*, edited by Ronald Cohen and Elman R. Service, pp. 161–186. Institute for the Study of Human Issues, Philadelphia.

Prigogene, Ilya

1984   *Order Out of Chaos*. Bantam, New York.

Rapoport, Amos

1969   *House Form and Culture*. Prentice-Hall, Englewood Cliffs, New Jersey.

1976   *The Mutual Interaction of People and Their Built Environment: A Cross-Cultural Perspective*. Mouton, Berlin, Germany.

1982   *The Meaning of the Built Environment: A Nonverbal Communication Approach*. Sage Beverly Hills, California.

1993   On the Nature of Capitals and Their Physical Expression. In *Capital Cities/Les Capitales: Perspectives Internationales/International Perspectives*, edited by John Taylor, Jean G. Lengellé, and Caroline Andrew, pp. 31–67. Carleton University Press, Ottawa.

Redman, Charles L., and Ann P. Kinzig

2003   Resilience of Past Landscapes: Resilience Theory, Society and the Longue Durée. *Conservation Ecology* 7(1):14.

Reed, Paul F.

2004   *The Puebloan Society of Chaco Canyon.* Greenwood Press, Westport, Connecticut.

Reed, Paul F. (editor)

2000   *Foundations of Anasazi Culture: The Basketmaker-Pueblo Transition.* University of Utah Press, Salt Lake City.

2008   *Chaco's Northern Prodigies: Salmon, Aztec, and the Ascendancy of the Middle San Juan after AD 1100.* University of Utah Press, Salt Lake City.

Reid, J. Jefferson

1997   Return to Migration, Population Movement, and Ethnic Identity in the American Southwest. In *Vanishing River,* edited by Stephanie M. Whittlesey, Richard Ciolek-Torrello, and Jeffrey H. Altschul, pp. 629–638. SRI Press, Tucson.

Reid, Jefferson, and Stephanie Whittlesey

2010   *Prehistory, Personality, and Place: Emil W. Haury and the Mogollon Controversy.* University of Arizona Press, Tucson.

Renfrew, Colin, and John F. Cherry (editors)

1986   *Peer Polity Interaction and Socio-Political Change.* Cambridge University Press, Cambridge, UK.

Reyman, Jonathan E. (editor)

1995   *The Gran Chichimeca: Essays on the Archaeology and Ethnohistory of Northern Mesoamerica.* Avebury, Aldershot, UK.

Richter, Daniel K.

1992   *The Ordeal of the Longhouse: The Peoples of the Iroquois League in the Era of European Colonization.* University of North Carolina Press, Chapel Hill.

2011   *Before the Revolution: America's Ancient Pasts.* Harvard University Press, Cambridge, Massachusetts.

Riding In, James

1992   Without Ethics or Morality: A Historical Overview of Imperial Archaeology and American Indians. *Arizona State Law Journal* 24:11–34.

2012   Human Rights and the American Indian Repatriation Movement: A Manifesto. *Arizona State Law Journal* 44:613–624.

Riggs, Charles R.

2017   Confronting Cultural Imperialism in Native American Archaeology. *Sapiens* 10 August. https://www.sapiens.org/archaeology/native-american-archaeology/, accessed August 10, 2017.

Rinehart, Melissa

2012   To Hell with the Wigs! Native American Representation and Resistance at the World's Columbian Exposition. *American Indian Quarterly* 36(4):403–442.

Robb, John, and Timothy R. Pauketat (editors)

2013   *Big Histories, Human Lives: Tackling Problems of Scale in Archaeology.* School for Advanced Research Press, Santa Fe, New Mexico.

Roberts, David

2015   *The Lost World of the Old Ones: Discoveries in the Ancient Southwest.* W. W. Norton, New York.

Roberts, Frank H. H.

1935   A Survey of Southwestern Archaeology. *American Anthropologist* 37(1), Part 1: 1–35.

Roberts, Heidi, Richard V. N. Ahlstrom, and Barbara Roth (editors)

2004   *From Campus to Corporate: The Emergence of Contract Archaeology in the Southwestern United States.* Society for American Archaeology, Washington, DC.

Rocks-Macqueen, Doug

2014   How Many Archaeologists are in the US? Doug's Archaeology (blog) 18 June.
        https://dougsarchaeology.wordpress.com/2014/06/18/how-many-archaeologists
        -are-in-the-us-more-than-a-couple-less-than-there-should-be/, accessed May 25,
        2018.

Rohn, Arthur H.

1983   Budding Urban Settlements in the Northern San Juan. In *Proceedings of the Ana-
        sazi Symposium 1981*, edited by Jack E. Smith, pp. 175–180. Mesa Verde Museum
        Association, Mesa Verde, Colorado.

Rothman, Hal K.

1988   *Bandelier National Monument: An Administrative History*. Southwest Cultural Re-
        sources Center Professional Paper 14. Division of History, National Park Service,
        Santa Fe, New Mexico.

Rothman, Hal K. (editor)

2003   *The Culture of Tourism, the Tourism of Culture: Selling the Past to the Present in the
        American Southwest*. University of New Mexico Press, Albuquerque.

Rushforth, Scott, and Steadman Upham

1992   *A Hopi Social History*. University of Texas Press, Austin.

Ryan, Marie-Laure

2007   Toward a Definition of Narrative. In *The Cambridge Companion to Narrative*,
        edited by David Herman, pp. 22–36. Cambridge University Press, Cambridge, UK.

Sabloff, Jeremy A.

2008   *Archaeology Matters: Action Archaeology in the Modern World*. Left Coast Press,
        Walnut Creek, California.

Sahlins, Marshall

2002   *Waiting for Foucault, Still*. Prickly Paradigm Press, Chicago.

2008   The Stranger King, or the Elementary Forms of the Politics of Life. *Indonesia and
        the Malay World* 36:177–199.

2017   The Stranger-Kingship of the Mexica. In *On Kings*, by David Graeber and Mar-
        shall Sahlins, pp. 223–248. Hau Books, Chicago.

2018   *What the Foucault?* 5th ed. Prickly Paradigm Press, Chicago.

Sassaman, Kenneth E.

2010   *The Eastern Archaic, Historicized*. Rowman and Littlefield, Lanham, Maryland.

Sauer, Carl O.

1932   *The Road to Cíbola*. University of California Press, Berkeley.

1952   *Agricultural Origins and Dispersals*. Bowman Memorial Lectures Series 2. Ameri-
        can Geographical Society, New York.

1954   [Comments on Paul Kirchhoff's] Gatherers and Farmers in the Greater Southwest:
        A Problem in Classification. *American Anthropologist* 56(4):553–556.

Saxton, Russell S.

1981   The Truth about the Pueblo Indians: Bandelier's Delight Makers. *New Mexico His-
        torical Review* 56(3):261–284.

Scarre, Geoffrey, and Robin Coningham

2012   Introduction. In *Appropriating the Past: Philosophical Perspectives on the Practice
        of Archaeology*, edited by Geoffrey Scarre and Robin Coningham, pp. 1–21. Cam-
        bridge University Press, Cambridge, UK.

Schaafsma, Curtis F., and Carroll I. Riley (editors)

1999   *The Casas Grandes World*. University of Utah Press, Salt Lake City.

Schachner, Gregson

2001   Ritual Control and Transformation in Middle-Range Societies: An Example from the American Southwest. *Journal of Anthropological Archaeology* 20:168–194.

2008   Imagining Communities in the Cibola Past. In *The Social Construction of Communities: Agency, Structure, and Identity in the Prehispanic Southwest*, edited by Mark D. Varien and James M. Potter, pp. 171–190. AltaMira Press: Lanham, Maryland.

2015   Ancestral Pueblo Archaeology: The Value of Synthesis. *Journal of Archaeological Research* 23(1): 49–113.

Schama, Simon

1995   *Landscape and Memory*. Vintage Books, New York.

Scheidel, Walter

2017   *The Great Leveler: Violence and the History of Inequality from the Stone Age to the Twenty-First Century*. Princeton University Press, Princeton, New Jersey.

Schelberg, John D.

1984   Analogy, Complexity, and Regionally Based Perspectives. In *Recent Research on Chaco Prehistory*, edited by W. James Judge and John D. Schelberg, pp. 5–21. Reports of the Chaco Center. National Park Service, Division of Cultural Research, Albuquerque, New Mexico.

1992   Hierarchical Organization as a Short-Term Buffering Strategy in Chaco Canyon. In *Anasazi Regional Organization and the Chaco System*, edited by David E. Doyel, pp. 59–71. Anthropological Papers 3, Maxwell Museum of Anthropology, University of New Mexico, Albuquerque.

Schiffer, Michael Brian

2017   *Archaeology's Footprints in the Modern World*. Salt Lake City: University of Utah Press.

Schneider, Wendie Ellen

2001   Past Imperfect: Irving v. Penguin Books Ltd. *Yale Law Journal* 110(8):1531–1545.

Schortman, Edward M., and Patricia A. Urban

1998   Culture Contact Structure and Process. In *Studies in Culture Contact: Interaction, Culture Change, and Archaeology*, edited by James G. Cusick, pp. 102–125. Center for Archaeological Investigations Occasional Paper no. 25. Center for Archaeological Investigations, Southern Illinois University, Carbondale.

2015   Networks, Cores and Peripheries: New Frontiers in Interaction Studies. In *The Oxford Handbook of Mesoamerican Archaeology: Villages, Cities, States, and Empires*, edited by Deborah Nichols, pp. 471–480. Oxford University Press, Oxford, UK.

Schroeder, Albert H.

1979   Pueblos Abandoned in Historic Times. In *Handbook of North American Indians*, Vol. 9: *Southwest*, edited by Alfonso Ortiz, pp. 236–254. Smithsonian Institution, Washington, DC.

Schum, David A.

2003   Evidence and Inference about Past Events: An Overview of Six Case Studies. In *Evidence and Inference in History and Law: Interdisciplinary Dialogues*, edited by William L. Twining and Iain Hampsher-Monk, pp. 9–62. Northwestern University Press, Evanston, Illinois.

Scott, Sascha T.

2015   *A Strange Mixture: The Art and Politics of Painting Pueblo Indians*. University of Oklahoma Press, Norman.

Scott, Tom
2012   *The City-State in Europe, 1000–1600: Hinterland, Territory, Region.* Oxford University Press, New York.

Scully, Vincent
1989   *Pueblo: Mountain, Village, Dance.* University of Chicago Press, Chicago.

Sebastian, Lynne
1992   *Chaco Anasazi: Sociopolitical Evolution in the Pueblo Southwest.* Cambridge University Press, Cambridge, UK.
2004   Understanding Chacoan Society. In *In Search of Chaco: New Approaches to an Archaeological Enigma*, edited by David Grant Noble, pp. 93–99. School of American Research Press, Santa Fe, New Mexico.
2006   The Chaco Synthesis. In *The Archaeology of Chaco Canyon: An Eleventh Century Pueblo Regional Center*, edited by Stephen H. Lekson, pp. 393–422. School of American Research Press, Santa Fe, New Mexico.

Sewell, William H., Jr.
2005   *Logics of History: Social Theory and Social Transformation.* University of Chicago Press, Chicago.

Shafer, Harry J.
2003   *Mimbres Archaeology at the NAN Ranch Ruin.* University of New Mexico Press, Albuquerque.

Shanks, Michael
2008   Archaeological Manifesto. http://documents.stanford.edu/MichaelShanks/112, accessed December 23, 2010.
2012   *The Archaeological Imagination.* Left Coast Press, Walnut Creek, California.

Shanks, Michael, and Christopher Tilley
1988   *Social Theory and Archaeology.* University of New Mexico Press, Albuquerque.

Shapiro, Jason S.
2017   The Talented Mr. Nusbaum: The Renaissance Man of Edgar Hewett's Circle. *Southwestern Lore* 83(1):1–10.

Shaul, David Leedom
2014   *A Prehistory of Western North America: The Impact of Uto-Aztecan Languages.* University of New Mexico Press, Albuquerque.

Shelach, Gideon, and Yuri Pines
2006   Secondary State Formation and the Development of Local Identity: Change and Continuity in the State of Qin (770–221 BC). In *Archaeology of Asia*, edited by Miriam Stark, pp. 202–230. Blackwell, Malden, Massachusetts.

Shepard, Anna O.
1937   Anonymous Review. *American Antiquity* 3(2):182–183.

Sheridan, Thomas E.
2005   Strategic Essentialism and the Future of Ethnohistory in North America. *Reviews in Anthropology* 34:63–78.

Shott, Michael J.
2005   Two Cultures: Thought and Practice in British and North American Archaeology. *World Archaeology* 37(1):1–10.

Shryock, Andrew, and Daniel Lord Smail (editors)
2011   *Deep History: The Architecture of Past and Present.* University of California Press, Berkeley.

Silko, Leslie Marmon
1996 [1986] Interior and Exterior Landscapes: The Pueblo Migration Stories. In *Yellow*

Woman and a Beauty of the Spirit, edited by Leslie Marmon Silko, pp. 25–47. Simon and Schuster, New York.

Silliman, Stephen

2010 The Value and Diversity of Indigenous Archaeology: A Response to McGhee. *American Antiquity* 75(2):217–220.

Silliman, Stephen W. (editor)

2008 *Collaborating at the Trowel's Edge: Teaching and Learning in Indigenous Archaeology*. University of Arizona Press, Tucson.

Silver Bullet Productions

2012 *Canes of Power*. Video. Silver Bullet Productions, Santa Fe, New Mexico.

Simmons, Marc

1979 History of Pueblo-Spanish Relations to 1821. In *Handbook of North American Indians*, Volume 9, edited by Alfonso Ortiz, pp. 178–193. Smithsonian Institution Press, Washington, DC.

Simpson, J. H.

1964 *Navaho Expedition: Journal of a Military Reconnaissance from Santa Fe, New Mexico, to the Navaho Country Made in 1849 by Lieutenant James H. Simpson*. Edited and annotated by Frank McNitt. University of Oklahoma Press, Norman.

Slater, Philip A., Kristin M. Hedman, and Thomas E. Emerson

2014 Immigrants at the Mississippian Polity of Cahokia: Strontium Isotope Evidence for Population Movement. *Journal of Archaeological Science* 44:117–127.

Smail, Daniel Lord, and Andrew Shryock

2013 History and the "Pre." *American Historical Review* 118(3): 709–737.

Smith, Claire, and H. Martin Wobst (editors)

2005 *Indigenous Archaeologies: Decolonizing Theory and Practice*. Routledge, London.

Smith, Duane A.

2005 *Women to the Rescue: Creating Mesa Verde National Park*. Durango Herald Small Press, Durango, Colorado.

Smith, Duane A., and William C. Winkler

2005 *Travels and Travails: Tourism at Mesa Verde*. Durango Herald Small Press, Durango, Colorado.

Smith, Duane A., Karen A. Vendl, and Mark A. Vendl

2011 *Colorado Goes to the Fair: World's Columbian Exposition, Chicago, 1893*. University of New Mexico Press, Albuquerque.

Smith, Michael E.

2008a *Aztec City-State Capitals*. University Press of Florida, Gainesville.

2008b Urbanism in the Southwest? A New Perspective. Poster presented at the Southwest Symposium. Arizona State University, Tempe.

2010a Archaeology Is Archaeology. *Anthropology News* (January 2010):35.

2010b The Archaeological Study of Neighborhoods and Districts in Ancient Cities. *Journal of Anthropological Archaeology* 29:137–154.

2011a Why Anthropology is Too Narrow an Intellectual Context for Archaeology. *Anthropologies* 15 May. http://www.anthropologiesproject.org/2011/05/why-anthropology-is-too-narrow.html, accessed May 25, 2018.

2011b Tula and Chichén Itzá: Are We Asking the Right Questions? In *Twin Tollans*, edited by Jeff Karl Kowalski and Cynthia Kristan-Graham, pp. 469–499. Dumbarton Oaks, Washington, DC.

2016 Were Ancient Societies More Egalitarian than We Had Thought? 10 October. http://wideurbanworld.blogspot.com/, accessed May 25, 2018.

Smith, Michael E. (editor)

2012   *The Comparative Archaeology of Complex Societies*. Cambridge University Press, New York.

Smith, Michael E., and Frances F. Berdan (editors)

2003   *The Postclassic Mesoamerican World*. University of Utah Press, Salt Lake City.

Smith, Michael E., Gary M. Feinman, Robert D. Drennan, Timothy Earle, and Ian Morris

2012   Archaeology as a Social Science. *Proceedings of the National Academy of Sciences* 109(20):7617–7621.

Smith, Sherry

2012   *Hippies, Indians and the Fight for Red Power*. Oxford University Press, New York.

Snead, James E.

2001   *Ruins and Rivals: The Making of Southwest Archaeology*. University of Arizona Press, Tucson.

2002   Lessons of the Ages: Archaeology and the Construction of Cultural Identity in the American Southwest. *Journal of the Southwest* 44(1):17–34.

2005   Paradigms, Professionals, and the Making of Southwest Archaeology. In *Southwest Archaeology in the Twentieth Century*, edited by Linda S. Cordell and Don D. Fowler, pp. 27–46. University of Utah Press, Salt Lake City.

Snow, David H.

2016   Pahos to Muy'ovi: Mytho- and Real History in Traditional Accounts of the Tano-Tewa Migration to Hopi. In *History and Archaeology: Connecting the Dots*, edited by Emily J. Brown, Carol J. Codie, and Helen K. Crotty, pp. 239–250. Papers of the Archaeological Society of New Mexico 42. Archaeological Society of New Mexico, Albuquerque.

Sofaer, Anna (producer)

1999   *The Mystery of Chaco Canyon*. Video. Bullfrog Films, Oley, Pennsylvania.

Sofaer, Anna (editor)

2008   *Chaco Astronomy: An Ancient American Cosmology*. Ocean Tree Books, Santa Fe, New Mexico.

Spaulding, Albert C.

1953   Review of James A. Ford's *Measurements of Some Prehistoric Design Developments in the Southeastern States*. *American Anthropologist* 55:588–591.

Spector, Janet D.

1993   *What This Awl Means: Feminist Archaeology at a Wahpeton Dakota Village*. Minnesota Historical Society Press, St. Paul.

Spielmann, Katherine A.

2005   Ethnographic Analogy and Ancestral Pueblo Archaeology. In *Southwest Archaeology in the Twentieth Century*, edited by Linda S. Cordell and Don D. Fowler, pp. 194–203. University of Utah Press, Salt Lake City.

Spielmann, Katherine A. (editor)

1998   *Migration and Reorganization: The Pueblo IV Period in the American Southwest*. Anthropological Research Papers 51. Arizona State University, Tempe.

Spinney, Laura

2012   Human Cycles: History as Science. *Nature* 488(7409):24–26.

Squire, John Collins (editor)

1931   *If, or History Rewritten*. Viking Press, New York.

Stein, John R., and Stephen. H. Lekson

1992   Anasazi Ritual Landscapes. In *Anasazi Regional Organization and the Chaco*

System, edited by D. E. Doyel, pp. 87–100. Anthropological Paper No. 5. Maxwell Museum of Anthropology, Albuquerque, New Mexico.

Steinberg, Michael P.

1995   Aby Warburg's Kreuzlingen Lecture: A Reading. In *Images from the Region of the Pueblo Indians of North America*, pp. 59–114. Ithaca: Cornell University Press.

Stensvaag, James T.

1980   Clio on the Frontier: The Intellectual Evolution of the Historical Society of New Mexico. *New Mexico Historical Review* 55(4):293–299.

Stirling, Matthew W.

1942   *Origin Myth of the Acoma and Other Records*. BAE Bulletin 135. Smithsonian Institution Press, Washington, DC.

Stocking, George W., Jr.

1960   Franz Boas and the Founding of the American Anthropological Association. *American Anthropologist* 62(1):1–17.

1982   The Santa Fe Style in American Anthropology: Regional Interest, Academic Initiative, and Philanthropic Policy in the First Two Decades of the Laboratory of Anthropology, Inc. *Journal of the History of Behavioral Sciences* 18:3–19.

1989   The Ethnographic Sensibility of the 1920s and the Dualism of the Anthropological Tradition. In *History of Anthropology*, Vol. 6: *Romantic Motives: Essays on the Anthropological Sensibility*, edited by George W. Stocking Jr., pp. 208–276. University of Wisconsin Press, Madison.

Stocking, George W., Jr. (editor)

1974   *The Shaping of American Anthropology 1883–1911: A Franz Boas Reader*. Basic Books, New York.

Storey, Alice A., and Terry L. Jones

2011   Diffusionism in Archaeological Theory: The Good, the Bad, and the Ugly. In *Polynesians in America: Pre-Columbian Contacts with the New World*, edited by Terry L. Jones, Alice A. Storey, Elizabeth A. Matisoo-Smith, and José Miguel Ramírez-Alaga, pp. 7–24. AltaMira Press, Lanham, Maryland.

Stottman, M. Jay (editor)

2010   *Archaeologists as Activists: Can Archaeologists Change the World?* University of Alabama Press, Tuscaloosa.

Stresser-Péan, Guy, and Claude Stresser-Péan

2001   *Tamtok: Sitio Arqueológico Huasteco*. El Instituto de Cultura de San Luis Potosi, San Luis Potosi.

Stuart, David E.

2014   *Anasazi America: Seventeen Centuries on the Road from Center Place*. 2nd ed. University of New Mexico Press, Albuquerque.

Stuart, David E., and Rory P. Gauthier

1981   *Prehistoric New Mexico: Background for Survey*. New Mexico Historic Preservation Division, Santa Fe.

Stuchtey, Benedict, and Echkardt Fuchs (editors)

2003   *Writing World History 1800–2000*. German Historical Institute, London; Oxford University Press, Oxford.

Swentzell, Rina

1991   Levels of Truth: Southwest Archaeologists and Anasazi/Pueblo People. In *Puebloan Past and Present*, edited by Meliha S. Durand and David T. Kirpatrick, pp. 177–181. Papers of the Archaeological Society of New Mexico 17. Archaeological Society of New Mexico, Albuquerque.

1992 Review: *Yellow Jacket: A Four Corners Anasazi Ceremonial Center. American Indian Quarterly* (Spring 1992):278.

2003 Anglo Artists and the Creation of Pueblo Worlds. In *The Culture of Tourism, the Tourism of Culture: Selling the Past to the Present in the American Southwest*, edited by Hal Rothman, pp. 66–71. University of New Mexico Press, Albuquerque.

2004 A Pueblo Woman's Perspective on Chaco Canyon. In *In Search of Chaco: New Approaches to an Archaeological Enigma*. Edited by David Grant Noble, pp. 49–53. School of American Research Press, Santa Fe, New Mexico.

Tainter, Joseph A.

1988 *The Collapse of Complex Societies.* Cambridge University Press, Cambridge, UK.

2005 Perspectives on Diamond's *Collapse: How Societies Choose to Fail or Succeed. Current Anthropology* 46(Supplement):S97–S99.

2006 Archaeology of Overshoot and Collapse. *Annual Review of Anthropology* 35:59–74.

2008 Collapse, Sustainability, and the Environment: How Authors Chose to Fail or Succeed. *Reviews in Anthropology* 37:342–371.

Tankersley, Kenneth Barnett, Nicholas P. Dunning, Jessica Thress, Lewis A. Owen, Warren D. Huff, Samantha G. Fladd, Katelyn J. Bishop, Stephen Plog, Adam S. Watson, Christopher Carr, and Vernon L. Scarborough

2016 Evaluating Soil Salinity and Water Management in Chaco Canyon, New Mexico. *Journal of Archaeological Science* 9:94–104.

Tattersall, Ian

2015 *Strange Case of the Rickety Cossack and Other Cautionary Tales from Human Evolution.* St. Martin's Press, New York.

Taylor, Frederick

1911 *The Principles of Scientific Management.* Harper and Brothers, New York.

Taylor, Walter W.

1948 *A Study of Archeology. American Anthropologist* 50(3, pt. 2): Memoir 69. American Anthropological Association.

Tennert, Robert A.

1987 Fairs, Expositions, and the Changing Image of Southwestern Indians, 1876–1904. *New Mexico Historical Review* 62(2):127–150.

Thomas, David Hurst (editor)

1991 *Columbian Consequences.* Vol. 3: *The Spanish Borderlands in Pan-American Perspective.* Smithsonian Institution Press, Washington, DC.

Thomas, Jeffrey Allen

1999 Promoting the Southwest: Edgar L. Hewett, Anthropology, Archaeology, and the Santa Fe Style. PhD dissertation, Texas Tech University.

Thomas, Roger M.

2015 Evidence, Archaeology and Law: An Initial Exploration. In *Material Evidence: Learning from Archaeological Practice*, edited by Robert Chapman and Alison Wylie, pp. 255–270. Routledge, London.

Thompson, Mark

2001 *American Character: The Curious Life of Charles Fletcher Lummis and the Rediscovery of the Southwest.* Arcade Publishing, New York.

Thompson, Raymond H.

2000 Edgar Lee Hewett and the Political Process. *Journal of the Southwest* 42(2):273–328.

Thurley, Simon

2013 *Men from the Ministry: How Britain Saved Its Heritage.* Yale University Press, New Haven, Connecticut.

Thurston, Tina L.

2002   *Landscapes of Power, Landscapes of Conflict: State Formation in the South Scandinavian Iron Age.* Kluwer Academic Publishers, New York.

Tobias, Henry J., and Charles E. Woodhouse

2001   *Santa Fe: A Modern History, 1880–1990.* University of New Mexico Press, Albuquerque.

Toll, H. Wolcott, and Peter J. McKenna

1997   Chaco Ceramics. In *Ceramics, Lithics and Ornaments of Chaco Canyon*, edited by Frances Joan Mathien, pp. 17–530. Publications in Archaeology 18G, Vol I. National Park Service, Santa Fe, New Mexico.

Townsend, Richard F. (editor)

1998   *Ancient West Mexico: Art and Archaeology of the Unknown Past.* Art Institute of Chicago, Chicago.

Traugott, Joseph

2012   *New Mexico Art through Time: Prehistory to the Present.* Museum of New Mexico Press, Santa Fe.

Trevelyan, Amelia M.

2015   *Miskwabik, Metal of Ritual: Metallurgy in Precontact Eastern North America.* University Press of Kentucky, Lexington.

Trigger, Bruce G.

1980   Archaeology and the Image of the American Indian. *American Antiquity* 45(4): 662–676.

2003   *Understanding Early Civilizations.* Cambridge University Press, Cambridge, UK.

2004   Cross-Cultural Comparison and Archaeological Theory. In *A Companion to Social Archaeology*, edited by Lynn Meskell and Robert W. Preucel, pp. 23–42. Blackwell Publishing, Malden, Massachusetts.

2006   *A History of Archaeological Thought.* Cambridge University Press, Cambridge, UK.

Turchin, Peter

2003   *Historical Dynamics: Why States Rise and Fall.* Princeton University Press, Princeton, New Jersey.

2006   *War and Peace and War: The Life Cycles of Imperial Nations.* Plume Books, New York.

2008   Arise "Cliodynamics." *Nature* 454(3):34–35.

2009   Long-Term Population Cycles in Human Societies. In *The Year in Ecology and Conservation Biology, 2009*, edited by R. S. Ostfeld and W. H. Schlesinger, pp. 1–17. Annals of the New York Academy of Sciences 1162, New York.

Turchin, Peter, and T. D. Hall

2003   Spatial Synchrony among and within World-Systems: Insights from Theoretical Ecology. *Journal of World Systems Research* 9:37–64.

Turchin, Peter, and Andrey V. Korotayev

2009   Population Dynamics and Internal Warfare: A Reconsideration. *Social Evolution and History* 5(2):112–147.

Turchin, Peter, and S. A. Nefedov

2009   *Secular Cycles.* Princeton University Press, Princeton, New Jersey.

Turner, Christy G., II, and Jacqueline A. Turner

1999   *Man Corn: Cannibalism and Violence in the Prehistoric American Southwest.* University of Utah Press, Salt Lake City.

Udy, Stanley

1958   Bureaucratic Elements in Organizations: Some Research Findings. *American Sociological Review* 23:415–418.

1970   Work in Traditional and Modern Society. Prentice-Hall, New York.

Upham, Steadman

1982   *Polities and Power: An Economic and Political History of the Western Pueblos.* Academic Press, New York.

1984   Adaptive Diversity and Southwestern Abandonment. *Journal of Anthropological Research* 40(2):235–256.

1987   The Tyranny of Ethnographic Analogy in Southwestern Archaeology. In *Coasts, Plains, and Deserts: Essays in Honor of Reynold J. Ruppe,* edited by Sylvia W. Gains, pp. 265–281. Anthropological Research Papers 38. Arizona State University, Tempe.

Vallo, Fred J.

2015   New "Origin" Publication Is Affront to Acoma. *Santa Fe New Mexican* 23 September.

Van Dyke, Ruth M.

2007a   *The Chaco Experience: Landscape and Ideology at the Center Place.* School for Advanced Research Press, Santa Fe, New Mexico.

2007b   Great Kivas in Time, Space and Society. In *The Architecture of Chaco Canyon, New Mexico,* edited by Stephen H. Lekson, pp. 93–126. University of Utah Press, Salt Lake City.

Van Dyke, Ruth M., R. Kyle Bocinsky, Tucker Robinson, and Thomas C. Windes

2016   Great Houses, Shrines, and High Places: A GIS Viewshed Analysis of the Chacoan World. *American Antiquity* 81(2):205–230.

Van Dyke, Ruth M., and Reinhard Bernbeck (editors)

2015   *Subjects and Narratives in Archaeology.* University Press of Colorado, Boulder.

VanPool, Christine S., Todd L. VanPool, and David A. Phillips Jr. (editors)

2006   *Religion in the Prehispanic Southwest.* AltaMira Press, Lanham, Maryland.

VanPool, Todd L., and Christine S. VanPool

2003   Introduction: Method, Theory and the Essential Tension. In *Essential Tensions in Archaeological Method and Theory,* edited by Todd L. VanPool and Christine S. VanPool, pp. 1–4. University of Utah Press, Salt Lake City.

Vansina, Jan

1985   *Oral Tradition as History.* University of Wisconsin Press, Madison.

Varien, Mark D., and James M. Potter (editors)

2008   *The Social Construction of Communities: Agency, Structure, and Identity in the Prehispanic Southwest.* AltaMira Press, Lanham, Maryland.

Varien, Mark D., and Richard H. Wilshusen (editors)

2002   *Seeking the Center Place: Archaeology and Ancient Communities in the Mesa Verde Region.* University of Utah Press, Salt Lake City.

Vasconcelos C., José

1997 [1925] *The Cosmic Race.* Johns Hopkins University Press, Baltimore.

Vellinga, M., P. Oliver, and A. Bridge (editors)

2008   *Atlas of Vernacular Architecture of the World.* Oxon, Oxfordshire, UK.

Venkatesan, Soumhya (editor)

2010   Debate: Ontology Is Just Another Word for Culture. *Critique of Anthropology* 30(2):152–200.

Verdesio, Gustavo

2010   Invisible at a Glance: Indigenous Cultures of the Past, Archaeological Sites, and Our Regimes of Visibility. In *Ruins of Modernity,* edited by Julia Hell and Andreas Schönle, pp. 339–353. Duke University Press, Durham, North Carolina.

Villela, Khristaan D.

2005   The Adobe Ambassador: The Curious Backstory of the New Mexico Museum of Art's Genesis. *El Palacio* 110(1):51–55.

2016   Controversy Erupts over Peter Nabokov's Publication of "The Origin Myth of Acoma Pueblo." *Santa Fe New Mexican* 15 January.

Vivian, Gordon, and Tom W. Mathews

1965   *Kin Kletso: A Pueblo III Community in Chaco Canyon, New Mexico.* Technical Series 6(1). Southwest Parks and Monuments Association, Tucson, Arizona.

Vivian, R. Gwinn

1989   Kluckhohn Reappraised: The Chacoan System as an Egalitarian Enterprise. *Journal of Anthropological Research* 45(1):101–113.

1990   *The Chacoan Prehistory of the San Juan Basin.* Academic Press, San Diego, California.

2001   Chaco Reconstructed. *Cambridge Archaeological Journal* 11(1):142–144.

2004   Puebloan Farmers of the Chacoan World. In *In Search of Chaco: New Approaches to an Archaeological Enigma*, edited by David Grant Noble, pp. 7–13. School of American Research Press, Santa Fe, New Mexico.

Vivian, R. Gwinn, Dulce N. Dodge, and Gayle H. Hartman

1978   *Wooden Ritual Artifacts from Chaco Canyon, New Mexico.* Anthropological Papers of the University of Arizona 32. University of Arizona Press, Tucson.

Vivian, R. Gwinn, and Bruce Hilpert

2012   *The Chaco Handbook: An Encyclopedic Guide.* 2nd ed. University of Utah Press, Salt Lake City.

Vivian, R. Gwinn, Carla R. Van West, Jeffrey S. Dean, Nancy J. Akins, Mollie S. Toll, and Thomas C. Windes

2006   Ecology and Economy. In *Archaeology of Chaco Canyon: An Eleventh Century Pueblo Regional Center*, edited by Stephen H. Lekson, pp. 45–65. School of American Research Press, Santa Fe, New Mexico.

Walker, William H.

1998   Where Are the Witches of Prehistory? *Journal of Archaeological Method and Theory* 5(3):245–308.

Wallerstein, Immanuel M.

1974   *The Modern World System, Vol. I: Capitalist Agriculture and the Origins of the European World-Economy in the Sixteenth Century.* Academic Press, New York.

Warburg, Abraham M.

1939   A Lecture on Serpent Ritual. *Journal of the Warburg Institute* 2(4):277–292.

1995   *Images from the Region of the Pueblo Indians of North America.* Translated by Michael P. Steinberg. Cornell University Press, Ithaca, New York.

Ware, John

2001   Chaco Social Organization: A Peripheral View. In *Chaco Society and Polity*, edited by Linda S. Cordell and W. James Judge, pp. 79–93. NMAC Special Publication 4. New Mexico Archaeological Council, Albuquerque.

2014   *A Pueblo Social History: Kinship, Sodality, and Community in the Northern Southwest.* School for Advanced Research Press, Santa Fe, New Mexico.

Washburn, Dorothy K., William N. Washburn, and Petia A. Shipkova

2011   The Prehistoric Drug Trade: Widespread Consumption of Cacao in Ancestral Pueblo and Hohokam Communities in the American Southwest. *Journal of Archaeological Science* 38(7): 1634–1640.

Washburn, Dorothy K., William N. Washburn, Petia A. Shipkova, and Mary Ann Pelley-mounter

2014   Chemical Analysis of Cacao Residues in Archaeological Ceramics from North America: Considerations of Contamination, Sample Size and Systematic Controls. *Journal of Archaeological Science* 50:191–207.

Waters, Frank

1963   *Book of the Hopi.* Viking Press, New York.

Watkins, Joe E.

2000   *Indigenous Archaeology: American Indian Values and Scientific Practice.* AltaMira Press, Walnut Creek, California.

2003   Beyond the Margin: American Indians, First Nations, and Archaeology in North America. *American Antiquity* 68(2):273–285.

Watson, Adam S. Watson, Stephen Plog, Brendan J. Culleton, Patricia A. Gilman, Steven A. LeBlanc, Peter M. Whiteley, Santiago Claramunt, and Douglas J. Kennett

2015   Early Procurement of Scarlet Macaws and the Emergence of Social Complexity in Chaco Canyon, NM. *Proceedings of the National Academy of Sciences Early Edition*, www.pnas.org/cgi/doi/10.1073/pnas.1509825112.

Watson, Patty Jo

2003   Does Americanist Archaeology Have a Future? In *Essential Tensions in Archaeological Method and Theory*, edited by Todd L. VanPool and Christine S. VanPool, pp. 117–141. University of Utah Press, Salt Lake City.

Watson, Patty Jo, Steven A. LeBlanc, and Charles L. Redman

1971   Explanation in Archeology: An Explicitly Scientific Approach. Columbia University Press, New York.

Watson, Peter

2012   *The Great Divide: Nature and Human Nature in the Old World and the New.* HarperCollins, New York.

Webster, David

2006   The Mystique of the Ancient Maya. In *Archaeological Fantasies*, edited by Garrett G. Fagan, pp. 129–153. Routledge, London.

Weideman, Paul

2017   The Center Holds: Enigmas Endure at Chaco Canyon. *Santa Fe New Mexican Pasatiempo* 21 April:28–35.

Weigle, Marta

1989   From Desert to Disney World: The Santa Fe Railway and the Fred Harvey Company Display the Indian Southwest. *Journal of Anthropological Research* 45(1):115–137.

1990   Southwest Lures: Innocents Detoured, Incensed, Determined. *Journal of the Southwest* "Inventing the Southwest" 32(4):499–540.

Weigle, Marta, and Barbara Babcock (editors)

1996   *The Great Southwest of the Fred Harvey Company and the Santa Fe Railway.* University of Arizona Press, Tucson.

Weigle, Marta, and Kyle Fiore

1982   *Santa Fe and Taos: The Writers Era.* Ancient City Press, Santa Fe, New Mexico.

Weiner, Annette B.

1985   Inalienable Wealth. *American Ethnologist* 12(2):210–227.

1992   *Inalienable Possessions: The Paradox of Keeping-While-Giving.* University of California Press, Berkeley.

Weinryb, Elazar

2008   Historical Counterfactuals. In *A Companion to the Philosophy of History and His-*

toriography, edited by Aviezer Tucker, pp. 109–119. Wiley-Blackwell, Malden, Massachusetts.

Weiss, Charles
2003   Expressing Scientific Uncertainty. *Law, Probability and Risk* 2:25–46.

Weiss, Harvey, and Raymond S. Bradley
2001   What Drives Societal Collapse? *Science* 291:609–610.

Weixelman, Joseph Owen
2005   Interpreting the "Anasazi Myth": How the Pueblo Indians Disappeared from the Story. In *Preserving Western History*, edited by Andrew Gulliford, pp. 128–144. University of New Mexico Press, Albuquerque.

Wells, E. Christian, and Ben A. Nelson
2007   Ritual Pilgrimage and Material Transfers in Prehispanic Northwest Mexico. In *Mesoamerican Ritual Economy*, edited by E. Christian Wells and Karla L. Davis-Salazar, pp. 137–165. University Press of Colorado, Boulder.

West, Geoffrey
2017   *Scale: The Universal Laws of Growth, Innovation, Sustainability, and the Pace of Life in Organisms, Cities, Economies, and Companies.* Penguin Press, New York.

Whalen, Michael E., and Paul E. Minnis
2001   *Casas Grandes and Its Hinterlands: Prehistoric Regional Organization in Northwest Mexico.* University of Arizona Press, Tucson.

2003   The Local and the Distant in the Origin of Casas Grandes, Chihuahua, Mexico. *American Antiquity* 68(2):314–332.

2009   *The Neighbors of Casas Grandes: Excavating Medio Period Communities of Northwest Chihuahua, Mexico.* University of Arizona Press, Tucson.

2012   Ceramics and Polity in the Casas Grandes Area, Chihuahua, Mexico. *American Antiquity* 77(3) (July 2012):403–423.

2017   Chihuahuan Archaeology. In *Oxford Handbook of Southwest Archaeology*, edited by Barbara Mills and Severin Fowles, pp. 397–409. Oxford: Oxford University Press.

Whalen, Michael E., A. C. MacWilliams, and Todd Pitezel
2010   Reconsidering the Size and Structure of Casas Grandes, Chihuahua, Mexico. *American Antiquity* 75(3) (July 2010):527–550.

White, Hayden
1973   *Metahistory.* Johns Hopkins University Press, Baltimore.

White, Leslie A.
1960   The World of the Keresan Pueblo Indians. In *Culture in History: Essays in Honor of Paul Radin*, edited by Stanley Diamond, pp. 53–64. Published for Brandeis University by Columbia University Press, New York.

White, Nancy Marie (editor)
2005   *Gulf Coast Archaeology: The Southeastern United States and Mexico.* University Press of Florida, Gainesville.

White, Nancy, and R. Weinstein
2008   The Mexican Connection and the Far West of the Southeast. *American Antiquity* 73:227–277.

White, Tim D.
1992   *Prehistoric Cannibalism at Mancos 5MTUMR-2346.* Princeton University Press, Princeton, New Jersey.

Whitehouse, Harvey, Pieter François, and Peter Turchin
2015   The Role of Ritual in the Evolution of Social Complexity: Five Predictions and a Drum Roll. *Cliodynamics* 6(2):199–216.

Whiteley, Peter M.

1993   The End of Anthropology (at Hopi)? *Journal of the Southwest* 35(2):125–157.

1998   *Rethinking Hopi Ethnography.* Smithsonian Institution Press, Washington, DC.

2002   Archaeology and Oral Tradition: The Scientific Importance of Dialogue. *American Antiquity* 67(3):405–415.

Wiget, Andrew O.

1982   Truth and the Hopi: An Historiographic Study of Documented Oral Tradition Concerning the Coming of the Spanish. *Ethnohistory* 29(3):181–199.

Wigmore, John Henry

1937   *The Science of Judicial Proof, as Given by Logic, Psychology, and General Experience, and Illustrated in Judicial Trials.* Little/Brown, New York.

Wilcox, David R.

1993   The Evolution of the Chacoan Polity. In *The Chimney Rock Archaeological Symposium,* edited by J. McKim Malville and Gary Matlock, pp. 76–90. General Technical Report RM-227. USDA Forest Service Rocky Mountain Forest and Range Experiment Station, Fort Collins, Colorado.

1999   A Peregrine View of Macroregional Systems in the North American Southwest, AD 750–1250. In *Great Towns and Regional Polities,* edited by Jill E. Neitzel, pp. 115–141. New World Studies Series No. 3. Amerind Foundation, Inc., Dragoon, Arizona, and University of New Mexico Press, Albuquerque.

2003   Restoring Authenticity: Judging Frank Hamilton Cushing's Veracity. In *Philadelphia and the Development of Americanist Archaeology,* edited by Don D. Fowler and David R. Wilcox, pp. 88–112. University of Alabama Press, Tuscaloosa.

Wilcox, David R., and Don D. Fowler

2002   The Beginnings of Anthropological Archaeology in the North American Southwest: From Thomas Jefferson to the Pecos Conference. *Journal of the Southwest* 44(2):121–234.

Wilcox, David R., David A. Gregory, and J. Brett Hill

2007   Zuni in the Puebloan and Southwestern Worlds. In *Zuni Origins: Toward a New Synthesis of Southwestern Archaeology,* edited by David A. Gregory and David R. Wilcox, pp. 167–209. University of Arizona Press, Tucson.

Wilcox, Michael

2010   Saving Indigenous Peoples from Ourselves: Separate but Equal Archaeology Is Not Scientific Archaeology. *American Antiquity* 75(2):221–227.

Willey, Gordon R., and Phillip Phillips

1958   *Method and Theory in American Archaeology.* University of Chicago Press, Chicago.

Wills, W. H.

2009   Cultural Identity and the Archaeological Construction of Historical Narratives: An Example from Chaco Canyon. *Journal of Archaeological Method and Theory* 16(4):283–319.

2012   This Old Trench: The Chaco Stratigraphy Project. *Archaeology Southwest* 26:21–22.

2017   Water Management and the Political Economy of Chaco Canyon during the Bonito Phase (ca. AD 850–1200). *Kiva* 83(4):369–413.

Wills, W. H., and Wetherbee Bryan Dorshow

2012   Agriculture and Community in Chaco Canyon: Revisiting Pueblo Alto. *Journal of Anthropological Archaeology* 31(2):138–155.

Wilshusen, Richard H., Gregson Schachner, and James R. Allison (editors)

2012   *Crucible of Pueblos: The Early Pueblo Period in the Northern Southwest.* Cotson Institute of Archaeology, Los Angeles.

Wilson, Angela Cavendish

1997   Power of the Spoken Word: Native Oral Traditions in American Indian History. In *Rethinking American Indian History*, edited by Donald L. Fixico, pp. 101–116. University of New Mexico Press, Albuquerque.

Wilson, Chris

1997   *The Myth of Santa Fe: Creating a Modern Regional Tradition.* University of New Mexico Press, Albuquerque.

2014   The Most Historic House in Santa Fe. In Chris Wilson and Oliver Horn, *The Roque Lobato House, Santa Fe, New Mexico*, pp. 41–70. Schenck Southwest Publishing, Santa Fe, New Mexico.

Windes, Thomas C.

1984   A New Look at Population in Chaco Canyon. In *Recent Research on Chaco Prehistory*, edited by W. James Judge and John D. Schelberg, pp. 75–87. Reports of the Chaco Center 8. Division of Cultural Research, National Park Service, Albuquerque, New Mexico.

Windschuttle, Keith

1996   *The Killing of History: How a Discipline is Being Murdered by Literary Critics and Social Theorists.* Macleay, Paddington, Australia.

Witmore, Christopher, and Michael Shanks

2013   Archaeology: An Ecology of Practices. In *Archaeology in the Making: Conversations through a Discipline*, edited by William L. Rathje, Michael Shanks, and Christopher Witmore, pp. 380–398. Routledge, London.

Wobst, H. Martin

1974   Boundary Conditions for Paleolithic Social Systems: A Simulation Approach. *American Antiquity* 39(2):147–178.

1978   The Archaeo-Ethnology of Hunter-Gatherers or the Tyranny of the Ethnographic Record in Archaeology. *American Antiquity* 43(2):303–309.

Wolf, Eric

1982   *Europe and the People without History.* University of California Press, Berkeley.

1999   *Envisioning Power: Ideologies of Dominance and Crisis.* University of California Press, Berkeley.

Wood, Nancy (editor)

1997   *The Serpent's Tongue: Prose, Poetry, and Art of the New Mexican Pueblos.* Dutton Books, New York.

Woodbury, Richard

1993   *60 Years of Southwestern Archaeology: A History of the Pecos Conference.* University of New Mexico Press, Albuquerque.

Woodward, Christopher

2003   *In Ruins: A Journey through History, Art and Literature.* Vintage, New York.

Woosley, Anne I., and John C. Ravesloot

1993   *Culture and Contact: Charles C. Di Peso's Gran Chichimeca.* University of New Mexico Press, Albuquerque.

Worldwide Indigenous Science Network

2015   What Is Indigenous Science? http://www.wisn.org/what-is-indigenous-science .html, accessed January 30, 2017.

Wright, Henry T.
1977   Toward an Explanation of the Origin of the State. In *Explanation of Prehistoric Organizational Change*, edited by James Hill, pp. 215–230. University of New Mexico Press, Albuquerque.

Wright, Henry T., and Gregory A. Johnson
1975   Population, Exchange, and Early State Formation in Southwestern Iran. *American Anthropologist* 77(2):267–289.

Wrobel, David M., and Patrick T. Long (editors)
2001   *Seeing and Being Seen: Tourism in the American West*. University Press of Kansas, Lawrence.

Wylie, Alison
2002   *Thinking from Things*. University of California Press, Berkeley.
2014   Community-Based Collaborative Archaeology. In *Philosophy of Social Science: A New Introduction*, edited by Nancy Cartwright and Eleonora Montuschi, pp. 68–82. Oxford University Press, Oxford, UK.

Yoffee, Norman
1993   Too Many Chiefs? or, Safe Texts for the '90s. In *Archaeological Theory: Who Sets the Agenda?* edited by Norman Yoffee and Andrew Sherrat, pp. 60–78. Cambridge University Press, Cambridge.
1994   Memorandum to Murray Gell-Mann Concerning: The Complications of Complexity in the Prehistoric Southwest. In *Understanding Complexity in the Prehistoric Southwest*, edited by George J. Gumerman and Murray Gell-Mann, pp. 341–358. Addison-Wesley, Reading, Massachusetts.
1997   The Obvious and the Chimerical: City-States in Archaeological Perspective. In *The Archaeology of City-States: Cross-Cultural Approaches*, edited by Deborah Nichols and Thomas Charlton, pp. 255–263. Washington, D.C.: Smithsonian.
2001   The Chaco "Rituality" Revisited. In *Chaco Society and Polity: Papers from the 1999 Conference*, edited by Linda S. Cordell, W. James Judge, and June-el Piper, pp. 63–78. NMAC Special Publication 4. New Mexico Archaeological Council, Albuquerque.
2005   *Myths of the Archaic State: Evolution of the Earliest Cities, States, and Civilizations*. Cambridge University Press, Cambridge, UK.
2015   Conclusion: The Meaning of Early Cities. In *Cambridge World History*. Vol. 3: *Early Cities in Comparative Perspective, 4000 BCE–1200 CE*, edited by Norman Yoffee, pp. 546–557. Cambridge University Press, Cambridge.
2016   The Present and Future of Counter-narratives. In *Social Theory in Archaeology and Ancient History: The Present and Future of Counternarratives*, edited by Geoff Emberling, pp. 345–357. Cambridge University Press, New York.

Yoffee, Norman, and George L. Cowgill
1988   *The Collapse of Ancient States and Civilizations*. University of Arizona Press, Tucson.

Yoffee, Norman, Suzanne K. Fish, and George R. Milner
1999   Communidades, Ritualities, Chiefdoms: Social Evolution in the American Southwest and Southeast. In *Great Towns and Regional Polities in the Prehistoric American Southwest and Southeast*, edited by Jill E. Neitzel, pp. 261–271. University of New Mexico Press, Albuquerque.

Yoffee, Norman, and Nicola Terrenato
2015   Introduction: A History of the Study of Early Cities. In *The Cambridge World*

History. Vol. 3: Early Cities in Comparative Perspective, 4000 BCE–1200 CE, edited by Norman Yoffee, pp. 1–24. Cambridge University Press, Cambridge.

Young, Lisa C., and Sarah A. Herr

2012   *Southwestern Pithouse Communities, AD 200–900.* University of Arizona Press, Tucson.

Young, Virginia Heyer

2005   *Ruth Benedict: Beyond Relativity, Beyond Pattern.* University of Nebraska Press, Lincoln.

Zaragoza Ocana, Diana

2005   Characteristic Elements Shared by Northeastern Mexico and the Southeastern United States. In *Gulf Coast Archaeology*, edited by Nancy Marie White, pp. 245–259. University Press of Florida, Gainsville.

Zeder, Melinda A.

1997   *The American Archaeologist: A Profile.* AltaMira Press, Walnut Creek, California.

Zimmerman, Larry J.

2001   Usurping the Native American Voice. In *The Future of the Past: Archaeologists, Native Americans, and Repatriation*, edited by Tamara Bray, pp. 169–184. Garland Publishing, New York.

2012   On Archaeological Ethics and Letting Go. In *Appropriating the Past: Philosophical Perspectives on the Practice of Archaeology*, edited by Geoffrey Scarre and Robin Coningham, pp. 98–118. Cambridge University Press, Cambridge, UK.

Zubrow, Ezra B. W.

1974   *Prehistoric Carrying Capacity: A Model.* Cummings, Menlo Park, California.

Endpiece: "Get off my lawn."
Hugo Rodeck Mimbres Archive,
University of Colorado Museum of Natural History.
Used with permission.

Index

abandonment, use of term, 132, 287n99
Abbott, David, 140–41
"Aboriginalism and the Problems of Indigenous Archaeology" (McGhee), 297n36
Acoma, 157–58, 276n26, 295n29
Adams, Charles, 44, 72
Adler, Michael, 276n25
agency, 120, 283n68, 283n70
agriculture: at Chaco, 77, 88–89, 127, 267n11; maize, 77, 268n11, 277n29; in urban contexts, 126–27, 286n89
Aguilar, Joseph "Woody," 296n32
Akins, Nancy, 263n3
Albuquerque, 16, 233n58
altepetl (altepemeh): Cahokia as, 107; Chaco Canyon as, 73–74, 81, 82–83, 261n57; defining, 126, 227n34; Meso-american, 73, 81, 270n23
America Before the European Invasions (Kehoe), 155
American Anthropological Archaeology: agency as popular theme, 120; and colonialism, 207; communalism as orthodoxy, 8, 79; and comparison as tool, 318n81; cultural connections biases, 108; and diffusion, 100; Ethnological Method as standard method, 65; as evolution of culture, 223n13; framing of questions by, 109, 280n51; and Glass Ceiling over Native societies, 7–9; and historical cycles, 132, 141; and history, 178–81, 311n46, 312n48, 315nn66–67; and History, 35, 36–37, 177, 310nn40–42; and Iron Curtain, 6, 9; and NAGPRA, 40–42; and pre-historiography, 177, 310n43; and science, 5, 35, 36–37, 38, 168, 223n15, 224n21; and Théorie,

170, 303n10. *See also* Southwestern archaeology
American Anthropology: Ethnological Method, 6; founding, 5; as Indianology, 222n12; and Native Americans, 151, 195, 222n12, 293n12, 324n103; as science, 5
American Association for the Advancement of Science (AAAS), 35
American Museum of Natural History, 28
Anasazi, "Mystery" of, 31
Anasazi America (Stuart), 163–64
"Ancestral Pueblo Archaeology" (Schachner), 52–53
Ancient Life in the American Southwest (Hewitt), 19, 277n29
Anderson, Benedict, 57–59, 252nn18–19
Anderson, David, 278n41
Anderson, Terence J., 199–200
Annales, 180
anthropology, *xiii*, 31, 253n22, 271n4
Antiquities Act (1906), 15, 37, 232n51
antiquities market, 173
Anyon, Roger, 275n25
Apache groups, 17, 222n9, 222n11, 234n67
"applied" anthropology, 32
archaeological historiography: absence of coincidences, 185–86; "everybody knew everything," 186; humanistic approaches, 180, 315n51; interactions spanned large distances, 186–87; Native American accounts in, 192–96, 320nn90–91; need to make causal connections and find patterns, 187–91, 318n79, 318nn81–83; style in, 191–92
"Archaeological Narratology, An" (Shanks), 312n48
Archaeological Resources Protection Act (1979), 37, 245n139

391